The Raped Vagina

A Military Prostitute's Story

The Raped Vagina

A Military Prostitute's Story

Suki Falconberg, Ph.D.

iUniverse, Inc.
New York Bloomington

The Raped Vagina
A Military Prostitute's Story

iUniverse books may be ordered through booksellers or by contacting:

iUniverse
1663 Liberty Drive
Bloomington, IN 47403
www.iuniverse.com
1-800-Authors (1-800-288-4677)

ISBN:978-1-4401-5772-1(sc)
ISBN: 978-1-4401-5773-8 (ebook)

Printed in the United States of America

For all the 'Comfort Women' of the world.

And for William James, who gave me the question I live by:

If all of humankind could be kept happy on the condition that one creature, at the far off edge of the universe, lived in abysmal, wretched misery, would it be worth it?

Contents

Brief Introduction

The Raped Vagina is partly autobiographical. I write about my own rape and about the time I spent as a prostitute. But a good portion of the book consists of my articles on prostitution and trafficking in general, particularly military prostitution.

I combine the personal with a great deal of research that I have done on prostitution.

Part one is my story. Part two brings together my articles on a range of prostitution/trafficking issues. These pieces grew out of my struggle to survive having been a prostitute. Putting it in words, in some form, helps.

Part three is my response to some of the scholarship others have done in the area of prostitution.

--Suki Falconberg, 2009

Part One

My Story

1

Rape

About thirty years ago I was gang raped by men who had served in Vietnam. They practiced on the Vietnamese girls and then came back and used my body as a rape playground. It was beyond brutal, lasted for hours, and tore me up badly. After that, I couldn't leave the house for months because the whole world seemed like a terrifying place controlled by male violence. Then I briefly ended up in prostitution near a military base because I felt I was a piece of public garbage fit only for more rape by men. After several decades, I'm finally finding the courage to write about all this, and it is incredibly frightening and painful and difficult. Once you've worked as a prostitute, you're always regarded as 'whoregarbage' and a 'sex toilet' for men.

One of the men who raped me was my boyfriend. A concrete slab of a guy, he could have been a poster boy for the military-commando type. The short haircut, the rugged face, the blue tattoo, like a streak of lightening, above the tricep. I found his strength, roughness, and maleness exciting. Long before the rape, he told me the story of 'Suzie,' a prostitute he and his friends brought to their barracks in Vietnam one night. About two dozen men in a row used her. My boyfriend said that "she enjoyed her work."

Through my 'commando,' I met other soldiers and one night, in a confusing, chaotic way, I ended up alone with six of them. I was probably raped about fifteen times since they all went more than once. While it's happening, you're not laying there making marks on the wall, like the Prisoner of Zenda, so I can only estimate.

Very few accounts of gang rape describe the physical aftermath. A torn, bleeding vagina, damage to my bladder and rectum, bruises all over my breasts and the front of my body from the weight of the men—that's just part of it. I even hurt deep inside, in my womb. Serial penetration by many men is not a mild form of torture. Just the tears at the vaginal opening feel like fire applied to a cut.

So, several months later, here I was with a messed up body and mind and life and no money since I was too afraid to leave the house. In fact, my favorite spot was a corner of my closet, where I crouched frequently, in a huddled ball, and cried as I tried to dig my way into the wall. When men rape us they really do a number on us. It goes deep.

Going into prostitution seemed like the only path. I know now that I was reenacting my own rape over and over, but at the time my motives were hazy and confused. I didn't think much about doing it. I just did it. There didn't seem to be any way to face the world. I couldn't be around 'normal' people, especially normal women. I couldn't think of any way to care for myself except for isolating myself in prostitution and hiding from the normal, 'decent' world.

And all my life, I had been moved by the plight of prostitutes so I think I did it to put myself in the place I feared most. At the time, I didn't know why I did it—these self –revelations have only come recently.

When I sold myself, it was very frightening, particularly since I am naturally timid. I was afraid all the time--of getting arrested, of getting a disease, of not knowing what this man was going to do to me. When you are in the room with him, he can do anything. Prostitutes are dirt with no recourse to the law. Or to any protection from the police.

My entryway into military prostitution was a man named Gerry I picked up one night. He liked sex, had a wife who didn't, did not want to cheat on her, so he bought women. He was an older man, maybe early forties, stationed at a nearby military base. That commando, concrete type I am so attracted to, the heavy male animal in his all his glory. Even the short, tough haircut.

Before Gerry, I'd been tentatively, with great terror, picking up a man here and there. I was still really new to the trade. But I figured a lot of things out fast. Like—charge a lot of money. If he buys you cheap, he'll treat you cheap. If they have to pay a lot, they will think you're worth something.

Gerry was willing to pay, and he became my regular. My only customer, in fact. He was kind to me. The big difficulty was that, despite his age, he liked a lot of sex and could pound me to pieces like someone half his age.

After several months, Gerry went off on TDY. But first, one Saturday morning, he introduced me to two of his military buddies and they took me to a motel near the base. As it was happening, this second, deeper entry into being with soldiers, I just seemed to fall into it, in this chaotic way. It was confusing and depressing because I felt as if Gerry'd just handed me on to them, without even asking me. So, passively, I had sex with one, for money, while the other one went out, did an errand or something. Then he came back, and I had sex with him. Then some kind of circus happened, because two cars drove up, and all of a sudden half a dozen or more GI's were there, potential customers. Word of mouth? There's a new whore around. Let's try her out. I don't know.

I finally asserted myself. Said, look, I don't go with a lot of guys, tried to work it out with them, said I'd go with two more men. (I was already sore from the first two, because my body was so resistant and I felt very mixed up. Very depressed by the way Gerry just dumped me and deserted me.) It didn't seem like a rape situation (they weren't that drunk, it was early in the day) and the atmosphere wasn't menacing. Most of them left, and I did do two more, and then the first two guys took me home. It was my first time having sex with that many men for money in one day, and I felt battered, scooped out, cried a lot. The whole incident, on that Saturday, just seemed to happen to this passive, timid part of me.

Prostitution. I only know it from my perspective. I simply didn't meet any others when I was selling myself. A few times, I saw others near the base. Scarred, or with abrasions on their bodies, hard faces, thin, sick-looking. It terrified me because I was afraid that's what I would become.

Gerry didn't come back—maybe they shipped him someplace else—I don't know.

I had calling cards. I was young and cute with long caramel-blonde hippie hair to below my butt, and I had a good body (voluptuous). Not pretty, but cute. And wholesome. The men couldn't believe I was a whore. I was too 'sweet' for that.

The drunken male animal was really difficult to get used to. For soldiers, drinking and buying a whore go together. Some men are rougher and meaner when drunk (not all, though). I learned a lot about how to handle men when faced with all these drunken young maniacs.

Overall, I just independently figured out whoring in my own fashion and thankfully never was threatened by some pimp-slime trying to get at me (although if I'd stayed in longer, one would probably have gotten hold of me). After I left the trade, I didn't seek out other ex-prostitutes to talk to, in therapy groups, because I just didn't want to hear their pain. I was having a hard enough time living with my own. Also, I'm not sure I really care if I fit some prostitute 'norm' or not.

I didn't even know the jargon of the trade. I still don't. I didn't call them 'johns.' I called them 'customers.'

When I do read about other prostitutes saying things like "I got paid to let men rape me," it hits hard. Practically every act of intercourse when I sold myself felt like rape. I was stiff, resistant, had to use lots of lube. I pretended warmth and I smiled a lot and learned how to make the men feel hot and manly and I was sweet and cute and wholesome. I didn't let them see how much I hated it. My purpose was to give them a good time and get money, as much as I could, out of them. It was not 10-minutes, that's it buddy, get out, and zip up. I made sure most of the encounters were like dates—dinner, etc. I cultivated 'regulars.' It was friendly. I was really lucky. Some Sex Guardian Angel watched over me, so I was not brutalized—usually.

One anal rape. I never did that kind of sex and most men did not ask for it—back then, over thirty years ago. I think the heavy emphasis on it in porn has caused a vogue. I said no and he forced me anyway. I didn't struggle much because I didn't want to get all torn up. As it was, it really tore me anyway. I remember bleeding and feeling ripped to pieces with the pain. I remember it took a long time to recover. It traumatized me so much that I was at the can't-leave-the-house-stage again. Finally, some of my regulars managed to reach me by phone (I wasn't answering it either). Gerry's friends stayed my regulars the whole time I was in prostitution, and they came over and comforted me. I was not just a little upset. I was ready to never go with another man ever again.

A few days later, my two faithfuls, Gerry's friends, called and said they'd taken care of it—he wouldn't bother me anymore—now would I please get back to work.

You see, the men knew each other. It was convenient since if one soldier hurt me, the others knew about it. I don't think protectiveness really motivated them, though. I just think they wanted me functioning and available for sex.

I only had one more violent incident. A man I didn't want to go with forced me. He got me alone and said he'd break my arm so bad I'd never use it again if I didn't take my clothes off. When I was naked, he took out his lighter and threatened to burn my nipples. I cried and begged and did exactly what he wanted. The sex was pretty rough. Then he put some money on the table and left.

Back to not being able to leave the house again—and the intervention of my two protectors, Gerry's friends. These men were really good to me, even though I was a whore. When I cried through my account of this miserable fearful nipple-burning awfulness, they seemed pretty disgusted that any man would do that. The same thing happened as with the anal-rape man. A few days later they called me and said the nipple-burner wouldn't bother me anymore.

Most of the men who bought me were pretty nice to me (the few that weren't are still the stuff of my sex nightmares). Gerry's friends, particularly, never treated me rough or crude and when I was with them it was comfortable, and I felt safe.

When one of them asked if he was hurting me during sex, I felt really touched, and cried. Here I was a whore, and this man was being so considerate. Mostly, though, I didn't cry. Men want an easy time of it with a whore—no big emotions, no upset.

But I hated the sex—although I pretended like crazy that I liked it, that it felt good. It wasn't too hard: the noises women make during sex—our moans and squeals-- these just come naturally when a man is inside me. It is pretty startling, being invaded in that area. I don't think men can tell whether the moans and squeals mean pleasure or pain for us. And just saying something like "you feel good" or "you feel big," when they ask if everything's going okay—something that simple will please them.

When you whore, you smile all the time and you please the men you go with. It is what is expected and what they pay you for. It is stupid to displease them. They could hurt you if they don't get their money's worth. The nicer you are to them, the less chance there is you will get hurt. You make them feel good about themselves. You make them feel manly and sexy.

I felt the difference between 'prostitution sex' and 'real sex.' I'd had good sex before all this rape/prostitution stuff hit. The kind where you melt under the man, in warmth, are so receptive to him, your whole body wants him. Prostitution sex was stiff and cold for me by comparison. My regulars didn't disgust me but the few times I went with sleazeguys, the repulsion of sex with strangers was powerful. Like throw-up powerful.

For one, you have to get used to a lot of different body odors. When you live with one man, your body odors mingle, become familiar. With all these different men, there's different groinsweat, armpit sweat. And men sweat. Bigger ones sweat even more. Most shower before going out to buy a woman but, still, men sweat.

Your body has to adjust to a lot of different penis sizes and shapes. Mine never did. I have a tender vagina and I tear easily. You also have to adjust to the different ways different men mount, angle themselves, keep their weight off you, or don't, as the case may be. With one familiar lover, he becomes known territory, and he learns how not to hurt your body. With a lot of different men on top of you, a twilight zone of sexual strangeness reigns.

Men are a lot bigger. This seems obvious. The bigness of the male. But when you have to lay down under a lot of them, you can feel bruised and crushed and pummeled. After a busy weekend, my whole body would be sore, not just my vagina.

I remember feeling sorry for myself when a nice, good-looking guy with polite manners would use me. It's like he came from a 'normal' world with 'normal' girls out there, and he was visiting my sad, dirty whore world for a few minutes, as he fucked me. And then he would leave my world, maybe feeling a little sorry for me, and I couldn't follow him into his world. I could never be his girlfriend because I was a whore. Forever.

I remember a lot of that time in fragments. Why some incidents stand out and others don't is a mystery. For example, one afternoon I had an appointment with a soldier I hadn't been with before. As much as possible, I saw men through them being 'vetted' by my other customers. As on all military bases, there was a high turnover of troops, so, despite regulars, I would see a lot of new men all the time as well.

He arrived. Nothing repulsive or too frightening about him—except that he was a guy and big and that's always scary when you've never been with a man before. With a new guy, I always made him take me somewhere—dinner, lunch, to listen to some music, something so we could get to know each other before the sex and I could feel more comfortable with the paid 'intimacy.' I tried to simulate 'dates' with these encounters. And to make it friendly. With the regulars, I would have sex with them as soon as they got in the door if they wanted—they usually did—they were pretty horny by the time they got to me, usually being stationed away from girlfriends, or sometimes even wives, and not having the chance to maybe take up with a girl near the base. I was their source for sex in place of dating, courting, etc.

I didn't charge by the hour—I gave them a flat rate for companionship and that meant sex more than once if they wanted it—which they always did, being young guys. I charged them a lot and didn't want it to be like a come in, unzip, fuck and leave thing. Too cold and I might get hurt more if I didn't 'humanize' them by them getting to know me. I spent time with them, and a 'date' could run several hours, depending if we went out to dinner, or took a walk, or watched sports on TV together, or whatever we did between the sex.

This guy had just been called on duty unexpectedly and only had a few minutes and he apologized and said he knew I didn't work that way and he had planned on taking me somewhere and we'd talk and get to know each other—but he had to get back and could I make an exception this time and he'd pay me the full amount and he was about to go nuts and blow his pecker or something like that and damn did he need to get laid. Like right now, this minute. He was cute and funny and nervous about it, and not at all threatening or mean, so I joked with him and said okay "instant sex, just this one time." So we got naked and had sex, quickly, he was pretty eager—a short hard needy fuck on his part. He only stayed a few minutes after that, to catch his breath, but I remember that he put his arms around me and kissed me on the cheek, while we were still in bed, after the fuck, and said, "Thanks." It was a nice thanks. Polite.

I didn't charge him much for that short time and told him to come back when he wanted a fuller job and more fuck and that I thought he was sweet.

All of this 'niceness' garnered me a regular who ended up treating me really well.

I don't want to sugarcoat that time in my life. A lot of the men were decent, like this one. Others were crude drunk idiots. I tried to avoid them—and I mostly could since I was not being pimped or held in a bar where I had to sell drinks and fuck to pay off some imaginary slave-debt to my 'owners.'

Overall, I think I was a dirty joke for many of the men and that attitude hurts to this day. I am very timid. Not at all armored against the crude rough drunk maleness in the world. I read a sad, sad account of a poor trafficked girl in Bosnia, in one of the bars/brothels that sprang up so that all the occupying 'peacekeepers' and NATO forces and American and Dutch and German soldiers could get their fuck and have fun on the destitute bodies of enslaved girls. This poor trafficked girl was plump, so her owners made her get up and strip so the men could jeer at her and have fun getting drunk and acting like cruel barbarians. (This sad miserable story comes from a book called *The Natashas* by Victor Malarek.)

I would not survive one night of that treatment. Just imagine the death of her spirit—after having to do that night after night. Get naked in front of an audience of drunk, jeering soldiers. And 'peacekeepers' having 'fun.' A big question I ask all through this book is why should any girl be treated like this? It is a 'norm,' this subjugation and humiliation of our soft tender feminine selves.

Did the men laugh even more when her face showed her pain and humiliation?

One of my male friends says I am a 'tough cookie' because I sound so strong when I write. I am not at all a tough cookie. The man with the cigarette lighter haunts me to this day. I have to cover my eyes and cringe when I think about him. I'd probably be a trembling, frightened, huddled, miserable creature forever if I'd been forced to strip and be jeered at by soldiers and NATO forces and crude military contractors and peacekeepers and all the other rough rapists who turned Bosnia into a brothel for their 'fun.'

I think the main reason I didn't get hurt more as a prostitute was that I didn't stay in it that long. Getting beat up, drinking, using, the whole picture would have hit me eventually if I'd stayed in. It seems to be part of prostitution world-wide, these things. (I almost hope they gave that poor girl in Bosnia drugs to help her through her humiliation and pain. How coercive and miserable most prostitution is can be seen in how girls have to be kept drugged to bear it.)

My connection with military prostitution has been more extensive than just selling myself to soldiers. When I was in my early twenties, my first lover, Vic, was ex-military. In his early forties, he was that huge, towering, hard kind of male that draws me, inexorably. He had the requisite granite-shelved triceps, rose a steep 6'5" above me, and had a roughish face with an appealingly warm smile. My huge blonde Viking. We met one rainy Friday night at a bus stop (his car was being fixed) and by Saturday night, I'd had my first lovemaking experience.

Vic had been stationed in Korea during the 1950's where he had used prostitutes. So what else is new in the world of male lust? All of the men bought bodies regularly, he said. It's what soldiers do.

Most of my boyfriends have been military. They buy bodies. It's what men do.

Vic was before the 'Suzie' Vietnam story that upset me so badly.

He was a good man. Kind, gentle (with as big as he was, he had to be or no woman would survive him). With Vic, I was glad he was buying the Korean girls, not meaner men. Yet the things he said were upsetting. Like that the girls were terrified of the American soldiers because of how big they are. That you could see they hated what they were doing. That some of them looked like they'd been hit by a truck and couldn't figure out why they were having to have sex with all these big soldiers.

Another soldier boyfriend I once had was not quite so sensitive. He said to me, "Korean girls don't care who they have sex with. They'd just as soon fuck as chew gum. That's why so many of them are whores."

Never mind that most were procured, seasoned, beaten, collectively raped to break them in, pimped, sold for the profit of others, the whole typical picture of prostitution. For him, they were simply whores who didn't care who went between their legs. His assumption, in a culture that prizes virginity to a ridiculous degree, is laughable. I read recently of a 40-year-old Korean woman, who lost her virginity to her bicycle seat, having her hymen resewn so she could feel 'pure' again.

I lived on a military base in Japan during my high school years, in the 1960's, and I was aware, every day, that, outside the gate, exploited Japanese girls were being forced to service our soldiers. It was as if I led a double life—the virginal, innocent, protected Caucasian girl that was me went to class, and the movies, and the snack bar, and talked with GI's who flirted with her. Then there was another body that was always feeling brutalized, somehow, because those girls outside the gate were being raped by our soldiers all the time: any form of enforced prostitution is the most terrible form of rape, since a girl is violated over and over again. At that time, in Japan, the poorest and most vulnerable of girls were the ones forced into the brothels, and held there, in debt bondage.

It also used to puzzle me, when I sat in the snack bar with the GI's, how they could be polite to me, and then go out and use one of those small, miserably hurting prostitute bodies. It puzzled me, how use by just one big American soldier didn't kill one of those fragile creatures, let alone violation by the thousands the poor girls were forced to service. And it still puzzles me how the exploitation of vulnerable women abroad, by our soldiers, is supposed to protect my freedom as an American woman at home.

I haven't been able to ask Asian women how they bear it physically. But my own experiences have made me incredibly curious as to how these tiny Asian prostitutes withstand intercourse with Caucasian males. I am a medium-sized Caucasian female (5'4", 125 pounds when I worked as a whore), and the rigors of intercourse as a prostitute practically killed me. It is very damaging to the body. I had constant tears. I bled. I was miserably sore everywhere, not just in the vaginal area. (My womb hurt all the time.)

Some of the Asian girls don't survive. In Thailand, girls sometimes bleed to death after encounters with American sailors, or so one sailor told me he had heard. Maybe he made this up, to shock me. I hope it's not true.

Given my tender, tearable vagina, it's no wonder I felt most of 'prostitution sex' as rape. The overuse of my body broke me down as much as the psychological harshness of being a whore, being a 'dirty' outcast. The few nice men I went with could not make up for the overall hardness of selling sex.

My own experiences have made me permanently terrified of assembly-line sex. Irrational as it is, I fear that I will be put in a 'comfort station' and used until I die, like all the poor comfort girls of history have done for centuries. Raped fifty times a day, insides torn to pieces, mind gone, spirit destroyed. It is still happening to comfort girls all over the world. Some of my recent reading has filled me with horror as to how the Russian mafia breaks Eastern European girls—a different man let in every fifteen minutes until she is docile and dead enough to never resist again. This is the norm for the broken, trafficked 'comfort girls' of the world—the same as it was for the Korean ones so long ago.

I write about assembly-line sex all the time because I am so terrified of it, and I don't know how else to get rid of the fear. I was only raped about fifteen times in a row for one day (this was my prelude to prostitution) and this almost killed me. A second day and I would have been dead. I would be dead right now if I had been broken like the Russian and Ukrainian and Moldavian girls are by the Russian mafia. Constant rape every day, starvation, burns to their bodies, the deep humiliation of being fucked in public, being allowed no dignity. There would be no me to write this book after one day of that treatment.

I really don't think I have suffered that much. I just sound really dramatic and intense in my writings—to make my point and move people. It must be working since all the articles I have published on the internet (collected in part two of this book) have garnered me a lot of e-mails—including professional people and a whole cadre of internet buddies.

To return to my excessive timidness and fear, I think I was born this way and even if harsh sexual things had not happened to me, I would still be this way. All my life, I have felt phantom rape pain between my legs because I am always aware of the ripped-apart vaginas of all the women and girls who have been sexually savaged over the centuries. And the ones who are suffering right now.

I have a terrible fear of bleeding to death between my legs. It amounts to an obsession. After lovemaking (not 'prostitution sex,' but the real kind with men who don't pay) I will sometimes go into the bathroom and check with a mirror to make sure I am not bleeding to death. I think this obsession is partly a legacy of the time in prostitution and how hard it was on my body,

I was in prostitution about three years and during that time I thought I would die in it. I saw no life beyond it. After being raped thousands of times by strangers, how could I go work at a Starbucks, go back to school, or be 'normal' ever again. I have never been 'normal' again. I can't sit down and eat an English muffin with jam, or take a dog for a walk, because I live in a whore body. A body that is a rape dump. These are some of the dark thoughts that circle in my mind when I feel that phantom rape pain.

How did I get out of prostitution? It was Gerry. He came back.

Toward the end of my time in it, I had more and more customers due to not really caring much about what happened to me. I was really wearing down, like a mechanism losing its last bit of energy. From that wholesome, sweet girl I had become something numb and used looking. During my last couple of months, I seemed to have a lot of customers. I'd go with maybe a dozen or so different men over a weekend and end up having sex twenty or thirty times since they all wanted to go more than once.

It was too much. Way too much. There wasn't hardly anything left of me to fuck with anymore. I think permanent insanity was just over the next cliff.

Gerry came back, came over, saw me, and was shocked. He said I looked hard and dead. Then he called his friends over, the ones he passed me on to, and they got in a big argument, and he was shouting at them about why didn't they take care of me better…I was in the bedroom at the time, where he'd put me, and I could hear them through the door.

I think he felt guilty. He had a good heart and I think he was shaken by seeing this worn-down me, so different from the shy girl who was just learning to prostitute herself when I first went with him. He'd passed me on to others--and look what happened.

Gerry helped me out of it. He was stationed at the base again, and he was with me all the time, to make sure I didn't slide back in. Prostitution is this pit that sucks you back in, without you even noticing.

I was off-limits to everyone but him and his two friends. I healed some physically. I slowly came out of complete numbness into partial numbness.

I am convinced Gerry saved my life. Even another year or two of prostitution and I wouldn't have made it. There would have been nothing left to 'save.'

I don't feel like writing about this too much more right now. I don't at all feel I am finding the words that express the reality of what I experienced. It's like when I try to talk about it—my throat tightens up, as if there is a block in there, stopping me. Usually I write elegantly, but now I sound awkward and clumsy. I have only stayed on the surface and maybe in future I can bear to go into more details. Just putting this chapter down has been incredibly painful. And I have much more book to go.

Even though, after several decades, I'm finally finding the courage to speak about all this, it is still incredibly frightening and painful and difficult.

Rape goes deep. Damage to that part of the body is far reaching. It has repercussions everywhere. No matter all I've done—travel, acquire college degrees, write, live, have lovers—there's a deep core of fear in me that never entirely goes away. It's the fear that it will happen again. Now, it's even more frightening because rape/prostitution can be a death sentence. It could come packaged with AIDS.

Even contact with 'civilized' men sometimes still terrifies me because I know that under certain circumstances, like war, those 'civilized' men are perfectly capable of rape, and of using women forced into prostitution due to wartime starvation, coercion, etc.

All sorts of aftermaths hit me all the time as a result of that time in prostitution. I panic at certain odd moments because I realize I am too old to sell myself anymore. No one will buy me, what I if I become homeless, what do I fall back on if no one thinks my body is worth purchasing?

I've always been sexually submissive. Prostitution made me more so. I love the tender side of sex but also respond strongly to the rough hard overwhelming strength of men that makes me feel helpless. I am always a confused mess when it comes to my own sexuality.

I am hyper-aware that I will probably never find my own sexuality. That precious side of me has been manipulated and twisted and ruined by condemnatory philosophies of 'whores' and 'good girls' and by the suffocating repressions that have destroyed female sexuality—probably for all time.

A huge positive that has come out of all this is that, after decades of silence, I am writing articles and books—lots of them--about sexual suffering, especially that caused by our military. I write about the girls currently being trafficked into brothels in Iraq for our men; about the ones trafficked into sexual slavery around our bases in Korea. Girls beaten, burned with cigarettes, girls broken beyond suffering and healing, and bought by our soldiers. And I have written novels, one called *Tender Bodies and Whore Stories*, a satiric fantasy set in KokoBang, military brothel capital of the world. I cannot stop writing. I am so enormously creative with all these books pouring out of me that I feel volcanic—and beautiful and powerful and fierce—at least for the moments when I write.

I also need to make it clear that I don't just dump on American soldiers. Sadly, within the spectrum that is military violence, they are by far not the worse. Other armies are even more savage. But they're my guys, the ones I know. That's why I want them to straighten up their act, never rape—and be nice to whores!

After all, it was a soldier, Gerry, who helped me. It took months, after he came back and got me out of prostitution, but I finally re-accepted myself enough to not feel the urge to go sell my body every weekend to a dozen or so men on base.

He was there for a year tour of duty. He kept tabs on me the whole time, to make sure I didn't go with anyone except him and his two buddies. When we had sex, he was more considerate and gentle than he had been when I first starting selling myself to him. I think he was sorry about all the damage and misery I went through.

His two friends had sex with me a few times a month—they had always been nice to me, and now were even nicer, in a slightly apologetic way, for letting my time in prostitution get so 'out of hand,' as Gerry put it.

I was in love with Gerry, but he kept me at a distance—no leaving of his wife, no me in his life forever.

When they shipped him out, he kept in touch with me to make sure I was not going to go back into prostitution. I saw his two friends for a few months after he left, and then they were stationed elsewhere as well.

Gerry called or wrote me for several years, and said he was there if I needed him.

After all my men were gone, I retreated into my apartment and read Tarzan books. It's a good thing that Edgar Rice Burroughs wrote so much. I couldn't face the world at all. Even TV was mostly painful, except for an old movie like *The Canterville Ghost*.

After Tarzan, there was the Mars series. And all of Agatha Christie again.

I'd saved from my time in prostitution and my needs were small—I have never lived fancy so I was able to stay in my cave for quite a while before the money ran out. I only left to go to the store for food, and even that was incredibly difficult. It was like there was a brick wall ten-feet thick at the threshold of the door that I could not push through. I would take the trash out at midnight or in the wee hours of the morning and breathe some gulps of air, to take in the outdoors. During the day, I took extreme pleasure in small things, like listening to the birds in the woods around my apartment, but never could go out to visit them without fear.

I still hate to leave enclosed spaces. I have a hard time facing the world. Life is frightening. People are frightening. They might find out I am a whore and scorn me. I have a lot of problems just making it through the day. I think my excessive timidness is a big reason. As I said, even without a speck of mistreatment in my life, I think I am too soft and feminine and naturally frightened to face the violent hard world that is this planet we live on.

I have one more story to tell you. One cold windy winter afternoon, back in the sixties, I was wandering around Tokyo, having taken the train in from the base, as I did every other weekend or so.

I was in the Shinjuku area, which, at that time, I think was near one of the red-light districts. I saw a couple of Japanese street prostitutes soliciting some American soldiers, all of them in a corner, discreetly, modestly, between two buildings, while they discussed their transaction.

The two girls smiled hopefully up at the men; the two men smiled hopefully down at the girls. From a distance, the meeting looked friendly. Nothing mean, or crude, or rough, which is what scares me most about encounters between the oppressor and the subjugated—the power the strong have over the helpless.

Both girls were dressed in that kind of tawdry way that a lot of Japanese girls, adopting Western styles in the 60's, looked, prostitutes or not. I remember both wore short, baggy skirts, over these kind of funny, pointed shoes. One's skirt was pink, topped by an orange blouse (a color pairing strange to Western eyes, but popular among the Japanese) and both were in these ugly, shabby-looking coats, open to the cold. What gave them away as prostitutes, other than talking to GI's, something 'decent' Japanese girls were very wary of at this period, was their heavy make-up—few young girls there in the sixties wore much make-up (although they do now, of course). My first reaction was pity for how 'funny' they were dressed, looking ill-at-ease, patched together in their cheap, Western garb.

But the detail I noticed most was their legs. Short, stocky—a build common to a lot of Japanese women—their small, bare legs looked blue and red and pale from the cold. Tokyo can be freezing in winter because a lot of chill winds blow through it. The two girls were also huddled in on themselves, shivering a little, as they talked to the GI's.

That moment, the sadness of their cold little legs, the encounter between two sexes—one weak and helpless, the other strong, the encounter between two different ways of being—he who buys and she who is bought—no matter how kind the buying—has stayed with me, in a haunting way.

Frequently, when the cold winter wind hits me, no matter where I am in the world, that moment hits me again, as if I were watching it, right then and there. I'm afraid, at that moment. Alone, and unprotected. And I relive the kind of sad pity I felt, back then, that afternoon in Tokyo—and the gratitude that I didn't have to sell myself on a street corner, in the cold. A deeper chill than the slicing wind goes through me, when that moment hits me full force. I wonder at the terrible mystery that made those two girls shabby little street prostitutes, and at the mystery that helped me escape from that sadness.

2
Yuki

I lived in Japan in the 1960's and went to high school there, on the American military base where my father was stationed. My first boyfriend was Japanese, a young man named Yuki, a translator. When I was fourteen (just about to turn fifteen), I saw him for the first time on a muggy summer day, in the shallow end of the base pool, playing with some kids, throwing a bright pink-and-orange plastic ball around with them. He smiled at me, friendly, curious.

He looked older, like maybe in his twenties, and I noticed he seemed to have an affinity with the kids as he joked with them, and rough-housed with the boys.

All summer, I was designated afternoon babysitter for Melissa, age four, a neighbor's girl—her parents paid me twenty dollars a week to take her swimming. She was a shy little thing and we hit it off well—since I felt like a fourteen year-old-version of her. One afternoon, Yuki came up, dripping with water from a show-off dive, and offered to teach her to swim, in pretty good English, a little thick in the accent on certain words but overall presentable, and way better than my barely existent Japanese. I guess he felt sorry for the poor thing, hovering in the shallow end, closing her eyes when the bolder kids, who could swim, splashed her. I couldn't swim either, and being as timid as she was, I was no help at all.

I remember that he patiently kept at it, every day, and how small and flyaway my tiny blonde charge looked as he held her in the water, tummy downward, his brown hands around her waist, letting her get used to stroking and kicking, until she felt secure enough, and he let her go. She learned to splash and dive with the rougher lot, and float on her back, and was soon looking like a skinny little fish, at home in the water.

Since I took care of her a lot, she was practically like my own child, and I guarded her with a fierce and deep tenderness. She was really my first love in this world, disregarding two hamsters, brown and white, that I had at age eight which my parents made me get rid of because "they smelled." I still can feel their warm, furry bodies, and see their tiny hands as they held peanuts in them. Anything small, soft, and helpless—hamsters, my fine-boned little charge—and my heart feels sore, because of how vulnerable they are, in this hard world. So, Yuki's gesture, teaching Melissa to swim, touched me.

Next, it was my turn. On breaks from his translating, he had passes to use the base pool. Every afternoon, he sat down on the grass, beside the lawn chair I was in. After a bit of getting to know each other, he asked me why I didn't go in the water much. He'd just see me, in the shallow end, along with the little kids. I told him I couldn't swim and he offered to teach me.

I really didn't want him to. I didn't want to feel like a dunce. After a bit of pressure--he really wanted to teach me to swim, it would be his pleasure to teach me, please, let me teach you—he let the subject drop when he saw how stubborn I was.

A few days later, there was an evening party at the pool. Typical little Japanese paper lanterns, in pink and orange and gold and blue dotted the area, and a typical American buffet—potato salad, fried chicken, etc. was laid out. Yuki came and sought me out, and sat at my feet beside the lawn chair—the way he did in the afternoons—this time watching me eat my fried chicken. (Later in life, I became a vegetarian, but I was still in my carnivore days back then.)

It was kind of a young person's party, with the other teens bobbing around to sixties rock songs, the girls in bikinis, revealing back then, but modest by the string- bikini, Rio-de-Janeiro, Victoria's-Secret standards of today. Back then, we thought the Bikini Beach movies were hot and that Sandra Dee was kind of wild. There was a goodly sprinkling of adults around, but mostly it was kids letting off summer steam.

Toward the end of the evening, when the pool crowd was thinning out, Yuki asked me if I had digested my chicken enough for him to give me a swimming lesson. Actually, the asking was suggestive. He came up behind my chair, put his hands on my bare shoulders, and leaned down so that his lips were close to my ear. He said that we could just pretend he was giving me a swimming lesson because what he really wanted to do was touch me.

Now, I was very shy, a social retard, and extremely afraid of men due to growing up with a brutal father in a household governed by an iron regime and harsh atmosphere. (My father had a kind side, but he was often violent, and being hit a lot, as I grew up, and shouted at, left me with a deep fear of anything male that I have had to struggle with all my life. End of mini-bio. More elsewhere on this.)

Yuki's hands on my bare shoulders gave me that proverbial shiver that I can't figure out how to express, except in this clichéd way. Strong hands, warm, on this hot, humid night, not just laying on my shoulders, but actually caressing them a little, just enough for me to feel his fingertips pressing into me.

I was too shy to say anything to this come on. He moved around to the front of me and held out his hand. When I stood up, he helped me slip off my blue terrycloth cover-up, and led me into the water.

We hung around in the four- to five-foot area, and I scooched down a little, so the water would cover my breasts. Even though I was in a one-piece, blue, cut modesty at the hip area, and no bellybutton visible, it still showed off my bosom, which was pretty well-developed, even at age fourteen (just about to be fifteen). I definitely blossomed early. That bosom was one reason I didn't go in the water much, just hung around in my lawn chair, with my terrycloth cover-up on, watching out for my little girl charge in the pool.

He took my hands and made me stand up in the water, so that he could see more of me.

We talked. A lot. This long conversation was the first intimate one I'd ever had with a boy (man), and something about being secluded, together, in the water, made me want to open up to him. It started with him telling me that everyday when I sat at the pool, all huddled into my terrycloth, he wished I would stand up, and take it off, so he could see more of me. Also, he wanted to see me happier. You look so afraid all the time, sitting by the pool, with that towel on your lap, he said to me. (I'm just going to recount, third hand, what he said, rather than try to capture his brand of English too much in dialogue. As I've said, it was presentable, but with certain Japaneseisms that I don't quite know how to record.)

It was true. In addition to the terrycloth that sheltered my bosom, I tried to hide my legs with a towel. He told me my legs were beautiful (they were pretty great legs back then, even though I didn't know it). He told me that I was beautiful and that whenever I finally crept into the water (trying all the while to hide myself), he loved to look at me.

Back then, it was impossible for me to see my teenage self, shy and fearful and cringing to a ridiculous degree, with any kind of objectivity. From my point of view, I was an ugly ducking (one of my favorite fairy tales when I was a tiny kid), all heavy and clumsy, wearing glasses, hair all untidy, in my unfashionable swimsuit—practically the only girl there that night not in a Beach Blanket Bingo bikini. In truth, I was not heavy at all, about a hundred and twenty pounds, and my hair was long and caramel colored and I had a cute, elfin face and 'arresting' blue-grey eyes (comments from future boyfriends who also helped me appreciate myself). Yes, my glasses were nerdy, and I didn't dress well, but the rest of me, the essentials, would pass muster, anywhere, for nubile, female desirability. I just didn't know it yet.

That time in the water, with Yuki, was a revelation, not to mention a revolution, a breakthrough, an earthquake (not quite on the scale of those that regularly hit Tokyo, but almost). A man telling me I was beautiful.

I need to stress that he was a man, not a boy, fully ten years older than I was I discovered that night. My fourteen-year-old self and his twenty-five-year-old self in the water, little blue-green waves swishing around us, he touching me, sometimes putting his hands around my waist, sometimes letting a hand wander, down to my thigh, or up, to rub my shoulder, or splash me a little—this was some kind of zone, wet, scary, yet reassuring, that I'd never been in before. Being intimate with a man, not being too terrified. It was the first time anyone had touched me, almost boyfriend-girlfriend stuff, someone courting me, coming on to me. No American boy had ever shown any interest in me at all.

I was flattered, afraid, dizzy with this first time.

Pool lights a few feet away, underwater, lit us up enough to see each other, along with the lanterns swinging in the warm breeze. Beatles music was playing in the background during most of our conversation. I was about five feet three (soon to be five feet four), he somewhat taller, maybe five eight. Oddly enough, he made me feel delicate, so close up to him, just a few inches between us, as we talked, even though he was not huge, the way linebacker-size Caucasian guys are. He weighed about 180 pounds and he had that kind of stocky build common to a lot of Japanese men, broad shoulders and very muscled arms (from a lot of swimming I later discovered), short, thick legs, big broad feet, thick toes. His hands were big too, flat and broad, with thick fingers. I was in a state of low-key arousal the whole time he was touching me in the pool, a sort of humming mild ecstasy all over my skin, every place his hands went. In the air, on my shoulders, his fingers had felt warm, big, delicious. In the water, they felt cool and delicious.

Then he gave me my first swimming lesson.

It took a while, but I was finally able to unstick my feet from the bottom of the pool enough, and trust my body enough, to do a rudimentary dogpaddle. He was all complimentary, encouraging, big smile, kind eyes, like a dad proud of his daughter for some little accomplishment.

Second lesson, float on my back. No way. Not only was I highly doubtful, I was adamant. Stuck my toes in—to the concrete floor of the pool.

He didn't bully or push, but, at some point, I was aware that he was holding me under my waist as I lay flat on the water, face up, trying to figure out how to float on my back and not drown. He'd been able to pry me away from the side (and bottom) of the pool enough to get me this far.

Trust and safety and feeling protected—all of this I must have felt because eventually I let him take his hand away—and I floated. He pushed and pulled me carefully around, sliding me over the silken water, holding one of my hands, and I felt like a privileged angel on the air, all gravity gone for the first time in my life.

Finally, I moved the wrong way, and went under, and came up, sputtering, clinging to his shoulder. Despite the water up my nose, it felt good, holding on to him, my arm around his neck. He picked me up, underwater, one arm under my knees, the other around my back, and walked with me over to the side of the pool.

Then he did that quick male thing—rapid leap from water to pool side, and holding his hand out to me, he helped me out. We dressed, and he walked me home. No goodnight kiss, but he did touch my forehead with the back of two fingertips before he left me for the night.

That time in the pool with him was a kind of emotional dividing line in my life. From feeling dumpy, too ugly for anyone to touch, hopelessly shy and frightened of everything male, I now felt touched, held, floating in this sensuous water, wonderful hands on me. Joy was possible. My homelife was pretty heavy, oppressive, thick unhappiness hanging in the air all the time. I jumped around like a startled fawn most days, afraid of being hit or yelled at. Until that time in the pool with Yuki, I don't think that I knew happiness was possible since I had no comparison. Reading, luxuriating in how much I loved other small helpless things, these were my big joys until that night in the water.

Fortunately, most of the time my parents ignored me, so, despite a rough home-life, I had a lot of freedom. To see Yuki—since my parents almost never asked me where I was going or where I had been--I didn't even have to make up tales.

Nevertheless, Yuki and I had to be careful. The prejudice against us was enormous. He limited the time he spent at my feet, on the grass, by the pool. We chatted only a few minutes here and there, so as not to give the impression of being close. Still, people noticed. Back in the sixties, the army was a peculiar fraternity of men who married women from all over the world—Japan, Korea, Australia, Europe, and had children with them, and took them to live on bases with them—yet strong disapproval against interracial mixing still governed a lot of attitudes. (It is probably still the same today.) It was oddly contradictory: the soldier next door to you in the housing area might have a Japanese wife, and you might go to school with his kids, but, still, these women were really only fit to be maids, and perform other menial tasks; and, of course, that huge population of small people, with dark hair, and slanted eyes, outside the gates, were nothing like us. Definitely different—and inferior, of course.

So, on base, we tried to stay as cool and distant as possible. Once or twice, we went to the snack bar, had French fries and milkshakes together. Once, we went to the post theatre together. We saw *The Pink Panther*, the original one with David Niven, my first movie with Yuki. Of course, to this day, I associate him with that film, and with Beatles songs, and French fries and chocolate milkshakes (now, rice-milk shakes for me, since I'm off dairy, as well as meat, these days). But that was all we dared, those few outings together, because the disapproving eyes were so strong--we could practically feel the glare. He was afraid he might lose his job, so we didn't try anymore on-base trysts.

Nevertheless, that summer, we found time to be together, in Tokyo, about a forty-minute train ride from the base, without anyone knowing. It was common for kids to take the train into Tokyo, in groups, act like American army brats, adolescent as we all were.

Yuki commuted everyday he worked, from Tokyo, and on off days he would commute, again, meet me at the station near the base (it was still summer and no school), and take me back with him—till I leaned how to navigate the train system on my own—then he met me at the designated stop in Tokyo.

Tokyo didn't offer too much in the way of being alone together time, but it was better than the contemptuous eyes of the base. The city also didn't offer any kind of take leisurely strolls together, holding hands, because, number one, Japanese couples didn't hold hands together back then, even non-interracial ones. (I think they do now, from what I can garner from Asian students studying at universities here in the U.S., but they didn't seem to do much in the way of any kind of public touching back then.) Number two, Tokyo was shoulder-to-shoulder crowds, moving with big-city urgency. It was also architecturally ugly, so picturesque strolls didn't jump out at one. A lot of the old city had been destroyed during the war, and the new Tokyo was a featureless place of huge concrete buildings, with little style, mixed in with older districts, full of mostly small houses, made of thin wooden frames. No soft, romantic stroll down a tree-lined Champs-Elysee, just a big mass of rushing humanity, all small and dark-haired, and looking at me, the *gaijin*, some with curiosity, others with suspicion.

He took me to meet his parents, whom he lived with. The few visits to them were awkward, I not knowing when to bow, or how much, or how low, and when Yuki translated for us, during disjointed conversations, we didn't have much to say to each other. They were neither friendly nor unfriendly toward me, but gave me the distinct impression that I was not particularly welcome. Hints Yuki dropped in conversations definitely made me think that the last thing they wanted for their son was a liaison with an American girl.

Even though they were only in their fifties, the couple looked very old, maybe because of hardships and illness and starvation during the war. His mother always wore the traditional kimono, her hair in a kind of grey-black bun at the back of her head, and his dad looked vaguely Western, and a little shabby.

Now what I would not give to go back, to talk to them, to ask them about the war, to try to understand them. I could have heard, first hand, about the conditions, the terrible poverty, the behavior of our occupying army. But I was simply an innocent, ignorant American high school girl, and all I knew was what stuffy, meaningless history books, written by stuffy, meaningless American historians told me about that time, and very little was included about the suffering of the Japanese people. In that decade, even Hiroshima and Nagasaki were minimized in my classes, almost as if we had never committed one of the great war crimes of all time, and back on base, I always seemed to be reading some clichéd truism about Thomas Jefferson, long before anyone bothered to mention his mulatto mistress and his many children from that union. A narrow, conservative, white-male perspective ruled American history. Still does, largely, for that matter.

Back then, I didn't even know there was any such thing as 'herstory,' since I grew up constantly being told 'his'tory. I didn't even know that one day I would long for a 'herstory,' so I could feel that my womanhood, my femininity, were somehow part of humankind, not just some incidental sidelight, on the margins, of battles and commanders and male names that shaped a destiny totally alien to me. Instinctually, back then, I knew the world story being taught me was fundamentally wrong, had nothing to do with the sufferings or aspirations of my girl body or my girlish mind. But I couldn't have put this into words or concepts when I was only fourteen.

I remember a picture, in one of my history books, of a huge invading mounted army riding into a town, with timid, ragged women peeping out from shadowed doorways, and skinny, ragged children running around the cavalcade, dogs at their feet. What battle, which era, which army, I don't remember, but I do remember wondering that I would like to know about the lives of the street children that were in the wake of the dust kicked up by the horses' hooves. And I wanted to know what happened to the horses, when the army finished with them. Did they find haven in a green pasture, with sunshine? And was anybody going to feed those hungry dogs? And what was going to happen to the shy women in the doorways? But at that time there was no way I could have expressed all this. Not the way I do now. I didn't even know what kind of herstory I was longing for, let alone how to write it.

So, I sat, awkward, in Yuki's house, before his parents, not knowing what I had missed.

Tokyo proved to be a place where we could be alone, in some sense. For one, we went to a lot of movies, where we could hold hands, although not too much else in the way of physical contact was possible. Couples in theatres didn't 'neck,' the way kids back in the states did. Even my hand in his was a bit risqué. And, of course, on the street, strolling hand-in-hand just wasn't done back then in Japanese society, let alone putting our arms around each other.

Those movies are still dear to me, sharp in my memory, my hand in his, because I saw them with him. In addition to the first *Pink Panther*, we saw all the fluff-and-tripe of that day—*The Great Race*, *Mary Poppins*, *Hatari*, *55 Days at Peking*, *Lawrence of Arabia*, *Ryan's Daughter* (a romantic killer), all the Sean Connery Bond flicks, and the Beach Blanket Bikini ones. Diligently, I still rewatch all of these whenever they come on TV, just to feel my hand in his.

A Hard Day's Night maybe remains my totem Yuki movie from that time, because our first touching was done to Beatles songs, floating over the water, and just because we both were Anglophiles. Francophiles, too. Japan was a mélange of pop culture, from both Europe and America, and I remember listening, on a portable radio, to pop rock songs from all over the world with Yuki. Slyvie Vartan, from France, was one of our favorites. We shared the same shiver when we heard her sing *Je le Vois*, a highly sensuous, moaning, raw ballad, that always brings up Yuki warm hands, and how good they felt on my back, rubbing me, as Slyvie rubbed us, with her voice.

Tokyo offered the subway, where we could be all squashed up against each other. Those subways are crowded and back them professional "pushers" packed people in (probably still do). So I could stand, breasts pressed up against him, head near his shoulder, with impunity, although I felt too shy to look at him, when he was experiencing my bosom, so clearly, pressing into him. And I could feel him, pressing into me. I knew an amused, hot look would be in his eyes if I looked up, into them. Before Yuki, any kind of crudeness from men, a hot, sexually raw look at me, at my body, would frighten me. He mixed that natural male crudeness up with his niceness, and taught me, for the first time, to not be so afraid of it.

In Tokyo, we shopped, usually on the Ginza, and ate out at little restaurants where the food was advertised through cute plastic replicas, in the window, even before you went in. Plastic food, in all the colors of the rainbow, shining under lights, and artistically laid out behind glass windows, struck me as some kind of Japanese art form, akin to flower arranging, and the tea ceremony.

As a result of our restaurant jaunts, I probably tried a lot of Japanese dishes, beyond the universally recognized tempura, that I would never have found on my own. Since this was our time together, we lingered over the meals, despite the crowding, the lunch-hour rush tempo of eating all around us. I learned to be calm, and to chew slowly, in the midst of lots of people shoveling noodles rapidly down their throats with chopsticks.

He taught me how to eat with chopsticks. He taught me Japanese phrases and words, although I never did quite make it to carry-on-a-conversation level with him. "Iki-mashoo, little *gaijin*," I can still hear him saying, jokingly, when I would be lingering during a shopping excursion, and he wanted to move on. From my understanding, *gaijin* had some slighting connotations, but he assured me he meant the word affectionately.

Sometimes we went to Pachinko parlors, but I had the impression he felt uncomfortable with me there because it seemed to be a man's venue—I don't remember many other women in them.

All that summer, and all the next year, we met in Tokyo. That summer, it was about once a week, but when my school started, I took the train in every other Saturday or Sunday or so to see him. Sometimes three weeks would pass before I could get in, and I would be all on edge, for his touch, his hand holding mine. ("I Wanna Hold Your Hand" brings him back to me so sharply that I can't listen to it without breaking into a long crying spree.) All on the quiet. All done as sneakily as possible, so that no one on base would know.

That first summer, something special happened, because of Yuki, on my birthday, which I had been bold enough to mention to him, in hopes he would buy me something. He did. We spent it, my fifteen birthday, in Tokyo, and he asked me what I wanted, as we wandered, shopping. I settled on a Japanese comic book with a female superhero, for a souvenir. Then, he took me to a park, and we sat under a tree, drinking cokes, and eating dried squid (kind of the equivalent of a potato chips or crisps snack in Japan—you buy them in little packets, the way you do rice crackers, to eat as you walk) while he read the comic to me.

A Japanese beetle, a species over there about the size of a woman's fist, and shaped like an armored tank, crawled up to us, and Yuki was going to attach him to a string, so I could take him home. This was a common sight, kids with red or blue strings, tied to this big beetle sitting on their shoulders. American kids adopted the habit of keeping these little battletanks, and you'd see their captors at school, dangling the poor things like yo-yo's, or swinging them around on their strings.

I thought it really cruel—I hated to see anything tied up—horse, dog, or beetle—so he let him go, but not without Yuki commenting on how "sensitive" I was. The comment wasn't meant as a criticism. He said that he was sorry that life was so hard on me sometimes because I felt too much sympathy, too much pain for other things. It was a revelation to me that he noticed this because I had known it about myself, deep inside, but never heard anyone put this trait of mine into words before.

Now, here is the special part, and it's going to seem unbearably corny, and adolescent, and like a cliché from a chick flick, but, yes, he did, under that tree, give me my first kiss. Sorry, I can't really manage to unmush or unsentimentalize this moment much. One girl's first kiss just isn't going to be all that different from another's. Very hard to make it original, in fiction, or film, considering how many times it's been done.

He started with the cheek, then moved to the lips. Slow, lingering, the touch of his lips so gentle and featherlight on mine that I didn't pull back at all. He simply let the kiss happen. No aggression, no roughness, nothing to scare me. He let me "come to him," because my lips were asking for more, seeking his, wanting something harder and deeper than just the featherlight. In my memory, that first kiss lasted a long, long time.

After it, everything seemed changed. I felt more intimate with him when we were just walking side by side, or eating out together. We'd kissed, we'd done this highly intimate thing, and I knew it, and he knew it, and this seemed to make every other contact with him, just light hand holding, almost unbearably and pleasurably intimate in a much deeper way.

If you were an American girl wandering around Tokyo in the sixties, stares followed you everywhere. If you were wandering around with a Japanese man, the stares were even harder. It may have been here that I developed my fascination with outsider status, being an exile, a rebel, not fitting in, in my own quiet, mousey way. I may look prim and mousey, but I have the heart of someone who climbs the fences, woman's the barricades, raises a defiant fist in the air, and sacrifices herself to some cause worth believing in.

Yuki didn't mind the stares either. Part of my appeal was that I was an American girl, and he wanted to show me off, no matter how much scorn people hit us with. We were exotic to each other. He with his mysterious Japanese aura, me with my mysterious American aura. Puzzles to each other. Meeting more as man/woman (or girl/man, to be more accurate), our ground for closest communication, than in other ways. Some things physical are universal. His male touch went far beyond any cultural differences or wartime hatreds.

Another way we found alone time was to occasionally take the train out into the country, where we could walk around the outskirts of some town, find trees to shelter us, and kiss and touch. In addition to the dried squid and soysauce-soaked rice crackers, I also remember we would buy, on these country outings, these little fried things on sticks, crispy on the outside, gushy in the inside, from roadside vendors, and stroll along as we munched. And we bought little glass bottles of milk, vanilla and chocolate, when we weren't drinking cokes, or orange soda, another Japanese favorite of that time. I remember the tiny Japanese school kids, in their little dark blue uniforms, with white shirts and blouses, buying orange soda pop, side by side, with Yuki and me.

On rare occasions, we managed some time alone in his parents' apartment. Those few times, in those few precious hours, my sex education took a big leap forward. We went from the handholding and kissing to an erotic venue which I discovered was of major interest to Yuri—my breasts.

The first time we were alone, really alone, inside the walls of his place, where no one could see us, where we felt free to do private things, we did. Here, he led the way, much more firmly than he had in the kissing arena, where he patiently let me explore, figure his lips out for myself. Usually slow and careful-not-to-startle, Yuki had my blouse and my bra off pretty quickly. At least, it seemed quick to me, because we went from kissing to semi-nakedness faster than I was prepared for.

How it happened was this. On the floor, on a mat, in his home, back propped up by pillows behind us, arms around each other, we were kissing. Then, all of a sudden, he went from kissing to reaching down my blouse, and inside my bra. Startling. That first touch of a man's hand on my breast felt like an invasion. A virgin breast and nipple, and then, all of sudden, his hand in that private area, inside my bra. With his left arm around my shoulder, he explored my breast with his right hand, cupping it, then playing with my nipple with his fingertips till it hardened into a tight rosebud knot. The other breast received similar attention.

Then he unbuttoned my blouse, slipped it down my shoulders and pulled it off of me completely. He looked at me, to see if all this was okay, but, after one quick glance at him, I kept my eyes lowered and kind of huddled in on myself. Some deep fearful shyness in me still reigns, to this day, whenever a man undresses me—not because of Yuki, who was careful and considerate, but just because the male, even the gentle male, is frightening to me. By now, I've been undressed multitudinous times, by large numbers of men (not all at once, of course); but even so, I am usually very passive, as he peels off the bra, slides down the panties, a frozen deer caught in the headlights, cringing in on my self. For all that men can be gentle beyond belief, there is some violence in them that I can never completely free myself from. I'm always just a little afraid, no matter how gentle the touch.

The bra wasn't that pretty—just utilitarian, plain white cotton, but it did have a cute little pink bow on it. This was the era before Victoria's Secret took bras to new levels of feminine seductiveness.

He reached behind me to undo that bra, and I put my head on his shoulder. Had I known it, in my innocence, the skill with which he unfastened my bra indicated a man of experience—it's not always easy to undo those little metal clasps. It's the true mark of a man who has undressed a lot of women—one who can handle those tricky little metal devils with boldness and confidence. His fingertips felt warm and fuzzy on my back as he undid me.

I replaced the bra he slipped off me with my hands and my long hair, and it took him a while to teasingly persuade me to bare my breasts to him. Finally, my hair pushed back, he took my hands away, holding my wrists, and had his first full look. It was a long one; he might have gone on staring away, but I pulled my wrists away, and covered myself again.

That afternoon, I basically discovered what my breasts were for. Until then, they had just seemed like two things just hanging there, and I didn't quite know what to do with them. Since I was already big, at fifteen, they weren't 'perky,' but full and womanly. (For about two weeks, when I was twelve, and just budding, my breasts could have qualified as perky. Then they just grew and grew and grew.) Hence, in their fullness, embarrassing. The rest of my body hadn't caught up with them yet. Until that afternoon, I had been ashamed and confused by these full, rounded things, just hanging there. During self-pleasuring sessions, I'd never played with them (the way I do now, realizing their sensitivity to touch), mostly just concentrating on my clitoris, since I had a maidenhead and couldn't pleasure myself inside yet.

Yuki showed me what my breasts were for. I'll never forget the sweet thing he said, before he began playing with them in earnest. "I could spend a lot of time on these." And he did. That afternoon, the first startling sensation of having my nipples kissed—a lot, and in many different ways—led to breast play beyond anything I had ever imagined—since I'd never really thought of them as erotic at all, till Yuri took possession of them. By the end of the afternoon, they were both thoroughly conquered territories.

I learned that there is a connection, what I call the golden triangle, between my breasts and my bellybutton, and beyond. When he kissed and played with my nipples, everything between my bellybutton and that other triangle, below, ached in a deep, hot way.

Yuki told me that most Japanese men are more fixated on genitals than breasts. This is understandable. Since most Japanese women have no breasts at all, there isn't anything to be fixated on. But contact with American women and culture, he said, was causing some men to branch out. Some of Yuki's sex symbols were Marilyn, and the two Janes, Russell and Mansfield

I teased him a lot, about only caring about my breasts and that was why he had courted me. He didn't entirely deny it. Given, I suppose that he could have flirted with any girl at the pool, I felt lucky he picked me, even if it was because of my boobs. But I also realize that many of the American girls would have rejected him, just because he was Japanese, no matter how handsome he was. By Japanese standards, I can't judge him too accurately, but his broad, flat, strong-featured face seemed incredibly handsome to me. And his big, strong hands on me, anywhere, drove me crazy.

Yuki adored my breasts so much--and my pink nipples, fascinating to him, because Japanese women, he said, had brown ones--that he made me think highly of them, too, as objects of desire. Thanks to Yuki, I have never underestimated the erotic power of my breasts.

Our few times alone in that apartment were spent in largely above-the-waist erotic play because he said he didn't trust himself to stop if we went into more intimate territory. I know that his hard, muscular arms and back and his broad shoulders held the same fascination for me that my soft breasts held for him.

I wish I could remember more about the room where I first became "sexualized," that precious place, but all I come away with is that sense of simplicity, uncluttered sparseness, that characterized the few Japanese homes I entered at that time. Maybe the people were still too poor to indulge much in luxury, in just buying things for the sake of buying them, back in the sixties. I know they no longer lived in the desperate poverty of the post-war years, but I also remember how grateful the maid, Yoko, who worked for us on base was when I gave her an old study lamp that I didn't need anymore, because my parents had bought me a new one at the PX. When she practically knocked her head on the floor, with gratitude, letting me know, somehow, in a combination of Japanese and almost unintelligible English, that her school-age daughter would be so happy with it, I felt really sad for her. The maids on base weren't treated with much courtesy—they were just there, invisible women with no needs, pint-sized cleaning machines, in baggy Western clothes, too big for them.

Back to Yuki. He was poor. His family was poor. My main income was from babysitting almost every Friday and Saturday night (when I wasn't off in Tokyo with Yuki), on base, and even that paltry income seemed to be more than he had. I paid most of the time when we ate out, went to our movies, because I wanted to. Yet another missed opportunity—to talk to him more about the lives of everyday Japanese people, about their privations and difficulties.

What did we talk about? It's hard to remember, so many years ago, forty years back, but I know we talked about food, and the movies we saw, and the books I was reading (I read all the time; I was a reading maniac). And we talked about sex, and life, and being American and being Japanese—we never seemed to run out of things to say. In fact, we never seemed to have enough time to say everything. It makes me wonder about all these artificial cultural barriers we create between humans. Barriers that lead us to regard someone as a lesser being because he has slanted eyes. Forty years ago, a twenty-five-year-old Japanese man and a fifteen-year-old American girl wandered around the streets of Tokyo, communicating as if they were telepathic soulmates.

One weekend that winter, we actually managed to spend time with each other, in a house on base, private, just us, body to body, exploring. That special gift of a weekend came about because Melissa's parents wanted to go off together—to northern Japan, to Yokohama, to Kyoto, I forget where—for a second honeymoon—and they trusted me enough to take care of their precious little girl. (I was flattered.)

Yuki there with me, that weekend--it was bold and risky and I was afraid (so what else is new, timid self), but we talked ourselves into it, and I didn't back out, the Friday the couple were set to leave.

So they could get an early start, the couple had left Melissa with a neighbor lady till I got off school. Late afternoon, I picked her up, and as soon as it was dark, Yuki came. In the backdoor, in hopes of escaping any detection from neighbors.

We had to be careful, about keeping the curtains closed all weekend, about not answering the door, about not feeling as if our breathing could be heard next door.

He was really patient with Melissa, helping to bathe and feed her and keep her entertained with storybooks. He didn't act like she was a bother, like she was something to be tucked in bed, so the grown-ups could get on with their life. Even though the last thing I wanted was to have a baby then, the image of Yuki as a wonderful father definitely gave me some cosy, domestic stirrings that weekend.

Melissa finally tucked in left us on the sofa, in front of the TV, alone and secluded from the rest of the world. Japanese TV back then was a funny hodgepodge of Sumo wrestling, variety shows, and imports from the U.S. That night *Bewitched*, dubbed in Japanese, was on, along with *Combat* (called *Combattu!* by a very forceful Japanese male voice). War and witchcraft. Would that Elizabeth Montgomery could have twitched her nose and eliminated all the weapons that hurt so many helpless creatures, like the way it happened in *The Day the Earth Stood Still.* I remember saying something like this to Yuri, and then being surprised that he understood the Michael Rennie reference. I thought I'd have to explain that to him, but it turns out he knew the movie.

That one weekend of privacy started on the couch. Our only all-alone, to-explore each-other, weekend. Since then, I've sat on many a couch, in the arms of lots of different men, watching TV, but of course the first time for anything has a precious newness and sharpness about it.

He took off my bra and blouse, and his shirt. I was kind of used to this part by now. How muscled his arms looked, how male and roughish he seemed. Exciting. Those wonderful, warm hands all over my breasts, all up and down my back. The incredibly leisurely journey his lips took, all over my nipples, up and down my body, across my shoulders, and down my arms. (His big warm hands spoiled me—I've always been disappointed with men who don't have hands like his.)

Meanwhile, I enjoyed how hard his arms and back felt, as I did my own slow, pleasurable touching of him. He taught me to take it slow and easy with pleasure. No rush.

When it came time to go in the bedroom, he didn't ask, simply held out his hand, and led the way.

By the muted light of a small lamp by the bed, he pulled my jeans down, and I held onto his shoulders as he helped me out of them. Those clumsy white cotton underpants of that pre-Victoria's Secret era were an embarrassment. I had rolled them down a couple of inches, so that at least my bellybutton showed, but there was still definitely nothing sexy about them.

These ungainly things he left on me, as he gestured me to get on the bed, and then he removed his pants, leaving only his shorts on, and laid down beside me. Lamp still on, I reached over to turn it off but he said, "No, I want to see you."

Then we talked, me in his arms. About whether to go all the way. I wasn't ready. My fifteen-year-old body and emotions just weren't prepared for this. I wanted to do everything but the intercourse.

I need to pause a moment, to let you know what a primitive stage sex education for girls was in back then. There wasn't any. My repressed home never mentioned the "s" word, or anything relating to the body, or even kissing, or dating. Schools had no classes in sexuality, not even any that would explain some basics of male anatomy to us.

Until a couple of months before this moment, our one weekend together, I had had only the vaguest of ideas about what men and women did together. That vagueness was still there, but I had read, since my first meeting with Yuki, two books that started to fill me in on this complicated picture. He had stirred me up so much that I sought out information in the only erotic works I had heard of by that young time in my life. I had gone to the base library and checked out *Lady Chatterley's Lover* and *Fanny Hill*—these, my first two 'pornographic' works of literature, finally gave me some notion of what happened when a penis met a vagina. Until then, I remember that my sexual fantasies were all full of kissing and caressing, but my imagination didn't even extend to a man putting his fingers inside me, maybe because I couldn't get inside my own self (I'd tried, when I self-pleasured), due to a tough maidenhead.

As for the penis, well, I knew what a baby boy's looked like, because I had changed little boys' diapers when I babysat them, but I'd never even seen a picture of a grown-up one and I didn't know what it meant for a guy to get hard. A kind of misty picture of this mysterious male thing, penis, would float into my head every once in a while, but not with any anatomical accuracy, due to complete innocence on my part.

Leaning up against Yuki in the subway taught me about the hard part—because he answered my questions, with no embarrassment, just a little amusement, about what happened to a man when he got excited (not right there in the subway, of course, but later).

I have yet to figure out much about the Japanese attitude toward sex, but it doesn't seem to be mixed up with any religious ideas about shame and sin and all that ridiculous garbage Westerners put on it. Being refreshingly free of religion back then helped me, somewhat, in trying to figure out Japanese ideas about sex. When Yuki explained things to me, about his body, about mine, he was straightforward, natural—it was not at all as if this were a forbidden subject. When I tried to figure out if sex was something 'practical' for him, something he did just for the physical side, without a lot of feeling involved, he said it could be that way but that wasn't the best kind of sex. "With a special woman, it's very special," he said. Then I tried to figure out if the Japanese are all romantic about sex, the way we are. He said it wasn't the center of everything, like Americans try to make it. But he said it could be very passionate. That was a deep part of what made sex special, he said, passion

Since that time so long ago, I have read that, despite a highly exploitative $30 billion dollar sex industry in modern Japan, the Japanese are quite reticent about sex—rarely discussing it with any openness. This fact surprised me since Yuki was quite frank about the subject. Maybe the Western influence was strong in him? Perhaps he was the exception to most Japanese? I don't know.

In my questions to Yuki, I was hampered by my knowing almost nothing myself, beyond all the romantic ideas wandering around in my culture, and beyond what I'd just learned from Fanny Hill and Lady Chatterley. I've since discovered that those two women do not contain all the possibilities of sex.

So, back to the penis. And Yuki and me, on the bed. We went about as far as you can go, that weekend, without actually doing it. I'm convinced that if we had had a place to be alone a lot, and had spent all our time together, boyfriend/girlfriend style, we would have had sex. His restraint wouldn't have held. So, it may be fortunate that we saw each other so infrequently and had such a hard time finding a space to be private in. I just wasn't ready. I listened to my body and it said to me, "Nope, you're not ready between your legs yet, and your emotions definitely aren't ready to do this important thing with a man." My body didn't say this to me, in exactly these words, but someplace deep inside, where my body knows me better than I do myself, it told me, "Wait."

Yuki accepted it. Wait. Okay. I understood. And he did. I was fortunate, too, that he didn't get angry, act all pissed, because I wouldn't 'do it.' He simply accepted that we would enjoy each other's bodies in every way but that. No going inside. Maidenhead intact. But that didn't stop us from doing practically everything else you could do, together, as a man and a woman. Once he had slowly relaxed me, helped me to not be so shy.

When he finally got those highly unattractive underpants off of me, after quite a bit of coaxing, I still tried to cover myself with the pillow. More coaxing, teasing, and I let him take the pillow away. It was hard, to just lay there and let a man see me naked for the first time. I felt afraid and vulnerable even though I wasn't afraid of him. It was like I was afraid of some basic essence of malehood, or manhood, or whatever you want to call it.

He slipped off his shorts, and I saw one for the first time. What made it fascinating was that I couldn't imagine being shaped that way. It looked so alien, sticking up, and out, with these floppy things that reminded me of cocoanuts dangling below it.

I was on my back, and he was sitting up, leaning on one arm, and he put his hand gently on my triangle, just letting it rest lightly on my hair. Hair. He said he had wondered what color mine would be down there. He didn't expect anything so 'blonde'—I was caramel-colored there, like the hair on my head.

Usually I go for hairy men, big, blonde Viking types, with coarse wire all over their arms, and coarse scratchy cheeks. And rugby builds. Or maybe one of those Australian Rules Football guys. The ultimate thick rough fearless male. Despite this, I loved Yuki's smoothness—very little hair anywhere, except he did have some between his legs. How he compared to his hairier Caucasian counterparts down below I couldn't, of course, know back then, since he was the first man I'd even seen naked.

He looked pretty thick and substantial even though I had no comparison for 'size'—since then, having been with so many men, I know he was about the size of an average Caucasian male. Since Yuki is the only Asian I have ever been with, in all my life, I can't make any generalizations about them. I know he had a pretty substantial mat of black hair around his member—I don't know if that is typical of Asian males or if he was simply a 'hairy exception.'

In terms of temperament, I think Yuki may have been exceptional—just for men in general, no matter what the race. He was patient and gentle and kind. Always understanding, no matter how silly and little-girl like I was.

He lay down beside me, the front of his body completely up against my side, and I could feel his hardness against my hip. He put his arms around me and, slowly, in no rush, he played with me, caressed me—breasts, stomach, arms, shoulders, legs, everywhere but the place I was waiting for. He circled around that area, never quite making it to it. The teasing was unbearable—like I was on fire. (Little did I know that he was setting up 'standards' in foreplay for me that I would later discover not many men met. Just a quick ram-in trip to the vagina was all many want—and they do not spend time on our bodies to arouse us. A woman's first sexual experience is incredibly important—it reflects on every sexual experience she has thereafter.)

The waiting worked since by the time he slipped two fingers between my legs, and spread me apart, I was moist. Way more than moist—absolutely dripping—I've always been brimming with wetness in that area. The sensation of his fingers invading me was more-than-startling. Even though I'd been playing with myself for years, it was nothing like someone else's hand down there. A combination of the shameless and the delicious. And an ease about it. I didn't have to do anything. Yuki was taking care of it all.

Only a light pressure on the maidenhead area, which was good, since if I'd felt in the least like I was being invaded, I would have panicked. It was too scary. Some deep archetypal feminine fear kept me from wanting that hard, alien-looking thing in me. Even when I got very wet and very hot, and so aching I was pushing up against him and kissing him like crazy, I still didn't have the courage to want him in me.

He concentrated on the essential spot (clit) and it only took a few minutes before I had a deliciously sharp orgasm; he kept his fingers pressed up against my maidenhead all the while I was gasping and squeezing my legs together, to make the pleasure more intense. In the aftershock time, lots of little ripples, mini-orgasms, were quivering around inside me, and I could feel the tissue at my opening throbbing against his fingers.

It was a good one—as good as most of the ones I gave myself.

Now, his turn. In my budding, virginal state, I leaned how to suck cock. First, he put my hand on his shaft and showed me how to stroke him. He felt warm and velvety. Then he pushed my head down toward it. I just did what came naturally. I don't remember it being all that hard to figure out. And he came in my mouth, that first time, for me, and I didn't mind. It was part of him, all this funny, slightly bitter tasting stuff, and if he could handle all the sticky wetness between my legs, I guess I could handle whatever came with owning a cock.

That first time, being all naked with a man, and all the sexplay, seemed natural (except for my fear of being invaded). I think his 'grown-up' attitude helped: he didn't make me feel pressured, or uncomfortable, or clumsy. It was more a just take it at your own pace, don't worry, this is supposed to be enjoyable. No apologies, if you're too afraid to let me inside yet. It's not the end of the world, and I'm not going to die if I can't 'do it' with you.

That first time also left me a little stunned, but in a nice way. After experiencing his cock for the first time, in my mouth, and after all the kissing and caressing, and being naked, I needed to just stop for a while. It was pretty overwhelming, all these firsts in a row. So, I slipped on a nightgown (shapeless, bulky) from the little kit I'd brought along, and he put his shirt and shorts back on.

The night was really chilly and it felt cosy in the kitchen. I made hamburgers for us, with lettuce and tomatoes on top, and potato chips on the side. We had pecan pie tarts for dessert, which I'd bought at the commissary and brought with me. They carried, for some reason, the best little miniature versions of pecan pies, and I wanted to share this, my favorite dessert, with him. I'd also brought some oatmeal and chocolate chip cookies and tangerines, for snacking. To this day, I associate these cookies and that fruit with him.

The only thing missing from that night was a fireplace, as we sat on the sofa, trying to find something on TV to watch. A variety show was about all there was, so he translated, as we held each other, and chatted about everything in the universe, as we usually did. Yuki opened me up when I talked so that I felt free to say almost anything,

It was cosy, sitting all close together, both of us sipping what he considered 'funny tasting' tea (Lipton's—this was way before the days of Celestial Seasonings, and Earl Grey on the local supermarket, or commissary, shelves).

That night, I felt completely comfortable all snuggled up beside him, a patter of rain outside. He generated a lot of body heat, against that cold Japanese winter; another first for me—how sleeping beside a man can be like having your own personal heater.

In later years, I rarely felt comfortable sleeping beside someone. Usually, I like my own space, and I'm kind of on-edge, that I'm going to disturb his sleep, or he mine. Of all the ones I've been with, there's been a few rare men that I loved sleeping beside. Yuki was the first.

Next day, all the cosy, domestic scene was there again. How good he was to Melissa. Most of the day was spent caring for her—she wasn't that demanding but Yuki really seemed to enjoy her company. I almost envied her. I wanted to be four again, and I wanted Yuki to take care of me. Forever. Like a father.

He showed the same patience with her as he had the day before. And he still found the time to come up behind me, put his arms around me, kiss me on the nape of my neck.

In the afternoon, I took her out for a walk and a ride on a little plastic truck on wheels, about her size, that she liked to scoot around on. I felt a little sad that Yuki couldn't be with us, making a cosy, domestic threesome. It struck me that the world was a pretty hypocritical and sorry place if a man who was great with kids couldn't take Melissa out to play because he was Japanese, and not supposed to be my boyfriend.

Her naptime was our time for more amorous play. This time we got naked on the couch and just enjoyed snuggling and rubbing up against each other, while watching a dubbed movie (I think it was *The Canterville Ghost*) on in the background. Being sensual with Yuri was so easy that I sometimes wonder why it couldn't have been that way with a lot of the other men I was destined to be with. With only a few did I have that feeling of sexplay as some kind of easy going gift from the stars, or the gods. No worry, no anxiety, about whether my thighs were too fat, or my butt too big. The way he accepted my body, admired it, made me accept it. Relaxing into sex, safe and warm, is the best way; and it has always been a mystery me to why so few men have made me feel safe.

We had an afternoon snack of grapes, and crackers with peanut butter, eating naked, side by side, on the couch. Where the grapes came from I can't say because I don't remember the commissary carrying them. How did they migrate from some Italian or Swiss hillside to that living room in Japan? To this day, of course, I think of him whenever I have that snack.

That night in bed was our big amorous time together, our last be naked with each other time—since the couple were coming back the next afternoon. I didn't know it would be our last time. Now the sadness of it hits me—so many years later.

Among other firsts, was the delicious sensation of someone laying on top of me. The first time he put his full weight on me, my whole insides caved in with desire. A deep hard burning ache everywhere. To this day, I almost always feel it, with that first "mount," but the absolute first sensation, with him, back then, seemed like a miracle to me. How could life contain anything so sexually beautiful as feeling a man's body on top of you, where it should be. Now, in middle age, after having been laid on top of by large numbers of men (not all at the same time, thankfully), I still don't feel jaded. It still seems like a sensual miracle, that precarious moment when he first presses everything into me, makes me feel small, taken, overwhelmed.

In my memory, this second night is full of magical tenderness. Maybe it's just the haze of years that's making it so special. But I think that the mystery of man and woman together, body against body, can create a sensual spiritual soft loveliness. I know that I felt some of that that night. It was not all in my imagination.

I also felt for the first time what I have had with other men in bed, when the magic is there—a sensation that the bed is an island where no one can reach us, and where no pain from the outside world can harm us.

He left mid-morning on Sunday since the couple said they'd be back early afternoon. He said he'd meet me, near sunset, in a park near the base where we liked to walk. I asked him what he'd be doing until then, and he said, "Seeing some friends."

There was an orange-red sunset that evening, shining though the trees in the park. We walked for a long time, holding hands, not really needing to say much. It was really cold so he held me close, up against him, when we stood still, to watch the last of the sunset.

That park is my most intimate and warm and dear memory of my time with him. We walked in it in the spring, too, when the weather was soft with the Japanese rainy season, warm rain, gentle, on our skin.

A few soft damp nights during the spring and fall with him in that park have stayed with me forever. When the air is soft and gentle on my skin, I think of him. It helps, but also saddens me, since most of this book is about how hard and brutal life is on our soft feminine bodies. The soft air on my skin is both a joy, and a sadness for me.

I knew Yuki for almost the whole time I lived in Japan, and when it came time for me to go back to the states, I considered staying—for him. I thought about going to the American University in Tokyo and taking one of those tiny Japanese apartments with him. But it was too scary for me—all alone, except for Yuki, in Tokyo and having to adjust to Japan—no longer being secure on the base, living my little safe American lifestyle. I wonder, of course, what my life would have been if I'd stayed—if maybe Yuki and I had had children, made a home together. All these ghost lives we can never experience.

Yuki and I didn't talk much about prostitution in Japan, partly because I hid from it whenever I could. It made me too sad to even let the idea of these poor women flit through my mind. I didn't know that much about prostitution back then, but, innately, I felt their misery. I think I must be a Reincarnated Comfort Girl.

When I was bold enough to ask him about it, he was vague, but when I pressed him about where and how and that I wanted to know some details, he took me one weekday afternoon to an area near the base where he said a lot of the soldiers went. It wasn't busy and I only have a memory of all those small wooden structures that are typical of Japan and that I saw a couple of women with sad eyes who looked surprised to see me. I saw no GI's that day, thankfully—maybe they weren't off duty yet. The second trip was to a red-light area in Tokyo—I think it was in the Shinjuku section—which he said was visited heavily by the American servicemen. Again, it was during a weekday afternoon. I think he chose these unbusy times on purpose so that we would not run into lots of GI's—there was a chance I might know some of them—even though it was a big base, I ran into and talked to a lot of soldiers all the time.

The area was bigger and more bustling than the one near the base, but I still only remember lots of small wooden structures and a few women with sad eyes. Most were in Western dress, but a few wore kimonos. Why my memory of these areas is so hazy I don't know. We only stayed a few minutes in each—so I only picked up a few impressions—only enough for a few images to come back to me. I know I felt uneasy and sad and depressed for even the brief time we were there. (I had the same reaction to the red-light area in Amsterdam when I spent a few brief 'touristy' moments there many years later and had to leave because the vibrations there were really disturbing me—they made me edgy and deeply sad.)

Later, I did discover, in one conversation with Yuki, that he had been to a prostitute that afternoon, between leaving me at Melissa's and our meeting in the park. During the very few conversations we had about prostitution, he said that he went regularly. It did not seem like a big deal to him, from what I could tell from his tone.

At the time, I didn't know what to make of this. I wasn't exactly surprised, or disappointed. It was the same I knew of all the men on base. None of them talked about it openly, but they dropped enough hints and veiled remarks that you knew that when they had leave, it was what they did—go find a Japanese girl/whore and have sex.

Now, many years later, after all of my own experiences of selling myself, and all the reading I have done about the wretched lives of most for-sale women, I consider what he did rape. At the center of prostitution is the rape of the girl's body. The Japanese women in the bars and brothels back then in the 1960's would have been no different from any others—all similar stories of coercion, poverty, vulnerability, debt bondage, all the trappings of sexual slavery—no matter how disguised the 'profession' is by Hollywood images and myths about 'choice' and happy whoredom.

It has been startling to know that this first man I loved, this first tender man who was so good to me, was a rapist.

3

Vic

What lips my lips have kissed, and where, and why,
I have forgotten...but the rain
Is full of ghosts tonight....

--Edna St. Vincent Millay

I grew up on military bases around the world. My dad was a big, tough, hard, relentless, unsentimental drill sergeant of a man who terrified me. The household always felt filled with violence because of his temper.

He had a kind side but it was hard for me to appreciate it since I was so afraid of him. Many years later, when he was near the end of his life, and had mellowed out due to age, I was able to talk to him—but I could never tell him how frightened I was of him.

It was simply normal to hit kids when I was growing up in the 1950's. I certainly was not beaten extensively, but even the few times a month that he hit me—with his hand or a belt—terrified me. I think I was born timid so even without this violence in my upbringing, I would be what I am—frightened, shy, scared most of the time. But he taught me young that male violence rules the world and that I am, as a female, helpless and small. In fact, I think this early 'training' made me feel permanently small. I am 5'4" and weigh about 130 pounds. I have always felt much smaller—tiny, in fact. Like about 5 feet and a hundred pounds. 'The bigness of the male'—this is a phrase I would repeat to myself when I worked as a prostitute since I felt so pummeled by male weight and strength.

Back to my dad. I do not mean to blame him too much. He did the best he could, poor guy, and he did take care of his family—which is way more than a lot of dads do. I always had a place to sleep and enough to eat and I was protected from sexual harm and had the opportunity to go to school. I was way more fortunate than most of the children of the world.

My dad was a career soldier, so we were stationed everywhere: Germany, Korea, Japan, Okinawa, all over the U.S. Since I grew up on military bases, the men I knew and was used to were soldiers. It is the type I have been attracted to all my life. I have always looked for the perfect soldier to protect me—a big strong hard wonderful man to shield me from the world.

Sex. It has always been an overwhelmingly powerful force in my life. As I grow restless with age, and my sex drive grows even more demanding, I find, in memories, some solace and stillness from this fire.

This chapter is about my first lover. It is about how I was before that extraordinary and painful time as a prostitute. It is about how confusing and beautiful sex is to me, even now, as I try to understand all my restless, sad longings.

Having a strong sex drive is probably what landed me in prostitution. I don't live in a world where a free and infinite and lovely sensuality is accepted in a woman. In my sadder moments, I think prostitution was my punishment for wanting sex, beautiful sex, on a planet where female bodies are so imprisoned and despised.

My first lover. My first time. I was in my early twenties, he was in his forties. He was a huge (6'5") blonde, rugged, rock-hard ex-Marine, now construction worker, named Vic (yes, I know I chose a concrete slab replica of my father). We met at a bus stop late one afternoon. He had that dusty, covered with dirt-and-chalk look that construction workers sport at the end of the day; and even though it was chilly, and raining a bit, he wore a sleeveless shirt, torn at the edges. His triceps took my breath away. I've always had a weakness for men's arms. Even his forearms, muscled, massive, and tanned and bristling with blonde hairs, would have been enough. The addition of all the other hard, gorgeous, sculpted parts of his body was almost too much. I admit I noticed the sheer animal muscled size of him first; then his face, kind of craggy and rugged, not handsome but interesting—full of cynicism and humor.

He had that thickness of the big muscled male past his youth who drinks and eats too much but who is still huge and hard and impressive and sexy, despite his belly and his face craggy with wrinkles from years in the sun.

I stared as discreetly as I could—I wasn't too subtle, and he caught me looking at him—especially at his arms—and he looked back at me and he came up, no shyness in him, and we started chatting. It turns out his van was in the shop, and what immediately occurred to me, young and romantic and silly me, was 'fate'! If his car hadn't broken down, we wouldn't be meeting now. I was immediately attracted to him. He seemed like that fantasy soldier I'd wanted all my life—even though he was a construction worker. When he told me he'd been in the Marines, it sealed the 'fate' mark of this chance meeting.

We ended up going off to eat dinner together and then to his place. That first night, we kissed and snuggled a bit, but not too much because my heart was beating so fast and I was so shy with him that I could barely look at him and I was afraid he would think I was some kind of retarded mute and he would never want to see me again.

My love life up until then was not too full. I'd tentatively gone out with quite a few GI's during my teens on the bases where we were stationed overseas. I didn't seem to have any connections with the boys I went to high school with. I was bumbling and nerdy and shy and shabby and didn't dress well. Not one of the popular types. The GI's were my substitute. But my dates with them were mostly pretty chaste, not only because I was shy and had a hard time even letting anyone kiss me, but because this was overseas—the men knew there could be consequences if they had sex with the dependent girls. And my growing up was back before the hippie era set us on the road to more liberal sexual attitudes. Those GI dates never gave us anywhere to be alone either—he was in a barracks, I had parents at home. So, my encounters with them were at movie theatres, in the PX, at the snack bar.

The romantic side of me was in full swing back then, before life jaded me. My construction worker/ex-Marine had Viking blue eyes, with centuries of pillaging in their depths, penetrating eyes, the kind that would make any virgin blush. They were intense, mocking, hard, full of humor, amused at me, at my shyness, but patient with my small fears. That first night in his arms I pretty much fell in love with him in the way that only a physically hot young woman desperately in need of her first time can. His impact on my senses, on my body, was overwhelming. I wanted him and I was terrified of him.

"Hey, we're really not so scary once you get to know us," he joked, when I was fumblingly trying to say all this to him. Back then, it was so important for me to be able to share every thought and feeling with him. Like a lot of girls, I had read all of Jane Austen and she set the standard for our romances—subtle and complex—not at all in touch with how simple and straightforward and impatient of nuance men are.

Saturday he had his car back and he picked me, little kit with toothbrush, nightie, all in tow and we were back at his place. It was a cosy, humble, slightly messy house, but clean and comfortable feeling. He started by slowing undressing me on the sofa, while we were watching TV. T-shirt first, then jeans, then bra, then panties. (Of course I remember the movie in the background—it was *The Ghost and Mrs. Muir*—and has been my totem movie ever since.) The way he was very unhurried made me feel hot, no rush, let her wait, I can wait. When he kissed and played with my nipples, a hot arrow of pleasure shot right down from them, past my belly button, to my vagina. It made me gasp, this golden-triangle, deep, sudden-ache sensation.

My naked body felt vulnerable to him, but in a pleasant, delicious way. He seemed amused by how I was trying to hide myself, particularly my lower half, behind the sofa pillows, and he kept taking them away from me in a teasing way.

I had a tattoo, a small daisy on my hip. He had a tattoo something like a cross between a jagged heart and a trident on his upper arm, a primitive pattern, of jungles and the deep blue sea. We compared tattoos, my small flower with his big trident. Tridents belong in the terrifying depths of the sea; a daisy is at home out on a windy grassland, homey, small and pretty, of this earth: our two realms met, his hard maleness, my soft femininity.

After my nipples, he paid some attention to the area between my legs, and the sensation of being touched there again after so long was like a highly embarrassing but delicious invasion. Since Yuki, no one else had touched me there.

We didn't spend too long on the sofa. Instead, he carried me easily into the bedroom (my 5'4" 125 pound self being a little feather for his 250 pounds of hardness), set me on the side of the bed, fetched a towel, and placed it in the center. I looked at the towel, he looked at it, and said, succinctly, "Maidenhead, I felt it on the couch, you'll probably bleed some."

He undressed in a leisurely way I was not even remotely prepared for how big he was. And his eyes looked so hard, too.

I turned away from his eyes and curled up into a seashell, feeling hollow inside and more than a little afraid. He slipped in behind me, cradling me in that spoon fashion that is so pleasurable, and began rubbing his scratchy cheek and chin on my shoulder, across my back, and on the nape of my neck, and then followed this up with slow kisses on the same spots, all the time encircling me completely in his arms, making me feel very small.

For some reason, the fates decided to grant me two men who actually liked foreplay and knew how to do it. I was later to discover that Yuki and Vic were rare in the world of men.

"Nothing to be afraid of, little girl, I'll be very careful with you." His bedroom voice was low and gentle and made me shiver. He moved his fingers lightly down my arm, barely grazing me, then the same soft fingertip touch, like a butterfly fluttering, down my hips and butt, across my tummy, up to my breasts, circling, barely touching me until I became yielding, purring, wanting much more. But he stayed, played, wandered lightly on the surface till my skin and my breasts and my nipples felt alive with sensation.

When writers say there is electricity between people, it is true. His fingertips felt like sparks and little jolts of hot fire on my nipples.

Finally, he climbed on top of me, lowering part of his weight carefully down on me. My stomach felt a cold hard pleasurable shock at this first "mount." He felt incredibly heavy but wonderful. While kissing me, deeply, he reached under me, slid his hand down my butt and between my legs from the rear, and then rubbed and played with me till I felt wet and hot. He spread my legs with his legs and put the tip of himself up against what now felt like the center of my being. He pushed. Nothing happened except a sharp pain and gasp (from me). A harder shove. Still nothing. A massively harder shove.

The first thrust is an incredible and impossible violation of a woman's body, of everything she holds secret, hidden, and fragile. He pushed so hard to break through the maidenhead that he went pretty deep into me. Incredibly painful. Then he didn't move at all. Just ran his hands up and down the sides of my body and kissed my shoulders and my face and my hair and murmured little sounds that seemed more like caresses than words. His hardness inside me and the gentleness of his hands and the murmurs made me ache and throb.

Taking his weight of me a little, he slid himself out of me a bit and gently rubbed my sensitive spot with his fingertip, for a long time, till I had an orgasm. I'd been pleasuring myself for years and had had lots or orgasm, half a dozen or so a day usually; but the sensation of one with someone inside me for the first time was extraordinarily intense—deeper, heavier throbs reaching out everywhere, then receding, a tingling pleasure all over my body, a feeling of almost wanting to pass out. I throbbed around him for as long as I could. It hurt from the stretching and from the torn maidenhead since I'd never had anyone in me before, but it also felt delicious.

He kissed me and I opened my eyes to find him looking into them, his almost too bright, too Viking blue. Slow, patient, slightly amused by the whole experience. Sardonic, teasing. A full spectrum of emotions seemed to pass across his eyes every ten seconds or so, various, mysterious, unreadable in its swiftness. (I've never had another lover with such eyes.) Right now, they were mocking and distant—as if he were thinking—"what is my little toy going to do next"—but also tender and caring. This whole thing with the eyes was a deeper penetration, a more disturbing intimacy than I was prepared for, since he was still so far inside me, so I closed mine, seeking privacy.

He cradled my head in his hands, still keeping himself inside me. We were kind of entangled in my long hair. He carefully untangled us. I was not prepared for what he did next. Up till now he had treated me like a fragile doll. He put his arms fully around me, and pulled my head to his chest. "The first time feels like hell for a woman—or so I hear—but I guess we might as well start breaking you in," he said in a practical voice—a job to do, let's get it done.

He started thrusting and it definitely felt like beyond hell. I gasped from the pain. Pain so intense I yelped. He held back, didn't go at me full strength. Still this first being thrust into was so awful that I gripped his arms and cried. He finished pretty fast since he could see I was in such pain and took it out as gently as he could.

He kissed my cheeks and smoothed my hair, making little murmuring sounds. There was a lot of blood—down my legs and on the towel—so he got up, fetched a wash cloth, wiped most of the blood off my inner thighs, folded the towel under me so I was on a clean spot, and lay down beside me again, putting his arm around me. I curled up by his side. His hand rested on my shoulder and arm and felt protective and warm. With his other hand, he reached over to shake a cigarette out of a pack and flip open his lighter.

I let him smoke for a while, and then said, "Can we talk about it." He laughed. "Of course we can. Why shouldn't we talk about it?" I didn't say anything for a while till he said,"Well?"

"I didn't think it would be so rough." Massive, quiet understatement of the century. I was still shaking inside from the impact.

"You'll get used to it pretty fast, believe me."

"I don't think I could ever get used to all that." It really scared me. I had no idea a man could do all that to me, could cause me so much pain between my legs, make me feel so helpless. That's what I wanted to say but I didn't know how, so I stayed silent and subdued. Sensing stuff unsaid, he came out with another "Well?" I stumbled out all my fears, about how easy and frightening it would be for any man to subdue any woman with that instrument they all had, what chance did we stand when men could do that to us, cause such terrible pain inside us. I felt more helpless and lost in the world of men than I'd ever felt before—do I have to be afraid of all men because they can hurt me in such an awful way between my legs. All of this came tumbling out, not too coherently.

He listened carefully, surprised. His response was that he wasn't used to being with women who were as timid and sensitive as I was. But he was kind about my fears. Held me. Kissed me.

The next thing I was aware of was something wiry against my nose. I'd apparently fallen asleep against him, and woken up with the bristly blond hairs on his chest tickling me. I felt so tired, but I had to drag myself out of bed to pee. A little blood came out, too, but I was too exhausted to shower or clean myself. Back in bed, I immediately fell asleep against him again. He was warm and comfortable to be beside.

In the morning, life looked different. Everything seemed unreal. My body had had a shock and somehow my perceptions were lagging behind. In bed, he was all sweetness to me, giving me pleasure by touching that magic button that never seems to slow down, keeping away from where I was still sore, but I was distracted by how hard his member was against the side of my body. I was afraid he'd want to do it again.

But he waited a few days until I had recovered. The second time was definitely not so scary. It was in there and it was big and formidable and he did move it around in me, but it didn't feel so searing and burning, the way it had the first time.

The problem I had the whole time I was with Vic was tearing. He was too big for me, and I never stretched enough to really take him full force without some bleeding. He didn't seem to mind taking it gentle and soft. We worked out compromises with lots of lube. He loved all the being naked with each other and kissing and touching, so the thrusting was not the only thing he cared about.

My Viking charged me up sexually to such a degree, made me feel like such an incredibly desirable woman, that I reveled in being physical, and pretty, and young with him. My caramel-blonde, hippie-girl hair tumbled like a waterfall to below my waist, and I wore low-riding cut-offs with abandon because I had great legs back then, and I went braless under tight T-shirts because my full breasts were firm enough to bounce merrily along under their own sail when I strutted my stuff. We flower-power girls walked in freedom, barefoot, naked in that freedom, loving the sensation of fabric rubbing against bare nipples.

I was so conscious of Vic physically that my sex drive, always strong, seemed to quadruple. I was always intensely aware of him near me, big and rough hewn, careless and lazy of his strength. He reminded me of a combination of a jaguar and a baseball player, a loose lithe lazy power, a lounging easy grace, a sureness of touch, strong arms holding me, making me feel small against his chest.

I moved in with him. We spent rainy nights by the fireplace, watched old movies together, listened to The Moody Blues. These were the sorts of things one tended to share in that time period. He liked jazz, a closed musical world to me, but I got used to it, especially the softer stuff, the kind so smooth it makes you slide out of your chair. The kind that is good to listen to in the middle of the night when the world looks bleak, and life seems lonely.

The house was comfortingly full of books, several thousand of them. Although not well-educated, like at a college, he read all the time.

He was one of the few men I've ever known who liked to stay naked for a whole weekend together, cooking, watching sports and movies on TV, cuddling, making love when we just naturally felt like it. No get in, get out, all done, now I can get on with more important things. He spoiled me for other men.

He made me feel comfortable being naked in front of him. He taught me that first open, uninhibited intimacy with a man when a girl loses her shyness and loves being naked and a little wild.

I felt at peace with him. I hadn't realized how easy and comfortable life could be between a man and woman.

We adopted a dog at a shelter, a sweetie with a big sloppy body and big floppy feet. He had been terribly mistreated and was still thin and bony from long starvation and tended to walk crouched with his tail between his legs, looking up and sideways in case a blow was coming his way. Everyone during this era was naming their dogs Frodo or Bilbo, so we decided on Boromir, the name we liked best from the books.

At home, we never argued much—for a big man, my Viking was quite a peaceful negotiator when differences arose. He did not believe in shouting matches. But we had to be careful to not even raise our voices a little bit because any small sign of roughness would send Boromir skittering behind the door, or trying to dig his way under the couch. We tried our best to de-flea Boromir but in the summer moist heat, every dog there had a few fleas. He slept in the same bed with us (where else is there for a dog to sleep?) and every once in a while we would see a little visitor hop from Boromir to us. That was okay. We loved him. We could share a few of his fleas.

Then we found Mindy, mange-ridden and matted, a Black Cocker mix, arthritic, limping, and half-blind from old age and neglect. She was wandering around a vacant, weedy lot, looking for food, one evening when Boromir was taking us for our evening walk. (I believe in letting my dogs take me for a walk, not the other way around; after all, it's their time out of the house, to explore, not mine.) I took her filthy, thin body in my arms without a thought that she would bite me and it was total love from that first embrace.

De-manged and treated by the vet, a holistic practitioner who gave Mindy some great homeopathic stuff for her old age afflictions and pains, our girl was a total, sweet-natured darling. She had a line around her neck from being chained for long periods of time. (I am haunted by dogs I've seen in rural Georgia and Arkansas, chained to posts, with only a couple of feet within which to eat, sleep, defecate, walk, exercise, dream, die, love, hate, long, go insane. Their eyes are so full of fierce despair that I can barely look into them, yet I must. How else can I put into words their pain?)

Mindy was, oddly enough, much bolder than Boromir, and despite being the half-blind one, and half his size, would take the lead during long walks, to give him confidence. He often followed her about, tip of his nose touchingly at her tail. Her old, half-blind eyes had a lot of life and spirit in them.

Vic threw balls for them in the backyard, and Mindy and Boromir both galumphed along, chasing them. While Boromir went after the long balls, Mindy went for the ones Vic tossed in close, so she could get to them. I loved to watch Vic's shoulder muscles ripple as he threw the long ones out for Boromir. I remember windy afternoons, with a chill in the air, and clouds gathering and the joy of that backyard as Vic threw out those balls.

So we now had two dogs in our bed. Two footwarmers during the winter. Two friends to share fleas with.

My Viking wasn't perfect. He drank and smoked too much. He liked to eat pasta with his fingers. He was subject to depression, deep and dark, and couldn't always dig his way out. He told me things I didn't want to hear, like, "Never put your happiness in another person. I could die tomorrow, Boromir could die tomorrow. So could Mindy. Always find your happiness inside you."

When he left me, he pretty much killed me forever. He took Boromir; I kept Mindy. The division of the dogs.

I remember him now, on this distant shore of a different time, far beyond my first time with him, when I was a trembling young girl who knew so little. I remember one spring afternoon swimming nude with him at a lake where hippies gathered. When it started to rain, a warm spring shower, we climbed up the grassy bank by the water and walked in the woods together, naked, clothes draped across our shoulders. He kissed me up against a big, rough-feeling tree, in the rainy, half-light, with other trees dripping softly all around us.

Sometimes when I'm alone at night in bed, feeling heavy with age and experience, and empty, I arch myself up toward him and I remember the feel of his light fingertips on my body. Even though he is now a phantom lover, his touch is still incredibly real.

Could I not have just one day of my life back with him, to touch him one more time? We'd always planned to take his van and drive to Oregon one day. Then we would park the van on a rainy afternoon, on the Oregon coast. And there he would make gentle love to me, once again.

After Vic left, I had dreams about missing Boromir and how I'd probably never see him again.

Vic was the one. There's never really been any one for me since, despite numerous lovers. Even though he, like Yuki, did the unthinkable—bought girls' bodies, I am still in love with him, after all these years. The few times he would talk about Korea, it was pathetic. He said you wouldn't find a guy there who didn't use the whores. First thing when you got stationed there, you went out and got laid. Initiation. He said the girls were terrified of him because of his size but he used them anyway. It was what all the guys did. He felt sorry for the girls, but that still didn't stop him. He said he was young and he'd changed a lot since then.

"What was for me a few minutes of pleasure, was for her a life sentence."

I know from being with him that he would never hurt a woman. Yet how can I reconcile this with the way he was part of the collective rape of those girls and how he hurt them beyond repair.

He said when Marilyn came and performed, it got the guys so horny they practically screwed the whores to death.

After he left me, I slept with a lot of men. I was trying to find love. And I went with these tough commando types in an effort to find another Vic. Wild stupid behavior led me to put myself in that gang-rape situation. I went to a house with two men, one of my boyfriends and another soldier, and did both of them—and got really turned on. Then they brought in some of their buddies and it turned into a rape party. "She's hot and likes to fuck" was what my boyfriend said, when he was passing me around.

I do like to fuck. But that doesn't mean I want to be raped. They could see I was crying. I think they must have noticed when I passed out from so many of them going at me. I think they must have seen how much pain I was in. I don't think they could miss that I was saying 'no'—in every way I could.

I am still bewildered by what happened that day. It was a huge betrayal by this man who I thought at least cared about me a little.

I never went to the police about it—or to the hospital, even though I was badly torn up. For one thing, I was in too much of a state of shock to go anywhere. And, later, I never talked about it since I knew everyone would say, "She asked for it. She was hot and went there to fuck two guys so if others came in, she got what she deserved. "

It's also been hard to talk about the prostitution since I wasn't trafficked or coerced or sold or held in sexual slavery. That, too, is an area where I can be blamed for what I did.

I have a lot of men I correspond with on the internet as a result of them reading my articles and e-mailing me about them. These men are very kind and understanding. They are polite and sensitive. They are a wonderful contrast to rude, hard men with no manners and no insights or clues about sexual pain. These good men are a joy after that world of rough sex that left me permanently terrified of men.

After I told one of them about my gang rape, with all the details of how it happened, he said to me: "You did nothing wrong, Suki."

That one understanding comment means a lot to me.

Part Two

Fuck for Food

Fuck for Food

A woman is a frail thing, for all of her courage.

--Daphne du Maurier

This section consists of articles that I have published on various internet sites over the last couple of years. Most of them deal with military prostitution, but I also write about prostitution in general. There is some repetition due to my coming back to certain core exploitations—the Korean Comfort Women, the Occupation Comfort Girls, etc. I chose to put "Sex Slaves for American GI's" first since it is about the situation that most touched my heart and set me off writing about this painful subject.

There are several pieces about Iraq and sexual violence and exploitation. I also touch on the current trafficking of women and girls into U.S. camptown bars and brothels in Korea. If any military men read these and can add to my knowledge, I would appreciate your communicating with me.

The title of section two reflects my view that most of the history of womankind has been a brutal "fuck-for-food" scenario.

Most of female history has also been a Rape Killing Field.

The dates below the titles indicate when they first appeared on various on-line sites and in various on-line magazines.

Sex Slaves for American GI's Accepted Mass Rape--"Peacefully"?

April 30, 2007

"There is no greater agony than bearing an untold story inside you."
--Maya Angelou

I just presented a paper on "Sex Trafficking and the Military" at a conference where I focused on the 'Occupation Comfort Girls,' sex slaves raped by the U.S. Military in Japan after WWII. The day after I came back from my trip, an Associated Press story, "U.S. GI's Visited WWII Sex Slaves" by Eric Talmadge (April 26, 2007), ran on a number of newswires across the country, and the world. It recounts how 'comfort stations' were set up for American soldiers in Japan in 1945 and stocked with 'Occupation Comfort Girls' forced into sexual slavery to service the men. Details beyond cruelty have emerged: the way some girls were raped sixty times a day; the way demand was so high girls had no time to eat or sleep; the way men stood two abreast, in lines a block long, at the Yokosuka 'Rape Station' (my word for it) to get at the girls imprisoned inside. The way the men were told to not pay more than ten yen for a short mount. Ten yen was less than a pack of cigarettes cost at that time. (Rape is economical.) The men were brought in by the truckloads and told to wear condoms no matter 'how good it felt.' I guess rape feels good for the rapist.

The above details are just a sampling of this atrocity.

Interestingly, Talmadge takes some of his article from the 'official' Japanese history of the enslavement and it reads like this: "As expected, after the comfort stations opened it was elbow to elbow. The comfort women… had some resistance to selling themselves to men who just yesterday were the enemy, and because of differences in language and race, there were a great deal of apprehensions at first. But they were paid highly, and they gradually came to accept their work peacefully." The rest of my article will definitely argue a very different point of view--that no woman accepts rape "peacefully"--let alone the mass rape that this was. It is a point that would not seem to need proving, but the notion that a prostitute cannot be raped because she is paid and because she asked for it and the idea that if she is Asian, it is part of her culture to be a whore—these ways of thinking predominate among the soldiers who frequent prostitutes. Someone has to express that it is not so. Someone has to express that paying does not make rape okay. I wish I could find another person to do this since it troubles me deeply to be only one voice in a world that regards the whore as a disposable non-entity who feels no pain.

And, by the way, I wonder what "paid highly" means. Can you actually pay a woman a sum of money that would compensate her for the serial rape of her body?

The way journalists refuse to express the pain of the tortured in the service of some imaginary 'objectivity' betrays the extreme suffering these women endured. And it leaves the reader with the idea that a woman will accept rape by sixty men "peacefully." Talmadge's article does not mention the unbearable pain the women experienced. Nor does he in any way refute the idea that the women came to accept mass rape "peacefully." So, it is up to me to add the view of the whore whose body is violated sixty times a day. There does not seem to be anyone else around to do it. All these journalists with their code of 'imaginary objectivity' in the service of a false truth are simply promoting the rape of the body.

For one, contrary to the above statement, the girls were not paid highly. They were held in debt bondage, as are almost all sexually enslaved girls, thus little of the money would have gone to them. Even if they had been 'paid highly,' how could this in any way make constant rape palatable to them? Let alone "peaceful."

That word "peaceful." What kind of askew definition of cruelty can possibly couple that word with "rape"? It would seem that the Japanese historian/chronicler of this event is so deep in his own male blindness that he can watch a woman mounted, serially, sixty times, and still not perceive it as rape?

From the point of view of the body being mounted, it is rape.

"Desire" is another troublesome word in this historical context. American officials reported that the women and girls "desired" to stay in this line of work because they had no other way to eat. How could "desire" possibly enter in to the women's choice under these circumstances? If it is survival sex, fuck-for-food sex, what cruel male lunatic could possibly think that the word "desire" applies here.

How can it be the desire of the starving and the homeless to fuck for food? That abysmal, brutal sexual imperative of all of human history: the fuck for food.

Of course, the big question is why did the military not help these girls instead of exploiting them? The answer to that one is easy: the soldier always has to have his cheap fuck dump.

Above I mentioned the "male lunatic." But it is the female lunatic who is also to blame. If MacArthur would not help these girls, then why didn't his wife? Why didn't the wives and daughters of all the other men who were stationed in Japan help these wretchedly in-pain girls?

As for the girls having "some resistance" to selling themselves to enemy men of a "different race," the resistance was major: the girls cried and screamed and tried to run away when the GI's entered the brothels. Terrified of these huge men, they held onto things to keep from being pushed down and mounted. Girls who tried to escape were shoved back in by MP's.

Yoshimi Yoshiaki's *Comfort Women: Sexual Slavery in the Japanese Military During WWII* contains the following assessment of the girls' fear: "The first comfort station, Komachien, was set up in the Tokyo-Yokohama area. It was opened as early as August 27. The women were petrified of the U.S. soldiers pouring in and began weeping. There were even some who clung to posts (holding up the roof) and wouldn't move."

How is crying and being terrified considered "some resistance." And note the cool phrasing of the official Japanese account: the girls felt "apprehension" due to "differences" in "race." This does not at all express the terror and disgust of lying down beneath bodies too heavy and penises too big and being torn apart. The girls were afraid of having their vaginas ripped to pieces. How is this "apprehension" over a "difference" in "race"? Utterly amazing, the way these men can hide the pain through language that lies to us.

How could the soldiers mount the girls if they were so terrified? One girl, completely inexperienced as a prostitute, tells how terrified she was to be mounted by twenty-three GIs her first day at 'work.' I am surprised she survived the savagery at all—how could she have withstood twenty-three rapes in row without bleeding to death? If the men saw how miserable she was, why did they continue to mount her? How else can you analyze this behavior except as rape? And I would like to ask the girls who were mounted sixty times a day if they came to accept this "peacefully." I would like to ask them how their bodies felt after sixty rapes and how they managed to not bleed to death in just one day, let alone being able to withstand this day after day after day. Were they stunned into shock the whole time? Were they even aware of who was mounting them, so deep would have been the ravaging of their bodies and minds? Hopefully, they did what other mass raped women report doing: become numb to bear the unbearable, and become indifferent to the disgust of intercourse with serial soldier rapists.

The male view that this activity can be accepted "peacefully" must be countered. Did the Japanese officials who observed the girls being raped into "acceptance" perhaps mistake the comatose state of the in-shock body for "peace"? Did they mistake the expression in the rape-dead eyes for "peace"?

Although the numbers are horrifying, it does not have to be sixty mounts a day to qualify as rape. Even one is too many—even one forced act of sex on a body is too many. Even one terrified girl forced to fuck for food is too many.

Someone has to ask the comfort girl what is was like for her. Talmadge's reporting does not include how she felt. How was she able to sleep at night with her torn body and how was she able to wake up the next day with only more mass rape to look forward to? As she slept, did she feel the stabbing between her legs in her nightmares? Most importantly, given that rape sixty times a day will cause severe physical damage—bleeding, bruising, and swelling of tissues, how could a woman possibly bear the pain of just one day of this to her most tender parts, let alone day after day, month after month, even year after year if she survives insanity.

The raped should tell her side of history.

And, of course, she cannot due to shame. It has never been brought out that it is the shame of the male that is the real issue—his shame for his raping cruelty. No shame at all should be put on the woman.

One group has told their stories. The Korean Comfort Women. (I would rename them Korean Comfort Girls since the average age was mid-teens, with many even younger. To call them 'women' is ludicrous.) These girls were imprisoned in brothels by the Japanese military and raped thirty or more times a day. By some miracle of the goddesses, a few survivors finally spoke up about their torment—fifty years after the end of WWII. Their testimonies report the bleeding, swelling, intolerable pain of ongoing mass rape to that area of the body, and the venereal diseases inflicted on them, and the extreme disgust and eventual insanity that results from being mounted all day by men you don't know. How could it be any different for the Occupation Comfort Girls, who were treated with identical savagery? How can that word, "peacefully," possibly apply to how they experienced this rape of their bodies?

Here are just a few testimonies from Keith Howard's *True Stories of the Korean Comfort Women*. These are the actual words of the women:

"Having to serve so many men made my sexual organs swell up" (53).

"My vagina was torn and bled for a week" (53).

"On Sundays, the soldiers came from 9 o'clock in the morning until 4 o'clock in the afternoon, without respite. Sometimes we had to serve…40 or more men without pausing for a break. We gave up counting" (61).

"On Saturdays, the Japanese soldiers formed long queues…The ends of the queues were sometime invisible….They came from 9 am till midnight on both Saturdays and Sundays" (99).

"Because I was forced to serve so many men, my womb became raw, red and swollen and began to smell badly….Even in this state I had to keep on serving men" (174).

"If I lay still wetting myself and with my womb bleeding…some men would just kick me and leave….I just lay like a corpse" (172-173).

"We had to serve countless soldiers….My abdomen, my womb, throbbed with pain. I had to serve so many men. Afterwards, I would be unable to walk…" (181).

"It was like a living death" (54).

Girls were transported, as needed for rape purpose, all across Asia: Rangoon, Mandalay, Thailand, and one says, "Wherever we went we were taunted and despised as comfort women" (112). The women of the cities would see where soldiers lined up to get at the girls and do nothing but scorn their suffering. Boys would throw stones and jeer at them. Let us hope that complete emotional and physical numbness hit these girls early in their rape life.

Of course, the aftermath, for the few who survived this unimaginable suffering, was also horrifying. One woman reports how even after many years her PTSD is so extreme that she is gets unbearable restlessness, then hot, then cold and she has to shout and scream and yell. Her fear is so extreme she has to lock herself away from people. She faints from fear when she meets people. She says she "stayed indoor for thirty years, crawling on my knees."

It's interesting that only the soldier is noticed as suffering from PTSD. The prostituted women he has inflicted his brute rapes on are never even credited with PTSD. As we can see from this woman's testimony, hers is far worse. This should not be surprising since she is subjected to extremes of suffering that the 'normal' person cannot even comprehend.

The girls in front of the rape lines at the GI comfort stations would have withstood identical ravaging to what the Korean Comfort Girls did—that torn, bleeding, insane, death-in-life that is the mass rape of the prostituted body. Mounted fifteen to sixty times a day, the women were the same brutalized destroyed whoreflesh as the Korean Comfort Women. American GI's were rapists as savage as the Japanese soldiers.

Another parallel: both the Korean Comfort Girls and the Occupation Comfort Girls had to say 'welcome' to their rapists and thank them afterwards for the rape.

And yet another: millions of Japanese soldiers and American GI's kept their raping behavior hidden for decades by making it a forbidden subject.

Since we do not have a surviving Occupation Comfort Girl to tell her pain, we will have to listen to her Korean sisters.

The Korean Comfort Girls are not exceptions in the world of prostitution. They are the norm. All prostitutes experience what they did.

I don't think that word "peacefully" can be applied to the girl lying there being sexually savaged all day. And I wonder that no journalist or writer focuses on the terrible physical pain. Don't they know that even one little tear to the vaginal area is excruciatingly painful. Just one little prick of roughness can make a girl cry.

It's hard to find even a word, an "accurate" word recorded from the raped Japanese prostitute in the last four centuries, the amount of time since Japan set up its first 'sanctioned' brothels. In 1600, Japan established what is called a 'licensed' system of prostitution: this means they made the sale and rape of bodies legal and confined it to red-light districts. At the edge of these areas were offices with signs that said, "Sell your daughters here"—and the poor did, in great numbers. The Japanese have offered 'comfort girls' to occupying foreigners since the Dutch. Enslaved girls were set up in 'kennels,' like dogs, in port cities and forced to service hundreds of foreign sailors. These girls were absolutely terrified of the huge men who constantly raped them. Only one quote have I ever read from a girl herself. Just one, as if in the entire history of prostitution in Japan, only one comfort girl ever spoke out. The word she used for her existence was "wretched." Perry's men would have taken full advantage of the 'sex slave' arrangement as well. (I found these descriptions of the prostitutes used to satisfy foreign sailors in *Interracial Intimacy in Japan*.)

Talmadge takes his material from two major sources: John Dower's *Embracing Defeat* and Yuki Tanaka's *Japan's Comfort Women: Sexual Slavery and Prostitution During WWII and the U.S. Occupation*. Dower's book came out in 1999 and Tanaka's in 2002, so the material is not in any sense 'hot off the presses' or the wires, so why Talmadge suddenly decided to 'reveal' all this in a news story is certainly a mystery, but I am glad he did. But, as with all news stories, it only contains the male point of view, and the sensitive bodies of the Japanese girls who were split in two by pain as they lay on their backs in the brothels is not touched upon. It is what I wish to touch upon in a very personal way since the Occupation Comfort Girls are my guiding spirits. They awoke in me the desire to tell my own story of being raped and prostituted, although it is nowhere near as tragic and devastating as theirs.

I think I feel their pain so deeply since they suffered so much more than I did. On a scale of one to a thousand, I would put their torment at the thousandth percentile, and mine down around one or two percent. Yet the rape/prostitution I managed to survive de-stroyed me forever. I am in no way a 'survivor.' I hate that phrase 'prostitution survivor.' There is no survival. There is no repair. There is no peace from rape.

Despite comparisons—and how few of us can lay claim to a torment as deep as that of the Korean Comfort Girl--I have discovered that I have to make peace with my own lesser pain. It, too, is important.

Military prostitution is a subject I have been writing on for about two years, and the pathetic tragedy of the Occupation Comfort Girls has been at the center of my consciousness the whole time. They have become the talisman for my search to understand how soldiers can rape the small and helpless, the little whore who is defenseless, as if it were his right, and a norm of military life.

(I need to pause and say a word about terminology. In my own writings, I use the word 'whore' not to degrade but to defuse the power to stigmatize and scorn and destroy that men have invested in it for centuries. To me a whore is a damaged, exploited, ravaged woman who can never heal. Thus, I ally myself proudly with all women who have been treated so. It is the only reparation I can make them, to try to take away the terrible suffering the word has inflicted by appropriating it for my own purposes.)

I am, of course, touched and moved by all those women, in all wars, who have been enslaved and raped by soldiers, but I cannot acknowledge the pain of all in one article, so I have to start somewhere. Why these particular Japanese whores, the ones given to the GI's in 1945, touch me so much comes from my own background. I lived on military bases for the first twenty years of my life, part of that time in Japan, and although it was years after WWII, I saw those tiny mincing timid prostituted Japanese girls and the big soldiers who bought them and this spectacle of helplessness and poverty tore at my heart. The sadness in the girls' eyes haunts me. The way they looked like small children, barely half the size of their GI rapists, hurt me and I wondered how soldiers could even contemplate forcing sex on a such a childlike body.

I felt guilty that I was a safe, protected girl while these girls lived in such misery and degradation.

Later, when I was in my twenties, I was gang raped by soldiers—this is a story I tell elsewhere in my articles so I will leave out the details here—and then I worked as a prostitute for several years near a U.S. military base. At the time, I went into prostitution due to despair and pain and a messed up body and a messed up life and a feeling that all I was fit for was more rape, but I now know that I re-enacted my own gang rape when I worked as a whore. And I must have unconsciously wanted to take upon myself the suffering of 'comfort girls' everywhere. I must have wanted to live their lives so I could understand what they felt. So I went into the place that terrified me most, the place of being violated every day, so I could 'understand.' One meaning of that word is to 'stand under,' to support and aid, and I wanted to lay to rest the troubled ghosts of those girls by becoming one of them. I now know that it was so I could write about them, many years later, but at the time this 'understanding' was hidden deep inside me. In fact, I did not know the details of any 'comfort' girl's life until much later since their stories were covered up after WWII. But I did see around me, in Japan, girls bought like meat, and my whole life I've been sensitive to how if a man rapes one woman, he also rapes me. Even without 'history' to tell me it happened, even before my own time of being raped/prostituted, my body had always felt the rape of all women.

My own rape and my whore life took place thirty years ago. After I left prostitution all those years ago, I simply buried the memory of that time, and tried to hide from the rape pain of others. I went to school, worked, traveled, always hiding from rape pain, not wanting to know about the ravaged girls in Vietnam, Bangladesh, Bosnia, Rwanda. These savage events happened, and I heard about them, but I tried to read as little about them as possible. As if there was much written—there wasn't since the least reported event of war is the sexual torture of women.

A couple of years ago the ghosts of the Comfort Girls (all of them—Korean, Japanese, Vietnamese, Bosnian, the list could be extended for miles of pages, and back into the centuries), and my own ghosts from so long ago, came back to haunt me. Two events triggered this haunting. First, I found myself in a situation where I felt threatened by several men. I don't need to go into the details except to say they were close to me, all of them, surrounding me, and they were big; and far from feeling protected, the way I do when big, kind men are near me, I felt the old rape fear hit me. I managed to get away from them, but for several days, I felt unreal and frightened and full of chills and nausea, almost as if I had a physical illness. For whatever reason, this small incident brought back the rape, and the time in prostitution, full force. I felt as if I was in a different dimension, not in my safe place and life anymore. And I felt very alienated from other women, the way I had felt so many years ago when I worked as a prostitute.

The second trigger that brought back the ghosts was a walk through a local library, where I passed a book on a table and glanced at the title. It was Tanaka's *Japan's Comfort Women*—about the extensive system of sexual slavery the Japanese instituted before and during WWII. I tried as best I could to simply pass it by.

I knew a tidbit of who the Korean Comfort Women were from some sketchy news coverage here and there, and sketchy numbers—about 200,000 had been 'conscripted' for brothel use by the Japanese army--but didn't really want to know more. For thirty years, I had tried to ignore any mention of prostitution or rape in the media. I was always in partial hiding from this subject. Not that there has been much written anyway, until recently.

I moved away from the book and then I kept circling back to it.

I took it home and read it in just a few hours and leaned of the terrible torture and extremes of sexual suffering the historians and journalists from WWII never tell us about and what the mainstream media still never tells us: how the Korean girls were virgins when procured and how they were raped 30-50 times a day; how their vaginas were swollen and bleeding; how their torn-up, infected wombs rotted in their bodies.

I made it through the Korean Comfort Girls' part without a nervous breakdown or irreversible trauma. (It is more accurate to call them 'girls' than women due to their extreme youth when first raped.) But when I read Tanaka's chapter on the behavior of American troops with the Japanese Comfort Girls given to them at the end of WWII, a heavy shocked haunted unbearable pitying sadness grabbed me and wouldn't let me go. I am not finding the words to describe the impact of this chapter about the Allied occupying forces in Tokyo and elsewhere and what they did in the brothels to the destitute girls conscripted for 'their' pleasure. It was identical to the way the Japanese had treated their 'comfort girls.' And it was far from 'comfort' for the girls. The word 'comfort' is such a cosy one. Comfort and joy. Holding a child or small animal tenderly, to comfort it. Did the girls hold the soldiers to their breasts, to comfort them, the way a mother would a child, as they were being raped?

It was the same rape of virgins on the part of the GI's--most of the girls had had no previous sexual experience: they were simply unprotected and living in the ruins, with no food and ragged clothes and some were barefoot when conscripted. It is no wonder some of the girls committed suicide. To go from being a virgin to having to 'comfort' big frightening men up to sixty times a day must have been a shock too terrible to survive. This is not to say that the other girls, including those who had already been prostituted, did not also feel the pain of constant rape. The prostitute, too, was once a virgin, and once had the life and 'purity' raped out of her as men turned her into a whore. And some of the original Korean Comfort Women, already raped beyond life and belief, were turned over to the GI's to be abused by their new conquerors.

As I have mentioned, some of the phrasing of the official American reports of the time, quoted by Tanaka, caused me extreme pain, for example, that the girls "desire to remain in this line of work" because it is the only way they can eat. (My big question is how come the army didn't feed them instead of raping them? But I guess that is an age-old dilemma: occupying armies need cheap bodies for rape fodder; starving girls will lay down to be raped more docilely than well-fed ones.)

The words we choose are important. "Desire." A "desire" to be raped, because of starvation? You cannot associate "desire" with "fuck for food." They do not belong in the same universe.

The way "intimacy" is used in the context of prostitution sex is equally troublesome. For example, Cynthia Enloe says that the sailors stationed in Hawaii during WWII only experienced three minutes of 'intimacy' on top of the prostituted assembly-line whores servicing them, at the rate of up to a hundred men a day-- where long, long lines formed in front of the brothels in Hotel Street. Although Enloe is sympathetic toward prostituted bodies, her word choice in this instance makes it sound as if this is a sad thing for the sailor. Poor guy. Only gets to mount and bang away for three minutes. Well, I guess if every guy were to take a ten-minute fuck, the whore's body would be even more shredded.

"Intimacy." It is a word that lives, in false security and splendour, in the likes of *Glamour* and *Cosmopolitan* magazine. It applies to all those safe girls who read the advice of safe sex experts on the joys of "intimacy" with a loving, tender man. For the whore, that man does not exist. Take the sex expert, proudly displaying her liberated sex knowledge in the safe pages of these fantasy publications and put her in a brothel and rape her all day, and she will maybe wake up to the way there is no safe "intimacy" for the blind, quasi-liberated readers of her articles. If you inflict rape on one body, then no intimacy is possible for any woman—until she liberates her enslaved counterparts, there is no freedom or safety for her. (This is, by the way, the reason I consider prostitution The Issue for all women. It is the lowest men can degrade us to. If these terribly mistreated women exist, there is no dignity for any of us. You have to liberate the most tortured to free the rest of us.)

"Intimacy." I read it recently in a description of a talk on "sex work" by an academic, where she frames her ideas in terms of "sexual commerce" and "intimacy" for customer and whore. She needs a stint of brothel time, as does the sex expert.

No, there is no "intimacy" for the raped body, or for the man who forces sex on her.

Back to Tanaka's book, there was one sentence that haunted me for months afterwards and still does. It was the sentence that set in motion all the writing I have done over the past two years on military prostitution. It is the center of my mission and my passion to free the ghosts of these girls, and all others, whose bodies have been murdered by brothel rape. The sentence was quite a simple one, written by an American officer who described how he saw "fifty men lined up to get at one girl—she was very 'busy.'" That was it. Just that simple sentence. The coldness of this description, of her being 'busy,' the complete indifference to her pain hit me so hard I became sick and couldn't leave the house for several days. My men did this? My noble soldiers? Fifty of them gang raped a small body? And one of them observed this and could only say she was 'busy.' That one sentence summed up for me all the hardness and cruelty of the military toward the women that it permanently places in rape hells.

It still sickens me to think of this sentence.

I think I must be a Reincarnated Comfort Girl, so hard is this pain that hits me.

So, I began to write. The book you are reading came out of this and two novels thus far: *Tender Bodies and Whore Stories* and its sequel, *Comfort the Comfort Women*. Both are erotic satires set in the world of military prostitution.

One of the Occupation Comfort Girls, a virgin, who committed suicide after several days of brothel rape by GI's, was named Takita. (I don't think she "accepted" her brothel rape "peacefully.") Since no one else has told her story, I have fictionalized it, in my novels. It is not the 'official' American account, of how she was 'busy.' It is not the 'official' Japanese history that tells me she found 'peace' through constant rape under the heavy bodies of terrifying soldiers. It is not the account in Talmadge's article, which is distanced from the pain of the women. It is not the male version of history and the media that controls our vision and narrows our reality, as if rape and enforced prostitution were simply a minor footnote to war. It is Takita's story, based on my own experiences of bleeding after servicing men. And it is the story of Yoko and Miki and Kasumi and Keiko and of all the other 'comfort' whores who perished without names under the gang rape of the Allied conquerors.

Talmadge's article leaves out the way prostitutes bleed when we service too many men. It leaves out the fact that we are like other women. Like those 'respectable' women without raped vaginas who would also bleed if turned into whores. And it only takes an hour or so, to turn a respectable girl into a whore. And hour of constant rape is the recipe the GI's used, as they raped some of the virgins into unconsciousness and into their new whore status.

(Then, by the way, we are not like other women anymore. We will never be like them again. There is no 'normal,' no recovery after mass rape of the body. I may not be like 'normal' women. But they can certainly become like me. All it takes is a few hours of rape and you are destroyed forever.)

Talmadge again quotes the official Japanese report from the time as to why the authorities set up the 'Rape Stations': "The strategy was, through the special work of experienced women, to create a breakwater to protect regular women and girls." "Special experienced women," as if the girls designated 'whores' are of a different species? As if they do not feel violated when stabbed between the legs sixty times a day? First of all, it needs to be said that even those previously prostituted, those 'experienced,' could not be thought of as engaging in 'special work' since there is really no training ground by which to become 'experienced' for this kind of work. Did the prostitute, when she was a virgin, walk into a brothel and say, "Rape me constantly, to give me 'experience' for this kind of work. Make me 'special,' by raping me. Make me different from 'regular' women. Rape me until you make me a whore." Then, did her rapists give her a certificate, which she proudly took to the newly opened Rape Comfort Station, where she said, "Now, I am a 'special, experienced' woman ready to lay down for more rape, much more rape, by the American soldiers"?

Do people really think the whore has a different kind of vagina from 'decent' women? It is supposed to be a cast-iron vagina? Do they really think she does not mind rape dozens of times a day as a 'special, experienced woman'? Where is the humane commonsense in this terrifying concept?

The male differentiation between 'regular' women and 'whore' women is highly suspect since it depends on the male action of raping a virgin body in order to turn it into a whore body. How is this action, which is beyond the control of the girl, a way of consigning her, forever, to the category of whore, that is, defining her as a disposable vagina, a dumping ground for excess testosterone? If the girl were not weaker than her violators, she would not let them turn her into an object of raped degradation. Cruel brute male strength is the only reason for the differentiation between 'whore' and 'regular' woman.

The rape stations were set up under the auspices of a fancy organization called the RAA (Recreation and Amusement Association) and it even had a head of Public Relations who reports seeing the hundreds of GI's lined up as soon as the places opened and that the men were so rough and noisy and unruly that the MP's could barely keep the men under control. An interesting position, a Japanese businessman who is Head of Public Relations for Rape, for places that sell young girls like insensate meat to rough sailors and soldiers. How rough and cruel must have been the intercourse these eager rapists inflicted on the terrified girls. And the girls must have passed out with fear, or vomited with fear, and peed from fear, when they heard the hundreds of men in the streets, waiting their turn. And did the Head of Rape PR then go home to dinner with his wife and daughter, after being paid handsomely off the earnings of the helpless raped occupation whores?

The entire mass rape system set up for the GI's in Tokyo and elsewhere had the full co-operation of the American military. Then, in late 1946, the Americans came out with some nonsense about prostitution being against women's rights and said they were closing the brothels.

Talmadge writes: "MacArthur's primary concern was not only a moral one."

Actually MacArthur's primary concern was not a moral one at all. If it were, why didn't he stop the setting up of the Mass Rape Stations in August 1945? He knew they were there. He knew about the long rapelines. By failing to stop the system at its inception, he tacitly condoned the rape of these girls' bodies thousands of times by thousands of men.

In fact, according to Tanaka, the reason for closing down the brothels was simple: the GI's had given the majority of the girls VD. It did not go in the opposite direction since most of the enslaved were virgins before they screamed and cried under the heavy men and the first rapes. (It makes one ask where the GI's were raping whore bodies before they landed in Japan. Some of the men had been in the European theatre and then were transferred over to the Pacific, so one can assume that that the starvation prostitution forced on the French, German, and Italian girls had infected them with VD as well. Again, I'd like to ask that big question—why didn't the commanders in the European theatre stop the rape of desperate, hungry prostituted bodies? For that matter, why didn't all American GI's and their superior officers set up true 'comfort' stations for the starving girls in Italy and Germany and France and Japan—instead of making them fuck for food among the ruins? It is a big question. Someone needs to answer it. I am going to keep asking it until someone does.)

Women's rights be damned. It is the old formula: you don't want an army of diseased penises; it lessens the effectiveness of the men. The same old story. Clemenceau's response to American commanders during WWI, when they complained that use of French whores was infecting their 'wholesome' boys, was, "I will give the soldiers clean whores." The Prime Minister of France offering women's bodies as rape fodder.

Women's rights has never had anything to do with it. It is purely a matter of VD. The welfare of the women is irrelevant to the 'hygiene' of the soldier.

It has always been this way due to the male idea that the whore is to blame for her own degradation and she is the carrier of the diseases. When a big whore industry flourished around U.S. bases in the Philippines, Filipina women objected to only the prostitutes being tested for VD, saying that it was the GI's who had brought AIDS to the country. Sure enough, there is strong evidence that American servicemen carried AIDS from Mombasa, a port city where militaries from around the world rape African whores, into the Philippines.

Talmadge writes that the U.S military knew of the plight of the Korean Comfort Women, knew fully what they had been subjected to, yet did not reveal this 'minor detail of war' to the world. And it is no wonder. As Tanaka, and another historian who writes on this subject, George Hicks, point out, since they needed comfort girls to service their own men all across the Pacific and in Europe, why would the Americans criticize the Japanese for setting up such an efficient Mass Rape System.

Talmadge also writes that the U.S. military commanders in Japan were aware that the girls were coerced into the Rape Stations. Now, how much intelligence it would take to figure this out, I don't know. A lot I guess, since it never seems to occur to the male military mind that no woman would ever, ever, ever invite the rape that is prostitution on her body if she had a choice. Please tell me what woman would actually lie down and invite sixty men to climb on top of her? With all of the bleeding and soreness and tearing and uterine and bladder damage and nausea and fear that this entails. And the indescribable disgust of being mounted by men you don't know.

Numbers are tricky. Some from the period say that the girls serviced 15-60 men a day. Even servicing five men a day against your will will tear you up pretty badly.

Did it never occur to these American authorities that if their own daughters back home would not want to service lines of GI's, why would it be fine for young Japanese girls to do so?

If the American commanders were capable of imagining how much the girls were bleeding, why did they not close down the rape stations? The big mystery, of course, is how all these 'wholesome' American boys could actually force intercourse on girls who were screaming and crying. When the girls lost consciousness from the extremes of pain, did the men keep raping them? Since it is obviously irrelevant to the man who buys an enslaved creature whether a woman is attached to the vagina or not, probably so.

What is really alarming is that Dower believes usage of prostituted bodies in post-WWII Japan by GI's was almost 100%. This means almost every father, son, and brother there was a rapist. How could these men go home and dare be allowed to ever touch another woman, given their rape behavior in Japan? When they had daughters, precious daughters, how dare they even be allowed to be in the presence of these tender girls after their rape behavior in Japan?

It seems that the civilian non-whore female mind also has a hard time figuring out that whores don't like the mass rape of their bodies. Japanese non-whore women knew about the rape stations. They saw the lines. Why didn't thousands of them form a barrier between the GI's and their sisters?

Supposedly, the whores were there to form a breakwater, a big dumping ground for oceans of menacing semen and lines of phallic spears, so as to keep the 'decent' women safe from marauding, pillaging GI's. This never works since men encouraged to regard bodies as cheap rape fodder in brothels will carry this attitude over to the civilian population. And the GI's did, raping thousands of 'good' girls despite the availability of cheap 'bad' girls.

Indeed, those GI's in the Yokosuka mass-rape lines set in motion a Culture of Rape that continues to this day. Those WWII soldiers who raped whores so freely passed this tradition on to their sons, who did the same in Vietnam, and now the current generation has inherited these rape values and this rape culture: GI's are currently using enslaved girls trafficked into 'entertainment' centers near U.S. bases in Korea. Raping whore bodies freely, and with impunity, has long-term consequences: American women live in this rape culture, struggle against it, all unaware of its progenesis--ongoing violation of the bodies of hundreds of thousands of prostituted enslaved bodies overseas, in war, and in peacetime (during occupation). The American woman's willful ignorance and lack of sympathy for the foreign raped body is part of the problem, but that is a topic for another article.

Details upon details, every one even more pathetic than the last, emerge from the documents uncovered by Dower and Tanaka (and Hicks as well). Above the rape area of each girl was a sign that read "Well Come" and below that her name. By the etiquette of enslavement, a Japanese whore is supposed to bow and welcome her rapist to her bed, and then when he is done with her, she is supposed to thank him for the rape. The Korean Comfort Girls had been instructed to do this with their Japanese captors and the Occupation Girls the same with their GI assailants. What ultimate submission of the female spirit to the entitled dominant male is implied by this brutal 'rape etiquette' even I cannot put into words—and I am a pretty good writer.

If the girls were unconscious after hours of rape, I am not sure how they could manage to stand up and bow, or to be aware they were supposed to thank the man for the torture of their body.

What kind of degraded submissiveness of womanhood could lead to this male version of enslavement etiquette is hard for me to grasp, given that I still try to hold on to some small measure of dignity in a world that turned me into a rape dump. To actually thank my rapist for raping me? I may be battered down by the male, and his terrible violence, but I don't think I could even imagine that level of submissiveness for myself.

Talmadge ends his piece with a note about the fund set up to compensate the Korean Comfort Women. Of the 200,000 or so, most were Korean but some Japanese women were enslaved as well. Talmadge quotes Haruki Wada, administrator of the fund: "The vast majority of women did not come forward." Talmadge writes: "Though they were free to do so, no Japanese women sought compensation." Wada concludes: "Not one Japanese woman has come forward to seek compensation or an apology. Unless they can say that they were completely forced against their will, they feel they cannot come forward."

The above statements by Talmadge and Wada do not even remotely approximate the psychology of the Japanese whore that would prevent her from coming forward. First of all, she is not 'free to come forward' in any way since she lives in a world that will scorn and blame her for her own rape. Of the few former Korean Comfort Women who told their stories of enslavement, they had to brave heavy censure from family and neighbors. One woman reports others calling her 'whore for the Japanese' and saying, "You must have been really tough to take on fifty men a day." 'Take on' as if she invited her own ravaging.

To come forward for an "apology." What kind of apology, in what realm beyond the universe, could compensate her for the loss of her body, her sexuality, her mind, and her life? "Apology." The word is a joke, right?

During WWII, as the Korean Comfort Women traveled, enslaved, with the troops, from city to city, they were scorned by local populations as whorefilth. Children threw stones at them, and local women objected to how unsightly the long rapelines were, objected to how the didn't want their daughters and children contaminated by the presence, in their city, of such dirty women. These objections took place while the comfort women were on their backs, being mounted, greatly against their will, for twelve to fifteen hours a day. Local civilian women were also glad the women were there as rape sites since they thought it would save their own vaginas from invasion. 'Decent' Japanese women thought the same in August, 1945, glad to have a 'breakwater' wall of raped girls for the semen to wash up against. But they were mistaken since the GI's raped 'decent' girls as well, and turned them into whores.

During WWI, European women on the way to church objected to seeing long lines of soldier in front of brothels. It was not 'seemly' and would be a bad influence on the children.

All this censure would also explain why one never hears the stories of the whores of Italy or France or Germany used by the Allies after the Second World War. Some of these 'comfort women' are still alive but I have yet to read of one coming forward. It is time. Your stories will be lost if none of you speaks. Those pimped on the streets of Naples and in the parks of Palermo to the Allies. Where are you? Say something! You continue to promote the dominance of the rapist; your silence kills us all.

Nothing has changed since WWI or WWII. Whores are still scorned and blamed for their own whore status and their own rape. (I know that I am frightened of my past being uncovered, of being degraded all over again once having been a rape dump and a piece of whore garbage: this can never be erased.) 'Decent' American women still regard whores as filth and dirt overseas seducing GI's and making the poor boys 'impure' by forcing them to succumb to temptation. At least this was certainly the attitude I heard on military bases as I grew up. When the American military wives and daughters would even talk about the subject—it was extremely rare to acknowledge the existence of the comfort women outside the gate, except to label them 'bad' and 'dirty' and 'sinful' and without 'morals.'

No censure of the GI was ever heard. Boys will be boys.

So, Talmadge's statement that any former Japanese comfort woman was 'free' to come forward does not hold up. What kind of freedom can she possibly have in a world that blames her for the rape of her own body? Neither can I puzzle out Wada's idea that the women didn't reveal themselves because they couldn't prove they were forced. How many rapes are needed to 'prove' force? One Korean Comfort Woman reports being raped 300 times over a period of eighteen hours. She had to pee where she lay. She 'took on' a different man every three or four minutes, and the men had to thrust very hard to come quickly. Would this number, and this amount of excruciating pain, be sufficient proof of force?

Since I have great difficulty talking about what happened to my own body, and the sexual violence inflicted on it was far less traumatic than lying down on a filthy mat and being mounted all day by brutal men—since I feel cold fear and misery and dread of being shamed when I mention my own experiences, how much worse must be the shame and terror of these other poor women, who were the object of a suffering so extreme, they kept silent for six decades. And the few who 'broke' silence, found no peace. To a woman, those Korean comfort girls who told their stories said: "No reparation is possible. The soldiers took our girlhood and womanhood away from us, they took our lives away from us."

As did the GI's take away the lives of the girls in the Rape Stations in Japan, 1945. Not one man has been punished for the murder of these girls' bodies.

Once the comfort stations were closed in 1946, the Japanese girls were not magically rescued from prostitution. Most stayed in due to destitution and due to feeling they were worth nothing after so much rape. In fact, Dower states that over 20% of the girls interviewed in the years after the war said they became prostitutes as a result of gang rape by GI's. After that event, they felt more rape was all they were fit for. It is a common sentiment among prostitutes and a major reason it is so hard to escape this rape prison. You cannot see beyond it while you are in it since you feel so ruined.

After the closing of the 'official' rape camps, brothels by no means disappeared. Rather, they flourished in even larger numbers and did, according to Tanaka, "a roaring business" among the GI's.

Japanese organized crime was heavily involved in procuring girls and running the brothels, so it is unlikely the women themselves made much money. As is common around the world, to this day, the whore's body bears the pain, the customer (rapist) takes his pleasure, and her owners take the money. If she survives, she usually has several STD's as well as other health problems, and life-long mental illness from the constant rape. Conditions are so brutal in this world for most prostitutes that CATW (Coalition Against Trafficking in Women) says that the average lifespan in many brothels is only twenty-five years. One reason for this startling statistic is the advent of AIDS. Due to heavy demand for 'clean' girls, child prostitution has skyrocketed. Girls are often sold so young (age ten or even younger sometimes) that they are dying of the disease by their 20's.

The sheer hopelessness of all this lies on me like a block of granite. And the hopelessness is compounded by knowing that all the 'whoregirls' in the world, if they had not been forced to whore, would blame their sisters for whoring. And even the female who has been raped into whoredom is without mercy for her sisters. The whore defines herself with such words as 'shame,' "filthy,' 'ruined,' 'worthless.' As long as she does so, she is part of the reason for her own rape—and the rape of those beside her in the brothel beds. You would think that a vagina would confer on a girl empathy with other vaginas. Not so— since women cannot see beyond the pernicious 'virgin/whore' split that is largely responsible for prostitution.

I blame women even more than men. On occasion, after WWII, a kind GI tried to rescue and marry a Japanese whore but this was strictly forbidden by the U.S. military. Extensive background checks were necessary and if she was even suspected of being a 'bad' girl, she was too impure for marriage with a clean American soldier.

The military has yet to explain to me how the GI's raping ways kept them 'pure' and 'spotless' while the men transformed the girls underneath them into dirt.

Cornelius Ryan, writing about the situation in Tokyo just after the war, complained that it was a shame all these American boys only got to know the Japanese woman as prostitute, as 'fake geisha,' rather than the 'real' Japanese woman, the 'decent' one with her gentle submissiveness and beautiful womanhood. Sorry for the GI's who took full advantage of helpless bodies? Sorry for the GI's who without mercy inflicted extremes of sexual torture on girls with no choice and no escape, except death, for those who managed to commit suicide? When I read this Ryan statement, quoted by a woman scholar who saw nothing amiss in the idea, I tried to pierce the kind of mind that can feel sorry for the rapist and have no sympathy for the raped. I wasn't able to.

Reading Talmadge's article bothered me due to the way the sheer unbearable misery of the girls was left out. It also bothered me because I had just come from a conference where a number of men and women read papers in favor of recognizing the terrible rape of the trafficked (the term now being applied to enforced prostitution). This handful of people think the way I do: that it is time to stop celebrating the rapist as courageous and noble and beyond reproach because he is a soldier. And it is time to stop shaming the women he rapes.

To actually meet a handful of people who share this view was special. It was magical. For one brief moment, I felt as if I was not alone. It was a shining moment that gave way, all too soon, to despair when I came home and read Talmadge's article.

Despair, not because of the article itself. As I said, I am glad he wrote it. I am glad the few people at the conference who heard my own article on the Occupation Comfort Girls are now not the only ones who know this. Talmadge's Associated Press piece went out to many papers.

The despair came when I read responses to the article across the internet. Attitudes such as this piece was not 'newsworthy' and 'leave the subject alone already,' it is in the past, it does not matter now, how can we criticize our noble GI's, and—this was the corker--the article is not 'accurate.' Talmadge makes reference to his sources, to the impeccable research by Dower, who is a Professor Emeritus at MIT, and Tanaka, an historian at an Australian university who is an expert on Japanese war crimes. I would like to add here that I have huge respect for both Dower and Tanaka, not only for uncovering this long-ignored topic, but because both men show great sensitivity as they write about it. They acknowledge and realize the girls' pain. Tanaka is even troubled by what he might have done if he had served in the Japanese army during WWII. Would he also have made use of the 'comfort girls,' he asks in his book.

Tanaka-san, thank you, you are my hero. As are you John Dower. And I would like to add George Hicks to the list, a third man who writes with compassion about both groups of comfort women and shows politeness and softness when he interviews these miserably wounded women.

But there were many attitudes in the internet comments that were incredibly disturbing. One woman was afraid she would be called a 'prude' if she thought it was disgusting for a whore to have intercourse with sixty men a day. The woman said that even after two men, that's enough, you get sore, so how can another woman do sixty? It is good that she objects to the mass rape of another woman, but why on earth and in all the heavens would she be afraid this objection would label her a 'prude'? Are we women so controlled by male entitlement to commercialized rape that we cannot see beyond it? Are we afraid we will seem 'prudish' if we stand up against the sexual torture of another woman?

The idea that all this had been covered before and that we should "leave it alone" astounded me so much that I had to do some deep breathing exercises. This subject has never been covered before. Of the hundreds of thousands of articles written on WWII, this is the first on the Occupation Comfort Girls. And the male voices out there think that one article on this subject is too many? U.S. servicemen have inherited the tradition of 'brothel rape' from the men who stood in the Yokosuka rapelines in 1945. Since no one has ever dared approach this subject until recently, I wonder how one Associated Press article can actually be considered excessive? And if we continue to silence and shame the victims of military rape, it will go on and on and on. And is doing so right now, anywhere militaries and NATO and UN Peacekeepers are stationed. There has never been a move to actually help the whores created by military demand. We are overdue on this one by about ten centuries. And we are doing nothing about it now in the latest brothel created by war, Iraq.

The attitudes of vets was particularly troubling, although I should have expected it, since I talked to many, many soldiers during the 1960's and 70's and 80's and they expressed the same ideas. In response to Talmadge's article, which reveals unbelievable brutality in the comfort stations, some vets were bragging about their own phallic adventures all over the world, as if it were fun and games to screw enslaved girls from Thailand to Morocco. "Line forms to the rear" was the attitude" and "horny guys off the ships gotta get in there and get drunk and find a whore to screw. " Comments like this, as if the men had not even read, or registered, the horror in the Talmadge article.

The inability to regard rape as rape sickened me to the point of despair. I reach out to try to understand. I would ask the soldiers, "If your sister or daughter or wife were on her back in front of the rape queue, would you say, 'Line forms to the rear,' as if it were all a joke?"

Other vets just took it for granted, that the soldier had to have his cheap sex, it is the way things are, boys will be boys, it will always be this way. At first, I wanted to say, "If you think this way, the rape lines will only grow longer." And they are, growing longer. Trafficking in humans is now more lucrative, according to the United Nations, than the drug trade.

Then I realized that the men who think this way want to. It is convenient for them to have whores to screw around the world. Why would they want to give up this centuries-old masculine privilege? I now see the reasons behind the joking about the girl's rape pain. I now understand how those GI's in Japan in 1945 could mount, one right after the other, despite the way the girls screamed and cried. The men are upholding an entitlement to sexual domination that is sacred to them. It is part of being a man for them.

The politics and privilege of soldier rape is still active.

It was interesting that some comments on the Talmadge article considered brothel rape a thing of the past. "Glad that's over with." I wonder what planet these people came from. Did they miss the whole 20th century? Are they not aware that due to trafficking; due to the huge presence of militaries and multinational forces around the world, creating customer demand; due to the strength and pervasiveness of transnational gangs; due to the low status of women in the third world; due to deep levels of poverty, there are more women and girls in brothels at this moment than there have been in the collective history of our species? And do these people from that other planet not realize that the attitudes of U.S. serviceman, far from having changed, are identical to those of the men in the Yokosuka rapelines? Badly damaged girls, girls held in debt bondage, imprisoned, beaten to make them compliant, service our soldiers near bases in Korea, and the men consider the degradations the girls are forced into, like dancing naked on the bars, the 'norm' because the girls are there for the man's pleasure.

Many of these GI's in Korea know the girls are enslaved. These men are not that dumb. But they use them anyway. Condoms sit in boxes at the gates of the bases as the men go out; and all the bars have what are called 'VIP' rooms, small squalid areas in the back where the men can take the girls for sex. And the few girls who escape describe how they cry when forced by the men. The situation is identical in Germany—maybe even worse since the country has about 350,000 'legal' sex slaves—most of them now from Eastern Europe, girls trafficked in by the Russian mafia after a thorough breaking in period of ongoing rape and humiliation and public fuck and being mounted by a different man every few minutes until the girls have no spirit or defiance left. The biggest red-light slave ground in Germany is the near the biggest U.S. base there. The soldiers must sample quite a few sex slaves since their owners rotate them around to different brothels so there will be 'fresh fuck meat' for the customers.

It is still puzzles me how the soldiers maintain the illusion that prostitution is always voluntary on the part of the girl, even when she cries, but then I am not a man. I am a gentle woman who has been raped. It would seem an absolutely necessary illusion on the part of the soldier so he can say, jokingly, "Line forms to the rear."

At my conference, I experienced a brief shining moment. I thought I could make a difference, because I was in the comforting presence of a few people who thought, as I do, that military rape is a terrible thing. I was with a few people who understood (stood under, supported) me. They even understood why I have to create my own vocabulary—'prostitution rape,' 'brothel rape'--since no words exist to reflect a reality that most of the world, and soldiers in particular, simply do not recognize. For them a whore is a whore and she invites her own degradation. No rape involved. It is a cherished illusion they must sustain, in order to enjoy the privilege of rape. Even if it is sixty men is a row, and she cries and bleeds, it is still not rape to them--since she is being paid. Remember the 'illusion' of the Japanese officials in the Talmadge article: that the girls were 'well paid'—as if money can compensate a girl for the eternal nightmare of being mounted sixty times a day.

The military vets on the internet expressed the idea that you couldn't blame the men for mounting the girls—after all, it was offered to them—served up on a rape mat, so to speak. What is a young guy to do? My response would be, "Take responsibility for his actions," but I now realize that would be impossible. The brief, shining moment at the conference dissolved when I read the responses to the Talmadge article. I had one wonderful moment, with a few people, of actually believing that the words I put down might reach some soldiers, and civilian non-whore women.

Not a chance. And in some ways I cannot blame the men. Biology is against them. If a man has a rapestick, he will use it. And all men have rapesticks. In Korea right now, our military brothers and fathers and sons are using rapesticks on trafficked girls. Girls so damaged from being broken they will never recover.

Young men have particularly brutal rapesticks since they combine power with no brakes on that power. And it is no wonder a young man can take pleasure in ramming a small, defenseless, crying whore. It must be the ultimate phallic experience for him. A proof of his superiority to the female, in all her weakness. Why would any man want to have intercourse with a confident woman who is his equal when he can enjoy overpowering a girl who is broken, docile, and completely helpless beneath his manhood? No higher proof of manhood exists than the soldier indulging in brothel rape of an enslaved body.

If you doubt me, then look at the Yokosuka rapelines. Fathers and brothers and sons were in those lines. No man held back. The comfort girls serviced all our men, and the men jostled and pushed and were 'elbow to elbow' to get at the enslaved bodies. No man held back. What but the driving power of his brutal noble phallic conviction could lead every father and brother and son to rape with such thoroughness? They knew no higher moment of manhood than when they mounted those terrified, crying girls.

I see non-whore women as heavily complicit in all this. I read feminist 'lists' of the types of rape: date rape, acquaintance rape, fraternity gang rape, etc. Not once, in the several decades that I have perused feminist literature on rape have I seen 'brothel' or 'prostitution rape' included as a type. The concentration is mostly on one-time rape, one man attacking one woman, as if the most raped beings in the world—the prostitutes—simply did not exist. So how can I blame the men in the Yokosuka rapelines when it has taken women all of eternity to even acknowledge that the prostituted body is a vehicle for constant, relentless rape? There seems to be massive sympathy for the body raped just once, and none for the body raped sixty times a day.

I talk to young women on college campuses who are so proud of their local rape crisis center. With happy, satisfied faces they tell me how, now, girls are no longer alone when they are raped. They can get help. Then I ask, "What about the prostitutes?" The college girls greet me with blank faces. "Huh, that's not rape, is it? The girls get paid."

Then I ask them if the prostitutes are able to go to the rape crisis center after a night of being climbed on by men they don't know? For "help."

Total blankness.

These privileged, safe college girls simply do not recognize that prostitution is sexual violence against women, let alone that it exemplifies extreme forms of oppression, suffering, and degradation. It is as if these safe girls are as incapable of empathizing with the massively violated bodies of prostitutes as the Yokosuka mass rapists were.

The ones who do regard prostitution as rape are those of us who have experienced it. But trying to tell others what it feels like is practically impossible.

At the conference, I had a brief hopeful moment of thinking my writing could make a difference. I remember talking to another woman from the U.S. and looking over at a group of three others, one from Iraq, one from Sri Lanka, and one from India, chatting together. In a small way, this seemed like an historic moment. Women from such different backgrounds all united against this extreme form of sexual violence against our bodies that has ruined us for centuries. A few minutes, in this space, with these other compassionate beings—what comfort. Although the moment was swallowed up in what the world considers far more important concerns, for me it had an historic significance on a personal level since it was so rare to share space with other women who care. It gave me hope.

I have abandoned all hope since reading the responses, scattered across the internet, to the GI rape-torture of the WWII Japanese sex slaves. Vets angry that we should criticize the GI's for this activity. "Boys will be boys." If we are not supposed to criticize them for the brutal mass rape of helpless, child-size bodies, then what can we criticize them for? Since no one stopped them in 1945, in front of the Yokosuka Rape Stations, this sexual brutality with impunity sanctioned the tradition of rape by GI's that continued into Korea, Vietnam, Thailand, the Philippines, Okinawa, etc.

Those responses tell me that that kind of rape is widely accepted and celebrated and practiced as necessary for male release in the military. It is widely approved, as tacit policy that cheap sex on enslaved bodies has to be available for soldiers. I now know that no change is possible. Men will always rape whores for fun, and 'decent' women will always be indifferent to this because their bodies have never known 'brothel rape.'

I now know that no healing is possible for me since I cannot help others to heal. If soldiers regard the rape of whores as a norm and a dirty joke, I can do nothing. I now know that I will always be a piece of rape garbage. No matter how many books I write, no matter how many words I put down, I can do nothing to lessen the suffering. I will keep writing, to release my own pain and tension. But I will always be only a raped whore, too dirty to live or have any dignity. Men raped all the life out of me a long time ago. I thought I could find new life in words meant to lessen suffering—but it is hopeless.

2

This article is a companion piece to the previous one. It gives yet another perspective on the wretchedness of the 'Occupation Comfort Girls.'

Australian Military Gang Rape of 'Fallen Blossoms'

November 11, 2007

Veterans' Day makes me uneasy. I wander from room to room, careful to touch each wall with my fingertips; if I do not complete this ritual, I become too jumpy to sit still. Years after I developed this strange rite, I discovered it was called an obsessive compulsive disorder. The final act of the rite is a visit to the closet, where I angle myself into the corner and place my forehead against the wall. It feels cool and soothing. In this corner, I am safe, at least for a few minutes.

Veterans' Day makes me jumpy because of Phantom Rape Pain. On this holiday, I hurt between my legs from thrusts, even though no one is raping me. A long time ago, when I worked as a prostitute, I was sometimes raped twenty or thirty times a weekend by soldiers. Since the U.S. military is never going to give me a Prostitute Star of Honor, I have to commemorate this part of my life in my own way on this day. Last year, it was by writing an article called "Flags of Our Raped Mothers." I decided that to write something every year would be my commemoration, a way to honor myself. A few days ago, I was in a used book store and my hand accidentally fell on a dusty, moth-eaten, mottled, out-of-print volume. I was going to pass it by, but some phantom force of phantom rape pulled me to it.

I bought the book. It is called *Time of Fallen Blossoms* by Allan Clifton and re-counts the author's tour of duty as an Australian soldier in Japan in 1946. The Australians call their military celebration of soldiers Remembrance Day, and, as in the U.S., they don't honor the women that their men raped and prostituted. Apparently, the behavior of Australian soldiers in occupied Japan was as savage, if not more so, than that of the American GI's. Clifton describes standing beside a bed in a hospital: "On it lay a girl, unconscious, her long, black hair in a wild tumult on the pillow....An hour before she had been raped by twenty soldiers. We found her where they had left her, on a piece of waste-land....The soldiers were Australians."

At first, Clifton tries to explain this away as the act of a few aberrant barbarians. But then, when he finds it is a regular occurrence, he can't.

Clifton's *Fallen Blossoms* is, in part, a fascinating portrait of a man struggling with what to make of the prostituted/raped Japanese women who were the sexual prey of Allied forces after WWII. At the Naval Headquarters where he is first billeted, he notices the street girls coming into the barracks at night, to share the bunks of the American GI's. Clifton writes: "Creaking beds and rhythmic movements made the night eloquent, as Japanese girls made the sacrifice, though with no great reluctance, to their country's conquerors."

Clifton seems to be intelligent and compassionate. If so, then I wonder how could he interpret lack of reluctance to hungry girls forced to lie down and withstand rape, night after night, from these terrifying, strange soldiers? I sometimes wonder if the only way to educate men about this horror is to have them raped as many times as the prostitute is violated—thousands of times during the few years she is able to survive this rough, unbearable life—if even that long.

Was the night 'eloquent' for the girls as the rhythmic thrust of rape killed them? I suppose you could see the girls as part of the Universal Rape Mechanism of War—a mechanism so common and necessary that the Rhythm of Rape controls Rape Planet Earth with 'eloquent' movements that imprison and define what a women is for—sexually--with brutal dominance. Clifton certainly has no insight, in this passage, as to what is means to be a woman in constant rape pain—which is what the prostitute is.

Prostitution is the rape of the girl's body. Why does Clifton not see this?

His picture of six-foot Australian GI's, reeling and drunk and rough, terrifies me. What if they had used me the way they did these poor Japanese prostitutes? But then I see every man I meet in terms of a customer/rapist, and my days are spent saying gratefully to myself, "I am so glad I am not a whore anymore—I am so glad I don't have to have sex with that!"

After the 'eloquent' rape of the girls in the barracks, Clifton notices the street whores huddling around the sentries' braziers for warmth at night. Having learned what he terms the "lists of love" from the American GI's, these pathetic girls, he thinks, are now all eager to lay down with their Australian conquerors: "Outside the flickering circle of the braziers' glow stood several disused refrigerating chambers, the floors spread with matting left by destitutes from Hiroshima. These became the scenes of the final consummation of love, and, like army latrines, were occupied and used by numerous people at the same time. The girls were a pretty, grubby dubious lot, as was to be expected. Camp followers are the same the world over. Nearly all were venereal disease hosts, a matter of supreme indifference to the soldiers."

That Clifton could even jokingly use the word "love" for this encounter is such a desecration of the pain of these girls. They were homeless and starving. Does he not see this as the reason for them being 'grubby'? And what pain too deep for tears they must have felt on these filthy mats with these rough, ugly men on top of them, one after the other. Until they became too numb to feel. It is the only escape—shock, numbness. When I was a prostitute, my body was in another place as I was being raped since it was the only way to keep insanity from taking over.

Next comes Clifton's struggle: "I could never bring myself to condemn these girls, whose immediate past experience could hardly have been conducive to observation of the niceties of the moral code." So, inside himself, somewhere where he will not admit it, he actually recognizes that this is starvation forced rape misery for these girls? Yet, he next calls the rape of these desperate prostitutes as "wandering down pleasant byways" for the GI's. He does not once seem to realize that the Australian GI's are the ones to blame. Their own 'moral' behavior is at the lowest level of cruelty and abomination if they will force sex on starving girls. There is another way—a quite simple way—one which the American GI's could have followed as well: give the girls food, protect them, set up shelters for them. Not one WWII soldier, in any way, can be pardoned if he forced a girl to have sex for food. And almost all of them did. So these men are all unpardoned, moral abominations.

Clifton's cruel phrasing continues as he calls the sex act forced on these girls "worship at Eros's inner shrines." Interesting in light of the fact that he has just likened the girls to latrines. And admitted that occupation of these portable toilets was 'numerous.'

One Australian lieutenant, he writes jokingly, "carried out his duties that night in a manner befitting an officer, if not a gentleman." To joke about intolerable pain is dreadful. The 'duty of war' is the duty to rape a woman turned into a toilet for common use? It is ugly, but it is the reality of war—an abomination and a cruelty ignored by everyone except the girl who is the toilet.

Clifton's sanitizes his own particular encounter with a 'fallen blossom.' His whore of choice is not a dirty-latrine camp follower. Instead, she is a prostitute attached to a hotel and he says she can choose her own 'companions.' Of the tryst, he says, "This was so far removed from the sordid squalor, the simulated passion, and the demand for payment…associated with the oldest profession…that no effort of mind could remotely relate the two."

Hum. Ho. Wow! How far from reality can the male military mind (Clifton's) stray in order to rationalize his own use of a communal toilet as something romantic, something far from the real dirt and cruelty of the experience. He imagines the girl as an independent prostitute who has choice—in order to justify his actions—as if to separate himself from the men who climb on the diseased latrines. Yet later he describes all these 'hotels' turned into brothels for the occupying soldiers as places where the owners beat the girls and hold them in debt bondage, taking 80% of their earnings. From what I have read, this debt bondage was typical. And Clifton calls the owners 'evil,' not once recognizing that this whole 'evil' system is the fault of customer demand: whether it be military or civilian rape of prostituted bodies, it is the male who demands sex without restraint; sex upon a subordinated, helpless being; sex without care or tenderness; sex without responsibility to the woman, or to the child he rapes into her body—it is this male who is to 'blame.' Big Time. All those GI's of all nationalities in Japan who were the 'buyers' created this misery. You can't condemn only the men who sell the bodies if you are the purchasers of these enslaved girls. The GI's were the biggest evil of all.

Clifton also excuses himself and the other soldiers by falling back on the old lie: prostitution has been an honored profession in Japan for centuries. Simply not so. For all those centuries of 'licensed' sexual slavery, the whore was, typically, a poor rural girl sold by destitute parents. At the edges of red-light districts were signs: "Sell your daughters here." The girl was broken through being caged and raped continuously in order to make her 'bestial' enough to take the bestiality of many men in a row. In other words, she had to be numbed to the point where she did not care what men did to her—or how many used her. Foreign sailors who used the whores described them as looking like chained dogs in kennels.

I guess the Australian and American GI's took care of this breaking in process in 1945 and 1946, and thereafter—since the typical whore for these soldiers was at first a destitute virgin who was coerced into prostitution and then raped an average of fifteen or more times a day in her kennel/brothel. I can attest from the misery of my own body, that the only way to withstand mass rape is to become as numb as a stone. (I was not raped nearly as many times as these poor Japanese girls, and I still found it unbearable.)

The Japanese prostitute is certainly not honored in any way. She is as scorned and outcast as her counterpart in every other country. She is particularly abhorred by the decent, modest, 'good' girls of Japan. These girls saw the whores given to the conquerors as a necessary barrier. The 'respectable' girls couldn't have all those gallons of semen washing up against their dainty pure ankles. Had to have a seawall for the seamen and their semen. Had to have a handy 'whore toilet' there, as a semen dump. (A GI once said to me, "The only difference between a whore and a toilet it that you don't have to flush her, she flushes herself.")

Clifton, by the way, is careful to distinguish between these gentle sweet wholesome Japanese girl-next-door types and the ones who are 'latrines.' He calls the good girls 'little dears' and sees them as all sweet and blushing. He does not seem to see that the girl lying on her gang rape bed in the hospital, tossing in fever and torment, may be destined for whoredom. About a quarter of the occupation whores had once been 'good' girls who were gang raped and then saw themselves as fit for only more rape, so they became whores. 'Bad' girls. The other three quarters of the whores were starving—so they didn't have to be raped into it.

Clifton seems in constant conflict throughout this book as he tries to reconcile the military male need for whores with the exploitation of the women labeled whores. At one point he writes: "In the immediate post-war period in Japan, because of economic hardship and starvation, young and physically desirable women offered themselves on street corners or railway stations in exchange for almost anything that was edible or capable of conversion into food." This same man says these girls have "tasted of the white man's exotic fruits," as if the rape of their body by thousands of strangers were simply all mocking fun and games.

Overall, he seems like a good man, not willfully cruel or brutal. Yet he says these unimaginably brutal things about bodies raped and raped and raped over and over by his own soldiers. I don't think that this man knows what to make of the pain of the whore, so he has to pretend it does not exist. Perhaps his male conditioning and biology are so powerful, they simply cannot be overcome?

One of his friends marries a Japanese girl, then the friend is killed, and the girl is raped by a group of drunken Australians. She contemplates suicide. Clifton loses track of her. Does he realize that she, this formerly 'clean' blossom, might now become a latrine, because of feelings of worthlessness?

Let's hope she killed herself first. Prostitution is too slow a death. It involves insanity from too much rape—if the diseases don't get to you first.

About the diseases, Clifton sees the girls as the source of the 'poison'—not recognizing that most were virgins when forced into prostitution, so they could not have been the carriers of infection. The soldiers were.

Clifton, also, interestingly, says that rapes of 'good' girls could not be prosecuted since it was assumed that she was offering herself for the chocolate bars. He calls these rapes 'numerous'—an affirmation of my contention that placing 'bad' girls in 'rape prisons' called brothels for soldiers will not protect the 'good' girls outside the raping grounds. So the semen wall against the seaman does not work.

Clifton's confusion and sexual conflict continue throughout the book. He has to maintain the good girl/bad girl paradigm, no matter what. Of 'romantic negotiations,' he writes: "With the professional ladies, money, gifts, and gesture overcame all language barriers, but the shy and virtuous ones had to be courted carefully and under great difficulties."

What is the difference between the virtue of the good Japanese girl being so carefully courted and the raped latrines available to all? Not much. Just get those twenty Australian soldiers to do a job on one of these virtuous girls and she will join the company of the toilets, just waiting for occupation by numerous males needing a semen dump.

This connection is one that it seems almost impossible for Clifton to make. Even though he sees orphaned girls in the streets, he seems to not understand that they will become the 'pom pom' girls he sees on the street corners—"amateur prostitutes who exchanged the dubious and dangerous pleasures of their bodies for anything of value."

What on earth is an 'amateur prostitute'? And how is she distinguished from a professional? Is it the number of times she is raped? After violation 5000 or so, do we up her into the next rank? Is this her hard 'training' that will turn her from amateur to professional? And what does he mean by 'dubious and dangerous pleasures of her body'? How can the word 'pleasure' ever be connected with the ravaging of the helpless, prostituted body—except with callous and ugly disregard of semantics.

Is the 'amateur' on the street corner automatically turned into a 'professional' when a pimps grabs her up and sells her to a brothel, a place that will sanction her 'professional' rape?

Clifton mentions the way many 'good' girls were screened for VD and how affronted their 'personal honor' was by this process. He also says that "any soldier's female companion was suspected of being a 'carrier.' Many an innocent was gathered into the net, but this was inevitable, and some of us learned to meet our respectable women in more secluded rendezvous."

What constitutes 'innocence' and 'respectability' under these circumstances? Going with the conqueror as a 'girlfriend' still means sex for food. It still means chocolate bars. I am reminded of how Vietnam vets told me about their Vietnamese 'girlfriends.' "She wasn't a whore. She really wanted to be with me." I always asked if the girl was hungry and if he gave her food and money. There can be no 'boyfriend/girlfriend' if the male has food and the woman has none.

No difference between men? So Clifton asserts—that the Japanese whores could tell no difference among the conquerors and so felt no revulsion. This is far from the truth: revulsion is extreme when a lot of men force themselves inside, where a woman is private and tender and where pain is at its most intense. Only turning to stone and leaving your body behind, on the bed, works. I huddled in the corner, and held myself for comfort and felt very cold with shivering, while the other me was on the bed was being raped.

The most disturbing line in Clifton's book is this: "With fifteen clients a night, and nothing to do all day, it was too good to be true." On the same page is his conclusion that starvation, economic hardship, and desperation are what drove almost all these girls into prostitution. That and of course being coerced and controlled by pimps—Japanese men heavily sold their own women to the conquerors. Not surprising since these men are so comfortable in a culture of rape. Their own system of military sexual slavery, instituted from the early 1930's until 1945, was one of the most brutal ever devised; and the current $30 billion sex industry in that country thrives because of the patronage of Japanese men: rape of the prostituted body is simply accepted—a norm inherited from their brutal and sexually vicious WWII fathers and grandfathers.

Reading *Fallen Blossoms* was full of deep sorrow for me. When I am in the realm of Caucasian men, my men, I want them to be different. I don't want them to be the horrible rapists that the Japanese were. It particularly saddens me that this good man, Allan Clifton, puts up so many screens against the horror of the prostituted life. If even a kind man like he cannot understand, then how much less chance will there be with the brutal ones of the world?

Clifton knows that these enslaved girls bodies are violated fifteen times a night. This man, who in many ways is kind and intelligent, does not seem to have even the remotest idea of what rape all night, every night, does to a woman.

I can tell you that it leaves behind a woman who never heals. Even though I left prostitution many years ago, I am still in it. "This is hell, nor am I out of it." No matter how many books I write, or how many Ph.D.'s I acquire, or how many allusions I make to plays of the past, I am always a whore. I know that if the people around me knew of my own past, they would spit on me. So I have to walk around everyday as if I were not me—as if I were not a whore body that had been underneath so many men. I also know that it is other women who are way more to blame for my 'shame,' if you want to call it that, than the men who raped me. The men made me bleed physically. These women make me bleed from a wound that I can't find a way to stop.

Far more cruel, to my mind, than the Australian and American Rapist Conquerors were the Japanese women themselves who scorned their sisters as whores. And far more cruel, to me, are all the American women who, in all wars, have ignored the conquered women their men have raped. Either because they do not want to know that the brother or husband or son who comes home has been inside a whore (or sex slave—term her what you will) or because the American woman simply does not care. Her indifference creates me, the whore. And my presence means she will never be safe or have any dignity—because I can have none. As long as one woman is deemed nothing more than a whore to filled up by men who rape her into pain and deadness, then all women are this whore. In their blindness, the 'decent' women of the world don't know this. I guess this is their protection from the truth.

3

This next article is my response to a holiday that troubles me deeply, Veterans' Day. It was written in 2006, when Clint Eastwood's *Flag of Our Fathers* hit the movie theaters around Veterans' Day. The advent of yet another war movie prompted me to write this piece. I'd like to reprint it—on every Veterans' Day—as a tribute to those that the wars of mankind leave out of our memories. I would like to make the reprinting of this a tradition on Memorial Day as well.

Veterans' Day: Flags of Our Raped Mothers

November 4, 2006

Just in time for Veterans' Day, I notice Clint Eastwood's *Flags of Our Fathers* coming out, yet another movie glorifying war and the men who make it. Just the previews indicate its 'John Wayne/war hero' slant: "More Congressional Medals of Honor…" blares the overvoice, as The Sacred Flag (Iwo Jima style) is raised. One reviewer (Dargis, "Ghastly Conflagration," *New York Times*, Oct. 20, 2006) writes: "It seems hard to believe there is anything left to be said about WWII that has not already been stated and restated, chewed, digested…."

Dargis's remark is so wrong, so off-base, no narrowly patriarchal, that I don't know quite how to begin to refute it. I will start by saying that 99% of 'war stories' have never been told: those of the women ravaged by the conflicts men create. Dargis finds Eastwood's movie full of the graphic 'horror' of war. The raped/prostituted women of war are its true 'horror.' Of the thousands of war movies, how many 'honor' and 'remember' their suffering.

As a rape and military prostitution survivor, I am always uneasy on Veterans' Day, and Memorial Day, because these two American holidays celebrate the ability of men to make war and the courage of the soldier and how glorious all this is for his manhood, etc. I remember that all of the year 2005, the 60th anniversary of the end of WWII, was like one long Veterans'/ Memorial Day in the U.S., with endless articles and TV shows and movies devoted to the nobility of the soldier and the magnificence of the wars he makes. The entire year, I only saw two mentions of the effect of WWII on women: some attention paid to the Korean Comfort Women, but only as if they were the 'big' exception--no mention that what happened to them (being raped 30-50 times a day in military brothels) has been the 'norm' for countless vulnerable and beleaguered women and girls caught in the sexual line of fire during wartime. And one mention of German girls raped by the Russians and then scorned as whores by their own men. The article (in *The Nation*) called them 'forgotten victims,' but failed to mention that they were just a small slice of countless other ignored women and girls whose wartime sexual plight means nothing to governments and news reporters. In fact, the article gave the misleading idea that the German girls, too, were some kind of exception.

The 'silence' of all these women is partly due to lack of journalistic/ historical attention to their experiences. But it is also due to 'shame,' the male term for the raped body, and how a woman is supposed to feel, after violation. In this way, women also collude in their own voicelessness, by buying into male notions of 'virginity/purity' on the one hand and 'uncleanliness/filth/ ruin' on the other. How else explain, I wonder, the complete lack of stories by women raped before, during, and after WWII by the war machines of all militaries? Only one group has come forth: the Korean Comfort Women. Where are the voices of the others? Where are, for example, the voices of the French girls, those still left alive, who were the object of extensive rape sprees by their American GI 'liberators'? What about the Italian girls heavily raped by Allied soldiers of all nationalities?

In addition to not coming forward, women are partly responsible in other ways for the vast silence that surrounds wartime sexual savagery. One example: certain Japanese feminists recognize the existence of the Korean Comfort Women, and have apologized on behalf of their men, and their government. (Source: *War's Dirty Secrets*, by Anne Llewellyn Barstow.) But these same feminists ignore their own sisters, Occupation Comfort Girls, handed out to American GI's and to Australian and British soldiers in Tokyo at the end of WWII. Truckloads of them, given to appease the conquerors. War-ravaged already, by the destruction of their homes and families. Now raped, sometimes into unconsciousness, by the 'entitled' soldiers, who must have girls' bodies as rewards. A noble soldierly deed, the virile rape of the conquered.

It is puzzling that MacArthur did nothing to halt the sexual carnage in Tokyo. The Japanese offered him a 'comfort girl.' He turned down this 'gift,' presumably because it would not look right for a general to take a sex slave, yet he did nothing to stop the setting up of brothels (euphemistically called 'comfort stations'—I would label them 'rape stations') for his men. The RAA (Recreation and Amusement Association), a joint effort of the Japanese and American authorities, forced girls (many of them teenage virgins, homeless and helpless) into the Rape Centers (my phrase for the places). Men bought 'tickets,' to make it all legitimate—after all, if you pay it can never be rape, right?

It was 'amusement' for the men. 'Recreation.' What was if for the girls? Pain and indescribable suffering. How their bodies, particularly those of the virgins, survived the constant assaults, without bleeding to death, is beyond me. I have a rape obsession—I admit to it, and a size obsession—since my own body was so heavily torn up by Caucasian and black soldiers when I was a prostitute. I live everyday from the perspective of a gang-raped body. It is my vision of the world. It is a rare one, in terms of writers, apparently, since I find few others putting their rapes on the page. (I do so with fear and with much cultural imposition of shame, but I am fighting to write in spite of the barriers that tell me to be quiet.) So my whole perspective on WWII is quite different from that of the historians. I do want to know the 'facts,' those kept hidden until recently—like how many times were the Japanese comfort girls raped a day by the Americans (on an average they each 'processed' 15 men a day—that was the military's phrase for this activity—'processing' GI bodies—the girls were regarded as assembly-line 'equipment'). But—and this separates me startlingly from the historians--I want to know what it felt like, for the girl—since I know what rape felt like for me. My historical questions are of this sort: I wonder how these tiny Asians withstood multiple rapes everyday by all these Caucasian men? How did their minds withstand it? The Korean Comfort Women report that some of the girls went insane. Most of my material on the Occupation Comfort Girls comes from historian Yuki Tanaka and he reports that one girl was forced 60 times a day. I want to know how she was even alive after so much rape? I want to know if she was even still conscious at the end of her 'processing' quota for the day?

I also wonder that the men did not see the pain in the girls' faces and the bleeding, torn genitals. Why did this not stop them? This is my history. The one no one tells. It is a history of shame and embarrassment. I have found it enormously difficult to come forward and reveal what happened to my own body. I have hidden it from myself for decades. Now that I have faced it by putting it in words, I die every day from fear that it will happen again. After all, I am breaking a silence imposed on the prostituted by the most powerful entity in the world—the military. Will I be punished terribly—with more rape--for daring to speak?

Tanaka's book on the comfort women shows a photograph of huge numbers of American sailors, a happy, grinning crowd, jostling together, waiting to enter a comfort station. I wonder if the girls inside were vomiting from fear, and peeing from fear, as they heard the coarse noises of the eager men at play, waiting their turn to buy a rape ticket.

Why didn't MacArthur stop them? If he had—if he had instituted a policy of setting up food centers for the girls, instead of rape centers, history would be very different for our fragile female bodies. Instead of a bunch of rapists, the military could have fostered soldiers as protectors. Men to make the girls feel safe, not girls dying from fear and sexual brutality.

We would celebrate our Veterans' and Memorial Days very differently if a policy of 'never rape, always help and nurture those poor, starving prostituted girls' were the norm. Just think of all the grateful, starving girls in other wars--Korea, Vietnam--who would have benefited from such a policy, one of humane commonsense. Just think of the monuments we could make to this true picture of soldierly honor and nobility. Not the fake one we now praise.

A first step is awareness. Celebrate the raped on Veterans' Day. Build monuments to them. Tell their stories. Where are those stories, I keep asking? Where is the Japanese girl that sixty American soldiers a day laid down on, and split in two, with pain (hers), pleasure (theirs)? If she is not dead from physical abuse or mental insanity (rape by one man can cause severe psychological disturbance—how do we measure the impact of sixty a day?)—if she is not dead, why doesn't she tell her story? She is a part of American history, and Veterans' Day, since American soldiers raped her.

Yet I know that it takes courage to come forth. The former 'whore' is heavily despised. As an ex-prostitute, I've experienced this first hand.

It was excruciating, the year 2005, to my own raped body, as if the whole year stamped into me, underscored, how little what happened to me mattered to the men of the world, and the wars they make.

How much WWII footage was shot of the raped? Did anyone bother to go into the Dachau brothels and film where girls, barely into their adolescence, were raped? Did any journalists mention that starving Jewish girls were brothelized by their own men in the Warsaw Ghetto? No. Rape of the Jewish women was not even mentioned at Nuremberg—not considered a war crime, since, after all, it's just women being screwed, and only the soldier matters. And the male. All we see of post-concentration camp footage is the skinny, skeletal males. Why didn't the photojournalists consider the suffering of the Jewish women worthy of note? Very puzzling.

Only once, in all of the thousands of hours of WWII footage endlessly spewed out by male-dominated stations, like the History Channel, have I glimpsed a raped being. A European girl, maybe eighteen, with long blonde hair all tumbling over her face, and that face was twisted in an agony of unbearable invaded pain. The camera gave us only two seconds, but the glimpse into the hell that was her mind, her body, her soul, haunts me.

I focus on the American soldiers (from all wars) a great deal because they are my men, and I care about them, care about what they do the women of the world. How they treat them is how they will treat me. If a man rapes in Iraq, he may come home and rape me. If a GI buys a fifteen-year-old in Bangkok, he might come home and buy a child here. But I know that other militaries are even more savage in their treatment of women. My men are practically saints compared to, say, the Japanese soldiers in Nanking. There, in that famous microcosm of war atrocity, the men ripped open the vaginas of pre-teen girls with bayonets, so they could rape them more easily. There is an account of an eleven-year-old girl, tied up and raped continuously, her ruptured, swollen, bleeding genitals terrible to look at, until she died. There are accounts of girls who could not walk for weeks, so severe were the gang rapes. As many as 100,000 females may have been raped—children, girls, women, even older ones, in their eighties, many of whom bled to death, because of their thin vaginal tissue. The Japanese soldiers also impaled vaginas on pitchforks, beer bottles, brooms—for fun. Girls lay in the streets, naked, their genitals stretched open by objects. And then the soldiers took pictures, for their photo albums. I wonder if they showed them to their wives and girlfriends back home? (Source for Nanking material: Iris Chang.) Where are the memorials for the women of Nanking?

And I know that compared to the savagery of the Serbs in Bosnia and the Pakistani men in Bangladesh, my own soldiers deserve to be crowned with laurel leaves of good behavior. At least when they rape, they do it more gently.

Gentle rape notwithstanding, we definitely need to stop celebrating the ability of men to make war. Our movies, particularly, need to call a cease fire. Hollywood continues to worship the John Wayne version of war in such sentimental, hypocritical slosh as *The Last Samurai*—nothing but one long paean to the male's violent, savage Homeric battle endeavors (albeit Japanese style). I think I've only seen one epic come of Hollywood that actually tried to celebrate peace—Kevin Costner's *The Postman*. Interesting, the critics panned this movie, with its gentle message, and highly praised the mediocre, battle-footage-ridden *Last Samurai*.

Instead of spending millions on more male-made war movies, we need memorials all over the world to the women and girls and children that the soldiers ravage and destroy, either through rape, or killing them, or forcing them into starvation prostitution. Men have a choice. They can refuse to go to war. Women who accidentally become 'collateral damage,' sexual and otherwise, during wartime, don't have that choice. It's not my battle, this masculine activity. I am a soft, feminine woman. And I don't make war. But we women are terribly damaged because you men place us in your line of fire. If men want to continue creating these savage conflicts, and then celebrating their ability to do so, they need to stop hurting women in the process.

I remember a long time ago visiting a war museum in London and seeing not one mention of this side of war, the ravaging of our poor, helpless female bodies. Every soldier's voice was there, but not one voice of the wretched, the prostitute. Why was there no exhibit of the girls forced to endure assembly-line sex in brothels on the eve of battles, because so many men crowded in, forming long lines to get at that one female body, that one last sex act, before combat. While the boys have their fun, she is knifed, over and over, between her legs. That is the terrible irony of prostitution: the man's sexual pleasure means incredible suffering for the woman. I would like to hear her story. All of this, the unbearable misery of the raped, is invisible, hidden, and will continue as long as no one talks about it. The few efforts of a few rare women to actually bring this up are always met with indifference, as if this were simply a trivial sidebar to the affairs of men.

What would war be, after all, for those 'courageous, honorable' men called soldiers, without the bodies of women to rape, break, violate, brothelize? The soldier "must have his fuck," as one vet said to me. What a hard irony: that the woman who provides the sexual service so necessary for the soldier's well-being is despised for it, as filth, as a toilet, as a 'diseased slut'—it is no wonder prostitutes rarely tell their stories—and he is glorified for his courageous noble deeds.

'Innocent civilians' is a common phrase for the 'collateral damage' of men's wars. Why not 'innocent raped body,' or 'innocent prostituted body'—to reflect the reality of that innocence being violated and destroyed?

It is not in the interests of men to remember the women ravaged by war. The Raped Body is the Soldier's Reward. (Could we get all these young American men to go to war without the Promised Sex Binge in Bangkok? After Vietnam, after the Persian Gulf War, and now--that's where the boys go, for the sex-fix reward.) Briseis's Tale doesn't matter. (To be crude, it is Briseis's Tail that is the territory of the war-savaged, not her story.)

Regarding any kind of accurate or sympathetic portrayal of rape or 'prostitution rape,' Vietnam style, or any style, movies simply don't show this side of war, the woman's side, the side of her torn and degraded body.

Oliver Stone's *Platoon* shows little in the way of rape when the men invade and destroy the village. A girl naked from the waist up is being attacked by a group of the soldiers and Charlie Sheen's character pulls them off her, says, "Don't do it," and holds her to him. The men say she's "just a gook." Sheen's character says, "She's a human being."

It's sad that Oliver Stone chooses to leave out this huge slice of realism in the destruction of the village scene--the gang rape of the young village girls—as if it were incidental, minor, barely important. Only a brief foray into that, and then he leaves it behind. But then he is a man, looking at the war from his male point of view, so of course the raped bodies of girls don't matter much. (I wonder if he bought the helpless and prostituted during his tour of duty there? If so, why did he leave this out of his movie?) It's as if the male is so much more capable of suffering, for Stone, so much more important in his maleness, that any female suffering is trivial, overlooked, barely there.

Another big element of realism Stone fails to note is that, after the soldiers totally destroy their huts, animals, property, men, way of life, etc., these poor village women and girls and children will now join a massive refugee population of starving people, and many, sadly, will be sold as whores. The little girl that Tom Berenger's character holds a gun to, now that her father has been taken away from her, and she has no protection, might end up on some GI's sexual menu in a year of two, when she's considered old enough to use. I wonder why Oliver Stone didn't see fit to chronicle this type of suffering. Even this liberated filmmaker obviously does not consider the sexual brutalization of women, girls, and children important. Only men's bodies matter, apparently. Only the soldier matters. Not the woman he hurts.

Apocalypse Now does show serial rape, but that of a blonde, glamorized Playboy playmate, not a Vietnamese woman. With all of the local women being ravaged, I've always wondered why this movie had to import a Caucasian. The guys could have raped her back home; they didn't have to bring her all the way to Vietnam to do it.

My lack of sympathy for 'the horror, the horror,' whether it be in this film, or its prototype, *Heart of Darkness*, derives from the fact that--of course, what else is new?--'horror' is couched exclusively in male terms. (Conrad was as patriarchal, and narrow, as the whole flotilla of male writers forced on me by the deification of the canon; nowhere in white Western male literature does the 'horror' reflect what happens to the gentle, fragile female body. I don't have to look very far to see Melville exploiting Polynesian women or the imperialist Kipling visiting an Indian red-light district. White male literature, about war or whaling ships [making war on nature], is meaningless to me. It is written from the point of view of the conqueror and the rapist.)

Full Metal Jacket (FMJ) is incredibly frustrating and painful because here, too, we are asked to only consider the suffering of the men, coarse and cruel as they are, and are given no insights into the suffering of the prostitute that is pimped to all the men, in one scene, at $5 a lay, for all of them to use her body. With a lot of crude jeering and shouting and joking, they call her a "little schoolgirl" and there's much amusement about the black soldier maybe being "boku," too big, for her, and the whole thing is played out like a savage farce from a male fraternity gang rape. (The black soldier refers to his member as "pure Louisiana rattlesnake," emphasizing the penis as weapon, something meant to punish, hurt, bite, sting, destroy the woman.)

The prostitute is pathetically fragile and her face is impassive, but she wears sunglasses, I presume so that the soldiers cannot see the suffering in her eyes. And if they saw it, would they care? It seems unlikely. The first one to take her shoves her very hard toward the door of the ruined building where they're all going to rape her and says, "I won't be long. I'll skip the foreplay."

If I were writing this scene, I would go inside the building, and record her pain, bear witness to the 'prostitution rape' of her body. But, apparently, Kubrick did not consider her story important enough to be told. (I do, and in one of my novels, *Pink Tiger*, I re-tell this episode from the point of view of her raped body.)

What prevails in almost all war movies is the time-honored, man-must-have-his-fuck, tomb-of-the-unknown rapist, buddy-bang theory of war—only the men matter. I hammer upon this point, ad infinitum, because no one has made it before. And no one is making it now. Ye shall know the truth, and the truth shall set you free—but not in war movies. Or in war coverage by journalists.

I saw FMJ in a military base theatre when it first came out, and the gang use of this poor woman made me feel sick and cold with fear and pain. It hit me as if my own body were being raped again. The audience, unfortunately, a combination of soldiers, civilians, and their girlfriends, thought this whole pimped-woman scene absolutely hilarious. Snorts and jeers and ugly comments bombarded the screen. That "$5-dollar boom-boom bang," as one soldier shouted at the screen, was apparently very popular in Vietnam. "Fun

Bang in Da Nang" was another comment I heard. My soldier boyfriend (he became my ex-boyfriend that very night) was among the jeering crowd. I heard not one sympathetic murmur for the prostitute's raped body.

Similarly, the audience found the pathetic street patois of the Saigon prostitute funny. They laughed at the "I'm so horny, I love you long time," which she wails out, like some lost victim of her profession, mimicking the language of the conqueror, like millions of women, in the centuries before her, have. Down through the raped-woman sands of the ages. Particularly sad is the irony in the word "love," since, in her subjugated state, she has been too used by men to tell the difference. For the men "love" means forced sex, rape of her body, so that is what it has come to mean for her, too.

"I let you rape-fuck me loooooong time." Funny, huh?

FMJ is typical of war movies in general, and their attitude toward sexually brutalized women. Look at *Gallipoli* (I could cite a hundred other similar instances), where the Mel Gibson character and his comrades visit the local brothel for some "horizontal refreshment," these soldiers all hooting and crude and drunk and hyped-up and amused, at flesh for sale, and then I'm supposed to feel sorry for these sorry specimens of non-manhood, when they go to war? No way.

I'm not sure what masculinity and manliness are, but I'm positive they have nothing to do with large numbers of men inflicting rape on a prostitute's body.

We find the sexual savaging of the prostituted body as a harmless 'norm' in war films from all eras. *The Big Red One* contains, of course, the obligatory brothel visit: all those fine young men have to have their last sex fix before going into battle. In this film, as in all others, the brothel inmates are smiling, happy girls, oh so willing to give that last sex fling to a gallant boy. This typical cinematic departure from reality reigns everywhere. Look at *To Hell and Back*, a 1955 Audie Murphy movie. In it, every French and Italian prostitute (sanitized by Hollywood for the blind hypocrisy of the 50's) is a 'happy hooker'—all painted up and smiling and just delighted to fraternize with the GI's. It's, apparently, what French, Italian and German prostitutes (Japanese ones, too) just delighted in during and after WWII—having sex with thousands of drunk American soldiers. At least, according to Hollywood--for the last six decades of its war movies, this pernicious place has made this portrait of the prostitute practically the only one we see. Never a glimpse into the hearts of starving girls, desperate for food. Never a hint that maybe all these young men should be giving the girls the food, instead of forcing sex upon them in exchange for it. That would be the humane, compassionate way.

Hamburger Hill follows the same pattern as *Gallipoli* (mentioned above): soldiers using girls—this time Vietnamese village prostitutes ("me, next," as they get in line) and then going off to fight in some battle where we're supposed to care, but only about them. Not about sexually brutalized women. Not I. I won't sympathize with the rapists. I am on the side of the raped body.

Gallipoli, also, presents the time-honored good girl/bad girl scenario, Gibson's blonde innocent farm girl back home set up as a wholesome contrast to the painted harlots he visits in his manly brothel forays.

The last two films mentioned—*Hamburger Hill* and *Gallipoli*--also glamorize the prostitutes—presenting them as voluptuous Hollywood versions of slave handmaidens. In truth, many of the village prostitutes in Vietnam were far from healthy, let alone glamorous, suffering as they did from TB, skin diseases, starvation, and, of course, VD, carried from one body to another by the GI's. (I don't think my mind wants to go into the *Gallipoli* brothels and the broken, diseased, non-Hollywood version of whorebodies the real soldiers there would have been lining up to use there.)

Over and over, we see war movies with Asian women in bars and brothels who are smiling, happy, flirting, made-up by Hollywood to look like brown Barbies, cute, slant-eyed sex toys. The image, overwhelmingly misleading, is that these women like what they do, and that it is voluntary. No one bothers to tell their side of the story. One common theme in testimonials of prostitutes: we smile on the outside, to make the money, or to keep from being beaten, if we don't bring in enough. But we cry constantly on the inside.

Air America, a Mel Gibson Vietnam flick about drug smuggling during the war, also plays into the happy-whore scenario, with a lot of smiling Vietnamese bar girls hanging all over drunken coarse American men, while others dance joyfully on a stage. The one Caucasian woman present seems to regard the whores with amusement, as a dirty joke; yet, she is an aid worker, supposedly there to help village refugees. Does it not occur to her that the step from refugee to brothel girl is pitifully short? Particularly, as pimps 'culled' girls from camps, broke them in, and sold them to the soldiers.

The men play a miniature golf game, with tiny Asian girls dotting the background, like decorative lawn furniture. The girls look like helpless little fawns. The men are roughhousing, fighting, shooting off guns with idiotic male bravado; and the tiny, painted-toy girls, all of whom look about twelve, with skinny, stork arms, are simply smiling cutely in the background. No fear of these crude men, no fear of the guns? The few testimonies we have from prostitutes say that the women fear the crudeness and violence of men very much. (I know I did.) Also, the big, heavy American men in this film weigh at least a 100 pounds more than their tiny concubines. Another big cause for fear on the part of the delicate, bought girl. (The few testimonies we have from Asian prostitutes—Vietnamese, Thai, Korean, Japanese--say how frightened they are of the bigness of the foreign men.) But, these little girls smile happily away, impervious to violence and rape, willing and brown and slave-like, per the Hollywood recipe.

The film was shot in Thailand, with Thai extras. What did these tiny Thai girls, barely looking twelve-years-old, with their tiny, skinny arms, think of the parts they were playing? Did they feel any revulsion at being turned into the typical Asian whore, for American men to play with? Or were they just grateful to have the money the role brought in?

What about the woman who played the field whore in FMJ? Did she feel the degradation of the girl she was portraying? Did the male actors treat her with any respect when they weren't filming? Or did they just see her as an extension of inexpensive 'cheap gook pussy' (in the soldiers' phrase of the time) since she was Asian? And what about the actress in the same movie who plays the street whore in Saigon, with her pathetic sexual litany of a come-on: "I'm so horny, I love you long time...." Her sad linguistic confusion of "love" and "forced sex," her inability to distinguish, in language, between the two, just deepens the pathos of the song that accompanies her entrance, Nancy Sinatra's "These Boots Are Made For Walking." Obviously, "these boots are gonna walk all over you," done, by Sinatra, in the sensual growl of the liberated Western woman, has little reference to the life of this sad, cheap, stepped-on street whore, bartering her body to rough, indifferent, drunk soldiers, only interested in screwing her as economically as possible.

(The Jessica Simpson redo of the Sinatra original, interestingly, echoes some of the Saigon cheap-gook-for-sale scene, although I'm sure unintentionally: the pure blonde-next-door Simpson offering herself for sex while she washes the car in a bikini ['Car Wash and Fuck,' could be seen on signs around Saigon during the American occupation--get your lay while you wait]. Simpson changes Sinatra's growl to a whisper, but Western liberated woman still reigns supreme. Simpson knocks a guy down, for patting her butt, and then all the men subdue each other in a rousing barroom brawl, leaving center stage to a bevy of unmolested, country-western dancing cuties. Blonde Western Liberated Woman, in complete control of her sexual destiny, and the boundaries of her body, no matter how sensual she is. I find the contrast—between the protected Jessica Simpson figure, made such a fuss over because of her dumbness and blonde American innocence, and what has become another archetypal cultural figure, the barely adolescent, frail Asian whore allowed no innocence because she is sold so young—inexpressibly sad. Simpson gets all riled at a butt pat; imagine the misery and degradation of laying down under 10 or 20 drunk men a day that is the everyday reality of many young Asian whores.

(Brownmiller, in *Against Our Will*, reports that young Vietnamese whores in the brothels adjacent to our military bases during the war typically worked in rooms furnished with three items: a bed, a chair [for clothes], and a picture of a pneumatic Playboy playmate on the wall, to stir up the horny young male customer, in case the ten-year-old size body of the Asian whore in the bed didn't do it. More than inexpressibly sad, getting raped all night beneath the symbol of wholesome, airbrushed, glossy, girl-next-door American sexuality. Maybe it's even sadder that some of these girls were grateful for the work because it meant they could eat. Soldiers really do have to start feeding these poor girls, instead of exploiting them.)

The image of the Asian painted toy whore is so pervasive it is insidious. There is also such inner emptiness, seeing them exclusively from the outside, as disposable surface creatures. Or ignoring their existence totally in a movie about Vietnam, as if this "female" part of the war were not worthy of note. Not even Oliver Stone thinks the stories of the sexually brutalized women important enough to be told, let alone Stanley Kubrick. (Even *Casualties of War* only shows the girl from the outside—this time as a raped, tortured, bleeding thing, rather than as a painted thing, but it is the same principle.)

In *Off Limits*, Gregory Hines and Wilhelm Defoe play two American policemen investigating the serial murder of Saigon prostitutes during the war. Despite their supposedly trying to help this most mistreated strata of Saigon life, the men themselves treat the prostitutes they talk to for information with scorn and contempt, as if they are dirt, filth, crap, flea dung, the lowest of the low. Not one polite or kind word to any of these women. Even the baby of one of the murdered prostitutes comes in for their scorn—as they take him to an orphanage run by French nuns, they make jokes about him and about all the abandoned Amerasian children they themselves have fathered around Saigon. This is particularly horrifying since, in the murder scene itself, after the gunshot that kills his mother, the poor, tiny baby starts crying.

At the orphanage, the men are polite, chivalrous, all gentlemanly with a nun who helps them with the investigation. In a cool fashion, but with a touch of compassion in her voice, she tells the men something of what she knows of the murdered prostitutes, because she had worked with them, tried to help them--"This one's specialty was sadomasochism, bondage"—"That one the officers lined up to use"—"This one her pimp exploited terribly—put her in the lesbian sex shows for the GI's." Her controlled compassion seems to have no impact on the hard attitudes of the men. Neither has it apparently ever occurred to these men that the reason the women leave their offspring with the nuns at night is so that they won't have to work in the same room, their babies and little girls right there, watching, while they're doing it with the soldiers in front of them. (The *Deerhunter* shows a similar situation—a Vietnamese bar girl taking the man to her room, where her Amerasian baby is crying.)

No more perfect picture of the virgin/whore dichotomy, created by the callous insensitivity of men, can we find than in *Off Limits*—treat those poor whores like absolute dirt and crap—after all, the sluts are getting what they deserve—and be all reverential and hushed and worshipful with the nun. To my mind, we should worship the prostitute for what she has had to endure from men. She is as worthy of respect as the nuns who care enough to help her.

One of the most disturbing scenes (again to my mind, in my own raped, battered body) in *Off Limits* shows a roomful of sweating, coarse, angry, crude American soldiers at a Saigon VD station; a prostitute comes in to try to identify one of them and she looks delicate, flyaway, vulnerable, and kind of sad in her ill-fitting Western outfit. It saddened me to think of these men using such delicacy and defiling her with their rough crudeness. It particular disturbs me because my own body, when I worked as a prostitute, was so damaged by drunk, rough men. In fact, I felt a chill of fear, and nausea, all the time I was watching this movie. A burning fear—all through my stomach, and down into my legs, similar to what I experienced when my own body was being raped. This movie is a rape of everything feminine and delicate in the world.

As in FMJ, the poor prostituted creature uses the vocabulary of her oppressors, calling herself a "number one blow-job girl." As if this were some sort of honorary position. The entire picture of the cesspool brothel of Saigon, created by our military, horrified and saddened me. I felt sickened at this Brothel World of misery and coarseness and roughness that the American soldiers created, through their sexual callousness and lust.

One of the most touching moments in the movie, again to my mind, is a glimpse we receive of the room of one of the murdered prostitutes. The little space is all cheap, pink finery, as if in imitation of what this Eastern women thought the sensuous workspace of a Western whore might be. Like the woman in the lesbian sex show, she was caught in a sad, Westernized version of sex-for-sale.

In fact, the opening scene of *Off Limits* pans over the naked, Hollywoodized version of a Vietnamese whore's body. Lying on her stomach, she's in a Playboy-like pose, with the silky curve of her spine and legs, the skin lush and taut, the butt rounded, everything undulating, bronze, ripe in the dim lighting of her room. The next moment she is shot. (The song "Pretty Ballerina," in the background as the whorebody is shot, intensifies the sadness.)

I didn't know whether to feel more sorry for her dead or alive. Alive that beautiful body was degraded by the roughness of soldiers, the coarse sadness of whoredom. Dead, maybe her beauty will find some comfort somewhere. In the arms of the angels, away from thieves and vultures. And American GI's. No comfort in their rough arms.

The movie ends with Hines and Defoe making a dirty joke about a woman with huge boobs. Apparently, even after contact with the sad, cheap, cruel world of Westernized sex imposed on these women, these men have learned nothing in the way of compassion. The horrifying coarseness of *Off Limits* filled me with pity, and made me cry with sadness. The fact that I felt sick with cold fear the whole time I was watching this movie because it reminded me of my own multiple rapes by drunk men seemed to me to be an anomaly. It is not accepted—for the prostitute to have a voice, or feelings, or a response to her degradation. We are not supposed to be part of the picture of war, except as silent, passive bodies. My feelings are not supposed to be part of the discourse of war.

Just look at how war is discussed night after night on CNN or Fox or *Charlie Rose* and you will observe the 'cool, detached, proper' discourse of the battlefield. And war is 'reported' this way by all the female journalists and politicians as well. I have written elsewhere that the most useful thing a Condi Rice or a Hillary Clinton could do is visit a brothel in Baghdad or Kabul—or anywhere else Allied soldiers are stationed and local militaries are making use of starving women. This visit to the true raped heart of war is much overdue.

But the hot sordid raped body simply has no place in the cool rhetoric of war.

To return to the movies, *Good Morning, Vietnam* sanitizes the world of the Saigon prostitute, showing only a clean American bar, again with the cute, painted-toy sex dolls enormously enjoying themselves, with big smiles on their faces, as the soldiers make fun of them because of the way they'll do anything for money. (My only thought as I see a tiny prostitute flirting with a huge Marine about four times her size, with arms far bigger around than her tiny legs--and her wrists so tiny, it would take half a dozen of them to fill his circled fist—is the awful damage it must to do her body to have sex with such large men.)

The whore/virgin idea is there, in full bloom, with Williams courting the chaste girl, protected by her family members, her cute little-girl, button-nose face all shining with innocence, in contrast to the cheap painted bar girl who will do anything for money. No hint that if this 'innocent' lost her family, she might be alone on the streets of Saigon, and vulnerable to pimps and soldiers. Do these filmmakers never think, or feel, or examine, or have any kind of congress with their own hearts, as to why a girl might become a cheap, painted, toy, desperate enough to do anything for money, rather than starve? Apparently not.

Hamburger Hill shows one soldier listening to a tape recording from his girlfriend. She says that she will always remain faithful, but she will understand if he can't. I wonder what could go through a woman's mind, not minding that her boyfriend is using an exploited, over-raped woman, not even caring about that other female's pain. Why does she have no sympathy for her, even though she shares a woman's body with her, one that can be sexually hurt and exploited? Is the temporary sexual pleasure of her boyfriend so important that the subjugated, violated body of the Vietnamese woman has no reality? Puzzling.

I know from personal experience that, overall, women on the homefront during the war exhibited no sympathy for the prostitutes their men were using in Vietnam. And, like women writers of this period, most of the time, the 'good girls' barely knew these highly subjugated female existed—or maybe did not want to know. These disposable people were, apparently, simply not important enough to come to the forefront of the American woman's consciousness. No feminists or anti-war activists paid any attention to them; they were invisible to Gloria Steinem, Jane Fonda. One exception was the woman historian Arlene Eisen, who wrote an essay on Vietnamese prostitutes in 1975 and who pointed out that our soldiers had turned Saigon into the Brothel of Asia. One voice. That's all. Millions with no voice, because this kind of sexual torture of women, then and now, is, apparently, only worthy of two or three minutes of coverage on CNN, every two or three months—if that. Major print media—magazines and newspapers, even the liberal and radical ones—show a similar indifference and disregard. Very small amounts of space, if any, are ever devoted to this issue. And it's not because all the journalists are male. Almost all women in the media ignore this extreme form of sexual torture as well--with rare exceptions. That 'dirty little secret' no one wants uncover: the same attitude the Japanese government had when the Korean Comfort Women tried to confront them with what had been done to them. It's too 'dirty' to talk about. (From the point of view of those ravaged, this is war's 'dirty big secret.') I never saw Christiane Amanpour go into the Serbian rape camps. Or even mention them. Lucky, privileged woman reporting male news from the male point of view. There are no 'women' journalists reporting wars. They all think like men.

I seem to be the lone female voice writing on this huge subject. Puzzling.

I find it startling that websites which tout themselves as non-mainstream—such as 'commondreams' and 'rense'--pay almost no attention to ravaged female bodies, trafficking, rape, military prostitution. Maybe a tiny inch of space now and then. The same goes for magazines like *Mother Jones*, which prides itself on being so radical—maybe a token article on underage Cambodian prostitutes every few months, but the rest of the time, our raped bodies don't exist for the MJ people. I don't know why I should be surprised since I am often disappointed by prestigious human rights groups like Amnesty International for the same reason. Yes, they do devote some of their space to trafficking, sexual slavery, exploitation of our bodies—but not nearly enough. It is peculiar that they've had a big, ongoing Guantanamo Bay campaign, yet never mention that girls trafficked into that base by military 'pick-up pilots' are being treated far worse by the soldiers than the detainees. What a strange world it is, when a group like Amnesty International focuses such heavy attention on the political prisoners (men) allegedly mistreated at Gitmo, yet they completely ignore the sex slaves (women) right on the same doorstep. Apparently being raped by soldiers is far less a violation of human rights than being detained as a political prisoner. Even for Amnesty International, men are, apparently, more important than women since they devote so much more space to their rights.

Back to war movies and prostitution—WWII ones show only the 'clean' American women, the Claudette Colbert types on the homefront, not the women their men were using. I remember one Memorial Day, when all the movie channels play their tributes to the soldiers. On one station was *Hamburger Hill*, with the men in their tub in the brothel, baby-faced little Hollywood whore-handmaidens serving and massaging them. (One ugly drunken shit GI threatening to hit one of the girls. I felt sorry for her that she had to fuck that.) On the channel right next door was one of those sentimental WWII jobs, with Claudette herself, along with Shirley Temple, welcoming the brave soldier home. I wonder how they would have reacted to knowing that those noble American soldiers raped their way across Europe and used Italian girls too starved to do anything but fuck for a can of Spam.

Overwhelmingly, in books about war, in movies about war, the lives and bodies of the raped and prostituted are ignored. There is one notable exception: *Casualties of War*. It is based on a true incident: a group of American soldiers kidnap, torture, rape, and finally kill a Vietnamese village girl. One soldier (played by Michael Fox) refuses to participate and later tries to report the incident, putting his own life in danger from fellow soldiers. One movie, out of hundreds, or thousands?? Just one?? Even here, there is a problem. Supposedly, the men rape the village girl because they can't get leave to go into the nearest town and get laid at the nearest brothel. Director Brian De Palma does not point out that the brothel girl's body is subjected every day to what the raped village girl endures only once.

So, we have all these monuments to that terrible endeavor, war, and the men who make it. We have, for example, the Vietnam Memorial, a big wall in Washington with a lot of men's names on it, celebrating the ability of yet another generation of boys to make war, be savage, rape and ravage. Beside that black wall, there needs to be another one. A wall that records all the bodies of the women and girls who died as a result of rape pain.

My archetypal memorial to men at war would not be that famous raising of the flag on Iwo Jima. That flag does not fly over raped bodies. My memorial, in stone, to all men at war, would be a group of soldiers, with their khakis down around their ankles, penises sticking out like weapons, surrounding a helpless, naked prostitute, who is crying.

Where is the Tomb for the Unknown Raped Woman? Where is the Monument for the Forgotten Prostitute? When will their voices (and mine) be heard, and remembered? Never, I'm afraid. Ye shall know the truth, and the truth shall set you free. Freedom. The word is empty for raped bodies...

The body is much wiser than the mind. Mine is telling me to tell my story. I am doing so. No more silence.

The above is what I wrote last year around Veterans' Day. I'd like to add a few thoughts apropos of this year. I want to note that what is happening in the Congo right now is more savage than what American men did to helpless women in Vietnam and at a level of unbelievable brutality similar to Nanking. And the numbers are on the scale of Rwanda--hundreds of thousands of Congolese women gang raped, some so severely that they are suffering with 'fistula': the tearing of the vaginal membrane so that the bladder and rectum contents seep into the vagina. Women torn from rape by bayonets and tree limbs. Soldiers are even shooting women in the vagina. And raping babies as young as a few months old to death.

There is medical treatment for fistula but not many women can make it to the country's few doctors. Those who do may have to walk for days, with bleeding and leaking between their legs, to get to a care center.

On all of the remembrance days and veteran and memorial days around the world, I'd like all of the news stations on this planet to carry full-size images of a Congolese woman with her insides ripped apart. Let's start right now. This November. Let's show what war really is. It is not the nobility of soldiers, believe me.

There is apparently a kind of 'remake' of *Casualties of War* coming out in the form of Brian de Palma's *Redacted*—his version of the rape and murder of 14-year-old Abeer in Iraq by American soldiers. It has already premiered in Europe, at the Venice Film Festival, and is slated for U.S. release this month. It will be interesting to see if it makes an appearance in this country. I have yet to see an ad for it. *Casualties of War* was not made until fifteen years after the end of the U.S. occupation of Vietnam. Will the American media, and the American people—particularly American women who believe their soldier sons and brothers and husbands are saints and never exploit the sexually vulnerable—will they even allow such a movie in our theaters?

What more can be done—other than the full-sized picture of the Congolese woman which needs to be carried on every front page in the world—and blazoned across Times Square? Not much. Once a year, a number of women in San Francisco honor the 400,000 Bangladesh victims of Pakistani rape camps. Does the day really do these practically forgotten women any good?

Universities faithfully put on productions of *The Vagina Monologues*. Maybe if one year all the money were donated to those raped and prostituted by war, it might cause a ripple in the media. It would be a minuscule step, but better than the absolute nothing that exists now.

We could vote for people who will do something. But who are those people? I can find no one to support for the 2008 presidential election in the U.S. Hillary has made a few token comments on trafficking; I have never heard Obama mention sexual enslavement/rape/military brothels/prostitution/trafficking. Nader never said anything about these subjects when he used to run for president. Once, a long time ago, I think the Green Party mentioned that war was not healthy for women due to sexual exploitation. But they don't seem to take up this cause with much fervor.

I could run but I'd probably be assassinated before I took the oath of office. Championing anything as shameful as the military whore body is not popular. After all, she is a disposable processing plant, not even remotely human by our high standards.

I don't see any possibility of getting politicians to notice the presence of women in war, and their subsequent rape/prostitution/exploitation. *USA Today* (Nov. 5, 2007) reports that of the 2.3 million refugees in Iraq, 83 % are women and children. (And there are another 2 million refugees in surrounding countries.) The article on these refugees made no mention of sex for food and survival. Since politicians and journalists are not interested in this topic—all the women journalists in Iraq apparently are looking the other way—where do we turn? Can Human Rights Watch, Refugees International, and Amnesty International tell us what is going on in Iraq? Information from these groups was invaluable when Kosovo was being turned into a military brothel. It was, in fact, the only source of information that we had—with the exception of one brave female military contractor who tried to blow the lid on the rape party and, as a result, lost her job.

Should Hillary be elected, I don't think she is going to spend a lot of time taking girls out of the brothels of Baghdad and Basra—and Kabul—and the other brothels attached to our military bases all over the world (in Korea, for example). The only way she might develop an interest in this topic is if it happened to her. Plant her in a brothel somewhere that the troops of the world pass through, and turn her into a rape processing plant, and I bet she'd put this on her platform very quickly. That is, if she survived long enough to do so.

In a world where women don't even care about the rape/prostituting of other women—and, in fact, even promote it through indifference--what is to be done?

Not much, as I said. I have actually found men better allies in this fight than women. More of them e-mail me and say, "You go, girl—these things need to be said" than do women. For every one rare woman who writes me, ten men offer their support. And many of these are vets—ex-military men who didn't themselves rape but didn't know how to stop what they saw happening around them all over the world—anywhere there is a military presence, they tell me, vulnerable women are sexually exploited. I even had an ex-Pakistani soldier write me an eyewitness account of what he had seen in a rape camp so many years ago. And done. And he asked me to forgive him. Not all men are rape monsters—even if they rape, I have discovered. But I do think that women are monsters if they do not help other women.

How can we combat what seems to be such hopeless and overwhelming "sexual terrorism" against women? Protest, awareness—these are first steps.

But they do not help the raped/prostituted unless they are followed by actions.

Here's a suggestion: let's replace all of those raping male UN Peacekeepers and NATO troops with women UN Peacekeepers and NATO troops. Then let us make these women (say, a feminine benevolent army of half a million strong) the sexual safeguards of the world. Anywhere there is conflict, they watchdog the militaries of the world. They set up safe camps and centers where women cannot be raped/prostituted and they distribute long-term aid and help to the millions who have already been caught in the rape mechanisms of war.

Where is the money to come from, you ask? Simple--we take it away from the multi-billion dollar business (probably trillion by now) called trafficking: confiscate every cent stashed away by every trafficker and procurer and brothel owner and every corrupt politician and border guard and police official who has enabled trafficking. Take back the money they have made through promoting rape and misery. The problem is, amongst such indifference to the sexual plight of women, who will do the confiscating? Who is watching the watchers?

Would women care enough to help other women on such a scale of benevolence and compassion? I doubt it.

"There is no right in war—only what's left." (Bertrand Russell)

4

The following article might be called my 'flagship' one. It is the first one I wrote—pushing the button on the computer to send it off took me several days. It took more courage than I have to send this out. Publishing it left me feeling cold and afraid. A raped whore woman, which is what I am, is not supposed to have a voice, or to write articles like this. As one of my readers said, "What is remarkable is that this kind of woman is finally speaking out."

Publishing "War and Sex" turned out to be an amazing experience. It brought immediate response from readers—most of them said they were overwhelmed by my passionate voice. They said I made them feel and understand the pain of the prostitute in ways they never had before.

What was even more amazing was that some soldiers wrote me. Some of them even apologized for having hurt prostitutes.

My many other articles seem to have branched out from "War and Sex."

I am still afraid. Every article I publish fills me with fear. But I am going to keep writing.

War and Sex

May 20, 2006

In all of the massive, ongoing coverage of the war in Iraq, one huge issue is left out, the sexual behavior of our troops. Recent coverage of the trafficking of Iraqi girls into brothels by gangs and pimps (*Time*, April 23, 2006) does not mention whether U.S. and British soldiers are their customers.

Iraq is like Vietnam in this respect. Silenced women suffering sexual brutalization. During that war, gang rape in the villages and the forcing of half a million hungry girls into prostitution to service our men was the picture, and we never heard about it. A tacit conspiracy on the part of the media to keep all this "dirt" from impinging on the attention of the "decent," privileged girls back home. (Sources for Vietnam material: Historian Arlene Eisen and my own conversations with Vietnam vets over a period of thirty years.)

An American woman reporter for *U.S. News & World Report* suggested that prisoners were being tortured in Iraq because our soldiers didn't have "reliable brothels" where they could "let off steam." (I wonder, what is a "reliable brothel." One where the women make no protest, no matter what is done to them?) Inmates in these places, violated over and over again, often by men who are drunk and rough, have it far worse than those prisoners. (A related issue: Are women being trafficked into Guantanamo Bay, for our soldiers? If so, why is no one protesting their mistreatment?)

Since Iraqi soldiers could not use their own women, for religious reasons, as prostitutes, Saddam Hussein trafficked in girls from Thailand and elsewhere to service his men. (Source: Gordon Thomas, *Enslaved.*) Where are these Thai girls now, those who survived the assault of Hussein's army? Have they been transferred over, for use by the Americans and the British -- in the same way that Korean Comfort Women were recycled for sexual use by our troops after WWII? (A related question: Is Hussein being prosecuted for this trafficking?)

A *New York Times* article mentioned "whorehouses in Basra." Are these being frequented by our men?

Filipinos are working on military bases in Iraq (source: Frontline). Have Filipina girls been trafficked in for sexual use?

I would like to know if vulnerable Iraqi women and girls are being trafficked/prostituted/brothelized for our soldiers. I would also like to know if girls are being brought in from countries with histories of exporting their women's bodies for sex-- like Thailand. If so, I would like to believe that our men are trying to help these sexually brutalized women, rather than adding to their misery. But I'm not too optimistic. Since the end of WWII, American soldiers have been among the largest consumers of exploited women and girls. Korean Comfort Women, sexually imprisoned by the Japanese, were not the only victims of the Second World War. In Tokyo, as soon as our men landed in August 1945, destitute, homeless, and unprotected girls were rounded up and forced into "Comfort Stations" by both the Japanese and American authorities. Most of these "Occupation Comfort Women" were teenage girls, and most were virgins. They were forced to service anywhere from 15 to 60 American soldiers a day. One dispassionate official's report describes a girl that 50 soldiers lined up to use as "busy," as if she were baking a cake or doing her homework.

When the girls tired to escape, they were pushed back into the brothels by our Military Police. Even when they cried and showed how terrified they were, the American boys still used them. Some were raped into unconsciousness. The conditions were so unbearable that some girls committed suicide. (Sources for Occupation Comfort Girl material: Historians John Dower, George Hicks, and Yuki Tanaka.)

During the Vietnam War, Thai and Okinawan girls were also sold to our men. The current multi-billion dollar sex industry in Thailand grew out of the heavy demand for flesh from our soldiers taking R & R in that country. In fact, Patpong, with its now famous fuck-and-pussy shows, blow-job clubs, and bar-girl prostitutes, was started by enterprising ex-U.S. servicemen, imposing a Western style of sex-for-sale on the Thai culture.

In *Let the Good Times Roll*, a book of interviews with Asian women and girls prostituted to the U.S. military, one Okinawan girl who saw heavy use under our soldiers on R &R during the Vietnam War recounts how, even many years later, she can find no peace from nightmares of mass rape by soldiers. "Rape" was how she saw her experience, of having to lie down under 20 or 30 men a day. As would any woman, not just those of us conveniently labeled "whores" for our army.

A girl trafficked into a Kosovo brothel begged American military men to help her escape, but they refused because they wanted to use her, too. (Source: *Amnesty International.*)

I have a solution: Educate our men about the misery of the women they use in brothels--although the soldiers may not realize it, many have been trafficked into these places which they frequent (Woman, Child for Sale). Consequently, the inmates are held in debt bondage, controlled by pimps, and beaten to make them compliant and to make them perform. Even if trafficking is not involved, other economic and cultural circumstances have led to the girl's exploitation. Instead of further hurting these already damaged females, our soldiers should try to help them. That would be a truly "honorable" soldierly act.

Educating the customers in compassion has to be a prime part of the campaign to end sexual exploitation. Men are not monsters (at least, not all the time). They can learn to protect instead of exploit.

It has always puzzled me, how the sexual exploitation of women abroad, by my soldiers, protects my freedom here at home. It doesn't. It erodes it, by teaching callousness toward women's bodies and that we can be used, as objects, without gentleness. Thirty years ago, I was gang raped by men who had raped in Vietnam. They had a lot of practice over there, and then came back and used my body as their rape playground. After the attack, I ended up in prostitution, near a military base, because I felt I was a piece of public garbage, fit only for more rape by men.

One thing that I garnered from talking to Vietnam vets about rape was how easy it was because the women were so small and fragile. Since Asian woman are about the size of ten-year-olds, it didn't take much to overpower them. It has always haunted me, how badly torn up these girls must have been due to their smallness. (It must have been like raping children.) I'm a medium-sized Caucasian woman and my attackers, all pretty big Caucasian males, almost killed me.

What's needed in media coverage of trafficking and enforced prostitution is more input from a sexually brutalized body, like mine, in order to make readers and viewers experience the full "horror and sadness" of all this. I can describe, in detail, what it is like to have the most intimate part of your body constantly violated. Forced serial penetration of the vagina is beyond miserable: just the physical damage to the opening, when it tears, feels like applying fire to a cut. Your genitals swell and bruise; you become raw inside, too, and everything hurts--your bladder, your rectum, your womb--and your breasts and hip bones because of the weight of the men. Almost no accounts of prostitution mention—let alone stress—how hard it is on the body. 'Hard' is too mild a word. It shreds the body. Girls who are raped 30 or more times a day report ruptured sex organs, like their ovaries. Abscessed nipples can result from the men 'playing' with them. Even one man, during lovemaking, can be rough on the nipples. Imagine dozens of men a day abusing your nipples. Deep disgust, at being used by strangers, is also part of the process.

The long-term damage to the mind and the spirit cannot be put into words.

The "customers" are the greatest puzzle. In Japan, did the American soldiers not see the terrible damage they were doing to that girl that fifty of them all lined up to use? They must have seen the misery in her eyes (if she was still conscious). Didn't they see the tremendous damage to her body and spirit? To her soul?

Or did they just make dirty jokes, as they waited in line?

Recently the Pacific Marines have issued statements about prosecuting men for using prostitutes, anywhere in the world. Although this is certainly a promising idea, I would be curious to see if it could ever be enforced. The Military Code of Honor already forbids the buying of prostituted bodies, but it has been completely ignored. One soldier I talked to when I lived in Japan called it "a joke."

When the U.S. Fleet visits Thailand, something like 10,000 women and girls are trafficked in, to service their needs. Many of these prostitutes are controlled by pimps, and roughly one third are underage. (Source: *Patpong Sisters.*) Do we arrest the entire navy? Do we arrest a third of them for statutory rape? There would be no one left to run the ships.

A shift in attitude--is it possible? Tailhook. Strippers and prostitutes were also at the convention, but not one article I have read on this incident draws any connections between the way the men treated these "for sale" women and the sexual barrage they subjected the female sailors to. Probably, the sexually "available" women were treated more roughly, and with less respect, than the "good" girls, but we hear nothing of their stories.

Women are all the same. There is something so fundamentally wrong about dividing the women of the world up into the "pure" and the "protected" versus those of us who have been dumped in the camp of the sexually brutalized. This division, into "good" girls and "bad" girls, "pure" virgins and "dirty" whores, degrades all of us, just as the rape and degradation of any female body threatens all of us. As long as military men think they can buy women's bodies, no woman will be accorded any respect. When I was growing up on army bases, it amazed me how the "good" military wives and daughters held the same coarse and cruel attitudes as the men; they referred to prostitutes as "the filth outside the gate" and had no compassion or understanding for the destitution or social or cultural circumstances which may have led them to sell their bodies.

On the hopeful side, it is amazing that the U.S. Military is finally recognizing that prostitution exploits and damages women and girls. It took them a while (a few centuries) but, as a girl who grew up on military bases, where it was simply considered the norm for soldiers to use what was called the 'filth outside the gate,' I find all this pretty remarkable. Moving from the view that cheap bodies for sale is a "necessary and harmless" recreational outlet for the troops to actually considering that those bodies have a humanity is a big step for the military mind.

International law is now defining the forced, non-consensual sex we find in most forms of prostitution as rape. It is now recognized that if any women, girl, or child is coerced, held against her will, forced to take customers without her consent, this is rape. (Source: Amnesty International.) It has always seemed to me that one-time rape, which we have paid some attention to, pales almost into insignificance beside the ongoing violation that forced prostitution takes. Although it is amazing that it took international law so long to even notice this most dreadful form of rape, this step still needs to be celebrated.

Another consideration is that, despite certain depredations, like the Kosovo, Vietnam, and Tokyo ones mentioned above, our soldiers often treat prostituted women far better than do most other armies. One reason for this, of course, is that American men accord some respect to their own women at home--and they sometimes carry this over into their attitudes toward prostitutes abroad. If these women are not sold to our men, they may have to service armies who will treat them with far more brutality than ours do. (My main source for the information in this paragraph is soldiers I have known and talked to over a period of thirty years.)

Another step in the right direction that I can suggest: Every time a high-profile woman like Condoleezza Rice visits any place our troops are stationed, or any place they land for R & R, she should also visit the brothels that service our men. She should talk to the women and girls, ask them about their lives, see if they can be helped rather than ravaged by more sexual mistreatment.

Hilary Clinton should take a world-wide trip with the specific purpose of visiting the brothelized, the trafficked, the sexually enslaved. She could call enormous attention to their plight. Would that I had her power to make the world notice the soft and the ravaged. As a former prostitute, I know that we are scorned as "filth" and considered "disposable." If high-profile women would accord us some importance and humanity, consider our lives worthy of notice, maybe others would not be so quick to despise us. I know that once you are in the camp of the brutalized and sexually mistreated, escape is practically impossible. World-wide, there is too much cultural barbed wire keeping you in that prison, blaming you for your own rape/prostitution. A recent Frontline show on "Sex Slaves" said that trafficked girls who manage to escape, return home, are shamed by their experience, turned into village whores

I wonder if the media overlooks the sexual brutalization of our bodies because they consider the topic "dirty." Such, for example, was the reaction of the Japanese press when the Korean Comfort Girls finally told their stories of sexual enslavement by the Japanese military. (I use "girls" rather than "women" because most were teenagers when they were held and raped continuously.)

Are the 400,000 women of Bangladesh who were held in rape camps by the Pakistani military over thirty years ago still considered too "dirty" for their stories to be told? It seems that this attitude still blankets the world--the raped woman must live in shame because of what was done to her body; the world media glance the other way because the topic is "dirty." Look at me. I live in a country where I have some small measure of recourse if I am violated. Yet it has taken me thirty years to find the inner courage to speak about my experiences, such has been the cultural imposition of shame upon me. And I write each word with fear--fear that I will be hurt again, for daring to speak. Fear that I will lose my job because I was once a prostitute--that word of hardness that hammers all the sexuality out of us, with its heavy connotations of shame, filth, etc.

There is a Jacobean play in which two girls are mass raped by an army. Their uncle blames them and says, "You should have kept your legs together." Great advice--except that so many men are forcing them apart.

When I try to speak up for the prostitute, I feel as if I stand alone. No one seems to care. Hide your raped body, Suki. It is too "dirty" to be defended, spoken for, even noticed.

I wish that some of the news accounts of Darfur would point out that Sudanese women are subjected to Female Genital Mutilation and that this makes rape all the more devastating. These poor women can barely handle any kind of 'normal' intercourse, given this 'cultural' damage to their organs, let along the violence of rape. When will this be in the forefront of women's concerns--rather than the latest Kama Sutra position in Cosmopolitan? (This is not to condemn the joys of the Kama Sutra or the pleasure that this magazine believes is our sexual birthright, merely to say that, as Western, privileged women, we hold a tenuous grasp upon out own sexual freedom if so many other female bodies are being enslaved.) When will the liberal media devote more than a few inches of space, every few months, to the ongoing misery inflicted on our bodies? When will it write long stories about the children fathered by UN Peacekeepers on prostituted bodies? (No peace for the ravaged.) Or notice the masses of Amerasian street children recycled into the prostitution their mothers had to undertake, to eat? When will it seek out and listen to the stories of the refugee girls that were "conscripted" and sold for $2 a lay in tent brothels across Vietnam because the soldier at war "must have his fuck," as one vet said so eloquently said to me.

I know from my own violation that a woman does not choose sex with large numbers of strangers as a way of life if she can escape. The degradation of this experience is tremendous. Sadly, the suffering of female bodies is rarely noted in the official accounts of war--obviously deemed of little importance, since war is told only from the point of view of the hard male, with his weapons. The soft raped/prostituted woman is, apparently, negligible. Is there any room in the media for the point of view of those of us who are tremendously damaged by this kind of sex at its most terrible, without tenderness?

From the pathetic Occupation Comfort Girls handed over to our troops in Tokyo after WWII to the destitute camptown girls of Korea and the starving tent-brothel whores of Vietnam, it is all the same picture. Occupying armies occupying the bodies of subjugated, conquered women. Men make war; women suffer its savage sexual consequences.

I don't have any solutions for suffering. I live inside a brothel/rape hell which is the everyday prison of my body. For temporary comfort, I write. To release, to forget, and to remember. And I watch pigeons. Because they are humble, and at peace with themselves. They calm me down, with their quiet ways. And I give my suffering to the mountains where I live. They tell me that they're big enough to withstand it, and that my helpless, fragile female body can rest, at least for a little while--from the pain.

I would like to see a Tomb for the Unknown Prostitute, and a Monument to the Forgotten Raped Woman. It's time their voices (and mine) were heard.

A word about terminology: I use the word "prostitute" or "prostituted woman" instead of "sex worker" because it seems ludicrous to me to term, say, a ten-year-old in a Cambodian brothel as a "sex worker." Not just ludicrous but callous and cruel, considering the rape that is being done to her body and life. Yet this is the phrase that is in vogue'no matter how brutal the sexual enslavement of the woman, girl, or child, writers are imposing the phrase "sex worker" on the victimized. Enforced prostitution is not "work" in any meaningful sense of the word. To put "sex" before "work" demeans the word "work" as well. That word should connote a fulfilling activity which adds beauty and compassion to life, not one which destroys a girl's body and spirit.

5

The prostitution situation in Iraq, and in neighboring countries, like Syria, where the refugees go, is what one would expect from a five-year war that has destroyed the lives and homes and families and fortunes of women and girls. Survival sex, fuck-for-food is rampant. Here are a number of articles I have written on sex and Iraq, many of them pointing out the typical situation: the abomination that is the sale and sexual enslavement of women—this abomination that is just considered a trivial byproduct of war. "Operation Iraqi Freedom"? What a joke that must be to the girl in the Baghdad or Basra brothel being raped for the tenth time in a day. Or for the six-year-old Iraqi girl pandered in a Damascus nightclub. "Good sex? Good fuck? One-dollar, please."

A different version of the following first appeared in *Off Our Backs* magazine, 2006, under the title "Where the Whores Aren't."

'Freedom' to Rape Prostitutes in Iraq: Fun and Porn for the Boys

January 9, 2007

My fury is high, and I am seeing red, and I don't quite know quite where to start in response to one of Newsweek's usual pieces: a sexist, patriarchal, overweeningly male, massively chauvinistic (that useful word bequeathed to us by the feminists of the 60's), on-the-surface story about how booze and drugs and whores are rampant in Iraq due to the American presence. Now young Iraqi men can easily have access to bodies. The author of this particular piece, called "Iraqi Vice" (Dec. 22, 2006), is Christian Caryl; and he tells of a typical journey from a village to Baghdad by a young male named Ali who, as soon as he gets off the bus, heads to a well-known alley where he plunks down $1.50 to buy 15 minutes with a woman. (Woman? What are the ages of the 'women' held here? Are they girls? Caryl does not bother to ask or to find out.) "The room is a cell with only a curtain for a door, and Ali complains that Abu Abdullah's women should bathe more often," writes Caryl.

Is Abu Abdullah the pimp, the 'owner' of the girls? Why didn't Caryl interview him to see where he bought the girls from?

Why didn't Caryl ask why the girls were dirty? There is a reason prostitutes don't bathe more often. The kind of filth they need to wash away is not amenable to soap and water. The filth that men like Ali deposit inside is so indelible and deep, that even scrubbing the vagina away, until it is raw and dead, will not take away the true dirt. The filth of being raped all day, for $1.50 a shot, can't ever be washed away.

Caryl's second enlightening comment on prostitutes in this piece is that the girls now have 'nothing to fear' since American MP's make the cops in this district release the prostitutes if they are arrested. Back to the pimps? That's not much of a release. And as for them having 'nothing to fear,' the prostitution-rape these girls undergo everyday is greatly to be feared. As is the ever-present possibility of physical violence. As is the psychological misery and destruction and pain that accompanies the violation of their bodies.

Why didn't Caryl go behind the curtain and interview the girl? Why was she so unimportaint that he didn't even give her a voice? Is she just an unwashed body, an unbathed whore, with no humanity or identity? I would ask this journalist: Is she just a hole that men stick it in for fifteen minutes at $1.50 a shot?

There is no female perspective in this article. But then there is no female perspective in the media. Every day journalists all over the world crank out articles just like this one—exclusively from the merciless, male point-of-view: without pity or empathy for the raped.

Ali is quoted as saying that the availability of these whores, unwashed as they are, is "a big improvement from Saddam Hussein's day. Back then, he says, the only establishment for a poor boy like himself was a Gypsy settlement on the capital's western outskirts. 'But now there are plenty of places,' he grins. 'Now we have freedom.'"

Okay, I guess this is a male version of 'freedom'—to be able to ram a hole for 15 minutes for $1.50. But does the girl he is ramming consider this 'freedom'? Why didn't Caryl ask her? (I'd also like to know what happened to those poor Gypsy girls.)

I would like Caryl to ask her other questions. Is she being rammed all day? Does she ever get to rest? What kind of physical and emotional shape is she in? How did she get here, in this brothel bed, behind a curtain? Is she hurting from the constant use by strangers? Does she have venereal diseases? Is she receiving any medical care? Does she have children? Does she get to keep any of the money or is she just a revolving sex-door for the men? Does she want to be here?

What woman or girl would invite this treatment, I wonder? Sexless, 'loveless sex,' sex without tenderness or caring, sex done anonymously, 15 minutes of being rammed by someone she doesn't know, and then the next man gets on. Why is this woman's point-of-view so negligible that this journalist did not go behind the curtain, to speak to her?

Is there never a journalist, anywhere, male or female, who asks these questions and writes about the world from the rape-battered woman's point of view? Why do we never hear the words of the millions upon millions of women and girls and children being sold every day for a dollar or two (or even less) a rape? I don't care which publication I go to—*Newsweek, Time, US News & World Report*, all the major papers—they only see the world from Ali's point of view. His 'grin' as he talks about raping a whore body is apparently a far more salient journalistic detail than is the pain of that raped body. Why this should be so is great mystery to me.

Caryl also reports massive attendance at porn films in Baghdad, now everywhere since the American presence took hold.

Girls have gone missing in Iraq? Have they been trafficked and put in brothels, for Ali's use? And, of course, my big question, are the American and British soldiers also taking advantage of these vulnerable, helpless girls? I don't have contact with military men anymore, but I would like to talk to those American MP's who make sure the prostitutes are released. I would like to ask them, and other soldiers who have been in Iraq, if they are buying bodies. (Is this the reason the MP's make sure the girls are let go—so they will also be available for our men?) If American men are buying bodies over there, then they're not really promoting 'freedom.' As I have written elsewhere, freedom does not exist for raped bodies.

I can't do much about the behavior of rapists like Ali, but I can definitely raise my voice in protest when I see my men exploiting girls—anywhere in the world. These American men belong to me, in a sense. They are my model of freedom and goodness, and they are my protectors from oppression. I want other men to emulate my men. It hurts me if my men are hurting girls in Iraq, or anywhere around the world.

Caryl's end note is quite puzzling. He quotes an Iraqi leader, Fuad al Rawi, as saying, "We can't forbid freedom." Then Caryl says, "Still, some people are always ready to try. That's how people like Saddam came to power." What kind of 'freedom' are these men (Caryl and Fuad al Rawi) talking about? The freedom of other men to traffic girls and make big profits off of them? The freedom of men to buy and rape girls for fun and sexual release? The freedom of men to sit and hoot at this spectacle we call hard-core porn, an industry that relies on Viagra-soaked men giving endless anal poundings to stiff, reluctant bodies (where is the foreplay, or anything like human interaction in all this male-designed porn?—but that is a subject for a whole other article).

A last question: Where is the voice of ordinary Iraqi women in all this? If we have liberated all these Iraqi women, and given them American-style 'freedom,' why are they not protesting the rape of their sisters?

Caryl's male window on the world is depressing and dark beyond belief. There is no hope for the women of the world as long as journalists record 'reality' in such a narrow, sad way—only from the point of view of the rapist, not of the raped.

Afternote: I assume from the name, Christian, that Caryl is a male. If I have the gender wrong, it doesn't much matter since all women journalists also record the world from the male point-of-view: they can't help it—it is how they have been taught. I recorded the world from the male point-of-view until I was raped and decided that there must be a better way of looking at reality.

After the rape and murder of the young Iraqi girl Abeer, there was some small media attention to sexual violence in Iraq. Here is what I wrote at the time of this young girl's death.

The following first appeared in *Off Our Backs*, the 2006 issue on "Women and the Military."

A Rape in Iraq

This is no distant story. It holds a personal note for me, this possible gang rape and murder of a 14-year-old Iraqi girl by American soldiers.

Thirty years ago, I was gang raped by men who had served in Vietnam . They had practiced on the Vietnamese girls, and then they came back and used my body as their rape playground. After the attack, I couldn't leave the house for several months because the whole world seemed like a terrifying place controlled by male violence. Eventually, I ended up in prostitution near a military base because I felt I was piece of public garbage, fit only for more rape my men.

That cold fear of male violence never entirely leaves raped bodies. Unexpectedly, things surface, and this event in Iraq is triggering those things in me--phantom rape pain, jumpiness, feeling startled if a man comes too near. Since I am used to reading about rape, living with it, writing about it, even experiencing it, why such an impact from this one incident?

It may be because of her age. I was a grown woman who was used to sex when half a dozen men attacked me—and it was still unendurable. The ordeal lasted for hours—I was probably assaulted about fifteen times since they all went more than once. Swollen, bleeding vagina, damage to my bladder and rectum, pain in my womb, bruises all over the front of my body from the weight of the men. This is just some of what gang rape means. The way it kills the soul probably can't be put into words. Abeer Qassim Hamza (that is her name) was most assuredly a virgin. Also, the vaginal membrane in girls is more fragile than it is in grown women. If the alleged rape took place, my imagination wants to turn away from what it must feel like to experience sex for the first time in this brutal form.

I am also disturbed because this is the first time the "R" word has surfaced in Iraq. In our three-year occupation of that country, is this the only time our men have raped? Given their war/rape record elsewhere, it would be hard to believe. It is a real puzzler to me that the U.S. Military is admitting to this possible rape of one Iraqi girl when they have done little, if anything, to acknowledge the rapes of thousands upon thousands of other girls by our soldiers during wartime. Widespread violation of girls took place in Vietnam. (One vet I know said it was so common the men called it SIMR, Standard Issue Military Rape.) After WWII, rape by American soldiers in Europe was "extensive," according to the *Oxford Companion to American Military History*. Rape of French girls by our men was so widespread that General Eisenhower actually had to acknowledge it was going on. He did nothing about it, of course, but he did admit it was happening. Our men produced roughly 200,000 Amerasian children upon the bodies of destitute Japanese girls after WWII—an indication that massive rape of prostituted/brothelized bodies was going on in the Pacific. (Source: Pearl Buck gave this estimate after her visit to Japan in the 1960's.) During the battle of Okinawa , our boys raped a whole village of women and girls too sick and weak to even run away from them.

Wartime rape/prostitution is common, the norm. Why is the military only taking note of this one incident, when the bodies of hundreds of thousands of girls have been sexually brutalized by our military?

According to the Oxford book mentioned above, in Vietnam, from 1970-73, thirteen marines and one navy serviceman were convicted of rape. The book goes on to say that this in no way reflects the actual number of rapes. According to some reports, and Vietnam vets themselves, the numbers probably ran in the hundreds, even thousands, per day. And, in Vietnam, the rape sometimes led to murder as well—a soldier would simply "blow away" a girl when he was finished using her. (Source for this latter: my conversation with a Vietnam vet.)

In the *New York Times* (July 7, 2006), we read of "a strongly worded apology issued by the top American commander in Iraq , Gen. George W. Casey, Jr." for the possible rape-murder crimes. "The alleged events of that day are absolutely inexcusable and unacceptable behavior," says his statement.

Associated Press writer Katharine Dunbar quotes Gen. Casey as follows: "Coalition forces came to Iraq to protect the rights and freedoms of the Iraqi people, to defend democratic values, and to uphold human dignity. As such, we will face every situation honestly and openly, and we will leave no stone unturned in pursuit of the facts....We will hold our service members accountable if they are found guilty of misconduct in a court of law."

All of these apologies and statements about human dignity hit me like blows since they have not been made before, to all those hundreds of thousand other women and girls. Nor to me. (The way I see it, the U.S. military owes me several million dollars in severe trauma damages for having trained men to rape, with impunity, and then setting them loose on me.)

In his long military career, Gen. Casey must have been aware of numerous rapes and instances of enforced prostitution. Why is this particular rape so important as to be noticed? A hint may lie in the way the New York Times article phrases Casey's response to the incident as "revealing the deep concern among American officials over the criminal episode's potential to damage the entire American project in Iraq." So, it is the American image in Iraq that might be 'injured'? The rape-murder of the girl, her agony, is not really the issue. Such a relentlessly male point of view "reveals" that what happens to the sexually vulnerable female body is still secondary, incidental, something off in the corner, never at the center of "male" concerns.

Along these same lines, I keep waiting for someone to suggest that there aren't enough brothels in Iraq where our men can let off steam—that's why they're raping. The same idea as in Okinawa when several American soldiers raped a 13-year-old girl and the politicians said, "They should have used a prostitute." Or when Occupation Comfort Girls were forced into brothels to service GI's in Tokyo after WWII so the men would not attack 'decent' Japanese girls. (Since most of the destitute victims were virgins before our army bought their bodies, were they at one point 'decent,' too?) Despite cheap bodies available in the brothels, American soldiers raped on the streets of Tokyo anyway, for fun and 'sport.' (Sources for Occupation Comfort Girl material: Historians John Dower, George Hicks, and Yuki Tanaka.)

Should the U.S. military traffic in girls from Eastern Europe, Thailand, and the Philippines for the troops? On a satiric note, I would say that these girls are already being trafficked by the truckload everywhere else in the world—why not to Iraq? Are girls already being imported for our men, I would like to know? It happened during Desert Storm—prostituted bodies were shipped in for our guys who lined up to use them. (Source: my conversation with a soldier who served in this engagement.)

The Iraqi rape broadens out into these other concerns—the entire picture of sex and war. If they have not already done so, it troubles me that military officials may start trafficking in girls (Filipinas, perhaps?-- Filipinos are already working on the bases over there) for sexual use in order to prevent further attacks on 'decent' Iraqi girls.

(The role of the U.S. military/government as pimp is not new. Agreements between the U.S. and Korea during that engagement in the 1950's ensured that prostituted bodies would be supplied to the American soldiers. [Source: Moon's *Sex Among Allies*.] Similarly, agreements between our government and Thailand during the Vietnam War set Bangkok up as a major R & R destination, with the inevitable sale of young girls to the soldiers. Instead of R

& R, the men called it I & I, Intercourse and Intoxication. One imaginative vet I spoke to said he called it D & D, Drinking and Dicking.)

Unfortunately, placing some girls into brothel beds, where they are subject to ongoing serial rape, so that girls on the streets won't be assaulted doesn't work. The men who violate the girls in the brothel beds learn that that the forcing of sex on a body is an accepted norm. They are far more likely to rape the girl on the street than they were before they raped the prostituted body. And far more likely to come home and rape those 'decent' American girls next door.

The *Casualties of War* incident has been haunting me since the Iraqi gang rape-murder announcement. That movie was based on a true event: a group of American soldiers kidnapped a Vietnamese village girl and kept her for several days while they raped, beat, and tortured her, including putting cigarettes out on her body. Eventually they killed her. One soldier, who refused to participate, tried to later report the event but no one cared to listen. Finally, a chaplain did, and the soldiers were tried, but given only light sentences—just a few months in jail. Similarly, the mass rape/massacre called My Lai drew only light sentences. Of the 13 marines and one navy man convicted between 1970-73 mentioned above, I wonder if any were subject to substantial punishment?

What will happen if the alleged assailants in the Iraqi case come to trial? According to a July 10, 2006 Associated Press story by Robert H. Reid, they have now been identified: "Sgt. Paul E. Cortez, Spc. James P. Barker, Pfc. Jesse V. Spielman and Pfc. Bryan L. Howard are accused of rape and murder and several other charges as alleged participants. They could face the death penalty if convicted. A fifth, Sgt. Anthony W. Yribe, is charged with failing to report the attack but is not alleged to have been a direct participant. The five will face an Article 32 hearing, the military equivalent of a grand jury proceeding, to determine if they should stand trial. They are charged with conspiring with former soldier Steven D. Green, who was arrested in the case last month in North Carolina . Green has pleaded not guilty to one count of rape and four counts of murder and is being held without bond." The article goes on to say that the soldiers had targeted the girl earlier and that they got drunk before the alleged rape-murder incident.

If they stand trial and are convicted, will a military-style gang rape finally draw a severe punishment, maybe even the death sentence? Why has this not been the case in the past? And why have all the soldiers who have raped girls forced into prostitution never been tried for this crime? The Iraqi girl's rape-agony was finite. With girls held in brothel beds, the rape goes on and on.

Particularly horrifying to me is the part our soldiers have played in the collective history of brothel rape. By now, we know about the Japanese rape torture of the Korean Comfort Women, but American history books never mention that our soldiers treated the girls given to them in post-WWII Tokyo with equal savagery. Japanese girls forced into brothels to service our soldiers were terrified of these huge men. They screamed, cried, held onto to posts to keep from being shoved down, but our men used them anyway. As many as 60 men would line up to use one girl. Some girls were raped into unconsciousness. (I use 'girls' because most were teenagers.)

Some girls managed to commit suicide: one such, Takita Natsue, walked in front of a train after being used for several days by dozens of American soldiers in a Tokyo 'comfort' station. Her rape-agony was disguised as a financial transaction: take a number, unzip, bang the girl, pay, and leave. No guilt, no accountability. "We will hold our service members accountable if they are found guilty…." says Gen. Casey. Isn't the ongoing serial rape of a prostituted body an act just as "guilty" as a one-time rape? Or more so, since the body is violated thousands of times, rather than just five, as is the case with Abeer. (I should say 'may be the case' rather than 'is' since nothing has been proven against the accused American soldiers yet.)

Perhaps the crime of raping the brothelized goes unnoticed because of the sheer numbers involved. During WWII, Korea , and Vietnam , access to cheap sex with starving girls was simply there—a fact of going to war. Historian John Dower estimates that almost 100% of the American soldiers stationed in Tokyo after WWII used Japanese prostituted bodies. It was considered such an everyday activity by the military that they refused to recognize it as rape. (It has always puzzled me enormously—how the use of sexually exploited bodies all over the world by my soldiers protects my freedom as an American woman here at home?)

What is the difference now, with this Iraqi case? Why is Abeer's rape-murder being taken seriously, whereas Takita's passed almost unnoticed? Six decades have passed since Takita, just a teenager, with a life ahead of her, couldn't bear the agony of brothel rape. Death was the way out that she chose. And, of course, every American soldier who used her is responsible for that death. Six decades in which some women have finally started talking about rape and forced prostitution as harmful to us. Almost never in my youth would a girl even bring up the "R" word, or the "P" word. Now I can log on to the internet and find other voices. I can actually find some women who care that I was raped. Some women who might be outraged at what happened to Abeer—and Takita. Amazing. Women who have finally recognized that not just what we term 'rape' is reprehensible but that enforced prostitution is actually the torture of gang rape—multiplied thousands of times.

Another difference between Takita's era and Abeer's might lie in the fact that in the early 1990's, the Korean Comfort Women finally told their stories. This was unprecedented. Woman actually admitting they had been raped/ prostituted. (In brief, for those of you who do not know the story, roughly 200,000 women were sexually enslaved by the Japanese military before and during WWII, held in rape camps, and violated 30-50 times a day. Those who survived were permanently crippled and broken, both physically and psychologically.)

This telling opened up awareness, following upon similar events like Bangladesh and Bosnia . Women finally speaking up. All the shame of WWII, Korea, and Vietnam that kept the raped/prostituted women of those conflicts silent was still there—but, despite it, women were finally speaking. Finally.

So, now we have the U.S. military forced to pay attention to Abeer. I'm sure they would just as soon hide it. I'm sure they're angry at whatever journalist decided to break the story. (The incident took place last March, so it was hidden for quite a while.)

Will Abeer's case be pivotal in the history of military rape? Will we finally recognize this as something serious, rather than men having fun?

In January 2006, the Pacific Marines issued statements recognizing trafficking/prostitution as harmful and exploitative and saying that, worldwide, the military would prosecute servicemen who bought bodies. Has this come about yet? Could it ever come about? When the U.S. Fleet visits Thailand , roughly 10,000 prostituted bodies greet them—roughly a third of the girls are underage. (Source: *Patpong Sisters*.) Do we arrest the entire navy? Do we toss thousands of them in the brig for statutory rape? There would be no one left to run the ships. Are there still stacks of condoms right beside the gates of our bases in Korea? Are our men still patronizing the 30,000 or so Korean women, girls, and children prostituted for their use? And, if our soldiers simply stop buying prostitutes, will the women be sold elsewhere, perhaps under worse conditions?

Still, that the Marines would make such a statement is a hopeful sign. From tolerantly regarding brothelized bodies as a 'necessary and harmless' recreational activity for the troops to actually realizing that prostitution hurts us is a huge step for the military mind.

To return to Abeer, her alleged rape stirs disturbing questions. In the Iraqi world, rape is too shameful to even be talked about. So, would other Iraqi girls even dare report their ordeals? Would a 'defiled' girl be killed to erase her shame and avenge the honor of her family?

Will journalists in Iraq ever tackle the other question I keep asking—are girls (Iraqi or of other nationalities) being prostituted for our men in that country? (With 130,000 young American male bodies over there, they must be doing something for sex other than handjobs. Hopefully, they're not raping their fellow female soldiers the way they did during the Persian Gulf War. How would I know? Journalists never cover this side of conflicts.)

Can Iraqi girls be prostituted is maybe the first question to be asked. Would this also draw forth the murder of the girl, to erase her shame, restore honor? Hussein trafficked in teenage girls from Thailand for brothel rape by his army since it was forbidden, under his rule, to turn an Iraqi woman into a prostitute. Is this still so?

Some Vietnam vets I've talked to have expressed the following ideas: The Vietnamese girls were really lucky getting to sell their bodies to the American soldiers because they were hungry and it was the only way they could make a living. Prostitution was good for the economy of Vietnam. That country made millions selling us their women.

Okay, I can sort of understand this point of view. After all, war is about death and sex, thanatos and eros. (I'm not sure if someone else said that, or if I just made it up, but it makes sense.) Men destroy towns and villages, crops and animals, and then the girls left alive are forced into survival sex with the conquerors.

Having worked as a prostitute myself, near a military base, I can see the destitution aspect. One incentive that pushed me into prostitution was that I was hungry. And I was afraid of being homeless. To survive, women will sell themselves.

Now, the case in Iraq seems to be rather different. Women are hungry in this war-ridden country. Malnourished, anemic was what I was reading about the majority of them. And their children are in bad shape, hungry, sick. One heavy reason women will sell themselves during war is to feed their children. Is this even an option for the desperate women of Iraq ?

Were the Vietnamese women 'lucky' because they could sell their bodies?

These may seem like heartless questions, but they reflect the hard reality of what hungry women, with hungry children, will do during war.

Despite my outrage at their sometimes savage behavior, I am not really down on men or soldiers. I can see why they might rape: young men, in a strange country, Iraq , which is completely alien to their American world. Young men angry when a friend is killed. Terrified themselves of death. At any moment, they could be maimed, disfigured, have their legs blown off. I am sorry for these young men, my American men, even when their fear turns to our brutalization. I saw too many men from my generation, the Vietnam generation, become savage and troubled for me to condemn what I don't understand—why men behave with such sexual brutality during wartime. My men, the ones I saw go off to Vietnam , were simply ordinary young boys pushed to extremes by that atrocity called war. The ones who came back were so damaged that they had to do terrible rape damage upon me, to release their demons and nightmares.

This rape in Iraq is not a cold act on the other side of the world for me. This whole Abeer misery has stirred up all these other miseries and questions in me. I always see the world from the point of view of a raped/prostituted body. Layers of shame and sexual battering will always be somewhere inside me. My collective rape pain is enormous. Rape one woman and you rape us all.

My hope is that Abeer's pain may lead to a huge shift in the attitude of the U.S. military. That there will be, from now on, for all time, a strict policy of soldiers never forcing sex on a woman in any form. A policy of respect for the vulnerability of our bodies. Give us food, protection, and money if we are in wartime need. Never rape us or force us to sell our bodies. I would revamp the whole 'core of warrior ethics' to include these as golden rules of compassionate conduct. True warrior values of honor.

Abeer, gentle sister, I am sorry for what men did to you.

This next article caused outrage. How dare she try to 'excuse' the men for having raped Abeer? Actually, this is not at all my point. I quote military leaders as to the stresses that lead to military rape. I admit that all human beings are capable of this terrible savagery. It is really a norm, not an exception—the horror of military rape. Anyone who has read my other articles sees this clearly. Not one of the readers who was outraged by this article and my alleged attempt to 'excuse' the men who raped Abeer saw the connection between the terrible reality of brothel rape and the one-time rape of the 'nice girl'—which Abeer represents. The girls in the brothels were nice girls as well, before they got raped into insanity.

Not one of these outraged readers seemed to have any sense of history at all.

All these outraged readers saw American soldiers as decent and wonderful—except for this small 'aberrant' bunch who raped Abeer. Never mind the *Casualties of War* precedent: all those Vietnamese girls raped and then killed by American men in Vietnam. (Apparently, there were many incidents like the one in this movie. It was based on a true incident and rape was an everyday commonplace occurrence in Vietnam.) Never mind their brute behavior toward women in all wars. Somehow the small group who raped Abeer were a one-time occurrence and a complete exception to the noble man who is the American soldier. These readers showed not one iota of historical consciousness or knowledge. They were only interested in the mistaken idea that I was somehow exonerating Abeer's rapists. Far from it. I don't exonerate any soldier who rapes. I don't excuse any of the millions of American soldiers who have been raping in wars for the past sixty years. They all disgust and horrify me. To them, I need to add the millions upon millions from other armies as well. There are too many historical incidents to list so I'll use one: Just the movie *Two Women* (based on true events) illustrates that those wonderful Allies of ours from Morocco gang raped the shit out of every Italian girl in their path during WWII. Whole villages fell before these rape-shit males. At least our men showed a little compassion and restraint.

Amazing that to these readers only Abeer, the 'innocent,' is important—and for them apparently those hundreds of thousands of other raped girls—some labeled 'prostitutes'—matter not at all.

Understanding Why They Raped

I can kind of understand why Marines in Iraq may have raped a 14-year-old girl and then killed her and her family. (I would like to stress the 'may have.' Nothing has been proven against these men yet. They have not been tried, or convicted. They are as innocent as you and I at this moment.)

It seems like a statement of the obvious, but the men are in a wartime situation. Full of the fear of being killed, the frustration of having to deal with this enemy they don't know or understand—Iraqi culture is incredibly different from ours. They see their friends killed. They could get maimed, disfigured, have their legs blown off at any moment. They're in the middle of this awful heat and loaded down with 50-100 lbs. of gear and angry as hell. Maybe rape and other atrocities are understandable responses? Maybe I would behave in a really savage way, too, if I were faced with what's hitting these boys everyday?

In a *USA Today* article (June 2, 2006), Brig. Gen. Donald Campbell, chief of staff in Baghdad, says: "It's very difficult to determine in some cases on this battlefield who is combatant and who is civilian." The soldiers, he goes on to say, are experiencing "stress, fear, islolation....They see their buddies getting blown up on occasion, and they could snap."

The *Christian Science Monitor's* "US Troops Weigh Impact of Stress" (July 7, 2006) by Mark Sappenfield reinforces these views. Sappenfield writes: "A number of current and former troops suggest that amid the daily calamity of war, everyone has their breaking point, and the seemingly endless nature of this war could, in some cases, cause frustration to boil over into criminal violence.

"They are quick not to prejudge fellow soldiers and marines implicated in the... murder investigations that have emerged recently.

"'War can make you do terrible things,' says Lawrence Provost," a man who has served in both Afghanistan and Iraq with the Army Reserve.

"Moreover," Sappenfield reports, "soldiers and marines resent what they see as the self-righteous condemnation of critics who sit thousands of miles from the fight and have little concept of what it means to fight an insurgency." And he writes of "the stress of a combat environment where friend and foe blur into uncertainty."

As a protected American woman sitting in my armchair, I am not likely to be called upon to go to war and to face the hardships and pressures of Iraq. About the closest I can come to urban warfare is watching Black Hawk Down. The movie was based on a true incident: on Oct. 3, 1993, young, untried Army Rangers, alongside more experienced Delta forces, engaged Somali militia in Mogadishu; due to poor intel, they didn't know the whole city was going to come down on them. As a result, a number were killed and wounded. (What the military learned about urban warfare on that day has carried forward, to places like Iraq.) The movie tries to recreate the stress, heat, carnage, and uncertainty of urban combat and does so with a tense, harsh realism.

Although it is not about the rape-murder of civilians, it does hit us in the face with the moral uncertainties of urban warfare, and the confusion. The Somalis used women and children as shields. Somali women would also dart out, in the line of fire, to distract the American soldiers. Telling friend from foe would have been impossible in the circumstances. Avoiding killing women and children would have been impossible.

If I put myself in the place of these threatened young men in Mogadishu, how would I behave? If faced with someone shooting at me from behind a line of women and kids, I would, if necessary, kill the women and kids to protect myself. If I saw my buddies being torn up around me, I might want to exact some revenge. Even though I don't have the male testosterone that would drive me to rape, I can imagine how men could use this act as an outlet for anger, wartime stress, frustration.

If the six soldiers implicated in the March rape-murder of the young Iraqi girl and her family are guilty, we should remember that they are ordinary men pushed to extremes. They are just like the men around us everyday—just like our boyfriends and brothers.

How can I condemn any soldiers for wartime rape-murder if I can't answer for myself? What kind of savagery might I inflict on a woman or child if war pushed me far enough?

Postscript: I think the readers who were outraged by this article did not like my idea that regular and normal and decent American soldiers can all behave like raping brute savages. Just put them near a whore, and they'll get drunk and roughly rape the shit out of her. Normal behavior for all these decent, normal, honorable, wonderful courageous men.

The Rape of Iraq and Other Sexual Matters

January 12, 2008

I just e-mailed the following paragraph to Human Rights Watch, Amnesty International, Refugees International, the United Nations High Commission for Refugees, Iraq Veterans Against the War, and two women journalists at CBS news, Katie Couric and Lara Logan (foreign correspondent in Iraq):

I would like to know more about the sexual assault on women in Iraq: rapes by American and coalition forces; rapes by the Iraqi police and military; rapes by Iraqi civilian men; rapes of women and girls detained in prisons; gang rapes; women forced into starvation prostitution—either for the occupying forces or for Iraqis; the increase of brothels in Baghdad and Basra as a result of the occupation; the trafficking of women and girls into prostitution by criminal gangs, either within Iraq or in surrounding countries; the way families are forced to sell daughters for survival; any 'survival sex' women and girls are engaged in due to desperation; 'survival sex' forced upon the refugee population (2 million in Iraq–2 million in surrounding countries); the trafficking, by U.S. military contractors, of Filipina and Chinese girls into brothels in the Green Zone; the role of the U.S. Military Police in the pimping of Iraqi women and girls; the physical and psychological state of the prostituted Iraqi girls trafficked into the Green Zone for paid rape; the rape of female military personnel by their own men—and anything else you may have seen going on in Iraq.

For Couric and Logan, I appended: "This aspect of Iraq has been overlooked by CBS news." For Amnesty International, I added, "I would also like to know about the trafficking of girls into Guantanamo Bay to service the U.S. military there. Your organization is involved in the rights of detainees there but has overlooked this other class of tortured beings."

2008. This is the year I would like to see the sexual exploitation of women in the wars America indulges in finally covered rather than ignored—in reparation for not having done so from the Revolution forward—the Civil War (with its wandering bands of syphilitic camp followers, mostly women widowed by the war); the Spanish American War and the two Great Wars and Korea and Vietnam and Desert Storm and Panama and Afghanistan and now Iraq—not a whisper from the whore in the dirty alley, offering it up for a few dollars due to hunger, or the hunger of her children. It is time. Katie Couric and Lara Logan (the latter journalist has been 'embedded' with the troops over there), it is time you report on all the women and girls, in Iraq, and all the Iraqi refugee women and girls in surrounding countries forced into survival sex. It is time you profiled the 14-year-old Iraqi refugee girl sold by her family to Dubai in order to feed her younger brothers and sisters.

It is time the 500 journalists 'embedded' with the troops focus, everyday, on this aspect of the war.

This is the Year of the Whore. And her woes in war. And her misery in 'peace' since she can never leave the battlefield. It is the year of her trafficked, ripped-apart vagina, and her shredded pulped womb, due to overuse. It is the year of the girl child prostitute whose anus is hanging out of her body due to too much anal rape upon a fragile being not even ready for a gentle act of intercourse. (I am not sure if there is a 'right amount' of anal rape—even one act forced upon an unwilling body is an abomination against the goddesses of mercy and tenderness. The thousands of rapes the prostituted body endures should make the planets drop out of their orbits and the stars go supernova.)

About the Rape of Iraq, information scattered across the internet is sparse, but it is there. Of 50,000 or so mainstream news articles on Iraq, only a handful even intimate that anything might be sexually amiss in the latest war rape zone, the one called Iraq; but the non-mainstream media give us a different view. In many ways, it too is sparse, but at least there is minimal coverage. Code Pink (Women for Peace), for example, at least make some mention (however slight) of the rape and sexual humiliation of Iraqi women by U.S. personnel in detainment centers and the way the girls are subjected to honor killings after release. And they report the kidnapping and trafficking of girls by criminal gangs who sell them into brothels in neighboring countries and the way "coalition forces and U.S. military contractors have committed horrific crimes of sexual abuse, torture, and physical assault." There are, according to Code Pink "copious accounts of rapes and gang rapes." All of this is quite hidden away on their site—as if this aspect of war were not really that important. And, unfortunately, Code Pink overlooks the starvation prostitution many Iraqi women and girls have been forced into. But, then, this does not surprise me. If you have read any of my other articles, you know that I am an ex-prostitute and that even women helping other women ignore my kind. We prostitutes are marginalized as disposable by the 'respectable' women of the world who regard the one-time rape of a 'good' girl as terrible and the thousands of rapes upon the whore body as not even an act of rape.

Iraq Veterans Against the War says that prostitution is now 'common' in Iraq, but they do not give details. This subject is not covered on their website—at least I cannot find it anywhere. The most brutal act committed upon a woman—the serial rape of the prostituted, degraded, humiliated body–is simply not important enough for them to comment on. The situation with the Winter Soldiers of Vietnam was similar. One description of a dead raped girl—naked and spread-eagled in a field—the insignia of her rapists plastered between her legs, as if it were a badge of honor. One more description of the way soldiers inserted an instrument in a girl and filled her with grease. A statement that female VC prisoners had live electric eels stuffed into their vaginas and anuses. And that their interrogators would set their pubic hair on fire. That's about it. No testimonies from these Winter Soldiers of the girls brothelized and raped thousands of times because they were labeled worthless whores and 'cheap gook pussy.' Maybe because these Winter Soldiers were also raping the brothelized? If you pay, it is okay? Did the Iraq Veterans Against the War take advantage of prostituted bodies? Is this why they say nothing about them?

As I search the internet, I come across photos (on Women's Space) that purport to be American soldiers gang raping a naked Iraqi girl. I say 'purport' since who can verify that this is not simply a 'staged' photo, for sensationalism. American soldiers in Iraq were carrying around these gang rape scenes, as fun, for porn and there was a website of Iraq rape pictures called something like IraqBabePorn. (I think it is now defunct.) There is also the by-now famous YouTube video of the imprisoned 15-year-old Iraqi girl virgin being pimped all day by her American captors until she hangs herself and they callously say they made $500 off of her. We do not know if this is a real video or if it was staged. Then there is the article by Ruth Rosen, a UC Berkeley historian, published in *Mother Jones* (July 2006) stating that the rape of women in our Iraqi prisons is quite real and extremely widespread, as is the sexual trafficking of women and girls in that country. In fact, her article gives the impression of extensive 'sexual terrorism' practiced upon the women and girls of Iraq. Not surprising, of course. So what else is new in wartime, I say. I have said many times that war never ever liberates women. It starves us and turns us into sex toys and whores and raped bleeding vaginas and objects of degradation. Put guns in the hands of horny young men and send them in as conquerors and they will rape, and buy every starving whore available who has to open her legs and fuck for food. It is what the horny young male soldier does. The supercharge to his virility must be tremendous. A gun in one hand and his other weapon out and ready and he is now a raping power stud, showing woman her place as fucked whore.

It's tough to come by information. The only rape to receive any mainstream media attention is Abeer's—the young girl who was also murdered, along with her family, after the assault. (See my article, "A Rape in Iraq," published in *Off Our Backs*, about this incident. The atrocity was also turned into a movie, *Redacted*, by Brian de Palma, now in theatres.) A major sexual agenda for me for 2008 is to enormously increase the coverage of all the sexual misery inflicted on women and girls worldwide. Even a magazine like *Mother Jones*, which pretends to be liberal, carries only one article on the rape of women in Iraq? And only one article, every few months, on other rape hot spots—like Cambodia and its child sex trade. Pitifully spare coverage for a magazine that styles itself 'alternative.' In fact, I scour the media for the sexual enslavement of women in Iraq, for the 'fistula' rape of women in the Congo, for the genital-mutilation rape of the women of the Sudan and am simply not finding it covered with any kind of depth or any kind of regularity on all the sites that style themselves 'alternative' or liberal. Common Dreams, Democracy Now, etc., will mention this sort of topic every once in a while, but almost as an aside to their 'real' news—all the stories written by men about the affairs of men. There is one article in *Glamour* by Eve Ensler on the 'fistula' rapes in the Congo. In all of its multitudinous coverage of the Iraq war, *The Nation* has carried one sentence about the rapes in Iraq. (*The Nation* is always sadly lacking in its attention to sexual savagery: a token article now and then, that's all.) Common Dreams and its ilk and all those magazines like *Harpers* and *The Progressive* are as blind as CNN and PBS and devote such a tiny tiny tiny amount of space to the rape and ravaging and prostituting of our bodies that they are worthless to me living in a perpetually raped body as I do. *The New York Times Magazine* will run one story a year on trafficking and think it has done its job. All these media so rarely cover rape/prostitution that they make it seem as if they care almost nothing about the whole frail female half of the species. They leave my rape-battered body out of their reckoning. They are all told from the point of view of the conqueror rapist. And they do not go into the misery of the raped/prostituted even when they deign to occasionally mention her. Almost all women journalists write from the point of view of the conqueror rapist.

Almost all history and journalism is told from the point of view of the conqueror rapist.

I just googled Common Dreams. Not one single mention in the long list of current articles of the ravaging and damage to our perpetually raped bodies. Not one! The articles on Iraq on the current board simply do not mention the prostituted women, as if we do not exist and have absolutely no importance to history, to journalism, to men. Or to women since the women who post on this site also ignore, for the most part, the ravaging of other women. I suppose it is not their fault. They spout the conqueror-rapist dogma that they have learned. There is no space in which to express the depth of the raped body. Certainly no journalistic space anywhere on Rape Planet Earth. I notice that the 'torture' articles on the current Common Dreams site all refer to the suffering of men. As if, within the space we call common dreams, there are no dreams for raped whore women—there is no reality for us, no caring, no place in which to breathe, or live—Common

Dreams is male space shaped by the conqueror rapist. How could that current board, with its emphasis on all male concerns, have anything to do with my raped body? These sites depress me far more than CNN—at least I know that CNN has no clarity of vision or compassion at all. They don't pretend to have any. They are not lying to themselves—the way Common Dreams does. CNN knows that no one believes their narrow lies. Maybe Common Dreams thinks someone does believe their lies?

There are a few sites that are not written by the conqueror rapists. MADRE, Polaris, and V-Day are three. Women's Space is another.

Some blogs from within Iraq contain helpful information. One by an Iraqi woman, Layla Anwar, mentions rape, rape, rape, rape so many times that it must be happening. She can't be making all this up. She also writes that "survival sex is rampant not only inside Iraq but also outside. It happens in alley ways, around shrines, in dirty beds and in bars...Bars in Syria and Jordan. They are there to make a bit of money to feed their hungry sisters and brothers waiting for them in some damp, dirty, cockroach ridden, room - where they are all amassed, one on top of the other, hungry and waiting.... Hungry and exiled because of YOU and YOUR fucking democracy. And this is exactly what it boils down to — a fucking democracy. Some of them are as old your teenagers - with one major difference. Our teenagers, forced into it by YOU, will remain stigmatized for the rest of their lives and they can already kiss their future goodbye. They have no future. So tell me, is that not criminal? So tell me, does that not make you a complicit criminal people? Our teenagers prior to their 'liberation' did not need to seek survival sex. They did not need to sit in bars in skimpy dresses waiting for the Mr. who will alleviate the hunger pangs of a whole family. Survival sex, the Iraqi-American version. Good, very good - $10 a shot. No make it $20- I have a hungry family. A $20 shot democracy."

Who is buying these girls? According to Ms. Anwar, both GI's and Iraqi men. She has a date with an Iraqi man who regards the buying of whore bodies as "fun." "Entertainment," he says, has become so "cheap and available" because there are so many poor Iraqi girls around.

I would hazard that customers for the girls are probably more their own men than ours, given that our American soldiers over there are up against a lot of cultural sequestering of female bodies, even whore ones. I don't know if the GI's are allowed to simply roam the streets in what have become 'red-light areas' since the occupation. I don't know how many of the trafficked Filipina and Chinese girls are available to them in makeshift brothels. I don't know if U.S. military contractors are making money off of trafficked girls, the way they did in Kosovo. I don't know if U.S. Military Police are getting payoffs for pimping Iraqi whores, the way they get payoffs for pimping girls to American soldiers in Korea. I would like to know. I can only speculate from what our sexual savagery has been like in other conflicts, and in other occupied countries. Have the men in Iraq completely broken the soldier mold and are they now rescuing whores instead of raping them or are they following the behavior pattern they have exhibited in all other conflicts? It is hard to find out, since, unlike Saigon and Bangkok, those Sweatbath Brothels of Asia, where a GI could buy a pimped fifteen-year-old right off a street corner (still can, for that matter), Middle Eastern venues are more covert about the exploitation. Does what is called 'general order one'—no sex and no alcohol—hold sway for our military in Iraq—or do they find ways to circumvent it? I would like to know from men who are serving there. Please e-mail me about this.

I would certainly like to know the numbers and condition of the women and girls imprisoned in those Baghdad and Basra brothels. Prostitution worldwide has a universal quality—whether it be Baghdad or Bombay or Dubai or New York, it involves debt bondage, coercion, control of the girls by owners and pimps—little of the money actually goes to the girl who is raped all day. It is an industry based, simply, on how profitable it is to rape a body over and over again—I doubt if the brothels in Baghdad are a humanitarian departure from the torture norm.

Ms. Anwar, the blogger, detests us fiercely—and rightly so given that we have destroyed her country. But, sadly, her sympathy for the whore body does not extend past her own countrywomen. She spits at Western 'hookers'—as she calls us—apparently not realizing that we too are condemned to no future and hopeless degradation. She seems particularly down on Russian whores—I wonder if she realizes most are trafficked, and what that entails? Just as Iraqi girls are being sold by their families and trafficked into Dubai (a major sex-slave destination) so are girls from the Ukraine—and all girls (despite nationality) are treated with the same savagery–they are burned and starved and filmed for porn, to break their spirits, through humiliation, and forced multiple times—sometimes raped up to 50 times a day–until they are either insane, commit suicide, or are 'willing' to submit to rape by customers up to twenty hours a day because they are too dead to fight anymore. I keep telling the world that basically when a customer climbs on a prostitute, he rape-fucks a piece of dead whore meat. When men climbed on me, they rape-fucked a piece of dead whore meat. I wish someone somewhere would believe me. But even if people did, would it matter? Men are never going to stop rape-fucking dead whore meat. Gives them a thrill to ram a helpless body into death and madness. In light of all this it is particularly painful to see Ms. Anwar wishing prostitution, in revenge, upon all American daughters.

If it is any consolation to her, many of us are prostituted. And we live in rape prisons as severe as those of Iraqi women. Many years past the time I spent in prostitution, I am afraid to leave the house. It takes me two hours to trick myself to cross the threshold. I am terrified I will be gang raped again, if I go outside. And that this time I will bleed to death, naked, in the middle of the road while passersby spit at me because I am a whore. Ms. Anwar can rejoice that I carry my own rape prison around with me. I am never out of it—there is no space outside where I can feel safe and free.

And I can certainly understand why she vilifies us Americans and wishes all us American women into whoredom. If my city were invaded by Iraqi soldiers who broke into my home and gang raped me and if I were forced to be a refugee who had to fuck for food, I would detest, for thousands of eternities, those who had hurt me this way. I would detest being prostituted to the enemy. To actually lie down with the invaders because of hunger and maybe to have his child, the child of the hated enemy inside me, would cause insanity and despair. You can see how hard this is for the whore 'occupied' by the enemy from the way women in previous wars abandoned the hated children born of the prostitution rape of their bodies. Japan, Korea, and Vietnam–tens of thousands of these detested Amerasian outcast half-breeds thrown away by their mothers. Are we now fathering a whole new group of what will be outcast half-Iraqi, half-American children? Will the abandoned girls be sold for whore-and rape-fodder, as has happened to the orphaned debris on the streets of Saigon and Bangkok?

Ms. Anwar appears to be one of the privileged who is not forced to fuck for food. She seems to be traveling widely within the Middle East and observing those Iraqi refugees who are forced to fuck for food. I wonder if she is in any kind of position to help them? And her descriptions of gang rape are only mildly accurate, and conventionally sensational—indicating she has not endured it first-hand but has borrowed her 'rape rhetoric' from reading about it. I can attest that it feels far worse than the conventional phrases used by the unraped.

Her blog reminded me of an entry on Riverbend's. Riverbend is a young Iraqi woman who has been blogging about the war for several years. (She is now in Syria and is still blogging.) She recounts a 20-year-old Iraqi woman being gang raped by the Iraqi military and then, when the woman goes to the Iraqi police, she is raped again—by them. The woman says, "How can you rape me. I'm not one of those prostitutes. I don't do such things." Which prostitute is she talking about? The 14-year-old Iraqi refugee being sold to feed her family since there is no other way? In Iran, the first thing a poor family does is sell a daughter. Is it the same in Iraq? Or is Riverbend's 'prostitute' the girl abducted and then trafficked into Syria or Jordan? Or is she one of the destitute Iraqi girls regularly let into the Green Zone to fuck for food? As long as this Iraqi woman thinks there is a distinction between a 'good' girl and a 'bad' girl, she is lost. She is also the rapist of her own kind. She brings violation upon herself if she refuses to break from this Rape Culture that rules Rape Planet Earth and if she thinks it is okay to rape "those prostitutes." I am sure the 14-year-old forced to fuck for food would not 'do such things' if she had a choice.

Riverbend is upset that the raped will be labeled 'prostitutes'—showing her complete lack of understanding as to what the prostitute is. The prostitute is a girl who is raped all day every day—not just once like the woman the Iraqi police mistreated. If anything, to be labeled a prostitute or a whore should be a badge of honor. It indicates the woman held in lowest esteem on earth, and still clinging to survival despite massive degradation. It indicates the courage to fuck for food, rather than starve. The only whores I do not esteem are those who despise and hurt other whores. And I do not esteem Riverbend if she condemns the prostitute.

Riverbend's attitude toward the prostitute makes her guilty of promoting Rape Planet Earth, as do most other women worldwide. I don't see massive numbers of middle-class Thai women marching on the brothels that hold their enslaved sisters. What I see is a bunch of 12-year-olds in schoolgirl outfits with hard raped faces and skinny raped bodies standing outside places with a big neon sign, Pussy Show, flashing above them. And should this hardened raped little schoolgirl ever escape her AIDS fate (doubtful) she too is likely scorn her raped sisters as whorefilth. I don't see large number of Cambodian women protesting the way the majority of Cambodian men (roughly 80%) visit brothels every night, and regard paying a few cents for a whore body of no more import than purchasing a bag of potato chips.

Even the Korean Comfort Women were blind. One was 'serving' beside a prostituted Japanese girl and the Korean girl said that the Japanese one 'could do' 40 men a day. 'Could do' as if it were voluntary on the part of the Japanese girl but not on the part of the Korean one. And this Korean Comfort Women said that the Japanese girl was a 'real' prostitute, as if there were some sharp moral distinction between them. Total ugly blind ignorance to the fact that the Japanese girl would have been conscripted in the exact same way the Korean Comfort Girl was under that famous 'licensed' system of prostitution in Japan where, in the typical scenario, a poor rural girl is sold, then broken through massive rape to subdue her and teach her her place and make her indifferent to laying down with so many men since she has no spirit left. (Our GI's, by the way, 'broke' the comfort women given to them in Japan the exact same way; traffickers worldwide break in girls the same way and they prize the ones who 'can do' 50 men a day since they have been tough enough to not commit suicide.)

I hate to tell the Korean Comfort Woman who thought she wasn't a 'real' prostitute this—but, baby, you are as much of a raped whore as your Japanese counterpart—as long as you condemn her as a whore, you condemn yourself as one.

There is the same self-censure on the part of women everywhere. When the Congolese women drag themselves or crawl back to their husbands, bleeding from severe gang rape, or from fistula, and they are kicked out, by that husband, to bleed in the road, and to try to crawl to one of the few doctors who can repair fistula, it is partially the woman's own fault for allowing her value to depend on virginity, chastity, fidelity, all these patriarchally imposed categories on our sexuality. These women are rapefilth in the eyes of their culture because they buy into these pernicious definitions of their own bodies and lives.

There has to be a radical revisioning of what female sexuality is. A sexuality completely divorced from morality and religion and fear and violence and repression—and war and poverty. These latter, in particular, have destroyed our sexuality. They have turned it into Fuck for Food. And great scorn of us when we have to Fuck for Food—even on the part of the women who are not forced to Fuck for Food. I never see a revisioning of our sexuality happening. We would not recognize it if it ever came about. Could you imagine me, Suki, with my highly powerful sex drive, actually liberated by a beautiful vision of my true sexuality? I can't. I wouldn't know what it would look like since my sexuality has been so defined—and 'conscripted' by men. Basically men taught me, through gang rape, that I am whore garbage. They punished me severely—through gang rape, for daring to express my own beautiful sexuality—since, of course, any girl who wants sex and men and pleasure is a whore—and must be put in her place—with rape. There is not even a vocabulary that could express a liberated form of my beautiful sexuality. The only word that applies to me, if I want to express my sexuality by taking on, voluntarily, many lovers, is 'promiscuous.' And if it is involuntary, then I am a prostitute. The two "P's." There is no vocabulary for sex outside of that pernicious institution called marriage. If sex is only defined as pre-marital, extra-marital, an act of infidelity (called adultery), it has no existence, in words or reality, free from the chains of religion and morality. There is no space or forum where a woman can express the beauty of her sexuality on this planet—to be free and hot and horny and loving it and dripping for it and to love sex and fucking and the heat and the beauty of it is impossible. As long as virginity is the only value the female body has, no sexual liberation is possible.

The only difference between me and the 'pure' virgin woman beside me is a few hours of rape. Then she will be raped whore garbage just like I am in the eyes of my culture. Not in my own eyes any longer. I am proud of that designation 'whore.' It distinguishes me from all those indifferent 'decent' women out there who ignore my kind. It distinguishes me from the billions of repressed women worldwide who can define themselves only within this prison we call marriage and can find no sexual self outside its bounds. It distinguishes me from the Congolese woman, pathetically bleeding from 'rape fistula,' who—even then–cannot, sadly, stand up to the husband who has kicked her into the road, since she is now called raped whore garbage, and say to him, "Go to a thousands hells you shitting brutal insensitive fucker." My vocabulary is not colorful enough to express what I mean, but you get the general idea.

The 'whore' label also keeps me a galaxy away from that abhorrent phrase 'sex worker.' Yet another sexual reform I would bring about in 2008 is the abolition of this dreadful phrase. That 14-year-old-Iraqi girl being sold would not regard what she does as work. Being raped all day is not work. It is beyond cruel, the way that all these cold, distanced academic sociologists and psychologists and anthropologists who 'study' the whore think they are 'respecting' the whore by mislabeling her rape 'work' when what they are doing is tremendous damage by using the phrase. They are imposing a 'normalization' on her rape as dreadful as any 'legalizing' of her rape would do. But then the vaginaless woman who is the typical academic can have no way of knowing that rape is not work. She is too distanced from reality, too soaked in the meaningless, dense jargon of her discipline, to know that prostitution is not a 'liminal reality for a body consigned to the spatial discourse of the forced intervention of penetration'—or whatever new ridiculous jargon-ridden definition she makes up to sound scholarly and publish her worthless articles. No, academic ladies, the prostitute is not someone 'consigned to a category of sexual disorder, marginalization, and displacement within the post-colonial phallic imperialist discourse of modernity.' She does not exist in that cold space. The prostitute is a body raped to ripe heat by searing misery. She is a vagina on fire with pain. There is a hot bleeding dying body in front of you. And how dare you 'study' her and then turn away from her pain. Your 'ethics of objectivity' is beyond objectionable and cruel. You cannot study a suffering being and then leave her to suffer. Another sexual reform I would make for 2008 is the elimination from the 'academic discourse on the whore' all academics who themselves are not whores. Before you write about us, you must undergo a brothel apprenticeship. You must lay there and be raped 50 times a night. And when your vagina is burning and bleeding and your insides are torn inside out, you will be so busy just trying to survive, just trying to find the strength to take the next breath that will keep you alive, that you will not have time to write those worthless articles anymore. Besides, I don't think your pimps and owners will have much patience with you sitting down at the computer to toss off a few cool pieces, MLA style, for scholarly journals, on the liminal whore body. They want you on your back fucking for profit, and the customers are not going to have any patience at all with a literate whore. They'll knock all that literacy nonsense right out of you. Burn it out with cigarettes on your body, starve it out of you, and rape it out of you.

When NOW (National Organization of Women) regards the rape that happens to prostituted girls as 'sex work' and thinks it is in some category of liberation for the female to be able to fuck all these men, there is so much amiss with our vision of sexuality that even a 5000 page book would not be enough to protest it.

A move back to the military realm, my main area of interest since when I whored I did it with American soldiers. First, I don't understand all this rape of American female soldiers by their own men: impossibly high sexual assault rates in the military—way above those in the civilian population–including gang rape. And very little is done to the rapists. You women soldiers are armed and you've had combat training. As a helpless civilian woman, I didn't stand a chance when all those soldiers raped me. But you women soldiers have weapons to counter their weapons should they take them out in a threatening manner. Why don't you just blow the balls off these would-be rapists? It is self-defense—if he tries to rape you, you have every right to incapacitate him. You have every right to stop him in any way you can. I bet the higher-ups would pay attention to your sexual grievances if you damaged a significant number of overly aggressive males. And, lady soldiers, you have to stop regarding the whore outside the gate as cheap throwaway garbage. If you do not champion her, your men will continue to rape you. Disrespect one woman and you disrespect all of us. Women soldiers–Go outside the gate, and take the whore out of her bondage, and blow the balls off of her pimps and owners. And while you're at it, enlist sympathetic male soldiers to help you. Only by extending protection to the whore will you yourself be protected.

In my impossible world of sexual change and beauty and perfection, I imagine our American military as setting a pattern for all others worldwide. I want all of them, men and women, to be noble rescuers of the helpless. And compassionate protectors.

As I have said, I want this (Iraq) to be the first war in which the sexual savagery inflicted on women is fully acknowledged—and we do something about it! This means every news source must cover the sexual humiliation and degradation of Iraqi women—fully, heavily, completely, all day everyday—until we stop this typical war-time sexual savagery forever.

And peacetime as well. I want to see our military involved in fighting trafficking, not supporting it through buying bodies. Germany is a good example. Since prostitution became legal there in 2001, Germany has become a major trafficking destination and our soldiers are among the customers using girls held in sexual slavery in brothels and places called "Eros Centers." Very few German women are involved in prostitution—they are too prosperous to be sold for sex. Eighty percent or more of the prostitutes in Germany are 'trafficked' beings—many from Russia and Eastern Europe and they go through the breaking process of burning, torture, starvation, gang rapes, imprisonment in rooms with bars on the windows, etc., that I have described elsewhere. There are about 350,000 trafficked girls now in Germany, and, of course, only a portion of the rapes upon their bodies are being committed by the troops we have there. But our military could set an example for all the men in the world, not just those in Germany

Let's get those girls out of there. Let's send our soldiers in to liberate them, rather than buy them. Bodily take them away from their owners. Then we can use the huge amount of money that the pimps and owners have brought in (trafficking/prostitution is a $4.5 billion dollar a year industry in Germany) to set up long-term care and healing facilities for the girls. And wonderful education programs for them. (I am hopeful that some of these girls can heal. I never did, but maybe some have tougher vaginas and psyches than I do.) Also use pimp money to prosecute those very pimps who have enslaved the girls. (Statistics on Germany come from Victor Malarek's book *The Natashas.*)

Let's do this liberating everywhere. Roughly 20,000 UN Peacekeepers and other multinational forces are still raping brothelized girls in Kosovo. Victor Malarek, a Canadian journalist, describes how girls are passed around at parties that soldiers give—and gang raped by all of them. Malarek describes the burns and scars and bruises on the girls' bodies and the hopeless emptiness in their eyes and the death of their spirits. Take our soldiers out of Iraq and send them into Kosovo—not to join the 'rape party,' as they have in the past, but to stop it.

Thousands of our military contractors in Iraq take R & R in Dubai, where the dead ghosts of the trafficked offer themselves in abundance. This is a huge 'rape-the-whore' hot spot. I need to mention to these contractors what a whore is. She is dead fuck meat. Her life and soul are gone. You are fucking a dead body. Rape-fucking dead whore meat. It is what I am, even years after I made it out of prostitution—I am dead whore meat and the men who mounted me rape-fucked a dead body.

Statistics are very tricky and unreliable. So I will do the best I can. According to the United Nations, 60% of all prostituted females are under age 15. Various sites across the internet yield these 'stats' (reliable? I don't know): in countries like India, Thailand, and Cambodia, 80% of all men and boys use prostituted bodies; in Japan the number is 99%. Europe varies from country to country but the numbers run from 15% of the male population to as high as 30% in Spain, Italy, and Greece. The number for the U.S. most often found is about 15% of men buy prostituted bodies. (Numbers for men in the military are much higher—sometimes 99%, depending on where the men are stationed and how available whore bodies are.) Given the youthfulness of the international prostitute population, and the way girls in Thailand and India and Cambodia are sold so pitifully young—even before they are ten years old–this makes large numbers of these buyers of bodies child rapists and pedophiles (including UN Peacekeepers and men in our military, who often purchase minors when they are available). As much as I deplore that Western pedophile who travels to Cambodia or Bangkok to buy a child, he is not the only 'sex offender.' It would seem that the millions of men on this planet who purchase the services of minors should also be listed as 'sex offenders.' They are raping child bodies.

Korea is another area where change is desperately needed. Between fifteen and twenty thousand prostituted bodies service U.S. military men there. Some few of the girls are Korean but most have been trafficked in from the Philippines, Thailand, Eastern Europe, and Russia. This is because there are no longer enough destitute Korean girls to enslave. And, supposedly, importing sex slaves will keep the 'decent' Korean women from being raped by all those horny GI's.

It's called the 'barrier' theory and it never works since the category of who is 'decent' and who deserves to be raped keeps shifting. From the 1950's to the 1970's, desperate poverty created the camp-town girls, Koreans sacrificed as 'rape scum' for the GI's. Now girls from the Ukraine are 'rape scum' for the GI's and all those 'pure' Korean girls are sipping mocha frappaccino lattes at glossy shopping malls.

Among the trafficked girls are women but also girls, age sixteen or even younger. U.S. servicemen make about two million visits a year to the bars and brothels where the girls 'work' (read 'sexual slavery' for work). The girls exist under those conditions of great misery that are typical in trafficking—held in debt bondage, brutalized, imprisoned.

They are literally slaves used for sex. The few girls who manage to escape report the degradations they are subjected to, like being forced to dance naked in the bars, and being beaten if they cry when a soldier takes them into the back rooms for paid sex.

Soldiers stationed in Korea say that boxes of condoms sit at the gates of the bases for the men. A soldier I talked to personally said that the girls he visited were definitely sexually enslaved.

In the U.S. military, the use of prostituted/enslaved bodies has long been a given. The prevalent attitude in Korea and elsewhere is: "We are here to defend democracy, not practice it."

Many American soldiers in Korea and elsewhere don't even know what trafficking is and, for a lot of those who do, whether the girls are enslaved or not is irrelevant. The soldier just wants his fuck. Essentially, U.S. servicemen are raping sex slaves, whether you call the girls 'trafficked' or 'prostituted' or whatever. The men see the girl as a convenience. In reality, she is a disposable rape dump.

Rape damage to the rape dump, should she survive, is forever. I rage in semi-madness at the memories. My own particular experiences of being gang raped by soldiers and of time spent in military prostitution have led me to huddle in the corner of my closet sometimes, and try to claw my way into the wall—and my sexual torture was no where near as traumatic as that of most girls in prostitution—yet the experience still destroyed me. I was not trafficked. No pimp controlled me. No one put cigarettes out on my body. I had a great deal of control as to who fucked me. The few times I did not (as for example, the gang rape) still haunt me miserably. No one hit me but I was anally raped once. Just once. That is burned into me in misery forever. I could say no to a man if I did not want to fuck him. Once a soldier I had fucked and hated, because he was so rough and ugly, came back. I said 'no.' He twisted my arm and said he would break it so bad I would never use it again. Then he took out his lighter and threatened to burn my nipples. I was so terrified that I let him get on and take his fuck. This was a rare instance—very few soldiers were such cruel sleazes as to treat me this way. Most were actually pretty decent.

Even that one experience still terrifies me. As I mentioned, I have a fear of leaving enclosed spaces. I am afraid that soldier is still out there, and that he will burn my nipples. It makes no sense, but there it is, irrational and ridiculous.

(I should append that Ms. Anwar, who wants to see all American girls prostituted, will probably be happy to know that I still suffer like this, imaginary as my fears are. And I would like to tell her and Riverbend that there is no recourse for the raped in America either. I never went to my police after my rapes—for fear they would make me a dirty joke in their macho world. And I did not go to a hospital, despite the way I was bleeding, because I could not bear having anything else stuck up in me—for 'examination' purposes. And the idea of actually 'telling' my story to anyone would have been impossible. All those cold eyes of policemen and doctors and nurses. There is no place anywhere in the world where the raped whore can find a soft comfort and nurturing tenderness from her pain. Iraq and America are the same. Raped by one set of men and then raped all over again by those you go to for help.)

With trafficked girls, what I rarely experienced is a norm for them. Look at Burmese girls trafficked into Thai brothels, for example. Very young, many of them, only 15 or 16, these girls are broken through rape and then violated again 10 to 20 times a night by the Thai military, the Thai police, Thai laborers, anyone who wants to buy them. Any protest is met with beatings. They have no rights. One was beaten for trying to listen to the BBC on the radio. They are not allowed to use condoms and are free to all for anal rape. Pathetically, they try to work off their 'debt' to their owners, in hopes the hell will end and they can go 'home.' After a year or so, the girls have AIDS, so they are shipped home (anuses hanging out of their bodies from the rape) where they are sometimes killed by their own families for the shame they have brought upon them—or killed because they have AIDS. New, uninfected girls are trafficked in all the time. (Information in this section comes from *A Modern Form of Slavery*.)

The one paltry anal rape inflicted on me and the threat to burn my nipples was nothing compared to what these girls endure. If I had been treated for one week the way those girls are treated for months at a time, I would be insane. As it is, I always feel like a piece of raped whore garbage and a piece of dead fuck meat. And this is from sexual roughness that was minimal compared to what the trafficked girls go through. Even that minimal roughness, on my prostitute body, practically destroyed me. Intercourse with those hundreds of men I did not want inside me destroyed me. And I whored before there was any AIDS. And I could insist on condoms. 'No condom, no sex' I even had printed, on a cute little sign, right above the bed. The death sentence that is AIDS which we are visiting on the trafficked is horrendous. That death sentence of AIDS on the child prostitute since she cannot negotiate condom use is horrendous.

The pain to the child whore body must be enormous—her vaginal tissue is not even developed yet to where she can withstand intercourse. I was in my 20's when I whored and the overuse still tore my vagina apart. I hurt all the time. I was swollen all the time.

To return to Korea and Germany and any place our men are climbing on whores, in January 2006, the U.S. Military came out with a new policy: that any soldier caught using a prostitute would be punished.

In the spring of 2007, a number of Department of Defense lawyers, some of them women, decided to put together training modules that will educate new recruits and defense contractors about trafficking and will inform the men that buying a prostitute could mean a year in jail. Perhaps I should be more hopeful that this signals a change, but my own response is rather despairing and cynical. I see so many difficulties in ever setting up our military as a model for all others—my big hope and dream. One big problem with this new policy, this idea of jailing the soldiers for a year, is that it is unenforceable. There are simply too many servicemen to jail.

And I wonder how the DOD will see any difference between the trafficked and the prostituted? It's the same orifice that's being raped–no matter whether you label the girl with this fancy new term–'trafficked'–or not. What prostitute is not trafficked in some sense? Prostitutes worldwide often work under very similar conditions, trafficked or not. Even those not terrorized and held as sex prisoners are subjected to violation by strangers, fear for their safety due to sexual and physical violence, control by pimps, exposure to STD's, etc., etc. It would be very tough to say where 'trafficking' ends and 'prostitution' begins.

Another consideration: there is no way the military could keep these men in service if they took away cheap fuck on enslaved bodies. And I do not think that the military in general regards the rape of whores as 'rape.' For them it is economics and common sense:

a) you have to keep the boys happy by providing fuck when they're off duty;

b) there is an endless supply of disposable, poor bodies for fuck purposes;

c) ergo, bring whore body together with horny soldier and he will serve out his term in the military.

Are you going to be able to keep all those boys floating around on ships in the Persian Gulf without the necessary sex binge in Thailand? A collective and willing blindness keeps their sexual activities hidden from us.

Another powerful problem: even if it were possible to stop our military from raping whores, the girls will simply be trafficked elsewhere. A really important point the DOD needs to consider is that arresting American military personnel will not remove trafficked girls from sexual slavery. In the Philippines, a huge whore industry grew up around our bases there (Subic and Clark) and when we pulled out, the enslaved girls were trafficked elsewhere—like into debt bondage in Japan. (The CATW—Coalition Against Trafficking in Women–descriptions of condition in Japan's sex industry are chilling.)

It is a dilemma: some American soldiers will treat whores far better than local men in Japan and Korea do. So, is it not better that the girls be sold to the men who will perhaps be nice to them—at least some soldiers are kind to whores—not all are monsters—I know this from personal experience. There are a few rare ones who even try to help the girls out of sexual slavery.

Rather than simply arresting the men, removing the girls from their enslavement and providing long-term care for them is essential. In a moral universe, we owe them this. Our military has long benefited from women defined as whores—recreational rape dumps. Therefore, we have to make reparation for all the rape our men have inflicted on them. (Gentle rape, sometimes, but rape nevertheless.) Setting up physical and psychological care facilities for the women on our bases, and schools and educational opportunities for them, is the only humane thing to do. It need not cost us a penny since we can use all the billions the pimps have made off the whores—once we arrest and punish all those rape murderers of women's bodies.

A big doubt I have about the education modules is whether it is possible to change male attitudes. Men have long created and benefited from a Culture of Rape. WWII soldiers raped whores freely and then they passed this tradition on to their sons, who did the same in Vietnam, and now the current generation has inherited these rape values and this rape culture. Using whores has long-term consequences: American women live in this rape culture, struggle against it, all unaware of its progenesis: ongoing rape of the bodies of hundreds of thousands of prostituted enslaved bodies overseas, in war, and in peace (during occupation). The American woman's willful ignorance and lack of sympathy for the foreign raped body is part of the problem.

Our government and military have never been sensitive to this subject before. Look, for example, at the role we played as Super Pimp in Korea in the 50's—agreements between the U.S. and Korean governments back then made trafficked girls available for 'recreational rape' for the soldiers. (See the book *Sex Among Allies* for a detailed account of this.) Similar agreements between the U.S. and Thailand assured a huge supply of enslaved flesh to our servicemen during the Vietnam War.

It is not, of course, just our soldiers or our military who are to blame. The Korean government was relentless in the forced 'recruitment' of whores to service the foreigners because they saw this as an economic bonanza. Under false pretenses, the girls were conscripted for 'jobs': they had no idea what was required was military prostitution. The Korean government was merciless in its policies toward the girls. Ideally, to work at what the government considered 'optimal' level, the girls were instructed to service 30 soldiers a day, one every half hour, for fifteen hours shifts, with no breaks, and they were supposed to do what was required to please the soldier. The Korean government told the girls it was their 'patriotic' duty to lie down as rape fuck meat. The girls, the rape fuck meat, probably did not appreciate the nicety of all the governmental politics that controlled their rape-excavated insides. It is the way of politics—men make decisions and 15-year-old girls end up as rape-fucked dead vaginas.

Certainly, when our military takes all trafficked girls out of sexual slavery there, the Korean government should help with the life-long expense of caring for these broken creatures. In reparation for their merciless sale of their own women, both to the Japanese during WWII, and to the Americans starting in the 50's.

It's kind of tough to know who might be exempt from reparation and guilt. The U.S. sets itself up as a 'judge' as to which countries are the worst sexual enslavers and the whole planet condemns the Japanese for their military Comfort Woman system, yet which country has not done the same to its own women—and women of other nations. I don't know of one. As we were putting Japanese war criminals on trail in Tokyo, our GI's were committing mass rape war crimes on their own brand of Japanese Comfort Girls, just a few yards away. Amazing. Don't just condemn the Japanese. Condemn yourselves and the whole world.

I have some personal knowledge about Korea. My first boyfriend, Vic, my first everything—lover, great love of my life, was stationed in Korea in the 50's. He said that the men who didn't buy camptown girls didn't exist. In other words, almost all the men indulged in raping enslaved bodies. Vic was a good guy. He would never hurt a woman. But he did buy the girls, just like his buddies did. And he said they were terrified of him and the other men. Terrified of how big the Americans were, and Vic said every girl he bought cried when he fucked her. He felt bad but he did in any way because that's what soldiers did.

It is still what soldiers do apparently. Is the DOD going to arrest the whole army and navy and air force and marines???? One question mark for each branch of the service. I don't think so. (Do we have to put the Coast Guard in there as well? I don't know anything about what they do when they dock.)

It has always been my impression that the men in charge in the military simply don't regard the use of prostitutes as any big deal. DOD lawyers says the push to change prostitution policies or rather 'non-policies of tacit consent,' as I would term them, came in 2003 when the Pentagon saw a Korean news show, taped in 2002, about girls being trafficked in from Eastern Europe, Russia, Thailand, and the Philippines for our serviceman; and part of the segment was about how our MP's were acting as pimps.

The Pentagon says it was outraged by this, but I rather doubt this reaction. For one, trafficking of girls into camp towns in Korea has been going on, as I said, since the 1950's, not to mention the other mass rape activities of our servicemen all over Asia, and Europe, and stateside as well (for example, border towns like Tijuana service the U.S. fleet in San Diego and El Paso has Fort Bliss—business for brothels and sex shows in Ciudad Juarez; Norfolk, Virginia, with its heavy naval presence, had long been a scene of exploitation). The Pentagon is full of military men who have seen prostituted/trafficked girls all over the world—and many of these men probably used enslaved bodies during their tours of duty. It would certainly come as no shock to any of these men that MP's pimp and that soldier freely purchase the bodies of vulnerable girls for sex. This situation has been a time-honored given in our military for ages and ages. (In all militaries, of course.) I wonder, for example, about Colin Powell and his time in Vietnam. He must have seen girls trafficked/prostituted all over the place. If he did nothing about it then, why would he and others associated with the Pentagon bother to notice this 'trivial' subject now. All of these military men in the Pentagon have seen girls forced to whore all over the world. It makes no sense to suddenly pay attention to this fact of military life now, as if the exploitation of women were something new and as if it mattered–it never has in the past.

The push is coming from the whole Pentagon, including the Secretary of Defense. Why, I ask? The military has nothing to gain from this policy. There is, apparently, no pressure coming from the outside in this country. This is not surprising. There have been anti-bases movements overseas, focusing on the degrading treatment of prostituted local women, but civilian women stateside routinely ignore the prostituting of women abroad by our military. What prevailed in Vietnam reigns now as well. The attitude back then was 1) when my boyfriend is stationed over there, he has to get his fuck. Can't expect a young guy not to get his fuck. 2) All I care is he doesn't bring any diseases home. And the women in the military also ignore the topic—assuming that the rape of their own bodies by their fellow soldiers has no relation to the Rape Culture soldiers promote in brothels.

A USO worker in Vietnam felt really sorry for the men when they had to go into combat because then they didn't have any base whores available to them. What could motivate a woman to actually feel sorry for men who rape little brown child-size bodies? Her notion that the man at war is entitled to his collective brothel-bang, his band-of-brothers fuck, and his buddy-bonding-gang rape is, again, time honored among thoughtless, vaginaless, non-whore civilian women.

So, why all the fuss now, if there is no pressure from women on the outside? It seems that a number of women DOD lawyers are concerned about the trafficked women in Korea. Could it be because some of these prostitutes are blonde (Russian and Eastern European) and therefore worth bothering with, unlike the Little Brown Fucking Machines (as the marines call Asian whores) we are accustomed to seeing our men rape? So accustomed that we American women make no protest—except for a radical, passionate, weird woman like me who has herself been raped and experienced a tiny brush with the horror that the trafficked experience.

It also appears that helping the trafficked girls was briefly brought up at the Pentagon, but that it was not stressed—as if this most important point were irrelevant.

To all of which I say, to paraphrase some lines from the movie The American President: "Congratulations! It's taken these guys—and women—five years to come up with a policy that has not the remotest chance of taking trafficked girls out of sexual enslavement."

These girls cannot walk away from their imprisoners. It is not a matter of our men buying the girls or not. It is a matter of the control their owners have to traffic them elsewhere. So, in despair, I ask again what good this new policy will do the girls?

And I wonder that the women lawyers at the Pentagon have said nothing about the new rape fodder playgrounds available to the military—Iraq and Afghanistan. Why don't these women lawyers from the Pentagon make collective trips to these hot spot raped-whore zones? I want to see every American female politician as well visit all the brothels all over the world that our military patronizes. If they don't care that trafficked girls are being mounted, and dying under rape misery, then let these women (Condi and Hillary and every American congresswoman) 'spell' the raped. Let all these privileged women politicians take the place of the destroyed bodies in the brothel beds.

Elizabeth Kucinich–wife of the man with a conscience. I was at an animal rights convention where she was one of the speakers. I wrote her a letter, not just about my animal rights agenda, which I would like to see her husband enact, but also about my concerns for the trafficked and prostituted. I had it delivered, by the front desk, to her room. I also e-mailed the same information to her and her husband. Not a peep out of them. If the Kucinich's don't care about the rape of prostituted bodies, then it is certainly not surprising that Hillary doesn't care. She has given brief lip service to the issue. And it is not included in her platform. It is in no one's platform. There is no one a whore, in good conscience, can vote for.

Back to those female DOD lawyers, I would say to them, you can't put a heart into men. At least, not through a training module. A man has a rapestick and he will always use it if the hole to be raped is there, is defenseless, is cheap, and is disposable and he suffers no consequences. As one Marine said to me, "A Marine will fuck anything with a hole in it. Hide the donuts."

And a year in jail is nothing for rape. How is that some kind of punishment? And would the man even serve out the sentence. The My Lai sentences and the ones in the Casualties-of-War incident were ridiculously short—and the men did not even serve out these. Murder, rape, sadism, incredible cruelty– not even deemed worthy of any kind of sentence commensurate with the crime. Disposable cheap gook pussy merits no consideration in the legal world of men.

Will the new DOD policy even result in a few 'token arrests,' I wonder, for show?

Another reason I don't think the modules will be effective: in addition to the difficulty of changing the rape behavior of men, it might be impossible to change the time-honored view that prostitution is the woman's fault, that she likes what she is doing, that it is 'fun,' recreation, not rape. It is a view held out in the civilian population, as well as in the military. In either area, to regard a prostitute as a human being is currently impossible, given prevailing attitudes of scorn, stigmatization, she's a filthy slut, etc. For one, to give her humanity would threaten every 'decent' woman in the world. (In my view, to deny her humanity does so.)

The confusion between 'trafficking' and 'prostitution' will also make the DOD policy impractical. Do we have to put 'forced' in front of the latter word to bring it up to the same 'victim status'? In my view, almost all prostitutes are 'trafficked,' that is forced in some way. If poverty is involved, then the activity cannot be considered voluntary. It can only be voluntary if the woman also receives sexual pleasure—but prostitution is only concerned with male satisfaction. The woman is in the position of having to please the man, so she is a lesser being, only there for him, not for her own needs and desires. Therefore, prostitution is always rape (her body is used by the man) and it is always enslavement (he buys her, rents her, as if she were a piece of equipment).

I wonder why I am the only whore voice on the sites that publish my articles. I do realize that I am not necessarily writing from the point of view of other whores since I don't really know it. I have never talked to other prostitutes, only read reports about them. Maybe all those Little Brown

Fucking Machines love being Little Brown Fucking Machines. But the few testimonies I do read express how wretched the girls are. In *Let the Good Times Roll*, a book of interviews with Asian women prostituted to the U.S. military, one common thread comes through: all the women struggle to maintain some small shred of dignity in the midst of the degradation of what they do. When you're kneeling in public in front of a GI, doing a blowjob on him, with a handkerchief over your head, dignity is a bit difficult to come by.

I would really like to speak for the whore, if I can, since no one else seems to be doing so. I can give reasons why whores don't like to be whores. For one, the sheer disgust of sex with strangers. The way you have to numb out and stop caring so you won't go insane. How prostitution cannot be considered a form of torture when it means cold, forced, impersonal sex with strangers is beyond me. It made me regard all men as potential 'customer rapists'—to this day, I size up every man I meet in terms of how he would treat me if I were a whore. Would I still be a human being to him, if he could buy me? And I think, often, with relief, with a sigh, when I look at certain men, "God, I'm glad I don't have to fuck that."

Women simply do not lie down with strangers and let them invade their soft bodies because they like it. When Master's and Johnson started studying sexuality, they at first used prostituted ones, since no 'decent' woman would be studied in this way. What M & J discovered was that the whores were too physically damaged to have any valid sexual responses.

When I peruse an 800-page college text on human sexuality and only two sentences pertain to the whore, I wonder why and then I think, "Well, she has no sexuality. It has been raped out of her."

I regard 'prostitution rape' as a central issue for all women because of the extent of degradation involved, and what is taken from us—our bodies, souls, lives, girlhood, womanhood.

Sex is at the center of a woman's identity. To invade that most private, sacred, intimate part of her, her vagina, her womb, against her will, is to destroy who she is—not just physically, but emotionally, spiritually, and in all other ways. To take what is meant for a very private use, a woman's vagina, and to turn it into what is essentially a piece of public property, has far reaching repercussions on a woman's whole being.

To turn what can be one of the most ecstatic, spiritual, and intense experiences of life—lovemaking—into something ugly, brutal, painful, crude, cold, is terrible beyond description.

Apparently none of this occurs to the soldier as rapist or to the non-whore woman, at least those who are 'vaginaless' and with no sympathy for their raped sisters.

Maybe the greatest tragedy is that the raped whore body is robbed of its sexuality. This beautiful gift called sex taken from her.

More statistics: by the year 2025, a quarter of the girls in India will all be prostituted. Will it reach critical mass at any point? The United Nations says that the profits from human trafficking now exceed those of the drug trade—and that the number of trafficked beings will only increase enormously in the future, since there are no effective measures to stop it. If by 2075, 75% of all human females in all countries are prostituted (provided men can still breathe the polluted air enough to rape) will the remaining 25% still ignore their suffering sisters?

An interesting science fiction scenario I will have to explore in a future novel—the prostituting of women to the point that it reaches 98% and the way the remaining free 2% do not hear the rape cries of their sisters.

Some suggestions for eliminating prostitution rape (now called 'trafficking'). First, set up 'fuckboxes' around the world, stations with artificial vaginas in them, where men can unload. It is obviously irrelevant, to most men, whether a woman is attached to the vagina or not. This is their only goal—to unload. I have come to the conclusion that for reasons unfathomable to me men can't do without our bodies. Unfathomable to me since all they care about is the fuck in the vagina. Why do you guys need the rest of us, if this is the case?

But–in some perverse way–men need more. They need to touch our softness. So, just fuckboxes won't do. But if they need to touch our softness, they can't be allowed to destroy it as they rape us.

We could also encourage men to simply use their fists to fuck themselves off. Those wretched, pathetic Occupation Comfort Girls in Japan are a perfect example of how well this policy could have worked after WWII. The girls could have been saved the unendurable misery of being raped up to 60 times a day by GI's if the military had simply suggested to the men that they do themselves. Since the soldiers were essentially masturbating inside the girl's vagina anyway—after all, her pleasure was irrelevant and her unbearable pain ignored–why the men actually needed female bodies is beyond me. (I've always thought that military gang rape was a form of public masturbation.)

When I see the famous footage of the huge American warships in the harbours off of Japan, with those thousands of men ready to go ashore, dicks out and at the ready for rape, I wonder why MacArthur didn't take the men aside and instruct them to masturbate instead of form rapelines in front of brothels.

But, then, I forget. For some perverse reason, men need our bodies.

Which brings me to another suggestion: worldwide Lysistrata. All my suggestions are practical, as you may have noted. The only drawback with this one is that it will take the combined effort of all the women in the world. All non-whore women, that is, they must shut off the sex supply—until all the men in the world stop raping the enslaved whore women—who are not free to shut off the supply. The rub is how do you convince 'respectable' women that whores matter? How can you convince such women to institute worldwide Lysistrata to free their enslaved sisters when they themselves do not see them as enslaved.

I would like turn to the men of the world for help. Those who do not buy bodies are a substantial number who could help girls out of sexual slavery if they would, physically, stop the buyers. Men of the world–don't let other men buy living beings. It is as simple as that. On occasion, on a blog somewhere, I will see an intrepid male, fed up with trafficking and the inhumanity of man toward woman, say, "Let's all get together, those of us who don't buy girls, and stop the ones who do. Let's take those girls out of those brothel beds." A wonderful idea.

Let 2008 be the first year in which no girls are sexually abused as part of the 'fun and games' at an Olympics. At all major sporting events like the World Cup and the Olympics, there is an underworld of dark sex happening—as the tourists party, pimps make huge profits off of sex slaves. The World Cup in Germany saw the trafficking of 40,000 girls into mobile brothels for fans to 'fuck party' on. A trafficked girl who escaped from her enslavers says that she was raped by thousands of customers during the Olympics in Athens. Sexual exploitation is as rampant in China as everywhere else. How many young girls will be served up as fun and games rape fodder for international fans in Beijing? No human rights activists ever focus on this aspect of the Olympics.

I would like more of those human rights groups to spotlight prostitution/trafficking during 2008. Refugees International, for example, lists the most vulnerable segments of the Iraqi population in wartime—but leaves young girls completely off the list! I don't know how much more vulnerable you can be than a young girl in wartime. Even your own family is against you since you are likely to be sold to feed the rest of them.

I'd like to see more movies on the topic of trafficking. *Human Trafficking* on Lifetime reached a lot of viewers. *Holly*, out now, is about child prostitution in Cambodia, specifically the trafficking of young Vietnamese girls into brothels there. It was produced by an investment banker named Jacobson who, on a trip to Phnom Penh, was followed around by prostitutes, some as young as five, who said if he didn't buy them they would be beaten. He was so appalled that he came home, gathered some funds, made a movie about the situation, and set up an organization to help the girls called Redlight

Children Campaign (redlightchildren.org). Amazing man. Let's have all investment bankers in the world follow his example.

I glanced at Sundance's offering for this year and only found one that treats sexual misery–*Greatest Silence: Rape in the Congo*. Not one film about the prostituted body. This is Sundance, the Great Social Conscience Film Festival? Apparently the dead whore meat of history has no importance for the privileged of Sundance.

Eastern Promises uncovers trafficking of adolescent girls into London by the Russian mafia. I have not seen it so I cannot make any aesthetic judgments but it looks as if it is more interested in the naked body of actor Viggo Mortensen than in the raped body of the dead, hemorrhaging adolescent whore that sets the plot in motion. Mortensen went to Russia to research the role. He says he is a social activist. If so, I would like to see him join forces with other activist celebrities (like Susan Sarandon and Angelina Jolie and Mia Farrow and George Clooney) in order to take trafficked girls out of brothels. Daryl Hannah can't do it all on her own. In so far as I know, she is the only one so far who has actually physically invaded a brothel and removed enslaved girls.

George Clooney made a big push for sending UN Peacekeepers to Darfur. Now that they are there, they are buying desperate refugees for a dollar or two a fuck shot. So what else is new? Those UN Peacekeepers always join in the rape spree. They regard cheap fuck meat at one of the 'perks' of the job.

I see that 3000 more Marines are going to be shipped into Afghanistan. Prostitutes worldwide say that the Marines are the roughest on them. They even hit the girls. In Vietnam, they raped the heaviest. Filipina prostitutes says the Marines were the ones they feared the most—because they were the most violent customers. What will the presence of 3000 more mean to the women selling survival sex in Afghanistan?

Quite frankly, I am sick of living in a world where 'man must have his fuck.' The Phallic Brutal Rape Imperative of all history. I am alienated from an entire generation of men—the ones of the Vietnam era—because of man must have his fuck. I cannot talk to a Vietnam vet without wondering how many brothelized bodies he rape-fucked into death and insanity. It was one of the reasons I could not vote for Kerry. I do not know if he climbed on any whores in Vietnam and rape-fucked them. I hope he didn't—but how can I know if he was exempt from this most dreadful of sexual crimes? As a Winter Soldier, he spoke against rape per se but he said nothing about the prostitutes—those raped far more brutally and terribly than the 'decent' Vietnamese girls. If a 'decent' Vietnamese girl got raped, there might be a tiny whisper of sympathy. But, of course, the whore deserves what she gets. After all, she's just a whore. A piece of dead meat.

I talked to hundreds of Vietnam vets (from around the mid-60's to the mid-80's) and 100% of them gave me the impression that 99% of the guys over there climbed on top of dead rape-fucked whore meat. It was what guys did. It was just 'cheap gook pussy' and you could buy it for about the price of a pack of cigarettes and who was going to turn it down when it opened up its legs and had to fuck for food, or so it wouldn't get beaten by its pimp, and you didn't care because you might die anytime so just get in there and fuck that cheap gook slantslut. She was just a whore.

I am really tired of living in a world where a woman's precious body is cheap cuntmeat.

I am alienated completely from the generation of my fathers, the WWII generation, because they raped cheap cuntmeat, hungry dead rape-prostituted whore meat, in Rome and Paris and Naples and Toyko and Berlin. Wherever the GI's went, the pimps offered the hungry young girls up, on fuckslabs, for rape.

I can't talk to an Iraq vet without wondering if he indulged in the universal GI taste for cheap raped cuntmeat in Iraq.

I go on a lot about numbers but it is not really about millions of raped girls. It is about one. If even one soldier in Vietnam turned one helpless girl into cheap gook pussy, it was too many. One girl who is cheap gook pussy means all women everywhere are disgraced and humiliated.

I will end with a story. While I was waiting in line at Target, I glanced through some of those luxurious, oozing-with-pampered-sex women's magazines. The ones who think women have some liberation and freedom. Lots of emphasis on 'positions,' as if the Kama Sutra were some key to the beauty of sex. Not one mentions that this famous sex manuscript is based on girls bought and sold in a 'pleasure culture' that had nothing to do with their pleasure. They were all whores and concubines, forced into the trade around age ten (or even younger) and forced into all those painful, uncomfortable positions for getting mounted by the male. In another one of these women's magazines, I came across a Romantic Love Bill of Rights. It was obviously a bill of rights that applied only to the normal, protected women of the world. It demanded all sorts of tenderness and understanding and gentleness. It was ludicrous in light of the dead meat whore enslaved body upon whom no tenderness is showered. As I read it, I thought how would a twelve-year-old girl sold into a Bombay (London, Tel Aviv, Istanbul—you supply the city) brothel, and ripped apart all day by rough men ramming her insides, think of this 'romantic bill of rights'? What does she think when she tries to see through the bars of her window? Are London women taking their dogs for walks? Does she see people sitting in parks, sipping their Starbucks lattes? Are young couples holding hands, and looking happy and warm and misty, all in love.

Can there be a bill of rights for the whore? The few whores in the world who are not in debt bondage, not pimp-controlled, not forced by men they don't want, where are they? They must be a tiny percentage. And how can they work for Whore Liberation if most of the other whores have no right to even protest what is done to them? Most are in the position of the Burmese girls in the Thai sex-slave brothels, or the 400,000 controlled without mercy by owners in Germany, or the ones trafficked into Japan's massive brutal modern-day 'comfort woman' system. None of these girls can march or protest or hold up placards, the way the few 'free whores' can. And if they cannot, then the free ones, how ever few, are in danger of being treated the same way. Whore Liberation will only work if all whores are free. Not just a tiny handful in a world of unbearable sexual exploitation. Only if all whores can chose their customers, refuse to perform certain acts, keep all the money (no pimps or owners involved), be treated with great respect since they are selling such a beautiful and valuable part of themselves, have protection from disease and dishonor and stigmatization—only then can any whore be free and safe.

The bill of rights I outlined above is just for openers. I would definitely add a $1000 Pussy Clause. No vagina sold for anything less than $1000. This part of our body is so precious and important that it is sacrilege to sell it cheaply. No more UN Peacekeepers getting their fuck for a few cents on a refugee body. No more girls in Bangladesh or Bulgaria having to fuck for a dollar or two. No more 25-cent fucks on pieces of cardboard outside migrant labor camps. In fact no more open-air brothel rape camps anywhere.

I dream on while still despairing that anything can be done. Maybe euthanasia for all trafficked, rape-fucked bodies would be the best thing. The raped-whore, dead-fuck meat that prostitution turns a girl into can never be 'normal' again. I have no self-esteem. I got a Ph.D. and I'm writing a ton of articles and books, but that will give me no self worth. The only thing that keeps me going is my proud alienation from all the 'respectable' women in the world who scorn whores. The Riverbends. I reject not only their ranks but the whores who degrade other whores. I am completely alone, one whore voice. I will never be 'normal.' I cannot take a dog for a walk. Or have a garden and grow a flower. Or look at a sparrow with wonder at how small and humble and fragile she is. Or enjoy an English muffin with raspberry jam and a cup of tea. I am always looking through the bars of the twelve-year old's room in that London brothel. As long as she is behind them, I see the world through her eyes. No romantic bill of rights or whore bill of rights applies to her or to me. Until all brothel beds are empty, every woman in the world is enslaved.

A word about the terminology used in this article: I like the word 'whore' since its harshness expresses the centuries of abuse to our bodies. It is venomous when spat at us as a 'label' (like 'slut'). But, at its heart, is means a woman who is raped, exploited, scorned, treated like a cesspool, a toilet, a piece of dirt. By using it, I try to defuse the scorn. Since I once worked as a prostitute and would, by the standards of many, be called a whore, I prefer to appropriate the word, make it my own, to soften the scorn. The phrase 'sex worker' I cannot abide: rape is not work. You may call me a whore, but never call me a sex worker.

I also have to make up my own vocabulary– Recreational Rape, Brothel Rape, Prostitution Rape, Whore Rape—since there are no words to express this reality. Hidden acts never spoken about. I might amend this last statement. These acts are actually receiving some media attention.

The Raped Prostitutes of Iraq: No Voice, No Hope

March 2008

After five years of war, there is finally one story on CNN about the prostituting of Iraqi women. "On Deadly Ground: The Women of Iraq" aired this last weekend (March 15, 2008) and in one short—very short—segment, reporter Arwa Damon interviewed a prostituted being, a woman selling herself to feed her children. The story was shallow and woefully inadequate and made me wonder why, after years of reporting from Iraq, Ms. Damon has just now decided to pay attention to this—scant as that attention is. And why did she have to begin her report with that ragged untruth: prostitution is the oldest profession. An ugly idea bandied everywhere—with not an ounce of accuracy in it. (Procuring and pimping are the oldest professions.)

The prostitute interviewed said, "I cannot imagine anyone would do this except to survive." And she said that women did not have to do this before 2003, and the invasion of her country. Both great revelations? Things we do not already know? Perhaps we really don't know these things—although it would seem that we should. And it would seem that the almost complete indifference of the American public, and of American journalists, to the rape and ravaging of the bodies of Iraqi women and girls is just par-for-the-course ignorance. No matter that in all conflicts, women suffer sexual torture, particularly the torture of intercourse with men they do not know, for money, due to starvation and desperation and, often, the need to feed their children. This is seen as standard military practice, in any war, as is the American ignorance of the fact. And the journalistic ignorance. Where are Katie Couric and Lara Logan, two other experienced women journalists with extensive, first-hand knowledge of Iraq, when it comes time to uncover the brothels in the Green Zone and the Iraqi 14-year-olds currently living in rape hell in Dubai—having being sold into that country's lucrative and merciless sex trade to feed their families. All these celebrated American women journalists—vaginaless, heartless, ignorant—when it comes to the wretched mass raped bodies of the survival sex whores that we apparently consider so unimportant that there is only one mainstream story in five years!

At least the military ought not to have been ignorant of this fact—that war means forced sex and the wretchedness of raped-for-money bodies. Almost every military man at the Pentagon has seen prostituted bodies—used them, probably, since it is the rapist- warrior way—is aware that sexual torture in the form of prostitution is a massive 'by-product' of war. Sadly, these military men consider it a trivial by-product of war. The 50,000 Iraqi women and girl refugees currently engaged in survival prostitution are apparently not even on their agenda of concerns. (This number comes from the Women's Commission for Refugee Women and Children.)

As is typical with war coverage, the sexual torture of women's bodies is so unimportant that it is relegated to the absolute lowest rung—even by women journalists. (This fact is indicative, by the way, of the second-class status of all women, not just whores.) In "Women of Iraq," Ms. Damon covers Yanar, a privileged, wealthy Iraqi woman, in extensive detail. But her extremely limited story on prostitution in Iraq just sweeps all the whores under the rug. After mentioning that these whores might be killed by the police and the military if found out, she just drops the topic. Too far beneath her consideration to even merit further attention, apparently—even though whoring may mean death. You would think Ms. Damon would explore this further—by interviewing the killers of these women. How many whores have been murdered by the Iraqi military and the police? How many whores are there now in the Baghdad brothels that have sprung up since the invasion? Where do these women come from? Who are their customers? Iraqi men? GI's? Iraqi police? Iraqi soldiers? Politicians? Are the coalition forces taking advantage of the starvation-sex whores available to them? Are these 'tainted women' automatically subjected to honor killings? If so, how can men keep the brothels stocked? If intercourse is so shameful for a woman outside of marriage, does any of this shame devolve on the Iraqi men who are raping the women in the brothels? Does any of the shame transfer to the men who rape the whore Ms. Damon's interviewed? After all, this is survival sex for her? What is it for her client/rapists? Do they see it as taking advantage of a destitute woman? Shouldn't their own shame be enormous? How does prostitution work in this war, given the culture? Is the Islamic culture as hypocritical and brutal toward the whore as is Christian culture—or Buddhist or Hindu culture—all of which condemn her for the sale of her body, even under extremes of starvation, oppression, and desperation.

It would seem that the hypocrisy is even worse in Iraq—the Iraqi police, notorious by now for their own gang raping behavior, are going out and killing whores because other men are raping them? The convoluted perverseness of that male logic is way beyond me.

And, if the military are killing whores for being whores, then how can they not condemn their own behavior—as with all militaries, these men rape—and use prostituted bodies. Look at their record in Kuwait—massive rape during their invasion of that country—along with forcing girls into prostitution to service them. Not Iraqi women—Hussein forbade the turning of them into whores—so he trafficked in girls from Thailand and elsewhere to service his army. All soldiers rape. I would like to know how Iraqi soldiers can kill whores for being raped in order to survive and eat when they themselves rape? They even forced the poor Filipina and Thai domestics in Kuwait into prostitution. And yet they are some kind of blameless, entitled male gods who can kill starving women in Iraq for daring to engage in survival whoring? Amazing.

These are some of the points Ms. Damon might have explored.

The brutal sexual primitivism of our thought is well illustrated by the Iraqi whore Ms. Damon interviewed. Terrified she will be caught, veiled, interviewed anonymously, so shamed by this debasement, by this daily rape of her body. What kind of perverse, beyond-cruel sexual world have we humans created—where there is blame and possible death for a woman who must engage in that most wretched of acts—intercourse with men she does not know—out of starvation desperation? What kind of world when the Pentagon knew this would happen—as a 'byproduct of war'—their thinking on it—and did nothing to prevent it? We could have saved all 50,000 of those women who, according to their culture, are irreversibly ruined due to daily rape. When even one rape ruins a girl forever in this culture, there will be no recovery for her from thousands of rapes. Her closed-in, culturally deadened mind will never allow her to see herself as a worthy being. Should she ever be able to escape from survival sex, she will be that walking dead raped ghost that is the ex-whore. How can she be otherwise when every country on the planet condemns her for her whoredom?

All ex-whores, those in America, too–walk around as condemned, vilified raped beings. The women of the world condemn the whore even more than the men do. In Iraq, those who aren't whores condemn those who are. In America, the non-whore women have not even a remote clue as to the wretchedness of being raped daily by men you don't know. If they did, they would put a stop to it immediately. If they did, thousands of women from American—and also Europe, since their men are over there as well—all these women would fly to Iraq immediately and demand, irrevocably, that not one more Iraqi girl be forced to whore for food. And they would demand that the $100 billion in oil revenue pouring out of Iraq this year be used to help all whores and raped beings everywhere.

It will never happen, of course. Not one war has called forth this kind of sympathy and solidarity among women. I lived through the Vietnam era, and for the ten long agonizing rape-filled years of that war, I could not find one American woman who had the remotest interest in the whores that war created. As with all wars, the massive rape of the whore body is an unimportant fact, dismissed as not even worth protesting or reporting on. I can understand the thinking behind this: since she is not a virgin anymore, she is worth nothing, and since she is so degraded by the invasion of all those penises, she will never be worth anything ever again. Why report her story? She has no story. Just as she has no life or soul or sexual beauty left. She is just the raped ghost of a whore. How could she possibly matter? Even one story on CNN every five years is far too many.

A couple of days ago, a young woman in Egypt e-mailed me. She is doing her dissertation on Prostitution and the Military in Iraq. She says that I am one of the only people she can find who is writing on this topic. I wrote her back—about how hard it is to find information. Every soldier I ask sidesteps the issue with 'excuses'—'oh, yes, there is prostitution there, but I didn't really see much'—or, they snigger when I ask, as if it were all a dirty joke. (So what else is new?—the whore is always a dirty joke.) I told her that I had sent several e-mails to Iraq Veterans Against the War, but no response from them. They have admitted there is prostitution there, but will say nothing more. 'The Pact' reigns. Rape the whore body but say nothing about it back home. As if the women back home gave a gnat's-butt-of-a-damn about this rape so far away, in that dusty country. (The rape will come home with the men. Transnational Rape.)

I'd like to say to this young woman in Egypt: I am really tired. I have been writing on this subject for two years—with almost no help. I have been doing the job of all those hundreds of journalists in Iraq who refuse to cover this issue–as they have in all previous wars. It is a journalistic tradition, apparently—hide the starving, war-created whore from view.

I am doing the job of millions of American and European women who refuse to foreground the issue of starvation sex in wartime.

My words are like smoke on the wind, but I will try to say it once again—

Let this war in Iraq be the first one where survival sex and the wretchedness of the raped whore are covered extensively—every night on every news station—and every day in every media outlet and publication—until millions of American and European women rise up and go over there, and put a stop to it.

A word on terminology: As in all my other articles, I use the word 'whore' with utmost respect for all the prostituted women who are gang raped daily. I see the word as a badge of honor since, for me, it defines the most wretched and suffering of women—those who can survive under the harshest opprobrium any woman has to face—blame and scorn for the rape of her own body.

I proudly call myself a whore, rather than a prostitute–and I would never label myself with that abomination of a phrase, 'sex worker.' Rape is not work.

6

Ken Burns did his usual masculine-centric job on history in his PBS series called *The War*. Here is my response.

A Letter to Ken Burns about *The War: An Intimate History*

September 28, 2007

'The War,' Mr. Burns, is the Yokosuka rape queues in August 1945, with GI's lined up for blocks, two abreast, to get at the Japanese girls enslaved in 'comfort stations' for them—with the full cooperation of the American and Japanese authorities. Destitute, vulnerable girls were raped into unconsciousness as the men joked and laughed and jostled in line, waiting their turn. Some girls bled to death. Some committed suicide—that is, the lucky ones who could escape. Not one 'comfort girl' has told her story—due to shame. Why did you not tell this particular 'intimate history' of 'The War,' Mr. Burns? Especially since 'usage' of the girls was almost 100%. Why has the small detail that almost every GI in Japan, 1945, was a rapist escaped you? Why his this big 'dirty secret' of war never been covered?

'The War,' Mr. Burns, is the men who lined up to use the prostitutes on Hotel Street in Honolulu: women were raped 100 times a day—a different man entered the girl every three minutes. Why should I mourn these rapists when they were killed in the attack at Pearl Harbor? They slaughtered the bodies of these women in a fashion far more brutal than any bombing could ever be.

'The War,' Mr. Burns, is the widespread rape of French girls by GI's after they 'liberated' Paris. Rape by American soldiers was so common that Eisenhower actually had to acknowledge it was happening, although he did nothing to stop it.

'The War' is the public parks in Palermo, where pimps considerately laid out mattresses so the GI's could fuck starving Italian girls comfortably, for a dollar or two a fuck. As one man got off, the next took his turn.

'The War' is homeless, prostituted girls in Berlin doing it in the rubble for a few cents and agreeing to 'share' a GI bed so they would simply have a place to sleep that night. This, after they had already had the insides raped out of them by the invading Russian army and then were labeled 'whores' since it was a convenient way for the authorities to deal with these 'ruined' women.

'The War' is the village in Okinawa where GI's raped every woman, girl, and child—the victims were too sick and starving to even try to run from their attackers.

'The War,' Mr. Burns, is the starvation prostitution forced upon tens of thousands of European and Japanese girls (some barely into their teens) by the ridiculous conflicts men create to display their phallic brutality. It is also the brothel attached to a military base in Arizona stocked with 'worn-out whores' and reserved exclusively for black solders, so that the white GI's would not have to 'contaminate' their penises by raping the same prostitutes. Thousands of black GI's passed through this brothel daily, and who knows what insane, pathetic creatures they left dead of rape and misery.

'The War,' Mr. Burns, is not your blind, masculine-centric vision of it, full of all these lies about valor and sacrifice and courage and nobility. There is little that is noble about the raping, war-making brute we call a soldier.

I was raped and prostituted by the U.S. Military. Why don't you tell my story, Mr. Burns? It is far more 'colorful' than that of these soldiers who raped their way through Europe and Asia. Don't you want to know what it's like to be mounted by a line of soldiers? It is a hell beyond any possible imagining. It has happened to me.

My PTSD, as it is so fashionably called, is far more intense than that of the men who raped the life and dignity and beauty out of me. The emotional damage to the soldier does not compare to the suffering he inflicts on the women he ravages.

War is never good for women. War sexually enslaves women. Men gain by war. They have the pleasure of rape: they mount starving women, 'cheap whores,' and take their pleasure, and the woman is silenced forever by her shame.

What a male abomination is not just your grandiose seven-part, tidy version of 'The War,' but PBS as well. You pretend to be enlightened but you are as blind and callous and cruel as the soldier rapists who destroyed the lives and bodies of so many women.

I looked at your so-called 'companion volume' to the series. The index carries not one reference to rape, prostitution, military brothels, or the sexual suffering of millions of woman. How can you overlook, ignore, dismiss a 'fact' so enormous? As if these women simply never existed.

What a betrayal of our raped bodies is your grand, masculine-centric version of 'The War.' Even your title indicates that you own this territory, this war, your war. It is, indeed, your war—since all wars are the product of your male phallic cruelty.

War never 'liberates' women. War sexually destroys us. It has never been otherwise. Briseis had no say in her fate as a 'captive' woman. No one asked her what she thought of the arrangement. No one has asked the Filipina women trafficked onto the fifty U.S. bases in Iraq what they think of their lot as the GI's line up for their five-minute shot inside them.

Men make war because they love war. Don't ask me to feel sorry for the way they 'suffer.'

Quite a few readers responded to my Ken Burns letter. I was really happy to see it picked up by a number of women's rights websites and was delighted with one reader's idea that women 'sign on' to the letter, and then we could mail it to him with thousands of signatures. Maybe the most heartening comment came from a reader who said, "It would be surprising if she were not outraged by this 'fact' of war. I was also cheered by the reader who said:

"Women like Suki have never spoken up before. They're not supposed to." (I assume I am the result when a prostitute finds her voice. I may have no 'empowerment' but I do have words.)

I wrote this follow-up article, due to so much reader response.

Ken Burns' *The War:* Deeper Areas of Conflict

October 13, 2007

"The latest research by the underground women's rights organisation the Revolutionary Association of the Women of Afghanistan (RAWA) reveals that as many as 25,000 Afghan women worked as prostitutes in 2001 - 5,000 of those were in Kabul alone - with stark predictions that the number will rise as women and girls resort to selling themselves to escape poverty."

--*South China Morning Post,* April 9, 2006

In the October 3, 2007 *Cyrano's Journal/Thomas Paine's Corner*, I wrote a letter to Ken Burns, creator of the PBS series *The War*, criticizing him for omitting the many women forced into prostitution by WWII (and by all wars, for that matter). I'd like to respond, with some additional thoughts, to some of the readers who responded to me…

First, I'd like to thank Robert Farrell, Kenneth, B. Lenner, Bolo, and MeganM for their compassionate and intelligent responses and contributions. I'd also like to ask the ex-military man, Kenneth, more about what he has seen. He writes: "I have been throughout the world; the amount of prostitution that is in lock-step with the U.S. military is mind-boggling." Please let me know, Kenneth, if you know anything about the situation in Korea (which I mention in the article below) and if 'the pact' (also mentioned below) still holds.

One reader asks for verification that almost 100% of the GI's in Japan after WWII took advantage of the sex slaves in the comfort stations set up for them. This fact comes from John Dower's *Embracing Defeat.* Dower is an emeritus historian at MIT. Another verification is the 200,000 Amerasian children abandoned by GI's. Pearl Buck reports this number when she visited Japan in the decades after the war. 200,000. To rape that many children into these prostituted bodies indicates a high amount of usage. That is enough rape-thrust power to send a space shuttle to the outer planets. Since girls who slept with GI's were outcasts (despite the vulnerability and destitution that led to their sexual exploitation) and so were their children, lying down with the soldiers was hardly a voluntary act on their part. 'Rape' is what was done to their bodies—despite the girls being labeled prostitutes to justify the act as innocuous—rape produced those 200,000 unwanted children. Hence, my conclusion that almost every GI in Japan was a rapist. Which brings us to a really big question: Why have those vets who are still alive not been tried and punished for this crime?

As a sad side-note, Pearl Buck also visited Korea and she writes: "There I saw the same child as I did in Japan–outside the gates of our military bases. She was dirty and frightened. These are the children of our sons and brothers. We have to do something for them." She might have added—"of our husbands and boyfriends" as well.

Another verification is a newspaper account from the time in which U.S. army chaplains complain about the long lines of soldiers outside the brothels. The same account says that the GI's were trucked in by the busload.

According to this article, once inside the brothel, the GI picked his girl. Demand was so continuous that the girls had no time to eat or sleep. Some were raped 60 times a day. I would like to ask the vets still alive how they could do this? Did you not see it as rape? It is time you took responsibility for this big 'dirty secret' of war. I can't understand why Burns made no mention of the GI's as mass rapists. Puzzling.

As for the "almost 100%" speculation, I think I can bring a personal note to the issue. Using prostituted bodies is simply what military men, in any era, do: I talked to many, many American sailors during the 1970's and 1980's and they all told me the same thing–when the ship docks in a foreign port, almost all the men go off and get drunk and find a whore to screw. Very, very few hold back. It is apparently still the same now, as, for example, when the U.S. Fleet pulls into Thailand, a major 'sex-binge' spot.

When I was younger, I had a soldier boyfriend who was stationed in Korea in the 1950's. He said that he never met an American soldier or sailor who held back from using the brothelized whores. Not one man. As far as he could tell, it was the same in Japan and on Okinawa, and in Germany and France and Italy. Any place the soldiers were, they used those whores provided for them. He said that when Marilyn Monroe made her famous trip to Korea and did all her undulating and flirting in front of those thousands of men, the men got so hot they went out and practically screwed those little Korean whores to death.

I am aware, of course, that all militaries behave with savagery toward the whores their wars create for their use. . I am aware of what happened to the Korean Comfort Women and that the Japanese soldier, not just in Nanking, but all over Asia, was one of the most efficient raping machines in the history of war. If there is a Purple Heart for Rape, he would win it.

I am aware that other allied forces raped during WWII. Apparently, the Australians behaved with even more savagery than did the Americans in Japan. According to historian Yuki Tanaka, the girls cried all night as the Australians raped them all night. (Answer for me, men of the world, how a man can get turned on enough to get hard if the girl is terrified and crying? Was every Australian soldier in Japan turned on by this hard, terrible act of rape? Will the Australian vets still alive answer me?)

Moroccan allied soldiers raped widely all over Italy, sometimes subjecting entire villages to this terrible brutality. (The 1960's movie *Two Women* shows something of this, particularly in the gang rape of a mother and daughter by 30-40 Moroccans.) But I am an American woman and these GI's are my men. I want to see them behave with compassion and kindness.

Another reader asks if I sent the letter to Ken Burns. Yes, I sent it to PBS. But, from what I saw of his series, Burns is so indoctrinated with the lies of war that I think it unlikely he could see war from the prostitute's perspective. This is what I try to do. She has definitely been left out of the history of war. That such a huge piece of war history could have simply gone missing is tragic. The reasons for ignoring her are obvious: the news and all of history are recounted from the point of view of the conqueror rapist, not from the point of view of the body in the brothel. As the prostitute takes her daily rape quota, she is not articulate enough to say anything—she is too busy trying to survive. And too ashamed to speak due to social censure. No one ever asks her what she thinks of all this war making and how her body got caught up in the sexual crossfire. If journalists (those who could tell her story) visit brothels, it is to sexually relieve themselves, not to stand as recorders of the injustice done to the brothel's inmates.

Our staggeringly large number of war films always tell the tale from the point of view of the soldier. Just one example from the Vietnam era: we never know what the field whore in *Full Metal Jacket* thinks as the men take turns on her. Significantly, she is wearing sunglasses so we cannot see her eyes. We know her only from the crude jokes the men make about her. This famous, lauded movie is supposed to uncover the horror of war? But Kubrick certainly made no effort to unmask the 'true horror'—that what happened to her body was far worse than anything that these soldiers endured. I would have taken the camera into the room where they gang raped her, and removed the sunglasses, and showed the dead misery in her eyes.

In all war movies, the prostitute is a dirty joke, a throwaway being with no humanity or importance—the focus is always on the soldier and his temporary 'lapse' as he buys a prostituted body in order to release his sexual tension inside her. His need to relieve himself due to the tensions of war and her necessary presence as a toilet, sewer, semen-dump, is simply a staple of this genre.

Even *Casualties of War* follows this pattern. Supposedly, the men gang rape the village girl because their leave is cancelled and they can't get laid in the nearest town at the nearest brothel. No notice does the filmmaker take of the fact that the prisoner in the nearest brothel undergoes on a daily basis what the village girl is only subjected to once.

Journalists all see the soldier's story as primary; the raped whore is incidental to his existence—just a convenience. A female journalist for *U.S News and World Report* speculated that American soldiers in Iraq are behaving savagely and killing civilians because they do not have brothels where they can drink and let off steam. Actually, there is evidence that Iraqi women have been brothelized for them. And relieving himself inside an already thoroughly raped whore's body does not make a soldier less savage. If anything, the license he takes upon this enslaved women will make him more careless and savage toward non-whore women—including the 'clean' ones back home. And I really wonder where this woman journalist from U.S. News mislaid her vagina? Can her imagination not extend to how she would feel if she were a body in a brothel, a woman on her back invaded by thousands of drunken men she doesn't know?

Yet another reader says that a gentle approach is called for. I think the time for a gentle approach is long gone. In fact, it evaporated when the first male raped and prostituted the first female. Historians will have to date for me the advent of war, since my primary expertise is in literature–but I do know that the first war epic in the West, Homer's The Iliad (850 B.C.), is purportedly based on historical events that took place around 1500 B.C. and that Gilgamesh, the first literary work of the Western world, dates from 2000 B.C. and is based on a Sumerian civilization from around 2700 B.C. The Sumerians created the first military empire, and Gilgamesh makes reference to sending sons off to war and to raped daughters. Twenty-seven centuries of raped daughters. Twenty-seven centuries of prostituted, sexually-enslaved women.

Enough is enough already.

Historians say that the first slaves were female: captive women taken during war and used for sex. And that both slavery and prostitution originated from men making war. Historians say that the practice of trading sex for money or food arose from conquered women trying to placate the enemy and to find a way to survive. Nothing has changed since pre-Homer or pre-Gilgamesh. Despite the emergence of numerous women's rights groups and organizations like Human Rights Watch and Amnesty International and Refugees International and the Coalition Against Trafficking in Women, plus dozens of others that document the conditions of prostituted women, girls, and children both in the civilian world and in conflict areas and around the bases of occupying military forces—and despite extensive coverage of the depredations of UN Peacekeeping forces and NATO forces who freely exploit sexually vulnerable women, girls, and children everywhere they are stationed—nothing, absolutely nothing, nothing, nothing, nothing has changed. Far more women, girls, and children are prostituted now, at this moment, than have, collectively, been exploited in the history of our species.

How will 'gentleness' protect women from being prostituted? It is our very 'gentleness' and softness that makes us vulnerable. Men can rape us because they are stronger—and rougher. Do you think 'gentle' girls would be in brothels if they were not weaker than the pimps who put them there for profit and weaker than the men who force themselves into the girls for pleasure? What girl would chose intercourse with men she doesn't know? What girl would chose to let one group of men rape her all day so that another group can take the money that she brings in? What girl would chose to work under the conditions that many prostitutes face: forced anal sex, for one, since that 'decent' girl back home won't do it and some one has to satisfy the male urge for this. After all, his sexuality is paramount, is it not? What girl would want to be treated like a dirty joke and a semen-release dump—as if her sexual needs were simply non-existent? And I can testify from my own experience that most military men are drunk when they buy a body. This means they are usually rough as well—sometimes just through drunken carelessness. It is not a great deal of fun to be banged into by a man who is not just smelly with groin sweat but reeking with beer breath and doesn't much care if he hurts the girl or not. Not to mention the soreness, tearing, bleeding, damage to the bladder and many other physical problems that are simply part of being used by large numbers of men in one day, or one night. I don't think that non-prostituted women, like some of the ones who responded to my article, really know what prostitution entails for the woman. What for the man is fun and games is for her a great deal of pain.

No, I don't think that the brutality visited on our bodies for so many weary centuries of 'prostitution rape' can be solved by a campaign of gentleness.

Another reader criticizes me for being graphic about sexual suffering. I don't make any apologies since this tactic is long overdue and apparently effective for some readers: I receive many e-mails thanking me for finally breaking silence and describing the harsh truth. It is time for someone to tell how deep the physical pain is. (I wish someone had listened to the Korean Comfort Women when they graphically described the horror of being raped 50 times a day, but apparently no one did—so I have to tell my story—in hopes someone will listen. It is not nearly as graphic as theirs—since I was not raped 50 times a day [I would not be alive to write if I had been]–but it will have to do.)

Concerning women and prostitution in Iraq, it is definitely hard to ferret out what is happening since journalists do not write about this aspect of the war and soldiers observe 'the pact'—that tacit understanding that 'what happens here, stays here' in terms of sexual behavior. (Yes, the famous Las Vegas advertising slogan comes from the military and dates at least as far back as WWI and the silence about collective visits of our soldiers to French brothels. I have this information from an uncle who is a WWII vet who, in turn, knew WWI vets.)

Information comes in snippets here and there, most of it from numerous women's rights groups scattered across the internet. All of them report the presence of sex trafficking in Iraq and that girls have 'gone missing.' All of them report that, of the 2 million refugees in Iraq, and the 2 million in neighboring countries, some women are turning to prostitution to survive. A *New York Times* article mentioned "whorehouses in Basra," but did not go inside the brothels to examine the lives and fates of the inmates—not surprising since this newspaper, like all others, is written from the point of view of the soldier and the conqueror rapist. I would ask the British soldiers in Basra if they are frequenting these whorehouses? If so, what condition are the women and girls in? Can you—British soldiers–help them? I would ask you to please rescue them instead of using them.

A Dec. 2006 *Newsweek* article by journalist Christian Caryl reports that booze, whores, porn, and drugs are now rampant in Iraq due to the American occupation. Caryl says that there are now brothels in Baghdad where young Iraqi men can rent a woman for fifteen minutes. It only costs $1.50. Apparently, according to this article, before our invasion of Iraq, only gypsy women were enslaved for prostitution. Most significantly, he reports American MP's are making sure that the women are released if arrested. Why would the MP's do this? Is it to make sure that the women are available for our soldiers?

Sadly, this journalist sees the 'right' to buy a body as part of 'Iraqi freedom.' Now Iraqi men can exploit enslaved women just the way Western men do! Caryl is identical to Burns in this respect: they both see the story from the perspective of the rapist—as do all other Western journalists, film-makers, etc. Since the whores' stories are never told, are the women simply brothel rape fodder and are the 'rape rights' of the male "all important"? When the *NY Times* matter-of-factly mentions 'whorehouses in Basra,' as if they were a given and a norm—no effort to ask the whores what they think of their lives—that 'revered' paper is on the side of the conqueror rapist.

Are the Iraqi military and the Iraqi police force visiting these brothels, as do militaries and police forces in almost all other countries with trafficked/ sold women (a few instances: Cambodia, Thailand, India, Turkey—there are many others)?

I would be incredibly happy if no American soldier in Iraq were using a prostituted body. I would very happy to learn that no Filipina women have been trafficked in to provide sexual services. I would be even happier if our men were rescuing Iraqi girls from brothels, comforting them, and setting up recovery programs for them.

I would like to know more about the Iraqi women and girls who are currently in the Baghdad brothels. How did they get there? Are they surviving, in any way, being raped every fifteen minutes by a different man? What will happen to them if they can escape their rape prisons? Is not 'honor killing' the way Iraqi men deal with 'wayward' women? If a 'decent' girl is tainted if she is raped only once—apparently the hymen is all that makes a girl valuable in Iraqi culture—then how much more 'unacceptable' must be a girl who was forced to whore and was raped thousands of times? How much greater must be her 'dishonor'? So great as to be immeasurable in a culture that judge's a girl's value solely by her virginity?

Are there any programs in Iraq to help the prostitute? Has any of the massive amount of aid money going to Iraq been designated to help her? Has Condi Rice visited any of the Baghdad brothels—to help the girls? Rice too is a woman. You would think she would care about the rape of other women.

I am just asking. These are important questions. They have not been asked before. They have not been foregrounded, front row center, on the first page of the *New York Times.*

Perhaps this newspaper, and all the others in the world, and all the magazines like *Time* and *Newsweek* missed their chance at a pivotal moment in history. This was the early 1990's. This was when the Korean Comfort Women finally told their stories. I had high hopes that this would be the continental divide in women's history. I had high hopes that every newspaper and magazine in the whole world, in all languages, would devote pages and pages and pages to this story, perhaps even entire issues. I expected the world to be consumed by the true horror of war that had finally been uncovered. For the first time ever, we had testimonies, dozens of them, about what war really was.

Every girl told the same tale: a virgin when conscripted; her body broken though hours of rape; her spirit destroyed through months or even years of use by 30-50 soldiers a day. Her whole life and girlhood and womanhood taken from her. Then fifty years of tormented silence, until finally a few incredibly courageous survivors spoke–in the early 1990's.

But it is 2007 and nothing has changed. The systematic sexual enslavement of women is more prevalent than ever. 'Comfort women' are still a staple, a norm for all militaries. Another group of 'comfort women,' in fact, now occupies a sad niche in modern-day Korea. Around U.S. bases there, roughly 10,000 girls trafficked in from Eastern Europe, Russia, and the Philippines service our soldiers. I don't know how many Korean women are similarly enslaved.

These trafficked girls receive about two million visits a year from the men so 'usage' is 'typically' high. The few girls who do escape and are able to speak (after so much rape trauma) all tell the same story: what 'trafficking' involves is beating, starvation, ongoing gang rape, and other terror tactics to break the girls and keep them docile and performing. The few who escape report the humiliation of being forced to dance naked for the soldiers and how they are beaten if they cry when the men take them in the back rooms for sex.

Apparently the militaries of the world have learned nothing from the stories of the Korean Comfort Women. You would think that these horrifying testimonies would change the history of women forever—and change the attitudes of militaries of 'free nations' like ours—Americans, to whom slavery is now horrendous—you would think that the whole fabric of history would turn itself upside down and all soldiers of all 'free' nations would say—"yes, we now know, how the prostitute suffers. We won't rape her anymore."

But nothing has changed. In 2007, the traffic in 'comfort women' is thriving and drunken GI's are partying on their bodies.

I thought, when the Korean women told their stories, that all 'free' women in America would rise up in enlightened outrage and say, "no, no more, now that we know the truth about the comfort women of war, now that we know the pain of all those forced into prostitution, you will not prostitute one more woman for our military or for any military anywhere." But if I ask the average American woman, she doesn't even know who the Korean Comfort Women were, let alone the Occupations ones served up to her father, or grandfather, in Tokyo or Paris or Berlin–and she has no knowledge of the ones now servicing our soldiers around our bases all over the world. She knows a lot more about the love life of Jennifer Anniston and whether Lindsay Lohan is once more re-entering her posh rehab spa than she does about the rape-fate of millions of women around the globe.

Is this rape-fate happening in Iraq? Since this kind of activity is always covered up, how can we find out what is really happening? Will American women soldiers tell us? They themselves are being raped. Our women soldiers in Iraq report being afraid to go to the latrines at night because of the possibility of being sexually attacked.

I have some corroborating evidence that might tell us what is happening from a book called *Afghan Women*, just out, by Elaheh Rostami-Povey, herself a woman from that country. The sexual misery of women in that country might give us a glimpse into a similar situation in Iraq. At least half a dozen times in this book, Rostami-Povey mentions that Afghan women, both in Kabul, and all around the country, are begging in the streets and selling themselves for sex to survive.

She gives the impression that this is widespread and commonplace. That country has 50,000 occupying allied forces, 25,000 of whom are Americans soldiers. Are these 50,000 men buying sexual services from these destitute women? If not, it will be the first time in the history of war that military men have not bought women forced into starvation prostitution. In every war, young men, trained to be hard and hyper masculine—war elevates male brutality to an intense level—have needed some place to put their penises. That place is the body of the cheap whore created by that very war: the destitute, vulnerable girl with no choice but to 'lay or starve,' as one Vietnam vet I talked to put it.

Is this also the situation in Iraq—women forced into starvation prostitution? Why should it be any different from in Afghanistan—where we now have an eyewitness account from an Afghan woman, Rostami-Povey, as to the pathetic circumstances of these women. With 4 million Iraqi refugees, the situation automatically creates starvation prostitution. It is so all over the world. In Liberia, young girls, some mere children, will sleep with the Peacekeeping forces just to have a bed for the night, so desperate are they.

Is Iraq the big exception to all war-time and refugee inevitabilities—no prostituted women, even though they are plentiful in every other conflict area in the world? And if women are being prostituted, are the allied forces using them? They seem to be doing so every place else. Why would Iraq be the exception?

I have a solution. It is a simple one. It is based on the remark of another vet. He said: "Instead of making useless wars, like the ones in Iraq, we should set our soldiers to doing something helpful—like knocking down all the doors of all the brothels in the world. And taking those girls out of there!"

It is so simple. Instead of raping prostituted bodies—in Korea, in Iraq, in Afghanistan—let's have our men rescue these poor girls. Let them put all the money they would have spent buying the girls to a much better end: take them out of the brothels and set up sanctuaries and refuges and long-term care facilities (to heal their physical and psychological wounds) and schools for these trafficked/prostituted girls so as to give their minds a different world from the rape they have known.

Just think. What if....What if, in Tokyo, 1945, the U.S. Military had set up 'comfort stations' for all the destitute, sexually vulnerable girls in Japan. Places where, instead of being raped all day, the girls were fed and soothed and given warm blankets and peace.

My last response is to the woman in the military who served in a combat zone and says the only prostitutes she saw were female military contractors who set up shop to take advantage of a 'captive market.' These women, she says, were fired and sent home.

Now, it is interesting that this apparently voluntary form of prostitution is frowned upon. What would be wrong with a woman, in an entrepreneurial spirit, exchanging sex for money? I don't think I would object to this if it were, indeed, completely voluntary. She would have to have complete choice as to customers and she would have to be treated well, and with respect—because she is providing a valuable service. The monetary reward would have to be substantial—since she is selling an inestimably precious part of her body. And no worthless, sleaze, pimp middlemen, taking the profits. And, of course, complete freedom to refuse anal sex or other services distasteful or damaging to her.

I could continue to lay out a Prostitute Bill of Rights, but I think you get the general idea.

Is this sort of voluntary form of prostitution possible? Would not the 'entrepreneur prostitute' be preferable to the 'starvation/war-zone' prostitute? If so, why not let these entrepreneurs set up sex shop in Iraq, or other combat areas?

Is prostitution always sexual slavery, given that, historically, the institution has depended on the strong (male, in power) taking advantage of the weak (vulnerable, hungry female)? Does setting up a space we call 'brothel,' where a woman is subjected to sex with multiple men, for their pleasure—certainly not hers!–imply that she is sexually subservient to the male, the dominant one, and his needs? If poverty is involved, there can be no question of 'choice.' Can there be 'choice' if the entrepreneurial woman offers sex without coercion, or is she simply colluding in her own degradation by acquiescing to the idea that the male, by his gender birthright, is entitled to buy a body just for his sexual gratification. Is she still degrading herself (and all other women) if she markets her own body and is well treated by her customers and makes lots of money?

I'd certainly find this form of entrepreneurial prostitution more palatable than the pathetic starvation prostitution of war.

On a crueler, satiric note, prostitution would certainly be a way of turning the Iraqi economy around: conscript all those war-impoverished females to sexually service those 150,000 or so horny young American men over there. Look what we did for Thailand. A third of their economy now depends on the sale of young girls—an industry jumpstarted by the massive presence of our soldiers during the Vietnam era. Prostitution would, of course, exist there without our war, so long ago, but considering that the famous sex-and-pussy shows were first set up by ex-U.S. servicemen and that the huge numbers of prostitutes we created during that era were, after the war ended in 1975, channeled into sex tourism (can't let all those prostituted bodies go to waste!)—well, just consider the possibilities for Iraq and Afghanistan. Baghdad and Kabul—Whore Capitals of the Middle East, like their sister city Bangkok, Brothel Capital of the World. Japanese and German tourists and the militaries of the world would have a whole new whore-destination to visit.

To return to being serious, I hope that not one girl or woman in Iraq is being prostituted to our military. I hope that not one American soldier there is forcing sex on a desperate, starving girl. If this I so, it will be a first in the history of war.

That's the end of my second 'Ken Burns' response. Below is another PBS response that I e-mailed that station after, in April 2008, they broadcast a show called *Carrier*, about life aboard the *USS NIMITZ*, an aircraft carrier with a crew of about 6000 sailors. It showed life on the ship and on shore during a six-month deployment in 2005. The *Nimitz* stopped at various ports in the Pacific, Australia, and the Arabian Gulf. Women were involved in the production of the film, among them director Maro Chermayeff and co-producer Deborah Dickson.

Here is a letter I wrote to PBS about the show:

PBS' *Carrier*: Why Didn't They Film the Rape-Stops?

I was disappointed that *Carrier* did not cover a basic fact of military life: when sailors move from port to port, they visit bars and brothels and rape the bodies of sexually enslaved women and girls. In its homeport, San Diego, sailors from the *Nimitz* rape the prostituted bodies of girls in that city and in Tijuana. These girls are subject to the harshness of the sex industry which treats women like modern-day slaves; girls are held in debt bondage, pimp-controlled, trafficked. Tijuana is in fact a 'corridor' city: girls are 'broken' there before being shipped to U.S. markets. To make them submissive, the girls are subjected to gang rapes, beatings, starvation, being filming for porn to degrade them, along with psychological terror tactics. This is the norm of what happens to prostituted beings. These are the broken bodies sailors buy and use.

I notice that during this 2005 six-month deployment of the *Nimitz* which PBS filmed, the ship docked in Thailand. When our navy visits this country, they dock off of Pattaya, a prostitution city created for the military. About a third of the girls trafficked to meet the sailors' sexual needs are underage. Numerous eyewitnesses have told me that the first thing the U.S. sailors do, when they hop of the boats that ferry them in, is head straight for the sex-for-sale enslaved girls. Why didn't the film crew document the men going with prostituted, enslaved women and girls and girl children in Pattaya? (My sources are military men themselves who have told me about what the fleet does in Thailand.)

During this 2005 deployment, the *Nimitz* also stopped at Dubai, a major trafficking destination in that part of the world. Large numbers of girls from Russia, the Ukraine, and Moldova are trafficked into this 'sex playground' by the Russian mafia. The girls are broken at nearby Pakistani labor camps where the pimps let a different man in every 15 minutes to mount the enslaved body. This goes on for days or even weeks until her spirit is gone. Until she is docile enough to accept rape by 30 or more men on a daily basis. These broken women and girls are the ones our sailors are using. The men see only the end product—the girl who must smile to survive even though she is no longer alive as a human being.

Another stop, Bahrain, is also a major trafficking destination. It was amusing to see the PBS crew filming the sailors visiting an orphanage under the guidance of a chaplain. I assume this behavior was staged as a PR stunt for the benefit of the PBS crew.

All the other port stops—Hawaii, Hong Kong, Kuala Lumpur, Perth, India—also offer enslaved, prostituted bodies. When the men left the ship in Hong Kong, there was a girl handing out cards to them saying "Happy Place." The sailors snorted with laughter, obviously well–acquainted with these 'happy' places. Then the film crew followed the men on a shopping trip. Why no film crew accompanying them into the brothels?

One young sailor aboard the ship did mention how, on a previous trip, he and his crewmates has visited a bar/brothel in Rio where, "it was insane, the strippers were really going at it, on the bar tops."

Usage of prostituted/enslaved/trafficked bodies is commonplace in the military. Of course, the navy is not going to voluntarily show a film crew this aspect of sailors' behavior. I am disappointed that the woman who directed the show and the female co-producer continue to cover up this side of the military—that they did not film the sailors and their typical 'sexual liberty' activities in Pattaya and Dubai. Closer to home, I am disappointed these women did not film the sailors visiting the red-light areas in San Diego which are full of trafficked, enslaved Filipina girls. This director and producer have betrayed the raped bodies of all these women.

I would like to know what the women sailors aboard the ship think of this rape of their prostituted sisters—do they make the connection? High rates of sexual assault in the military are directly related to the time-honored rape of for-sale women by sailors. Train and allow men to rape one group of women, and they will rape others as well.

I read that the *Nimitz* is planning to dock in Hong Kong this month. Perhaps PBS could do some 'postscript' filming--follow the men into the brothels. As a woman who was raped and prostituted by the U.S. military, I would like my side of military history to be told. What is 'fun' for the sailors is life imprisonment in rape hell for us prostitutes. I wish women journalists and filmmakers would cover what happens to us.

Cordially, Suki, rape/prostitution survivor (except that I didn't survive)

Author's Note: I learn from a reader in Thailand that the Nimitz docked in Phuket. Since the PBS site simply listed 'Thailand' as its port of call, I did not know which city—I just assumed it was Pattaya since that is a frequent stop for navies.

Phuket is the place where, in the mid-1980's, a number of girls lost their lives in a brothel fire because they were chained to the beds and could not get out. Are girls still being held against their will in Phuket brothels? What girl, I wonder, would be in a brothel 'with her will,' given what brothel life entails...

I'd like to add an afterword to the above article--one that attempts to explore the sex scene in Thailand.

Some Thoughts on Prostitution in Thailand

June 14, 2009

It is very hard to determine the conditions that prostituted girls work under in Thailand since so much contradictory information comes out of the country. Of course, this is true of all countries since prostitution is so hidden and such a forbidden topic. Mention it in any serious fashion to the average person and they titter and look away and make dirty jokes. It is an inherently embarrassing topic. No wonder I have trouble talking about my own time in it. Why we women who are prostituted should be ashamed is the big puzzle? Does a fear and hatred of female sexuality lead to prostituted women—and to the scorn of them?

Leaving the above philosophical consideration aside, I have found information about the Thai sex industry on the internet from 'farangs' and Western women who call themselves 'sex workers'--and I find information in blogs from sex tourists who have been to Thailand or from men who have been there and not used the girls and I have had a few men e-mail me about the sex tourist scene in Thailand. And I have had a few accounts from eyewitnesses. And then of course I have read the academic studies of the sex industry in Thailand. What is largely missing is first-hand accounts from the Thai prostitutes themselves—unmediated by Western writers and observers--although these are starting to surface very, very slowly. One piece of information is that many of the girls come from rural areas and are not literate due to no chance to go to school. This would of course account for their inability to write down their own stories and why they have to rely on Western observers to do it.

The result of all my sources of information is quite a welter of contradictions. What I say about prostitution in Thailand in the rest of this piece is derived from all those contradictory sources. It is what I will have to rely on since I am not likely to go to Phuket or Pattaya or Bangkok or Chiang Mai myself. (These are some of the major sex- tourism destinations in Thailand.) I will admit cowardice. Too painful. The very few encounters I have had with other prostitute have been devastating. The sadness in their eyes is overwhelming. If prostitutes in the West receive no respect, it is hard for me to imagine that ones in Thailand do, given that sexual attitudes there are even more narrow than they are in Europe and the USA. To say prostitution is 'no big deal' for the Thai woman implies that she has no discrimination when it comes to her own vagina and her own sexuality? She will let anyone in? She does not mind being pawed by drunk sex tourists or drunk Marines? Does she belong to a different species of woman? Who wants to be pawed by drunk men and who is completely indifferent as to who enters her body?

I trust my own body. No drunken men pawing me, if I have control over what happens to me. No strangers inside me, disrespecting me and treating me like a dirty joke. Are the prostitutes of Thailand respected in their own society? Do 'normal' women make friends with them and help them go to college and take them home to dinner? For that matter, would prostituted women in Europe or the USA be treated as 'normal,' mainstream members of society? Are they treated that way anywhere?

What are the backgrounds of the girls who come to work in the bars in Phuket or Pattaya or Bangkok or Chiang Mai? Are they from poor rural areas? Were they subjected to any kind of sexual or physical abuse before they entered prostitution?

How many of the bar girls have college educations? High school educations? Are there other job opportunities for them that will pay as much as the bars and sex with farangs?

How many girls voluntarily do the pussy-and-sex shows that are so famous in Thailand? It is funny that they are considered such a part of Thai 'culture' that tourist buses include them on their routes. I have this information from a Caucasian female who took such a tour in Bangkok. Her conclusion about the whole Thai sex scene was rather callous: "Well, I guess those Asian girls will do anything for money." She was surprised when I told her that stuffing things in your pussy on stage was not a hallowed part of Thai culture. She was astounded to learn that Western/Military demand for sex shows has brought all this about.

I wonder what all the other Caucasian women tourists in Thailand think. They must see the sex scene in sex-tourist destinations like Phuket and Pattaya. Does it trouble them in any way? If they see the bar girls being pawed and mistreated by drunk men, does it bother them in any way? Do they think it is okay for girls to be disposable sex objects? Do they just assume that the smiling bar girls like what they do? (You have to smile all the time when you sell yourself and that outer smile is often quite disassociated—quite a distance--from what is happening inside you.) And, of course, some may like what they are doing—if they are not mistreated. But it is hard to separate prostitution from violence and danger and disrespect, even under the best of circumstances.

Attitudes toward prostituted women seem to lead to violence toward them: men do not ordinarily consider prostituted women in the same category as 'normal,' 'real' girls—so they feel as if they can treat them with contempt and roughness. Judged by patriarchal standards as used and dirty, it is no wonder prostituted girls often find that men are violent and callous toward them. Lack of protection under legal systems also leads to violence toward the girls. Where can the girls go for protection if the police and courts are part of the problem? In some places, corrupt police take kickbacks from brothel owners and traffickers and the police themselves use the girls--and will return them to the brothels if the girls 'escape' and go to the police stations for help. (This has happened to trafficked Slavic girls in Korea and Turkey and India—probably many other places as well, but these are places I have read accounts of.) It is 'no-win' for the prostituted girl—violence and disrespect from all sides—customers, police, courts—and from the 'normal' women of the world who despise her for being filth. 'Normal' women are protected from the roughness and ugliness of men by certain rules, at least in Western society, that impose politeness and courtesy on the men. The prostituted girl is defined as not only 'unprotected' but also not worthy of protection—since she is so dirty—since all those men have used her. The men who use the girls and make them 'dirty' (by patriarchal definition) are of course deemed noble knights of purity and pillars of the community and--in the case of military men—rescuing heroes and defenders of democracy, etc. Any old sex slave or dirty bar girl anywhere will do to satisfy the noble soldier's manly needs—till he gets back to the clean, pure girl-next-door. Given all these contradictions and cruel inequalities, it is no wonder that prostitutes have incredibly low self-esteem.

Even a Ph.D. has not been able to lift my self-esteem to the eye-level of an ant. Ph.D. Post-Harlot Depression. In graduate school, I was shy, frightened, and introverted—and no wonder. I kept thinking, 'What if they knew I was a whore—would they throw me out? Would all those "decent" girls refuse to sit by me in class and would the boys make dirty jokes and just consider me fit for nothing but rape?' I still feel this way. Many years later. Ph.D. Post-Harlot Depression. It never ends. Sigh.

Do those Thai bar girls and other prostitutes all over the world feel the same lack of self-esteem due to being defined as dirty by society?

To return to the main train of thought, how many girls are in brothels in Thailand, as opposed to ones who work in bars? Are the girls in the brothels trafficked, underage, subjected to slave-like working conditions—as seems to be suggested by Human Rights Watch in its *Modern Day Slavery* report. If so, are the bar girls also in danger of being forced into this kind of prostitution? A show on PBS, *The New Heroes*, presented by Robert Redford, featured a segment on Sompop, a Thai man who tries to help prostituted girls. The show revealed that a third of the prostitutes in Thailand are underage and half of those girls have AIDS. I do not know how accurate this is. Contradictory information surfaces on the internet: like the claim that the Thai government has gotten rid of all brothels that contain underage girls and trafficked ones. I doubt this piece of knowledge: for one, large numbers of Thai men frequent brothels—one estimate is that at least 80% of Thai men use prostituted girls and that the average Thai male goes with around 30 prostitutes before he marries a 'pure' girl. If this is the case, an enormous number of prostituted girls would be needed to service these local men. You could not find enough girls who would be willing to undergo this kind of sex—brothel work in Thailand is very harsh with girls sometimes servicing large numbers of men a night. One big reason for trafficking (in Thailand and all over the world) is the unwillingness of girls to withstand this kind of sex. And, of course, what girl would want to work under conditions where she has to fuck all day while someone else takes most of the money? No 'free sex worker'—if there is such a thing—would agree to this—ever, under any circumstances, if she had 'choice.' So, it is really hard to see brothel work as freely 'chosen' in any way.

Another internet claim is that the government has eliminated all police complicity. No corruption in this area. No allowing of brothels to operate by the police for kickbacks and no use of girls by the police. If the brothels are all gone, where is the Thai military getting serviced? They have in the past been large patronizers of the brothels? And spreaders of AIDS to the girls.

If people who live in Thailand could let me know if all the brothels have been closed by the government and no girls are being exploited or trafficked, I would appreciate knowing.

Bar girls average about 15 different customers a month. That is of course better than 15 a night, which might happen in the brothels, but that is still a lot of different men who could hurt the girl. A lot of physical and psychological damage can arise from so many men using one girl. I would have no objection to prostitution in Thailand or anyplace else if you can prove to me that it does no damage to the girls to go with so many different men. And if the girls are never subjected to violence or mistreatment.

Violation and degradation can never be part of the job description for it to be 'voluntary.' Neither can poverty or coercion by family. If a girl is expected to sacrifice her body to support a family, it is not her choice. A man who had been to Chiang Mai told me that he talked to a bar girl who said that her father forced her to work the bars. He beat her to make her do it. At first, she hated it but now she preferred it to working in the fields and to being at home, getting beaten. Her hands, he said, were very rough from work.

What kind of choice is that?

How many times do the bar girls have to go with men they find unpalatable? Even one unpalatable male inside your body can mess you up for life. I know this from my own time in prostitution. Do the bar girls feel good about themselves after having men inside them they do not want there? Are some of the bar girls forced to do this from financial desperation, not just due to lack of other palatable jobs. Are the girls faced with choices between factory/sweatshop labor and prostitution? If so, it is certainly logical and understandable that they choose prostitution. I would. The torture of factory/sweatshop labour would be as bad as prostitution. Are the bar girls subjected to social scorn? Are their customers ever violent or rude? Can the girls fit into mainstream society after being whores? Are the girls coerced by their families to do this? How difficult is it for them to become hardened so they can deal with drunk, crude farangs in bars? For that matter, does a woman ever get used to crude drunk men? We women are essentially soft. I like polite men. A man should behave like a gentleman at all times. I feel happy inside when someone opens a door for me. Are any of my sensibilities shared by Thai girls? Or are they really that 'different' species that farangs and soldiers and chaplains have told us about: girls born to be whores since it is part of their culture. Girls born to love crude rough drunk men. After all, it's 'part of their culture.'

I think all of the above needs to be considered in terms of how 'voluntary' bar-girl work is. I remember talking to a non-whore girl from Thailand in a local Thai restaurant. She said that the girls who become bar girls just to 'party' are considered trash. Those who do it to support their big, demanding families are not considered total trash—just partial trash. These were not her exact words, but this was the gist of what she said. Now, I ask you—what kind of attitude is that? If the girl enjoys herself, she is trash because she is having fun? All female sexuality negated by the needs of the male and the ugly censure from 'good' Thai girls who do not whore.

The more I hear attitudes like this, the more resentful I become that a patriarchal world has completely robbed me of my own sexuality. This is why I made the whores in my novels the way they are: even the most liberated of my whore characters are pathetic in that they must function under a patriarchal system that has destroyed all female sexuality. Women are simply handmaidens and byproducts of male needs. There is no way we can envision a pure female sexuality. There is no place for it to exist on this planet. My novels are by no means paeans to prostitution.

Prostitution would seem to be so entrenched that we cannot eradicate it in its present form. *Glamour* carried an article called "When Prostitution Is Not Sexual Slavery." The title is revealing since it implies that most of the time it is.

Setting all my idealism aside, I realize that for the 'free' whores in Thailand—the bar girls—this 'profession' if far more lucrative than any other. I would never think of interfering with their 'right' to make money in this way. I am on the side of Empower. Improve their conditions. Make sure they are safe. I think all the bar girls should control the bars. No bar fines. And they should have a network of men who 'guard' them from violence and harm. No pimps, just protectors. If brothels still exist, they should be completely 'co-op.' Run by the whores. And no girl under age 25 in prostitution anywhere in Thailand. A template for 'free' prostitution worldwide, perhaps.

I don't think you can have a 'safe' form of prostitution anywhere if situations happen where girls are chained in brothels and a fire breaks out and the girls die since they cannot get away. This happened in Phuket in the mid 1980's. Are girls still being held against their will in Phuket brothels? What is the background of the girls in the brothels? Were the girls placed there by someone else? Does a girl ever voluntarily enter a brothel—would she if she knew that the working conditions mean sex with men she does not know and debt bondage and control by an owner—typical of brothels worldwide. Are the Thai brothels an exception? The trafficking of underage girls takes place all over Thailand. Are young girls trafficked into Phuket? It is a sex-tourist destination, and this attracts traffickers.

What is the truth behind prostitution in Thailand? Is it now completely free and safe for all the girls in it? Are there no underage girls in it? Are there no 'adult' women in it who were coerced into it when they were minors? Were the Thai girls in prostitution subjected to many of the situations that prostituted girls around the world face even before they enter the 'trade': rape, incest, poverty, deprivation, financial desperation—there are many factors that typically accompany the entry into prostitution. Of course, not every girl who is raped enters prostitution—but large numbers of those in this profession do seem to have been subjected to previous sexual abuse. If Thai girls with college educations and no background of abuse or coercion enter the profession by choice, for fun and money, I would be all for it. But any circumstances that might force the girl in that direction makes the choice no choice. If there is any coercion—and any disrespect and violence toward the prostitute, then this profession is not voluntary and it is a form of sexual slavery. Only in a non-patriarchal, non-condemnatory world can we have 'voluntary' prostitution—in Thailand or elsewhere.

If the majority of girls in Thai prostitution are from poor rural areas—as I have heard they are—and the girls are making money for themselves and gaining independence and able to fund an education for themselves and set up businesses for themselves—all without any mistreatment or violence or disrespect from customers, then I would be all for this. It is a sad fact that in many poor countries prostitution is the only lucrative 'profession' available to girls with little opportunity or education. If this is so, then let us make prostitution as safe and palatable for them as possible.

Another of my great ideas it to put bars and brothels, worldwide, right beside universities and churches (those two great patriarchal institutions) so that nothing is hidden about the 'profession.' No brothels way out in the middle of the desert. Instead, recruitment tables in the universities and churches—for girls who want to work as whores. Lay out the working conditions. Take away violence and humiliation. Add pensions and health insurance.

Let's face it. Any buying of bodies anywhere in the world—by sex-tourists, military men on leave, local men—contributes to the global sex trade. That trade is often exploitative and many times is even a 'sex-slave' trade. Even under the most benevolent of conditions, there is a degradation involved in buying the female body. Under the best possible scenario for Thai girls, they would work and do well at selling sex and keep their own money—until they reach an age when they are no longer marketable. Then they will either set up their own businesses, or go to college, or in some way make a different life—with the help of the money they have made selling sex. Is this the way it works in Thailand for these girls? If so, there might be an aspect of financial empowerment for these girls. How many Thai prostitutes actually follow a scenario similar to this one and end up with a secure future after prostitution?

The real world intervenes. Or a fantasy version of it. To keep up with the cruder aspects of life, in order to know they are there, and avoid them, I will sometimes watch a show on a channel alien to me—like Spike TV. Three in the morning. Insomnia. I accidentally come across a martial arts-type movie from Thailand. It is full of gangs and blood and fancy violence and all these whores standing around smiling in tight dresses, for decoration. On the arms of the men who are violent and nasty and dreadful. As if this were their natural place—decorative, standing beside men who will be violent toward them next. The movie presents an ugly brutal sick world. One where there is no softness, or protection for softness. Just painted toy whores cheering on violence—not realizing, apparently, that the violence visited on them is a continuation of that which they are lauding. Movies like this make me think we are an insane, sick, dark, brutal species. Spike TV styles itself 'for men.' Most of the fare bears a resemblance to the above movie. If this is what men are—brutal, ugly, crude, violent--we are in trouble. It scares me to watch this channel.

(In fact, it scares me to even think of a place called 'brothel'—what a sick, dark, perverse concept this is: a place where women have sex with men they do not know. Even the word itself sounds brutally ugly: 'brothel.')

Is there any accuracy in this martial-arts movie? It also came equipped with vicious farangs, to match the vicious Thai men. Ugly slimy brutes with mean eyes and hard fists and no mercy. All muscle and no brain. And what appeared to be a really worn-out blonde whore—a Slavic girl? Do Thai bar girls have to deal with men like this? Do the Slavic girls trafficked into Thailand?

Even a small amount of crudeness killed my softness. I cannot even watch bar scenes with drunk men or drunk soldiers. Even the scene right at the end of *Jarhead*—with the really crude Marine and his prostitute (apparently no girl will go with a man this hard and slimy by choice—he has to pay some unfortunate creature) depresses and disturbs me. What if I were these poor girls? Could I ever become hard enough to survive such a harsh world?

I switch the TV channel and find that fluff movie *Irma la Douce*, the *Pretty Woman* of its time. Sugar-coated prostitution complete with a cute alcoholic poodle.

7

Now, a bunch of miscellaneous articles, all centered around prostitution, some dealing with war, some not.

War and Civilians: A Few Swiftian Modest Proposals and Random Musings at Year's End

December 29, 2006

Atrocities are the norm during wartime. So are civilian casualties. In the twentieth century, women and children comprised 80% of all wartime deaths. Yet when U.S. Marines allegedly kill a handful of unarmed civilians as, for example, in the Haditha incident in Iraq, it makes the cover of Time magazine. It is a peculiar human mindset: note the death of a few and blank out the millions.

Can making war and moral behavior co-exist? Probably not. Train men to kill, and behave savagely, and they will. I always wonder why we act surprised and outraged when civilian casualties, like those at Haditha, happen? I would ask: Why punish these Marines for what we have trained them to do? If *Jarhead* is any indication of the savagery military training inculcates, then it's evident our soldiers are not going to behave like well-behaved tea-party participants when faced with an elusive enemy, in Iraq, trying to kill them. It is also evident that the stresses of war will cause savagery in men.

Instead of pretending morals in wartime are possible, let us simply celebrate how brutal the male can be. This celebration would be a window into a reality we rarely acknowledge, a reality that is the true picture of war. Not the fake one inherent in pretending men at war can behave morally. Not the hypocritical one inherent in showcasing a few dead civilians in Haditha, yet ignoring the inevitable savagery of men at war. Why have we singled out this one incident, Haditha? Are we looking at a phenomenon similar to My Lai, that 'one' atrocity in Vietnam? In retrospect, we now know that My Lai was only one of many such incidents.

We make Marines so we can worship tough, muscled commandos, warrior gods. We don't create this species of the male for his morals. Besides, I sympathize with these men if they act a little crazy and wipe out a few hamlets or housefuls of civilians. I mean, it's not as if they're in Iraq for some noble reason, like to defend freedom or promote human rights. Frustration must run high in men engaged in an utterly useless, futile war. It happened in Vietnam, too—that even greater exercise in atrocity, stupidity, and misinformation. Guys got crazy. Killed and pillaged and ravaged. Compared to ones in Vietnam, the Marines in Iraq are behaving with the height of civility.

Some of their leisure-time activities in that other Age of Insanity included throwing beer bottles at the heads of Amerasian beggar kids trying to eat out of their garbage cans. They would bet on who could kill a kid. It was good target practice, and it served another purpose—rid the landscape of the 'evidence' that the men had been fraternizing with the bodies of the indigenous females. Read *Spoils of War* for a rousing account of this 'killing-two-gooks-with-one-beer-bottle' recreational activity.

"Core warrior values" figured heavily in that other war, too. The upholding of high ethical standards. *Spoils of War* tells of a Marine in Vietnam who fell in love with a prostitute and wanted to marry her. His buddies soon set him straight. They all raped her, to show him she was garbage. Men at war. There is strong evidence that this is their core value of behavior, not the fake, glossed-over one we see on CNN every night.

"Ethical standards"—a military given? *Spoils of War* says the soldiers force fed explosives to village dogs so they could watch them blow up, from the inside out.

I hope the Marines in Iraq aren't hurting any dogs. We know they are raping, but we don't know how much since only one incident has come to light, that of the 14-year old girl allegedly gang raped and then killed in March 2006. We don't know if our soldiers have raped women prisoners since the journalists don't mention this sort of thing. Neither, apprarently, do Iraqi women, since to be raped in their culture is beyond shame. When it happens, the women are very reluctant to report this insupportable indignity. (Even in my country, the USA, girls are reluctant to report rape attacks since the American court system spends most of its energy trying to discredit the victim.)

On the other hand, I suspect Iraq is a low-rape war since the women are so hard to get at. The women are kept sequestered, and swaddled heavily in clothes—they look like they're wrapped in yards of big sheets. Not easy to strip, and get at, for rape purposes. Vietnam was a lot easier. All those flimsy little pajama outfits—guys could just rip them off with one gesture, and mount. And the girls were so tiny, didn't even need to break a sweat while holding them down. The Iraqi women look pretty big, closer to Caucasian size.

Why pretend rape is some exception during wartime? The alleged rape-murder of the 14-year-old Iraqi girl (whose name was Abeer) by American soldiers spawned a *New York Times* article (August 7, 2006) about atrocities against civilians in Vietnam that went unpunished. It said that newly released archives report fifteen substantiated cases of sexual assault by American soldiers during the Vietnam War. Fifteen? Fifteen?! Fifteen???!!! During ten years of American occupation???? It might seem like some kind of beyond ridiculous understatement, but that number appears ludicrously low—beyond ludicrously low. Vets I spoke to during and after the war said that rape was a daily occurrence. The paltry 'official' ones recorded are nothing beside the real numbers. "By the hundreds, everyday, maybe by the thousands" was the consensus of men who had been there (and either participated in, or witnessed, the attacks).

That girls were raped in Vietnam seems too obvious for comment. I wonder why the military is now kindly informing us of this 'fact'? Since they are 'embarrassed' by the alleged rape of Abir, why are they even bothering to rake up Vietnam? According to the article, Retired Brig. Gen. John H. Johns (a Vietnam vet himself) was in favor of keeping the Vietnam records secret, but now thinks they should be disclosed because "we can't change current practices unless we acknowledge the past." So, this 'official' soldier cared nothing for the ravaging of the girls while it was going on. Since he was on the spot, he must have seen the savagery. Back then, he did nothing about it. Now that the military has been caught with its alleged pants down in Iraq, he is being forced to actually admit that this was not the only rape ever committed by our soldiers? And, if he is so concerned with changing soldierly behavior, why didn't he pull the men off the Vietnamese girls 40 years ago?

My answer would be that soldiers aren't really supposed to care about these sorts of things. Women raped, damaged, prostituted, pregnant with GI babies, 100,000 or more Amerasian children left fatherless after Vietnam—all of this sort of activity is simply trivial compared to the true world of the warrior; and he is the center of our media war attention, not the many helpless women and children he destroys, physically and psychologically. Our whole media circus is a huge, cloudy, hypocritical lie, as it spouts ideas about ethical standards and moral values. Like some big squid curtain of black ink.

An interesting sidenote: after the big Pentagonal release of the Vietnam archives, they took them back. Covered them up again. Un-released them, so the public can no longer have access to their big truth: that all of fifteen times, during the 10-year sexual carnage atrocity we call Vietnam, women were raped. Apparently that number would seem so startlingly high, given the moral values and unbreakable ethical standards of our military men, that the American public, and all the American journalists, would faint dead away at the mere thought: fifteen girls assaulted by American soldiers. Never. It just couldn't happen! Not with their 'core warrior ethical moral standard values,' or whatever lying bunch of words these journalists and military spokesmen string together to blanket the raw reality of rape.

There have also been reports, not well publicized, that our men are raping our women soldiers in Iraq. If the military wanted to face the sexual frustration problem over there, I supposed they could traffic in a bunch of those blonde Eastern European girls. These girls are being trafficked by the truckload to every place else in the world—why not to Iraq? They'll arrive already broken in, completely seasoned from beatings, starvation, torture and terror. Ready to install in a tent. Place for the guys to release all their wartime frustration. Is she not every American boy's dream—a docile blonde, completely passive, completely available.

There is precedent for trafficking in sex disposal-sites (called prostitutes) for our boys: one long-time theory is that men at war will rape 'good' girls unless 'bad' girls are made available to them. In Iraq, are there any 'bad' girls being made available? I wonder if Iraqi girls--hungry, needing to engage in wartime sex for food, like millions have done before them in all the others war men have made—I wonder can these Iraqi girls become prostitutes? Would their men kill them before letting them indulge in this "shame" (society's italics, not mine)? In Asia, the body-for-sale has kept many a war-torn girl and her family, many a destitute mother and her children, from starving. It is perhaps a shame that Iraqi girls cannot sell themselves as freely as Asian ones have done to our soldiers—hunger is terrifying and these poor Iraqi girls cannot even assuage it by bartering their bodies. How much soldiers suffer is a prevalent theme of warfare. Personally, I don't really feel too sorry for these guys since I think that men like to make war. Gives them a chance to play with their phallic toys. All those rifles, knives, bayonets, submarines, torpedoes, missiles, bombs, whatever—every single one of them crafted in the shape of that weapon a man carries between his legs.

Rape, one of the essentials of wartime. It may be a 'core warrior value' but what it lacks is 'sporting' values. What's the challenge of overpowering some unarmed civilian women, match-thin from malnourishment? I think the soldiers would have more fun raping each other. A fully-loaded fellow soldier—now that's an opponent worthy of a rapist. Add some danger to the endeavor. Could get those nuts and berries and twigs blown off if you wave them threateningly in the wind, at one of your buddies.

I have a solution to end the civilian casualties: Isolate all the male combatants, maybe off in the middle of the Gobi desert, and let them have fun out there playing with their phallic toys and slaughtering each other. This would leave all the non-combatants, the women and children, out of the line of fire. (Except that I'd worry about the animals in the Gobi—all the lovely snakes and furry little desert rodents.) Except for the GI Jane's. But any woman who wants to fight has to sign a disclaimer that she won't whine if she's raped. Part of the job description for female soldiers—Standard Issue Military Rape, expect it. I have no patience with those wimp women soldiers (actually sailors, to be accurate) at Tailhook. All upset at having to run a little gauntlet or two. All flustered over a tidbit of 'sexual harassment.' Tailhook took place at a Las Vegas hotel. Sex was on the menu. Strippers and prostitutes were being treated crudely and roughed up all over the place. Did the female soldiers expect the men to all of sudden shift gears, treat them with tea-party politeness, while they were hooting at bare boobs, and screwing bought bodies?

I also have a solution for stopping wartime rape. Film it as it is happening, and show it every night on CNN, wherever the conflict area: Iraq, the Congo, Darfur. Wartime rape is the Cinderella stepchild of all these battlegrounds--ignored, hidden, glossed over. Let us show the world the raw misery on the girl's contorted face, as she is violated. It will, maybe, touch the somnolent indifference of all the complacent viewers who assume war is great and noble and that nothing terrible ever happens to women in war zones.

Of course, this sets up some ethical problems for the journalists—do you help the screaming girl or do you just record her agony? I don't have an answer for this one.

In the case of the American soldiers mentioned above, if they did hurt and kill the young Iraqi girl, what if a journalist had filmed the entire episode, everything from her violation, to her murder? This might stir up a ruffle of outrage and maybe even some questioning—are other American soldiers also raping over there?

How would I know?—no journalist ever tells me about this particular 'deed of misconduct.' (Note the overly polite phrasing, as if the men were involved in a bit of illicit fun over a beer.) We Americans can't know if rape has happened only once in Iraq, or zero times, or many thousands upon thousands of times, as it did in Vietnam.

I urge journalists covering all conflicts—Iraq, Darfur, the Congo, Israel's ongoing battles—to regularly film rape and to blazon the woman's agony across the CNN screen, night after night after night. Give wartime the rape the coverage it has never received, and badly needs, to wake up the world to its existence.

(I always used to wonder, when Christiane Amanpour was covering Bosnia, why she didn't talk about the rape camps and Muslim women being stripped and staked to the ground. Serbs climbed on while other Serbs watched, and some of this was videotaped. At least we have this one record of rape agony. We need more. Why was Ms. Amanpour not highlighting this ravaging of other women?)

The only problem I see arising is that the nighttime CNN rape films might be mistaken for a new form of pornography. You'd have to be careful to label it—'actual gang rape and murder of a woman by (American, Serbian, Congolese, whatever) soldiers' rather than 'snuff film gang rape and murder of a woman,' etc.

It's worth a try, this filming of the ravaging while it happens. I don't see anyone else making any helpful suggestions about the tradition of wartime rape.

Note: Since I wrote this YouTube has carried footage of a Marine in Iraq throwing a puppy off a cliff while he and his buddy laugh about it, and of American soldiers there shooting a dog in the rear and then laughing and joking as she pitifully tries to crawl off.

A different version of the below appeared in *Off Our Backs* magazine, 2006, under the title "Where the Whores Aren't."

Prostitution and AIDS

November 4, 2006

AIDS coverage in the media pays little or no attention to the prostituted women, girls, and children who suffer greatly from this disease's impact. *Frontline's* two-part series, "The Age of AIDS" (May 2006), is a good example. The show's point of view is relentlessly male, even though one of the co-producers and writers is a woman, Renata Simone. The show praises "the condom king" of Thailand for slowing the spread of AIDS, but fails to note that the policy of putting 100 condoms by every brothel bed continues to enslave women, girls, and children in that country's multi-billion-dollar sex industry. (The selling of young bodies generates 25% of that country's income, according to the PBS series, *The New Heroes.*) *Frontline* also fails to note that the Thai military are heavy consumers of trafficked girls and that the soldiers' high AIDS rate spurred the campaign, not any concern for the prostitutes themselves. Frontline totally overlooked the fact that handing out condoms will not relieve these victims of the misery of prostitution and the ongoing rape of their bodies, not just by their own military, but by local men, by sex tourists, and by militaries from around the world who continue a precedent set by U.S. servicemen during Vietnam with their sex junkets to Bangkok. (Our boys are still banging away with every shore leave: roughly 1/3 of the girls who serve them are under age 15, and half of them have AIDS--Stats from PBS's *New Heroes.*)

Although *Frontline* is often to be commended for its thoroughness, its gender attitude is usually as patriarchal and narrow as that of the mainstream media: the world only exists from the male point of view. Its women writers and producers are no different from men.

The episode gives us a few glimpses of Patpong bargirls, all looking about twelve years old, pathetically thin, scantily clad and painted up like sextoys. But why no interview with one of these girls? Why no mention that these are, sadly, the 'lucky ones' in the Thai sex trade—free to move around, with some choice of customers. Why didn't the camera crew go into the brothels, where, hidden from view, are the trafficked, the ones sold by their parents who went through harsh training—beatings, rape--to make them compliant. As if the twenty or thirty men they must service a night are not rape enough. Some of these girls are never allowed outside. Why didn't Ms. Simone even bother to interview a brothelized Thai prostitute? Well, I have seen them and their eyes are full of desperate sadness. No condom will protect them from the serial rape that is their lives.

Simone does not mention the Rwandan mass rape in the mid-1990's which led to roughly a quarter of a million women now finding themselves HIV-positive. As co-writer/producer, why would she leave out such an enormous event?

Maybe because she and her cohorts chose to endlessly interview older gay males from the San Francisco bathhouse culture that initially spread the disease among that community, I suppose in reparation for so heavily stigmatizing them before AIDS became 'acceptable,' a fashionable cause, via Elizabeth Taylor and Rock Hudson. (As an ex-prostitute, I can tell you that gay males don't even rate on the stigmatization meter when it comes to the opprobrium, scorn, disgust, hatred that is heaped upon us. We are regarded as 'filth,' disposable bodies.)

And why didn't the *Frontline* crew interview the prostitute in the Bombay brothel who said she was forced to be there? Why didn't they take her out of that sex hellhole? As privileged Westerners, they have enough money to do so. They could have bought her out of her debt bondage. I wonder, would Renata Simone want to be left in that brothel, forced to service dozens of brutal men every night? (As an ex-prostitute, and I know that customers are not careful with our bodies.) Wouldn't she beg for someone to help her? If she were in a Bombay brothel bed, she wouldn't be making any more documentaries. She would be too rape traumatized to do much beyond barely survive.

In the filthy sweatshop stew of this brothel, there was a child beside one of the prostituted women. She, too, will likely end up in the 'trade.' When her mother is too sick to work, she will be forced to sell her. It's called 'intergenerational prostitution.' (You see it in Thailand as well—grandchildren of girls forced to serve our military during the Vietnam era are now themselves prostituted.) I wonder why the camera crew did not take the child out of there?

The episode also left out trafficking, and the connection with AIDS. Trafficked girls--broken through beatings, burning, starvation, and collective rape--are often forced to have unprotected anal sex (a prime recipe for contracting AIDS) with customers because they have no choice and because 'independent' prostitutes won't. Trafficked girls cannot negotiate condom use because they are slaves.

Also ignored was child prostitution and the inevitable connection with AIDS. Part of the explosion in this trade worldwide is the result of the mistaken idea that a child will not have AIDS because she is 'fresh.' Mistaken because girl children have more fragile vaginal membranes than do adult women. And they are smaller—for these two reasons they tear more easily and become infected more easily. Also, the myth that having sex with a child virgin will cure AIDS has increased the procuring of girl child bodies. All this female misery and not one whisper about it from Frontline and its woman co-writer/producer.

Outside of South Africa's goldmine barracks, prostitutes ply their sad trade on pieces of cardboard in the surrounding woods. Many are women with children, and no husbands, forced into this degradation. Frontline's camera followed a few shy ones into their 'retreat,' carrying their pieces of cardboard. Such sadness and hope in those shy faces, knowing they were being filmed. But no effort to help them on the part of these privileged Westerners with their cameras. Or to talk to them. Apparently, these women are not 'high' enough on the scale of AIDS sufferers to merit a voice. (There is something despicably 'unethical' about the 'ethics of objectivity' in filming the suffering of others—and not helping.)

Frontline, instead, asks us to feel sorry for the miner, the man who buys the prostituted body, and then spreads the AIDS. Frontline shows us a specimen of this rapist, with his 'important' AIDS case, filming him as if he were some victim. Victim of what? His own raping lust?

It is a terrible truth, and almost completely unacknowledged by AIDS media coverage: Men spread AIDS through rape and the use of prostituted bodies. Consider: If there were never any women or girls or children forced into prostitution due to hunger, poverty, parental coercion, grasping procurers and greedy pimps, not to mention the biggest 'force,' customer demand for flesh, there would be no AIDS explosion. In Africa and India and Southeast Asia, men spread the disease among the sexually enslaved, since transmission usually goes from male to female. Then other men use these infected bodies and carry AIDS out into the general population--taking it home to their wives and girlfriends.

Interestingly, the pattern seems to be the same as it was with syphilis: destitute camp followers infected by soldiers during all those endless wars raging across Europe in the Middle Ages; diseased soldiers taking the 'pox' home to their wives. Even the male rhetoric was the same: the whore is blamed for her filthy ways; the man is the victim, like those poor South African goldminers away from their homes, lonely, having to buy a whore body to keep them company. Poor guys. And, of course, it's all those dirty little Thai girls, more-than-willing to sell their bodies for Yankee dollars, who are the real 'demons' in the AIDS scourge—not the tourists and sailors and soldiers who purchase them. Never mind that the young Thai prostitute is sold by her parents, seasoned by her procurers and pimps, raped every day by her customers, and sees little of the money herself. She is still the archetypal brown submissive femme fatale, the little willing 'brown sex machine,' as the US Marines call her. (The men substitute a less-polite word for the 'sex' part.)

Even the origins of syphilis and AIDS are similar: transmission from animal to human. There is strong evidence that AIDS was passed from chimps to humans. Some accounts of syphilis I've read say it was likely that human males acquired it from sex with animals. The role of the military is the same: Sailors spread syphilis worldwide by using women forced into prostitution in foreign ports. It may have entered Japan , for example, as the result of infected European sailors using girls sold into the sex trade. (These girls didn't leap into the chance to have sex with thousands of rough, large, terrifying foreign sailors on their own—unlike all those mythical accounts of the willing, subservient Asian female.)

Soldiers and sailors taking AIDS from infected prostitutes back to their families has a scary sound when you consider the way American servicemen frequent prostitutes all over the world. And there is strong evidence that US servicemen carried AIDS from infected prostitutes in the port city of Mombasa to the women forced to sexually serve them in the Philippines (and perhaps into Thailand and other Asian countries where they use prostituted bodies). How much have they brought home with them?

No notice taken by *Frontline* of any of this military connection. And nothing about the role of UN Peacekeepers raping sexually enslaved prostitutes and spreading the disease. The presence of 100,000 of these men in Cambodia in the early 1990's caused a massive explosion in the sex trade, and in AIDS. Wherever they go, these 'Peace Keepers' are 'Violence-Bringers' to the bodies of women: they have money, pimps cultivate them, young girls serve them.

So, how do we solve this problem? It's simple, really. We eliminate, completely, customer demand? No men anywhere ever buy prostituted bodies ever again? As if that would ever happen. And, it's too late, boys. You've already given the women of the world AIDS.

A *Newsweek* issue (May 15, 2006) devoted to AIDS is not quite as remorselessly sexist as the above *Frontline* show. It at least carries some small sympathy for the prostitute in an article about African ones refused medical treatment for gonorrhea, syphilis, herpes, and AIDS, due to their being considered such 'filth.'

Melinda Gates actually mentions 'sex workers' in this *Newsweek* issue, acknowledges they are part of the AIDS picture, although it is in the context of focusing on the 'decent' women of Africa, the ones she apparently thinks are worth saving from AIDS.

During the recent AIDS conference in Toronto, Melinda Gates pointed out that "the ABC approach— which stands for Abstinence, Be faithful and use Condoms — does not always work.

"'Abstinence is often not an option for poor women and girls who have no choice but to marry at an early age,' she said.

"'Being faithful will not protect a woman whose partner is not faithful. And using condoms is not a decision that a woman can make by herself; it depends on a man.'

"Melinda Gates said condoms do not encourage promiscuity, and she said people have to get over their embarrassment about helping sex workers, who are key to fighting the pandemic." (Quoted material from Reuters News Service, 2006, and *ABC News* Internet Ventures, 2006.)

For all that she and her husband, Bill, are trying to help in the war on AIDS, note that Melinda Gates promotes the very attitudes that have allowed heterosexual men to widely infect hetero women. "Promiscuity" is based on that most pernicious of sexual notions, the virgin/whore split: some of us on the side of damaged goods, the sluts, the others all sweet and pure with that strip of pink tissue intact. (Damaged by whom? Men make 'sluts' by screwing women, and then blaming them for being screwed?) And she uses that equally damaging phrase, 'sex worker.' I shudder every time I hear it. I shuddered when I saw a Western woman reporter for Frontline applying it to a tiny painted-harlot four-year-old in a Bombay brothel. How what that little girl does could be considered 'work,' by any stretch of the word, is beyond me. Is a pension plan in the 'works' for her, that trusty 401K, and maybe she's lined up a plush job as a Starbuck's barista after she gets done with her fun 'sex work' stint. (When I write, I use 'prostituted woman, girl, or child,' as most accurately reflecting the sale of bodies; I use 'whore,' unabashedly, in an attempt to defuse the male-derived negativity it carries---scorn, hatred of us, etc.)

In her tour of Africa, Gates focused on the 'normal,' non-whore women as being important. Did she even visit a brothel? Did she talk to the open-air rape-camp whores on their strips of cardboard?

Why does Gates see the 'sex workers' as key to fighting the pandemic, when it is the millions of men who rape them who are the true key, blind as we may be to this?

Even though she mentions the helplessness of the adolescent girl forced into marriage, why does she not mention the far worse enslavement and rape of the prostituted one?

Blindness. As if whore bodies, needs, lives, are invisible, totally marginal to the concerns of 'respectable' women.

Another practice, 'dry sex,' also receives no coverage anywhere. Turning the vagina into parchment with hot peppers, so the male will have a tight fit, is widely practiced in Africa. And, of course, the more the vagina bleeds, the more likely the male is likely to inflict his STD's on the woman. Both wives and whores practice 'dry sex' because of the demands of the male.

I cannot even imagine one act of dry intercourse forced into me, let alone the thousands the whores must endure. Dry intercourse would be unbearable. Just the tearing would make me cry. When I whored, I used lube—lots of it. Even at my lowly rung of existence, no customer dared tell me to dry out my vagina for his pleasure. He took his pleasure in a lubed tunnel, or not at all. Those poor African whores really make me see how fortunate I was to have mildly enlightened, only semi-barbaric American male soldiers for customers. What kind of man could take pleasure inside a vagina that is torn and bleeding from being dried out? He must see the pain in the girl's face.

America and Europe advertise lubes of all sorts—luscious fruit-flavored ones and silky sensuous warming ones and ones for both male and female that, when they join, are supposed to ignite galactic sweeps of golden passion across our bodies. How come the African whore with the vagina dried out by peppers is suffering so intolerably in the service of male 'pleasure'? I think an advertisement for a fancy lube must seem a cruel joke to her. But then I never understand the contradictory ways of the world. Why one girl is a pampered princess gently made love to, lube in her protected tunnel, and another whore is dying in agony as her dry vagina gets ripped apart.

In the eyes of the world, it would seem, the 'normal/decent' women, the good wives and good mothers, those upholding family values, have merit, and we abject whore outcasts are lesser beings. Are the whores of Africa receiving any AIDS drugs, I would ask? *Frontline* only spotlighted 'decent' non-whore women taking the drugs.

In my eyes, I find the whore has far more value than the decent woman since she has suffered the lowest degradation men can inflict on her, and somehow survived. But where is her monument? All our magazines (*Cosmo, Time, Essence*, etc.) carry stories about the 25 Strongest Women, all those business corporate types, all those 'successful' tough, independent sorts, as if they were the heroines of our civilization. No, the 15-year-old whore, still alive despite the torture of her vagina, and the death of her spirit, she is the only heroine I recognize. But I stand little chance of anyone listening to my own whore voice. Even worse, I may be labeled a 'sex worker,' consigned to the same tier of 'labour' as the little painted four-year-old harlot. Her AIDS body will not make a ripple in anyone's mind.

A Message to George Clooney: When 'Peacekeeping' Equals Rape

November 13, 2006

The actor wants to send UN Peacekeepers to Darfur, or so Clooney said in a recent speech in front of the UN Security Council. Be careful. Wherever they go, these 'Peace-Keepers' are 'Violence-Bringers' to the bodies of women. The head of the peacekeeping forces in Bosnia requested that a girl from the Serbian rape camps be delivered to him for his pleasure. On the streets of Zagreb, peacekeeping forces were asking women how much they charged for sex.

The litany of this sex horror goes on. Refugees International reports that in Liberia peacekeepers patronize a club called Little Lagos, where they have sex with girls as young as twelve and also take porn photos of them. The poor children do all this for a few bucks, or food. Sex with the vulnerable and the exploited is routine for these men all over Africa, and the world. An article in the UK Independent recounts how UN Peacekeepers in the Congo offered food to women and girls in exchange for sex. It was a pathetic picture. Already raped by warring factions, refugee women with children to support would visit the men at night for food. So would young refugee girls—gratefully, some of them, because they were so hungry. One girl reports the soldiers being kind to her and not hurting her, the way the other soldiers did. I guess that gentle 'prostitution rape' is preferable to wartime gang rape, but 'kindness' cannot exonerate peacekeepers from taking advantage of damaged, financially desperate women. (I have always held that in wartime, soldiers should simply give starving girls food, instead of making them lay down on their backs for it. Would it be possible to train soldiers to think this way? The old saw—"it could be your mother or sister exchanging sex for food"—doesn't seem to be working.)

Refugees International details a number of Danish peacekeepers having sex with a 13-year-old Eritrean girl, an Irish soldier making a porn movie of an Eritrean woman, and several Irish men using girls as young as 15 in that country.

Their report on Cambodia is especially disturbing. A UN Peacekeeping force of 100,000 invaded Cambodia in the early 1990's, causing the sex trade to skyrocket. Brothels, massage parlours, the sale of girls from rural areas into these torture 'palaces of pleasure,' a massive increase in child prostitution, and AIDS—this rosy picture accompanied the advent of these misnamed 'peacekeepers'—they need to be called what they are--UN Rapists, or, if you want a fancier title, UN Emissaries for Rape. Maybe we need a UN High Commission on How to More Effectively Rape the Women of the World.

In Cambodia, the peacekeepers were reported as being "drunk and disorderly." As an ex-prostitute, this conjures up awful pictures in my mind of how rough drunk men can be during sex, and of those pathetic, tiny, underage Cambodian girls having to withstand this brutality. The response of Yasushi Akashi, the Special Representative to the Secretary-General at the UN, to all this 'fuss' about sex and 'fun' in Cambodia was "boys will be boys." I guess he has a fancy title and a high salary, and I guess it does not occur to him that his own wife, daughter, sister, could be in brothel bed, under a 'peacekeeper.' (Peacekeeper Rape. A catchy oxymoron, no?) I guess the doctrine of the "band-of-brothers gang bang" still rules. I am reminded of how, during WWII, US, British, and Australian troops raped side by side, particularly in the Pacific. That glorious bonding ritual of everyone climbing on the same body as a symbol of International Sanctioned Rape by Warriors has now taken a new form in that so many more nationalities--Danish, French, German, Irish, Moroccan, etc.—can band and bond, be "boys," get their entitled act of sex upon the destitute, under the auspices of the UN. Was ever rape so sanctioned as now, when we label its perpetrators 'peacekeepers.' But then 'violence' upon women's bodies has never held any sway or court in international affairs. Why not just set up a UN Commission for Sanctioned Rape and be done with it?

Kosovo. The 'fun' continues in this hot sex spot "littered with brothels," in the words of Human Right Watch. "Littered" as a result of the presence of 40,000 of those gallant rapists (both UN and NATO forces, as well as civilian military contractors from the U.S.) who have transformed the place into their own special whorehouse. Trafficking and its attendant horrors—the drugging, "breaking in" (read rape), and imprisonment of girls as young as eleven, girls "forced to service international soldiers and police" (in the words of one UN/NATO whore who escaped)—has increased enormously due to high demand. Eighty percent of the customers of these trafficked girls are these multinational forces. One trafficked girl reported begging US military men to help her escape from her brothel, but they used her anyway. Some soldiers are themselves involved in the trafficking and selling of the girls. US Military police are in the pay of brothel owners, and they take 'freebies' off the already heavily raped bodies of the girls. (Source for Kosovo material: Amnesty International.)

(I remember seeing a sugar-coated *National Geographic* picture of a German peacekeeper in Kosovo—presented in the text as all noble and courageous--looking at a picture of his girlfriend, misty, romantic, longing to be home with her. If his behavior was typical of that of his cohorts, I wonder if he raped any of the enslaved girls in the local brothels set up for him after this picture gazing? If this particular soldier abstained, many others did not. Why didn't *National Geographic* present this typical side of the behavior of these occupying forces?)

The response of the UN? Well, troops are immune from prosecution in Kosovo and nothing has been done to even reprimand them in their home countries. (Not that a "reprimand" will mean much to the raped bodies of their victims. What amounts to a few minutes of sexual pleasure, for the soldier, on top of a prostitute, means a life sentence of misery for her.)

According to Refugees International, in 2001, the UN "effectively halted an investigation into allegations that UN peacekeepers in Bosnia were recruiting and enslaving women in brothels." Jacques Klein, the UN Secretary-General's special envoy to Bosnia, says that focusing on the customers of the brothel-enslaved is "inappropriate." (I wonder if he would use such cold, stiff words as 'inappropriate' if it were his body being raped all day in a brothel? Or that of his wife, daughter, sister?) Instead, he says, we need to concentrate on the procurers, corrupt officials, etc. Well, of course, there is some truth in that. But this attitude is a cover up, and a continuation of the "boys will be boys" caveat. After all, if the man takes out his rapestick in a brothel, well, he is a rapist. And needs to be labeled as such, tried as such, castrated as such, etc. Otherwise, "boys will be boys" and "man must have his sex fix" will reign and flourish, as they do now. No matter what the misery of the body he 'occupies,' as an occupying military force, somehow, this rule has been sacred to the soldier—"man must have his quickie, his lay." Well, as a rape survivor and ex-prostitute, I'm sick of "man must have his sex fix," no matter what the pain to my body.

An *A & E Investigates'* show on trafficking followed a very old Tel Aviv street whore into an alley littered with garbage and piles of used condoms. "This is where the man comes to have his orgasm," she said succinctly. I saw ectoplasmic ghosts hovering in that alley—the dead bodies of all the women upon whom man "took his sex fix."

No more.

George Clooney, I'm sure your intentions are humanitarian. And if you want to go to Darfur and stop the UN Peacekeepers from their usual rape rituals, and the AIDS and misery they bring, fine. But don't recommend sending in these sorry, rapist excuses for human beings on their own, free to buy exploited brown bodies, free to force them to exchange sex for food. Please go over and supervise them. Better yet, visit their haunts all over the world and take the suffering girls (brown and white) out of the brothel beds these men have created. You have enough money to set up a Whore Sanctuary for these raped, miserable, suffering girls. And realize, also, Mr. Clooney, that Sudanese women are 'genitally mutilated.' What sexual misery your projected force of 20,000 UN Sanctioned Peacekeeping Rapists will inflict on these already terribly damaged women is unimaginable. These poor mutilated women can barely withstand 'normal' intercourse, with their shredded vaginas and ragged, chopped- off sex organs, let along prostitution rape by a bunch of drunk 'peacekeepers.'

Afternotes: I did not even touch on the thousands upon thousands of children fathered and abandoned by these multinational forces. I have yet to see one word in the media about this issue.

I shuddered when I heard a proposed force of 15,000 peacekeepers, mostly from the EU, was destined for Lebanon. The EU forces have money, pimps cultivate them, young girls serve them. Will Lebanese women have any protection from them?

Currently, in 2008, American soldiers are still stationed in Kosovo. How are they treating the brothelized trafficked girls? Are they buying them, or trying to help them? The total number of all multi-national forces still stationed there is 20,000. Is the whore situation still the same—with trafficked girls in brothels for their use? If there are any soldiers there now who can tell me, please e-mail me.

A word on terminology: As an ex-prostitute, I use the word 'whore' freely, to refer to myself and others forced to sell sex, in an effort to defuse the heavy, negative, male-generated burden of 'shame' and 'filth' the word carries. I would never use the word 'sex worker' since prostitution is not work in any meaningful sense. Probably the most offensive application of it I've seen was by a female Western journalist who applied it to a four-year-old girl, in heavy harlot make-up, in a Bombay brothel. Was the women simply being 'fashionable' with her terminology, or did she actually think that this child was engaged in work? Was a cushy 401K in the tiny whore's future, and maybe a job as a barista at Starbuck's, after she finishes up her 'fun' stint as a 'sex worker' in Bombay?

Caring About Sexual Slavery

November 18, 2006

Last year this time I wrote a letter to *Glamour* magazine about its "Women of the Year" issue, commending the editors for including a raped woman on the list, and suggesting that next year they include a 'typical' prostitute. If you take all the for-sale females in the world, and extract a typical profile, it would probably look like this: she is 15-years-old; she was sold by her parents around age twelve; she now has AIDS; she is held in debt-bondage; she is controlled by a pimp.

Glamour came through in its current (Dec.2006) issue, at least part way. Somaly Mam is profiled A former sex slave in Cambodia who was sold by her parents, Somaly now runs a center to help girls and children escape from sexual slavery. According to the *Glamour* story, during her time in the brothels, Somaly saw other girls caged and beaten. When she saw her best friend killed by a pimp, she was inspired to escape and help others. Somaly tries to give the girls she rescues, many of whom have AIDS, a lot of love. She says she tries to "help them heal, physically and emotionally" (255). One big difficulty she faces, in all her compassion, is that brothel owners threaten her life daily.

I want to pair this up with another recent article, by *New York Times* columnist Bob Herbert, in which he asks why outrageous acts aren't receiving the outrage they deserve. Herbert concentrates on the massive violence toward women, sexual and otherwise, that is simply a part of everyday life all over the planet: bride-burning, trafficking, ritualized gang rape, women beaten as a matter of course in societies where this is still the norm for controlling them, etc.

I wrote this response to him:

"Mr. Herbert, look on your own doorstep for the reason why outrageous acts stir little outrage. Lack of media coverage. You yourself write for a paper that devotes little space to these issues. A few brothel columns every once in a while by Kristof and a few lines by you and an occasional comment on a rape in Darfur—and that's about it. Not even any mention that the women of that country are genitally mutilated, so rape is even more devastating to them: apparently the male perspective of the *NY Times* does not consider the abomination called FGM worthy of note.

"Kristof is admirable in that he at least pays compassionate attention to the trafficking/sexual slavery issue, but I wonder why he is the only one of your columnists actually engaged in an ongoing attempt to educate the world about the miseries of brothel life, given the scope of the problem. (Some think that the sex trade now exceeds the drug trade in profits for mafias in Asia and Eastern Europe and for transnational gangs worldwide.)

"I am a professional writer and I have submitted numerous Op-Ed's on many aspects of sexual violence/trafficking/prostitution to the *NY Times*. Not one printed. Your Op-Ed section should have a sign on it—'For Men Only'—since I never can find female voices raised in alarm, or anger or passion, in that space."

That said, to Mr. Herbert, I am grateful to him for at least devoting a column to the violence (sexual and otherwise) against women that is a pandemic, not just an epidemic, across the globe. (Many of my other articles detail this problem, and its many facets, so I don't need to pause to give examples here.)

Glamour could have gone still farther and made one of the trafficked, one of the still sexually enslaved, a part of its pantheon of influential women. I see this trafficked/raped/enslaved being as even more admirable than activists, or concerned women politicians, or businesswomen with power because she is surviving, without power. She is enduring the deepest humiliation and pain that can be inflicted on our bodies as women: ongoing serial rape, day after day. And she is surviving.

With not much help from the rest of us. That is my point in pairing up these two pieces from very different sources, *Glamour* and the *NY Times*. Where's the rest of us? Why aren't women's voices all over the world raised, in outrage, with passion, with deep anger, over this abomination called prostitution (sexual slavery, trafficking, they are all the same). And men's, too (those of them who aren't customers of the enslaved).

I'd like to see a Million-Woman March on Washington (and London, and Paris, and Bangkok, and Las Vegas, one of the major sex-for-sale centers in the US). No, a Ten-Million Woman March. (And let's add Manila and New York and Berlin and Amsterdam, and all other trafficking destinations. And let's invite caring men to join us.)

Glamour's biggest "Woman of the Year" was Sandra Bullock. She received a lot more space than little Somaly Mam. That's understandable. Bullock's a big celebrity and little Somaly is barely known. And how many *Glamour* readers actually want a long article detailing the miseries of the sex trade for children and girls sold into it in depressing, poor countries like Cambodia. They'd rather read about Bullock telling little girls they can do anything if they try. (The problem is, if you're in a brothel bed, you really can't. Being raped all day makes it tough to become an actress, or a writer, or even a barista at Starbuck's. There is not much left, physically or psychologically, to try with. And mostly, even if you escape, you're going to be battling severe PTSD and AIDS for the rest of your life. Not much recipe for inspirational maxims and success stories here. Sadly, for every Somaly Mam who escapes, there are thousands who will die in their brothel beds.)

Glamour, after all, is a sanctuary. We women know we won't be raped in its pages. It gives us privileged few of the world a place where our sexuality is celebrated and reveled in, not degraded through rape, sexual slavery, prostitution. Where would we go for sexual sanctuary if this magazine detailed the harsh sexual reality outside of its safe boundaries? It is too difficult—to really know what happened to Somaly's child body in that brothel.

I think that the Fabled Pages of Angel Space called the Victoria's Secret Catalogue performs the same function—sexual sanctuary in a hard world. There girls can revel in being outrageously provocative, without punishment. No one is going to rape these thonged girls, with their shining, taut, naked expanses of tummy (and bellybutton), for flaunting cleavage, and rounded buttocks.

It is a beautiful fantasy, and one we women all need—sexual freedom without fear of punishment for taking the license of our own sensuality. No "she deserved it because she dressed so shamelessly" in this sacred, innocent catalogue space.

But I think there is a way that the glamourous world of the safe, pampered woman can interact with the wretched space of the sexually enslaved one. Activists like Bullock, and Charlize Theron and Susan Sarandon and Angelina Jolie, could all get together, in one big powerful group, and go into brothels enslaving women, girls, and children (whether in Cambodia, or India, or in Europe or the US) and publicize the wretchedness of their inmates. And, of course, physically, take those girls out of there. (I wonder why Jolie has not done this yet in Cambodia since she has adopted that place as her second home. I also wonder why she did not adopt a girl child there, to keep her out of sexual slavery, when she adopted her son.)

These celebrity women have the power to do all this because they are so high profile. I would also like to see every high-profile woman politician (Hilary Clinton and Condi Rice, for example) do the same. On their political trips abroad, they could greatly serve the cause of suffering women, girls, and children if they visited red-light districts and our major media (like CNN, the *NY Times*) gave full coverage to this. Show the conditions under which the women work. And then take them out of there, set up sanctuaries for them....

This is not a radical idea. It simply makes humane commonsense to me. I wonder that women in power in the world (actresses, political leaders) have not thought of it before.

Even we ordinary, low-profile women could do so much—if we all united, with the celebrities and politicians. Just imagine, all of us, marching by the millions on Washington and Paris and London and Bangkok. Marching, and taking all those girls out of sexual slavery. And marching and marching and marching--until all the brothel beds are empty.

Sex Trafficking at the World Cup

June 29, 2006

Fans party as raped girls suffer. A (London) *Guardian* article (May 30, 2006) reports that roughly 40,000 girls from Eastern Europe, Russia, and Asia are being trafficked into mobile brothels in Germany to serve the World Cup fans this month. Since there has been little mention of this in the U.S media (but quite a bit on the European front), it seems it's up to me to bring this up. The Guardian piece gives a depressing portrait of the 'stalls' in the 'Mega-Brothel' set up beside the Berlin stadium: these small spaces, where the girls are doing the sex, are called 'performance boxes' and they're about the size of 'toilets,' according to the Guardian. Cribs of the old American West all over again. And 'toilets'—how appropriate since prostitutes have been called 'toilets.' I once heard a joke from a soldier—"the only difference between a toilet and prostitute is that you don't have to flush her—she flushes herself." (Military humor tends to be a bit rough.)

Since prostitution is 'legal' in Germany, the *Guardian* says it is difficult for anyone to help the trafficked girls, even though they have been through the 'works': in case you're not familiar with trafficking, the procedure involves beating, burning, starvation, and collective rape, to make the girls submissive and compliant. (See, for example, Italian writer Paola Monzini's recent book, *Sex Traffic*, for descriptions of what trafficked girls endure.) Apparently, a lot of London police are going there, but since the event is taking place on German soil, they can't bust British men for using prostitutes where it's legal. Not even if the girls are enslaved? Or underage, as many trafficked girls are? Is there some international agenda of human rights that transcends the rights of nations?

So, while the World Cuppers party, these most vulnerable and tortured of human beings are suffering. (And their 'owners' are pulling in the money.)

All of this buying of sex is simply regarded as 'normal' fun, a recreational activity for the horny male fans—but in reality it is the sanctioning of legal rape. Now, I wouldn't take work away from the legal German prostitutes at the World Cup, but isn't there something pathetically brutal about drunk, crude World Cup fans partying around the raped bodies of the trafficked? (And what do the women fans think of all this?)

The *Guardian* article says the customers are not always able to tell the difference between the 'trafficked' and the 'free.' (The ones crying are the trafficked.)

When I lived in Tokyo during the Olympics, it was rumored that prostitutes (mainly indigent girls held in debt bondage) were given as 'gifts' by the Japanese government to athletes. Shades of the Korean Comfort Women.

What will happen in Beijing in 2008, with the heavy increase in the sexual enslavement of women which we are seeing in that country? No one ever talks about this underside of big sporting events.

Anderson Cooper Tackles Child Prostitution and Animal Rights in Asia

April 6, 2007

CNN journalist Anderson Cooper and his news crew recently spent a week in Cambodia and Bangkok reporting on the trafficking in humans and animals. One extremely good aspect that came out of all this was the profiling of Somaly Mam, a Cambodian woman who was sold into prostitution as a child and who escaped and now rescues other girls, many just five or six years old, and most of them, sadly enough, already infected with AIDS. It is hoped that this publicity may garner her beyond-courageous, one-woman effort some financial support from women elsewhere whose lives are so much easier than hers has been. It is also hoped that the international publicity may afford her more protection since her life has been threatened by brothel owners.

Cooper is also to be commended for highlighting child prostitution in an American city, Atlanta, where, he points out, young girl children may be raped as many as 40 times a night by grown male customers. This segment suggests that the men we call 'johns' or customers are really rapists—a useful contention since, in my view—as you may know from my many other articles on this site--any buying of any body, no matter what the age of the female, is an act of rape. Prostitution always involves exploitation of the weak by the strong and it reinforces the idea that a woman or girl is a piece of property and that she is worth less than a man. Whether it be Atlanta or Bangkok, it is the same orifice being raped, and the same attitudes that degrade women apply. So, it was with great happiness that I found some echo of my idea that the 'buyer' is a rapist, even though the idea was just being applied to this one situation—the child prostitute as rape victim—rather than more broadly.

Unfortunately, Cooper only focused on child prostitution. He failed to mention that many girls in Cambodia and Bangkok were sold into the trade as children, making them just as much victims as the younger ones. And there was not one profile of or word from any of the older girls forced into this industry due to the usual reasons: poverty, coercion from family members, lack of alternatives, lack of education, exploitation by pimps who misrepresent the work the girl is being hired for—the picture is familiar by now—a depressing situation of taking advantage of the most vulnerable entity in the world: a young, poor, often unprotected female.

I sent Mr. Cooper feedback at CNN. I always like to offer journalists--and the world--large, idealistic solutions to problems. Solutions that have a sure-fire chance of success—if anyone would listen to me. One solution: Instead of waging a futile war in Iraq, why not have our soldiers out there doing something useful, like breaking down the doors of Cambodian pimps, and taking these little girls out of sexual bondage?

I also mentioned to Mr. Cooper that, although I appreciated his efforts to cover a taboo subject, the analysis of the situation was rather on-the-surface. It was not the 360° that the title of his show implies. Rather it was a tiny slice. He should have also gone into the heavy frequenting of brothels by local men in Thailand and Cambodia. The average Thai male rapes at least thirty different brothelized prostitutes before he marries a 'nice' Thai girl. As in Japan, in Cambodia visiting a brothel and raping an enslaved body is simply a commonplace night out for roughly 80% of the men in that country—of no more importance than buying a bag of potato chips or fish chips. I wish, too, that Mr. Cooper had covered the practice of 'bauking,' in Cambodia: purchasing of one prostitute by a group of young men (any where from 3 to 10, many of them college students) and then they all serially rape the girl—usually more than once. The girl screams and cries but the men don't stop and the poor girl may be raped 30 times a night. I would say to Mrs. Cooper: Don't just target Western tourists—or pedophiles, but also, as in the case of Thailand, visiting militaries—mostly a lot of drunk rough servicemen out for a good time. Please enlighten the public about all these other aspects of the sex trade in Cambodia and Thailand, Mr. Cooper.

At one point, Mr. Cooper expressed great surprise that children were being sold in brothels. As a well-educated and experienced journalist, surely, he must have seen this going on around the world: the current exploitation extends far beyond Southeast Asia. Saudi Arabia has roughly half a million children being held in sexual slavery; Dubai is another hot spot in that part of the world for child prostitutes. And Mr. Cooper must have witnessed, in

Bombay, the four-year-old whores painted up like sad little harlots in that city's huge red-light district. In the many war zones he's been in, he must be familiar with the prostituting of the vulnerable (women, girls, and children) to occupying soldiers. What surprised me is that he expressed surprise. This misleads the public into thinking that the plight of Somaly Mam's charges is unusual—whereas it is, sadly, commonplace. In the aftermath of the Tsunami, Mr. Cooper must have noted the trafficking and exploitation of homeless children. What was surprising about finding child prostitution in Cambodia?

What is surprising, of course, is that so little is being done about it, or about the enslavement of females of all ages. Cooper's crew could have put hidden cameras in their shirts and gone into brothels and filmed the girls being raped by customers. Better yet, they could have taken the girls out of their rape prisons. There is no justifying the 'ethics of objectivity.' You do not leave a girl's body suffering under the cruelty of serial rapists everyday.

I also asked him about the sexual behavior of journalists abroad. One I know personally who is currently living in Malaysia says that journalists frequently take advantage of the 'sexual perks' offered in Southeast Asia. A journalist may do a story about sexual exploitation in Bangkok and then turn around and buy a bargirl. I am not saying, of course, that any specific member of Mr. Cooper's crew may be buying girls. I hope they are not, and that their compassion for the enslaved extends to the grown-up prostitutes as well, who are also horrendously exploited. But, if his men are typical, I would like to know what they're up to when they travel the world, uncovering 'exploitation.' If any journalists anywhere, on any news crews, buy girls, they are contributing to the suffering they are supposed to be trying to reveal. If they buy prostitutes who are eighteen or older, the girls may have been sold into the trade as children and--if they have survived the rape, diseases, beatings, roughness of customers, etc.--they are massively damaged, both physically and psychologically. They have never known another life so that 'choice' of any sort cannot be presumed about their lifestyle. Buying them is as terrible as buying the children.

It has always puzzled me that, up to age 17, 11 months, and 29 days, the girl is an exploited victim because she is underage; and then when she turns 18, she automatically becomes a 'whore' who deserves her fate, even though she was forced into the trade many years before any age of consent was possible. It makes no sense—compassionate, humane, or otherwise.

One of his reporters, Dan Rivers, a British journalist working for CNN in Bangkok, has also traveled with the Royal Navy. All navies move from port to port and from brothel to brothel. If Mr. Rivers saw this kind of exploitation, as he went from port to port, I would like to have this kind of reporting from him, about the sexual suffering of the enslaved when navies dock, as well as what he says about child prostitution in Cambodia. This would have broadened out the prostitution picture in a necessary direction.

For the Cooper team, Mr. Rivers covered the story of Srey, a six-year-old ex-prostitute rescued by Somaly Mam. Unfortunately, he called Srey a 'sex worker.' I can assure Mr. Rivers, from personal experience, that having the insides raped out of you is not work.

This term, sex worker, is in common use, fashionable, and it should be abolished. It is an abomination to classify little Srey and all the rest of these girls with their rape-battered bodies and destroyed lives as 'workers.' The phrase 'sex work' cannot convey the reality that Srey experienced. It is not remotely accurate to call having rapists shove their penises in you 'work.' The term 'sex worker' is cold and sterile and inaccurate. I also object to 'trafficking'—another sterile word that parades around as if it were something 'new' on the scene. Trafficking is prostitution, enforced sex, sex performed on an enslaved body, and this is nothing new. Men and poverty have inflicted this form of rape on us for centuries. Why pretend that prostitution is something new by disguising it behind a fancy new word like 'trafficking.'

Mr. Cooper also paid attention to the plight of animals in Bangkok and Cambodia. These creatures are as helpless as the trafficked girls. I was, however, surprised to see, in one segment, a bull hook being used on an elephant at a place that was purported to be a 'sanctuary' for these animals. The bull hook is a heavy stick with a curved thick nail-like sharp projection at one end that is used to control elephants through pain and fear. Trainers jab the elephants in sensitive areas—inside the ears, in the genitals. Mr. Cooper could have pointed out that all captive elephants in Thailand, and around the world, have been broken through pain and terror. As babies, they are separated from their mothers, tied down, starved, terrorized by fire, beaten for hours--and they also have nails driven into their feet. He could have pointed out that every time tourists ride an elephant in Thailand, they are on top of a beaten animal who has had her spirit broken in this way. That would have been immeasurably useful in his 'trafficking' in animals segment. Every captive elephant is trafficked: taken from her home in nature, broken, and enslaved.

All elephants, worldwide—in Thailand, in the USA in circuses--are trained through pain and fear—it takes hours of beatings to break their spirits so they will 'perform.' They won't do those stupid, degrading tricks on their own.

No true 'sanctuary' would use a bull hook, so I wonder about this place Mr. Cooper visited in Thailand. Go to the web and look up the Elephant Sanctuary in Tennessee and PAWS in northern California—no hooks of torture in these 'true sanctuaries.' The animals are terrified of them, bear scars all over their bodies, not just in the ears and genitals, from them. You cannot give an elephant peace, in a sanctuary, if there is a bull hook in sight.

Don Imus and His Whore Comment

April 14, 2007

The controversy over talk show host Don Imus and his 'ho' comment has been on the news everywhere over the past few days. My take is so different on this whole incident that I have to share it with at least the one or two readers who might want to hear what this author, Suki, who is an ex-whore, thinks of the furor. Or maybe I should say 'ex-ho,' to reflect the parlance of the times.

Imus called the girls on the Rutgers' basketball team ho's, whores. If you examine what a whore is, she is a person whose sexuality is sold, usually by a pimp or owner, to a male who regards her as a piece of equipment that he unloads himself into without feeling or care or tenderness. A whore is a trafficked/prostituted body, the most abject, degraded, oppressed creature on this planet. She is constantly raped for money-- sold for money, like a piece of insensate meat—and she is scorned because she is treated this way. She is the most exploited and brutalized member of the human race. It would be hard to imagine being raped every day as a way of life—or death. This is what she experiences. She is a being clinging to life at the outer edge of extremes of pain.

In light of all the privileged girls who ignore the plight of the whore, I would much rather be identified with her than with the fortunate ones. The Rutgers girls are the fortunate ones. Please call me a whore if it means I am one of the hurt and oppressed and dying of rape degradation. I would much rather be a whore than part of the brigade of 'decent' women who ignore whores and do nothing to help their sexually brutalized sisters.

This opinion will never be aired on CNN or MSNBC or Fox, or accepted as making any kind of humane commonsense, but I had to let at least a few people know what the an ex-whore thinks. It causes me extreme pain to hear a privileged Rutgers basketball player say she is 'scarred for life' by Imus' comment. The Rutgers girls have enough to eat, and a place to sleep, and the chance to learn, and play sports, at a prestigious university. They are not in the position of, say, the Manila street child, sniffing glue to deaden her hopeless world. The kind of girl who is 'scarred for life' is the 10-year-old sold to a Bombay brothel who has to lie down on a filthy stained mattress every night until she contracts AIDS from constant rape. This is 'indignity.' This is 'scarring.' And no one even notices her plight. Unlike days upon days upon days of coverage of Imus and his apologies to the Rutgers' girls. Who apologizes to the ten-year-old Bombay whore after she has taken her nightly quota of rape? (I could have substituted any number of places for the city of Bombay: Bangkok, London, Atlanta.)

The girls on the Rutgers basketball team are strong. They have to be to reach this level in athletics. Tough and strong and disciplined. I have a hard time believing that one of these strong, confident women could be 'scarred for life' by this one comment. The vagina of the child prostitute in Bombay (or Bangkok, or London, or Atlanta) is 'scarred for life.'

Another side to what a whore is: Any non-prostituted woman who takes her sexual freedom and assumes she has choice as to how many sexual partners she shares her body with, any woman who wants to express the beauty of her sensuality in this repressive culture is also called a 'whore.'

There is no 'complimentary' word for a woman who has multiple sexual partners. In the realm of sexual rape torture, the poor creature is called a whore, or a prostitute, or she is sanitized with that abomination of coldness—that viciously inadequate phrase, 'sex worker'—a phrase that can in no way reflect the rape reality of her life. Rape is not work.

If a woman voluntarily takes multiple sex partners she is a 'slut' or 'promiscuous.' The closest our culture has come to finding an alternative word is 'non-monogamous.' It is awkward and ugly sounding. 'Non-monogamous.' It sounds like the ailing cousin of a sadly dying mongoose.

I feel guilty I cannot take upon myself all the pain of all the ten-year-old 'whores' being raped around the world this moment. I would be honored to be in their company.

Under the circumstances, I would be proud and pleased to be called a whore.

Mr. Imus—you may call me a whore—but never call me a 'sex worker.'

8

These next two go into sex in Nevada, in various forms.

The Sex Industry in Nevada

January 13, 2008

Sin City. Skin City. Las Vegas is flesh city. Billboards everywhere display tempting bodies. At one posh nightclub, the Tao in the Venetian, near-naked girls greet you in perfumed bathwater, roses floating on its surface. Girls shadow dance behind screens at Caesars Palace . The Palms has its Playboy Club. A Penthouse Pet Club has just opened. The city is the haunt of the Implant Babe, Pamela Anderson, and of Carmen Electra, and the cavorting Pussycat Dolls. Rows of topless showgirls in big-stage extravaganzas have been a staple for decades, and the city is famous for its strip clubs—like Crazy Horse and Cheetah's. Newer clubs are springing up all the time. Topless, and bottomless, venues abound and the city flaunts the beauty of the female body—glossy, shining, naked, or near-naked—images of women as sensually pleasing and arousing objects are everywhere.

As a highly sensuous woman, I like sex and nakedness and the beauty of our lovely soft bodies. We women are lovely and sensual and soft and delectable. I do not connect sex with outmoded notions of 'lust' and 'sin' and I do not link it with morality. To do so denies an experience that at its highest can be beautiful and emotional as well as physical. And I would see nothing wrong with Las Vegas as a sexual playground if it did not involve exploitation. Unfortunately, this harsher aspect is a big part of the $6 billion dollar industry of sex in Nevada . This exploitation side makes me object to the name of the gentleman's club, newly opened, at the Luxor . It is called Cathouse.

What really happens inside Nevada's legal 'cathouses' is not glamourous. Psychologist Melissa Farley's recent book, *Prostitution and Trafficking in Nevada: Making the Connection*, the result of a two-year research project sponsored by the U.S. State Department, uncovers some of the less savory side of the Nevada sex industry.

"No one really enjoys being sold," a woman in a Nevada legal brothel told Farley. "It's like you sign a contract to be raped." From interviews and first-hand observation, Farley says that "many of the women in the legal brothels are under intense emotional stress; many of them have symptoms of chronic institutionalization and trauma." Farley found mentally ill women in the brothels, ones who had been beaten, and ones who has been trafficked in by pimps, who took the majority of the money they earned. She found 'debt bondage conditions' in some brothels: girls being charged enormous amounts for food and cigarettes and even the condoms they needed—these latter items are supposed to be supplied, free, by the brothel in a legal establishment.

Prostitution is not legal in Las Vegas or Reno: the brothels are in adjacent rural counties. To get to the ones outside Las Vegas, in the area surrounding the small town of Pahrump, is quite a trip--they are way, way out in the desert—and, once there, it is very difficult to get to talk to the girls. Why, I wonder, if it is legal, is there something to hide? Are these girls 'inmates' in a prison?

Legal prostitution is only a part of the picture. Farley reports that the links between illegal and legal prostitution and between trafficking and prostitution are the same as one finds every place where legalizing it has been tried. The Netherlands, Germany, Australia —in all these countries trafficking skyrocketed after prostitution was legalized. It made it much easier for the exploiters to operate, for the 'johns' to get at the enslaved, and it did nothing for the girls themselves, the victims of the exploitation. Only a tiny handful of Dutch, German, and Australian prostitutes might benefit from the health and pension systems that legalizing brings. The majority of prostituted beings in these countries are sex slaves with no access to benefits, or any rights whatsoever. Even the few 'independent' German/Dutch/Australian prostitutes often report pimps taking their money, so I even wonder if they are 'free' to prostitute themselves or whether this 'trade' involves a universal form of coercion visited on all the women in it.

Maybe Farley's most shocking find is that "Las Vegas is the epicenter of North American trafficking and prostitution. Women are trafficked into this city from all over the world, including Korea, China, Mexico, Russia, El Salvador, Guatemala, Ukraine, Czech Republic and others."

According to the U.S. State Department, prostitution and trafficking are heavily linked. Whether you call the girl 'trafficked' or not, prostitution is inherently harmful. To quote a pamphlet from the State Department: "Few activities are as brutal and damaging to people as prostitution…victims meet the criteria for post-traumatic stress disorder in the same range as victims of state-organized torture. Shocking abuse of the body, a myriad of serious and fatal diseases, such as AIDS, higher rates of cervical cancer….Prostitution leaves women and children physically, mentally, emotionally, and spiritually devastated. Recovery takes years, even decades—often, the damage can never be undone."

I have written two articles on the sex industry in Nevada. I think they can add to Farley's insights as to what goes on in this lucrative business. Here is the first, called "In the Las Vegas Sex Industry, the Rapists Go Free"—date May 15, 2007--

Two dozen girls were picked up in a raid on a Las Vegas brothel last month. The customers present were questioned and released. This particular raid, the result of something called Operation Doll House, came after two years of investigation, and it yielded the arrest of about half a dozen exploiters with ties to Asia who had trafficked the girls in. The first news article on this raid (in the *Las Vegas Review-Journal*, April 25, 2007) was entitled "Women Facing Deportation" and made it sound as if the girls were the criminals since they were in the U.S. illegally. The second article (also in the *Review-Journal*, May 4, 2007) did an about face and said the girls would be eligible for "T" visas (ones available for trafficking victims) and they would receive help locally from the Salvation Army and WestCare, a facility with a newly established trafficking program.

The article mentioned the conditions the girls were found under: dirty mattresses on the floor, separated by sheets strung up; the rooms reeking of cigarettes and feces and urine; gallon containers of lube and hundreds of condoms in the brothel. While the brothel was running, neighbors reported seeing customers vomiting and urinating in the street before going in and they reported huge numbers of used condoms rolling down the street on trash days.

The article also, thankfully, pointed out the campaign of terror and physical and psychological abuse, not the least of which is the daily rape of their bodies, that girls who are trafficked endure.

These articles prompted a number of questions on my part. The biggest one: why were the customers not arrested for the ongoing rape of these girls' bodies? Were the girls put in jail cells right after the raid, further traumatizing their already shocked minds and bodies? If they are indeed the victims of this terrible rape of their bodies, why would anyone even consider putting them in a cell, or 'arresting' them, for even a moment?

Who termed this Operation Doll House? It makes the pathetic situation of these poor girls sound like a dirty joke at a bachelor party—as if a brothel were a place full of live dolls to play with. Another such operation in Las Vegas a number of years ago was called Operation Jade Blade, carrying sad, 'exotic' associations with the knives brothel inmates feel between their legs everyday. Words are important. I would like to know if male police officers named these operations, unaware of the insensitivity of phrasing.

Since the Las Vegas police must see the pathetic conditions that prostitutes live under, why would they use such a sadly callous and sexist title for this operation? The Las Vegas police report that the city has as many underage street prostitutes (most trafficked in by pimps) as bigger cities like Los Angeles and New York. Given this, they must see the misery of these girls. Sold girls are not 'dolls.'

Other questions about the raid: Why did it take two years to release the girls from their sexual slavery? Is not the fact of all those used condoms rolling down the street enough of a clue that something is terribly amiss? Two years while the girls were raped thousands of times.

A local aid worker who helps trafficked victims says she was not aware of anyone being sexually enslaved in the U.S. until she herself began helping victims in 1997. Although I have great admiration for what she does, I do know that I have been aware of sexual slavery since I was quite young. I am not sure there was ever a time that I didn't know that the sale of female bodies is one of the most lucrative businesses on the planet. It is rather hard to miss it. When and where have women and girls not been sold for sex? Why would anyone think it does not happen in this country? Is there a city, a place, a haven, anywhere, in the history of our species, where sexual slavery has not been practiced? I have always been aware that my own safety exists at the expense of those less sexually protected in some terrible equation of unfairness and pain.

How many other brothels full of trafficked girls are operating right now in Las Vegas? It is one of the major sex-for-sale venues in the world. Wherever sex is a massive industry, as it is in this entertainment capital of the world-

-as it styles itself--there will be exploitation. In recent years, Las Vegas has seen a massive proliferation of Asian massage parlours, and the numerous escort services advertise many girls from both Asia and Eastern Europe. The phenomenon of selling more girls from these areas parallels the rise in trafficking worldwide.

Setting up services for trafficked girls in Las Vegas is very recent—only within the last year have organizations and women's groups actually recognized the problem—this despite the fact that Las Vegas has been 'Sin City' for decades.

Operation Jade Blade took place in 2000, Operation Doll House this year. Two stings within a period of seven years in a city where sex-for-sale is a commonplace? The Las Vegas Yellow Pages runs 150 pages of ads under the caption "Entertainment." Girls are offered under such headings as "Barely Legal China Dolls and Asian Centerfolds and Asian Beauties." "Direct to you, petite and willing, you no happy, you no pay, wild, ready to have fun with you"—these are some of the promises. Along with that famous phrase "full service," as in "Full Service Japanese and Chinese Teens." "Exotic European Girls" are there, along with "Chinese Teens in Short Skirts" and "Sizzling Asian Teen Strippers" and "Chinese Take-Out, Asian Girls Are Better." "Affordable Asians" is yet another ad. Some present the girls as docile and submissive, in the traditional stereotype. "No attitude" is the promise. They will do what you want.

There are, of course, plenty of ads for home-grown girls, but I do note that the marketing of Asians, and Eastern Europeans, in Las Vegas has increased enormously over the last few years. It would seem obvious that a link with trafficking is the reason.

Little cards with near-nude, provocatively posed girls and brochures are other ways that the escort and massage and entertainment services of Las Vegas advertise. One girl for $35, two-girl special for $60, etc.

Yet another aspect of the Las Vegas sex scene is an increase in 'Gentleman's Clubs,' some displaying just topless but others offering full nudity. Crazy Horse and Cheetah's and others have, of course, been a part of the Las Vegas scene for a long while; but around the city there now seems to be an explosion of nude entertainment. Many girls may be quite happily making lots of money in these clubs—if so, I would be really overjoyed to know this is the case--but we do not really know much in the way of their stories. Nor do we know much about the connection between these establishments and prostitution per se in Las Vegas. In fact, how much sexual activity is voluntary, and how much 'forced,' on the part of girls engaged in the various aspects of the sex industry in this city is impossible to tell. A local investigative reporter who has interviewed Las Vegas and Nevada prostitutes on-and-off for many years says that almost every girl he talked to stuck him as damaged in some way. The few who might actually benefit from selling sex were rare in his opinion.

How many of the escorts are independent operators and how many are controlled by pimps? Prostitution is illegal within Las Vegas itself, but legal in the adjacent county. Girls are sometimes trafficked into the legal establishments by pimps, who take the money. They are also trafficked between the escort services and strip clubs and brothels so as to provide fresh merchandize.

If the women and girls working in the Las Vegas and Nevada sex industries were there because they wanted to be, and were indeed making money, instead of it being siphoned off by pimps, owners, procurers, traffickers, it would be fine by me. I would like to envision a form of prostitution where the girl has control over her body and her finances. But I wonder if this is the case for many of them? Particularly with the huge increase over the past few years of Asians and Eastern Europeans being marketed. In addition to the two dozen rescued during Operation Doll House, how many more girls are being held in debt bondage and sexual slavery around the Las Vegas valley and in the adjacent county with its legal establishments? I doubt if this tiny handful of girls rescued in the raid is even the tip of the sexual misery going on out there.

Trying to get to talk to a girl in one of Nevada's legal brothels is tough. The places are way out in the desert and resemble prisons. If the activity is a prosperous and beneficial one for the girls, why are the places so hard to get into, or out of? And where would a girl go, out in the desert, if she did escape? There are only jackrabbits and coyotes out there.

Back to a question that I raised at the beginning of this article—since it is the one that troubles me most deeply: Why are the 'johns' who rape the girls not being arrested? Since I have been raped/prostituted, I know that what johns do to us is rape. They pay to rape an already thoroughly raped body. Why are these attackers going free? Please call johns what they are—rapists. And punish them for their sexual brutality.

It puzzles me why one girl raped by her boyfriend is considered so important and 'special' that she has rape crisis centers and counseling and prosecution under the law at her disposal; but if a girl is trafficked, broken, tortured, terrorized and raped over and over, on a daily basis, the many 'customers' who violate her multiple times are not even considered criminals.

And--could a trafficked girl even use the local 'rape-crisis' center? Or would they throw her out because she wasn't really 'raped.' After all, the guys paid her.

If anyone reads this and knows about how the law operates, please let me know if the 'johns' are culpable under a new move in international law to regard any man as a rapist who uses a girl forced into sexual servitude. How does international law intersect with local law?

As you may know, Las Vegas has a famous slogan: "What happens here, stays here." What you may not know is that the phrase comes from the military. An uncle of mine, a WWII vet, told me it referred to the GI's buying and raping starving prostituted girls all across Europe and Asia. Obviously, the men did not want their wives and girlfriends back home to know about the way they took advantage of women and girls and the way they forced conqueror sex on a destitute population, nor did they want the many babies they fathered and abandoned to come to light. So they all formed a 'pact' around that phrase, "what happens here, stays here." My uncle (who bought prostituted bodies in Japan) says he thought the phrase went back at least to WWI, when soldiers in that war behaved the same in France and elsewhere. And, of course, the same soldier/sailor mentality continues to this day, as our military stops off for the regulation sex binge in Bangkok, or our men buy girls trafficked into brothels for them near bases in Korea and Germany and other places overseas. "What happens here, stays here." An appropriate 'slogan,' no?—for Las Vegas, a major sex-for-sale city.

It seems unlikely that Las Vegas will ever tackle the exploitative aspect of its sex industry. There is too much money to be made. It is also too much a part of the 'glamourous' aspect of Sin City. My temporary solution would be to at least not treat the girls as criminals, no matter if they are 'trafficked' or not. I would set up extensive services (physical and mental health care, job training, mentoring by ex-prostitutes) for those trying to escape prostitution, including actively seeking out enslaved girls since the truly oppressed are often not in a position to escape on their own—too beaten down and terrified and broken. For those who are in the profession voluntarily, I would advocate 'protective' services for these girls that really work in their favor, including decriminalizing it totally for the women, and punishing exploiters and pimps as slavers and rapists. 'Legalizing' has been a failure. It is time to envision a completely different path for protecting girls involved in selling sex. This is matter for a whole article, or book, on its own, for a later time.

I would like to conclude by saying that I hope these poor 'doll-house' girls receive nurturing care for many years to come. They will need the kindness of the generous-hearted people at the Salvation Army, and WestCare, for a long, long time. It takes a whole lifetime to heal from being raped everyday by johns. And even then the sexual scarring is inside forever.

That's the end of the first article. When the 'Doll-House' case surfaced in the Las Vegas news again last month, I wrote the following in response to the coverage of it--

According to the *Review-Journal's* latest coverage (Dec. 11, 2007) of "Operation Doll House," a brothel sting that rounded up a number of Asian girls, it appears that the rapists/exploiters are going free. One man indicted has received a suspended prison sentence and 5 years probation. That's all—for his role in the rape of these women's bodies. The article also reports that this was not a case of 'trafficking' and that the girls were not coerced. The RJ's previous coverage of the event, a number of months ago, described the rooms where the girls were found: gallons of lube, hundreds of condoms, filthy mattresses on the floor, the rooms reeking of feces and urine. It described drunk men urinating and vomiting outside before they went in to use the girls. Yet, according to the current RJ article, the FBI investigators found no evidence that the women were being 'forced.'

Now, would a woman 'choose' to have intercourse with men who have just vomited in the street? Would any woman choose to be penetrated multiple times a night by men she doesn't know on a dirty mattress on the floor-- in an apartment reeking of urine and feces? No forcing???? Who would ever choose to work under these conditions?

Which male universe do these FBI agents come from? Do they think that their own wives and daughters would ever invite sex with drunk strangers, night after night, on filthy mattresses? If not, then how can they possibly assume any other woman would want to be treated to a nightly dose of serial rape in an atmosphere of filth and misery? In what way is the situation of these girls not 'coercion' and force? And rape—of the most terrible kind.

It took the authorities two years to investigate this situation. Their attitude is well illustrated by what they labeled it: Operation Doll House—what a degradation to imply these raped girls are 'toys'! Why did it take them two years to get the girls out of the brothels? Two years while their poor bodies were being raped thousands of times. And then when they get them out—the people who put them there are let go, on 'probation,' and the customers (the real rapists) are not even punished at all? The girls have no 'probation' from the permanent hell that will be their life after years of being gang raped every day. As a rape/prostitution survivor, I can tell you that the prostitute never heals. I never healed. I never will. I am always in that rape prison.

Were the women held in debt bondage? Are any of these Asian women in brothels not being held in debt bondage? This is not just a form of coercion—it is enslavement.

The FBI agent called it a "straightforward" case. How so? What is "straightforward" about women being treated this way--except that it's rape but that word did not surface in the article. Who makes up the definition of 'force' that the FBI and the courts use? I think I must look at reality very differently from the way the courts and the FBI do. I look at reality from the perspective of a body that has been raped thousands of times—the way these women have been.

The RJ article could have covered this so differently. It could have recounted the extent of the girls' physical injuries. Serial rape, night after night, leaves tremendous damage. The article could have found out what the girls said—that is, if they were able to speak. Ordinarily, due to shame and deep trauma, prostituted women are only capable of saying what they think they have to in order to not be hurt anymore.

The article reports the girls are being sent back to their countries. What it does not mention is that there it is likely they will be re-trafficked: they will probably end up back in prostitution not just because of this but because they will be seen as unfit, as whores, to go back into their society. Also, their self-worth will be so low, due to the thousands of rapes, that they will probably not see a way out of prostitution. I know that when I was in it, I thought I would die in it. I could not picture a life after or beyond it. Who can ever be 'normal' after thousands of rapes? Who can get a job at Sears or Starbucks after thousands of rapes?

I can't see a whole lot of difference between 'forced' prostitution and prostitution/trafficking. Is this Las Vegas case another example of the TIP (Trafficking in Person's Act) not working because the women are too terrified to speak? Their abusers are free to still hurt them if they testify. Is what is happening in this trial an example of women too frightened and damaged to testify? Too fearful of future reprisals? Why didn't the RJ cover this aspect of the case?

I also know that speaking out for these women may be impossible. If faced with the men who hurt me, now, in my current life, there is no way I could ever testify against them. If I were in the same room with them, I would vomit and then run away as far as I could and hide in the nearest closet for safety. There is no police force that will protect me from them, and no court, not anywhere in America on any place else on this Rape Planet that I can go to. The legal system is designed to discredit the 'mass-rape' victim that we label 'prostitute.'

I really don't understand why rape/forced prostitution/trafficking are the only crimes where the victims are blamed for what happens to them.

That's the end of my second article. It indicates what we are up against in terms of tackling prostitution—in Nevada or across the planet. Attitudes and systems that keep girls enslaved and that do little to punish those who inflict extremes of torture on other human beings. 'John' = 'Rapist' and 'Pimp/ Owner' = Rapist Murderer of Women's Bodies.

Farley has interviewed hundreds of prostitutes all over the world and she concludes that most are desperate to get out. That investigative reporter I mentioned earlier has interviewed about a hundred girls and come to the conclusion that almost all of them are in terrible shape. A former prostitute in Las Vegas who runs a 'john's' program—designed to educate the customers about the harm they inflict, comes to the same conclusion—that these are highly damaged women. And she should know. Being one of the damaged ones.

Farley presented a panel on prostitution shortly after her book came out, and a number of former prostitutes spoke. One said that Las Vegas is greatly lacking in services to help prostituted women, girls, and children. (The city has a thriving business based on the sale of young girls, ages 13-17.) She said that local charities would not help the prostituted. Once they discover you worked as one, they throw you out.

I know that the Salvation Army, nation-wide, is now getting involved in helping the trafficked. They are receiving federal funding to do so. Will they help the prostituted, or do they see a distinction between the two? (For me, the trafficked and the prostituted are the same tortured being.)

At the panel, one prostitute came up with a startling fact: that very few women, girls, or children actually make it out of prostitution, and, of the few who do, life expectancy is short. Most are dead two or three years later. From insanity, suicide, disease?

Her remarks made me stop breathing for a few seconds. I now realize that I was incredibly lucky to actually survive the three-year stint I spent in prostitution and that the odds of my being alive now are amazing. When I was in it, I saw no way out. Esteem so low and a body and mind and emotions so battered that I could not see past the next hour or so. I felt as if I was in a ten-foot pit and could not see the rim. I smiled all the time, as if everything was okay. But I simply assumed I would die in prostitution. I gave up. What life is there after being raped thousands of times by men you don't know?

There is none. I have no courage, no self-worth—all these must come from inside and there is only empty cold space inside me. I am afraid to leave the house. I am terrified of everything. I am not a rape/prostitution survivor. I didn't survive. I have no 'support network' since I have never spoken to another prostitute. I am always afraid I will see the same sadness in her eyes that I see in my own. The only way I know what other prostitutes think is through people like Melissa Farley, who has talked to so many all over the world. With surprise, I found many similarities—whether it's Bangkok or Bombay or London or Las Vegas, the raped body feels the same. Through Farley's interviews, I have also found ones who are 'true' survivors. Hope and peace and safety they have found. That's not me. No hope, no peace, and certainly no safety—since I am terrified to go outside the door. This is a big deal for me since you can't do much of anything else if you can't cross the threshold, into the outside world.

I pretty much live in spite of this. The beautiful things in the world--I know they are there--but I can't reach them for comfort. I am still ten feet down, in that pit. I love sparrows. So small and cute and sweet and fragile, yet also so cheeky and spirited. I wish I could appreciate the beauty of a sparrow again.

Hope. Sweden seems to be doing something that works! They have decriminalized it for the women and made it a felony for the men who buy the girls. Their attitude is simple: Prostitution exploits women—all women. The 'demand' side, the way men 'must' be allowed to purchase bodies, is the result of male dominance and exploitation of the female. Prostitution hurts women. Period. Sweden has reduced trafficking to almost nil and they provide many services for women who are either in prostitution, or who want out, or who have gotten out and are struggling to survive. No blame on the woman in Sweden. Finally, a paradise on earth that really includes women? I have to blink to believe it. And sit inside a warm blanket, safe, in a small space away from how cold and huge the outside world is—to believe it. I hope it's true.

When Sweden's new laws started really working, traffickers shifted more business to Norway. Norway has passed laws similar to Sweden's. Now, Denmark is currently working on going the way of the 'Swedish model.' The latest news I have is that the women of Denmark are pressuring the men who do not buy prostitutes to vote for legislation similar to that in Sweden. All Western European countries, except for Sweden, and now Norway, are major destinations for impoverished girls who are imported from third world countries and from Russia and the Ukraine for sex.

Could the United States follow the Swedish model? It would entail a sweeping change of attitude within our borders—that the prostitute is not a depraved immoral sex fiend addict and a threat to all decent pure women everywhere but that she is a terrible victim of rape and male dominance. Following the Swedish model also involves 'tracking' men who buy sex in other countries. Sweden is working on this side of the problem: it is tackling the Swedish men who go as sex tourists to Thailand and also the sexual behavior of its military abroad. During the World Cup in Germany , Sweden was the only country that 'policed' its players and tourists to make sure they did not buy any of the 40,000 enslaved bodies that Germany made available for rape 'fun and games.' I will be interested to see if Sweden can do similar policing of its own men at the Beijing Olympics where massive numbers of trafficked Chinese girls will be on sale.

The 'policing' of men will only work in the long run if we change men's hearts. They have to realize that to buy us destroys us. It harms the men as well since it reduces women to slaves.

Non-Prostituted Women and the Loneliness of the Long-Distance Whore

Over the last few months, I have seen a number of articles in the Las Vegas press that fill me with sadness. The first by local journalist Kristen Peterson is called "Glamour Girls of the Streets" (*Las Vegas Sun*, 4 Dec. 2007) and recounts how photojournalist Jonnie Andersen heads out to take pictures of Las Vegas street prostitutes. According to Peterson, "The girls in Jonnie Andersen's recent photos emit joy, dignity, sensuality and strength."

Among other things, Andersen dressed the girls up in wedding dresses for the photos.

Peterson writes: "At first, Andersen says, the pimps (or 'boyfriends') wouldn't let her near the women, fearing she'd talk them out of the lifestyle or that the photos would boost their confidence."

Andersen says she "saw universal similarities between these women and everyone else." The basis for this claim, writes Peterson, is that "the models are presented as humans and not as stereotyped or glamorized drug addicts working the street."

Peterson's conclusion is that "the photos don't gloss over reality and they don't exploit misery." She thinks that the "photographer spotlights prostitutes' 'humanity.'"

In response, I (the prostitute with the inside track on the subject) would first address the title "Glamour Girls of the Streets" and the phrase "glamorized drug addicts." Street girls report little glamour: their heads are banged against dashboards so much they sometimes suffer permanent damage; they kneel in alleys giving blow-jobs to strangers; they are stripped and left naked in the streets by clients (read 'rapists' for this last word).

I don't know how Andersen would have talked these girls out of this lifestyle when there is no place for them to go. No social services and open arms and tender understanding. And escape is very difficult. Fear of pimps is overwhelming according to former prostitute Rachel Lloyd, who started a service called GEMS in New York to help other girls out. She says you learn to keep your eyes down in front of your pimp, in docile surrender, so fierce is the punishment meted out for the slightest infraction of 'pimp rules.'

There is no "sensuality" in being raped all day and in taking the penises of men you don't know in your mouth in a dirty alley, as you kneel, subservient. No woman subjected to this "emits joy and dignity." As for "strength," it is all on the side of the pimp who beats and rapes submission continuously into his property.

A photo of Andersen accompanies the article: a picture of a woman all bright and smiling and sane since she is not raped all day.

We whores are not "similar" to you in any way, Ms. Andersen. We are raped all day. We do not have your "universal humanity."

Did you dress up the whores in wedding dresses as a grotesque masquerade of the protection and dignity they will never know?

Not only do your photos "gloss over" reality—but they present no reality whatsoever.

A moment of reality does creep accidentally into the article when Peterson describes the girls' "hardened faces" and the bruises and scar tissue over wrists. (Suicide rates are astronomical among whores and ex-whores due to the extreme torture of the lifestyle.)

Two clean safe women, journalist and photojournalist, without a clue about that extreme torture. Journalists such as these are parasites on the prostitutes' misery. How else explain that Andersen thought it was okay to photograph women who are rape-tortured by this sanctioned system called 'prostitution'—as if taking pictures of this were a 'norm'—and then she walked away from their pain. Also a 'norm,' that walking away: safe women all over Las Vegas, and everywhere in the world, who live in comfort and dignity, while next door, or in the next street, invisible women suffer terrible sexual violence and degradation. We have so accepted that some women must be sacrificed for the needs of 'the client'—and the profit of the pimp–that we do not even seem to question the act of taking pictures of this, and displaying them proudly in books and newspapers—works of 'art' based on unbelievable psychological and physical misery.

The girls cannot escape, Ms. Andersen. They are not like you. They do not share in your "humanity."

I wonder how many hundreds of times these girls have been raped over the last few months, since she took her pictures of them?

Abigail Goldman's "Bewildered Academics Pore Over Sex-Trade Hysteria" (*Las Vegas Sun.* 31 Jan. 2008) exalts two female sociologists at the University of Nevada who study the sex industry in that state. Goldman also cuts down San Francisco psychologist Melissa Farley for presenting a grim picture of that industry.

Goldman's stance is very odd. She asks why should Las Vegas, with its girls "direct-to-your-room," advertising, buy into Farley's ideas. Quite frankly, I don't think Goldman need worry about Las Vegas ever trying to combat prostitution and the trafficking that is such a huge part of the industry. Sex-for-sale brings in so much money in Nevada that it is untouchable by those who see the exploitative side. An article or two in the newspaper favoring Farley's side will not make a dent in the exploitation.

"Full-service girls, direct to your room," is an accepted norm in Las Vegas, no matter how many of us point out the enslaving side of prostitution.

Goldman also writes that "*New York Times* columnist Bob Herbert… swallowed Farley's thesis—that sex work is violence against women." (Actually, Bob Herbert has long taken a stance that prostitution exploits women in dreadful ways: he doesn't really need Farley to make up his mind for him on this. His highly sensitive articles on the subject in the *NY Times* are small miracles that I look forward to–they give a whore like me hope—there is a man who understands! Just his view of the meat-market line-up in the brothels as extremely degrading shows his humane commonsense. And his idea that prostitutes are the "least empowered" women he has ever seen. I'm a great example. I have no empowerment at all. It all got raped out of me and there is no 'power shake' of magic ingredients I can drink to bring it back.)

That prostitution is sexual violence toward women does not seem to be just Farley's thesis. The evidence everywhere is overwhelming. (The entire country of Sweden holds this view, by the way.) In preparation for a book I am finishing up called *The Raped Vagina: A Military Prostitute's Story*, I have read about 400 other books on prostitution over the past two years—so I would know what I am talking about. I have been overwhelmed by the amount of evidence that supports Farley's thesis–worldwide the picture of prostitution is very similar to what has now been termed 'trafficking': women and girls subjected to rape, violence, and terror tactics. Women and girls with few alternatives since corrupt police systems and paid-off politicians and patriarchal legal systems offer them little help. Escape from the brothel and go to the local police—and they drag you back to your owner, for a pay-off. Women and girls held in debt bondage, a modern form of financial slavery. The majority of prostituted women in the world are subjected to these conditions—horrifying and unbelievable as it seems, this torture and degradation are simply the norm for this 'profession.'

As Nicholas Kristof, another caring man who writes for the *NY Times*, points out Kristen, the pampered call girl of former governor Spitzer, is not at all typical of prostituted beings. (See his excellent piece, "The Pimps' Slaves," in the 16 March 2008 NY Times.) When even the 'high-priced' girls report violence several times a year from clients, you can imagine that for the majority of 'lesser' women in the sex industry, it is a grim picture. As Kristof so beautifully phrases it, for them, "selling sex isn't a choice but a nightmare." To promote the idea that 'choice' is involved, as do the UNLV sociologists, misrepresents the circumstances of the majority of women and girls caught in this cruel profession worldwide. It is irresponsible to give the impression that the few who might have some freedom and dignity are representative. Far, far from it.

The two sociologists criticize Farley's work, saying it is not 'peer reviewed.' As an academic myself, I know what that empty, high-sounding phrase means–in this context. It means a bunch of non-whore women sitting around putting a stamp of approval on jargon-ridden prose that has no relevance to the heat and rape and pain of the brothelized whore. No connection to the bruised, beaten-down street whore with the near-death eyes.

I have said elsewhere that we need to remove the non-whore women from the discourse on the whore. Only sociologists who have been brothelized and degraded in the line-up and then set to work on the streets, on their knees, sucking the filthy dicks of guys they don't know–only these women should be allowed to write on the whore. Except their pimps will knock them around so much they won't have enough of a brain left to write with. Or enough spirit. That part of you is as dead as your body.

(I would subject all journalists and women's studies professors and other academics to the same brothel apprenticeship. Male journalists and academics included. I would make a few exceptions: scholarly women like Farley who already have sympathetic hearts and journalists like Herbert and Kristof—and a rare women's studies professor here and there who actually has a clue about the extreme suffering of the prostitute.)

At a "quiet academic gathering," as Goldman phrases it, the sociologists sat around, along with some women's studies professors, discussing the whore. (There is nothing "quiet" about rape, by the way– is a hot noisy inferno inside and the vagina is a place that bleeds and is in pain. I think that sociologists can only be allowed their self-indulgent, safe, rape-free "quiet gatherings" when no whore anywhere is ever again in the middle of the noise and chaos of rape-pain.)

Goldman writes that the "commodification of intimacy" is not all that simple. Actually, it is very simple. You cannot turn 'intimacy' into a commodity—except in the distanced vocabulary of the intellectual. Goldman favors these academic women. She seems to believe that you have to "elevate the discussion" to the intellectual level to get at the root causes. Well, the root causes are there and evident: a body is bought and sold, according to an historically sanctioned rape system called prostitution. The root cause is as clear as the bleeding vagina. I don't think we need any more academicians to point out the obvious in 'scholarly' prose no one can read. Goldman laments that no one will listen to the sociology professors since their format is "erudite dialogue." She is certainly right about the 'erudite.' Of those 400 books I read, a goodly number were written in this abysmal language we term 'academic' and 'peer-reviewed.' You would never know that the author was writing about a suffering, raped being, so distanced is the language from any reality. Even the few scholars out there with hearts become lost and ineffectual in this abominable way of writing.

A women's studies professor at the same "quiet academic gathering" believes that the way "sex workers" (her phrase, not mine) are presented as "universally exploited, trafficked, raped and coerced" goes well with the media's tendency to sensationalize. I would say the media is not 'sensationalizing' enough. They are not really uncovering the raw truth of what prostitution is. They need to follow the example of actress Daryl Hannah, who went into brothels to film the misery and also to take girls out.

More 'raw' reality is needed, not "quiet academic gatherings." Raw reality of the sort that actress Emma Thompson has brought to the table: she stars in a PSA video called "Trafficking is Torture" in which she portrays an Eastern European girl trafficked into the UK who is forced to have sex with 40 men a day. It is emotionally and physically wrenching. Bravo to Thompson for not "quietly" covering up reality but instead presenting the red-hot inferno of rape that prostitution is for most who are snared and trapped by this trade.

I don't think there is any excuse for "quiet academic" approaches to this misery. Even *The New Yorker*—a cool, distanced, and safely ensconced magazine if ever there was one—does not entirely hide the suffering from its readers. In a recent piece called "The Countertraffickers" (May 5, 2008) William Finnegan, writing about the flourishing trafficking of girls from Moldova, describes how the "trauma and sorrow are intense." *The New Yorker* is usually pretty cool and intellectually distanced about pain. Yet Finnegan describes a prostituted girl covered with "knife scars and cigarette burns." He says the stories of the girls are ones of "desperation, violence, betrayal." If the girls are ever rescued, they "seem broken. Beatings, rape, and torture are common forms of labor control among pimps."

The majority of prostituted beings around the world undergo some form of violence and humiliation. For the academics who study these girls to actually give the impression that the profession usually involves 'choice' is false. It rarely does so. And who would chose a profession where beating and sexual violence are a possibility, even if not an everyday occurrence.

I'd like to use myself as an example again. Once I entered prostitution, I simply assumed that there was no way out. It was so damaging that I didn't have any will or commonsense or intellect or brain left—to fight it or to make other decisions for myself. I had no way of seeking help from others since I was such an outcast, due to my prostitute status. And, although not burned with cigarettes, I did once face a client who threatened to burn my nipples with a cigarette lighter if I didn't do what he wanted. I only faced two acts of violence the whole time I was in prostitution. This cigarette lighter incident was one of them. (The other was an anal rape.) No one hit me. No one slammed my head against a dashboard. I was not broken and controlled by a pimp. I could leave my apartment at any time I wanted, unlike the trafficked girls who are under constant surveillance lest they try to escape. (Never mind that I rarely did leave my apartment due to agoraphobia and a fear of leaving enclosed spaces that troubles me to this day.) I worked as a prostitute under optimal circumstances—compared to most of those poor wretches out there in the sex industry. But even those two acts of violence were too much. I am still haunted by them. If I had been beaten and burned and anally raped everyday, I would not have survived even a week or two.

The sociologists at that quiet safe academic gathering bring up the idea that to object to the sex industry in Nevada is reactionary in someway—it "recalls a time when pornography was widely seen as exploitative and dangerous. That was before it became accepted that some adult starlets had chosen their path and enjoyed it..."

The parallel between porn and prostitution is striking, but not in the way these sociologists think. The few porn stars who have made it big are not at all representative of the industry. Even ones who have prospered, like Belladonna, often tell of horrific experiences. Her first porn shoot was gang rape by a dozen men and she was torn up badly. Jenna Jameson herself criticizes the direction porn has taken—the desire to stuff the woman's orifices to breaking point. It is a shock to a woman's senses—and her sensibility—to watch current-day porn and see another woman stretched to ultimate pain by two penises in her vagina and two in her rectum. Many standard practices in mainstream porn are dangerous and degrading to all of us—like the idea that sex is simply the endless pounding of the penis into the female body—with little foreplay or human interaction. I am not prudish. I am not anti-sex. I love porn that has foreplay and tenderness and sensual dimensions and imagination. But, as with 'voluntary' prostitution, non-exploitative porn is very rare. Just the heavy emphasis on 'anal' in mainstream porn degrades and damages us all. There is a big myth out there, promoted by porn, that we women 'like it.' Take a poll, folks. See how many girls like anal. Then look at the way 'trafficked' girls, who have no choice, are torn up by anal. Anal popularized by porn. (I can't get my wife or girlfriend to do it, so I'll go buy a trafficked girl and force it on her.) And then tell me porn 'liberates' women in any way.

Only a sex industry that never hurts and degrades anyone will work. You cannot have a few pampered women who have by some miracle bypassed the usual enslaving conditions of prostitution and set them forth as the 'norm,' when the majority live in great misery. Even one woman enslaved destroys the freedom and dignity of us all.

Goldman ends her article by saying that these sociologists want to "study" the girls, not "save them." I don't think it is morally possible to study "suffering" without helping those who suffer.

It is interesting that the photo that accompanies this article has, in the foreground, a page from the Las Vegas yellow pages open to the section called "Entertainers." This particular page advertises "Barely Legal Teens"—pointing to yet another dangerous trend in pornography—the eroticizing and 'commodification' of children. (For my purposes, a teen is a 'child' as far as sex goes. I am quite old-fashioned in this respect—teenage girls are too young for sex. They have not figured out their bodies and emotions enough to engage in this incredibly important and beautiful act. Not only no sale of teens [children] in my world of kind and non-exploitative sex, but no sex for any girl until she's in her 20's.)

In the photo, behind the page open in the phone book, sits Chong Kim, an ex-prostitute who spoke on a panel in Las Vegas hosted by Farley. Ms. Kim was trafficked into Las Vegas, imprisoned in a storage locker, raped up to 50 times a day, and had her arm damaged so badly by her pimp that she is partially crippled.

Not a great photo to accompany an article on prostitution as a 'choice.'

The next article is by Henry Brean and is called "Love for Sale 101: Brothel Tour Part of College's U.S. Culture Curriculum" (*Las Vegas Review-Journal*, 11 April 2008).

Love for Sale 101? Hum.

This one details a group of women students from ivy-league Randolph College in back-east Virginia who visit the Chicken Ranch Brothel. (I wish that journalists would be more accurate. "Rape for Sale at a Battery Fuck Factory" reflects what is really going on.) The photo accompanying it shows one of the wholesome college girls in the brothel room of a prostitute. This poor prostitute looks like a sad caricature of extreme sexual degradation. She has a huge artificial bosom, cleavage like the Grand Canyon, stale dead blonde hair, and heavy heavy heavy make up–all the whore paint trimmings she must dress up in to survive and hide herself from her deeper self. And to 'distinguish' her from the 'decent' women around her. The badge of dishonor—the heavily painted whore must look like a whore. If, as the sociologists imply, this is such a benign and non-exploitative institution, why must the prostitute look this way—cheap and sad and degraded. If you want to bring the sex industry into the realm of the safe and respected and the acceptable, then the woman should not be a composite of layered artificiality. She should look wholesome and sweet, if prostitution is so good for her as a career. This poor creature is in the requisite high high heels and her dress is practically up to her pussy. Sad. Cheap and sad and depressing. What we, the human, race, have turned women into and labeled "for sale." And in this same photo, this college girl is observing her surroundings. This "field trip" to the rape ranch, to the "sex battery farm," disguised as an outing to study 'culture.'

Studying rape culture and doing nothing about it. Making the simplicity of 'prostitution-rape' 'complex' by studying it and denying that a brothel is a rape prison.

I wonder if these ivy-league students know that the prostitutes are not allowed to sit in local restaurants during certain hours for fear their presence will contaminate the local schoolchildren. I wonder if these students see the double-standard contradictions involved here: the customers, all respectable fathers and sons and brothers, can visit the brothel to unload, but the women they unload into are too dirty to be in the presence of 'normal' society?

Eleven women students were given a PR job by a spokesperson and by two prostitutes who talked to them. Were the prostitutes 'coached,' as in HBO's *Cathouse*? How can we know? The brothel PR machine shows the public what it wants them to see.

Then the students left with plastic bag of souvenirs. All of this is presented as if it were harmless, just fine, and the author of the article calls the two prostitutes who were interviewed by that ugly misnomer 'working girls.'

On occasion a truth slips through. One prostitute says it "'takes courage' to stand in a line-up and take a customer back to a room to negotiate a price."

Nothing as degrading as the 'line-up' was ever forced upon me during my time in prostitution. I could not have done it if I had been trapped in that grotesque imitation of 'independence' called the line-up. If the woman is truly an 'independent contractor,' the smokescreen phrase for every brothel inhabitant—trafficked or pimped, or not—then there would be no line-up. There can be no freedom or choice in the life of the 'independent contractor' if she has to face a line-up where any sleaze can pick her off the auction block. This used to be called 'slavery' when whites did it to blacks—and it was as sanctioned and acceptable as the slavery of the brothel is now. 'Decent' women in their go-to-market finery would pass indifferently by the slaves in their shackles, just as these ivy-league college girls visit the rape factory without even recognizing what it is. It is a place where a women stands, displayed, in the cheapest, saddest way while a man she has never seen picks her to go back into a room, where she has to let him inside her body. No customer choice. This means no independence and no freedom and no dignity. I had customer choice. I could say no. I would not have lasted a day in prostitution if I had been put on an auction block. Did not the Randolph college girls see anything wrong with this auction block?

If the prostitute has been put in the brothel by her pimp, then she doesn't even get the money for this degradation.

I wish these girls had spoken to the local investigative reporter who has interviewed about 80 prostituted girls in his career and he says that almost all of them seemed damaged. I wish they had talked to Eve Pouinard, an ex-prostitute who helps run a johns' program for Metro. She uses the same word the investigative reporter does: she says prostitutes are 'damaged' women.

The author of the article, Brean, writes that the "field trip was downright scholarly, touching on psychology, commerce and feminism." Feminism? He quotes a student asking if "legal prostitution is a feminist industry?" What? How? Who? I don't quite know how to express the outrage this question stirs in me. This student has obviously not read any literature about what happens when prostitution is 'legalized'—trafficking skyrockets. Of the 400,000 prostitutes in Germany, the majority are trafficked. Over one million German men per day visit these enslaved girls, not to mention the sex tourists and U.S. military members that use them. Nevada brothels are advertised on the internet, and German tourists come here and rape our prostitutes after they have raped their own.

Another student says that before this trip she did not have an opinion on prostitution. No opinion on it? The most important aspect of female liberation in the world—the fact that no female liberation is possible without the eradication of prostitution as we know it—in its current horrifying form—and this supposedly educated young woman has no opinion on it? (I can see why WHISPER, an organization in New York that helps prostitutes, says that prostitution will be the last bastion feminism will have to face and dismantle—it is that difficult to get 'feminists' to see the harm it does.) The student then says "it's hard to condemn the industry after seeing it in person." What was she condemning? The women in it—for letting themselves be raped everyday? And what has she seen? Nothing—but the outside. Nothing but a slick PR job.

The trip was organized by the college's "experiential learning coordinator." I guess that everyone at the college can now congratulate themselves that the students have seen the rape animals in their cages, have pretended it is not rape–per their 'cultural experiential' expectations–and have gone back to their café lattes and cups of tea at their ivy-league ivory tower without a clue. Gone back 'culturally enriched' by rape.

Brean writes: "One of the four faculty members on the trip said the students will discuss what they observed at the brothel and write about the experience in journals they are assigned to keep."

Now, isn't that nice. All tidy and neat and orderly. It's a shame they're not taking notes on where the average prostitute in America comes from: she typically enters the 'profession' at age 14 and is broken into her new whore status by a pimp. She is terrified to raise her eyes to him for fear he will 'discipline' her through violence and psychological terror. She is terrified that she will not bring home her fuck-quota money from a night spent on her back as disgusting beer-sweat truckers screw her at the stops in Arizona and California where the men pick up their fresh young whore-meat fix for the night. (The students also need to take notes on the 'stats' that relate to sex at too young an age for the female body: increased cervical cancer rates, for one—and the pain is terrible since young girls' vaginal tissues are thin and not ready for intercourse yet.)

It is not unlikely that this grim picture is the background of many of the prostitutes in the rape factory that these ivy-league girls visited, that they have so comfortably and safely observed as part of "experiential learning 101."

The only way to learn about this is to put your body in the brothel bed. Rape 101. Then I bet these college girls won't be so sanguine and distanced. And they will be too busy surviving rape to take any notes or write any term papers.

About the brothel trip, one of the accompanying faculty members says, "The really important thing is for them to see how this works. You can read about it, but it's not the same as being here and seeing it face to face."

What have they seen? Nothing. They obviously have not read anything either. Those 400 books on prostitution that I read over the past two years build up an appalling picture that far exceeds any of the torture and pain I went through as a prostitute. They are available in all college libraries. This is no longer hidden information. The massive ignorance of college girls as to the suffering of their prostituted sisters must be deliberate.

Did these college girls ask themselves how these other girls got here—in this place called 'brothel'—rape space and playground for men? Did they ask if the girls were 'willing' to lie down and fuck men they did not know? This is a revolting thing to have to do. You have to be 'broken' in order to bear it. You have to be raped so much you are now numb to it.

The college girls did not seem to understand even a tiny tiny tiny ounce of the disgust of this act. They took a sanitized PR trip through a rape factory and came away with nothing. Except a bag of plastic souvenirs.

I think these girls need to look up the stats and the facts. Overall, prostitution is full of abused, raped, broken human beings. They are not happy campers, let alone happy hookers. The instances in which a woman might actually enter this so called profession on her own, eyes open, aware, happy and thrive in it, without any physical and psychological damage, are so rare that maybe they do not exist. Prostitution does not exist for the benefit of the prostitute. It exists for the benefit of the client who rapes her. And the owners who make money off her body.

I think part of my disgust at this article, and the women in it, was my imagining them 'studying' me. Are you going to put me in front of your fancy ivy-league classes and observe me, the rape-fucked whore with no dignity and no place in your safe, soft, protected world? It would repulse me to be interviewed by you. No one interviews me. I interview myself. No sociologist—or ivy-league college girl—better ever try to 'study' me. I am not a fuck-rape specimen for cool, academic observation. That would degrade me far more than the whore-rape I experienced.

Thirty years after leaving prostitution, I cannot be interviewed. To let you into the place where I have suffered inside would be impossible. I don't think any prostitute can really be interviewed. You have to keep what happened private, to protect at least one tiny spot inside.

My last sad, depressing article is from the *Las Vegas Weekly*, last Valentine's Day. The title: "Love at the Chicken Ranch: Visiting the Brothel on the Most Romantic Day of the Year." On the cover of this issue is a very slick photo of a young whore girl in those platform heels. She is naked and holding a teddy bear across the front of her body.

The authors Benjamen Purvis and Aaron Thompson go to "the Chicken Ranch for a day of…romance?"

"On the day dedicated to all things love, photojournalists Aaron Thompson and Benjamen Purvis hit the road to find at what life is like at Pahrump's world famous Chicken Ranch," says this jaunty, fun piece.

Basically, at this point I don't have too much to add. Just deep, deep depression at the 'gimmick' of this article: to hunt for romance at the least romantic site on the planet, a rape playground miscalled brothel, and to pretend it is all in good fun.

A couple of truths slip out, past the fun and jolliness. "It's difficult when you hide your life all the time," says one prostitute. And, when the journalists ask another prostitute if this is hard life, she responds: "If you're mentally strong, you'll be all right."

At that point, I cried.

(Note: "I found the phrase 'battery sex farm' in an article by UK journalist Janice Turner–"Brothels are Booming," *Times Online* 23 Feb. 2008.)

9

In the following article, **Sex Battery Cages,** I draw parallels between torture of animals and torture of humans. I mention the battery-cage hen several times. In case you don't know about her she is sad, miserable, fragile little creature. Of all the animals that humans torture, she especially touches my heart since she is so small and defenseless.

She is the source of all those supermarket eggs labeled 'farm fresh.' *Silent Suffering* on the Mercy for Animals website is one of the best videos on her. Her life is hell from the moment she leaves her shell.

As soon as she hatches from her egg, there is no mother hen in sight to shelter her. Instead, along with thousands of peeping others, she is 'sorted' on a conveyor belt by rubber-gloved factory workers. Her male counterparts--useless to the egg industry, and not genetically enhanced to be 'broilers,' the chickens humans eat—these tiny peeping fluffy males are either shoved into plastic bags to suffocate or put into meat grinders.

The tiny peeping fluffy female next goes to the de-beaker. When she is just a few hours old, and should be snug under a mother's wing, she has the tip of her beak sliced off by a red-hot blade—so that she will not peck her fellow prisoners to death when it comes time for her permanent confinement in a battery cage, where she will reside for her whole life crammed in with several others in a space too small for her to even spread her wings.

In the videos of this de-beaking, the chick's little eyes look bewildered with the pain. Severed nerve endings in that area keep her in constant pain for the rest of her short life.

Other kinds of pain vie with the hot misery in her mutilated beak. On the Mercy for Animals website, we see undercover footage taken of a typical battery-cage warehouse. A worker is stomping and stomping on a struggling bird who has escaped her cage until he kicks her into the manure pit beneath the cages. Another worker takes a near-dead bird and spins her violently around to break her neck. When he can't do that, he throws her, hard, against a wall. We later see her still feebly kicking in her efforts to die.

Even one bird treated like this is too much, let alone the millions of laying hens whose suffering is commonplace.

When it comes time for new hens to be 'inserted' into their cages, where they will 'live' with 7 or 8 other birds in a space the size of newspaper, the workers simply shove and stuff them in as if they were insensate things—the process is "forceful and violent," says MFA. In the videos, the noise of the suffering hens screaming and crying is a constant background.

The hens spend one to two years in this battery cage, which is about ten rungs below the hell of a concentration camp. The MFA footage is without mercy. We see insanity, birds driven crazy, sick and dying birds, ones with no feathers and bloody patches from rubbing on the wire of the cages, ones with deformed bleeding feet from standing on wire constantly (no soft mercy of bedding for these disposable little girls). The eyes of the birds are hopeless, dead, and dazed with pain. We see one little de-beaked girl with a horribly prolapsed uterus from being forced to lay such an abnormally large number of eggs.

"Not one single time did I see any vet," says the MFA worker who went undercover to get this footage. If the hens manage to escape, they are too weak and injured to stand—having broken wings and legs. They are just left in the aisles to kick and die slowly, unless a worker comes along and uses the animal as a football for fun.

Maybe most pitiful and grotesque of all are the eye injuries: lacerated corneas from the manure fumes--helpless attempts to rub their eyes with their wings in the small space--huge swollen sores and abscesses around their eyeballs.

'Spent' hens, those too worn out to lay any more, are yanked out of their cages roughly, sometimes breaking legs and wings in the process, and thrown into metal bins as if they had no more feelings than pillows. These 'lowest' of birds with tough stringy meat go into baby food and chicken noodle soup. If you have ever wondered why the chicken in that bowl of 'comforting' soup is like a piece of dead matting, that's why.

I have often wondered if maybe these hens end up as whatever is processed into those breaded squares in the McDonald's Happy Meal?

All of this torture is the norm—just like those downed cows being electric shocked in their ears on the mainstream news were the norm. 'Banality of evil' run rampant.

(Material courtesy of the Mercy for Animals website.)

Sex Battery Cages

May 2006

I see a strong link between our treatment of animals and the way we also enslave people. The intensive confinement of 'food' animals and forcing women and girls into prostitution seem to involve similar levels of brutality and degradation.

It is all the same picture, when we torture something helpless, whether it be an animal or a human. The factory farming of bodies is one similarity: the way girls are confined to brothels and their movement restricted. In the worst scenarios, they are never allowed outside, and their lives consist of the hopelessness of constant, serial rape by customers. They have one reason for being: to sexually serve men so other men can make money off their bodies. I don't know what kind of hopelessness a battery-cage hen feels, confined for her one purpose, but it must be similar. Pigs raised for food on our intensive-confinement hog farms also suffer greatly. Imprisoned in spaces so small they can barely move, the poor creatures go insane.

Cheapness. Another similarity. The girl in the wooden-shack brothel in Cambodia offered for $2 a lay. One Vietnam vet I talked to said that a guy in that country never wanted "to pay more for a fuck than he did for a pack of cigarettes." It was just "cheap gook pussy and not worth any more than that." That 99 cent burger at McDonald's, which came from the cow that may have been dismembered while still alive, since the kill line goes so fast. Assembly-line sex goes along at a brisk pace, also. The end result is the same: 'Cheap meat' in both instances.

'Cheap meat' is the operative word. Assembly-line sex is one of the staples of sexual exploitation. The Romans practiced it: soldiers in Britain raped prostituted women until they bled to death. The Korean Comfort Women, teenage girls, virgins before their ordeal, were forced to service 30-50 Japanese soldiers a day.

Our soldiers behaved no differently. Destitute 'Occupation Comfort Girls' in Tokyo were forced to sexually served anywhere from 15 to 60 American soldiers a day in brothels set up for our troops after WWII. The physical torture of the girls' bodies was disguised as a financial transaction. The conditions in the brothels were so unendurable that some of the girls committed suicide. (Sources: Historians John Dower, Yuki Tanaka, and George Hicks.)

The pathetic girls in the tent-whore brothels of Vietnam withstood man after man, for very little money. 'Cheap fuck meat' was the attitude of the soldiers.

Recently, I saw an ad for an escort service which calls itself The Meat Market, offering one girl for 39 dollars, two for 60, etc.

Brothels in Paris where turnover is especially high—women sometimes servicing as many as 160 men a day, each, according to Kathleen Barry (*Female Sexual Slavery*)—are called *abattoirs*, slaughterhouses.

As with the sale of bodies as flesh for sex, so is it with the sale of animals for our food: torture disguised as a financial transaction.

Incredible physical pain is another similarity. It needs to be described by someone, what all this feels like. No media coverage seems to be devoted to the sheer fact of physical pain. When I was in my twenties, I was gang raped by men who had raped in Vietnam . It went on for hours, and they tore me up badly. After this attack, I couldn't leave the house for several months, and the whole world seemed terrifying—a heavy, harsh place controlled by male violence. Eventually, I ended up in prostitution, near a military base, for a time, because I felt I was a piece of public garbage, fit only for more rape by men.

Serial penetration by many men is not a mild form of torture. Just the tears at the vaginal opening feel like fire applied to a cut. Your genitals swell and bruise. Damage to the womb and other internal organs can also be tremendous. Physical pain is not a minor matter. How do we imagine what the battery hen with her depleted, fragile bones and her uterus falling out of her body due the massively unnatural egg producing she is subjected to, feels? She must be in pain all the time.

Degradation. The 'rape rack,' as it is jokingly called in animal husbandry. Animals defined as 'for human use' are allowed no dignity. Neither is the prostitute, defined as 'for male use.' She must withstand the disgust of being forced to allow strangers to invade that most private part of herself. Signs around Saigon during the Vietnam War read "Car Wash and Fuck"—indicative of the contempt that a woman's body can be held in, reduced to. Her 'cheap gook pussy' was of no more import than getting your car hosed down. (Source: My conversations with Vietnam vets.)

The killing of the spirit. The 'learned helplessness.' The Korean Comfort Women said that the Japanese soldiers who continually raped and beat them, sometimes for years on end, took away their girlhood, their womanhood, their lives. What must it be like—to wake up knowing that the only thing you have to look forward to is sexual pain and abuse of your body? What does the battery-cage hen, in her tortured state, wake up to, since she's gone insane from confinement?

Ignorance—as to why they are being tortured in this way. Does the battery hen know why this is being done to her? Does some invisible, phantom part of her spirit know that there is sky outside—even though she's never been allowed out of her cage? Since the Korean Comfort 'Women' were mostly 'girls,' teenage virgins completely ignorant of sex and men, when they were first raped, sometimes for hours, during their 'initiation' sessions, to 'break them in,' did they ever figure out why this painful, violent act was being inflicted on their bodies?

The hurting of the weak. A battery-cage hen is so fragile, with those thin bones of hers, so breakable since the demands on her body have depleted them of calcium. Or the way just-born chicks are sorted by sex: females heading toward the battery cage, males disposed of through suffocation or meat grinders since they're useless to the egg industry. It's because they're small and helpless that they can be so hurt. I didn't stand a chance against a group of men climbing on top of me. Even one could have hurt me so easily with his male strength.

Shame, another connection. Karen Davis, of United Poultry Concerns, says that it's difficult to look at the hens in such pain in the battery cages since suffering is essentially a private thing. I know from my own experience that being used as a public dumping ground by those men left me with deep shame that I still feel in the pit of my stomach—it's like a hard, heavy, sick feeling that never entirely goes away. They saw not just my completely helpless, naked body, but they heard me beg, and cry. They reduced me to something low and disgusting that suffered miserably in front of them.

Even years later, it has taken tremendous courage for me to put these words on the page, so deep is the cultural shame imposed on me for having a 'filthy,' i.e., raped body. There is a Jacobean play in which two girls are mass raped by an army. Their uncle blames them and says, "You should have kept your legs together." Great advice—except that so many men are forcing them apart. It has also taken me so long to speak because of fear—that I will be raped again, for breaking my silence.

My last connection: compassion, and the compelling need to feel ashamed that one feels it for the animals and the prostitutes—after all, they're just animals, aren't they?

I read of an experiment where male mice were hyped up on a drug so that they would rape female mice. It was a *Newsweek* article, which coolly reported that the males raped the screaming females for hours—while distanced scientists (some of them women) looked on. Maybe the 60 American soldiers queued up to use that prostituted Japanese body regarded their 'rape' task with the same dispassionate and impersonal calm—in between the dirty jokes they must have made, to pass the time, in that long line. Maybe my rapists felt nothing for my pain.

I never have any solutions for pain. I like to watch pigeons. They are small and humble and seem to go about their business, hurting no one. I give my pain to the mountains where I live. I figure they're big enough to absorb it.

(Note: "I found the phrase 'battery sex farm' in an article by UK journalist Janice Turner–"Brothels are Booming," *Times* Online, 23 Feb. 2008 and it suggested to me the title for this article two years after I wrote it. The original title was "Affinity." I don't know if 'battery sex farm' is a common term in the UK. I know that I recently heard a European woman refer to brothels with trafficked inmates as 'sex farms.')

10

In 2006, five murdered prostitutes in England drew heavy response in the British Press. I wrote the following after reading a lot of British journalists on the topic at *Times Online*.

Are Prostitutes Human?

January 3, 2007

The recent murder of five prostitutes in Ipswich, a small port town in England, prompted varying responses in the British press. As I followed these articles, I became increasingly annoyed. As an ex-prostitute, I found myself resenting all these journalists making easy, specious pronouncements upon a subject they know nothing about. A 'popular' view, supposedly liberal and open-minded, on their part, was the advocating of legal brothels to 'protect' the women. As I read their views on this topic, I grew from being merely annoyed to deeply offended and angry. Alice Miles, *Times* journalist, is all for these establishments in her "How We Let Gemma and Tania Down" (Dec. 13, 2006). "Brothels: proper, clean, large-as-you-like, licensed knocking shops, with medical checks and protection for the girls" is what Ms. Miles proposes. What she fails to consider is that legalizing prostitution makes it easier for procurers and pimps and customers to exploit women. Look at Germany and Holland, where sexual trafficking is massive and the few 'independent' prostitutes (those who actually benefit from the health care and protection) are extremely rare.

It is the same situation in the legal Nevada brothels in the USA: girls are trafficked in by their pimps, who take the money. Ms. Miles envisions 'clean' safe brothels but I'm afraid that these only exist in some fairyland somewhere where men don't control the actions and lives of the prostitutes. Such places don't stand a chance on this patriarchy of a planet.

It would be nice if they did: establishments controlled entirely by the women, places where they have complete say as to working conditions, number of customers, etc. Places where no men make money off their bodies: take all the owners and procurers and pimps and drop their greedy deadweight off a huge cliff and then let women define how brothels should operate. They would not resemble, for example, the current ones in Nevada, with their degrading meat-market line-ups. They would not resemble the ones, worldwide, full of trafficked girls fighting to survive the brutality of beatings and terror tactics to keep them compliant and performing so as to bring in the money for their 'owners.' They certainly would bear no resemblance to the flesh markets with enslaved youngsters in them, practically babies, that are standard fare in Thailand, India, Cambodia, etc. With 60% of the world's prostitutes being minors, brothels are places where millions of girls who are mere children are gang raped everyday—by local men, by sex tourists, by the world's militaries, and by UN Peacekeepers ('Rape-Bringers,' I call them) who significantly fuel the sex trade wherever they go since troubled, war-torn places and conflict zones create destitute, vulnerable girls.

The entire sex industry, globally, would be quite different if we prostitutes completely controlled it and no men made money off of us.

What does Ms. Miles mean by a 'proper' brothel, I wonder? And in what way does this sort of 'sex-for-sale zone' protect the women who work there? What does Ms. Miles mean by 'protect.' She only mentions 'medical checks.' I'd like to inform Ms. Miles that the sort of protection women really need—the psychological protection from sex without tenderness or love--is not available in a brothel.

In Germany, 'legalizing' means that abomination they call a 'drive-thru brothel' in Cologne. I shudder when I think of a 'fast-food' sex establishment—yet another meat-market endeavor, this time woman reduced to a 99-cent burger on the menu.

Another *Times* woman journalist, Minette Marrin, also advocates legal brothels ("Now End the Hypocrisy on Prostitution," Dec. 17, 2006). Doesn't she even consider, for a moment, that these places promote the cruelest of double standards: women regarded as 'flesh/meat,' roped off in a 'sanctioned' space, where men are licensed to rape them. (Prostitution is a particularly dreadful form of rape, by the way, Ms. Marrin. Any time the man's pleasure matters and the woman's is negligible, we have rape.) The entire idea of a place that contains bodies solely there for male pleasure, while the woman is merely a sex-deposit site, strengthens the notion that men are the entitled and dominant ones, while we women are there to serve them. Why would these otherwise sensible women journalists want to continue to rope off this space, called 'brothel,' that enslaves our bodies? That space, called brothel, has been hurting your sisters for centuries, ladies. Why are you promoting the rape of your sisters? Serve up one woman, this way, put her on the menu as sex meat, and you degrade all of us. I think these women journalists need to work in a brothel for a while—just a few nights will do, to totally break their bodies and spirits and give them the true perspective on these rape prisons.

Some of the articles touched on the linguistic dilemma of what do we call these 'lost' women outside the domain of society, and presumably, therefore, outside the domain of language. Calling them 'prostitutes' demeans them, writers like Matthew Parris claim ("They Were Women, Weren't They," *Times,* Dec.14, 2006). I definitely have my views on this issue: as an ex-prostitute I am fine with being called a 'prostituted' woman since the sex I endured was forced upon me and felt like a form of rape. But I detest the phrase 'sex worker' since violation of a woman's most intimate, vulnerable self, in the paid rape that we call 'prostitution,' is not work like any other. It is ludicrous and cruel, for example, to call the four-year-old girl, sold to a Bombay brothel, and painted up like a tiny harlot, a 'sex worker.' Does she have a 401K retirement plan, and a job as a Starbuck's barista all lined up for her, after she finishes her fun stint as a 'sex worker'? I freely call myself a 'whore,' in an effort to diffuse the male imposed stigma of 'slut,' shame, etc. which clings to the word. I also call myself a whore to distinguish myself from all the non-whore women out there who would label me a 'sex worker' and who do not have the remotest notion of the ineradicable damage that selling the body inflicts on a woman.

I realize that the 'w' word causes some strong reactions in non-whore women. That's good. It makes them acknowledge our presence, and what we are there for—to be used and degraded by men. 'Whore'=degraded, raped, rented genital space, a woman reduced to vagina and its function (place for male to take his pleasure) and our humanity matters not at all. I call myself a 'whore' because I felt like all of the above (degraded, raped, rented genital space) when I sold my body. If 'whore' makes non-whore women uncomfortable, it should. But at least it might set them to thinking: what does the existence of whores mean for the rest of the women on the planet? If a man can buy the body of the girl labeled 'slut,' the 'bad' girl who can be subjected to unfeeling sexual use, then he can also mistreat 'good' girls. He does not become a gentleman when he switches bodies.

I also like the word 'whore' because I make it my own when I use it. I take away the power to degrade that its very presences has inflicted on us women for so long.

There was yet another *Times* article ("How the Dutch Protect Their Prostitutes," Patrick Jackson, Dec. 14, 2006) that set up the 'legal' system in that country as a shining model of cosy whoredom. This piece puts forth a 'cosy' picture of 'cosy' car parks with 'cosy' counselors, and 'cosy' cups of coffee and 'cosy' showers for the whore bodies, in between sessions of being climbed on by men they don't know (or having to take the sex organs of men they don't know into their mouths—a particularly raw and disgusting act). Articles like this one, which make the car parks sound so 'cosy,' depress and sadden me because they do not tell the full story. Some of those girls in the Amsterdam car parks are servicing up to a hundred men a night—with devastating impacts upon their bodies and emotions. If I were to go back into whoring (a scenario I devoutly hope I will never have to face), the last places I would want to be are the countries where prostitution is legal because here transnational gangs and mafias and traffickers control a massive trade in enslaved bodies. It would terrify me, knowing the traffickers could get hold of me, too.

Sweden is, I think, the only place that would not terrify me. There they have decriminalized prostitution for the girls and criminalized it for the johns. This law extends to their military abroad as well, since they are now arresting Swedish servicemen who buy women in foreign countries. I do not know if this has also been applied to the sex tourist arena since Scandinavian men, like many others from around the world, take advantage of the young girls available in Thailand. Sweden's policy has had a marked affect on reducing trafficking into that country.

I was glad to see one woman writer in the *Times*, Helen Rumbelow ("Who Buys These girls? It Could Be the John in Your Life," Dec. 18, 2006) pay attention to those to blame for all this ravaging and selling of the body: the customers themselves. She pointed out that johns are pretty much everyone.

How many men buy bodies? The figures vary. In countries like India, where it is the 'norm' for young men to lose their virginity on top of a prostituted body, numbers may be as high as 80%. In Cambodia, the same, since local men regard a night out together as a collective visit to the brothel: according to the men, it is no big deal. Buying a body is like buying a bag of potato chips (or fish chips, or peanuts). In America, perhaps 6% of men buy bodies. In Europe, it varies by country from 5% to 20%. Roughly 12% of men, worldwide, buy bodies? I don't know how accurate any of these numbers are: they are scattered gleanings from various sources across the internet. But anyway you look at it, the money being generated by the sex industry, globally, is massive. So that's millions and millions of girls forced onto their backs. That's millions upon millions of rapists out there, doing the buying.

I can say from personal experience that Ms. Rumbelow is on the right track: customers are ordinary men—brothers and fathers and sons and husbands. Ordinary men bought me. I sold myself near a military base after soldiers gang raped me; I thought I was a piece of public garbage, fit only for more rape by men. My gang 'rapists' were just ordinary soldiers; so were all the men who bought me, my 'other' rapists, as I call them. (Prostitution is a particularly miserable form of rape. I keep repeating this in hopes someone may understand this someday.) Enlisted men bought me; so did officers. Some were cruel and rough and treated me like a disposable piece of rented genital space. Other men were kind. Some were curious: why are you doing this for money? Some guys were lonely and had girlfriends elsewhere and didn't want to 'cheat' on them with another girl while they were in the military. But they needed sex. So they rented a whore body. A lot of the officers were married. Bored with their wives, wanting diversion. Some men wanted to talk. Some just wanted to get in there and drill the hell out of me to get their money's worth. Some guys had no interest in anything I felt or thought; I was just a piece of meat to be used for quick sex. Others were actually thoughtful and considerate, and the experience resembled a 'date' despite the impersonal anonymity of the sex. My point: all kinds of men buy bodies.

In yet another piece, Yasmin Alibhai-Brown in *The Independent* ("Where Are the Men in This Horrific Story," Dec. 18, 2006) astutely says of the Ipswich murders: "It isn't just the killer who is invisible; so are the male pimps and the customers....As with drug addiction, suppliers are the focus of public and police attention, not the consumers, without whom there would be no trade and destruction."

"Dismantling demand" is the phrase some activists are now using in order to focus attention on a good, old-fashioned fact: male attitudes (we can buy bodies, it is what we do, as men) are largely responsible for the sex trade.

Ms. Alibhai-Brown also mentions that the few women in the trade who actually make a great deal and are doing what they like are in the minority. She calls the johns "purchasers of loveless sex." She focuses, as I do, on how, overall "this profession demeans and endangers young girls." And she brings up the hard-to-argue with fact: "trafficked women—big business now—have no protection at all."

Except for briefly touching upon the subject, there was, elsewhere, inevitably, little coverage of the johns, the ones actually fueling the industry by raping the bought bodies. It seems evident that they both create the misery and keep it going--and it is no wonder: men are the ones who benefit from a world where they have easy access, with no emotional consequences or responsibilities, to young, vulnerable female bodies. The consequences for the girls who are being raped are enormous. They bear the stigma of being sexual filth while, for the male, use of a bought body increases his manliness and heightens his prestige with his buddies, the men he makes his collective visits to the brothels with (as is particularly the case in military society).

Many years ago, I talked to a military chaplain who said that he feared for the morals and wholesomeness of his boys when they were faced with the temptation of all these 'bad' girls in foreign ports. Why, I asked, was it the fault of the girls? His answer: man must follow his penis. It's how he's made. (KPIP?)

I would ask is not the male responsible for his sexual choices and the consequences of his sex drive? Perhaps the soldier, as male, and all other males as well, need to be more 'moral' and not less when faced with girls who resort to prostitution because alternatives are limited. Perhaps the ones in the military need to spend their shore leave exploring how the girl got into this way of life and searching for ways to help her out of it, rather than satisfying themselves at her expense. After all, these men can always resort to manual stimulation—and give her the money without making her have sex for it. I always think my solutions are sensible and humane. I just wonder why men don't follow them. Probably because, as the chaplain said, man must follow his penis.

Men need to develop a conscience and some sexual imagination. They need to realize that it's just a few minutes of pleasure for them but it is a life sentence for the girl. Men need to realize that prostitution destroys girls in ways they never recover from.

Another article ("Out of Darkest Suffolk, Enlightenment," *The Times*, Dec. 15, 2006) by Ben MacIntyre contains an amazing revelation: that prostitutes are actually human beings. A humanity inside us, just like the heart that the bodies of decent women harbor, and maybe a brain, and the ability to express ourselves? How many centuries has it taken for this delayed reaction to receive a few lines of coverage in a newspaper? That the same heart beats in all of us women—whore and 'decent' one alike.

I find the anomaly that Mr. MacIntyre points out extremely interesting: that these murdered women are actually being regarded as human beings with lives and feelings rather than as disposable bodies, and as filth. During my time in prostitution, I was looked upon, by my crueler customers, as a dirty joke and a hole that a man poked himself into without regard for my pain. Even at my busiest, I only serviced about a dozen men a weekend. It felt like several hundred. Not all were mean. Most were, in fact, pretty decent. Despite this—limited numbers, half-way civilized johns--I always felt like a raped, shredded, fragile woman with a torn vagina and a lot of bruises from the weight of too many heavy bodies.

Because of my personal experiences, Mr. MacIntyre's own attitudes about prostitution are painful to me. He calls what we prostitutes do "a grimly ordinary trade." No, it is not 'ordinary,' the sale of the body. Widespread, yes, since so many men demand 'sexless sex' (my phrasing). But 'ordinary' in the sense that the lives of what we call 'decent,' non-prostitute women are 'ordinary,' no. 'Ordinary' is shopping for a treat for your dog, or having a peaceful latte with a friend, or enjoying the Christmas lights strung all over houses once a year. 'Ordinary' is far, far away from the sexual violence the prostituted body endures. When I was in prostitution, I couldn't enjoy Christmas, or even buying a cup of fancy coffee because I knew I was alienated from ordinary life. Christmas looked different. The Christmas lights didn't apply to me because I was walking around in a rape-battered body. A cup of fancy coffee at a Starbuck's was so normal and wholesome that I cried when I saw people sitting outside, sipping those comforting cups. Such comfort was not for me because I was not 'ordinary.' I was a raped body.

Even a soft day, one with a light breeze, and sunlight, when nature seems especially gentle, made me cry because life was not being gentle with my body. The air on my skin, soft and kind, was a sharp contrast to how it felt to be banged and bruised in order to satisfy men and their impersonal sex drives.

Mr MacIntyre writes that "Germany and the Netherlands do not share British anxieties about paid sex; both countries have regulated brothels—and levels of violence against prostitutes have dropped significantly." Now, where is this information coming from, I ask? Both countries are destinations for massive trafficking of women, girls, and children from Asia, South America, and Eastern Europe precisely because the 'legal' situation makes it almost impossible for the victims to receive any protection at all. And these trafficked girls comprise the majority of bodies being sold. I think it is all the male customers who don't have any 'anxieties' about paid sex. The prostitutes themselves, the girls whose bodies are being raped, these girls have plenty of anxiety--and misery.

Mr. MacIntyre suggests that society must 'make provision' for this 'activity' called prostitution (note the coolness of his phrasing—all distanced and polite and intellectual is he about 'making provision' for this 'activity,' as if prostitution were on a level with leaning how to bake brownies after school). Well, Mr. MacIntyre, due to the damage it does to a woman, there is really no way for 'society to make provision' for this 'activity,' as you so neutrally phrase it. The 'activity' is rape, of a particularly cruel sort. Men paid to rape me. I wonder how on earth, on in all the hells that this earth contains, Mr. MacIntyre could 'make provision' for rape of this kind, the lowest kind, serial rape, the kind a woman never recovers from. In one-time rape, it happens, then you heal. With the ongoing, massive battering and violation of the body that is prostitution, there is no time to heal because the body is raped over and over again.

Empathy on the part of men like Mr. MacIntyre might lead him to perhaps not so easily believe that society must 'make provision' for this sort of rape. Does he have a wife or daughter, any feminine vulnerable being who is dear to him? If so, would he like her body to be the one that is sacrificed, the body that is used to 'make provision' for this 'activity'?

I am particularly sensitive to language and the cruelties it implies. Mr. MacIntyre's cool, neutral phrasing is on a par with that of those academic women who write about prostitution and talk about 'reading the liminal space of the bartered body,' and all that sort of distanced nonsense. Women who do not have the remotest idea of the pain of that bartered body. I call these sorts of academicians 'vagina-less' women.

I call the refined *Times* women journalists who are in favor of legal brothels, vagina-less as well. I do not usually make a practice of attacking others in my prose; in a discussion, you attack the person's ideas, not the person. But I'm having a tough time refraining from ad feminem here because so many vagina-less women overrun journalism. They talk about 'sex workers,' thereby sanitizing the raw ugly reality of the raped vagina; they advocate 'legal' brothels without ever having had their own vaginas shredded in one of these places.

They write without passion and pain. They write 'objectively' in a way that degrades the pain of all of us who have suffered.

(The *Times* informs me that many of its columnists opining about the Ipswich prostitutes are 'award-winning' journalists. Actually I write as well as these people. I wonder why they are the ones making the money and earning the accolades.)

One day I want to meet the women who espouse legal brothels face to face. I want to sit down to a refined cup of tea with them, and a plate of scones with Devonshire clotted cream and raspberry jam. Over this civilized repast, I want to tell them that I was not a 'sex worker.' I was a 'whore,' and I am now rather proud of that designation since is distinguishes me from all the non-whore women out there who don't have the remotest idea of the unimaginable damage selling the body does to a woman.

To continue with the articles, there was of course a "Confessions of a Mad Call Girl" style piece. It was shallow. But out of it came a truth: that you are never safe when you sell yourself because you never know what cruelty or brutality a client who is a stranger (not a regular) may inflict on you.

The article, however, that I found most difficult to take was a tea-and-sympathy Christian piece by Libby Purves called "Once They Were Lost… How the Church Rediscovered Its Humanity in the Prostitute" (*Times,* Dec. 16, 2006).

The title says it all. The Church is the lost soul, cast out by its own brutal condemnation of the prostitute. Not to mention its own hypocrisy vis a vis these 'temptresses' and fallen women. The Church owned brothels during Elizabethan times. And those holy fellows in Rome, in centuries past, used to organized orgies where they hired dozens of prostitutes and had marathon sex sessions to see who could stay on the longest.

As one of those pieces of prostitute filth cast out by religion and society, I definitely think that dividing women up into 'pure virgins' and 'dirty whores' is certainly one of the more pernicious miseries Christianity has inflicted on us women. In the Middle Ages, under Church law, the scorned whore could not even bring a charge of rape against her attackers since she was regarded as 'public' property. Never mind that a common way to turn a virgin into a whore was to gang rape her and then declare her body too filthy for anything but whoredom. This time-honored tradition continues to this day—look at the numbers of prostitutes who have been subjected to previous sexual abuse—they are staggering. Rape her and then turn her into a prostitute so as to rape her even more in order to punish her for being raped in the first place, seems to be the way male logic works.

(I followed male logic myself, not knowing any better at the time. I entered prostitution after being gang raped because I had a really messed-up body and a messed-up mind and a messed-up life and I saw whoring as all I was fit for.)

A recent judge in America ruled that a whore could not be raped because her body was already so abused she couldn't tell the difference.

The only useful thing Mary Magdalene did was to be a whore, so the rest of us whores would have someone to look up to, but the Church stripped her of that honorable title in the 1980's.

I think we whores are better than non-whore women because we have endured the worst men can do to us. Instead of being scorned, we should be embraced and comforted.

Too little, too late from the Church, all this tea and sympathy. You have made our lives a torture for centuries. You treated us as disposable outcasts and scorned pariahs. You cannot erase this with a bit of tea and sympathy now.

The high-flown and pious and well-meaning but very limited views continue with "Red-light Reform? Sorry It's Not That Easy" by *Times* writer David Aaronovitch (Dec. 19, 2006). His article wanders quite a bit, so I can't pick up on a central point, but he does talk about women who 'chose' to become drug-addicted street prostitutes and how they are not going to set themselves up in "nice, comfy brothels." Instead he says that there are "already plenty of massage parlours and cheap flats they could use, if they could get together." His point here eluded me totally. So, I guess I'll pick up on his rhetoric, what I can hold onto in this slippery article. I'd just like to tell him that there is no such thing as a 'nice, comfy brothel,' as he so jovially and cruelly calls these sex prisons. A brothel is a place where a woman's body is gang-raped on a daily basis. Mr. Aronovitch also uses the term 'sex work.' I always have to respond, emotionally, to this phrase since the violation of my most intimate part was not 'work'—it was rape.

He refers to an "inner self," that mysterious realm inside which 'chooses' prostitution, if I am reading his meaning right. I'd have to say that I really don't think any woman's 'inner self' is going to choose sex with large numbers of drunk, rough, crude men (yes, many customers are like this—they think if a woman is a whore, they can be at their savage, ugly worst). Maybe Mr. A. needs to go out and whore, go out and get penetrated by a lot of men he doesn't know before he writes another cruel article like this one. I don't mind writers being misinformed; but I cry with sadness when they are cruel about our raped bodies. And prostitution raped the life out of more than my body; it killed my heart and soul. His words show he understands nothing of this.

In all of the coverage, I also found little mention of a salient fact of prostitution: although some women sell their bodies to support a drug habit, others take drugs, and drink, in order to bear the pain and degradation of the work.

I know that I wandered in this article as well, but I think that one clear point came through: You cannot create a 'safe' brothel. At least not safe for the women in any meaningful sense. As long as the male is the dominant one, the buyer, and the female the body bought for his pleasure, there is no such thing. A brothel is, pure and simple, a 'rape zone.'

A second major point I tried to make is that all of you non-prostitutes out there talking about us women who have sold sex, you people have to realize that the damage to us is massive. Prostitution was letting men pay to rape me. To this day, I have physical problems from overuse; my emotional problems will fill a book. That fabled "PTSD" which psychologists have discovered and popularized seems to exist in me in neverending layers of depression, sadness, pity, heaviness, sleeplessness, and terrible dreams. When I was in prostitution, getting out seemed impossible because my sense of self worth was non-existent. I was only fit for more rape by men. I have no solution as long as men will pay to do this terrible thing to us. Financial help, a few encouraging words, drug counseling won't do it. Sticking us in 'tolerance zones' won't do it. I think the main point of my missive (letter to a world that is slowly starting to care) is that we prostitutes are so damaged that psychological support for us will have to be extensive if you want to really help us out of our rape prisons. Maybe ongoing psychological care, over a period of many years, will help. I don't know. Maybe there is really no solution for this terrible rape called prostitution

One last point: In any discussion of prostitution, trafficking has to be at the forefront, since it is the major form. The majority of bought-and-sold bodies, worldwide, are trafficked. In this sense, there is currently little distinction between trafficking and most forms of prostitution. I was glad to see so many people writing about the Ipswich situation. Misguided as many of these writers are, at least they are now talking about prostitution in open and helpful ways. I would like to see the same coverage devoted to the trafficked. They are the real victims of this pathetic and brutal industry, far more so than the Ipswich women, or me—I did have 'choice,' in a limited way. The trafficked have no choice at all.

A recent book I find particularly enlightening is Italian writer Paola Monzini's *Sex Traffic.* It is short and concise, and not riddled with fancy academic jargon. From it, I take much of my knowledge about the pathetic lives of the trafficked in Europe. It lays out, in a stark way, how, to train them and break them, the girls are mass raped and beaten and burned and psychologically terrorized. Particularly disturbing is her description of how the Albanian mafia operates: a girl may be broken by one set of pimps, and then sold to another set of pimps, who break her again, to keep her completely passive. The Albanian mafia traffics girls into London. Amnesty International reports the case of one 14-year-old Albanian girl held in a London brothel who was forced to have sex 20 hours a day.

No one can argue that this, the most prevalent form of prostitution, amounts to sexual enslavement. Other London examples are equally appalling. Poppy, a London-based group trying to help the trafficked, reports that one woman who'd escaped her traffickers had been routinely used by 50-60 men a day in a Soho brothel. How her body is still alive is beyond me. My imagination cannot even extend to this level of sexual torture.

This sexual torture isn't just hidden and overlooked in London. This hidden activity is going on all over the world. In my own city, I know that two miles away from where I live, there is a network of massage parlours full of girls trafficked in from Asia and Eastern Europe. I look at the whole world differently, now that I know this underside of sexual cruelty runs side-by-side with 'ordinary' life.

I'll end with a suggestion for a solution. Don't put brothels and massage parlours and sex clubs in 'zones' or out-of-the way places. Those Nevada brothels, for example, are way out in the desert, not right in the middle of the Las Vegas Strip. Whether it be Las Vegas, or London, or New York, or small-town America, we should put brothels and massage parlours and sex clubs right beside schools and universities and shopping malls and churches, so we can see all the customers going in and out. 'Ordinary,' non-prostituted women could go in and talk to the girls, find out if they are trafficked, help them if they are. No more hiding away of the sex industry. Make it open and accessible so that all of us can see what is going on. Under the gaze of us all, most of the cruelty and exploitation would evaporate.

11

The Governor Spitzer/Kristen Sex Scandal offered me a chance to make a few points about prostitution from the prostitute's point of view.

A Prostitute's View of the Spitzer Sex Scandal

March 2008

As an ex-prostitute, I read with dismay the initial coverage of the Governor Spitzer sex scandal. "Romp with a high-priced call girl" was the racy way the press stated it. All the focus was on family values, betrayal of middle-class morality, apologies from him for not living up to his own high standards.

The focus should have been on the prostitute herself rather than all the narrow, prudish marriage-and-family garbage and the puritanical rhetoric attached to it. Maybe what was wrong was that he bought another human being.

Having opened my body to men I don't know, I am aware it is difficult, this intimacy with strangers–no matter if the sheets are silk, and the girl is fucking in a luxury suite at the Ritz. I wondered why no one asked about the welfare of the prostitute–instead of extending misplaced sympathy to the woeful, betrayed wife. Is this prostitute exploited by the ring that rents her out? Is she keeping the money or are they taking a hefty chunk? Who are these people? How do they recruit the girls? How do they treat them?

What do we know about "Kristen," the call girl he bought? In titillating terms she was initially described as a "petite brunette." That first description was about as relevant to what led her to selling herself as what she ate for breakfast.

What ran through my head were the usual questions I ask about a prostituted being: Did she come from the typical scenario that leads so many kids into the trade, one that ought to be familiar by now to anyone with a half a brain and half a heart. I quote from a *U.S. News & World Report* article ("Young Lives for Sale," 24 Oct. 2005) detailing the background of one young American whore: "She was raped repeatedly by her stepbrothers when she was 6 and 7, and she fell in with a pimp who convinced her to start prostituting herself when she was 13."

Runaways, very young, who fall into whoring as a way of finding love, acceptance, and survival, are the norm, not the exception in America. You don't have to go to Bangkok or Cambodia to find girls exploited by the sex industry. A thriving child prostitution business in Atlanta, Georgia sells ones as young as 11 and 12 and these girls (mostly black) report being raped up to 30 times a night.

It is often a grim picture, prostitution. Admittedly, not all prostituted girls have horrifying backgrounds but there seems to be a fair amount of previous abuse in many cases. A severe gang rape precipitated my entry into the business.

The image of the "high-priced call girl" as a pampered being can be misleading: we need to investigate the lives of these women in the Emperor's Club VIP (the ring that sells Kristen) and see what led them into prostitution. Now, from what I have read of Kristen's life, she seems to be somewhat in control. When told that Client 9 (the number id attached to the governor) would ask her to do some things that were unsafe, she said she could handle it. No one seems to have forced her into this-insofar as we can tell. What happens underground in the sex trade is a whole other picture. (There is the bigger issue of whether prostitution can ever be considered 'voluntary' in a culture that promotes the woman as bought sex object and the man, with power, as the dominant purchaser.)

I am fine with Governor Spitzer (or ex-Governor, as the case may be) buying a girl if he treats her well, as he seems to have done. Kristen says she liked him. And I am fine with this if the girl is not exploited in any way. This latter point is hard to determine since so much prostitution does just that. Many times girls profit little from the use of their bodies--it all goes to third parties: procurers, pimps, owners.

I am also fine with Spitzer buying a non-exploited girl if he finds this an acceptable way for his own daughters to make a living.

"There is no sliding scale in the exploitation of women," says Tania Bien-Aime, executive director of Equality Now, an organization that has fought against a sex tourism business in Queens, New York called Big Apple Oriental Tours. Actually, there is, Ms. Bien-Aime. A huge sliding scale. When I whored, I was not pimp-controlled and no one forced me, but the whole business of selling sex left me damaged in ways so numerous-physically and mentally-that I am still dealing with the repercussion thirty years later.

Despite my own difficulties, I would not even compare my life in prostitution, or that of Kristen, to the raped child whore in Atlanta. My relative freedom was the way I survived and made it out. No choice as to clients and a pimp beating and raping me if I failed to fulfill my own daily rape quota-this would have been unendurable for even one night. I would not be alive today. So there is a distinct 'sliding scale.'

Kristen is on top of things. She is not being serially raped in a brothel every night. She lives in a posh Manhattan apartment. She has choices if a client proposes unsafe sex. She is, hopefully, not being hit with the violence that brothel and street prostitution often bring. (We have no way of knowing.) Presumably, she is making money with her vagina-if Emperor's Club is not taking an unfair cut. $4000 for a sexual encounter would be about right-we women are worth it. She is 22, not 12. If this is how she wants to make a living, that is fine. Instead of prosecuting her for this, let us create an environment where it is safe for women like her (note, I say, women, not girls), and me, to prostitute ourselves. I am not proposing any inane notion of legalizing prostitution-this just makes it easier for someone else to sell the girls. No, we should both decriminalize and de-stigmatize the profession of selling the body for the women involved. No scorn attached to a lovely lady who wants to sell her sexual beauty. Just enormous respect and admiration for her. And protection from all sexual violence. And complete choice as to customers. And heavy prosecution and long, long jail sentences for any pimp, procurer, trafficker, owner-and for any client who hurts a prostitute. Only when the woman makes all the profits from her body, and can sell herself under completely safe and protected circumstances, will prostitution be acceptable to me.

I wonder why the federal government concentrates its efforts only on a glamorous prostitution ring like the Emperor's Club. I do think we need to find out if its girls are exploited and offer them ways to exit prostitution, if that is what they want to do. But, first, let's focus on that 'sliding scale' of prostitution. Let's remove all those 11-year-old whores in Atlanta from their rape beds and give them protective services and long-term therapy and care. And let's raid the truck stops in California and Arizona where 13-year-olds are pimped to grown men. Then we can tackle girls held in sex slavery for migrant farm workers. And all the pathetic street whores on drugs. And then we can concentrate on the sex trafficking of Asians and girls from other countries into massage-parlour brothels in New York and other big American cities.

Another sex scandal reported from the narrow puritanical prudish American viewpoint. Reporting that will never help the truly exploited escape prostitution.

12

The last few articles are my latest. I start with rape in the Congo and then continue on with the subject of military prostitution, adding some new material to areas introduced in other essays, like what is going on in Iraq and Korea. Then I move to some musings on female sexuality with the last piece, "The Magic Vagina."

The Padlocked Vagina

January 21, 2008

> Go where you are least welcome; it is where you are most needed.
>
> –Abigail Kelley Foster

Of the many rape zones on Rape Planet Earth, the Congo is currently the most savage. After gang raping women and girls, soldiers are piercing their labia and padlocking their vaginas shut. Hot plastic as well as sticks and bayonets are being inserted into the women. Six-month-old girls have been raped to death.

Gang rapes are so severe that many women are suffering from fistula (the tearing of the vaginal wall so that the contents of the colon and urine seep in). Unable to reach medical care, some women are dying of massive infections. Even if the women do reach a doctor, fistula is very hard to repair—few practitioners can do it.

To intensify the cruelty, soldiers are even shooting women in the vagina, destroying their systems so completely that numerous operations are necessary—and even then repair may not be possible.

Despite how horrifying all this seems, there is nothing new Under the Rape Sun. 'Fistula Rape,' I call it—needing to find my own vocabulary for a reality rarely written about. The Romans, at one time, inflicted it on women in wartime. The Japanese were masters at it—the soldiers own photos of Nanking show naked, dead Chinese women in the streets, objects like pitchforks shoved into them.

Nothing new, either, about "sexual terrorism," the use of women's bodies as battlefields for male cruelty, for political ends—we have seen it all before, in Bangladesh, Rwanda, Bosnia, Darfur. (And now in Iraq.)

Anderson Cooper, reporting on the 'fistula rapes' in the Congo on a recent *60 Minutes* (Jan. 13, 2008) asks why men do this? It is a huge question. As a gentle woman, I have no answer. Do you men hate us women so much that you have to destroy our vaginas and our wombs, the very source of life itself?

But this article is not really about fistula rape or the Congo or that huge question in the previous paragraph. It is about the Padlocked Vagina and about my place in this confusing world. I am what is called a 'dissident' voice. I am a woman who speaks against those who inflict sexual suffering (whether it be in the Congo or in Iraq). As such, I am, according to my government, a terrorist.

Previously, the American Congress labeled me one when they passed the Animal Enterprise Terrorism Act. It condemned me for speaking up for the other animals species we torture by the billions (in factory farms and in labs, for example). Now the "Thought Police" are promoting a Homegrown Terrorism Bill (H.R. 1955/S. 1959) that tells me my 'dissident' voice is a danger to my country.

My take on all this is hardly original: A democracy is strong precisely because of its dissident voices. All Americans should nod to me, in approval, or maybe even clap for me–with high rejoicing–that I speak up. I don't want my vagina to be padlocked next. It has been through enough.

To not sound too corny, as an American I cherish my rights. That first amendment is precious beyond gold and diamonds to me. (Never mind that I never buy gold and diamonds because of the exploitative way they are mined and marketed—it is the metaphor I am after here.) Being a woman of little courage, I tremble every time I exercise my first amendment right to be a dissident voice. But I am aware that I live in a country that, so far, has let me speak—loudly, dissidently—without imprisonment, torture, or execution.

When I saw a photo of a Congolese woman being held down, the most sensitive area of her body being pieced, it was like having cold water thrown on me. It was a wake-up call. I don't want to be that next padlocked vagina. I sit in comfort, in front of my computer. I am relatively safe—no immediate threats of physical violence, no one beating me up. Despite having known some severe sexual mistreatment in the past (like gang rape and being a 'dirty joke' to a lot of men since I sold sex, once, a long time ago), I realized, when I saw this picture, that at least I was not having my vagina padlocked. What a joy! To sit here, with the freedom to write–and an unpadlocked vagina, too! This is true happiness.

After I write this article, I can get up and take my dog for a walk. No bleeding, infected, padlocked vagina holding me back. Then I can come home, to a warm, safe room, out of the winter chill, and give Boromir (that's my dog's name) a treat and we can both sit by the fireplace—me with a (vegan) buttered English muffin and hot chocolate (vegan) by my side–and watch an old movie on TV. I can sip my cocoa and pet his big, comforting body (having a big dog makes a cowardly woman like me feel safe).

I have to keep being a dissident voice in order to keep Boromir safe and myself safe and my vagina free from being padlocked.

Prostitution and the Military

April 2008

Can it be stopped, this use of enslaved bodies by American soldiers and sailors? Is there any reason to stop it? These are a couple of the issues that this article deals with, along with delving into our current war, Iraq, and its devastating sexual consequences for women.

A first step in dismantling demand would be to actually admit that servicemen buy prostituted bodies. This has always been a hidden subject in the military. I grew up on military bases for the first twenty years of my life and we were stationed in Asia for several long tours of duty. Among the dependent wives and daughters, it was tacitly acknowledged that camp towns and GI-towns and red-light areas packed with bars and brothels for the soldiers existed, but few ever spoke about it. On occasion, I would hear a military wife mention "that filth outside the gate," referring to the prostituted girls, or they would joke and snicker about the women. Overall, the attitude seemed to be, "my husband would never do that" combined with "but if he does, I hope he doesn't bring any diseases home."

I lived through the Vietnam era and found the same indifference on the part of all American women to the many other women and girls prostituted to our troops in both Vietnam and in Thailand and Okinawa, where the men took R & R or, as they jokingly called it, I & I--Intoxication and Intercourse. Only one woman, historian Arlene Eisen, actually wrote about the turning of Saigon into one big, sweat-bath brothel for the troops during this time. Journalists in Vietnam—ones like Peter Arnett and Dan Rather--routinely ignored the prostituting of the country's women as an unimportant and inevitable sidelight of war. Rape was also dismissed as a trivial matter. Arnett reports routinely hearing the screams of girls taken off into the jungle and gang raped and simply ignoring this (Brownmiller 89-91).

During that era, I think that American woman did know something about the sexual savaging of Vietnamese women. It was hard to be completely ignorant given the dirty jokes the returning vets made about "field whores" and Saigon bar girls. But I came to the conclusion that the women did not care. Not once did even an activist like Fonda make mention of the brothelization of Vietnam. At the anti-war rally's I attended, it was impossible to get anyone interested in the topic. It was simply considered 'trivial.'

The same situation of ignoring sexual abuse as part of war prevails in Iraq—including by American women. If I try to talk about it, I get blank faces and "I didn't know that was going on"—with a big shocked pretense of ignorance (real or pretend?—it's hard to know).

One way I would tackle dismantling demand in the military is a strong campaign to foreground the turning of women into prostitutes as a result of war. If you don't know what is happening, if it is always hidden, you can do nothing about it. A great deal of this article is, therefore, not so much about 'dismantling' but informational, particularly as regards Iraq, since I think bringing this subject out in the open, in a big way, is essential.

After five years of war, there is finally one story on CNN about the prostituting of Iraqi women. "On Deadly Ground: The Women of Iraq" aired March 15, 2008 and in one short — very short — segment, reporter Arwa Damon interviewed a prostituted being, a woman selling herself to feed her children. The story was shallow and woefully inadequate and made me wonder why, after years of reporting from Iraq, Ms. Damon has just now decided to pay attention to this — scant as that attention is.

The prostitute interviewed said, "I cannot imagine anyone would do this except to survive." And she said that women did not have to do this before 2003, and the invasion of her country. Both great revelations? Things we do not already know? Perhaps we really don't know these things — although it would seem that we should. And it would seem that the almost complete indifference of the American public, and of American journalists, to the rape and ravaging of the bodies of Iraqi women and girls is just par-for-the-course ignorance. No matter that in all conflicts, women suffer sexual torture, particularly the torture of intercourse with men they do not know, for money, due to starvation and desperation and, often, the need to feed their children.

At least the military ought not to have been ignorant of this fact — that war always means forced sex and the wretchedness of raped-for-money bodies. Almost every military man at the Pentagon has seen prostituted bodies — used them, probably, since it is the rapist warrior way.

I would like this conflict in Iraq be the first one where survival sex and the wretchedness of the prostituted are covered extensively — every night on every news station — and every day in every media outlet and publication. It is a radical idea and one that has never been tried in all the history of western warfare.

The first step is trying to find out what is going on. American military men have this thing called 'the pact'—what happens overseas, stays there, particularly in the realm of taking sexual advantage of starving populations of women. In an effort to find out more information about the sexual situation in Iraq, I have e-mailed many groups, among them Human Rights Watch, Amnesty International, Refugees International, the United Nations High Commission for Refugees, and Iraq Veterans Against the War-- and women journalists who have spent time in Iraq, like Katie Couric and Lara Logan of CBS.

Here is what I wrote to all these people:

I would like to know more about the sexual assault on women in Iraq: rapes by American and coalition forces; rapes by the Iraqi police and military; rapes by Iraqi civilian men; rapes of women and girls detained in prisons; gang rapes; women forced into starvation prostitution—either for the occupying forces or for Iraqis; the increase of brothels in Baghdad and Basra as a result of the occupation; the trafficking of women and girls into prostitution by criminal gangs, either within Iraq or in surrounding countries; the way families are forced to sell daughters for survival; any 'survival sex' women and girls are engaged in due to desperation; 'survival sex' forced upon the refugee population (2 million in Iraq--2 million in surrounding countries); the trafficking, by U.S. military contractors, of Filipina and Chinese girls into brothels in the Green Zone; the role of the U.S. Military Police in the pimping of Iraqi women and girls; the physical and psychological state of the prostituted Iraqi girls trafficked into the Green Zone for paid rape; the rape of female military personnel by their own men—and anything else you may have seen going on in Iraq.

Over 2 million refugees are currently living outside of Iraq, in countries like Syria and Jordan. About 50,000 of these Iraqi women and girls are currently engaged in survival sex, according to the Women's Commission for Refugee Women and Children. Several sources--among them MSNBC, the *Guardian* and the *New York Times* --

have covered the prostituting of young Iraqi girls, mere children, practically--only 14 and 15 years old—in Damascus bars and brothels. Some as young as 6 are being sold to feed their families, and girls are also being trafficked to Dubai, a major 'sex-playground' destination.

Inside Iraq, information is harder to come by. A blog from an Iraqi woman, Layla Anwar, is helpful. She writes: "Survival sex is rampant not only inside Iraq but also outside. It happens in alley ways, around shrines, in dirty beds and in bars...Bars in Syria and Jordan. They are there to make a bit of money to feed their hungry sisters and brothers Our teenagers prior to their 'liberation' by America did not need to seek survival sex. They did not need to sit in bars in skimpy dresses waiting for the Mr. who will alleviate the hunger pangs of a whole family. Survival sex, the Iraqi-American version. Good, very good - 10 $ a shot. No make it 20$- I have a hungry family. A 20$ shot democracy."

Who is buying these girls? According to Ms. Anwar, both GI's and Iraqi men. One girl trafficked into a Baghdad brothel says Americans were among her customers. A Dec. 22, 2006 *Newsweek* article by Christian Caryl says that American MP's make sure that Iraqi prostitutes are released from jails. Why? So they will be available for American troops?

According to the Organization of Women's Freedom, 15% of Iraqi women within the country are either engaged in prostitution or seeking 'pleasure marriages'—these are temporary arrangements for the advantage of a male wanting another partner. Yanar, the Iraqi woman who heads the organization, says: "There is a huge population of women who are the victims of war and who have to sell their bodies, their souls. It crushes us to see them." Her team of activists pounds the streets trying to find these women who are too humiliated to come forward. There are no safety nets now in Iraq, no funding for widows.

A big question, as an aside, is where has the money gone? Oil revenues for Iraq for 2007 and 2008 will be about $100 billion, but no one knows where the money is. It is outside the country, hidden in foreign banks. (This is from a recent *New York Times* article which says the GAO [Government Accountability Office] is trying to find out why the money is not going into social services, hospitals, all the things these devastated people need. The UNHCR (United Nations High Commission for Refugees) says it does not have enough funding to help those 50,000 prostituted outside the country. The United Nations is a corrupt institution involved in the money laundering of hundreds of millions of dollars in funds: one of the reasons Kofi Annan stepped down—he and his son were part of this corruption. The money appears to be there—it is just not being channeled toward the needy, prostituted women. (Again, that handy *New York Times* is my source for articles on corruption in the UN—they ran some pieces at the time Annan stepped down.)

IVAW (Iraq Vets Against the War) say prostitution is very common in Iraq but they won't give more details. Journalist Patrick Cockburn says that Iraqi prostitutes make regular visits to the Green Zone, where these sad girls who must sleep with the enemy for food write anti-occupation slogans on the walls in a language their enslavers cannot understand.

Yet another sad story is of an Iraqi women who works out of her one-room dwelling and has her children stand in the corners, faces to the wall, while she has sex with customers, since she has no one to care for the children. (Source: Organization of Women's Freedom.)

In a 2007 article, "Is the Iraq Occupation Enabling Prostitution," Debra McNutt, a feminist scholar researching this topic, quotes an army reservist as saying that in Baghdad you can buy a prostitute for an hour for about a dollar.

McNutt sees that our war there has jumpstarted the sex trade and increased trafficking astronomically all over the Middle East--in the same way we did in Vietnam and Thailand during that era when so many girls were forced into sexual service for troops in the war or for those going on R & R—and in the same way that the military presence of 100,000 UN Peacekeepers stationed in Cambodia in the early 1990's caused trafficking to skyrocket and massage parlours full of underage girls to spring up like mushrooms after a rain. We saw the same scenario in Kosovo, with the multinational forces, where brothels with trafficked girls sprang up to service them. There are still 20,000 UN and NATO forces in that area and they are still using trafficked girls. This is another area of dismantling military demand where little has been done. Peacekeeping forces currently in Darfur are buying girls for a dollar or two, and ones in the Congo are raping, alongside the other militaries there.

Back to Iraq, are the military contractors trafficking in women in that country, the way DynCorp did in Bosnia? asks McNutt. From her research, there seems to be every indication contractors have imported women in the guise of maids and office workers to work as prostitutes. A Kuwaiti contract company has smuggled women into the Green Zone. Brothels disguised as restaurants with Filipina and Chinese prostitutes have opened and closed in the GZ, as the media found out about them.

McNutt tells us that contractors brag on sex websites about their contacts who supply them with "Iraqi cuties." Those same sites indicate that Chinese, Filipina, Iranian, and Eastern European women are being prostituted to the Americans and other westerners in Iraq. There are also reports, by the way, that Chinese and Filipina women are being prostituted in Afghanistan—which has 50,000 troops—25,000 of them American, 25,000 from other nations. Survival sex is also rampant in that country among Afghan women. If there are 50,000 men there, well…some of them must be doing what soldiers do when cheap sex is available.

The contractors take R & R in Dubai, a major trafficking destination, and also in the northern Kurdish region, where the girls are genitally mutilated—which makes prostitution much more difficult for girl since their vaginas are already so destroyed by this cultural practice.

McNutt says that girls in Iraq are kept inside for fear they will be kidnapped, raped, and trafficked and that there are many homeless girls vulnerable to the sex trade.

"Our occupation," she writes, "not only attacks women on the outside, but attacks them inside, until there is nothing left to destroy."

Of course, there is nothing new in this. It is a story as old as we are, the conjunction of soldiers and starving women forced into survival sex.

I wonder when will women's rights groups mobilize in huge numbers over this issue of prostitution in wartime for the military? Or not just women's rights groups—but women in general? I rarely hear any discussion of this from the women around me, and when I tell them about it, they are vastly surprised. "I didn't know that was going on in Iraq." Or-- "I thought all that sort of thing stopped a long time ago."

Code Pink (Women for Peace) is aware of the rape and sexual humiliation of Iraqi women by U.S. personnel in detainment centers and the way the girls are subjected to honor killings after release. And they report the kidnapping and trafficking of girls by criminal gangs who sell them into brothels in neighboring countries and the way "coalition forces and U.S. military contractors have committed horrific crimes of sexual abuse, torture, and physical assault." There are, according to Code Pink "copious accounts of rapes and gang rapes." But this is all that CP says about this topic on their website. And there definitely needs to be more coverage in depth.

Another aspect of dismantling demand is the rape of women soldiers by their own men. Rape and prostitution are identical in my mind, except that prostitution is far more severe since the woman is reduced to nothing from ongoing, daily rape. The one-time victim has recovery time; the prostitute has rape upon rape heaped upon her—a devastating and destructive scenario. Soldiers who rape prostituted bodies are encouraged to think that all women are targets for rape. Sexual assault rates are very high in the military—since they are being reported with more frequency over the last few years, we are getting some picture of the extent of the problem. It now has a name—MST—Military Sexual Trauma. Women soldiers in Iraq report being afraid to go to the latrines at night due to the possibility of being raped.

One woman vet said to me: "A female soldier in Iraq has a much greater chance of getting raped over there than of getting killed."

In Kuwait, which is a launching point for troops into Iraq, American women officers raped there report lack of medical treatment following the assaults; being left in the same units as their rapists, where they were harassed and humiliated all over again by their assailants; and not receiving sexual-trauma counseling. The pattern is the same we see with prostitution, covering up the subject and trying to ignore it—this is only slowly changing now as a result of there being more women in the armed forces and more of them reporting it. Whether the military will really pay attention to it and take effective measures remains to be seen. That same woman vet is not too hopeful. When I asked her if the sexual mistreatment of women soldiers would ever be a top priority, she said, "No way in hell."

Until military women recognize the exploitation of prostituted women by the military, their own sexual position will continue to be precarious. Tailhook is a good example. At that Las Vegas convention, the sailors and Marines were buying prostituted bodies and strippers. Typical LV sex shows at bachelor gatherings are raw and raunchy: girls get naked with each other, they go down on each other, they use dildos on each other, they simulate sex acts with the men in the audience, they put their naked butts in the air and invite the men to shoot rubber-tipped arrows into their cracks. I don't know how the women sailors at Tailhook could expect any respect when the men were in an atmosphere of drunken wildness with these 'for sale' women. Yet not one single account of Tailhook ever makes the connection: it is as if there is a 10-foot brick wall between what are considered the 'good' girls and the 'bad' girls.

Now I am going to switch to Korea and a move on the part of the military to address trafficking and dismantle demand in that country. About 5000 girls, most of them trafficked form Russia and the Philippines, work in bars and brothels around U.S. military bases there. That is a very conservative estimate since, until recently, something like 7000 E-Visas (those issued to girls imported, supposedly, as 'entertainers') were being given out a year to 'legitimize' the activities of criminal elements trafficking the girls in.

The reason for the importing of these foreign girls is there are no longer enough destitute Korean girls to enslave. And, supposedly, importing sex slaves will keep the 'decent' Korean women from being raped by all those horny GI's.

It's called the 'barrier' theory and it never works since the category of who is 'decent' and who deserves to be raped keeps shifting. From the 1950's to the 1970's, desperate poverty created the camp-town girls, Koreans sacrificed as 'rape scum' for the GI's. Now girls from the Ukraine are 'rape scum' for the GI's and all those 'pure' Korean girls are sipping mocha frappaccino lattes at glossy shopping malls.

Among the trafficked girls are women but also girls, age sixteen or even younger. Up until recently, U.S. servicemen made about two million visits a year to the bars and brothels where the girls 'work' (read 'sexual slavery' for work). The girls exist under those conditions typical of trafficking: debt bondage, humiliation, physical and psychological abuse. (A good article detailing this is "Base Instincts," by Donald MacIntyre.)

Again, using enslaved women in Korea is not new behavior. For decades, boxes of condoms have sat at the gates of the bases in Korea. The men call this area 'condom land' (Moon 130).

Recently, the military has actually recognized and made statements about the prostitution situation around our bases in Korea. They are amazing pronouncements: I quote from Lt. General Charles Campbell: "Prostitution and human trafficking are demeaning acts toward women and by participating in this buying of women, soldiers are participating in the enslavement of women and girls from all over the world." (What I wonder is where did he get this rhetoric from?—a military man would not think this up on his own: no military man is going to think of prostitution as 'enslavement.')

The reason I call these pronouncements amazing is that they are unprecedented in the history of the military—its typical attitude is that using prostitutes is a "harmless and necessary recreational activity." Brothels are places where men 'let off steam.' And you have to have them to keep the boys happy.

To demonstrate just how remarkable this shift is, I want to roll through a bit of military history. Many historians think that prostitution actually arose as a result of warfare. Conquering and occupying armies forced destitute women into exchanging sex for food and goods and money. It is a pattern we recognize almost as iconic in modern conflicts: the post-war GI offering chocolate bars and nylons to the starving post-war Italian girl (or substitute German or Japanese or whoever) for sex. There are legions of jokes about this 'chocolate-bar' sex situation. And 'Spam.' Lots of jokes about that. She'll fuck for a can of Spam. Slaughtered dead meat in the can; slaughtered fuck meat on the hoof—the whore forced to fuck for food. Fun stuff for the GI's. Stuff they joke about. Snort, snort.

Women as sex slaves for militaries goes back as far as the first 'civilization' (if you want to call it that) in the Western world—the Sumerians. They date to about 3000 BC, are also the first 'warrior empire' and what little we know of them indicates that military prostitution was a part of their 'civilization.'

The first war epic in western culture, Homer's *Iliad*, was written around 850 BC. Although a work of literature, archaeologists have found evidence that it reflects a civilization existing around 1500 BC, a warrior culture where captive women were passed around to the troops. Prostituted women as the booty of war had a reality in the 'real' Troy. There was a Briseis, even though her tale was not told. (It was her tail, sadly, that was of more interest to the soldiers.)

This has been military reality for a long, long time. The soldier's sexual needs are paramount. Captive, trafficked women are necessary to satisfy him. Moon's *Sex Among Allies*, about military prostitution in Korea, quotes a U.S. officer there in 1991who says, "If a soldier is that far away [from home], and his sexual appetites are met, he's feeling pretty good, and he'll serve better" (85). Whether it is 1500 BC or 1991, it is all the same picture.

That same officer in Moon's books calls prostitution a "real source of U.S.-Korean friendship and friendliness." Since when is the rape of our bodies a friendly act? How amazing that this is the norm: What is pleasure for the male equals rape pain for us.

According to the military, use of whores is supposed to 'soften' men within the hard sphere of their public duties, etc. (Moon 85). A weird way to look at it since there is nothing 'soft' about having a hard object shoved in an unwilling female body.

The prostituted women are the losers in all of this diplomatic 'friendliness.' The Korean government supplied women and called it a 'patriotic act' on the part of the women to 'sacrifice' themselves to keep the foreign soldiers happy and the American military condoned this as necessary and the women were left with diseases, misery, madness, half-caste, outcast children, and every other commonplace of military prostitution.

Here are some selected sections from Moon, to fill you in on what we did there. (And are still doing.) I also add my own comments about the language used in some of Moon's descriptions and also some of my 'prostitute' responses to her information. I put many of my comments in parentheses after selections from her text.

One prostitute Moon interviewed says that although she helped the Korean government get rich off of the sale of her body, she was always in debt due to outrageous charges by the bar and brothel owners. This prostitute says she knew the whole patriotic thing was a load of crap. She calls the work she did 'disgraceful. ' All the prostitutes Moon interviewed says economic need drove them to it, not a sense of patriotism (155).

The prostitutes have the typical trauma of not seeing themselves as normal. (When I read this in Moon's book, it helped me a bit in my own dilemma. Feeling completely alienated from non-prostituted women has guided my life. I remember sitting in the lobby of a posh Parisian hotel once with a number of academic women, all of us at a scholarly conference, reading papers. Polite and well-meaning women. But in their neat blouses under their neat suits, and with their calm, safe, educated, upper-middle- class lives, it was incredibly hard for me to feel as if I came from the same planet as these women. Even more difficult was it for me to see them as in any sense being of the same species as the abattoir whore in an immigrant section of Paris, at that moment trying to survive her 60th or 70th rape for the night. [Or maybe trying to not survive it—to die from it, to end the torture.] How could they just sit there, unaware of the abattoir whore in her sex-slaughterhouse, in her rape torture bed? Adjacent to them was unthinkable sexual agony being inflicted on another woman. Yet they just sat there.)

Moon defines one of the camp towns, "American Town" as a "town built on and for prostitution" (18).

Moon describes some of the conditions the girls work under. They are controlled by owners and pimps and must sell drinks and mingle with the soldiers and be 'fondled' by them. ['Fondled' would not be not my word since there is nothing gentle about these rough bar environments.] Since they cannot make enough to satisfy the debt-bondage slave owners just by selling drinks, they are "expected to sleep with GI's for the bulk" of the money (19). The owners and pimps take 80% of what they get paid when they have to get laid by the soldiers. (Sounds to me like the typical debt-bondage scene you find all over the world—a system of economic enslavement. Charge the girl so much for basics that she can never get out of debt to you, no matter how many men she has to fuck.)

"Most women do not come into the clubs equipped with 'hostessing skills' and the willingness to share flesh with GI's," Moon writes (20). (I'm not sure I'd call what they do 'hostessing' and as for a 'willingness to share flesh,' I don't think that any of them are really willing to get raped by strange drunk crude soldiers all the time. The few times Asian prostitutes do speak out they talk about "fear of the men's big bodies" (see, for example, the interview with Ms. Pak in *Let the Good Times Roll*).

"Most of the women have taken to alcohol or drugs to help them get through their sex work, " Moon tells us. (I would not call what is done to them 'sex work.' Rape of the debt-bondage held body is not work.) Moon reports that some GI's are mean enough to say that the girl did not "put out," even though she had sex with him (was raped by him is the way I would phrase it). Moon says the girls are held prisoners to make sure they do not run away and that there are "pimp holes" in walls so that their owners can hear and see into the room in case any of the girls try to get help from a possibly sympathetic GI.

There is one hopeful story in Moon's book of a soldier who works to buy a girl out of her debt bondage and then marries her. He then works right alongside his 'buddies' who had raped her as a prostitute. (This latter is my phrasing. I try to be careful with my words in order to reflect the true reality of what is going on. We have used neutral words like "service" for far too long to mask what really happens to the prostituted body: rape.)

As much as I am grateful to Moon for the information she gathered, I wish that she, and other academics, would emphasis the rape-shredded vagina. I cannot even find one place where she mentions that the girls bleed or are in pain from all this rape by GI's.

She does say that it was very hard to find women to talk to because of "ill health and loss of memory as a result of years of physical abuse, drug and alcohol intake, and psychological stress" (14). She also says that it was difficult to get the women to talk due to "shame, pain, fear, and mistrust" (x). (At this point, it is might be worthwhile bringing up the lack of accountability on the part of the GI's. One wonders why the rapists are not the ones in deep 'shame'? I find it baffling that women enslaved in this way and continuously raped are held 'responsible' for what has happened to them. It is as if male sexual privilege is so powerful and so important that complete blindness rules our attitude toward the victims. We simply label a woman 'prostitute' or 'whore'--and then this allows all kinds of dreadful abuse to be visited on her? And the men who sexually murder her body are simply allowed to get away with this—forever? Astonishing. I think that Ms. Moon's use of 'psychological stress' is a bit mild in its phrasing. Let's try something like 'complete psychological disintegration after continuous rape by rough, hell-raising soldiers.' All those buddies out for a 'good time.')

Moon says the prostitutes are "objects of extreme contempt" (7). She gives a history of how they have been slighted by other women in Korea. Local women activists ignored them as not worth bothering with. One says that as women they are "too different from us" and she cannot see how they are exploited. (Where did this woman mislay her vagina, I ask?) What they did was long considered voluntary by other women. They want to live this kind of life, the 'decent' women believe, because they are 'bad' girls. (And, of course, I find it really pathetic that the girls are held in 'contempt,' not the GI's who use them. But then I find all of prostitution pathetic and terrible—from the way a girl can get fucked by a 'customer-rapist,' who will then say she didn't give him his fuck or didn't give him 'good service'—therefore, he refuses to pay—to any attitude that regards a portion of the female population as disposable, any attitude that regards any girl as dirty--who is only valued as 'a fuck machine'--dirty because so many men have been inside her, etc. The whole situation is impossible. Where is it not pathetic?)

What I find really astonishing is the pattern: whether it be Japan after WWII or Korea or Vietnam, or current-day America, according to the 'good' women of the world, the whore is always a whore by choice, no matter what the abuse, rape, beatings, deprivation, desperation, poverty that may have preceded her 'choice' to get fucked all day by rough drunk shits she doesn't know. Some kind of vicious perennial blindness rules the world of 'decent' women. I would call them 'indecent' in the obscene cruelty of this attitude. Would they want to be treated the way these girls are? Raped, spit at, climbed on by drunken shits, fucked to pieces and then someone else takes the money. Who would want to be subjected to this 'voluntarily'?

Yet another twist on this: if, by some slight chance, a girl might actually 'like' to work as a prostitute (under non-abusive circumstances), she is triply scorned. If she went into it for 'fun,' she is quadruply scorned. Not that too many women would find the abuses of prostitution 'fun,' but I am referring to the rare scenario where a girl who has independence, protection from pimps, and completely safe working conditions might actually operate for her own pleasure. According to the 'decent' women, that's even worse, even more 'sinful,' than being forced. Boy! No sexual pleasure for the female body. Apparently, it's all reserved for the male.

Moon cites one woman as saying that "she and her coworkers had never placed the kijich'on prostitutes [those who 'service' the foreign soldiers] in any framework of exploitation or oppression."

Yet more fascinating facts from Moon:

U.S. military officials have always enthusiastically promoted prostitution in Korea and have even 'owned' women in some of the bars and taken the money off of the rape of their bodies. This information comes from as recent as 1993 (27).

"Some former comfort women also worked as GI prostitutes among the first generation of kijich'on sex workers" (Moon 46). (Again, I would not call it work in any sense. I wonder that Moon can label these poor women 'sex workers' who had been raped up to 50 times a day by the Japanese military in preparation for their 'job' of being raped by the GI's.)

Anyway you look at it or label it, camp towns, according to the information Moon gathered, are ugly brutal places for women, where sanctioned rape and sanctioned brutality are the norm. (My point of view.)

I have given this information from Moon's study in some detail since a bit later in the article I am going to explore what is currently going on in Korea and show that it is similar to what has been going on since 1945—when the first Korean girls were turned into whores for the U.S. soldiers. The business continued and grew throughout the 1950's to the 1970's with the collusion of both the American and Korean governments.

More recently, in January 2006, the U.S. Military came out with a new policy: that any soldier caught using a prostitute would be punished.

In the spring of 2007, a number of Department of Defense lawyers, some of them women, decided to put together training modules to educate new recruits and defense contractors about trafficking and inform the men that buying a prostitute could mean a year in jail.

Since this new attitude came about, there have been several hundred arrests of servicemen in Korea, but little has been done to them. Minor penalties. The arrests seem to be for show, to let the government know that the officers over there are 'serious' about this. There have also been many bars and brothels—about 600, in fact—put off-limits to U.S. personnel because they are suspected of imprisoning trafficked girls. Whether this off-limits policy is being enforced is another matter. I cannot find out for sure if the new policy is just lip service and high sounding rhetoric or if all the U.S. soldiers in Korea are actually being dissuaded from buying prostitutes.

Bars put off-limits are opened up again, and when the GI's can't get into bars and brothels in one camp-town area, they go to another. Also, girls are trafficked from the 'off-limits' establishments to other bars, so they are no better off than before. Being trafficked elsewhere doesn't get them out of their sexual slavery. A question I would ask a man in the Pentagon is this:

If you had a daughter imprisoned as a sex slave in one of these establishments, would your first concern be to 1) get her out of there or 2) arrest the men using her.

Rather than simply arresting the men, removing the girls from their enslavement and providing long-term care for them is essential; and this does not seem to be focused on at all by the Pentagon.

Due to all this attention to prostitution/trafficking, the Korean police have gone around to bars to advise girls of their 'rights.' They have supposedly talked to about 700 girls. I would ask: how can you 'advise' a trafficked girl of her rights since under the imprisoning, degrading conditions of her employment she has none? The girls cannot get away from their owners. How can they have any rights? Are their owners going to let them go out on a picket line, with placards? These girls are locked away and not allowed to go out when they're not fucking to make their owners money. I don't think those owners are going to look kindly on the idea of 'rights' for sex slaves.

The Korean government did a major crackdown on prostitution in 2004, but it only resulted in large numbers of Korean prostitutes in Seoul losing their livelihood and having no place to go. Several thousand of these women, faces covered by handkerchiefs for anonymity, took to the streets in protest. The trafficked girls could not join them since they were still being imprisoned. A few months later, the girls returned to work and it was business as usual. The Korean government is, however, suppressing what are called E-visas, those issued to trafficked girls so they can enter the country as 'entertainers.' Korea seems to be making some move toward setting up services and infrastructures to help girls exit prostitution. But this is in its early stages, and seems to be low on the list of what to do about trafficking—actually helping the girls themselves. (This, too is a pattern worldwide—almost no countries have any kind of substantial programs that might help women and girls [and children, too] out of prostitution. The U.S. certainly doesn't. It is the same old pattern of arrest her and treat her like the criminal.)

One suggestion I have would be to set up services on our bases for the trafficked girls who have serviced our men. After decades of exploiting hundreds of thousands of girls so GI's can get their fuck, it is time we make reparation. We owe these women—big time. Services would have to be long-term, since we are dealing with extremely damaged beings. I don't know how you help and counsel a sixteen-year-old Filipina who has been forced to strip naked on a bar eight or ten times a night, as rough men jeer at her and try to poke her in her hole. And then she has to go off and have sex with these ugly drunk maniacs. I think psychological scarring is probably permanent, and I don't think I want to think about the shape her poor body is in. But I guess we can at least try to care for her.

Long-term means education for the girls, and college, and good jobs that don't involve sexual degradation. We owe them this. We could do this on bases all over the world. Part of the money could come from confiscating the billions of dollars all these rape-shit traffickers and rape-shit bar and brothel owners have made on the girls' bodies over the years. It's easy. Just put all these rape-shit pimps and procurers and traffickers and owners out of business. And regard the girls as worth something, not as fuck-dumps for horny GI's.

So it would go in my fantasy world of humane commonsense. I know I have just about as much chance of bringing this about as I do of ending war as a male pastime, but I have to at least dream.

Does this new Pentagon policy really signal a major shift in the military and finally the means to help all those prostituted by our servicemen? Is it meant to apply to men stationed everywhere? A *Stars and Stripes* article by Jessica Inigo quotes soldiers in Germany saying it should not apply to them since prostitution is legal there and all the German girls are working of their own free-will. This shows a woeful lack of knowledge on the part of the military about the trafficking situation in that country—of the 400,000 prostitutes in that country, around 80% are trafficked in from elsewhere. Only a small number of German prostitutes actually benefit some from the system there. (Even these are often pimp-controlled—it takes coercion to force fuck by strangers on a woman—we don't like men inside us we don't know.)

Currently, large numbers of these trafficked girls are from the Ukraine and they have been broken by the Russian mafia in typical brutal fashion. Rape every few minutes by a different man for hours, or for days even, is typical. Making the girls fuck in public to humiliate and demoralize them is typical. Beating and raping girls in front of other girls to render all of them docile and terrified is typical. What the customer sees is the end-product. The soldier visits the whore in the Eros Center in Germany--or the drive-thru brothel--and the whore smiles and fucks and does what she has to to please him and bring in the money. She has no choice. She is property. Owned. "Legal sexual slavery" is maybe the term we should call it in Germany.

Once our military there frees all of these girls in Germany, we can use the 4.5 billion a year the pimps and traffickers have been bringing in to set up all sorts of healing services for these poor girls.

In terms of numbers, it would seem that the German Eros Rape Camps are a lot larger than the Korean Rape Camp Towns. One in Cologne alone, the Pasha, is a twenty-story brothel full of rape prisoners. Time to zero in on Germany, along with Korea.

Our government and military have never been sensitive to the subject of girls enslaved in prostitution before. Look, for example, at the role we played as Super Pimp in Korea in the 1950's—agreements between the U.S. and Korean governments back then made trafficked girls available for 'recreational rape' for the soldiers. (See *Sex Among Allies* for a detailed account of this.)

DOD lawyers says the push to change prostitution policies or rather 'non-policies of tacit consent,' as I would term them, came in 2003 when the Pentagon saw a Korean news show, taped in 2002, and carried on Fox television, about girls being trafficked in from Eastern Europe, Russia, Thailand, and the Philippines for our servicemen; and part of the segment was about how our MP's were acting as pimps. The MP's boasted that they knew the girls had their passports taken away from them as soon as they landed in Korea, that the girls were put up for auction, and that they had to work off their debts by having sex with the soldiers. The MP's sounded as if it was all a big fun dirty joke.

The Pentagon says it was surprised and outraged by all of this—a highly doubtful reaction since the trafficking of girls into brothels and camp towns and red-light areas for our soldiers has been going on in some form since the late 1890's—military brothels were established in the Philippines for our men there during the Spanish-American War. The men must have frequented them heavily since VD rates were enormous.

Stateside, the Pentagon must know about military prostitution. For example, towns like Tijuana service the U.S. fleet in San Diego and El Paso has Fort Bliss—which provides business for brothels and sex shows in Ciudad Juarez. Norfolk, Virginia, with its heavy naval presence, has been a scene of exploitation for decades. There are many other instances too numerous to mention, stateside.

In addition, the Pentagon is full of military men who have seen prostituted/trafficked girls all over the world—and many of these men probably used enslaved bodies during their tours of duty. It would certainly come as no shock to any of these men that MP's pimp and that soldier freely purchase the bodies of vulnerable girls for sex. It makes no sense for them to suddenly pay attention to this fact of military life as if the exploitation of women were something new and as if it mattered--it never has in the past.

Some congressmen saw this Korean footage and wanted action taken by the Pentagon. Again this surprises me since the vets in Congress know about whores. All vets know about whores. There are vets in Congress who were in Vietnam. Surely, they must have seen the whores. It was kind of hard to miss Ms. Saigon and her sisters—she was on sale everywhere. How could these men have possibly not known that in Korea girls have been pimped to GI's for the last 60 years?? It didn't just all of sudden come about one Friday night in a bar outside one of our bases in 2002.

Why the sudden interest by Congress—they've never cared about whores before either. Even the liberal women in Congress largely ignore the plight of these most outcast of women.

It seems that the strong impetus was also a number of women DOD lawyers who were concerned about the trafficked women in Korea. Could it be because some of these prostitutes are blonde (Russian and Eastern European) and therefore worth bothering with, unlike the Little Brown Fucking Machines (as the Marines call Asian whores) we are accustomed to seeing our men rape?

Will the training modules do any good? In addition to the difficulty of changing the rape behavior of men, it might be impossible to change the time-honored view that prostitution is the woman's fault, that she likes what she is doing, that it is 'fun,' and 'recreation,' not rape. It is a view held out in the civilian population, as well as in the military. In either area, to regard a prostitute as a human being is currently impossible, given prevailing attitudes of scorn, stigmatization, she's a filthy slut, etc. For one, to give her humanity would threaten every 'decent' woman in the world. (In my view, to deny her humanity does so.)

To really dismantle demand we would have to practically dismantle 'civilization' as we know it—completely get rid of antiquated ideas of virginity, of 'good' girls versus 'bad' girls, completely lift all the sexual repressions that have destroyed female sexuality for centuries.

I also hold the unpopular view that biology plays a huge role in all of this. Men will rape prostituted bodies because they can. They are born to rape, just as we women were born to be raped. Anatomy is destiny, as Freud says. Of course, cultural and social conditioning play a small part, but physical strength and testosterone and getting drunk and acting like those lunatics in *Jarhead*—this is normal, natural male behavior. As someone (a man) once said to me, "Men are a great deal simpler than you give them credit for." Horny young guys in the military want pussy. And pussy shows. And they want to get drunk and shout and jeer and act crazy, while they watch pussy. And then they want to fuck pussy. It's 'fun'—and natural for them to degrade us women to "bought pussy." No great thoughts of female liberation and the rights of women go through their heads. They just want pussy.

I have some personal knowledge about Korea. My first boyfriend, Vic, my first everything—lover, great love of my life, was stationed in Korea in the 1950's. He said that the men who didn't buy camp-town girls didn't exist. In other words, almost all the men indulged in raping enslaved bodies. Vic was a good guy. He would never hurt a woman. But he did buy the girls, just like his buddies did. And he said they were terrified of him and the other men. Terrified of how big the Americans were, and Vic said every girl he bought cried when he fucked her. He felt bad but he did in any way because that's what soldiers did. He also said it made him feel powerful, in a funny way, to have a girl so terrified of him—even though he felt guilty about it.

In the 1960's, about 85% of all the men stationed in Japan, Korea, Okinawa, Vietnam, Germany, etc. had used a prostitute. That's millions of rapes.

I talked to a lot of GI's from for about 20 years (from the mid-60's to the mid-80's), many of whom were in Vietnam and Korea. These men told me of the prostitutes they used. Men in the navy said that going from port to port meant going from brothel to brothel. One guy told me the only man on board they couldn't get to go to whorehouses with them was a Mormon.

Moon says that a sailor she spoke with in 1991 told her that before the ship docked anywhere--in Korea or the Philippines or Thailand--the medical officers would gather the men for health briefings and "throw condoms at them as if they were cards."

There seem to be a lot of reasons for how common brothel and whore usage has been, and still seems to be, to some extent. (It's hard to tell if the current military is actually dissuading this behavior in any appreciable way.)

I have heard and read these reasons in so many places, there must be some truth to the fact that military men believe them:

1) The girl is there and available to be bought and I need sex. No big deal.

2) It is part of her culture to be a prostitute.

3) She is poor and needs money so I am doing her a favor by buying her so that she can eat and support her family.

4) She is lucky she has this way to make a living since no other one is available to her.

5) She doesn't mind doing this. She is not like an American girl, who would mind. I once had a soldier say that a Korean girl would just as soon fuck as chew gum. It didn't really mean anything to her. (I think it probably didn't 'mean' anything to her because she was numb from taking on so many guys. You just fuck with indifference when you are overused—it is the only way. To feel anything is deadly.)

6) Other soldiers buy them and it is expected of me as a soldier to join in and do the same.

7) I don't have much else to entertain me when I'm off duty except to go to a bar and drink and buy a girl.

8) Life as a soldier is tough and I need relaxation in the form of drinking and sex.

From my experience, I don't think the men know what they're doing to the girl in terms of damage. And I don't think they want to know--if a girl is trafficked or not—since they just want their sex. One of the most moving things anyone has ever said to me came from an older man who'd used prostitutes in his youth. "I didn't know back then that what was a few minutes of pleasure for me was a life sentence for her."

The military men in charge have encouraged thriving prostitution scenes worldwide, in peace and in war, for American soldiers, since they know the men 'need' this release. (After all, 'man must have his fuck'—no matter what.) It is practical for there to be prostitutes available for the men. (The life and body and sanity and feelings of the prostitute are irrelevant—only the sexual needs of the soldier—and efforts to keep him disease free by 'controlling' the prostitutes—have been important.) Her health has only been important as it impacts the soldiers and the effort to keep them from getting VD. Hygiene campaigns take precedence over her humanity. As an aside, I have a theory that the real, hidden reason behind the Pentagon's "humanitarian" concern for the prostitutes all of a sudden is AIDS. Large numbers of infected troops would be disastrous. Although the impetus to curb prostitute use by our troops seems to be because of the link with human trafficking, it is more likely that the AIDS spectre is the real reason.

If the men knew how wretched the lives of the girls are, would it stop them? I think a lot of these soldiers in Korea have to be aware that trafficked Russian and Filipina girls are working under the same conditions as their Korean counterparts used to—sex with drunk rough men, pressure and mistreatment from their owners, taking drugs and drinking to bear the work. Women smile when they sell sex. If the men could see beneath the smile, would they care—or would they prefer not to know since it might interfere with their right to buy sex?

What I have been able to find on the internet about Korea, and about the new policy of discouraging men from buying girls, and whether it is working, is scattered. The information covers about five years—most of it is from around 2002 to now. One article says they are training the soldiers to 'report' abuses. If men over there are doing this, I would love to know about it. Once they report the girl is trafficked, does she get any help? In the articles, some soldiers seem to know the girls are trafficked, some don't care, and others are disgusted. One man says that a lot of soldiers may know that there is something amiss or exploitative going in but they may not know the extent of it: the debt bondage, the pressure from pimps to bring in money, or the terrible, slave-like conditions the girls live and work under. I think this is probably understandable since it would make it hard for the more compassionate ones to buy sex—so the men may pretend nothing is wrong.

Perhaps there is a necessary blindness involved. The soldiers know that this is sexual slavery. But admitting so would interfere with their sexual pleasure, so they hide this fact from themselves. I think this psychological 'hiding' must apply in many circumstances where a girl is obviously in pain or distress or trauma from sexual mistreatment, yet the men go ahead and have intercourse with her anyway. I wonder if this was the case with the Korean Comfort Women and their 'customers'? Those millions of Japanese soldiers must have seen the pain and terror and misery on the faces of the girls. Yet millions upon millions of these men used the girls anyway. The 50 GI's lined up to get at one 'comfort woman' in Tokyo, 1945, must have seen her deep pain—but they went ahead and inflicted even more pain with each mount. In the UK, currently, there are trafficked Slavic teenagers being forced 40 to 60 times a day by British men. Are all these British men simply so determined to get a few minutes of sexual pleasure that they completely ignore the obvious enslavement and pain of the girl? This ignoring of the pain of the girl is one of the great mysteries of male sexual behavior for me.

I do not know if a girl is still conscious after being mounted so many times. At what point does she pass out? If the girl is unconscious after 20 or 30 mounts, surely the next 20 or 30 men can see this? Do the men in the UK just climb on these Slavic girls even though these girls have passed out? We know from the testimony of the Korean Comfort Girls that some of them passed out due to the unendurable pain. And the men just kept mounting anyway. Did the 50 GI's in 1945 Tokyo just mount the girl, even though she was unconscious? Did this not bother them in any way—to be raping an unconscious girl? Did it not bother them to be standing in line, with all these other rapists? Did they make jokes about the rape they were going to commit, while they were waiting 'their turn'?

These were just ordinary guys. You could substitute any young man from today—anyone's brother or boyfriend or cousin—and put him in that line back in 1945 Tokyo and he too would be raping a girl in terrible pain. Apparently, usage of prostituted bodies was almost 100% by the GI's in occupied Japan. Would your boyfriend or brother have held back--or would he be in that rape-line, joking around, waiting his turn?

I know that I passed out after just a few rapes. I think 50 in one day would have killed me. I would have not been alive to 'take on' 50 the next day. And, indeed, in the testimonies of the Korean Comfort Girls, we are only hearing from the few who survived.

These testimonies, by the way, are invaluable since they are among the few documents we have in which girls actually describe some of the physical and psychological torture of prostitution. Current accounts by girls who have escaped trafficking are not usually as detailed. It is understandable since it is very difficult to speak about all this. I know that my throat closes up if I try—and I was not damaged nearly to the extent that the comfort girls were. The camp-town girls in Korea over the past 50 years have felt such shame and degradation, it is no wonder no one ever hears their story. They are effectively silenced by male sexual need and the indifference of 'decent' women.

I am hampered in my current coverage by no longer knowing soldiers. The ones I prostituted myself with opened up to me about the other whores they had used, both in Asia and Europe. Since I was on the other side of the divide, no longer a 'good' girl, the men were frank about their dealings with other 'bad' girls. Also, my life brought me in contact with a lot of soldiers from about the mid-60's to the mid-80's, even when I was not in prostitution.

So, I had a lot of firsthand knowledge and stories back then that I do not have now. My attempts, for example, to find out information from soldiers about prostitution in Iraq have been met with a lot of walls. The 'pact' still seems to be holding: what we do overseas, stays overseas. Soldiers and sailors do not tell their sisters and mothers and wives and girlfriends about the prostitutes they buy and the bars and brothels they visit. It sometimes slips out as a dirty joke, but the wives and sisters and girlfriends don't pursue this knowledge: perhaps they do not want to know? From my experience growing up on military bases around the world, as a dependent girl, this underworld of buying sex on the part of the soldiers was very, very hidden. I only heard wives refer to it in dirty joke terms, sparingly. So, when the current sailors have liberty in Thailand or Hong Kong or Rio or Mombassa or Bahrain, all places replete with women who are sold to navies from around the world, they don't necessarily tell the women back home about the girl who stripped naked on the bar for them, or that they got drunk and purchased a body. Nor do they talk about this, apparently, where they homeport. San Diego, for example, where the sailors have access to trafficked girls in bars both in that city and in Tijuana.

Any information from soldiers or sailors currently in the military would be greatly appreciated. Does the U.S. military really seem serious about helping trafficked/prostituted girls, I would ask you servicemen? Is this problem highlighted on armed forces radio and in the *Stars and Stripes*? Is it dealt with on an ongoing basis, or is it just given a few minutes of attention and then forgotten? Is there any move to provide 'exiting' strategies and programs for prostituted/trafficked girls around the bases in Korea and Germany? Any information you soldiers have I would be most grateful for.

Similarly, if women lawyers at the Pentagon read this and can tell me what is going on, I would appreciate it. Since you women lawyers are part of the reason the U.S. military paid attention to this, are you still interested in tackling the problem? What is being done about those 'exiting' strategies and programs to help the prostituted/trafficked? Since the majority of prostituted girls in Germany are trafficked, GI's using girls there are most likely buying sex slaves—many of them from Russia and Eastern Europe. Is there any strong move, on the part of the USA, to help these girls? Is there any way for the USA to work with the EU on this?

The next part of this article is my summary (and response) to a few of the sources I have found. As it usual with me, I don't just quote. I get mad, I interpret, I do what used to be called "deconstructing" the text—getting down and dirty to uncover the lies and cruelties.

Here goes.

There is a remarkable 300-page blog by a man named Kalani O'Sullivan who is stationed at Kunsan AFB in Korea. It runs up until 2005 and reveals a great deal about the prostitution scene in the Korean camp towns around our bases. Although not without compassion, a lot of his blog seems to try to justify keeping the Russian and Filipina girls in sexual slavery without admitting it is sexual slavery. The blog unintentionally reveals conditions of extreme mistreatment and humiliation visited on these girls. So disturbing were the insights that I got from his descriptions of their lives that I cried and cried while reading the blog. The girls are not treated that differently from their camp-town Korean counterparts of the 1950' to the early 90's. (This was about the time Korean girls grew prosperous enough to refuse camp-town degradation and so bar owners began substituting trafficked girls from abroad.)

O'Sullivan goes into the history of Korean camp towns—this section is lengthy and fascinating and I don't have room to quote from it extensively, so I'll give a couple of samples:

A Marine, Ron Stout, "vividly remembers in 1953 the sight of a young girl with an Amerasian baby covered with sores begging for food in exchange for sex. At that time, things were so desperate that people were living in holes dug out of the side of the hills."

"A retired ROK general decided to profit from [prostitution] by creating A-town as a 'special tourist zone' specifically for American GIs. In this way, special tax advantages would be given to the bars. Korea would benefit from the earning of much needed foreign exchange. The benefit to the Americans was that by moving the 'red-light' district closer to the base in a 'controlled' area, the U.S. military could better 'protect' their troops. This had been a problem of how to control the troops had plagued senior commanders on the base since the late 1950s. With the concurrence of base officials, construction was started in 1969.... Since that time American town has been the play area for the GIs."

"A-town" as Moon tells us, is a camp town built for prostitution. What is fascinating about the above passage from O'Sullivan is corroboration that the American military authorities fully co-operated in its 'official' construction. What is even more fascinating is that this sanctioned sex playground had to be well known to many—back then—and must be so now—since so many hundreds of thousands of GI's have used its inhabitants over the years. Many,

many American women must know about it by now—all those who have had brothers and boyfriends and husbands stationed there, all those who have themselves lived on bases in Asia, where similar camp towns are. Yet, not one American woman has ever made a protest that this 'entertainment' system for their men was based on military sexual slavery--identical in brutality to any 'comfort woman' system? (I cannot find words strong enough to express my absolute contempt and disgust for these blind, privileged American women.)

More from O'Sullivan's blog:

"For the South Korean government, these camptowns and the regulation of camptown women have been crucial to maintaining smooth relations with the U.S. government. Katherine Moon points out that making sure that the camptown women played their proper role as entertainers and sexual playmates would foster goodwill among American soldiers was essential for the South Korean government. A-town was the only place the personnel of Kunsan AB could blow off steam. By and large, it was simply a place to get drunk and raise hell with your comrades."

(This was one of the passages that really started the tears—I felt sick when I thought of all those poor girls pawed and raped by these young ugly brutal horny crude rough GI's. We women are small and fragile and delicate. We are not meant for rough drunken abuse.)

He tries to draw a big line between trafficking and prostitution. Here is his effort to distinguish between the two: "First, I'd like to point out that there is a wide gulf of difference between the two. Prostitution is the direct result of a government's inability or disinterest in ensuring that decent jobs are available for all of its citizens. Prostitution is a direct result of economic necessity.

"Human trafficking, on the other hand, is the direct, hands-on exploitation (either by force or coercion) of one person by another for economic gain.

"I won't spend any more time on that explanation. Either you get it or you don't."

I guess I don't get it. And I'm glad I don't get it: such 'logic,' based on no compassion, is not the way I would care to 'think.' In my view—in any compassionate view--the poverty the girls come from makes them vulnerable to trafficking. And there is no 'voluntary' entry into prostitution if any kind of coercion—economic or otherwise--is involved. O'Sullivan tries to draw an imaginary line between two kinds of exploited, vulnerable women: both are subjected to similar 'working' conditions--sex with men they do not know, violence toward the girls, humiliation of the girls since they are in this 'profession' called prostitution.

O'Sullivan devotes a lot of time trying to prove that the Russian and Filipina girls were "whores" back home so any protestations of "purity" are in vain—when the girls get to A-town how can they complain about their servitude—they're already whores. Interestingly, he gives Angeles City as an example of where the Filipina girls were already whores. Well, Mr. O'Sullivan, the girls were coerced into that profession in Angeles City back home, usually very young, usually coming from backgrounds of abuse, usually for the same reasons we find all over the world: poverty, rape, incest, being sold before they are even old enough to resist or know what sex is, or—in the case of older girls--having babies and being deserted by husbands and needing to feed their families...all the typical scenarios. It is interesting how he tries to use their lack of "purity" when they get to Korea as a justification for continuing to mistreat them.

From here on out, I am simply going to quote some sections from O'Sullivan: they are very revealing in terms of the glimpses they give us into the lives of these women--the humiliations, the harshness of the bar-fine system, the psychological and physical torments that are simply part of prostitution, whether you call it 'trafficking' or not. O'Sullivan's tone is chillingly neutral about this way of life imposed on women—this thing called prostitution that has been inflicted on us women for so long--men apparently cannot see its deep, deep cruelties. These cruelties have become an acceptable norm, not just for the men who use the girls, in all of their male privilege and entitlement, but for the millions of other men who don't—but ignore the girls' plight--and it is a norm for all the 'safe' women who turn a blind eye to this damaging institution of selling female bodies.

So, here is more from O'Sullivan's very revealing document:

"Filipina bargirls are frequently locked in their apartments during the day."

"U.S. military police officers are accused of extorting valuables or sexual services from businesses in Gijichon - or red-light districts that spring up near U.S. garrisons."

"Most of the Korean bar girls have racked up heavy debts to the bars and cannot leave [the establishments]."

"The worst case scenario is that the Korean 'girls' will be 'sold' to another bar -- not necessarily in A-town. "

"The brutality inflicted on the bar girls by bar owners has always been a lively topic amongst the GIs. However, to be frank, A-town is much more humane in its treatment of the prostitutes than any other area in Korea. Verbal abuse is common with a lot of yelling…."

"As to the Russians in other camptowns, there appears to be some girls from Russia, Uzbekistan, Kazakhstan and Moldova who were lied to and were devastated when they found out what was expected of them according to news reports. We have not heard such tales from Kunsan. Allegedly many of the Russians from Muslim upbringing found the sex routines a shock. Education levels range from some college to barely able to write."

"The Russians have expanded their prostitution network throughout the country from Pusan to Inchon to Yeosu to Tonghae. The Russians are everywhere as the Koreans have shown a preference for sex with caucasians. In July 2004, it was found the Russians were being pimped in Yeosu over the internet."

"Have the bar girls in A-town been coerced to become prostitutes? For A-town we believe the answer is -- NO!!! (For other Korean camptowns, we cannot speak.)"

"Even at the thought of human trafficking, the hair on the back of people's neck starts standing on edge. We believe that people are lumping A-town in with the abusive bars in other camptown areas which is not fair. A-town is NOT the same and has worked to treat its bar girls humanely."

"From all accounts, the bar girls became prostitutes of their own volition simply over the economics of the matter. Whether they were lied to or dazzled with a prospect of fast money is irrelevant."

"Our assumption is the bar girls in A-town KNEW that they would be performing sexual services before they even signed the contract….If the girl is an effective "juicy girl," the women can pay off their airfare and agent expenses within three months -- WITHOUT resorting to prostitution. However, to do so would place them in the bare subsistence level with very little money to send home. Prostitution is a much more lucrative proposition."

"It appears at first that the local 'managers' did not take the passports of the girls as was done in other camptowns."

"Problem girls were ultimately transferred to places even worse. How are PROBLEM bar girls in A-town handled? Through penalties and transfers. Penalties are standard for a bar girl as they must make a 'quota' in order to 'earn their keep'....the problem bar girl is transferred to a less-desirable club -- most likely a Korean bar using foreign bar girls....Those opposed to human trafficking often use the term 'traded' to refer the problem girls being moved to more hellish bars....the Korean police will return a runaway foreign bar girl to the bar if caught...."

"At other times, when a club is placed off-limits for an infraction of the 'prostitution' rules, the bar girls will be 'loaned' to other clubs....For example, in July 2004 the Stereo and Long Beach were placed off-limits and their girls were sent to other clubs."

"The bar girl's contract is a double-edged sword. It may coerce the woman into prostitution because of the monetary imperatives....Note that the amount of money provided in the contract was very small and food allowances also minimal without promise of lodgings....After the expenses are paid and a meager amount is sent home to the families, the girls are subsisting at a poverty level. Thus the imperative is to also engage in prostitution to earn more money. "

"To compare A-town with the standards prevalent in the red-light districts of Kunsan City is like night and day. In Kunsan City, the violence can be fatal. However, in the red-light districts areas most deaths are written off as suicides -- simply because in our opinion, it saves paperwork. However, more realistically, no one cares one way or another about the death of a prostitute -- except a small and vocal civic activist group. The police turn a blind eye to many incidents of abuse of women simply because they are prostitutes.... Thus when compared with Kunsan City, A-town is a paradise. In Kunsan City, many of the women are locked up in brothels, while in A-town they walk freely about. In Kunsan's redlight district there are places where they are displayed in storefront windows and treated like pieces of meat to be bought by any passing male. In A-town, they work in bars with at least a moderate amount of choice in their partners. In Kunsan City, they are forced to sell their bodies or face beatings. In A-town, they push "juices" as the top priority and engage in prostitution as a secondary goal…In other camptown areas of Korea, girls are forced to work 16 hours a day without a break according to some journalists. In A-town, the girls work 8-9 hours -- more or less."

There is much more. This is just a sampling of this document. As you can see, it reveals every abuse imaginable visited upon these girls—with O'Sullivan's many equivocations that this is not really slavery. Peering into this document, reading behind the tone of 'acceptance' that he gives to much of this prostitution world, we see debt bondage; the physical misery of sex with strangers; pressure to earn money through prostitution or be punished; corrupt local police and corrupt America MP's; insights into why the 'no-prostitution' policy of the USFK will never work—the girls are trafficked elsewhere for use if an establishment is placed 'off-limits'—and the GI's just follow along. We see conditions in other camp towns that are even worse than the humiliating and harsh ones in A-town. In short, we see every abuse that was visited upon the original 'camp-town' girls, the Korean ones, being inflicted on the Russian and Filipina ones.

What we don't seem to see is any help for the girls themselves—despite all the new proclamations about 'zero tolerance' for prostitution and all the fluff rhetoric about violations of human rights and dignity, etc.

As I read O'Sullivan's blog, I kept saying OMG, OMG, OMG—Oh, my god—I was so horrified and yet fascinated by the picture of incredible cruelty toward these girls he presents, seemingly without even knowing what he is revealing. This man has the gall to say that the Russians are 'girlfriends' of the GI's. There is no boyfriend/girlfriend 'relationship' when one is doing the buying and the other is bought. This is slavery.

A question that ran through my mind was what would he think if a daughter, or sister, of his were treated this way? Would he not consider it a severe form of abuse? Apparently that dividing line between the 'good' girl and the 'bad' has to remain brutally and sharply etched for him. (You might want to take a look at my "Australian Military Gang Rape of Fallen Blossoms"—also in this book—for a similar viewpoint from an Australian soldier about mistreated Japanese prostitutes.)

Another idea that ran though my mind as I read about the hell that is camp-town Korea for these trafficked girls: my time in prostitution was some kind of shining paradise compared to this—yet it still felt like rape to me.

All the basic misconceptions about prostitution seem to be in O'Sullivan's document. The idea that girls 'know what they are getting into,' they know they are going to be sold for sex. I can attest that there is no way a girl can know what this will be like—the devastating misery of intercourse with drunk men she does not know. And even if there were some way she could know 'what she is getting into,' does this excuse the tremendous physical and psychological abuse inherent in the prostituting of her body? It is these sorts of attitudes that will keep us women sexually enslaved forever.

Every thing I have read and heard about the 'breaking' of Russian trafficked girls is horrendous. (I use 'Russian' as an overall term to cover any girls from Russia itself or from countries formerly of the Soviet Union, the Ukraine, Moldova, etc., any place in Eastern Europe, etc.—'Slavic' would be more accurate, I suppose.) Letting a different man in every few minutes to use the girl, raping her in front of other girls to keep them all terrorized, beatings, filming the girls for porn to further humiliate them—these are the typical ways these girls are broken. (A good, short, readable account of what goes on in trafficking can be found in Paola Monzini's *Sex Traffic*. She goes straight to the point and also shows great compassion and understanding about how horrible this is.) Richard Poulin, a Canadian expert on sex trafficking, tells us there are "Submission Camps" in the Balkans where girls are raped to break them in (117). 'Russian' girls are now shipped all over the world: they are prostituted in Korea, Japan, China, Turkey, India, all over Europe, in Mexico, Canada, the USA. This is just a partial list.

If GI's are using girls who have been so treated, what can one say? I really can't find words to express how painful this is. I cringe when I think of these broken, submissive, terrified girls being raped all over the world. I especially cringe to think of them being raped by American soldiers since these are men that I know.

If any men stationed in Korea read this, I would appreciate knowing what is going on there in terms of these poor girls. Are they being helped out of prostitution? Is the new policy doing anything to rescue and protect them? My inside knowledge of why there was some move to help the girls comes from a medical doctor who was on a committee on human trafficking. He says that a number of female lawyers in the Pentagon were upset at the selling of trafficked bodies in Korea. I don't know if these female lawyers have been able to do anything other than raise the issue. Have they taken any concrete steps to help the girls leave their enslavement? Are they putting any 'exit strategies' in place? Were these American female lawyers at the Pentagon troubled, in the first place, by the trafficking in Korea because it involved blonde Slavic girls and not the usual Asian ones? I am just asking.

If the bars and brothels around the U.S. bases are indeed being policed and shut down, are the Slavic girls simply being trafficked elsewhere—either within Korea or to Japan or China? Are the U.S. military and the Korean government setting up long-term therapy/ rescue programs for the girls?

Has the Korean government changed its attitudes toward selling girls to the American military? Since the 1950's, when they agreed to supply prostituted bodies to U.S. soldiers, they have been very gung-ho in terms of making money off of Korean girls. At the expense of the girls, whose lives and bodies were simply disposable. Yet another set of 'comfort women.' Has the Korean government undergone any kind of attitude change? If so, are they willing to offer any kind of reparation to the 'comfort women' they have forced to service the U.S. military for so long? What is the Korean attitude toward prostituted women? Are the women still the outcasts they have always been? Is corruption within Korea aiding and abetting trafficking?

Just asking.

Any information from people in Korea, civilian or military, or at the Pentagon would be greatly appreciated. I cannot know what is going on inside. I am hampered by only knowing what I read or what eyewitnesses tell me. And eyewitnesses, being people, put their own slant on information. It is only natural. Kalani O'Sullivan will see very different 'facts' in a bar/brothel where female bodies are being sold from the ones I would observe since I know what is it like from the point of view of the girl being sold. His privileged male lens or 'filter' will screen out the female pain. His privileged position will accept that the prostitution of females is necessary for male use. My female raped body will find this position not only unacceptable but I will feel outraged. One venue: bar/brothel. Two very different points of view: privileged male; controlled female.

I quoted this from O'Sullivan above: "From all accounts, the bar girls became prostitutes of their own volition simply over the economics of the matter. Whether they were lied to or dazzled with a prospect of fast money is irrelevant." These statements reveal more of the reasons why prostitution will never be eliminated: the idea most people hold that there is a 'voluntary' form of prostitution caused by poverty. It seems obvious to me that there can be no 'voluntary' if poverty forces the girl into this. O'Sullivan says the girls "being lied to or dazzled by the prospect of fast money is irrelevant." What could be more relevant, I ask, than poor girls desperately reaching after some kind of economic survival and then finding themselves in Korea or China or Turkey or India with no passports and being raped all day by strangers while their 'owners' take the money? Are we to blame these girls for wanting some kind of better life? Something beyond just subsistence or starvation? The privileged Western female and the privileged Asian one, in Japan or South Korea or Singapore, lives her life of soft luxury with her pretty outfits and her little techno-gadgets--all shining and appealing and dazzling is this world where girls are pampered by luxuries. Why shouldn't the poor and destitute and deprived girls of the world reach after their 'material' dreams?

All the 'working conditions' O'Sullivan describes would be intolerable to any 'normal' woman. Can you imagine any normal, middle-class American or European woman 'putting up with' being held a prisoner without a passport and forced to have sex with men she does not know, under threat of beatings and terror and pain? Yet these are the 'normal working conditions' for trafficked girls. Would O'Sullivan want a wife or daughter or sister of his treated in this way, I wonder? O'Sullivan minimizes the misery when he writes: "A-town is much more humane in its treatment of the prostitutes than any other area in Korea. Verbal abuse is common with a lot of yelling…." I just wonder what normal, average, 'decent,' protected, privileged woman would 'put up with' constant verbal abuse in a harsh barroom setting from crude drunk men and from coercive bar owners? This is a work environment that would destroy most women. This is not 'humane' treatment of any woman in any way—despite O'Sullivan's claim that the A-town bar girls are treated 'humanely.'

There have been hundreds of thousands of American soldiers stationed in Korea since the 1950's. There have also been dependent wives and daughters there. Has no one at all ever noticed the ongoing sexual enslavement of girls in these camp towns—first Korean girls and now Russian and Filipina ones? It would seem obvious that a population of women imprisoned, held in debt bondage, locked in rooms, not allowed to go out, forced to have sex with men they do not know—women 'traded' or 'sold' from bar to bar, women 'punished' by being sent to 'hellish' bars—women abused in ways so far beyond what any dependent wife or daughter can ever even imagine, let along consider 'acceptable'—it would seem that someone somewhere over the past 50 or so years would actually have noticed the suffering of these girls. But you never hear any of the dependent wives or daughters say anything about the girls—except as underground dirty jokes. At least that was my experience—as a dependent daughter in Asia on American military bases. I went to school with all these 'clean' safe American girls on base, all of us there as proponents of 'democracy,' and right outside the gate sexual slavery was flourishing. Amazing. As the GI's were raping the sex slaves, didn't it occur to them that it could be us, the American girls, being raped--if we were vulnerable and starving and exploited? There are not two kinds of women in the world. We are all the same.

So, after 50 years of girls being sexually enslaved for U.S. soldiers in Korea, in 2003 or so the Pentagon and Congress are 'surprised' and 'shocked' that prostitution is going on in Korea around U.S. bases? This has to be one of the biggest cover-ups of female suffering in history. An enormous piece of history gone missing—not just the story of these prostituted girls but of all prostituted girls over the past 5000 years of human history. Attitude must have something to do with it. The dependent wives and daughters are magnificently blind to the suffering that is prostitution. They have been brainwashed into thinking these other girls are 'bad'—'whores' and 'sluts' who get what they deserve. I am always astonished that these privileged, protected women make no link, no connection, have no compassion in their thoughts—they cannot see the connection between starvation and the prostitution of the female body? They cannot see that poverty pushes the vulnerable girl into prostitution? They completely ignore those who exploit her—the pimps and bar owners and men who buy her. Amazing.

I am aware that I mostly offer knowledge of what American soldiers do. There are other militaries around the world, and I do not have time to offer evidence from them about rape and prostitution. That will have to be for another book. Soldiers who behave far, far more savagely than do the American or British ones are out there. I am not sure I want to research them. The pain would be too great. I have stayed with the Americans partly because there are actually some articles and books available about their sexual behavior with prostitutes. Some American men and women have cared enough to research this hidden subject. I am not sure I have the courage to venture out, and find out about sexual savagery far beyond what the Americans are capable of—either in the civilian or military world. After all, American men do have some respect for women. It is part of their culture. I cannot imagine how savage must be the treatment of prostituted girls in cultures where women in general are held in low esteem.

Without even researching the treatment of prostitutes by men other than Americans, I am having enough trouble just digesting the material from Kalani O'Sullivan. Particularly haunting to me are his descriptions of Kunsan City: it seems to be a place where imprisonment and sexual violence and beatings of girls are the norm and, as he writes, "no one cares one way or another about the death of a prostitute." A very sad sentence. O'Sullivan also mentions 'news articles' about what happens to the prostituted girls in the camp towns in Korea, but those are hard to come by. If there are ones being published in Korea—by local media or by the military--I would like to know about them. The information in the *Stars and Stripes* is very sketchy.

The conditions the girls work under haunt me so deeply, I don't know how to get rid of them in my mind. They stay there, like a pain or a dull ache. "In Kunsan City," writes O'Sullivan, "[girls] are forced to sell their bodies or face beatings....girls are forced to work 16 hours a day without a break according to some journalists." From my point of view, whether it is Kunsan City or A-Town, it is still men getting drunk and being noisy and raising hell and pawing girls and buying bodies. I would never survive even the mildest camp-town bar. I would be broken for life by the rough atmosphere. What girl would not be? Would the 'normal,' protected, privileged women of the world actually want to work under these conditions? Would you not have to become hard and coarse and near dead with numbness to survive being pawed by rough, drunk men and being forced to have sex with them? So ugly—and yet taken for granted as a norm. As O'Sullivan says, "A-town was the only place the personnel of Kunsan AB could blow off steam. By and large, it was simply a place to get drunk and raise hell with your comrades." Frightening for the poor girls the men let of steam with and raise hell on. We women are delicate. We are not made for this.

Where are the dependent wives and daughters? Safe inside the gate? Why are the dependent wives and daughters not saying anything? If Russian girls are battered and raped and degraded, then there is no safety for the ones inside the gate either. Men will treat all women as they are allowed to treat prostituted ones.

I cannot even watch movies with drunk rough men in bars. I don't know how to forget even the small amount of roughness that 'customers' inflicted on me. Nothing like the verbal abuse and yelling and beatings and violence that O'Sullivan describes. But enough to kill me for life.

Military attitudes of soldier don't make changes seem too likely. Here are a couple of articles from the *Stars and Stripes* that illustrate this. "Troops Mixed on Anti-prostitution Proposal," by David Allen is the first one. He interviews soldiers at Camp Foster in Okinawa. Here are a few samples of what men on base said:

"It's [cutting down on visits to prostitutes] a good thing....It will help prevent a lot of the younger Marines from going out and catching diseases..."

"Look, young guys aren't going to change their behavior....let's face it, part of seeing the world is seeing the girls."

"A 44-year-old civilian contractor who spent 13 years in the Marines said, 'It's just crazy. It's going to be damn hard to enforce.' "

"A 21-year Navy veteran [says]: 'I know that when young sailors and Marines get liberty somewhere like the Philippines or Thailand, they'd run amok like pirates and then come back to Okinawa still in that mode and wind up getting into serious trouble.... Maybe this will prevent some of that.'"

A Kitty Hawk sailor: "You go to sea three months, your wife is in the States or you don't have a wife, or you go to war … most of the people, when they got back, they were drinking and hiring [prostitutes]. "

"Something like this — who's going to listen? A man has needs …"

Damn, I say. Only an emphasis on the guy getting VD, on the way a man has to have his fuck. The next *Stars and Stripes* article, "Troops Say Proposed UCMJ Change Unfair in Prostitution-Legal Germany," by Jessica Inigo, is every bit as depressing. It's written from Rhein-Main Air Base, Germany, "only minutes from one of the largest red light districts in the world." Here are some excerpts:

"Those interviewed largely agree that Germany is not the place to enforce such a law….Unlike other overseas military installations across the world where sex trade and human trafficking runs rampant, in Germany, prostitution is legal. There are licensed brothels, called Eros Centers…. German women choose prostitution as a profession…"

Comments by the soldiers: "It would be different if it were some third-world country that had no jobs and no opportunity, and women were forced into it….if it's an issue of safety, there are condoms and stuff like that that soldiers can use."

A woman soldier concurs, saying that the women "are regularly tested, so there should be nothing stopping troops from using Eros Centers if they choose to…. It's a legal job, and if a girl wants to make money that way, she should be able to get her customers."

"Hormones build up," says a male soldier....I've talked to soldiers who have gone to these places and it doesn't badly affect their military career or badly affect the prostitutes' career….Soldiers say this is [BS]."

Then we have the wife of one of the servicemen contributing this comment:

"It seems like we can spend our time worrying about more important things."

For me, it's kind of hard to know where to start regarding the woeful lack of information these people have about prostitution in general and the industry in Germany specifically. For one, even many of the 'independent' German prostitutes there are pimp-controlled and tend to come from backgrounds of abuse—as is typical worldwide—and since Germany is the largest trafficking destination in Europe due to the legal climate that makes exploitation easy, we have roughly 350,000 foreign girls in those Eros Centers and who knows what kind of 'training ground' they were subjected to to make them docile and accepting of their 'trade'? As I stress, fuck by strangers is a really rough road. Fuck by drunken strangers is even rougher. Debt-bondage fuck doesn't benefit the whore.

The facade that the clients see is in no way the hidden reality of prostitution—whether it be Germany or Cambodia or the U.S. Abuse of these trafficked girls has been so tremendous that both Germany and Holland (the other European country that has unfortunately legalized sexual slavery) are now back-tracking on their policies. This has come about partly because of a concerted effort on the part of women's rights organizations across the European Union. They noticed the huge influx of Slavic girls into the brothels of Western Europe and cared enough to listen to the stories of the ones who escaped—stories of how the Russian mafia, and other criminal organizations, controlled the girls through torture and stories of how the girls were forced by 30 to 40 men a night.

Another reason Europe is starting to listen is Sweden, where legislation in that country is based on the idea that prostitution degrades and exploits women. Period. No silly, fabricated lying equivocations—as we saw in good old Kalani O'Sullivan, with his efforts to justify the entitlement of the military male to rape the enslaved.

Sweden assumes that the raping shit male we so politely call the 'customer' is at fault. If a man cannot control his rapestick, it still does not make it okay to rape. (This, at least, is my interpretation of the Swedish position.) Sweden makes perfect humane commonsense to me (as it should do to all of us). As a result of this wonderful country, Norway and Denmark are considering similar legislation, and even the UK, long a bastion of outer darkness and ignorance when it comes to prostitution policies, is finally starting to wake up to the light.

I don't know if the military male (and female) will ever wake up to the light—given what we have seen as typical of their attitudes in the above articles. Particularly disturbing, in all the darkness and ignorance of these soldiers, is the comment by the wife of one of them, that we should "spend our time worrying about more important things."

<u>The</u> Issue for all women is prostitution. As long as it exists in its current coercive form (and is there a non-coercive form, one should ask)--as long as

the torture and degradation of women's bodies for profit is a norm, this young sheltered military wife cannot stand anywhere on this planet with dignity.

"A man has needs…" says the soldier in the Allen article from the *Stars and* Stripes. Do those 'needs,' I ask, involve the sexual destruction of female bodies? Are men's sexual needs so paramount, so important, so privileged, that the trafficking of hundreds of thousands of girls, the extreme sexual misery of wretched women forced against their will, is simply irrelevant—is this the way it has to be—because men 'have needs'? It has been this way so far—U.S. servicemen have used hundreds of thousands of coerced, vulnerable women and girls all over the world for decades. Is this changing? If it is, what reparation can we make to the girls who have been destroyed? How do we make reparation to the Okinawan girl used by 20 to 30 GI's a night for years, held in debt bondage, a being with no rights and no dignity. After thirty thousand rapes, how do we give her her life and body back? There is no way, of course, but some reparation for rape horror this deep must be made, in some way. If only the acknowledgement that this was actually not just rape, but beyond rape, what these men did to this girl—as a norm. Is this still happening to prostituted girls on Okinawa? Are dependent wives and daughters there ignoring this, as they always have ignored the rape-pain of the 'whores' that men need--to 'let off steam'? What is this 'let off steam' thing? We women matter not at all--as long as they get to 'let off steam'?!

It does not seem to matter whether we exploit Little Brown Fucking Machines or Big Blonde Fucking Machines. Both are soft and tender and can be so easily destroyed by sexual roughness. But—after all—'men have needs.' That is what is important.

William H. McMichael, bureau chief for the *Navy Times*, has some enlightening comments on the situation in Korea:

"The trafficking is so open and widely known that one Air Force sergeant at Osan Air Base said any commander who didn't know about it is an 'ostrich.'"

McMichael tells us that Russian girls are held in debt bondage near the base, they work 7 days a week, and must go to nearby hotels with the men for paid sex. They are confined in small apartments when not working with 8 or 9 other women and are monitored by a camera so they will not escape.

"Soldiers and airmen in South Korea say that only the newest or most naïve troops could be unaware" [that the women are trafficked], McMichael tells us.

McMichael's comments are interesting since they seem to reinforce my idea that even if men know that girls are trafficked and enslaved, they will use them anyway. Male sexual needs are so powerful that destruction of the female body and life is irrelevant? This is the huge puzzler and mystery for me—how men can use us when we are in such pain. It is my main source of despair: if it is true that male sexuality can never be controlled, then how will we ever stop prostitution/trafficking?

K. Heldman's article on Itaewon, a GI camp town in Korea, is full of horrors. He describes drunk soldier yelling and vomiting up against walls and a fight outside the clubs between a prostitute and a man with him yelling 'bitch' and 'asshole' at her. Hostility, hatred, violence, ugliness, crude hard sadness. (Kind of like Spike TV, the station for 'men'—if this is what men are, we are in real trouble.) It would kill me to work in an environment like this. I am too soft and gentle. I think these poor prostitutes were that way, too, until men forced them into being coarse, to withstand the ugly brute side of these soldiers. (I wonder if soldiers know how frightening and ugly they are to us prostitutes when they behave like *Jarhead* barbarians. The rough crude brute on the town.)

The women soldiers in Korea are, in their own way, even worse. They mock the Korean girls: "Buy me drinkee, I give you something." Damn, the female soldier is even crueler than I thought. It is no wonder she is reaping the side benefits of the raping male soldier so heavily—she stupidly and with great insensitivity refuses to protect or help the defenseless of her kind. She is getting the by-product of the rape of the prostitute visited on her own body because she is too blind to see the horror that is prostitution. Too blind to see that the degradation a man visits on a prostitute's body he will visit on any woman's body.

Heldman interviews a soldier who has "75 cents to his name because he spent about two hundred dollars the last two nights on longtimes (as in 'GI want long-time?') with a Korean prostitute in the Sunshine Club....The only Korean he knows is 'Suck harder.'"

Contrast this with how General Leon J. LaPorte, Commander of the Republic of Korea-United States Combined Forces, describes the GI's in Korea in front of the House Armed Services Committee: "The overwhelming majority of them embody the very best attributes of our national character…."

Boy!

I wonder what the prostitutes in Korea would think of this statement.

The Magic Vagina:

Thoughts on that Remarkable, Feminine Sacred Space

March 14, 2009

The *vagina dentata*. It is a mythological construct, a vagina equipped with sharp teeth, supposedly reflecting the male's fear of losing his member if he invades that mysterious place, a woman's insides. It is an ambiguous fear since blow jobs are so popular and the male has to brave a whole phalanx of teeth to get one of those. Maybe our vaginas are more scary than our mouths?

The film *Teeth,* just released, is based on the *vagina dentata* theme. Dawn (Jess Weixler) is an insecure virgin who is raped and then, for revenge, she castrates her lovers with her deadly vagina.

The vagina as dangerous is not a new theme. Ages ago, I read a science fiction story (the title eludes me) about women who punish the sexual brutality of men by wearing needle-tipped diaphragms.

The fantasy/science fiction realm finds a counterpart in modern day South Africa where a doctor has invented an anti-rape female condom called RapeX. Inserted into the vagina, it has hooks that latch onto the attacker's penis. It can only be removed surgically, at a hospital, thereby tagging the man as a rapist. (For a longer description of the device, see www.rapestop.net.)

Out of desperation, it is being tested in South Africa, which has the highest rape rates in the world, outside of a conflict zone.

Could this really be the Eden of Non-Rape we women are all looking for? Install one in every vagina? Problems with the device I see are that it can only be worn once and costs about $8 U.S. dollars, a hefty sum in a poor country. Can the average South African woman afford this every day, when she steps out of the house and becomes vulnerable to attack? How many other women around the world could afford an $8-a-day rape barrier? Also, girl children in

South Africa are frequent targets of rapists, due to the belief that sex with a virgin will cure AIDS. With her maidenhead, a child could not insert it. And the device looks pretty big—designed for a woman's body, so I don't think a child could get it in anyway, even if she didn't have a hymen.

When I first read of the device, I felt such sadness for its need, and fortunate that I live in a country where, ordinarily, I can step out the door without arming my vagina for a possible attack.

Despite having been raped a great deal, in my past, during a less protected time in my life, the idea of a *vagina dentata* is not very appealing. I am not out for revenge on all the penises in the world. I don't want to sport a mini-guillotine at my vaginal entrance. I don't want to see rows of severed members, like flaccid sausages, laid out like trophies. Upon the many kind men in my life--those who support me with loving care and are patient with all my neurotic female frailties—upon them I would never wish a *vagina dentata.* But it is seductive to think of inflicting revenge castration on those who deserve it.

Who deserves it? I could name millions of men—and I do in my other writings—but since this article is going to focus mainly on musings on the vagina, I will be brief. Let me just target one group. I recently read *Dancing Girls of Lahore*, an account of a Pakistani red-light district by a British scholar named Louise Brown. She mentions girl children kept drugged in brothels so they can withstand the pain of large numbers of 'clients.' ('Clients' is Brown's word. I would substitute 'rapist monsters.' We have to be careful with our terminology.) She says that the girls who 'enter' the profession so young are often left with lifelong physical problems: infections, infertility, totally messed up insides. ('Enter' is Brown's word, as if this were voluntary. I don't think the average 10- year-old is going to apply for a job where she has the insides raped out of her every night.)

The Pakistan rape-shit males who shove themselves into helpless girl children are not alone. There are Indian rape-shit males and Cambodian rape-shit males and Thai rape-shit males and Mexican rape-shit males, not to mention American rape-shit males. Just one example of the latter: there is a thriving child prostitution business in Atlanta, Georgia, USA, mostly taking advantage of young black girls. Girls as young as 11 or 12 are being raped 30 or more times a night by monster rape-shit American males. Sex tourists having fun on our own soil. I guess it costs too much to take their rape-shit penises to Thailand. Not that I would wish them on the pathetic Thai child sex slave either. I assume that grown men in London and Paris and Athens and Dubai and Las Vegas--and any other city in the world you mention—are climbing on girl children and destroying their lives and bodies. There is a

Universal Rape-Shit Male. He is those millions out there who add to the nightly rape quota of the shredded whore vagina—whatever the victim's age: the 8-year-old whore will one day be an 18-year-old whore, if she survives. (Whether it be India or Cambodia or Thailand, the world turns girls into whores pitifully young.)

Grown men raping children. A universally accepted phenomenon. Brown's description of Pakistan reflects what I have read of all other brothel cultures, from Bombay to Bangkok. Average age of first sale: 12. Brown says the teen years are the peak ones; then the girl's desirability fades in her 20's. Whores who do survive end up in cheap brothels taking on many clients for a few cents. Or they end up begging on the streets.

What kind of twisted sexual world have we created where young, completely unsuitable for sex girl child bodies are considered 'prime' for sex? And the girl in her 20's, just barely starting to become a woman, has no sexual value at all? Damn. Women are barely aware of the infinite beauty of their sexuality by the time they hit 40 or 50. A child cannot have no concept of hers—especially when it is raped away from her.

All of which leads me to this question: what is the appeal of the Lolita child whore vagina? Why would a grown man want to climb on top of a child? 'Child' is not just a 12-year-old. Child is, to me, a 15-year-old, or an 18-year-old. Young, unformed, immature. What is the appeal of sex with girls so young? In my mind 18 is far, far too young for sex. If I could rule the world, no girl under 25 would have sex. By then, the body and the emotions are ready. The girl is slowly becoming a woman.

The child and teen body are not equipped for sex. Young girls have thinner vaginal membranes and so they tear easily, as well as that other obvious fact—they are smaller in size. What an abomination to consider 12 the 'normal' age for deflowering. What an abomination to only consider the teenage body desirable. Women are not even interesting enough to talk to, let alone have sex with, until they are at least 25 or so. What turned-upside-down view of female sexuality has the rape of the whorechild vagina created—in Pakistan and India and Thailand—and Atlanta, Georgia?

Is it all the usual 'excuses' that makes the whore child vagina desirable?--she is helpless, she is small, she is frail, she is innocent. A man does not have to be a man with a child. He can do anything he wants to her. He does not have to respect her, or listen to her. In a world where most women are still second-class sexual citizens, it should not be surprising that men who are not men like to dominant helpless prostituted children. The child whore is an extension of the way men dominate all women. Why else would all these Pakistani or Indian men line up to use the drugged child whores in those brothels? Or why else would the American man mount the heavily raped child whore in Atlanta?

Frail and small? Is that the appeal? When I worked as a prostitute, I weighed about 125 pounds. I thought that was plenty frail and small enough considering that the average male is so much bigger than we are. It seems that all those hefty 200-pound guys (or even 180-pound guys) would be satisfied with the smallness of the average woman and not have to go to the child-size range for their kicks.

AIDS, of course, has been a big factor in increasing child whore numbers. There is the illusion a child will be 'clean' but, of course, she is far more likely to be diseased due to the fact that she tears more easily. It is not a recent illusion: child whores in previous centuries, when syphilis was feared, were also sought after.

A startling fact: at one time, the average age of an inmate in an Indian brothel was early 20's. Now, since the advent of AIDS, it is 13. (Source: Coalition Against Trafficking in Women.)

All those rape-shit penises shoving themselves into pitiful whore bodies--these I would gladly subject to the *vagina dentata*. It would be satisfying to see the dead weapons hanging in long rows in the air, like empty sausage wrappers. Instead of Vlad, the Impaler, Suki, the Flag-Pole Flyer.

I have to admit some prejudices in the area of whose members I would like to see flapping from those poles. I recently read of how, when the Russian mafia renders a girl 'suitable' for trafficking/prostitution in Dubai, they take her to a nearby Pakistani labor camp where they let a different man in every 15 minutes to mount and break her. I want to see those Pakistani rape-shit males castrated. But only after they have been spread on their stomachs, tied down, and mercilessly raped anally as many times as the Dubai Trafficked Girls are.

I have had bad feelings toward Pakistani men ever since Bangladesh. 400,000 women held in rape camps by them for months and degraded and sexually savaged beyond places where the human imagination can even go?

But, to be fair, the Rape-Shit Male comes in all nationalities. That famous red-light area in Lahore, Pakistan was once frequented by the British. It is where Kipling visited whores. "A man is a man, for all that," or however he phrased it.

One of the worst rape-shit males now is the German one. Over one million Rape-Shit German males per day visit the pitiful trafficked whores of their country and shove their merciless rape-shit penises into these miserable, helpless girls. In a country where prostitution is legal, the industry has grown hugely due to it being easy for pimps and traffickers to operate; and the majority of the 400,000 prostitutes there are trafficked. The largest number of these at the moment come from the Ukraine, brought in by the Russian mafia.

I don't know how to get rid of the rape-shit male. I guess if the rape-shit trafficker male has no customers to buy his product, this means no women for sale. But how do we eliminate the customer rapist? All the millions of men who don't buy the enslaved have to physically stop those who do.

Having a vagina makes a woman vulnerable. She has no place, or home, or country—since everywhere she goes, she might be raped. There is no country without rape-shit males. So woman is not a citizen of any land, to borrow from Virginia Woolf. She could only be a citizen of a country without rape.

To return to the vagina, and another area that troubles me. Late at night, I see TV shows with Implant Babes, girls sitting around with their jello-mold bosoms jutting into the air, discussing the virtues of The Big Penis. (I want to make it clear that I have nothing against cleavage, or scanty clothing, and I love to see and display skin—but I recoil from the artificial plastic unreal breasts that are now such a huge fad. They don't even move normally. No softness or sway to them and men tell me they feel like concrete. Ugh.)

These Implant Babes, sitting around talking about The Big Penis, say that the penis can't be too big. Big is never big enough, for them.

Yes, it can be too big. Big ones hurt. These implant girls do all women everywhere harm if they extol The Big Penis.

(The loveliness of foreplay, by the way, has it over The Big Penis. The touch of a man, patient and tender, that melting warm gentle ecstasy of the pleasure he gives, touching and tender—that is way, way above The Big Penis.)

When I worked as a prostitute, over a period of several years, I slept with about 500 different men. (I can't be entirely accurate as to numbers since you lose track. I learned, surprisingly—by the way--that this number is quite small, in comparison to the average of 800 a year that some say is the 'norm' for a prostitute in the U.S.) Of those 500, most were Caucasian, but a handful were black. All of the black males were too big for me. I know there must be 'normal' size black men out there, but it was my misfortune to come across the ones with the big ones.

As a non-prostitute, I also have slept with a number of black men. All of them were too big for me. I always tore, even when aroused. As a prostitute, I was never aroused, so perhaps that might account for the bleeding and pain.

Even using a lot of lube did not help. And I know that I tore all the time with other customers as well. I was always in pain. It wasn't just the big ones that hurt me. It was overuse of a vagina that tears easily to begin with. (It is no wonder that so many prostitutes use drugs—it eases the pain of a torn-up vagina.)

Back to those black men, the way I tore even when sex was voluntary and I was excited (as a non-prostituted woman) tells me that the vagina can only stretch so far. Which brings me to the problem I have with all these women's magazines who say it can stretch endlessly. An article called "Va-Jay-Jay—Fascinating New Facts about your Lovely Lady Parts" in a recent *Cosmopolitan* (March 2008) tells me that the vagina can accommodate even really big ones. It can't. The dimensions quoted in the article are confusing. At rest, the vagina is only a tiny little thing—a couple of inches long and one inch wide at the opening. Aroused, it balloons to about 5 inches in length. So how can it stretch to withstand 8 inches (this was about the size of the black men I had inside me)? Where does the rest go? It went into banging my cervix very painfully, if I read the diagrams of my insides correctly.

And the opening doesn't get any bigger, during arousal, in so far as I can tell. I never stretched enough to comfortably take the really thick ones. All these myths about how we can happily accommodate huge dicks do such a disservice to our tender bodies and tender parts.

I want to make clear that this is not a criticism of black men—just their penises. When I was non-prostituted, I seemed to run across black men who were fun and open and light-hearted and not afraid to show affection--character traits I found refreshing and pleasing. My suggestion to you black guys—and to well-endowed white guys—is, don't get any bigger. Don't use any of those 'extend your member' products. Instead, trim a few inches off those whoppers. Have some mercy on the women of the world.

I always have to draw a distinction between my prostituted and non-prostituted self, and my prostituted and non-prostituted vagina. During prostitution sex, I was stiff and closed up tight and frightened. During 'real sex' (the non-commercial type that has some tenderness to it) I can melt into a pool of ecstatic warmth between my legs if the man—and the circumstances—are right. There needs to be a new vocabulary for sex. 'Prostitution sex' is not really sex: it is a brutal forcing ramming shoving miserable act inflicted on an unwilling body. Men don't really buy 'sex' when they buy a body. They buy the financial right to rape. (I get tired of only having this limited pool of words at my disposal.)

While I am on the subject of distinctions, I want to draw one between the vagina that is raped once, and the vagina that is raped thousands of times. Condi's visit to Japan recently will serve as a handy example. She apologized to the Japanese government for a recent incident—the alleged rape of a Japanese adolescent by an American Marine. The Japanese sputtered about the incident being an 'outrage' and 'unforgivable'—all the usual rhetoric. This from a government that not only allows but promotes, through inaction, a 30-billion-dollar a year sex industry based on trafficking girls (some just children) in from the Philippines, Columbia, Thailand, and Taiwan—among other countries—and holding them as debt bondage sex slaves who are subjected to any sadistic act any rapist client wants to perform on them, including cutting their genitals with knives, as one poor girl who escaped reported. If Condi really wanted to do something useful about rape, she would launch a long-term, determined campaign to release these girls from slavery. She would demand to visit the brothels were girls are being held—wherever she goes—Japan, Pakistan, Afghanistan, Korea, Iraq (particularly the ones in the Green Zone)—and she would use our considerable military might to release these girls—immediately. And she would not leave it at that—she would make sure the girls received the long-term trauma care they need.

There is yet another military rape case pending in Japan—this one involving four Marines accused of raping a Japanese girl. Again, I would ask why her body is valued and the bodies of the prostituted girls these Marines may have used as release sites not? I do not mean to belittle these 'nice' Japanese girls who may have been raped by these Marines. They, too, are important. But why are they so much more important than their suffering counterparts, the prostituted adolescents, who are serially raped every day in Japanese brothels—and other brothels all over the world--under circumstances far more devastating and horrifying than any these 'respectable' girls will ever know? The one-time rape of the 'good' girl is a hallowed incident; the mass rape of all those 'bad' whores is a norm.

The Japanese are dredging up the famous case on Okinawa in the mid-90's when a group of Marines allegedly raped a young teenager. At that time, the response of a high-ranking American officer was, "Damn, why didn't those guys just go out and buy a whore?" (!). No realization, of course, that the whore was probably an imported Filipina who had been broken in to her trade, as a young teenager, by being drugged as she took on her long line of 'clients' for the night. (These Filipinas really get it from all sides--pardon the terrible sexual pun--since we have turned them into the Whores of Asia—open to all comers, victims of all traffickers. Only their Thai sisters hold higher Whore-of-Asia status.)

I want to draw another distinction—one between the Pampered Vagina and the Raped Vagina. Western female journalists (the kind who write for *Cosmo*) and trendy sexologists (the kind who are quoted in *Cosmo*) give the misleading idea that the Pampered Vagina is the norm. That it is Sacred Feminine Space. That it is a Tender Lotus Blossom and a Precious Treasure. They overlook the irony that, say, in India, this Sacred Yoni Blossom Space is worshipped by selling young girls into prostitution to appease erotic goddesses. It certainly is a huge irony to worship an erotic goddess by destroying a girl's sexuality. They overlook the horror that entire nations of women (like those in the Sudan) are genitally mutilated. They are subjected to "infibulation"—the most severe form of 'cultural' female mutilation, where all outer genitalia—clitoris, labia--are razored off and the remaining tissue is sewn shut, permitting a tiny opening for pee and menstrual fluid. Should the girl survive the razoring (some bleed to death or develop infections they die from)—should she survive, her legs will be bound together, for several weeks, until the wound starts to scar over. Peeing for these girls is beyond any pain zone you will ever go into. As a result, they hold it as long as possible, and develop bladder infections. In fact, infections of all sorts are rampant throughout their lives, as a result of the mutilation, not to mention that intercourse for them is pure hellish suffering—can the Pampered Western Female Vagina actually imagine what it must feel like to be rammed into when your hole has been sewn to a tiny pinpoint and your whole genital area is an infected mess? This is the norm for 120 million women (and growing, since this practice is inflicted on 4 million more girls a year). The Pampered Vagina in not the norm. And I don't think that the 8-year-old child in the Pakistani red-light district, drugged to endure her long line of 'clients' every night, would even remotely see her vagina as Sacred Feminine Space. There is no Sacred Feminine Space left after genital mutilation, or after long lines of rapists mounting you every night.

It is very depressing for me to go into a drugstore because there I see all these dainty pink boxes with flowers on them labeled, Gentle Glide Tampons. I see magazines called *Teen Prom* with sweet wholesome pampered safe girls in pink dresses on the covers. What good will a Gentle Glide Tampon do a child whore with a vagina ravaged by thousands of rape-shit males? What could these protected girls on magazine covers possibly have to do with the torn mutilated vaginas of all those other millions of girls around the world who are not safe, who are not cherished and pampered and who have had all the Sacred Feminine Space raped or razored out of them?

Fancy pampered Western sexperts, writing for pampered editors of glossy, safe, happy women's magazines, turn out books about the vagina and call them cutesy things like *Vagina, Your Owner's Manual.* Actually, my vagina does not belong to me. It got raped away from me a long time ago. There is no way I will ever get it back, or be able to protect it—because it is still being raped away from me everyday, as I read about the extreme oppression of other women's bodies. The Pakistani whore child in front of her long rape queue does not own her vagina. Fancy glossy safe happy blind pampered Western women experts and sexperts need to include the child-whore vagina in their sexual scheme of the universe. The whore body, of whatever age, I have noticed, is invisible to them.

Given what I have seen of the blind insensitivity of the 'decent,' protected women of the world, I am really proud to be a whore. Ages ago when I was one, I was mostly a dirty joke to the men who bought me and I never went near 'respectable' women due to fear of rejection and scorn. Under this double censure, it was hard to overcome feelings of being dirty and worthless. I got a Ph.D. mostly to affirm myself in the eyes of the world, not really because I thought that this imaginary patriarchal construct called higher education was of any value. When people 'respect' me because of this degree, I feel fake. (Ph.D.—Post-Harlot Degree?) They should respect me for having been a whore—I was worth way more back then, as a I tried to survive in that harsh reality of rape. I have no value conferred by this worthless degree granted by a bunch of blind academics who teach nothing but lies.

I mostly see the world from the point of view of a powerful truth—that of the Raped Vagina. POV—but in a different sense from the porn meaning. I can't write on the current issues in the EU without asking what they are doing about that 20-story brothel in Cologne, German stocked with debt-bondage sex slaves trafficked in from the Ukraine. Rape is all tidy and legal in Germany, the Modern-Day, Sexual-Slavery State.

I read article after article on Darfur and all of them seem meaningless to me since they leave out one of the cruelest practices ever inflicted on woman: these writers never note that the thoroughly raped women and girls of the Sudan have already been subjected to a far greater rape—the razoring off of their genitals in an act of massive cultural blindness. It is, by the way, why so many girls in Darfur are dying of the gang rapes—their already damaged, infected vaginas cannot take the additional assaults. Yet these gang rapes are mild compared to the way these girls were mutilated to rob them of their sexuality. Female Genital Mutilation is permanent, irreversible rape and an abomination to all women on planet earth. The most atrocious cruelty of all in Darfur passes by completely unnoticed. All the fancy celebrities like Mia Farrow, with their Save Darfur rhetoric, fail to mention this 'minor' fact of female oppression. As if it mattered not, or did not even exist. The great puzzle is that the women do this to their own daughters, feeding the savage practice new victims all the time. I wonder why we feel any sympathy for the women of Darfur when they continue to razor off the genitals of their own girl children. This is my Raped Vagina POV on that conflict.

My Raped Vagina POV controls my vision of history. I can't see pictures of ragged Afghan women, widowed by all the wars inflicted on them—homeless women, sitting in the snow--without imagining their desperate sadness. I hope they are able to sell sex for food to all those rich NATO troops over there. At least it gives them a way to eat. Starving takes more courage than does selling the vagina. The really brave (and foolish women) starve. The smart ones figure out they have this valuable thing between their legs. I am one of the cowards. Put me in the place of the ragged Afghan homeless woman and I would choose daily prostitution-rape over starvation. I'd be hopping all over those occupying troops, saying, "I let you rape me long time—just feed me!" And I'd choose prostitution with the enemy over being cold. I would fuck to be allowed inside, where it's warm. Being cold is like a premonition of death. (I want to be warm on this planet since I will have all eternity to be cold in the grave.)

As I ponder survival sex, I wonder how come our species evolved in such a way that this beautiful place we women have between our legs has to be turned, through rape and prostitution, into a wound that never heals.

"These old whores are really smart. They'll offer it standing up, to the soldiers on duty at the gates." Thus said an American soldier stationed in Italy after WWII. He was referring to women who had been starvation prostituted during WWI and were still desperately trying to open their legs so they could continue to eat.

A vagina is an asset. It will earn you food. We women are really lucky. If you're willing to fuck anyone who wants you, you will never go hungry.

The latest news out of Iraq is that oil revenues in that country have been in the billions over the last five years and no one knows where the money is going—it seems to be in non-Iraqi banks, and not being used to help the people of that country with social services, medical facilities, food, etc. ("GAO Asked to Audit Iraqi Oil Revenues," Associated Press story, March 9, 2008). This same article says that projected Iraqi oil revenues will be about $100 billion for 2007-2008. That is enough to rescue and aid all the 50,000 Iraqi women, girls, and children who are currently involved in selling survival sex as a result of the war. (This 50,000 figure comes from the Women's

Commission for Refugee Women and Children.) That's plenty to save the vaginas of all Iraqi women and girls from more sexual exploitation. With that kind of money, Iraq can even go to Dubai and rescue all the Iraqi girls sold by their families into the sex trade there. Helping them to live normal lives may be another manner. Brown's book, referred to above, recounts how Pakistani girls are also sold to Dubai—they go expecting good working conditions, but some are taken advantage of by their 'agents.' Once there, the girls are faced with long lines of 'clients' (rapists) and even have to be tied down to withstand the pain. If they survive and return home, they can say nothing of their 'ordeal' since the mass rape would bring shame on them! (The weird workings of the female mind. She blames herself for the terrible abuse of the own vagina?)

If tender Iraqi virgins have been sold to Dubai, to feed their families, and long-lines of rapists using them are the result--it will take a lot of that $100 billion to help them recover—if any recovery is possible. But with $100 billion dollars—well, it is a start toward making reparation for what these girls have suffered.

I am currently obsessed with the Iraqi whore vagina since its raped misery is the result of our current "Operation Iraqi Freedom" campaign and I wake up every morning feeling Phantom Rape Pain between my legs because of all those Iraqi women and girls who have to fuck to survive. I lived through the era of the Vietnamese whore vagina, the result of our other protracted campaign to 'free' a people, and felt the same rape within my body every day for the ten long brutal years of that war.

I have felt the rape pain of women from many centuries past.

'Vagina' comes from a Greek word meaning 'sheath for a sword.' As if it is secondary to the penis. As if its only function is to be 'put to the sword.' The etymological origins of 'fuck' are similarly brutal: it is derived from words meaning "to strike" and "to pierce with a weapon" and "to beat." Brownmiller, and many other feminists, say that men rape us because they can. Because they are stronger. Will the vagina ever be safe? As long as men can take it by force, I don't think so. Such a simple fact—a difference in strength, has governed all of human history. It has determined that the female half of the species will always fear the male half. And that she will always have to fuck for food. All of female human history is governed by the doctrine of fuck-for-food. Fuck-for-food is the reason for marriage, a rape prison almost as terrible as prostitution.

Fancy women's magazines designed for pampered safe women regard the vagina as Sacred Feminine Space—what a huge cruel joke for the millions of prostituted women and girls and children.

In my erotic fantasy novel *Tender Bodies and Whore Stories*, one of my heroines, Shaylin, is getting a Ph.D. in Sexual Misery Studies. I want to establish such Ph.D. programs everywhere, not just in the imaginary university I create for her. (Read the novel—there you will see how I replace Sexual Misery Space with Sacred Feminine Space.)

In that novel, I also work out, through fictional catharsis, one of my greatest fears: assembly-line sex. I subject some of my poor heroines to it in order to get rid of it from my imagination.

My first introduction, in writing, to this terrible practice came in my teens when I accidentally stumbled across a passage in a book (now long forgotten, I don't even remember the title) about how Roman legions in ancient Britain lined up to use Saxon girls until they died from exhaustion and bleeding. This same passage mentioned Napoleon's troops doing the same on the island of Elba. Why just these two instances were cited I don't know. I imagine that in whatever real Troy there was, the Greek troops, camped on the beach in front of the city, were doing the same to captive Trojan girls. When the Goths sacked Rome, they practiced it. At Masada, the soldiers were inflicting this terrible mass rape on captive girls. Every army and navy throughout history has probably practiced it. And every male civilian population.

That first passage, read in my teens, horrified me because until then my imagination about sex had not extended that far. I didn't know it was possible to rape anyone to death since I knew nothing about rape. I was protected, the whole time I was growing up, from anyone hurting me sexually. And I grew up in an era when sex was so forbidden as a topic of conversation for 'nice' girls that I only had the vaguest idea about what intercourse was until I was fifteen. That was the year I read *Fanny Hill* and also *Lady Chatterley.* Until then, I knew men had this thing called a penis, but I didn't know quite what they did with it. And I certainly didn't know what one looked like, never even having seen a picture of one. (When I first put my hand around one, later in my innocent young life, it looked and felt like this alien instrument. Damn, how could anybody be shaped like that?)

Those two novels—*Fanny* and *Lady Chat*--were a big illumination since they contained graphic descriptions of intercourse. I had not even looked at my own vagina in a mirror yet since I was rather afraid of what I would find--and this kind of exploration was not encouraged in my growing-up era. So the way Fanny described hers was very helpful—as was what she experienced when men were inside her. Until Fanny, I didn't even know men went inside women, let alone what it felt like. (Fanny has always been one of my favorite literary heroines, along with Jane Eyre. I am kind of a combo of those two women.)

Shortly thereafter--now that I knew what happened between men and women (thanks to Fanny)--I came across the passage about the Roman legions. Then I dipped into another book about Bar Girls Around the World. How this racy volume ended up in the chaste military-base library where I did my reading, I don't know. (I was a military brat and the whole time I was growing up, we were stationed on military bases around the world.)

It was a small library with lots of comfortable chairs and cosy nooks and a colorful corner for kids full of Dr. Seuss and *Peter Pan* and a cardboard Tink hovering over one area, dangling from a string, and stuffed animals with big pink-and-blue bows and little red-and-green wooden trains. I spent a lot of my free time in that small library, and what I read on that one rainy afternoon about the bar girls of the world saddened and depressed me. The danger to their vaginas was a blow to my safe little library world, with its trains and stuffed animals, and to my protected vagina. The Roman legions had already destroyed my safety and now the bar girls completed that destruction.

I don't remember too much of that bar-girl book except a few really depressing sections. One was in a Thai bar where a really sluttish older whore (the book's way of describing her) was trying to get some big, ugly rough coarse German sailors to use her and she was hiking up her skirt (no undies) and pointing to the area between her legs and licking her painted lips in a crude way and saying "yum yum." It made me think of how she must have looked at twelve, which seemed to be the average age of the rest of the girls in the bar receiving the crude attentions of the ugly German sailors. It made me think of how she was once fresh and sweet until the men turned her into something as crude as they were.

This Thai bar girl sent me into such a tailspin of a depression, that I abandoned the book for a while. I went over and sat in the kid's section and read some *Peter Pan*, with Tinker Bell hovering above me like a Guardian Fairy. On that wet afternoon, I remember that her wings looked pale bluish from the rainy half-light coming from the window.

When I went back to the bar-girl book, I read a section on Japan, the country I was currently sitting in—an innocent teenage protected girl--on this rainy afternoon, reading about rape and sadness in a military-base library. This was the 1960's, when I was sitting reading on this wet afternoon. The book said that the older Japanese bar girls dated from just after WWII when they had been broken by pimps and criminals as soon as the American and

Australian GI's landed since the Japanese saw a big, big source of profit in rape-broken bodies. Pimps and criminals seasoned homeless, war-destitute girls through assembly-line rape in the bombed-out buildings and then turned them out, all ready for rape and fun, for the ready-to-party conquerors. And the pimps, the book said, were right about profits. Huge amounts of foreign currency flowed through the vaginas of the girls, right into the hands of pimps and profiteers and corrupt police and politicians and businessmen. The Japanese could not keep the rape factories stoked up at a high-enough heat. They had to run 24-hours a day, with vagina served up piping hot by the slice, for the hundreds of thousands of conquerors. (Vagina by-the-slice was also being served up piping hot in post-war Italy under identical conditions: pimp- and criminal-controlled vaginas serving as conduits for cash. GI's brought the idea of pizza by the piping-hot slice back from Italy, too—along with learning the fun of the war-time rape of piping-hot vagina slices.)

The Japanese whore vaginas were a windfall—without them, no economic recovery would have been possible. These women's raped bodies formed the basis of the prosperity of modern Japan.

That was enough for me. I put the book in a corner, behind other books, in hopes I would never find it or have to look at it again. Then my eye fell on *The World of Suzie Wong*. I read it that night and it was not too depressing except when the hero cruelly makes fun of her for pretending she is a virgin in her fantasy world. I have never re-read the book, but I do remember the way Suzie says she hated 'short times.' I later learned that all whores hate short times and the disgust of instant sex with crude ugly men who just climb on and don't care.

Ever since I was tiny, I'd been aware, in some dim way, that there were these girls outside the gates of the bases where I lived that everyone made fun of for sexual reasons I didn't comprehend in my innocent childhood. The bar-girl book, along with Fanny's filling me in on what men and women did together, made it clearer. I'd always felt sad for these girls, and now that I knew what sex was, at least through reading, I felt sadder. It really puzzled me how I could sit in the snack bar and have French fries and a milkshake with a GI who was being nice to me, and then he could go outside the gate and be mean to one of those girls.

After the bar-girl book, I resolutely stayed away from reading about prostitution. It was depressing enough seeing all the GI's around me going outside the gate to hurt the girls.

Then, in my late teens and early 20's, I accidentally came across several more pieces of assembly-line sex information that have haunted me ever since, just like the bar-girl book. I read a news story about how worn-out French whores from Marseilles were shipped into North Africa to service the French soldiers there. The girls were raped 60 times a day. For some reason, the pimps who shipped them in were prosecuted and imprisoned, but the article said the girls were not imprisoned for what they had done. What had they done, I wondered? It said they were returned to Marseilles. To where? Back to their brothels? The article didn't say.

I came across the enlightening information that Marseilles was also the source for worn-out French whores used in assembly-line brothels for local men in Morocco. These places are called *abattoirs*, slaughterhouses, and the women are subjected to rape every few minutes by a different man for 15 to 20 hours a day. They can be raped a hundred or more times a day.

The last piece of information that I imbibed, back then in my more innocent years, was from a book called *Female Sexual Slavery*. It opens with the description of an *abattoir* brothel in the immigrant section of Paris where worn-out French whores are sent to service (dreadful cold word) 80 Middle Eastern men a day, 160 a day on weekends, so their pimps can get some last fuck money out of them before they die of rape exhaustion.

In so far as I have been able to determine, this is still going on, decades after it was uncovered in *Female Sexual Slavery*. These poor *abattoir* whores are described as 'apathetic' when they're not working. When they are working, a buzzer goes off every 5 minutes so one man can get off and the next can get on. Timed fuck.

The women are not allowed to leave the house. Where would they go if they could? (Can the women even still walk after all this physical abuse?) Laughing, joking policemen stroll by the gates, taking kickbacks, knowing full well what is going on inside. Not caring, I assume, since the imagination of those not being shoved into by crude sadistic rapist shit males cannot extend to the pain. I assume the imagination of other French women cannot extend this far either. They must know what is going on? It is no secret anymore, what is being done to our bodies. If I could find out easily, and if the Sources section of the book I'm currently finishing up (*The Raped Vagina*) consists of over 400 entries (and this is only a portion of what is in print about prostitution/trafficking), everyone on the planet who can read should know—what is going on.

But way back then, in my teens, information was scarce and what little I read about assembly-line sex terrified me. It intensified the Phantom Rape Pain between my legs, something I have felt all my life, even before I knew what sex and rape are. I was seemingly born with a body that is being constantly raped, as a tribute to the history of the female body for the past 3000 years.

It is a real liability—to have a vagina. As long as you do, you are never safe. Men can rape and break you at any moment. They can reduce you to nothing. Once broken, that's it. I cannot fathom this fashionable, trendy word: empowerment. Where did this ridiculous notion come from? Women have no 'empowerment.' As long as we can be raped and broken and reduced to nothing, we are nothing. Men are the superior, dominant beings on this planet. We women are nothing but rape sites.

After those terrifying pieces of knowledge about assembly-line sex, ages ago in my teens, I once again resolutely stayed away from any mention of prostitution in print. I didn't want to know anymore.

In my 20's I was gang raped and this experience had a deep impact on me. Even though it was a continuation of the Phantom Rape Pain that had plagued me all my life, this event drove the fear of assembly-line sex so deeply into me that this fear rules my life. Since that rape, I have had agoraphobia, a fear of leaving enclosed spaces. It takes me forever to force myself across the threshold in the morning. The possibility of dark hard humiliating rape is always out there. Having to face people in all my shame and sadness is out there. I hate facing 'normal' people. I hate facing unraped women. They are so bright and happy and safe. It is unbearable to be with them in their sunshine normality.

If I don't force myself to leave the house everyday, things can become impossible. When I have been sick and out of work, I have stayed home with my animals and loved and cared for them. A great comfort but this seclusion made facing people impossible. During these times, the only trips outside the door would be for food. Those days were terrible. I'd feel cold and shaky the whole time I was at the supermarket, and the faces of all those normal, safe, unraped women made me feel hopeless and sad beyond repair. All those shining lovely glowing sexy girls on the covers of *Cosmo* and *Glamour* and *Teen Prom* on the magazine shelves made the ordeal of the supermarket even worse. All these happy protected women who live in a fantasy land where there is no rape and degradation and terrible forcing of men into our bodies. All these women living in this happy illusion that we are 'empowered.'

I have to force myself to leave the house everyday, for fear I may never get across the threshold again. Thus, this is what having a vagina that got badly raped does to a woman.

That gang rape was just one of a number of rapes I've been subjected to, but it was the worst in terms of numbers. It was half a dozen men and they all went more than once so I was probably raped 12 to 15 times. I can't know the exact number. And I passed out a lot toward the end. And I couldn't walk after the ordeal was over with. How does the *abattoir* whore in Morocco get up after her 100 a day? Does she just pee where she lays, like the Korean Comfort Women report doing during their daily rape quotas? One says that when she would wet herself and bleed too much, the men would just kick her and leave.

It's a real puzzle as to why women have to be reduced to this state of extreme pain and degradation because they have vaginas. I don't think that magic space should be treated this way. Apparently the rapist shit males of the world and the indifferent protected respectable women of the world do not agree with me. Apparently all those millions of Japanese soldiers would not agree with me. Japan, Land of Monster Rapist Males. But, then, it is hard to find a country without Monster Rapist Males. No such place exists. All nations are Rape Nations. Those millions of Japanese soldiers just made assembly-line rape an accepted norm. One wonders if any of those millions of young men felt anything for the girls? And when the men went home after the war and married and had daughters—was there not even a second of self-awareness—that the daughter could have been the body in the rape-torture bed? These Japanese men inflicted rape that was Beyond Rape on the comfort women. They turned it into a fun, sanctioned, leisure activity. And they tied the girls down and got in line and heard the girls crying for hours—but the men still kept raping and raping them. These men are beyond monsters. What kind of collective psyche are we dealing with in the Japanese male? A Monster Rapist Psyche. It is no wonder. Called 'licensed prostitution,' the 'legal rape' of the female body arose in 1600 in Japan. The Comfort-Woman system was just an extension of that. And the massive trafficking of girls from Thailand, Columbia, Taiwan, and the Philippines into current-day Japan is an extension of that. So is the massive use of prostituted bodies by modern-day Japanese men. It is all the same picture. The same reality.

Even that mild, mild gang rape that was inflicted on me—nothing like what happens to the *abattoir* whores in Paris with their 160 a day on weekends, and the buzzer going off every 5 minutes for the next rapist shit to get on—even that mild rape terrified me forever. I am broken. Men don't need to make me submissive anymore. I am completely docile—and have no dignity, or existence, beyond a raped being. You have proven your superiority over me.

Over the past couple of years, I have been writing a book—*The Raped Vagina: A Military Prostitute's Story.* It's almost done and will be out shortly. It has entailed my reading vastly in the area of prostitution/trafficking since the book combines autobiography with research. Sadly, this reading made me aware of yet more assembly-line sex instances. There are two that haunt me: one is a description of a trafficked girl in London who was raped 50-60 times a day and over 80 times on Christmas Day. She escaped and found refuge with Poppy, a London group that helps trafficked girls. What haunts me is not so much what happened to this girl but what a Poppy volunteer said about this girl. Poppy says this girl is now fine and doing well. This was a real puzzle. Surely, the women who help at Poppy must be aware of the long-term effects of mass rape? They are, by now, becoming quite well documented since we now accord to the prostitute the same PTSD that we do to torture victims. How can Poppy think that all is fine and dandy with this woman who was forced 50-60 times a day, 80 times on Christmas Day, day of gentle peace and sweetness and giving--and I guess the men who forced her went home to play with their daughters and kiss their wives. Given the normal women (wives and daughters) outside the rape-room, and the trauma and disgust of crude ugly rape-shit males on top of you, 80 times on Christmas Day, believe me, you will never be fine again. I am not 'fine' after only 15 rapes in one day. It did not 'empower' me.

The second instance that haunts me is finding out how traffickers break girls. They all operate similarly but apparently the Albanian and Russian mafias are particularly brutal. The girl I mentioned above, the Russian one trafficked into Dubai and set up by the Russian mafia as a portable brothel in a Pakistani labor camp, where the men were let in every 15 minutes—apparently she is typical of how the traffickers work. I have read similar descriptions in Tijuana, a border city for breaking girls before they are sent into the U.S. The gangs who break the girls in Tijuana prize the ones who can take 50 rapes a day, docilely, without insanity or suicide—that is, they are 'prized' until they wear out and are thrown away.

I have come to call in my mind the prostitute broken in the Pakistani labor camp the Dubai Girl. Her counterparts are all over that 'pleasure' city, with its enormous wealth. They come mostly from the Ukraine and Moldova—two desperately poor countries whose chief export is the Raped Vagina. Unprotected girls from orphanages in the Ukraine are a favorite source for traffickers, but other girls are also pimped and procured by their own countrymen and relatives. People are sometimes surprised that traffickers can treat girls in such unimaginably brutal ways, but looking at it from their point of view, it would be foolish to not take advantage of this replaceable, incredibly lucrative form of making money.

For one, there is no prosecution or punishment anywhere for the traffickers so they run no risks. They operate with complete impunity worldwide thanks to corrupt police, border guards, and politicians and to the indifference of other politicians and of practically everyone else, including all the respectable women whose vaginas are not being raped inside out all day.

The only ones subject to punishment are the girls themselves. Should they actually be arrested in a brothel raid, they will be taken to a police station and treated like dirt, like the 'dirty whores' they are. Should they be deported, they will return to a Ukraine or Moldova where they will again be treated like the dirty whores they are: rejected by the families that sold them, turned into public whores for the men of the town, blamed for now being public filth.

Should a girl dare try to prosecute her procurer or trafficker, the judge will tell her she is a dirty whore who got what she deserved in Dubai and her traffickers will threaten to mutilate or kill her if she dares say a word against them. Such is the fate of the vagina in the Ukraine, or Moldova.

(It is also the fate of the dirty gang raped vagina in America. I did not go to the police after my own assault since I did not want to be treated like a dirty joke by another group of macho men—and maybe even raped again, by this new 'entitled' to be rough bunch. And, besides, I was so sick and in such shock, I was barely conscious. I was too damaged to go anywhere, for help.)

The mass-raped whore vagina fares no better than the gang-raped one in the U.S. Of the many girls trafficked into massage parlour brothels from Asia and Eastern Europe, if they are ever 'rescued' in a brothel raid, they are jailed and treated like the whore filth they are by police and judges and their owners get off with a light fine or a probationary warning and the rapists called their clients don't get anything done to them at all. The girls have no escape since if they try to prosecute, they are threatened by their still at-large traffickers and owners with death or bodily injury.

Such is the fate of the whore vagina in America. I saw this operating on an episode of that ridiculous show *Law and Order: SVU.* They raided a New York brothel full of trafficked Chinese girls and the girls were handcuffed and shoved roughly into police vans, as if they were the criminals. But then this show is always on the side of the respectable vagina. It apotheosizes the 'normal' girl who is raped once and ignores the massive rape of throwaway street walkers and other undesirables. In one episode, a poor porn star was getting double-banged--both the vagina and the rear end--mercilessly and she was being set up for one of those gang-bang porn fests where 300 slimes shits would use her in a row while it was being filmed and then her porn pimps would put her on *Howard Stern* so she could tell how much she enjoyed the experience. The *Law and Order* cops treated her like dirt. It's peculiar that on this show a girl gets raped once and she's all upset and nervous and full of PTSD and ready to cut her wrists and she has sympathy and counselors at her disposable. But the whore/porn vagina is garbage.

One-time rape is nothing. Before I got gang raped, I was raped by individual men. It was nothing compared to the torture of gang rape. I cannot even imagine how any women can survive 'mass' rape—what I would call the gang rape of the body on a daily basis.

To return to why traffickers cannot be stopped. Who would pass up so much money for no work (except the energy required to beat and rape a girl into submission) and with no possible punishment or repercussions. And it is so easy. The girls are available and unprotected everywhere—and no one gives a damn what happens to them, particularly the relatives who sell them, the sex tourists who seek them out, the navies who need them for R & R, and the indifferent prosperous pampered women who read *Cosmo* and live in a fantasy world where rape will never happen to their special protected bodies.

Besides, for the traffickers, it is a renewable resource. Wear out one vagina and there are thousands to take its place. Traffickers can purchase a girl and make hundreds of thousands of dollars off of her vagina by slotting thousands upon thousands of men in there before it wears out. That is the magic and beauty of the vagina—the amount of tremendous abuse it can take before it breaks down completely and has to be replaced by another slot hole. It is no wonder trafficking is now bigger than the drug trade.

Traffickers will never be stopped since there will never be a shortage of customer rapists. As a British man who uses whores on his business trips to Dubai said to me: "It is so easy. There are these young, really young prostitutes everywhere. No man is going to turn down this. It's what men think is owed them. Young girls to fuck. Men don't see it as doing anything wrong. It's just young girls available to fuck and you think you're doing them a favor since they smile and flirt to get the money. They get the money and that means it's okay." When I asked if he knew that it was mostly the girls' pimps and owners who got the money, he said that most men didn't want to know that and that there were girls there who worked on their own. He said he tried to pick ones who worked on their own. I asked how could he tell and he was vague in his answer.

I don't know if this businessman knows how his whore was broken in to the trade. Even if she is now 'independent,' it is likely that she was once turned into a whore by traffickers. A woman doesn't choose to do this on their own. There is a tortured path that leads to such a miserable fate for her vagina—men she doesn't know, British businessmen, slotting themselves in there for rape fun on their trips to Dubai.

The Dubai Girl I mentioned earlier, after her breaking in by the Pakistani rape-shits, is set to work to service businessmen, tourists, religious men, mechanics, other laborers, military contractors, soldiers, and the navies of the world, since this is a major docking port for them. American sailors are among the Dubai Girl's customer rapists. What haunts me about the Dubai Girl is not so much the breaking-in process—the letting in of a different Pakistani rape-shit slime monster every 15 minutes. Or even the way her shredded vagina is shoved into by rape-shit, slime-monster American sailors. And rape-shit American military contractors, since this is a major sex playground city for all of those highly paid Blackwater/Halliburton KGB men—it is their R & R stop off to and from Iraq. All of this is, of course, troubling. But what really bothers me is the way an American woman journalist asked a Dubai Girl who had escaped her traffickers, and was now working as a prostitute on her own in that city, why she didn't go work in a shopping mall. Dubai is rich. It has lots of malls.

So the female journalist from American sits there in front of the Dubai Girl, who has been broken—forever, by a session in a Pakistani labor camp, and by businessmen and tourists and religious men and sailors and military contractors—and asks her why she doesn't go work at a fancy mall, instead of still prostituting herself. (If I were the Dubai Girl, I think I'd be afraid of pimps getting a hold of me again—and setting me up again for assembly-line sex.)

Even though I am grateful to this journalist—it takes much courage for her to put herself in danger in order to interview these women (a courage I do not have)--the fact that the journalist did not understand the girl and how she can't go work at a mall is what haunts me and troubles me deeply. There is no shopping mall after being broken so brutally. There is no shopping mall after a succession of businessmen and tourists and mechanics and laborers and military contractors--and let's toss in a few UN Peacekeepers along with those sailors from America and Britain and France and every other navy in the world—there is no shopping mall after all these men climb on to get their crude ugly fuck on your dead body.

There is no café latte at a cosy little coffee shop either. There is no normal ever again. There is only a rape-dead body and a rape-dead mind and a rape-dead soul. There is no recovery after this kind of torture. There is no way to block out the crude sweat slime ugliness of the male and his filthy dick when he shoves it in. This is your reality—forever. There is no shopping mall.

The journalist who interviewed the Dubai Girl also takes photographs. She says she does not want to show the cigarette burns and cuts and abrasions and bruises on the trafficked girls' bodies because she does not want to portray them as victims. To that, I say, why not? They are definitely victims. There is no 'empowerment' or 'survival' after this kind of treatment. We have as proof the testimonies of the Korean Comfort Women—they were broken in the same way as the Dubai Girl—raped 30 to 50 times a day, sometimes even more. Even those still alive did not 'survive.' They tell us so. They say their spirits are dead—60 years after they escaped. They say, "Give me back my girlhood, my womanhood, my body, my life."

The Dubai Girl is no different from any other 'comfort woman.' I don't think she has a cast-iron vagina that would make her immune to the horrors of assembly-line sex. Here are a few testimonies from the Korean Comfort Girls from a book called *Comfort Women Speak: Testimony by Sex Slaves of the Japanese Military*:

"I worked from 8 in the morning till 10 at night….I was forced to have sex with 20 to 40 soldiers a day…we all ended up having venereal diseases…. Some girls became hysterical and crazy."

"The most painful thing was continuous, forced sex act with soldiers. Saturdays and Sundays were the worst, facing 30 to 40 men a day I felt like a living corpse. When soldiers came to my room and did it to me one after another, it was done to a lifeless body. Again. And again. And again…"

"I was forced to service sex to…40 to 50 on Sundays. We were exhausted, weakened, and some of us could not even eat meals. We were in the state of the 'half-dead.' Some girls became really sick and could not recover from the ordeal."

"I became ill soon after I became a sex slave and started to bleed severely through my vagina…I frequently thought of killing myself…I had poor health. I was still bleeding, and it became worse when I received many men."

I think the above can help us to do a simple equation: Korean Comfort Girl = Modern Day Comfort Girl in the form of the Dubai Girl who had a different Pakistani laborer climb on her every fifteen minutes. She is definitely a victim. I don't know what more has to happen to her to make her one. Does the rape quota have to be 300 rape-shit destroyers and murderers of the female body, to make her a victim? The poor Korean Comfort Girl who reported being used 300 times in 18 hours, peeing and bleeding where she lay, is a victim. I'm not sure how it would be possible to rape her any more than that. Does it have to be a man every 3 minutes for 24 hours for her to qualify as 'victim' status? (Source for this terrible fact about the '300 Comfort Girl' is Ryang's *Love in Modern Japan.)*

All this refusal to see as victims the deeply damaged, those subjected to extremes of rape torture, troubles me deeply. I only went through a fraction of the rape hell that these other girls do—I was on the outskirts, the very mild mild edge of rape hell, with my paltry little gang rape. (These other girls are in the searing center of this hell.) But I was definitely a victim. And my time in prostitution was so much less harsh since I could pick men, shield myself from rough ones, walk around and leave my house, and not be chained in a room with bars on the window and subject to terror and humiliation. Even so, I feel destroyed by intercourse with men I didn't know. Sex without tenderness.

Just the sheer physical pain that the Korean Comfort Girls describe is beyond my imagining. The one who reports bleeding and bleeding from her vagina yet she must still 'service men.' (Why should any girl be reduced to this level, to this thing called 'servicing'? What kind of monsters are men—what kind of monsters were these millions of Japanese soldiers?) I would never have made it through one day of that. Three or four acts of intercourse a night with 'customers' and I was beyond sore. And bled and tore sometimes. The trafficked girls in the UK, 'taking on' their 40 to 60 customers a day, the 14-year-old prostituted Balkan girl in Greece, being raped for the 100th time in a day—all these girls and bodies are the same. It is the same body being raped. It was the same body being raped 2000 years ago, on hard stone slabs, in the public brothels of Athens, where all the 'free' men of the city went to get their cheap fuck and the girl was mounted continuously. There is nothing 'cultural' about this—as in, oh, yes, that was part of 'democratic' free Greek 'culture,' instituted by the Great Pimp Lawgiver, Solon, who decreed that we 'place' slave girls in brothels so no male citizen of Athens has to go without his fuck. There was no protected temple harlot living the good life back in Sumeria—Shamhat got fucked by The Brute. End of story. Calling her by the cutesy academic phrase 'temple harlot' does not change the rape of her body. Don't give me any 'cultural' commentary crap for rape.

If she has also serviced many other men—businessmen, tourists, military men—then the Dubai Girl will have had to numb out, even die inside, to survive. This is why there is no other life outside prostitution. Once you are in, you can never get out. Even if you leave it, you go back. There isn't any place for you in the normal world after the disgust of all those men inside you. I think that is the big fact that is left out: the nature of this sex act--this terrible fact that you have strangers inside you--is revolting—and yet this aspect is never written about or mentioned.

After I accidentally, by some miracle unknown to me, got out of prostitution, there was no shopping mall for me. I have never felt that I left prostitution in any true sense. I'm still in it because I can't walk around like a normal woman. After I got out, I couldn't even face the idea of going to the store to buy some English muffins and apples. Facing customers at a store in a shopping mall—clean respectable shining safe protected women in all of their fantasy-world ignorance and indifference--would have been unthinkable. And I was not even broken the way the Dubai Girl was. She probably had to lie there under those Pakistani rape shits for weeks till she got properly broken in. From what I have read, the traffickers **really** break you—they make sure every last corner of the vagina is scoured with pain, every last naked inch of you inside is invaded, every last ounce of rape fuck is shoved into you, and every last inch of dignity is raped out of your hole. They make sure you have your insides raped right out of you. They really break you.

No polite shopping mall full of 'normal' women after that. How could you face the favored and protected women of the world after that? How could you sell one of them a fancy silk scarf after that? You can't ever look in their eyes since they are so protected.

You know there is no protection or gentleness for you. You can't sit at a café and have a cup of coffee and a cookie. You can't look at the normal women around you and know they are protected and you will never be shielded from the harsh raped pain of your body. No arms around you can keep you safe--ever. Even the gentle soft air on a beautiful day with a light cool breeze hurts. That gentleness in the air does not belong to you since your body no longer belongs anywhere except in the middle of rape pain. That gentle cool wind hurts when it caresses you since you are still being raped.

I struggle with words to express this and fail.

How, I wonder, would one of those sweet protected girls on the cover of *Prom Girl*, in her pink sweet dress, respond to having the insides raped out of her?

This has been the great mystery of life for me, ever since I can remember. What is the difference between the girl who is a piece of shredded raped whore garbage and the sweet protected one in her pink dress? I could never understand how one girl got to be a whore vagina with no dignity or safety or tenderness visited on her, and how the other girl is so precious and valued. Why isn't every girl's vagina sacred space? When that trafficked *abattoir* whore in Morocco was a tiny baby, did she have 'destined to be a whore raped a 100 times a day in a foreign land' tattooed inside her little vagina as she kicked her tiny pink feet in the air. It is a real puzzle that she is on her back underneath a 100 filthy rough rapists everyday, being laughed at as they mount her and kill her with their filthy penises, and another girl is sitting and laughing and flirting with her boyfriend at a coffee shop and then they take a stroll and he puts his arm around her and kisses her forehead with affection. As if she too had some dignity. She has none if the Moroccan *abattoir* whore exists. The *abattoir* whore makes life and tenderness and freedom impossible for all women.

There is a question I live by. It comes from the philosopher William James. He asks: "If all humans could be kept happy in exchange for the unbearable suffering of one being at the far edge of the universe, would it be worth it?" His answer was 'no.' That such a moral exchange would be 'abhorrent.' I agree with him.

It seems no matter where I travel, I cannot rid myself of Phantom Rape Pain. In London, when I go off to eat at my favorite veggie restaurant in Soho, I am aware that trafficked Albanian adolescents are working in upstairs brothels, maybe one right above where I'm enjoying my meal. When I walk around Paris, the beauty of the architecture is ruined by the incomprehensible pain of the *abattoir* whores. How can it call itself the city of light and love?

I know that I became a prostitute because of Phantom Rape Pain. I was driven to find out what it felt like for real. I know that I became a prostitute in order to re-enact my own gang rape—and the mass rape of women for centuries of rape time. I had to venture into the territory I feared the most.

As a writer, I go into the territory that the academic woman usually ignores when she writes on prostitution: I want her to realize that what is at the center of prostitution is a sex act so revolting and degrading that she would not survive, mind and sanity, intact, if she had to experience it.

I want the normal woman who browses at the local fancy mall to know that if she were treated the way the average trafficked prostitute is—burned with cigarettes, terrorized, on her knees with a penis forced into mouth for money—this would be considered a crime if it were perpetrated upon her, yet it is the reality that the street whore a few blocks over lives through everyday. And that street whore is considered the 'criminal'--for 'allowing' such deep degradation and torture to happen to her. Nothing happens to the real criminals--her pimp and her customer/rapist. And the 'decent' woman who ignores her. Indifference to suffering is a criminal act.

Would the average woman—academic or otherwise—really 'put up with' being treated with such brutal ugliness and cruelty? If this average woman had to do for a few minutes what the street whore has to 'put up with' every day, would she not be outraged, traumatized, go into a state of shock, maybe become dazed and half-insane, to hide from her everyday torture.

I don't think the ordinary average woman has a clue—about what the torture of the vagina feels like in prostitution. Where did all these ordinary women mislay their vaginas, I wonder?

I have come to the conclusion that the greatest sin we inflict on the prostitute is not just the physical pain but the destruction of her sexuality. What a precious thing to destroy.

I always write about such dark, tortured things—to rid myself of my overwhelming fears. Words are the only place I can find to contain them. But there is a light shining humorous not-so-frightened side of me that I have managed to find over the years—largely due to kind men. A kind man helped me to get out of prostitution all those years ago. I could not have freed myself on my own. I probably owe him my life and the fact that I am free to write and walk around and find some peace now.

In my more cheerful moments, I think my vagina—used as it is-- is a sacred, special place. Maybe that is what has made it special—so much use. Not overuse, but I mean when sex is chosen and voluntary and I can exercise my right to lay down with the men I want—and however many men I want. A tough freedom to find in a world that condemns female sexuality so heavily. The vagina is made to fuck and make love and be lusty and joyful—and then we are scorned and despised for the very joy of our bodies.

I have a very conflicted relationship with my own sexuality. I have experienced the worst men are capable of in terms of sexual violence. Yet their strength and power are also what make them appealing, when I am willing, not forced. I am frightened of the very power that attracts me.

Is my vagina Sacred Feminine Space? Sometimes. Although it has been heavily overused, it does not seem dirty or defiled. It still seems like a precious mystery to me. What's going on in there? Despite diagrams, I can never seem to adequately map my insides. All sorts of little mysterious nooks and crannies. It is a miniature mythical treasure cave. The mystery of how does it feel to a man, when he is inside me? I have asked many of them. Maybe the most poetic description was like "crushed, rolled velvet."

Men say it is how warm we are inside that makes coming quickly so seductive. They don't want to wait when the rawness of heat combines with slick wetness, and a pink rush of tight friction squeezes them to ram it deep and hard…

Men tell me that we women are not all the same inside—something I would never have known since I am not into other women. My only knowledge of what other women look like is through porn and I have never touched another woman between her legs. Men tell me that some vaginas are softer, some rougher, some tougher, some more tender. Size is a big consideration. Tighter is better. (It was a selling point I had as a prostitute—a small one, or so they told me.)

I always find it funny that the men I go to bed with know a lot more about the vagina than I do, since they are acquainted with so many different ones. Mine is the only one I know.

My vagina is special now since I am no longer prostituted. And it is special when I become intimate with patient, gentle men who don't frighten me. There are a lot of those men out there. No *vagina dentata* for them. Instead I have another fantasy. I would like to offer them a Magic Vagina. *Vagina Magicus.* A supreme tight wet hot beyond delicious magical place. Every time kind men enter me, I would like them to visit warm, orgasmic, intense, melting, ecstatic galaxies. The good men of the world deserve this—our Feminine Sacred Space.

13

Afterthoughts (Wandering Ones)

I had intended "The Magic Vagina" to be the last of the articles in this section. But it seems as if the pain of writing this book never ends. Ideas keep coming at me, more thoughts that need to be put on the page, as a result of a chance reading of an article, or a passing remark by a stranger that shows insensitivity toward prostitutes.

These afterthoughts are an effort to bring this part, "Fuck for Food"—at least temporarily—to some kind of close—by reflecting on what I've already said and by responding, one last time, to the many cruelties that hit me in the media and on the internet, everyday.

Just as I am about to send this book off to the publishers, I accidentally come across a 'farang' blog from Thailand (there are a number of these written by expatriates in that country) telling me about the visit of 5,800 American sailors and Marines taking liberty in Pattaya, major brothel port and sex-tourist destination. The blog also mentions those ever-present prostitute-buyers, the contractors, who seem to take their 'liberty' in Pattaya as well.

Now, this is June 2008, when I am reading this blog about the sailors and Marines landing in Pattaya. If you have been reading this book, you will have learned that the U.S. military kicked up a big fuss in 2004, and again in 2006, about making all prostitution off-limits for servicemen, all over the world, and about how there was now an absolute, 100% 'zero-tolerance' policy toward our military men buying prostituted bodies.

The 'farang' blog also mentions seeing the U.S. military men in the bars, and how in one bar a group came in, had a drink, and immediately 'bar fined' a bunch of the girls. This means they bought them out of the bar so they could take them elsewhere for sex.

Pattaya, Phuket (another brothel docking port in Thailand), wherever the ships are landing, it seems as if the boys are still in there engaging in the traditional navy thing—booze and purchased sex. It seems as if the sexual imperatives of history--"Man must have his fuck" and "woman must fuck for food"--are still in full force.

It's not a big secret, that they are engaging in this illegal activity harmful to women. I found out about it easily on a 'farang' website. The site even helpfully told me the names of the ships: it's the U.S. Navy's Essex Strike Group (*USS Essex, Juneau,* and *Harper's Ferry*). I could also easily find this information by simply asking the few sailors and Marines I am in contact with. So, where is this 'zero-tolerance' policy?

To explore the issue more deeply, I must respond to those who will say that this is not 'harmful' to the women. They make lots of money off these guys. I know that. I also know this is in many ways 'natural' behavior for these men. As one sailor so thoughtfully told me, "You're on ship for a month or more and it's like a prison: when a guy goes ashore, he'll go after pussy in any way he can."

Supposedly, the U.S. military made some motions toward forbidding prostitution usage because of the link, recognized by our government, between prostitution and trafficking. As Preston Jones, former Navy man, now a professor at John Brown University, says in his article, "We're Still Supporting Slavery," [when the] Navy guys hand over their money, they are promoting a global catastrophe."

Actually, to agree fully with Jones, what they are promoting is a system of global exploitation and trafficking that is not just confined to a bar-fine sex fix in Pattaya. I try to look at the big picture. I realize that for rural girls in Thailand who come out of deep poverty, and who are pressured or sold by families into the sex industry, and for women there who may have lost male support, have children, have no education—for these women and girls, bar-girl prostitution is an overwhelmingly lucrative 'choice'—given the alternatives—of which there may not be any. And bar-girl prostitution, if the girl is not pimp-controlled, must be thousands of times better than confinement in the Thai debt-bondage brothels, which are essentially sex-slave prisons: no choice of customers or freedom, and extremes of degradation and mistreatment visited on the girls.

This, I have read, is the most common form of prostitution in Thailand—and the places are not much frequented by sex tourists or foreign militaries but by Thai men—who buy 90% of the prostituted girls in that country. Which brings me to another path to wander down. How can so many Thai men use prostituted girls, especially since they are visiting brothels where the inhabitants are utterly pathetic—little sad sold creatures with no life, no choice, just rape visited on them all day. Debt-bondage rape, not allowed to turn down customers, raped a dozen or more times a night, beaten if she is disobedient—or wants to listen to the radio for few minutes. One statistic I came across was that 80% of men in Thailand, Cambodia, and India buy poor wretched sold girls enslaved in brothels. If this is true, how can so many men be so deeply evil? If this is true, it makes it hard for me to meet a man from one of these countries without prejudice: I wonder if he is part of the horror that is the accepted, everyday rape of young enslaved girls back in his country. Of no more importance than buying a bag of potato chips for the Cambodian who goes off with his buddies to 'socialize' and rape-fuck at the nearest bargain-basement brothel. And how can anyone meet a man from Japan knowing that almost 100% of men in that country buy the rape-enslaved, as a norm. These local men make the phenomenon of sex-tourism rape and the military tradition of raping brothelized girls seem numerically insignificant in contrast. If one million German civilian men a day are visiting rape-enslaved trafficked girls in that country's legal, battery-sex rape farms, the horror of the German rapist male must rent the very fabric of that supposedly 'civilized' country.

Statistics. Another bypath. I came across many as I was researching this book. It is impossible to know if numbers are accurate. Of course, when you keep reading the same ones in many different sources, you think, maybe there is some validity to them. The "80%" brothel usage for the local men in India, Thailand, and Cambodia, popped up a lot. As did the one million German men taking advantage of legal rape in their homeland.

When numbers of trafficked beings varies, in many different sources, from 800,000 to 10 million, worldwide, annually, it is impossible to know how many there really are. After all, trafficking is an underground activity.

There seemed to be a lot of consensus that at least 50% of trafficking is for sexual exploitation. Probably a lot more. As high as 80% came up in some sources.

I am not sure how important numbers are. Even one person trafficked for sex is too much. Even one German man visiting a brothel with trafficked girls is too many.

Back to those Thai bar girls, those icons of Asian sex-for-sale since American military demand created them, and the famous pussy shows of

Patpong: to look at the micro-picture, these bar-girls are really 'lucky,' at least within the brutal picture that is prostitution worldwide. On the other hand, they live in a country where the majority of women are below the poverty level and where there is a large discrepancy between male and female income, and where there are far more well-paying jobs for Thai men than for women. They are working in a system where men from the outside—whether they be sex tourists or sailors—are financially and sexually privileged: the girls have no money; the men do. The girls have only their bodies as a way of 'making it.' The tourists and military men take full advantage of their own privileged sexual 'entitlement' (that useful word the feminists have come up with). The girls have to have sex with men they don't know—many times rough and crude drunk men. Getting pawed, mauled, and banged by strangers is not a fun activity or one designed to up a girl's self-esteem and dignity. (Can the bar girls turn down customers, I wonder? This is a crucial question.)

No matter how 'lucky' the bar girl is, in the prostitution picture, any pawing or mauling or banging of her means yet more men who think they can paw and maul and bang me against my will. Her presence hurts us all. Frankly, I think the debt-bondage, brothel-imprisoned Thai girl hurts us far more—she is subjected to levels of sexual humiliation and horror so deep, my mind cannot even go into the hell that is her everyday life. But we do not see her pain since she is not 'tourist visible,' the way the bar girl is. We can see the little cute painted toy whore smiling away that is the bar girl—she is an icon by now due to media and movie exposure—so she is our symbol of what prostitution is. (I have never seen one picture or film of the tortured Thai girl in her brothel rape- bed.)

Still, this 'lucky' bar girl does not seem so lucky to me. She wears the painted whore make-up mask that 'marks' her and that she must hide behind. I just ran across a few pictures of the toy-whore Pattaya bar girls on one of those 'farang' websites. They look so tiny. Such skinny little-girl arms and no hips and tiny ten-year-old stick figures. What is the appeal, for a 200-pound Marine, to buy a girl who is barely bigger than a ten-year-old? Makes no sense to me. I had a grown-up body when I sold myself, and I still died with pain from the sex with these men. It is beyond me how a fragile Asian girl, only ninety pounds and tiny beyond belief, can even endure one act of intercourse without severe pain and damage. It must be like raping a child for these military men and sex tourists. This has always been a huge mystery area for me—physical survival for these child-size bodies. The second big mystery is the appeal raping such a tiny body has for men. You would think guilt and shame would overwhelm the sailors and sex tourists who hurt these tiny, defenseless girls.

And I wonder how the men can see buying a helpless little miserable whore as some kind of simulated 'girlfriend' experience. As I have said elsewhere, when the man has money, and purchases a girl who has no money, as if she were a slave—this is not a 'boyfriend/girlfriend' dynamic. This is raw exploitation—no matter what the illusion the man tries to sustain.

You can only call a woman you are intimate with a 'girlfriend' if she is willing, if she does not have to do this for money under coercive circumstances, and if the sex is for her benefit as well as yours. A 'girlfriend' is not purchased, like a thing, and then obliged to abdicate all of her sexual needs in favor of the man's. A 'girlfriend' is a beautiful, feeling responsive sexual equal, not a numb, dead convenience for the man's sex drive and sex needs.

Despite the ugliness and cruelty of prostitution, I would never even consider taking any prostitute's 'job' away from her, or 'rescuing' her. This is all she has. Terrible as it is. When I worked as a prostitute, I would have been furious if anyone had tried to 'rescue' me. After all, this was my private pain, this was the only thing I thought I could do, there was no place for me to go, if 'rescued.' There was no life after prostitution. How dare anyone try to 'rescue' me? If any 'normal' woman had tried to come near me when I was a prostitute, I would have spit at her. I deeply resented all the women in the world who were not being raped every day. I still have deep resentment toward normal, non-raped, non-prostituted women. I reserve the most contempt for the indifferent—those who simply go their own way, in neat little suits, sipping lattes—those successful safe ones who are businesswomen and teachers without a clue that they too could be broken and turned into whores after a few hours of rape. My next level of contempt goes to those who 'study' the whore and understand nothing of her reality and her pain.

When I was in prostitution, I was having enough trouble just dealing with the indignity of 'no privacy' for my poor miserable body, due to having to fuck all of these men—and the terrible physical pain from overuse. I could not have handled any 'do-gooder' with good intentions and no clue trying to invade my mental pain as well.

I don't know if any of these ideas are also in the bar-girl's head, about being 'rescued.' After all, if she is able to make phenomenal amounts of money in a third-world economy, maybe she considers herself really 'lucky' and fortunate as well. (But, again, how on earth and in the heavens, does that tiny body survive all that rape?)

I certainly cannot pretend to know what other prostitutes think. I am fairly certain that many of them, even the 'free' ones like bar girls, must, to some extent, regard what is happening to their bodies as rape, even after the necessary numbing process that allows one to bear sex with strangers. It would be impossible not to feel some kind of violation, ranging from the unpleasant to the absolutely revolting, given the conditions they work under: drunk, noisy men; crude jokes; public, humiliating nakedness when they strip; even more humiliation showing pussy and inserting objects into themselves; stigma and scorn because they are 'whores'; selling sex, an intimate act; being bought—which smacks of slavery—any way you couch the transaction. I know that not all do pussy shows, and not all strip totally naked, but, still, in this bar-girl world, every girl is there to be bought. She is available to strangers who might hurt her. I cannot help but think these girls must be afraid of big men who might hurt them during sex just the way I was. Or do they belong to a different species, immune to sexual pain? The myths their sex tourist and soldier and farang customers weave around them seem to put them in a different category.

It is really difficult to see any difference in prostitution no matter where it is happening in the world. The factors seem universal: stigma upon the girl (and not the man who buys her); low self-esteem because of the attitudes toward her—she is 'sleaze' and 'trash'; the possibility of violence; the danger of diseases, particularly the life-killing one, AIDS; other physical problems from too much sex (some of them considerable, like an increased chance of cervical cancer); PTSD if she ever gets out. In fact, prostitutes seem to be in permanent PTS while they're still in the trade. So great are the stresses from fear of physical violence, from living as an outcast, from violation by strangers, that their bodies undergo pre-mature aging. Their systems wear out to such an extent, prostitutes go into meltdown.

In cases of severe abuse, such as Comfort Women, it is no wonder so few survive. Of the 200,000 or so Korean ones conscripted during WWII, only a handful made it. Of the karayuki-san, Japanese girls exported for prostitution all over the world in the late 1800's, almost none made it home. Sold at age ten or so and worked until their late teens—that was as far as they got. Death from disease, madness, and exhaustion. I point to these two instances to show the tragic continuity through time of prostitution. It would have been the same in ancient times, for the women put in slave brothels to accompany Greek armies and for captives divided among the men; and for the slave girls Solon placed in brothels in Athens so every 'free' man could get his cheap sex fix. Such is the foundation of our 'democracy.' (It is the same picture in 2008 by the way.) The women in ancient times did not have 'different' bodies. They were not more suited to be prostitutes than women are now.

Others making money off of their bodies seems also to be a universal fate for prostitutes. I cannot find firm numbers as to how many work completely independently, taking all the money. Holland, Germany, and Nevada have some women working in legal brothels who are supposedly free and receive state-supported benefits. But if you talk with them, many say pimps are still taking their money—sometimes it is boyfriends, sometimes a family member, like a brother or even a father.

How many girls are truly 'free' from financial coercion? Are the ones on the internet working completely for themselves or is their a pimp/owner in the background? We know that pimps now hawk their stables of girls on the internet to an international array of customers. (See Victor Malarek's *The Natashas* for a description of this.)

I would have no objection to prostitution if the girls were safe, well-treated, respected, never hurt. I have no silly 'moral' objections to it. I do not think it is 'wrong.' But where does this safe kind of prostitution exist? In a different galaxy perhaps?

I tried to carve this form out for myself, when I did it. I worked under conditions far freer and safer than do the majority of prostitutes. I still could not make it beneficial for myself. Too much fear, too much stigma, too much sex with men I didn't know.

One of the sad things about writing on this terrible subject for so long is that I have come to understand the point of view of the traffickers—and why stopping them is probably impossible. It is such an easy way to make money. All a man has to do is grab a girl and rape and break and terrorize her and put her on her back to make money for him. What could be easier than that? No punishment will even devolve upon him since it's her fault that she let this happen to her. Finnegan's recent article in the *New Yorker* (May 2008) on trafficked Moldovan girls was a real wake-up call. The few girls who return home and try to seek justice are scorned by the judges and legal system as whores and sluts who got what they deserved. This is what greets the few brave enough to try to seek redress.

Change the locale to America, or Turkey, or Dubai, or Thailand—or anywhere. It is the same picture. No one is on the side of the girls. They are, after all, only 'sluts.' Corrupt police and politicians and employees in embassies facilitate the trafficking. I was, in fact, stunned to learn of the extent of corruption, at all levels, in all countries, that allows this to go on. The traffickers cannot do it all on their own. They get lots of help. No matter what the country, if the girl 'escapes' and goes to the police, she will be returned to her owners. Or deported—which means 'returned to her owners' in another form since they can re-traffic her. Any attempt to go up against her traffickers could mean death. And who is she to go up against them with? The courts and police and legal systems will not protect her. She is just a 'slut.'

Another big problem is that she often cannot speak for herself due to trauma. 'Opening up' about the degradation that has been visited on her body may be impossible. The emotional conditioning and torture inflicted on her, to 'train' and 'break' her, mean she may not have anything left inside to speak with. She will say what her owners have trained her to say: I am fine, no one is hurting me, I want to be here.

You will say anything to prevent more beatings and rape.

I am not at all sure any prostitute can be interviewed. She has to tell too many lies to herself to survive. So, there is no way she can tell you the truth.

I cannot be interviewed. It would be impossible for me to speak. And I am not even severely traumatized, like a trafficked girl. The prison I walk around in is in my head.

One can see the impossibility of helping the girl. We give her no protection at all from those who harm her. Even the millions of men who do not hurt her—those who are not traffickers or procurers or customer/rapists—even these good men will not help her. They outnumber the exploiters, but do nothing to protect women who so desperately need their help. And as long as the female universe is divided up into 'sluts' and 'good girls,' there can never be change. And can you even imagine lack of corruption and bribes and payoffs—in any country, or any system of government? Nothing will ever change the greed and cruelty of the human heart.

Women who sell or procure other women are of course the supreme puzzle. Given that many of those doing the selling, the *mama-sans*, or whatever you call them, were themselves sold at one time makes it more understandable. Extreme mistreatment will cause hardness. But those who were not sold are as much of a dark mystery as the men who do this.

Before I embarked on this book, men were the bad guys. I am discovering, however, that the good men of the world are tremendous allies. They help and support women in their fight for liberation and dignity. Of those who contact me about my writings, the majority are men—outraged and shocked and with much compassion in their hearts. For every one woman who writes me, ten men do.

It was a shock to learn that women can hurt other women as much as men do.

So many factors work to disguise the harm that is prostitution. There is almost no recognition that prostitution is sexual violence toward women. I can find illustrations of this blindness everywhere. For examples, as I am writing this, I have the TV on in the background. Currently playing is a show on the Travel Channel with a perky little hostess visiting Amsterdam.

Reluctantly, squeamishly, she visits the red-light district. Her professional guide is a woman who apparently takes tourists through the area. The perky hostess asks about it being legal and the guide says, yes, it is and what a good thing that is because it means the girls are all there because they want to be and there is no 'trade' in women, whatever that means.

I'm not sure how inaccurate information can be, but this certainly is in the running for a prize. Does the guide genuinely not know that the girls in the windows are trafficked, that in underground brothels Ukrainian girls are being forced 30-40 times a night, that there is a drive-through brothel on the edge of town where immigrant trafficked women are forced 100 times a night? Perhaps she really does not know this. After all, her counterparts in London and Bangkok and Las Vegas have not a clue. Middle-class London and Thai and American women go indifferently about their business, without a thought, or even a 'nod' of recognition to the hot, cruel world of sexual slavery running side by side with their own sanitized reality.

If the guide does know of the conditions, perhaps she is simply hiding them from us, to increase tourism.

Once upon a time, most of the windows were filled with Dutch girls. How 'voluntary' was their participation in the sex industry, I do not know. But now the windows are full of the trafficked. And some aware women all across the EU are starting to recognize and fight against the massive influx of Eastern European sex slaves broken and destroyed by traffickers, and held right in the middle of London, or Brussels, or Amsterdam, or wherever. In fact, both Amsterdam and Germany are re-thinking their 'legal' stances since they have seen the horrendous consequences of this policy. Maybe the guide in Amsterdam should have known something of this.

When the perky hostess visited Copenhagen, a female guide mentioned to her how the waterfront tourist area was full of prostitutes at one time, girls who serviced the many navies of the world that docked there, and the perky hostess giggled. How wretched the lives of these girls were is hard for us to realize. No different from any port where girls are pimped to navies from around the world. Certainly not a cause for giggling. The drunk raping the helpless. I don't think I'd giggle at this.

I realize this show with the perky hostess is meant to be enjoyable fluff, not social commentary. I thoroughly enjoy it myself, when I can rid myself of the shadows of the raped.

I enjoy all the luxurious hotels the perky hostess stays in and her safe trips to art museums and picturesque castles. She eats and shops and enjoys the glitz and beauty of places. She takes us to snowy Swiss mountains and charming little shops full of cuckoo clocks. She is witty and cute and her little 'summary' at the end is always profound enough for this kind of show and gives me insights into countries and cities I myself have visited.

In fact, she now has a new show on the Travel Channel that is every bit as enjoyable. We see her not just as perky, but tough, and a little wild and still very witty—and the way she is revealing more sides of her personality makes for an appealing journey around the world with her.

My point is that she should not contribute to the screen that hides the pain of prostitution, even if this is a light show and she brings up the subject in a light fashion. She should at least acknowledge that it is not fun and giggles for the women. Just one small, sober comment, and then she can move on to the more pleasant and kind aspects of her show. I welcome being able to escape into her luxurious reality—but not at the expense of others.

I ran across a blog that displays photos of cute sweet Asian girls—beauty queens and prom queens and movie stars—all of this showing the overwhelming surface value of women (Asian or Caucasian or whatever race they are). We are worth something because we are pretty or cute. This blog emphasized the wholesome sweet Asian girl as opposed to her 'trash' sister, the whore.

When value systems are so twisted as to see only the surface of a woman, and to divide women sharply as to 'pure' versus 'trash,' it makes the cause of dignity for women even more hopeless.

As I have said, this whole prostitution misery is a hopeless cause. I keep writing since there is nothing else to do with hopeless causes except face them.

To cheer myself up, I go back to men like Preston Jones, ex-Navy, savvy about what's going on the sex-trade world. Running across his article "We're Still Supporting Slavery," at least makes me feel not so alone. There are at least some men who have humane views on women, prostitutes or otherwise.

I quote a few passages from him:

"Near the back of one of my Navy cruise books—roughly analogous to a high school annual—is a photograph of a girl no older than 15 years old. Index finger on lower lip, she's scantily clad and posing provocatively. She's a Thai prostitute….her customers we can identify, at least on this occasion. They are American sailors assigned to the now-defunct *U.S.S. Ranger*….When Navy ships aren't anchored off the coast of Pattaya Beach, the girl's customers are Australian, Belgian, German, Canadian, Japanese, British, and American tourists. Whether she knows it or not, she is part of a global economy. And when American sailors hand their money to her (or to her pimp or *mama-san*), they are casting a vote in favor of slavery." (I kind of think some sailors must know this. But the need to get sexual gratification and to get drunk and 'have fun' is simply what matters to them. The girl's circumstances are secondary to the male's sexual needs—perhaps even irrelevant to his needs.)

Jones says that when he was in the navy, all he heard before they docked in Korea was how the country had "great and inexpensive hookers" and he says these girls were transported from Pusan to Seoul "to accommodate an aircraft carrier's thousands."

Jones partly blames those in power who ignore this slavery. "The drunken deeds of America's unwitting freckle-faces in the brothels of Bangkok are bad enough. The willful refusal among the powerful to acknowledge that each year American troops pump millions of dollars into Asia's vicious skin trade is criminal," he writes.

He's not too hopeful that any new laws in place about forbidding patronage of prostitutes will work. How could they be enforced? He writes: "If nothing else, when a carrier pulls into a port, some 6,000 sailors and Marines hit the beach. Melting into the labyrinths of Bangkok is easy...."

"For the law to be effective," he says, "a fundamental shift in the moral culture of the Navy would be necessary....the long-standing eye-winks of high-ranking officers, the open encouragement by senior enlisted men, and the silence of chaplains over the years have created the sense that, by right, young men in uniform from Nebraska, Maine, and California should have easy access to the bodies of girls and young women from Korea, Thailand, and the Philippines....it is easy for the mainstream to ignore or minimize the experiences of bar and brothel girls." (I would say that the mainstream has not a clue about what those experiences are. The collective mainstream imagination is incapable of realizing the disgust of sex with drunk crude men and the low self-esteem and misery that attend being regarded as 'just a whore.' Just a disposable woman. Maybe 'the mainstream' don't want to know all this. Maybe they want to stay collectively blind.)

Silence on the part of all those dependent wives and daughters who have ignored the 'prostitution culture' right outside the gate should be added to his list. And he is certainly dead on-target about 'minimizing' what the bar or brothel girl goes through. As I've written this book, I've been continually stunned by how the majority of 'mainstream,' middle-class men and women, and all those politicians making their moral campaign speeches, never even acknowledge what is for me one of the greatest miseries there is—forced sex.

More from that great guy, Preston Jones: "In Iraq we promote democracy. In ports-of-call on the way home from Iraq we toss our coins into a system that locks girls in the clutches of pimps in Pattaya Beach, Bangkok and Phuket....for the past several decades American servicemen in East Asia have horrendously exploited powerless women and girls with the consent of their superiors."

I like to be in touch, at least on paper, with a man like Preston Jones since it makes the world seem a little less frightening. He makes sense, in that way of humane compassion that is so appealing and soothing. He is a counter to a world I really fear, the one those poor bar girls live in. It is a world of rough, impersonal sex I hope I never have to live in again. It is a place where I had no power since the ultimate power resided in the man on top of me, hurting me. He was too strong for me to have any power—or rights. People forget—at the center of prostitution is this rough, impersonal sex act that hurts the girl. This reality gets disguised in all kinds of ways—debates about 'choice'; images of cute toy Asian whores in movies; ideas that because the man pays, it does not harm the girl.

My fear of that world means I can probably never help these girls. I am terrified of bars and drunken men and men treating me (or other girls around me, like bar girls) crudely. Even one harsh word from a man and I cry. Roughness in a bar would kill me. I had to become very, very numb to survive prostitution, no feelings inside at all, and years later, now that I have feelings again, I am very vulnerable. Even a scene with a bunch of drunk soldiers on TV at a bar and I have to turn it off. Men really terrify me when they are rough. I'd be scared to death to go into these bars and see all these men (sex tourists or sailors or whoever they are) being rough and drunk and crude and pawing these poor girls who by now must be so used to it they don't have any feelings left either. So, I cannot help them. This really saddens me, my lack of courage and my deep fear making it impossible for me to help these girls. If they can be helped at all. For a prostitute, the only way to survive is to smile and 'play dead.' Is the numbness involved permanent?

I have gained some kind of dignity and elegance and safety in my life now, and I would be terrified to lose all that again in bars with rough men. Even being near men who might hurt me again terrifies me. I have trouble leaving the house many days—it takes forever to get across the threshold, due to fear of rough men hurting me again. I have lost work due to fear. I have almost been homeless due to fear and not being able to work. And I know if I become homeless, I will kill myself right away since 100% of homeless women are raped. I am afraid every day because I am now old and broken down and no one will buy me when I become desperate enough to sell sex. I am full of contradictions and fears, and the pain of writing this book about them has practically killed me. I am pretty much still a hooker who is an emotional, terrified wasteland of a human being forever. And all this from minimum mistreatment. I was never beaten up, even once, and only once feared for my life—in one incident where a man was very threatening. I did not face the degradations of the bars and brothels where many girls 'work.' I was not imprisoned and yelled at and 'broken.' Still, my time as a prostitute emptied me of hope and life. Prostitution in its mildest form—the kind I knew—practically killed me. My mind cannot even reach into the realms of pain and misery the trafficked girls know. Or the poor Thai bar girls pawed by drunks—how must they feel being treated so roughly and disrespectfully day after day, with no escape?

Western men are fond of saying, "Prostitution is different in Thailand (or Korea) or"—pick an Asian country. Then will follow a remark like, "It is no big deal there." Or-- "It is an honored and traditional profession." Or --"The girls don't mind." Or--"It is like a 'girlfriend' when you buy her. It's not like the way Western hookers operate, like it's a business." Or—make up some more fairy tales, I say.

Now, I know there is some validity (however small) to all of these observations—made for decades by sex tourists, and all those farangs in Bangkok, and all the servicemen on 'liberty.'

But, what is peculiar is that I notice the Asian prostitutes subjected to the same scorn and dirty jokes and dangers and lack of respect as we Western ones go through. So, how is it so different, if she is Thai, or Korean? She is not 'honored' in any way.

Cultures may be different, but prostitution is the same everywhere.

And, universally, the picture seems to be the same as regards male/female dignity, and privilege. The prostitute, whether she is a bar girl in Pattaya, or me, here in the U.S.—the prostitute is there as a convenience so horny, 'needy' young men, too rude and cruel to control their testosterone, can use a body for a while. She and I, me and the bar girl, we are branded 'whores,' we are 'sleaze' and 'trash,' and nothing happens to the men. Does the sex tourist or the Marine go home with a mark on his forehead or a sign on his chest: "Bought a body in Bangkok, contributed to the global sex-slave trade"?

Or does that horrifying typical Thai man, and all 80% of his raping compatriots, receive any kind of condemnation for his brothel activities of the previous night, when he killed with pain a young girl's body already almost dead, but not dead enough to be beyond all pain. Why is he not in prison, for his rape of the helpless? And if prostitution is illegal in Thailand, why is the girl in a brothel to begin with? Why are not her owners and pimps and the customers who use her being stopped?

Under legal systems world wide—those systems made and controlled by men and by conservative women with power—the whore has no importance.

You see. It is the same picture everywhere. Thailand, Germany, the USA. Man, entitled to rape for fun; prostitute ends up with death, disease, madness.

For men a few minutes of 'pleasure'; for the girl, a life sentence in brothel hell.

There is something really wrong with a world where male pleasure equates to terrible pain for women.

The bar girl, not imprisoned in a brothel, may seem like a different case. But she still has to survive sex with strangers. Maybe 15 a month instead of 15 a night, but that is still a heavy, heavy rapeload. Way more than the one-time, finite rape of the 'good' girl who has recourse—and resources to help her if victimized.

Even if the bar girl is a free agent, she might be in danger of being pimped. In the fluid prostitution world, men could get hold of her, just because she is a whore and put her in a brothel, where she would have no choices at all. 'Free' prostitutes can never be safe if other prostitutes are enslaved and mistreated.

The bar girl has to survive male crudeness and rudeness. This is no small thing. I don't think I could survive it if exposed to it again, as I once was. My customers may not have hit me but treating me like a dirty joke left some deep wounds.

I am not used to the crude, hard, harsh male anymore. I had to numb out totally and become like rubber to deal with that kind of male once upon a time. I have gotten spoiled over the years—knowing so many polite men. I am getting spoiled right now since a lot of men who are very compassionate about prostitution e-mail me. It gives me the mistaken idea that all men out there understand. Boy, do they not!

Prostitution set up a dynamic and a measuring instrument in me that never goes away. Whenever I meet a man and he is polite to me, I wonder, "If he knew I was a whore, would he be so courteous?" If he wouldn't, I don't consider **him** worth much.

I measure the worth of men by how they treat the helpless. I have enormous amounts of respect for the many good men I know who are sensitive to what prostitution really is. And for the ones intelligent and sensitive enough to treat whores just like other women. These men are rare. For most men, we whores are just a dirty joke to be scorned.

I really appreciate it when one of the polite, good, sensitive ones opens a door for me, and treats me with respect. That time in prostitution, having to be around the drunk and the crude, has, if anything, made me stand on my pride. I have regained some dignity—and I exercise it. And I revel in how polite the good men of the world can be.

It would be unfair for me to end this section without once mentioning the many boys who are also sexually exploited. The numbers are not small, and they are the truly forgotten ones, since most of the media attention (for sensationalistic reasons) goes to the girls. I am not just talking about the sex trade in boys in Asia or Mexico or the Middle East. It is much closer to home for me. I have been touched that some men who have read my articles on the internet have e-mailed me about how sexual abuse in their childhoods has had a long-term impact on their lives. I am not insensitive to their pain. I know it is as real and deep as what any trafficked girl goes through.

And, of course, the prison rape of men in America is an abuse so horrendous and ignored, I don't know where I would begin to try to help.

All I can do is inadequately apologize for not writing more about these areas. It is not that I consider them less important than the prostitution/trafficking issue. It is just that I cannot do everything. Maybe the next book.

Since so much of this book is about military prostitution, I need to say another word or two about what is happening currently. I think the higher-ups, the officers and commanders and captains of ships, etc., probably just consider all this 'zero-tolerance' stuff an annoyance. They know it can never be enforced. When called upon, they will say a few words to the contrary, to keep the State Department happy. They know young military men need sex, whether it's the crew of the *Essex* flooding Pattaya, or all those horny single soldiers stationed in Okinawa, or Korea, or Germany.

In Korea, soldiers frequenting the trafficked girls in the camp towns have been arrested, but nothing much has been done to them. Hand slap, don't do it again for a while, week or two later, back to a bar to get a girl. What I have not been able to discover at all is if the new military policy has made any difference in the lives of the trafficked girls. Since some American soldiers are capable of compassion and kindness when they find out girls are trafficked and mistreated and enslaved, are not the girls worse off if their owners ship them to venues where they will be even worse treated—like into the sex industry in Japan, a horror camp of sadistic customers. Japanese men treat prostitutes like total shit. (Apparently, so do German men.)

So, what good will eliminating all the U.S. military men from the prostitution scene do, if it means the girls will be even worse off? Damn, if I were still a whore, I'd rather fuck an American soldier than a German or Japanese tourist any day.

I hope that if any American soldiers and sailors read this book, they will let me know what is going on in Korean and Germany and any other places our men are stationed. At one time, I knew a lot of American servicemen, and they were an invaluable source of information about the prostitutes they had met all over Asia, and in Europe.

As an ex-prostitute who was not really all that exploited, I am very confused sometimes—as you may notice in my writings. I feel as if maybe I have no right to write about this since I did not go through what so many girls do—none of that pimp exploitation, drug addiction that so many of these girls manage to survive. (How did they survive is my question—I would never have.) I feel too humble and like I have not really suffered enough to know what it is all about. I have it good now—I am safe, I am doing what I love—writing. It's hard to know if I have any right to try to be a spokesperson for others who have gone through hells I cannot imagine.

A wise friend once said to me, "It's foolish to compare 'plights.' Yes, there are those who are far worse off. But you have to deal with your own 'plight.' Just because it's not as terrible as others doesn't mean it's unimportant." So, to deal with my 'plight,' I try not to be ashamed of being weak and frightened. I let myself feel like a 'victim,' since I think it's okay to be afraid and vulnerable in a world full of so much violence. If others scorn me for feeling worthless and helpless, so be it. It is my coping mechanism, it is the way I am. It is my 'plight' and I am doing the best I can.

I know I am fortunate compared to the crippled and the mutilated, so I have no right to complain about anything.

I know how fortunate I am compared to most of the sex-tortured girls in the world. I sit here safe, at least for the moment, at my computer. I can write every day, a great joy. I think of a show I saw on PBS called *The New Heroes*. It said a third of the prostitutes in Thailand are under age 15. It showed footage—very clear and undeniable footage--of large numbers of young girls—most looked about 12 or 13—outside those Patpong Pussy Venues. These were the unhappiest looking adolescent girls I have ever seen. Very hard, sad faces. They did not look at all like they were having any fun selling their bodies.

One of the biggest shocks I had when researching this book was finding out how bad things are. In those 400 or so sources at the end of this text, I discovered searing rape prisons with walls of hell fire—all over the world. You would think that the screams of these millions of women would rent our peace and make all of us vibrate with pain. Not so. The next biggest shock I got was the way women scorn whores for being whores. Before researching and writing this book, it had never even occurred to me that respectable women are far more responsible for the existence of whores than the uncontrollable, raping penises of their men. I had thought women were the 'good guys.' But the respectable women keep themselves deliberately and blindly isolated from their suffering raped sisters. They choose to believe the lies that hide the rape pain, so they can feel superior and accepted and part of hypocritical mainstream reality.

"They treated us like hookers," I overheard a girl say at a restaurant. Maybe hookers should not be treated like hookers. Unfortunately, a whore is still just a whore for most women. She is a source of dirty jokes, a cliché 'hooker' puppet in high heels and a skirt up to her butt who leans into cars to negotiate her next rape price with a customer. She is 'funny' and 'dirty' and she is never a human being who needs to be understood—and will never be unless we can completely retrain and re-indoctrinate all these 'normal' women who have put her in this place of rape and pain. My disgust with 'normal' women is so deep that it even overrides my revulsion toward the men who have made our planet a Rape Killing Field.

"Women have to earn respect. I could never respect a woman who sold her body. Every escort I've been with is trash." I heard this jumble of remarks at an adjacent table in another restaurant. They reminded me that the third biggest shock was learning the attitudes of the world. How a man can buy a body and he is still full of dignity since he does not have to earn 'respect.' But the girl he buys can never be 'respected.' Makes no sense to me. Neither does the remark of the man who says he is sure no girl in a brothel is raped because her owners and pimps would not allow it. She would not be in good enough shape to fuck ten or twenty men a day if her owners 'allowed' rape.

Another big shock was how all the millions of men who don't rape are doing nothing to prevent those who do. Where is their protectiveness toward us if they can let these women and girls and children die in misery in brothels?

The 'respect' issue still troubles me. Earn what kind of respect, I would ask? Do I play by rules invented by men to control and destroy my sexuality? Is that what is meant by 'earning respect'?

Yet another shock was how the multitude simply regard prostitution and trafficking as unimportant. Even telling them about how it destroys women makes absolutely no impact on them.

Elevating the harm that prostitution does is not a way of devaluing other kinds of suffering. Torture and mutilation are not made any less terrible because I also want some recognition for sexual pain. The main problem is that this kind of pain is simply accepted as a norm. The sexual violence against women that is prostitution is never questioned. It would be hard to justify this kind of attitude toward mutilation and torture.

The only parallel I can think of is the everyday torture we humans subject animals to. We cause them to live in unthinkable pain in labs and factory farms, and never even question the necessity of this—in the same way we never question that female bodies must be available for mass rape in brothels because men must have sex.

I definitely recognize other kinds of pain in the world, other than sexual. But this subject has been so thoroughly ignored for thousands of years that it is time….It is time to liberate all of us (men and women) by taking the last bedraggled body out of its brothel. Men will be liberated as well. We women are a lot more interesting if we are not slaves.

I definitely recognize the pain of not being able to protect the ones you love. The most painful 'war' photos to me have nothing to do with grimed-over soldiers, looking weary. The ones I cannot bear are of women holding children in their arms as they try to escape bombs and gunfire and mortars and whatever else the grimed-over soldiers are hitting them with.

I have moments of panic when I look at the animals I have rescued and think, "What if that little fellow was tied down and being cut up by a vivesector?" It's the same pain as the women fleeing war violence with her child desperately held to her chest. The violence out there is so powerful, how can I protect the helpless? This thought causes me as much pain as sexual cruelty.

As I have written this book, I have found myself overly troubled by the attitudes of others. By their assumptions that I am some sort of prude who thinks prostitution is morally 'wrong' or how, as a whore, I cannot possibly be worth listening to. I do not buy into the conservative religious moral stances that have created the very idea of 'whore.' Without these stances, there would be no division between women into 'good and cherished' versus 'bad and despised.'

There would be no men willing to buy women since the idea of forced sex would be repugnant to them. Get rid of religion and 'morality,' and you will rid the world of the narrow, harmful views of female sexuality that have led to prostitution in the first place.I would never say prostitution is 'wrong' if it celebrated female sexuality instead of destroying it.

Just as I think I am finishing up this section, I receive an e-mail from an Iraqi woman who has seen the plight of the Iraqi prostitutes in Syria. So I have to put down what she saw. Some girls, she says, are choosing to stay in Syrian prisons because the abuse of their bodies by Saudi, Kuwaiti, and other Gulf States customers is so severe due to these men wanting to 'get back' at Iraq through its women for the 1991 Gulf War. She says little eleven-year-old girls are being sold. She says the UNHCR is doing nothing, except lining their own pockets. The massively funded UN is not helping the girls at all.

As I read this e-mail, a news story comes through about the United Nations "denouncing rape as a weapon of war." Didn't we already do this after Bosnia and Rwanda? Condi Rice is making declarations at the UN about stopping all rape in conflict zones immediately. That 'zero-tolerance' phrase, of course, makes an appearance.

This sounds like a great idea but I wonder how she plans to do it. For one, the UN simply makes no effort to police its own troops and these men are notorious, all over the world, for raping the shit out of women, girls, and—yes—even children who are helpless, in those savage conflict zones, and have to fuck the 'peacekeepers' for food. The UN, a highly corrupt, unprincipled institution, is going to 'correct' and halt the ways of corrupt, unprincipled armies, and governments—in order to stop men from raping? Ha! I say.

I have suggested elsewhere that we arm and train half a million or more female peacekeepers—and set them down in all conflict areas. Draw these women from the ranks of the starving, helpless, raped, prostituted, and disenfranchised all over the world. Cambodian women—and ones from Thailand and Iraq and the Ukraine and the Congo, etc. Mix in a few Swedish women, who seem to have dignity and strength, so the poor raped ones can have an example to gain strength from.

All those millions of UN dollars that are going no where useful should go to this arming of women

Condi should act rather than speak. You know my theory by now. If there is one hurt woman anywhere in the world, all women are in danger. The rapists might get Condi next. She might get kidnapped by one of those brutal mafias and get broken and turned out like the Dubai Girl. Then she won't be able to speak because she will be too rape-dead. A few empty pronouncements in front of the UN will do no good.

I find yet another area that I have not dealt with. It is the end of June, 2008, as I write this, and in August, the Beijing Olympics will see sexual trafficking of girls to entertain the tourists. Some will be Chinese but there are also large numbers of other nationalities involved—girls trafficked from Vietnam, Thailand, and Tawian, for example, are forced to service Chinese men. And China is the largest 'importer' in Asia of enslaved Russian girls. At least 15,000 (probably more) have been trafficked into the country. Will these girls be put to use in Beijing by their owners? Of all the human rights violations being leveled against China in order to discredit the Olympics, this particular one which involves all the nations of the world in a spirit of rape and violence and degradation of women is being ignored—as usual.

What is the rhetoric of the Olympics? Higher, greater, purer? Is it not about the best in the human spirit? I don't think the event is supposed to promote yet another Rape Killing Field venue in the world.

Toward the end of *Gulliver's Travels*, the narrator says, "I've shown you everything that's wrong—how come you haven't fixed it yet?" (Paraphrase of Swift's words—you get the general sense of what I mean.)

I don't think I am writing this book with the hope anyone will fix what is wrong. It is probably impossible since, due to biology, I don't think men will ever stop hurting us sexually.

I also know that my persona, that I am a victim, is not popular. I am supposed to be all tough and empowered like Lara Croft, Tomb Raider. This is not the body I write out of—that of the warrior woman. I write out of a body that is crushed and vulnerable.

My sense that no woman can have any dignity, that all power for women is an illusion, as long as one girl any where is being sexually hurt and degraded—this idea is not one that I have found other women share. I cannot seem to make them understand that her presence endangers us all.

And I am aware that any kind of 'help' I might extend to the vulnerable women of the world could be unwelcome. They live their own lives and think their own thoughts and, hopefully, have their own dreams. Who am I to try to 'help' them? I am a mass of confused sexuality. I don't have any wisdom.

I have a hard time caring about the people of the world in general. India promotes itself as a spiritual nation—but any country that visits such sexual cruelty on its own girls has no wisdom at all, in my estimate. Paris, city of light and love? Hardly. For centuries it has practiced a system of prostitution so ruthless that even Renoir said the brothels were places of "indescribable sadness." My own country's depredations are too numerous for a brief mention here. It would be hard to know which sexual cruelty to address first in the 'land of the free.'

Besides, I sometimes have a hard time caring about these supposedly mistreated prostituted girls when they themselves mistreat the other group of sentient beings on this planet who are far more deserving of my help—the animals. The animals are the true victims on this planet. A Thai girl watches the breaking of a baby elephant in her village. It is the way it has been done for several thousand years: tie the baby down, starve her, terrorize her with fire, drive nails into her feet. Break her spirit forever. The little Thai girl laughs and plays around the elephant, along with the other children. Why should I care if this girl is sold, after she has participated in such unimaginable cruelty?

But my compassion dies hard. I am haunted by so many ghosts. I am haunted by yet another Dubai Girl. Louise Brown describes her in *Dancing Girls of Lahore.* She has been brought up to be a whore. Raised in the profession by her mother. This is all she knows. It is going to be her first trip to Dubai, to whore. And she is excited. She puts together a fancy outfit, home-made finery that she thinks is sophisticated but that just makes her look sad and shabby.

Her 'agent' takes the excited girl to Dubai. She has been told she will be pampered and treated like a princess and make lots of money. She does make lots of money. For her agent. He subjects her to long lines of 'customers' until she almost dies.

When she comes home, she can tell no one since it would bring shame upon her and her mother.

As with all the girls in pain in this book, the poor hopeful Pakistani girl with her hopeful, shabby finery is not someone I can help. I can't help anyone. I sit here safe and well-fed. I can get up and make myself an English muffin with strawberry jam. This is no small thing. I don't take the little joys of life for granted. Or the big ones: I have a home to sleep in and an education and an incredible gift—the freedom to write without censure. I am in good enough health to walk around and I can breathe the fresh air and enjoy looking at trees and dandelions. And I am free to look at the birds I love so much as they fly free of gravity, at ease on roof tops, on trees, way up almost near the clouds. What luck and beauty is my life right now. But I cannot help the Dubai Girl to my place of freedom and beauty.

Writing this book and all of these articles over the past two years on this unbearable subject has driven all that beauty out of my life.

Part Three

Vaginaless Women, Cruel Men--and Some Good Guys

Vaginaless Women, Cruel Men--and Some Good Guys

Must one suppose oneself mad because one has the sentiment of universal pity in one's heart?

–Victor Hugo

In all the reading I did while writing *The Raped Vagina*, I ran across many insensitive female scholars and journalists—ones who write coldly about the raped, shredded, brutalized, degraded, swollen, bleeding prostituted body. Vagina-less women. Ones who obviously have no tender hole that can be raped. I also ran across men who wrote about the prostituted body with such brutal insensitivity that I had to cover my eyes with pain when I read them.

Fortunately, there were many—both men and women—who did have a clue—about what it means for the whore body to be a whore.

I also gathered huge amounts of information from all these writers—even the insensitive ones without a clue as to what the rape of the whore body means.

I read far more than I can find space for in this section, so I have selected a few books that represent the points I want to make, and also ones that I consider very important if you want to learn about prostitution/trafficking.

This section is my version of an 'annotated bibliography': informational but also containing my personal commentary on and responses to what is being written on prostitution/trafficking. Some writers I praise highly and others I find much fault with.

The very, very few voices of actual prostitutes writing about what it was like for them are the ones who make the most sense. These seem 'right' to me, in a deep place felt in my own body.

A word about setting off long, quoted material, in this section and earlier in the book. I do not like the method of double tabbing on the left margin, so I choose to do it this way: introduce the quote, put it in quotation marks, then put the attribution at the end. It simply looks better to me this way, and I use the quotation marks to make sure you see it is quoted material. I figure I can make up my own form if I like—if it suits me better. I am not writing an 'official' dissertation for anyone in order to earn a degree, as I did in the past. At this point, I can please myself in the world of scholarship and citation. Scholars have done enough harm inflicting their complicated forms on us.

We are so caught up in all these crazy rules for MLA, APA, etc., that we lose sight of what is important.

I looked up copyright rules and discovered that as long as you do not quote more than ten percent of the work, you are not infringing on copyright. I do not quote anywhere near that amount from any work.

I typically introduce the author and source of the work and then put the material from him/or her in quotes after this—sometimes setting it off, if the material is long. After quoting others, many times I put my own comments in parentheses afterwards. It should be obvious from the context and my phrasing when I am doing this.

What is lacking is a few page numbers here and there (in this section and in other parts of the book) for one reason and one reason only: I found reading all this material excruciatingly painful just the first time through. I could not make myself go back and read it again in order to find a page number I missed.

I try not to be 'scholarly' and objective—while at the same time letting you know I have read more than enough to see what is happening in the world of trafficking. I would rather not be associated with scholarship. I think that all of Western knowledge took a wrong turn with Aristotle: classifying and counting at the expense of the heart.

Enough is enough already. We have statistics and 'studies' and all the information we need about how terrible trafficking/prostitution is. The information is, of course, invaluable since it has never happened before in history that the prostituted was considered important enough to write about. Now we know. We know what happens to her. Hundreds of books and articles tell us what happens to her. Mostly with coldness do the writers write—nevertheless, the material is there. Now it is time for the next step—ACTION.

I think I will start with a remark by some non-prostituted women that makes sense to me, in the world of pain that is prostitution. *Legacies of the Comfort Women of World War II*, edited by Margaret Stetz and Bonnie B.C. Oh contains a valuable perspective. At a scholarly meeting where the authors speak on the Korean Comfort Women, a white American male asks them, "How are we to make sense of this uniquely horrible exploitation of women's bodies? Was it attributable to some flaw in the Japanese character? What made Japanese men so different, that they were able to do this?" (xiv).

Their answer: all you have to do is look around at those who are "forced to provide sex for standing armies in the many 'camptowns' surrounding military bases throughout the world" (xv). A point I make over and over in my writings is that the Korean Comfort Women are typical. Prostitution is a form of rape. There have been countless other 'comfort women'—ones in Kosovo and Bangladesh and Rwandan—ones now in brothels is Germany, that great Nation of Traffickers; ones brutally broken by the Russian and Albanian mafias using methods identical to the torture visited on the Korean Comfort Women; ones in massage parlours all over the U.S., held in debt bondage. To see the Korean Comfort Ones as some sort of anomaly is utterly ridiculous.

The testimonies of the Korean Comfort Women are useful in order to counter someone like Dr. Harold Cross who, in his book *Lust Market*, makes one of the most extraordinary statements I've ever heard. He holds that even if a prostitute takes on fifty men a day it will only cause mild irritation of her mucous membranes. He says that this is easy to recover from. He pays absolutely no attention to the devastating psychological effects on the woman of being invaded in such a merciless and brutal way.

"It must be realized" he writes, "that a prostitute, even though she takes upwards of fifty men *per diem*, in no way jeopardizes her sexual potency and reproductive power....there is only a temporary strain on her mucous membranes. With rest and adequate treatment these...are easily restored to their normal state."

He calls the girls he examines "merchandise" and says that one half have inflammations of the cervix but he dismisses this pain as trivial. The pain the poor things must have experienced during the constant intercourse they endured must have been tremendous with inflammations in that area. Even one man going in too deep, even if you are not inflamed, can be beyond painful. A man not realizing at all the everyday horror and torture that is intercourse for the prostituted body. It saddens me beyond words.

In yet another heartless passage he describes German ships docking in Portugal: "Business was so brisk that the police—always so helpful here—arranged the seamen in queues outside each house." All of this is a joke to him, apparently. I wonder what would happen if we put him there, to be ravaged by the rape queue. I know that I would die after one hour of being used by a rape queue. Absolutely no attention to the pain, mental or physical, of the girls on his part. Of the prostitute taking on fifty men a day, and then returning to being physically 'normal' after rest--that he mentions, he pays no attention to her psychological state at all. He pays no attention to the way entry by fifty different men in one day, let alone by fifty day after day, would render her insane. And I dispute that returning to even being physically normal is possible. I was only raped a few times a day and I have never been 'normal'—both the physical and psychological damage are permanent.

I wonder how these poor girls imprisoned in the Portuguese brothels mentioned above, servicing lines of German sailors, felt? Why does Cross not ask this question? Doesn't he realize that servicing one crude German rapist sailor is devastating? I cannot even imagine how these girls survived lines of these men. Prostitutes forced to perform assembly-line sex must service men who are complete slime. Even one man touching a woman if she does not want him inside her is unbearable—can you even imagine what dozens of crude male slime inside you would be like? I wonder why Cross never considered this side of prostitution when he was joking around.

Did this man have a wife or a sister or a daughter, or any woman dear to him? Could he imagine any woman dear to him returning to 'normal' after fifty rapes day after day after day?

A wise friend once said to me, "Attack the ideas of the person, not the person himself." I have found this very, very hard to hold onto as a principle while writing this book given the way I see all these 'ideas' as expressing supreme and callous indifference to the pain of the raped body.

I was only raped fifteen times in one day and believe me it was not a 'mild irritation' to my mucous membranes. It was a burning tearing swollen bleeding hell of pain. And there was no recovery and it definitely 'jeopardized' every inch of my being, physical and spiritual. How can this man Cross think there is no damage to a woman after this rape that is not just rape—it is meta-rape, hyper-rape, rape upon rape. If Cross's attitude is the prevalent one—and I think it is—there is no hope for our bodies. I have found the world at large deeply insensitive to the raped body of the prostitute—I have found most of the world not even regarding this most horrific form of rape as rape at all.

I find this sort of insensitivity even more reprehensible when it is a woman holding these sorts of 'ideas'—as you will see when I tackle some of the women writing on prostitution.

Cornelius Ryan in *Star-Spangled Mikado* stuns me into a pain beyond soothing when he writes about what a shame it is that the GI has to miss out on "the charm and dignity of the Japanese woman, her delicacy and graciousness....It was regrettable that the G.I. had been introduced at the beginning to the fake geishas and prostitutes." The massive and cruel insensitivity of this remark makes me writhe with pain: as if those miserably exploited women, conscripted for the degradation of sexual service, were so many throwaway pieces of garbage. These are the women who should be highly honored, not scorned. And how 'regrettable' is the position of the GI who is raping these poor enslaved creatures. The overwhelming arrogant masculine insensitivity of the remark tears my insides to pieces with pain. It makes me realize why fighting for the bodies of women, fighting for the right not to be raped, is a complete lost cause.

In *Women on the Verge*, Karen Kelsky, an anthropologist at the University of Oregon, stresses the politeness of the GI's in Japan, particularly just after the occupation started. She says that Japanese women talked about how courteous American soldiers were. This is very odd. Would these girls feel the same if they were put forcibly into the comfort stations?

Kelsky is aware of the comfort/rape stations. She writes: "Within days of Japan's defeat, the Japanese government established a system of official government brothels to serve the Occupying forces. Considered a lower class 'female floodwall'...protecting the chastity of 'good' middle-class women, thousands of Japanese women—most not professional prostitutes but homeless, destitute, orphaned, and desperate teenagers—were hired as Occupation comfort women to work in these brothels. When this official system was abolished by MacArthur only one year after its inception due to skyrocketing rates of venereal disease...the young women by and large found themselves even worse off, having lost such official protection as they had been accorded and reduced to walking the streets as panpan girls." Now, how could the extremes of rape and physical and psychological torture that the girls experienced in the comfort stations be considered 'protection' of them in any way? Also, Kelsky terms what happened to them in the rape stations as 'sexual oppression.' Continuous rape of the body, such as they experienced, is so far, far, far beyond 'oppression' that is an abomination to use this mild word for it.

Those girls lived in the middle of a brothel rape hell. I don't know how you can possibly call the GI's polite when almost 100% of them were raping these poor defenseless little whores. (I wish I could rid myself of this terrible image, the lines of GI's waiting to get at the 'comfort whores.' I always feel as if it is happening to me, all the time. It haunts me with a pain I can find no peace for, this phantom rape pain my body feels. I am probably a reincarnated 'comfort whore.')

Book after book after book about Vietnam, even ones written by women, even ones written by nurses who were there, either completely ignore or minimize the sexual exploitation of Vietnamese women. I'll just give one example—but I could point to hundreds on the library shelves—rows and rows of them with no mention of the raped bodies: James R. Ebert's *The American Infantryman in Vietnam, 1965-1972*. Exclusively told from the male point of view, it is as if the soldiers never even raped and used and destroyed all of those helpless Vietnamese girls turned into whores for them.

I will say that he does mention torture of animals: "the handler of a mine-sniffing dog…fed C-4 (plastique explosive) to some ducks and a dog in one of the villages. 'They started foaming at the mouth and went into convulsions…It ate them up something fierce," according to soldier John Meyer. Men would also take their brutality out on pigs, macheting them to death. It is frightening to think how they must have treated the helpless whores given to them, seeing how they were so without mercy toward the animals.

I cannot find one interview with a brothel whore from the ten-year American occupation of that country. Are they too ashamed to come forward, as are all of their war-raped counterparts around the world? Are they all dead? Most of these women in Vietnam would be about my age now—yet not even their ghosts seem to trouble the wind and the water.

Leslie Ann Jeffrey, *Sex and Borders: Gender, National Identity, and Prostitution Policy in Thailand*, is very cold, chillingly so. This is how she talks about the hardships of prostitution, as if they were something so mild, like maybe having to put in a long shift at a restaurant : "Working conditions within the sex sector…are often well below acceptable….Work hours could be extremely long, and the pressure to receive many customers could be very intense." This kind of 'distancing' does nothing to express the rape arena that is this 'job.' She also has a fixation on 'agency,' that faddish word that is supposed to express how the prostituted really has control over her life, despite the constant rape.

We don't have lives to speak of, Ms. Jeffrey. We are just raped bodies—there is no 'agency' for the raped body.

This is a good time for me to go into the 'choice' debate that rules among the feminists: they waste endless time and words on trying to either prove or determine a 'voluntary' aspect to the prostitute who gets raped all day. That she invites it in some way, is 'willing,' 'knows what she's getting into.' As if she would ever invite this searing misery to her insides. There is no choice in the world of rape and degradation.

Jeffrey writes: "I view 'the prostitute' as a subject-position constructed in discourse and imposed on a shifting reality' (xvi). No, I don't think she is anything as rarefied and abstract as this. Men don't rape the air. They rape a body—and it is an ugly, painful act. Jeffrey has all these fancy phrasings, like how women are "positioned" in prostitution. I have noticed that academics love these vague abstract ways of describing pain. "Re-positioned" is another word they love. In a non-abstract real flesh context, the poor creature is either 'positioned' on her back, legs up and apart, getting rammed or 're-positioned' on her stomach with her poor butthole getting ripped to pieces.

The saddest thing about Jeffrey's book is her tone that what happened to the impoverished helpless girls of Thailand as a result of American military sexual demand is some kind of myth. It is very puzzling when she talks about it being "the usual story": stationing American troops in Thailand or sending them there to take R & R. Her tone implies it did not happen. Yet she says the number of prostitutes in Bangkok alone skyrocketed from a mere 20,000 to over 400,000 as a result of the men taking their sexual leave and doing their sex bingeing there. Women, she says, "migrated" to areas where men were. "These women were to provide sexual services in the mushrooming bars, discos and massage parlours built to cater to the military...." Her phrasing gives absolutely no indication that this was involuntary in any way. No indication of the trafficking and sale of helpless hungry young girls. "Were to provide services," she writes. Such coldness in her phrasing. As if this were just an ordinary 'service,' not the terrible rape of the body.

At least I learn a few interesting stats from her—like the fact the about 90% of Thai men visit prostituted girls (xiv).

She really likes the idea of 'agency'—it is her pet fad word. It is the pet fad word of all these feminists who have not a clue that there is no 'agency' involved in the helpless suffering body subjected to hot rape and pain.

Jeffrey has another book, *Sex Workers in the Maritimes Talk Back*, in which she takes this 'agency'/choice' stance as well. What is interesting is that the lives the women reveal as she interviews them are horrifying. Just the physical damage and illnesses as a result of this 'job' are at a level of extreme torture. Yet Jeffrey persists in this 'agency' myth, as if women would really choose this level of physical damage as a way of life.

Jeffrey and her kind do so much more harm than good by making it sound as if this 'job' were 'normal' in some way. There is nothing normal about the raped whore body. I should know. I have one. And I have absolutely no desire to be academic, distanced, objective, or analytical about it. To write about this and really reflect the reality—that is my goal. We have enough distanced, cold accounts of prostitution. It is time for anger and emotion.

In both books, Jeffrey thinks she is making a contribution by interviewing the girls, but in my view, you cannot give a real voice to women who can't be interviewed due to the lies they must tell themselves to stay alive.

I would have been incensed if anyone had tried to interview me when I worked as a prostitute. How dare you invade my pain.

Another woman I find chilling is Teela Sanders. She is full of the jargon of 'commodifying intimacy" and in her *Sex Work: A Risky Business*, she says, "this book moves beyond stereotypes of 'the prostitute' to look at the mundane and ordinary activities of the female sex worker." Yet she gives a lot of information as to how they face violence and soul-destroying scorn.

If so, how can this be an 'ordinary' job? One of her sub-headings is the "Normalization of Violence."

Let's roll into some testimonies by the Korean Comfort Women. Maybe this will convince the feminists determined to find 'choice' in the unbearable torture of rape that there is none. Please remember that these comfort women are the rule, not the exception, in the tortured world of the body that we call prostitution.

Here goes. The first passages are from David Andrew Schmidt's *Ianfu—The Comfort Women of the Japanese Imperial Army of the Pacific War: Broken Silence.*

After servicing men all day, the girls say we ate our dinner in the evening "with tears dripping on the food in our hand" (149).

One of the few Dutch comfort women, Jan Ruff, says, "they stripped me of everything, my self-esteem, my dignity, my freedom" (152).

A former Japanese soldier testified: "There were 5-6 rooms and one woman per room would have 10-15 soldiers lined up outside. Those lined up would shout and jeer, 'Faster, faster. Hurry up.' I was 23 years old at the time and I recall being very rough with the women" (155).

Schmidt's conclusion: "Life at the comfort stations was a living hell. They were beaten and tortured in addition to being raped by 15, 20, or 30 soldiers a day and officers by night, day after day, for periods ranging from three weeks to eight years....When they were brought to the comfort stations they were virgins, healthy in body and spirit. They left the comfort stations diseased in body and crippled in spirit" (176).

What is even worse, when the Americans came to places like Mindanao and Okinawa and the Philippines, they also used the comfort houses. These poor women, raped to death and then raped to death again by new rough men. (Only tenderness should be visited on a woman during sex, never roughness.)

Schmidt writes: "The Allied Powers had full knowledge in 1945 that these atrocities had been committed. They did nothing to bring the offenders to trail or to obtain reparation for the victims. Clearly they owe a duty to explain this..." (179).

What happened to the Comfort Girls is much worse than just the brief 'facts' above. I started out with a mild account.

This next is from *Casting Stones: Prostitution and Liberation in Asia and the United States* by Rita Nakashima Brock and Susan Brooks Thistlethwaite:

"The Japanese authorities figured that one girl would be able to handle 29 men a day....Some comfort girls died as they lay...[there was massive] swelling of the genitals...Sometimes a woman had to serve 50 soldiers in a row in one day...Some lucky enough to survive never dared return to their native land because of extreme disgrace. They roamed aimlessly with ill—health and mind until they died" (71).

[Girls were] "raped by as many as 60 soldiers a day, as frequently as every 3 minutes" (73).

(In my experience, just one penetration by a man you don't know is terrible. How measure the effect of what a comfort girl lived through in just one day? There can be no healing for this. I also wonder about the male mentality that can numerically decide that one woman can 'handle' 29 men a day. What kind of hard, dead, non-human mind can actually make this sort of decision about living bodies with vaginas that tear and living beings with souls that will die from sexual murder? I refuse to be 'objective' about such monstrous decisions on the part of men about my female body. Anger is needed. Deep, outraged anger.)

Casting Stones makes some astute observations about military prostitution:

"The sexual exploitation of women by soldiers is an expected fact of military life...the military exploitation of women goes largely unnoticed most of the time because it is so pervasive...it is an integral part of the military construction of masculinity and aggression...."

"That an international women's movement has formed to demand that sexual exploitation by a government's military be treated as war crimes is an important step towards exposing such exploitation....The U.S. government might eventually be required to take responsibility for the behavior of American troops abroad. " (This is a great idea, I think, but it also strikes me as too little, too late. How can one make reparation to a fifteen-year-old Korean girl who, in 1952, was seasoned and broken by a Korean shit-male pimp and turned out for sex entertainment for the GI's and then she became diseased and died from the harshness of her life before she even reached age 20? There is no way any government—Korean or American—can make reparation to her. There is no way you can restore her life and her sexuality—a sexuality taken from her years before she was even ready to have sex. There is no way to punish or hold accountable the Korean shit-male who sold her and the GI rapists who bought her.)

In 1990, according to Brock and Thistlethwaite, there were about 30,000 prostitutes in bars and brothels around U.S. military bases in Korea. Also, "a large number of Filipinas have been trafficked to Okinawa to meet the demands of the sex industry around American bases there. In addition, virtually every US military base anywhere has a sex industry near it" (74).

The authors point out the high rates of violence against prostitutes by their military customers and say that "sex industries around U.S. bases are an accepted fact of military life. When the military is engaged in conflict, the sexual use of women at R & R stops, along with drug and alcohol abuse, is regarded as a necessary pressure valve for troops to let off steam" (76).

They informed me of something I did not know: In the 1991 Gulf War the U.S. military sailed 'entertainment' ships into the Persian Gulf for the troops, and the men docked in Manila for brothel visits on the way home. I had heard that the military trafficked whores into the desert for the men, and that lines formed to use them; but I did not know about the ships. I would like to find out where the girls were trafficked from, how they were treated, what happened to them? All these great 'mystery questions' that are never answered, never even allowed to be asked—as the servicemen keep their pact of silence about the sex slaves who 'service' them.

I also did not know this quite interesting fact: "the government of Athens supported itself partially by funds obtained from slave brothels that were forced to follow Greek armies" (Brock and Thistlethwaite 72). Add to this the fact the Solon, the revered Greek lawgiver, set up brothels stocked with slave girls so that every citizen of Athens could get his cheap sex fix, and you can see why prostitution is so sanctioned both in military and civilian life: Western civilization was founded by pimps and rapists.

Keith Howard's *True Stories of the Korean Comfort Women* contains many horrifying testimonies from the girls:

"Having to serve so many men made my sexual organs swell up…my vagina was torn and bled for a week" (53).

"On Sundays, the soldiers came from 9 o'clock in the morning until 4 o'clock in the afternoon, without respite. Sometimes we had to serve…40 or more men without pausing for a break. We gave up counting" (61).

"On Saturdays, the Japanese soldiers formed long queues…The ends of the queues were sometime invisible….They came from 9 am till midnight on both Saturdays and Sundays" (99).

Girls were often too weak to get up to pee, even if they were allowed to. One says: "If I lay still wetting myself and with my womb bleeding… some men would just kick me and leave….I just lay like a corpse" (172-173).

(Painful bladder infections can result from not peeing after intercourse. This is not a small thing when you have 50 men a day ramming your insides. The pain to the bladder during intercourse can be excruciating.)

"Because I was forced to serve so many men, my womb became raw, red and swollen and began to smell badly....Even in this state I had to keep on serving men" (174).

"We had to serve countless soldiers....My abdomen, my womb, throbbed with pain. I had to serve so many men. Afterwards, I would be unable to walk..." (190).

"It was like a living death" (54).

"Return my youth to me," says one girl. "Give me back my life" (88).

Other hardships reported in Howard's book: some girls starved to death because of being too weak to eat after twelve to fifteen hours of rape a day.

They were injected with a liquid that contained mercury which induced abortions and the girls describe being massively sick for a week after being forced to drink this.

They were taunted and scorned wherever they were transported by the 'good' women of the towns who saw the soldiers lined up to use them and thought it was fine, just so long as their 'decent' vaginas were not being raped. Children threw stones at them for being so filthy.

One girl describes her PTSD many years later: how she is restless, then gets hot, then cold, and how she shouts and screams and yells and how she is so afraid of people that she locks herself away. "I got scared when I met people, and shuddered when I heard any loud sound. I stayed indoors for 30 years, crawling on my knees."

Howard's book is invaluable. What amazing insights these testimonies give us into extremes of sexual torture. Raping girls until they cannot walk! Sexual torture similar to what modern-day sex slaves, comfort women, trafficked/prostituted women—whatever terms you want to use—also undergo. Adolescent girls from the Balkans, forced to 'take on' a 100 Greek man a day; abattoir whores in Paris and Morocco raped every 10 minutes by a different man; Slavic Girls trafficked into Dubai and 'trained' by being mounted by a different man every few minutes. As with the Korean Comfort Girls, these girls would not be able to walk either after so much rape. It is the same vagina and same body being tortured.

Distressing as the accounts of the Korean Comfort Girls are, they are a major document in the history of female sexuality. Or non-sexuality might be a better term since prostitution negates female sexuality. No testimonies since the ones of the KCW have come close to telling us what prostitution is like. Currently, girls who have escaped trafficking are telling their stories—

but not in the detail we have from the KCW. I am trying to remedy the lack of detail by going into my own story in some detail. But, fortunately, I lack the background of extreme sexual torture that these women went through. I have to make do with recounting the quite mild sexual torture inflicted on me, and how deeply it affected me. How, when I first go to bed with a man, I am so scared he will hurt me I get a burning sensation on the back of my neck and a cold feeling in my stomach. How I am jumpy and timid and how it takes me forever to leave the house since I know that girls outside, in my very city, in cities all over the world, are being sexually brutalized—and I can do nothing for them. I have to literally trick myself to cross the threshold, everyday. How can I feel safe in a world where even one girl is being used as a 'comfort woman'?

We have these magnificent, courageous documents from the Korean Comfort Women, and, seemingly, the world is ignoring them. Traffickers and pimps and brothel owners and customer-rapists all over the world are 'manufacturing' comfort women in greater numbers than we have ever seen. These girls are all over Germany, imprisoned in Eros Centres (what a cruel joke of a phrase); spread all across Western Europe is the modern-day comfort girl: the Slavic girl broken by rape, reduced to such a level of terror, she does not exist in any human form anymore. She is just pure raped fear.

She smiles like a wind-up doll and fucks like a machine, so she can survive. Meanwhile, the privileged Western European woman sips fancy lattes at cafés and goes shopping at glossy boutiques and dresses up to attend the ballet or the Proms. Meanwhile, her enslaved counterpart fucks away in a torture bed of pain.

Why, I wonder, should any woman be reduced to this? What is the difference between the safe woman sipping her coffee at a café in Paris and the girl in the abattoir whore slaughterhouse in the immigrant section of the city being mounted without mercy 80 times a day?

I wonder, too, how people can approve of prostitution, or ignore it, when most of it involves conditions similar to what the comfort girls went through. Trafficking, coercion, debt bondage, beatings are all part of the ordinary everyday picture of prostitution. Small numbers of independent prostitutes may exist but most are coerced and mistreated in some way. Even the high-priced call girls, as we label them, report some violence from their customers. Even those well-paid girls are often subject to humiliations that ordinary women would find it hard to deal with.

It's also odd that no one who writes about it focuses on physical pain and how even one little prick or roughness in that area can make a girl cry. Even one rough male can cause not just physical damage but terrible psychological pain.

The thing that is so hard for me to fathom is surviving what the comfort girls went though for even one day. I was only raped fifteen times in one day during my ordeal and I couldn't walk even after that one time of roughness and misery and pain. It would not have been possible for me to survive two days of such treatment.

And I ask why would anyone choose this as a 'profession'? Since so many prostituted girls are mistreated, many of them miserably, it really renders the 'choice' dialogue that so many feminists are stuck on as meaningless.

And the real puzzle is why girls who are treated this way are the criminals, not their traffickers or rapists. It is peculiar that millions of Japanese soldiers kept quite about their participation in their mass rape of comfort women before and during WWII and then these men went home as heroes and touched wives and had daughters and held them and were considered 'respectable' members of society, and the comfort girls went home to nothing—to hatred and revulsion from 'normal' women and men if they dared tell their story, or to the death-in-life of silence if they kept quiet about the 'shame.' (Whose shame, I always ask? Certainly not theirs. They did nothing wrong.)

(Isn't it about time women stop buying into this I am-a-whore-therefore-worthless crap and you-are-a-man-and-therefore-worth-everything-because-you-rape-me crap. What insanity we feed ourselves.)

The Russian mafia and the Albanian mafia apparently break girls in ways quite similar to what the comfort women went through. Elsewhere in this book, I have mentioned the Dubai Girl: trafficked into Dubai by the Russian mafia, she is seasoned at a nearby Pakistani labor camp where a different man is let in to use her every fifteen minutes. There is the fourteen-year old Albanian girl controlled by her mafia in London who is forced to have sex twenty hours a day in a Soho brothel.

It is all the same picture. The Dubai Girl is a comfort woman. So is the Albanina girl.

Here's another example, of the brutal comfort-woman phenomenon from *A Modern Form of Slavery: Trafficking of Burmese Women and Girls into Brothels in Thailand* by Human Rights Watch.

To summarize some of what HRW found happening in Thai brothels to trafficked Burmese girls: Passive and broken from the beatings and rapes, these poor girls were mostly illiterate peasants sold, held in debt bondage, raped up to fifteen times a day. One poor thing worked and worked even though she was 'sore' so she could pay off her imaginary debt faster. Another was beaten when she tried to listen to the BBC on the radio. Even one small pleasure not allowed her. If girls tried to escape, they had no where to go and would end up coming back to the brothels on their own. They did not know how to use a telephone and who would they call for help? The Thai police were in on it—corrupt rape shit males who also used the girls freely, for kickbacks.

"Powerless to negotiate condom use" (170), when the girls contracted AIDS they would be sent home—to die or to be killed by the Burmese government as infected filth. The poor things didn't even know what AIDS was. And since they were just babies most of them, fifteen or sixteen, or even younger, their poor young bodies suffered greatly. The "mucous membrane of the genital track in girls is not as thick as that of a grown woman" so the poor things would tear very easily (170).

Pathetic. Again, I ask why should any girl be treated like this? And what girl would chose this as a way of life? We never ask the obvious questions about prostitution.

Let me give you another example of how the comfort-woman paradigm is alive and well and killing girls in the modern world. This time let's go to India and to information in *Guilty without Trail: Women in the Sex Trade in Calcutta* by Carolyn Sleightholme and Indrani Sinha.

Here's what the authors say about what these women suffer: "The work and lifestyle take their toll on women's mental health, and their psychological problems and low self-esteem are expressed in acts of self-mutilation such as scarring their own arms with knives, alcohol addiction and tolerance of violent relationships…" (73). Physically, almost all have Pelvic Inflammatory Disease which causes extreme pain in the lower abdomen. When I read facts like this, it hurts very deeply since I could barely withstand intercourse with the men who bought me when my reproductive system was relatively healthy; it is unbearable to think of 'taking on' men when that area is in acute pain. (I also know from personal experience that bladder pain can be severe due to too many men inside our bodies. And I ask—again and again—why should any girl or woman be subjected to this kind of pain during intercourse just because men have to have sex—no matter what. Why does our pain not matter?)

Of the "child sex-workers" (as these authors call them), they write: "Notwithstanding the mental strain, the physical effects of sexual abuse on minors are horrific. From doctors we receive accounts of…what child sex-workers…have suffered: the internal injuries are so severe that repair is difficult; they suffer from rectal fissures, lacerated vaginas, poor sphincter control, foreign bodies in the anus, perforated anal and vaginal walls, chronic choking from gonorrheal tonsillitis, and by asphyxiation. CINI (ASHA) came across a fifteen-year-old whose anal muscles were hanging outside her body after repeated anal rape. To make matters worse, the risk of catching HIV is increased in children because of the higher incidence of abrasions and bleeding when sex occurs" (84-85).

This next passage may be the hardest in the book to take: "Although rarely spoken of, most sex workers have experienced violent inductions into the business….Those women who are forced into sex-work might be raped many times before they resign themselves to what is happening and then, given their powerlessness to refuse, cooperate with what is seen as consent….It is not too far off the mark to talk of sexual abuse and rape as a daily occurrence that the women, being powerless to resist, have grown used to….Sex workers have experienced this abuse in many forms and often deeply internalize a sense of worthlessness after being treated as a mere sexual commodity, as less than human. It is not unusual to find women who have mutilated themselves, for example by slashing their arms, as a way of expressing self-loathing after experiencing years of abuse from others."

What is so astonishing about the above passage is that is it not confined to Calcutta, a city, by the way, where prostitutes have to some extent been able to 'unionize,' at least in a rudimentary form. If things are this bad in Calcutta, just think about what they must be like in Bombay, where the women and girls and children are even more powerless, and where middle-aged men climbing, in full view, on top of seven-year-old girls trafficked from Nepal is simply a commonplace.

What is astonishing is that the violence and rape and powerlessness are not at all confined to India. They are typical of conditions for prostitutes around the world.

In addition, the distinction between the child and adult prostitute is very hard to draw, not just in the violent filth of Bombay or Calcutta: you will find girls age ten or twelve working side by side with older prostituted beings in bars and brothels outside plantations, outside military bases, in migrant farm worker sex prisons, in large glamourous cities. Often, according to CATW, the 'adult' prostitute, should she live so long, was coerced into it as a child. I often wonder why up until age seventeen years, eleven months, thirty days and twenty-three hours, she is a 'child' to be pitied and then after midnight, at age eighteen, she is suddenly a grown-up whore who made a 'choice.'

Sleightholme and Sinha also make a great deal of sense when they write: "The sheer numbers of men visiting sex-workers every day means that clients cannot be considered abnormal. The whole point of the sex trade is to cater to the needs and desires of men. It is likely that the sex trade exists because patriarchal societies give undue emphasis to the male sexual urge and to gratifying men's desires....and while the class of women who gratify these needs are branded as public women and are ostracized from society, the men...find approval from other men and continue to lead a publicly respectable life....It must be remembered that the sex trade, where survival and gratification meet in such diverse ways, has as its objective the gratification of the needs of men" (123).

From my point of view it would only be possible to see a free and beneficial form of prostitution for women if their sexual needs were met by the transaction. Emotional needs as well. Given the extraordinarily violent and coercive climate of prostitution, I don't really see how this can ever come about. There is overwhelming evidence that this is not a great 'profession' for the majority of women and children in it. Therefore, it is difficult to envision a kind form of it, as for the few, the very few, who might actually operate independently of the coercion and cruelty of pimps, the degradation of the brothels, the ever-present danger of violence, and the stigma and scorn that cause low self-esteem, self-mutilation, etc. These few privileged exceptions are also in danger due to the nature of the sex industry.

The people of the world need this drilled into them: that privileged minority is not representative of the tortured beings who make up the bulk of the prostitutes worldwide. There has been little 'choice' in the lives of most prostitutes. After all, what woman or girl would actually choose rough, impersonal sex with men (often drunk) she does not know? Would not she run screaming away from this if she could? Her most tender cherished beautiful part used so cruelly, so a pimp or owner can get rich off of her. I really don't see 'choice' here.

Even one drunk man using me roughly scarred me for life.

Before I began writing this book, I was not quite prepared for how much of prostitution is conducted in an atmosphere of violence and torture. When I read things like brothel owners cutting out syphilis sores with scissors and knives and then cauterizing the wounds with fire, I wonder how prostitution could ever be 'good' for the women and girls in it.

Now that I know all this, it is even more difficult for me to envision a form of prostitution that would be safe and non-coercive for women.

My only caveat about Sleightholme and Sinha is that they still use the term 'sex worker' even after what they have seen of the horrors of this 'non-work.' And how they can actually use the phrase 'child sex worker' is beyond me. Is it 'work' when a girl child's anus is hanging out of her body from continuous rape?

Let's return to the Korean Comfort Girls. Maria Rosa Henson tells her story in *Comfort Woman: A Filipina's Story of Prostitution and Slavery Under the Japanese Military.* Taken when she was just a child, she had no pubic hair, and calls what the brutal soldiers did to her 'rape.' She is quite clear about this. She was a virgin and then a dozen used her in a row, and then another dozen. She was so swollen and bleeding she was in deep pain. When she speaks of another comfort girl, she says "a hundred a day lined up to rape her." It is very, very clear from her wording that this was rape. Oddly, many who write on the Comfort Women have tried to call it 'prostitution'—as if that were not rape as well. They are identical. Prostitution is rape. (It is none the less rape if the man pays.)

These are Henson's own words:

"Twelve soldiers raped me in quick succession, after which I was given half an hour rest. Then twelve more soldiers followed. They all lined up outside the room waiting for their turn. I bled so much and was in such pain, I could not even stand up. The next morning I was too weak to get up…I could not eat. I felt much pain, and my vagina was swollen. I cried and cried, calling my mother…Every day, from two in the afternoon till ten in the evening, the soldiers lined up outside my room…At the end of the day, I closed by eyes and cried. My torn dress would be brittle from the crust that had formed from the soldiers' dried semen…"

Later when she escaped, she could not stop slobbering from fear and mental derangement.

When she finally told her story to the world in the early 1990's, she was taunted and teased by neighbors who said she must have been really tough to service battalions of soldiers and a woman journalist accused her of coming forward for money and even her granddaughter was against her, saying she had brought shame on the family (87).

This is typical, by the way, of what happened to the other Korean Comfort Women who finally came forward in the early 1990's. I have often wondered why all the other sexual victims of WWII have never come forward. For example, the ones that Brownmiller reports being so savaged in Palermo by GI's; an eyewitness said: "Business boomed when the Yanks…were here…. The American troops set up their camps in the parks. Husbands brought their wives to them, and took the money. As soon as one man came out, another went in; they waited in line. *Ol rait. God fuc. Uno dollar.* The park keepers provided the mattresses so the Yanks would be comfortable" (75).

Where are these Palermo girls, the ones mass raped by GI's in the name of starvation and prostitution? Are they slobbering with mental derangement and nightmares from all the laughing soldiers who climbed on top of them, one after the other? Are they crawling on their knees in misery, not able to leave their houses for fear of men? For fear they will be mass raped again.

If a reception of scorn and shame and taunting would greet them for having such filthy bodies and for daring to get themselves mass raped due to starvation, then it is no wonder they have not come forward.

I always think of these things. When the Athens Olympics started commemorating all the Allies soldiers in some kind of remembrance ceremony, all I could think of was the poor Italian, German, Belgian, French, Greek, and Dutch whores who were sold to them. And I zero in on the coverage of this, when it actually surfaces, which is rarely. Like when a woman historian, in a article on World War II, briefly mentions how 'entrepreneurs' in Naples sold their 'merchandize' to Allied soldiers from Morocco, Algiers, and America. That's all she has to say. And this is in a big woman's history book purporting to tell our side of the story—I guess 'our' does not include us whores when it comes to women's history.

I wonder why the women historians either never deal with this, or call the transaction one that deals with 'merchandize' and 'entrepreneurs,' not raped starving girl and their pimps.

I think we really need to make clear that we are dealing with rape. I don't feel strong enough to do this all on my own. I need some help. One of my male friends says I am a tough cookie. I am not at all a tough cookie. One of my women friends says she feels ferocious after she reads what I write since she is so stirred to go out and do something. I wish I could find some of that power inside me that these other people see in me. All I feel is timidness and hopelessness—how can I deal with women historians who see nothing of the truth of history?

At the moment I am most troubled by the Dubai Girl, the one broken without mercy in the Pakistani labor camp, the one living in the same rape hell as the comfort girls—and when the navies of the world dock at Dubai, and the military contractors fly in, on R & R. to use her, they are raping an already raped beyond pain body. She is haunting me. And when all the businessmen go there to combine pleasure and work, and all the tourists flock in for horseracing and other events, these men are contributing to the torture methods of the Russian mafia.

I am scarred easily. I don't think my sensitivity stems from being raped. I think I was born this way. All things seem connected. Pain seem to hit from all directions. Now it is hard for me to watch a Sharapova or a Kournikova or all the other Russians on the tour and wonder why these glamourous tennis greats do not help all of their suffering sisters trafficked by the Russian mafia. I have a Russian male friend, formerly in the Russian army when the country was the Soviet Union. I love this man for his goodness and compassion but it is now hard for me to not associate him with his countrymen who have apparently become as ruthless as the Yakuza mafia. He adds to my concern when he tells me how brutal the Russian men he served with were.

I am really sick of reading about life from the masculine/decent women point of view. Somehow it is never told from the point of view of the helpless and scorned and hated and despised. I can give numerous examples—too many for the space I have—so I'll limit myself to a few

Vietnam vet Robert S. McKelvey dedicates his book, *The Dust of Life: America's Children Abandoned in Vietnam*, to his wife and daughter. This after he says he may have fathered children in Vietnam. Why no dedication to his other daughter, or daughters, the ones scorned as the children of whores, outcast from Vietnamese society, begging street girls prostituted and raped? Half-breed disposable daughters. If he may have fathered children in Vietnam, has he gone to look for them? Were any of them girls and are they now prostituted? These are big questions that need to be answered.

He makes a joke about the pornographic filth and exploitation that was Vietnam: when he returns to the country long after the war, he says he is "greeted by the smiling face of a Vietnamese boy offering to sell me a pack of pornographic playing cards. Some things have changed little in the past twenty years" (xx). The ugly dirty joke male filter that ignores the reality of degradation for the Vietnamese women on those cards—perhaps his forgotten daughters are on those cards? Half-breed flesh is considered prime erotic barter and rape fodder all over the world.

Then he writes about "Freedom Street…Here GI's once walked arm and arm with their Vietnamese girlfriends dancing and drinking the night away at 'Maxim's' nightclub, before returning to many nearby hotels for liaisons that may have produced some of the Amerasians I had come to interview" (xvi).

I wish to point out that there is no girlfriend/boyfriend relationship possible when the girl is starving and pimped and the soldier buys her for rape purposes. I think that men must be able to lie to themselves about the rape of these helpless destitute girls by pretending there is a 'girlfriend' aspect. I'm not sure how that lie fits a pimped girl who has sex forced into her continuously by men she does not know. It must take some kind of male mindset to believe that her raped little body is that of a 'girlfriend.'

But, then, the female mindset is every bit as brutally insensitive. For example,

Le Ly Hayslip, author of *When Heaven and Earth Changed Places: A Vietnamese Woman's Journey from War to Peace,* scorns her own sisters for 'entertaining' GI's—apparently she too has no sympathy for those who must fuck for food. When an American soldier calls Vietnamese whores 'that filth,' she makes no protest. Who turned the girls into whores and 'that filth,' I ask? Do the men who raped the bodies of starving girls sold and pimped to them get away with their own 'filth' of behavior and are the girls simply tossed aside as garbage? Why did Le Ly Hayslip not object to girls—vulnerable, abused girls—being called 'that filth'?

A fancy ritzy scholar, safe at her university, writes of the outcast status of Amerasian children because their mothers "were stigmatized as being lower class prostitutes or bar girls…and the offspring of a passing relationship with a GI" (Iijima Hall 219). However, she says this stereotype was not true because "the majority of these Vietnamese women were in relationships with these military men for an average of two years…" (As an aside, this information really puzzles me since the average tour of duty in Vietnam was only one year.)

Note her thoughtless, without-mercy attitude from her lofty academic perch toward these women she calls "lower class prostitutes" just because of the way she phrases herself. What exactly is a "lower class prostitutes"? Is the definition dependent on volume of rapes? Is the comfort girl who had to take on 300 men in one day, peeing and bleeding where she lay, a "lower class prostitute"? Is the poor debt-bondage whore forced to service 20 or 30 Vietnam GI's on R & R a day, even when she is sick and exhausted, a "lower class prostitute"? Why does the designation not apply to those in these imaginary long-term relationships since these were also a fuck-for-food situation? There is no 'relationship' in wartime when the girl has to fuck for food.

I really think that this scholar needs to rethink her system of values. Pride of place should go to those few who survived the "degradation of the brothels," (as Eisen calls it)—to those used a dozen or so times a day and called 'filth.' Being raped all day because you have to fuck for food should not be a badge of shame. It should, instead, be a badge of honor.

Sad to say, whores do not even understand the suffering of other whores, even though they may have been treated miserably themselves. Whores will condemn other whores as filth, too. It is all women who are to blame for keeping others in this miserable sex prison called Rape Planet Earth. We women keep ourselves enslaved and enchained—the scholars who place women in the category of 'lower class prostitutes'; the trafficked girl who says, "I am not a bad girl, I am not dirty like those prostitutes.' Her sheer lack of understanding and heart is astonishing. The blind trafficked girl can be raped all day and still think that those we label 'prostitutes' invite the same rape on their bodies? Astonishing, the blindness of women. And I am not sure I can find words to express the blindness of the women who genitally mutilate little girls in the name of 'custom' and 'culture.' How ignorant can we as humans make ourselves—to allow all kinds of sexual torture as a norm? It is as if we work—full-time—to make our species as brutal and stupid as possible.

Another heartless, vagina-less academic is Kelly Foreman in her article "Bad Girls Confined." For some reason, she expends her energy on trying to prove geisha are not primarily "sexual playthings" (36) as Western men perceive them to be—yet why would she consider the sexual aspect so shameful? This is yet another implied condemnation of the prostitute, from the conservative moral majority family values crap perspective.

"There was some justification for this assumption," she writes, "because earthquakes, war, and bad economic conditions forced many women into prostitution." If this is the case, then why would it be shameful in any way? These women should be praised for refusing to die of starvation. It takes a lot of courage to fuck for food.

Foreman writes: "Following WWII, the United States heard much about 'geishas' and 'geisha-girls.' The American Occupation (1945-1952) and the anti-prostitution law of 1956 triggered a shift in meaning for 'geisha' once and for all away from performing arts, to mean a woman devoted to sexual services. Unlike prostitutes, geisha were allowed to continue working after the 1956 law was enacted because selling sex was not an official part of their cache, and prostitutes often refereed to themselves as 'geisha' to avoid arrest. These 'geisha' were numerous because there was good money to be gleaned from foreign servicemen stationed in Japan" (37). My god. Or maybe I should say OMG. Or 'my goddess.' Does Foreman actually think there was a voluntary aspect to this fuck for food? Unbelievable. She says nothing about the brutal pimped, debt-bondage most of the girls would have been held in; the violence and humiliation inflicted on them, let alone the 200,000 abandoned, scorned Amerasian children who would themselves be vulnerable to sale when they were old enough to be turned into whores. And does she think all of sudden, with the passage of this imaginary act, that no more girls continued 'working.' Their pimps would damn well make sure the girls they controlled continued to fuck these 'lucrative' GI's. The girls rarely made 'good money' off the soldiers. Pimp-controlled, like most prostitutes around the world, the girls got rape-fucked and others took the money. Basically, disease, misery, long-term mental and physical problems—this is the lot of the prostitute if she survives. Not 'good money.' Not good anything. From the day that the fist American soldier stepped on Japanese soil in August, 1945, Japanese pimps were there, seasoning and breaking vulnerable starving girls for rape-prostitution.

These girls are pitiful, raped beings. Why does Foreman completely overlook this? All this suffering seems to have escaped her in her efforts to prove the sexual 'purity' of the geisha. She should see the misery in these women's eyes – the two times I saw prostituted girls during my time on bases in Japan, there was a terrible sadness in their eyes. Those rape-dazed, hit-by-a-truck eyes that Vic, my boyfriend, described when he used the young prostitutes in Korea in the 1950's—and ones in Japan during that era as well.

(By the time I met him, 20 years later, Vic was in his 40's, and mature enough to see the girls in a different light. Back then, in his youth, he says, he just saw the girls as fuck conveniences for him and the other men. He still says he would have used the girls, numb and rape-dead as they were, because he needed fuck and that was that. He felt sorry for the girls—both back when he was using them—and when he told me about them many years later—but he says that he needed sex, and that was that. Rape-dazed eyes or not underneath them, the guys fucked the girls because they needed sex. Such is life, I guess—much as I would have it be otherwise. There's nothing I can do about it. Write this book. Won't make a difference, won't make anyone give a damn. Write it anyway—since what else can I do? The world will always be full of girls with fuck-dazed eyes: prostituted ones; trafficked ones; and all those millions upon millions of child brides, forced to have sex years before their bodies are ready. At least I can decide to not contribute to the cruelty—at least I can say something.)

More sad passages from Foreman's article with unintentional hidden realities of misery: "In Kyoto, the word geisha smacks of the wrong type of article. It is not forgotten that [foreign] soldiers of the Allied Occupation Forces after the war used to refer to the kimonoed camp-followers and masseuse and club waitresses as 'geisha girls.'"

"Within a matter of months after American occupation forces arrive in Japan in the summer of 1945, thousands of the troops and officers were supporting full-fledged mistresses. By 1949 it was estimated that over 80 percent of the Occupation force has at least a part-time mistress…"

What exactly is a 'mistress' in this context, I wonder? Given that there were 350,000 soldier there, and over 80% of them were raping prostituted bodies, that certainly makes for an overwhelming amount of starvation prostitution, or 'survival sex,' as they call it nowadays. Is this is what is meant by a 'mistress' in this context? Hungry girls with no choice? I always think of a mistress as some pampered girl with choice, like in *Gigi*. I am not sure the word choice is accurate here, given the starvation-reality of these girls. Poverty was acute in Occupation Japan. Girls were literally starving. How could they be 'mistresses' under these circumstances? One man stationed there after the war told me that, due to hunger and poverty, families sold their daughters to the Allied soldiers. Families were actually homeless and living in train stations. I don't know if girls sold under such conditions of privation could be called 'mistresses.' And the numbers Foreman quotes are staggering. "Over 80 percent of the Occupation forces" with these 'mistresses.' Didn't the chaplains or the women back home or the commanding officers notice such a large amount of glaring prostitution of vulnerable girls? If they did, why were the girls not helped—with food and support—instead of being forced to sell sex? Foreman's presentation of this issue does not address all of these underlying exploitations and oppressions. She should not give the impression that starvation-prostitution is voluntary in any way. It misleads—and promotes the 'normalization' of prostitution during occupation—whether in Japan or elsewhere.

Moving to a later time period, Foreman tells us that "Some [Olympic] athletes insisted they be provided with geisha for bed partners. I understand that street girls dressed in kimono were finally made available to them."

She also tells us that "Ignorant American servicemen were not interested in making social distinctions…[for them geisha meant] "passive whore"… [this was] "essential to the American understanding of Japanese women as a group (despite how inaccurate it was)."

Why this disclaimer, I wonder, in the face of the huge number of girls raped and turned into 'passive whores'?—why do they have no importance for her—what kind of rigid sexuality have they transgressed in her book that she must disregard them as 'representative' of Japanese women. The whore is representative of all of us—a concept apparently unfamiliar to the protected, ivory-tower mind. Turn one girl into a whore and you rape-fuck all of us. We are the whore. When the men serially rape her body every day, they also rape all the 'decent' women in the world.

Where is the rape reality behind Foreman's analysis? Lost, sometimes, in the mists of jargon: "The existence of non-Western institutions of bought-and-sold, pitiful women such as the supposed 'geisha girls,' have the potential to assist comparative analysis of 'modern' and 'enlightened' women, and these images cannot avoid clouding any Western understanding of actual geisha." What?? What? What?

Historian Arlene Eisen is one of the few to give us any insights into the misery of the brothelized in Vietnam. The "degradation of the brothels" she calls it. The GI's turned Saigon into one huge brothel with half a million prostituted beings. Eisen points out that the inmates were refugees: "The women had no means of support." Some half a million became prostitutes." VD was rampant. Three million cases inflicted on the prostitutes by the GI's in 1975.

Sad facts emerge. Like the way girls who wore 'tags' in bars were clean, those without were considered diseased filth. 'Car Wash and Get Screwed' read signs in Saigon. "As GI's left Vietnam, the prostitutes remained trapped in cycles of heroin addiction, poverty, and self-hatred....their most dangerous diseases were spiritual. Their social personalities were destroyed."

"Centres of Leisure" were the brothels called and the Saigon regime took 80% of the profits, and the remaining 20% went into maintaining the girls in imaginary debt bondage, Eisen tells us.

Soldiers I knew took full advantage of the starvation and misery of the women. "Fun Bang in Da Nang." "I love you long time." "I let you rape me long time." Put it on your T-shirts and baseball caps. The Marines were reportedly rough and brutal when they hit town for 'leisure.' Those poor, soft, small women. The 'normalization' of rape. Not a peep did I hear from the women back home, in America, about this terrible, everyday, commonplace exploitation of Vietnamese women. All around me, ignorant, safe American girls with no hearts—and, apparently, no vaginas. Mislaying the vagina. Seems to be what privileged American women do.

So troubled was I about American female indifference to this commonplace rape that I wrote a little piece, way back then, called 'The Mislaid Vagina.' Made no more impact than this book, but I had to do something. Inaction is intolerable and unconscionable.

Susan Brownmiller's *Against Our Will* has, of course, become a classic, since its publication in 1975. She went where few had gone before in this study of rape. She broke ground and moved into territories that many women after her, myself included, are still exploring. Her section on rape/prostitution in Vietnam still remains very useful, largely because so little has been written even now about this aspect of the war. Given how indifferent journalists who covered the war back then were, and how indifferent they are now to war-time prostitution, it is not surprising that this side of the conflict still remains largely ignored.

Brownmiller tells us that CBS correspondent Dan Rather said it never crossed his mind to do a rape story—it simply wasn't important enough. Rather comments: "Everybody who passed through a village did it—steal a chicken and grab a piece of ass…Vietnam was a loosely organized gang war and the women caught it from all sides." He adds: "When you see women crying and you see that universal look of bitterness and anger, you find out about rape" (91). Now, this is interesting. Despite the way he was at least minimally aware of the suffering of the women, he was still not touched or moved enough to devote even one story to this in ten years of coverage? No outrage on his part? No sense of the women's personal misery? No link to any woman in his life he might have held dear? No connection that if she had been the raped one, it might have upset him—greatly. I guess not.

Women journalists in Vietnam were every bit as callous and indifferent. And continue to be so in the Iraq conflict. They report on everything in Iraq but the girls selling sex to eat and the ones being gang raped in prisons, and by the Iraqi police. Absolutely no connection with their own vaginas and their own lives. Absolutely no realization that if you put them homeless and starving in a war zone, they too will have their vaginas ripped to pieces and their souls destroyed. The vaginaless, heartless, blind women journalists of America. They also covered WWI and WWII and Korea—and completely left out one of the most important aspects—how women suffer abysmally from the wars men make. Only the soldier who 'suffers' is important to them---not the women he destroys.

Back to Vietnam, Associated Press correspondent Peter Arnett spent eight years covering the war there and heard the screams of village girls being gang raped in the forest and did nothing. He never even reported it (Brownmiller 89). Not one rape story filed in all the years of the war?

These are the journalists we celebrate and give literary awards to? Where is my award, I wonder, for the service I am performing in writing this book—despite tremendous personal pain?

Speaking of the girls in the brothels that the men serially and brutally climbed on, Arnett describes the sexual service as "quick, straight, and routine" (Brownmiller 95). It is hard to imagine the humiliation and the physical pain and the destruction of the soul that lies beneath this "quick, straight, and routine" sex.

Are Vietnamese girls so different that they have no need for tenderness or consideration during sex? What is this "quick, straight, routine" sex that men have invented? Surely, it satisfies only the men. Prostitution can never be anything but rape if the woman's sexual needs are irrelevant. "Routine" seems accurate. War-time rape and occupation rape of the helpless prostituted body are truly "routine," the accepted norm, simply standard practice. Don't the men call it SOP—Standard Operating Procedure? And SIMR—Standard Issue Military Rape?

"Quick, straight, and routine." The brutal cruelty in that phrase is beyond fathoming for me. The 5000 years of male war-time rape privilege in it is beyond fathoming. The degradation of the girl being used in this "routine" rape is something I can't stand to think about without extreme pain.

Did Arnett use the raped whore girls as well, or did he go without sex for his eight years in Vietnam?

Brownmiller's book is, overall, a useful chronicle of rape, but even she often leaves out the point of view of the raped. Here is what she writes about the whores of Vietnam: "I am sorry that it is not within the scope of this book to explore the lives of the Vietnamese women who became 'Occupation: prostitute' as a direct result of the foreign military presence in their country. It is a story that should be told in detail, from the tremendous source of revenue that prostitution provided their beleaguered country, to accounts of Saigon brothels filled with ten-year-old girls, to the incidence of work-related details from tuberculosis and venereal disease, with a special nod of recognition to those who survived" (96).

Now, I ask why is it beyond the scope of her book to tell their stories? Are they not the 'raped'? Her section on Vietnam is told solely from the point of view of the soldier and the journalist. She does not interview one single whore. Why was the rape of the whore not as important to her as the rape of the 'decent' girls she chronicles elsewhere in her book? The rape of the whore is meta-rape. It is rape beyond rape.

I cannot, in fact, find one single interview with a whore in any of the thousands of books on Vietnam. I cannot find commentary--and acknowledgement--that what happened to her body was rape. The closest we come is a beyond-pathetic whore girl on Okinawa who was raped 20-30 times a night for seven years by GI's on R & R from Vietnam. (This is in *Let the Good Times Roll.*) How she survived to even tell her story is beyond me. How she is even capable of speech any more after such an experience is beyond me. Over 30,000 times she was raped. Thirty thousand different men ramming her bleeding hole. How did she make it? And I wonder what the 'good' girl who is raped only once and is all 'traumatized' would think of this kind or rape?

I don't know how we measure the distance between one rape on one body, once, and the relentless torture of a woman being climbed on by thirty thousand different men. Thirty thousand GI rapist monsters.

"The distance in the mind"—inexpressible. The distance in the soul—like galaxies from different universes.

Rape is the norm on Rape Planet Earth. Not an exception to the behavior of men.

Brownmiller wants to give a "nod" of recognition to those Vietnamese prostitutes who survived. What good on earth or in the heavens or on all the planets in the galaxy will a "nod" do these sex-tortured beings???? Damn! There is no giving this girl back her life with a "nod." There is no way the GI rapist monsters can give her back her body and her sexuality—and her beauty and her spirit. She was a girl that some man should have been tender with. Instead, she was raped by 30,000 men.

Where are they, the girls who lay down and were thoroughly raped day after day after day in the brothels by rough GI monsters? Why has not one woman come forth? They would be about my age now. Where are they?!

We know where their rapists are. These GI's came back home and went to college and did things like become teachers. We currently have vets--ex-GIs who were rapist monsters in Vietnam, and on Okinawa and in Thailand, where they went to drink and sex binge and climb on helpless little whores—we currently have these GI rapist monsters doing things like teaching at American universities. Teaching young college girls that they have no right to even be in the same room with. And these rapist monsters have had daughters. How dare they cradle their daughters after raping those tiny whores 20-30 times a day?

Other GI rapist monsters have become politicians. And businessmen. And they have asked us to feel sorry for them for what they 'suffered'? I say, you did not have to go to war, you did not have to pick up the guns.

Men love to make war, and then pretend they "suffered." They have been making war for at least the 5000 years of recorded history—and probably before that. Why are they asking us to feel sorry for **them**, and what **they** suffered, when they have savaged the bodies of women for 5000 years?!

I don't think they would have been making war for 5000 years if they didn't love it.

We women don't love it. We get raped. You men love violence. We women do not love the violent sex that is rape.

How dare the soldiers set themselves up to martyrs of some exalted PTSD? You monsters raped. You destroyed a country. Now some of you go back to Vietnam and have all these sentimental tourist trips to Da Nang. Fun bang in Da Nang. "I let you rape me loooong time," wails out the whore. Are you still buying their bodies? You go back to Vietnam and pretend all this contrition. Why did you go there and destroy their country, and all those women, in the first place?

Don't put me in the same room with a Vietnam vet. I would be too terrified to move, or run.

I would like to ask one of the whores they mass raped if she feels sick when she hears the sound of a belt buckle being undone. It's a heavy sound. The metal clangs. I always remember rape of my body following that sound of the man taking off his belt.

A book that caused me extreme pain to read is by a woman at an Australian university, Elaine McKenon. Her work is called *The Scarlet Mile: A Sociological History of Prostitution in Kalgoorlie, 1894-2004* and is partly about goldfield prostitution. It just might take the grand prize for insensitive cruelty. This is a woman who seems to consider the rape-torture of the female body that we call prostitution all fun and games and humor. A norm without pain or trauma for the prostituted girl.

I would not want to meet McKenon. She would frighten me as much as the Vietnam vets.

She tells a 'funny' story about a girl gone mad and naked and screaming during a "particularly hectic week because of a firemen's convention in town."

When there are lines of men outside brothels, her comment is "these peak times…were no doubt welcome because of the increase in income they brought." Australian prostitutes subjected to Korean Comfort Women circumstances—to the tremendous pain of servicing lines of men and the only understanding McKenon brings to this is an economic one? Unbelievable.

A similar coldness is in her description of the brothels during WWII: eyewitnesses say "long queues" formed in front of them. Her comment: "This seems to have been related to the deployment of hundreds of American servicemen stationed on the goldfields."

We have seen ample evidence of what these long lines of men shoving into one fragile female mean in the case of the Korean Comfort Girls—the bleeding, swelling, life-in-death insanity of rape torture. Yet McKenon seems to see nothing of this. She is puzzlingly neutral.

It is an ugly world, this brothel goldfield life, with rough drunk men and dead animals thrown at the prostitutes for fun and women shattered by assembly-line sex, yet McKenon is oblivious to the pain.

Her treatment of the karayuki-san, the Japanese prostitutes imported by pimps to service the goldfield men in the late 1800's and early 1900's, is also disturbing. She quotes a poem from the time period:

"There's a little tawdry damsel, who grins behind her fan,
She's a dealer in commodities exclusively Japan...
She does a thriving business..."

She does note that the Japanese women were brought in "often against their will" and that they "suffered the ravages of disease and exhaustion." Now, if she can recognize that there was mistreatment of these girls, then how can she not see that the rape queues of GI's during WWII waiting to painfully ram the Australian prostitutes would bring about the same ravaging from disease and exhaustion? It is the same female body being raped. There is no difference between the enslaved karayuki-san and her enslaved Australian sisters.

The saddest passage maybe in the book is the testimony of an Australian nurse who treats one of the karayuki-san suffering from diseases and exhaustion. The girl, whose name is Oyoni, says to the nurse, "I not want to get better, nurse, I want go to sleep and no more wake up."

Despite this, the hospital sends her back to her pimp and the terrible rape existence of her life. Later the nurse finds her dying in a Perth Hospital. To the other nurses in the hospital, says our nurse, she was "'just one of those Japs from the houses' who had to be screened away from the other decent patients."

It does not seem to matter where I look or what I read. I find that rape reality is all the same. The goldfield men mercilessly torturing, with their penises, this little Japanese girl into rape exhaustion and eventual death. The 'decent' women refusing to recognize the misery and torment of continuous rape and needing to be 'screened' from her contaminating filth. It does not seem to matter if the rapists and the 'decent' women are American or Australians or whoever—they are all the same mercilessly brutal and blind people.

How could those men have continued to rape and rape and rape little Oyoni when they saw what pain she was in? Australian rapist monsters. The norm in the Rape Killing Fields.

There was one cheerful note in this book. A customer, a goldfield man, who does seem to recognize something of what is wrong with the prostitute life. He says that the girls "do the hard work; they can't pick and choose who they go with…I hear they don't have much choice. They're forced. They need some sort of regulation, something to help control who they see. Because you don't need some drunken asshole come in and say, 'Here's a hundred bucks. Let's go.'"

I like this guy! What a sweetie. And his summary of the prostitute's dilemma and misery is masterfully done: 'some drunken asshole comes in' and says here's my money, now let's fuck. Ugly, to understate it. In brothels from Bangkok to Berlin to Nevada, that drunken revolting asshole comes in, pays, and says 'let's fuck.'

I wonder if he ever realizes how disgusting he is to the girl he rapes?

Those karayuki-san are, by the way, the predecessors of the Korean Comfort Girl system of sexual slavery. Japanese girls were shipped all over the world—sold by parents and relatives to procurers who took them to brothels in Australia and America, and all over Asia. Apparently, they were always taken "against their will," and their lives were full of dreadful suffering. The Japanese consul in Singapore has this to say of them: "their miserable lives are too wretched to look at."

Karayuki-san were shipped to the U.S. in the late 1800's and early 1900's. Like their Chinese counterparts, some ended up in San Francisco brothels or in mining camps, raped numerous times in tent brothels. One girl who escaped from her U.S. torture in the early 1900's returned home to Japan and became a fiery activist. She says the anger and outrage and pain raged so deeply in her that she wanted to burn to death every man who had raped her.

I think the desire to murder their rapists is common among prostitutes. From reading this karayuki-san's remark, I now see why my anger burns so brightly in me. I also think that that McKenon must live in some kind of deep blindness to not see that the long rape lines—and they are precisely that, rape lines—that these lines of men being let in, one by one, to use the Australian girls are identical to the men who raped the karayuki-san. The same diseases and exhaustion are being visited on the Australian prostitutes. Yet McKenon can only see the economic aspect of this—that the girls 'welcome' their rapists since it means more money. Does McKenon have absolutely no idea what man after man after man shoved into you means--until you die of pain. First every thing else dies since the disgust of any man being allowed to shove himself into you is overwhelming. It kills everything tender inside you even before your body dies. When you are rape-dead from rape-exhaustion, you can't even see or walk, let alone care that your rape brings your owners more money.

An entire book—McKenon's—on prostitution without any realization that this was enormous sexual violence being visited on these women.

Prostitution is rape. Prostitution is sexual violence visited on women.

Those academic women with no clue as to this should not be writing about it. My upset while reading McKenon was so extreme that I had to simply stop reading completely--and stop writing this book--for a few days. It haunted me so much and so deeply, the terrible pain hidden under the surface words, that I felt too sick and sad to work again right away. As it is, I cannot go back and re-read any of this book. Too painful.

Tomoko Yamazaki's *Sandakan Brothel No. 8: An Episode in the History of Lower-class Japanese Women* recounts the lives of a number of karayuki-san, poor girls sold into overseas prostitution from the 1860's to 1930's. It focuses on a girl, Osaki, sold to North Borneo by her brother around 1915. She's only ten and her first sex act is forced upon her when she is twelve—she is terrified and disgusted by the gigantic native man forced upon her: "It was so horrible I could hardly believe it." This was a typical age, by the way, for a karayuki-san to be sold and set to 'work.'

That horror became her everyday reality. At the worst, it was thirty men a night and the girls had to work even when sick from exhaustion. "When a ship anchored out in the harbor, every brothel in town was filled. While we were busy taking care of one customer, others would be lined up waiting outside the door."

The norm of rape again—amazing how the navies of the world have gotten away with it over the centuries—with no protest, no one seeing anything wrong with this forcing of drunk men into the bodies of helpless girls. And it still goes on and on and on and the fuck rape ports do a roaring business: from Pattaya to Dubai to Mombasa, it's still the same picture.

Osaki is only about 4' 6 " in a photo of her in the book, so it must have been excruciating to take thirty grown men. I am always puzzled as to how the girls do not bleed to death. Prostitutes do suffer from holes torn in their vaginas and they bleed profusely from these wounds. Just one tear of the vagina is miserable, but it can heal if the girl, the 'normal' privileged girl not forced by thirty men a night, is left alone by her kind boyfriend. But how does a girl whose vaginal tissue is punctured over and over again not bleed to death during just one night of this treatment?

Maybe the greater mystery for me is one I have expressed before: how could these sailors climb on and rape these tiny, fragile, fine-boned girls over and over and over again when they saw the unbearable misery and pain in their eyes. Man without mercy toward the helpless is the biggest mystery of all.

The karayuki-san was held in debt bondage—a common form of financial slavery in prostitution. What money Osaki earned went to her owners and to her brother back in Japan. When she did return home, her brother and family rejected her as impure.

Very few karayuki-san made it home. Most died of diseases and mistreatment and exhaustion and insanity before they even got out of their teens. McKenon, in her book, says that when a Japanese girl is brought into the Australian brothels in her teens, she can work for the next thirty years—another indication that McKenon seems to know nothing of the torture and death-in-life of the constantly raped whore body.

Who would choose this life? Why should any girl be treated like this? These are the questions I would ask—instead of taking for granted this honored tradition of sexual brutality, as McKenon seems to.

Jeremy Seabrook's *Travels in the Skin Trade: Tourism and the Sex Industry* is a useful window into the Thai sex world. He says that the average Thai bar girl goes with about fifteen different men a month. He writes of the pain: "One young woman spoke of the agony of being expected to have frequent intercourse, even with a condom: the sores and wounds which the friction caused subjected her to continuous pain" (135). At least there is this one mention of the physical misery. I was sore all the time. I had abrasions all the time. It bothers me dreadfully when so many writers, especially women, fail to mention the physical torture of the bed for the whore. It as if the most salient fact is simply left out of consideration.

My question would be how can the men go inside her if they see she is in such pain? I can to some extent answer my own question—I have noticed that in bed many men are not very observant. Only their own thrusting matters and their own grunts and groans and growls or whatever noises they make when they are on top of a body. Pretty much the woman does not exist except as a space to thrust into. Thus, they can get hard and can have intercourse even when the woman is in deep agony. They are made very differently from us.

Of course those bar girls who only go with about fifteen men a month are the privileged few. Unfortunately, Seabrook does not go into the cheaper brothels where the girls who must handle high volume are (these girls would easily be raped by fifteen different men a night, rather than just fifteen a month). The ones for whom 'condom burn abrasions' would not be a problem, since they are not allowed to suggest that the 'customers' (read 'rapist shits' for this word) use them. But every other sort of rape abrasion--pain, bleeding, swelling--will be there.

I think that even fifteen a month is a huge number. I probably did not average that many men a month I did not know during most of the time I worked in prostitution—partly because of regular men I saw, and partly because I was not subjected to the ridiculous harsh and insane world of 'bar fines' and debt bondage and being 'bought out of a place' and whatever other rules of cruel and ugly slave logic govern the harsh and restricted lives of these girls so others can make money off of them.

Seabrook has some insight into what the girls go through: "To confront farangs, sometimes drunk, often old, not infrequently dirty, with a serene smile…is a constant violence against them" (94). He recognizes that "it is difficult for the young women…in the sex industry. It is not that the constant mauling and penetration by strangers does not reach them: to be subjected to continuous assault in this way must have its effect" (115).

But, unfortunately, he does not want to see them all as damaged, as victims. He borrows a lot of ideas from Empower, a group that helps the girls with self-esteem and confidence—for me, impossibilities for a girl who is raped by strangers fifteen times a month. He quotes Siriporn, a woman who helps the bar girls and who spouts all kinds of 'empowerment' rhetoric, and all of this trendy 'agency' stuff and has this idea that the girls are in control of their lives. For me, as you know, no one who is raped fifteen times a month is in control of her life.

One objection I have to all this empowerment rhetoric is that it is ridiculously impractical and far-fetched for the girls in the cheaper brothels who are sometimes chained to the beds to keep them there and who work under "conditions of abusive wretchedness" (Seabrook 150). "Duty" to parents who sold them will resign them to the torture and keep them from suicide long enough to earn money for their families.

(Those chains, by the way, can be fatal, as when a number of girls died in a brothel fire in Phuket in 1984 because they were chained to the beds. I have some solutions for this. Dismantle this ridiculous pernicious institution called 'family.' If all it can do is destroy its daughters, and get them chained to beds, then 'family' needs to be done away with.)

Seabrook says that when he suggested ideas of 'empowerment' and possible confidence of 'sex workers' at a "meeting at the University of Leicester in June 1996, one woman, a former sex worker…disagreed strongly. She insisted all women are wounded, damaged by such experiences." She is right. I am the most disempowered person you are every likely to meet

I would agree with her one hundred per cent. But then I make no pretense at 'objectivity.' For me, the ongoing rape of the body is not 'empowering.' There is no possibility of confidence or healing for the girl who has only been raped by fifteen rough crude dirty men a month, let alone that many in one night.

I call rape rape. I don't disguise it as a 'client/prostitute' transaction, and I do not attribute this academic imaginary 'agency' to the raped body. There will be no confidence or power or healing for these girls. Only a lifetime of rape nightmares.

In a world full of rape, I do not lie about what is happening through words that do not reflect the brutal physical reality of prostitution. To let fifteen crude dirty men inside you a month is rape.

At the same time, I can see the value of Empower. If there is no other way of life, then help those who are in it as much as possible. There is a huge difference between rape by fifteen men a month and fifteen a night. Mild wretchedness is preferable to the insanity brought on by assembly-line sex.

I would, however, object to counseling for the girls in the cheap brothels where they are terribly overworked—for example, the trafficked Burmese girls who are subject to abrasions and sores and pain from too much intercourse and beatings if they ever dare refuse a client, or ask him to use a condom. Or if they try to do something simple, like listen to the BBC on the radio. (Burmese girls who escaped their Thai brothels report all these terrible abuses. See *A Modern Form of Slavery* from Human Right Watch.) Some NGO's think that if they can get at these girls in the brothels, counseling will help them. What? The only way the girls can survive is complete numbing. To counsel them would be to take away that protection. If you make them face the pain, they will die.

Quite frankly, I don't see how you can counsel a girl for a half hour, and make her 'open up,' and then send her off to eight straight hours of rape. It is like a report I read that the Korean government is sending police to "'advise' trafficked girls in brothels of their 'rights.'" What could those rights possibly be for a girl held by terror and physical torture in a venue where her owners will make sure she has no rights? If the girl is being held in debt bondage, without a passport, and locked up in a room when not working so she will not try to escape, what can she possibly do with this 'advice' that tells her she has rights? What could those 'rights' possibly be if she cannot escape her owners?

In both cases, it is puzzling to me that the NGO's and police don't take the girls out of their rape hells. In the case of trying to counsel girls held prisoner in brothels, it would be the height of cruelty to make a girl self-aware. Whores can only survive by telling necessary lies to themselves. Never take a whore out of her numbness. She will die of the pain. You cannot be a whore and have any sensitivity. Any awareness there is a difference between men. You have to be completely blind to the slime who mount you. Otherwise, you die of pain and disgust.

All my ideas on prostitution are sensible. I can even envision a form of it that is safe and beneficial for the woman, even if it is only in a fantasy realm. The forces of patriarchal (and matriarchal) oppression are so powerful that to bring that form about would be impossible. No man wants to do without his fuck time on the powerless and no 'respectable' woman will of course grant the whore any rights or humanity. Both patriarchy and matriarchy are against her and make my lovely shining visions of a free sensual spiritual tender prostitution world a complete impossibility.

I have read a ton about prostitution/trafficking over the past couple of years and the picture that emerges is a worldwide one of exploitation where the girl actually gets little and her buyers and sellers benefit and she is at risk of AIDS and other life-long physical problems (not to mention mental ones from this dreadful profession) and she's often the victim of violence, degradation, etc. The picture is pretty awful for the majority of girls. Kristen, the Spitzer prostitute, the 'call-girl' kind who might actually be making money under fairly safe circumstances, is just a small part of a much bigger picture of girls who are coerced, forced, mistreated, etc.

If I were to envision a safe, wonderful form of prostitution that actually benefited the woman, it would involve some of the following:

1) The girl goes into it voluntarily as a fun and pleasant and exciting way to make money.

She is not really a 'girl' since I would prohibit prostitution for anyone under twenty-five or so in my perfect sexual world. By then, a 'woman' has a bit of an inkling as to her sexual being. It really takes much longer—well into her 40's and 50's, for a woman to discover her full and beautiful sexuality, but by age twenty-five, she is at least leaving the baby stage.

And I could only let her go into prostitution if she had already experienced wonderful sex with a number of wonderful men. Never in my perfect prostitution world would a poor drugged-to-bear-the-pain twelve-year-old have her body and soul and life ruined by 'client rape.' Unthinkable.

2) She has complete choice as to customers and is never in danger of being pimped or exploited by a third party. She takes all the money.

3) She is never paid less than $1000 for the sex act. Her beautiful sacred vagina space is worth that—and much more. The $1000 pussy minimum, I call it.

4) She is not regarded as a criminal who has to scurry from the law but is respected for what she does—sell sex (this envisions prostitution as a 'real profession,' not 'sex work,' which simply means a woman sells her vagina, no matter what the terrible circumstances she must 'work' under. I hate the term 'sex work,' by the way).

5) She has protection under the law if a customer mistreats her.

6) She is respected enormously for this generous act of sharing her body.

7) She is to be treated with gentleness, kindness, and tenderness at all times.

Contrast the Comfort Girls of all eras with my tender, gentle portrait. One girl wrote of her time enslaved to the Japanese military: "When it is busy, I just lie down on my back, eating rice balls with my legs apart, and the soldiers come and mount me and leave, mount me and leave. Finally, I am beyond pain. From the waist down I get numb and lose feeling. It's a struggle just getting up each day. When the feeling [in my lower body] returns… my legs cramp up and my abdomen gets cramped as well. There's a heavy dull pain that lasts all day….When people talk about a living hell, this is it" (Yoshimi 148). In Singapore, the comfort girls had their legs and hand tied to the brothel beds. The soldiers report hearing the Indonesian comfort girls crying all night as they took their rape quota. The women were regarded as "communal latrines" (Yoshimi 135).

Japanese historian Yoshimi says the girls were "terrified of the men who lined up" and the girls would "curl up" in "fear of the men who were drunk and violent."

To say a concluding word about Seabrook's book, it is a really useful look into the minds of many of the 'farangs' who buy girls in Thailand; and Seabrook himself is a sensitive and caring man who writes very perceptively about this world.

Gary P. Leupp's *Interracial Intimacy in Japan: Western Men and Japanese Women, 1543-1900* is useful for its informativeness but I strongly object to his word 'intimacy.' There is no intimacy in the relationship between a whore and her 'client.' Intimacy is a tender work, with no resemblance to the burning rape pain of the sex inflicted on the whore.

He tells us that the Japanese prostitutes were "frightened and disgusted by both the hirsuteness and intimidating stature of…the foreigners" (141). Dutch men 6'3" must have ripped those little vaginas to pieces but no where in the book does he mention this discrepancy in genital size. This omission really amazes me. Do men think that we're not afraid when they are too big for us? We are terrified.

He describes the girls like dogs in kennels. Their function is to deal with drunk foreign sailors. They were used by hundreds of them. Only once in the book do we hear the voice of a prostituted being. She calls herself "wretched." Otherwise, it is exclusively the male point of view, as usual.

Leupp's conclusion: "To the family, brothel owner, and authorities—perhaps even to the woman herself—the foreigners capacity to pay compensated for this distasteful otherness." No, not to the girl. Money cannot 'pay for' her pain in any sense. Money cannot pay for the 'distastefulness' (what a mild word)—for the massive disgust and torture of sex with hundreds of drunk sailors.

But, then, the male point of view rules the world, in this book as elsewhere. 'Distasteful' indeed!

Speaking of word choice, even thought I like the insights into the Pakistani sex world that British academic Louise Brown gives me in her *Dancing Girls of Lahore*, I really object to the way she phrases herself when she speaks of the very young girls who are drugged to withstand the pain of constant rape: "those girls," writes Brown, "who are not yet out of childhood who enter the business and entertain too many clients too often….They become infertile through injury, infection, and botched abortions."

I don't think politely calling the men clients will do it. It masks the brutality of what they do. And to use a work like 'entertain,' as if this drugged child knew what she was doing voluntarily….

Brown also calls Lahore a "Pleasure District." As much a misnomer of a rape zone as the "comfort" hell holes were for the "comfort" girls. Whose pleasure? Their pleasure is our rape pain.

We have to be careful with our language. For far too long words have been used to lie about the rape of our bodies.

Brown gives the impression that many of the girls in Lahore are sold as early as age twelve and are considered washed up by the time they reach their twenties. Therefore, I would imagine that a lot of those bodies are ruined early. And it seems inconceivable to my mind that such young girls are considered sexually desirable. A girl is not even a woman when she hits her mid-twenties—the earliest age, in my opinion, when any girl should have sex. What kind of world have we created when a twelve-year-old child is the height of sexual desirability and girls in their twenties are regarded as 'old'? An incredibly sick one, at least in Pakistan and in other parts of the world where girls who are not even out of childhood are sold and also forced into marriages with older men.

Women like Yasmin Alibhai-Brown, who writes for *The Independent*, make a lot more sense to me than do all the 'patriarchal' and 'matriarchal' voices that leave out the reality of prostitution pain. She calls the johns "purchasers of loveless sex" and says that "all across the world, this profession demeans and endangers young girls. Trafficked women—big business now—have no protection. Few females are physically stronger than males; few of the men who use prostitutes feel genuine affection or respect for the women they paw and enter." Bravo! Clear, to-the-point, and completely on-target as to what is wrong with the 'prostitution world.'

I am always impatient of the endless useless feminist debate about "choice." We need action instead of covering the same ground over and over again. One of my favorite moments on the internet was reading a comment by an ex-military man. He said he had been all over the world and come to the conclusion that instead of going to war in Iraq our army would do better to knock down the doors of all the pimps in the world. Action!

(The internet, by the way, can be a real source of military male knowledge about the prostitutes they have seen. One sailor who said he had visited girls from Liverpool to Bangkok called their lives "terrible." Another said if you want to see sexual slavery go to the brothels near U.S. bases in Korea. He says condoms sit at the gates. [Sad--that the soldiers head out for their sex 'fun' with the debased, beaten, and enslaved.] The internet is helpful for civilian information as well—as, for example, the American man who has lived in Japan three years and says you cannot find a Japanese male who has not visited a prostitute. This must mean hell for the 200,000 or so sex slaves from Thailand, the Philippines, Columbia, Taiwan and elsewhere who must service those millions of men.)

Endless debate that does more harm than good characterizes the academic approach, and the splits in what's called this 'movement.' The splits seem irreconcilable. Leah Platt, for example, in "Regulating the Global Brothel" views 'prostitution sex' as a "repetitive task that can be as unerotic and downright boring as cutting pork shoulders on an assembly line...."

Donna Hughes of the University of Rhode Island begs to differ and says when a man buys sex, it is not like going through a car wash. I would add that violence and rape are not 'boring' for the girl being subjected to them. I wonder if Platt would like to be 'regulated' in the 'global brothel'? What a title of coldness and hardness.

Jo Bindman of Anti-Slavery International wants to see the abuses as the same as other workers experience. She thinks you can fix the brothel workplace the same as you can fix a factory. My view, of course, is that you cannot make rape palatable or ethical or good for the girl being raped. You can of course change factory conditions so they are more humane: shorter hours, longer breaks, higher pay, treating the workers with respect. This intention simply does not transfer over to prostitution since sex is such an integral part of identity and integrity. You cannot really carve out a space called 'brothel' that does not involve sex with men the girl does not know. That's for openers. Such sex necessarily involves coldness, impersonality, humiliation of the 'used' female by the privileged male. It is of course infinitely preferable to only be raped by five men a day as opposed to fifty. In the latter case, no recovery is possible for the woman. In some essential way, she is permanently destroyed. But rape by five men a day in the space called brothel--whether you term it 'legal,' or not—is still rape. All women everywhere will suffer from this degradation if it is inflicted on even one woman.

The problem with non-prostituted women writing on the subject is that they seem to have no conception of the degradation involved in sex with men you do not know. Can they imagine themselves having intercourse with a man after knowing him for only a couple of minutes? Doing this incredibly intimate and sacred act, being invaded in this most private of places by many men—and some of those men will treat you roughly and with no respect or tenderness at all. I don't really see how one can legitimize and normalize paid rape. Do the Platt's and Bindman's have any idea of the lifelong damage to the lives and sexuality of these women that prostitution inflicts?

Prostitution is the sexual humiliation of the female body and psyche imposed on us women by a male world that sees our female bodies as disposable dump sites for the penis to unload in. What a concept of sex. It is not even 'sex' in any way I can recognize the word. The Platt's and Bindman's of the world promote this male-centered rape agenda.

Platt wants to legalize it-- "sex work is here to stay and by recognizing it as paid labor governments can guarantee fair treatment as well as safe and healthy working conditions." How, I ask? I don't see how sexual enslavement can ever be made healthy and safe? You will only legitimize not just the degradation of the prostitutes, but of all women. People like Platt and Bindman will be setting themselves up to be next in the "global rape assembly-line." Make sexual slavery a 'legitimate fuck-factory job' (my phrasing) and you will make the world infinitely more dangerous for all of us women. And that move would still not eliminate the procurers, traffickers, pimps, owners of the girls—after all, you have to have middlemen to force the girls into the fuck factories. No girl is going to want to open her legs to the disgust of men she doesn't know, shoving themselves into her. You're going to have some pretty empty factories if you leave it to the girls to show up.

Platt's idea that "sex work is here to stay" is yet another promotion of the male rape order. Women have to be on the bottom—getting rammed for male fun? Does this woman seriously think that women are the sexual inferiors of men and that men need to have some place to stick it in, no matter what—therefore, we can do nothing about stopping prostitution? Her idea that "sex work is here to stay" sounds perilously close to legitimizing a 5000 year history of sanctioned rape. Instead of accepting the prostitution—i.e., that the paid rape of the female body is inevitable, why don't we adopt a stance like this one: this horrible practice of cold, impersonal sex performed on the vulnerable, poverty-ridden, destitute women of the world must stop. Right now. Immediately. There is no way we women can allow such sexual atrocity to continue any longer. You degrade all women when you degrade even one this way. If every woman in the world thought this way, just think what a revolution we would bring about!

I know the practical side of having to prostitute since there is no other way. I know that you cannot take this 'job' away from girls who have no alternatives. I know that helping to improve the conditions they work under is invaluable. I am aware that if I had worked under the brutal oppressions and beatings and humiliations that most girls in prostitution suffer, I would not be here today. Yet all of this practicality cannot make the systematic sexual degradation that is prostitution alright.

When an ex-prostitute writes about the subject, as Jane Anthony does in "Prostitution as 'Choice,'" it rings true to me. She writes: "One might expect that feminism, which has dragged out of the closet issues such as rape, incest, and battering—all of which are frequently part of the prostitution syndrome—would target commercial sex as the beginning and end of women's exploitation." She says that those who "attempt to portray prostitution as a 'career choice'" are not themselves prostituted. Of the ones who actually work in prostitution and see it as a career choice, the numbers are remarkably small, "given the millions of women worldwide who live as prostitutes in silence" (416).

"If a woman faces poverty, hunger, sexual abuse, homelessness...her possibilities of establishing herself in mainstream culture, or merely surviving, are well beyond the traditional concept of 'choice.'"

"No doubt it is easier to view prostitution as a 'choice' than to address its implications. This institution has been with us for millennia, has no prospects of disappearing anytime soon, and is often...a source of cruel and insensitive jokes about women's condition. It is no wonder that women would prefer not to ask themselves what this means about their own lives and relationships, and their own struggle for freedom. In 'Confronting the Liberal Lies about Prostitution,' Evelina Giobbe of WHISPER (Women Hurt in Systems of Prostitution Engaged in Revolt), in Minneapolis, has noted, 'Dismantling the institution of prostitution is the most formidable task facing contemporary feminism.'"

"It may be comforting for some women to see prostitution as a 'career choice.' But when they promote this message to an all-to-eager male-dominated media, they may be sentencing other women to years of dehumanization and numbness. Or, in some cases, death. *Real* death, unlike some 'choices'" (418).

In so far as I can tell, feminists don't seem to be addressing the issue of prostitution at all. In fact, I can't see anyone addressing it. Female politicians never say anything about it. Good old Hillary, as she runs for president, is certainly supremely indifferent to the main problem on Rape Planet Earth, namely, rape, in all its forms. She will never fight for the women who need her the most—the women no one fights for, the ones who are in too helpless a position to fight for themselves. Those tough female soldiers never say anything about it, except to scorn and despise the whores near the bases, thereby empowering men to rape them even more since they do not question the male soldiers entitlement to rape outside the gate.

My view is that countering prostitution is the primary battle for all of humankind since no woman can be respected if even one degraded prostitute exists anywhere. It is an instance, again, of that famous William James thought I live by: If all of human kind can be kept happy by the acute misery of one wretched being at the far edge of the universe, is this a fair moral exchange?

Quite frankly, I don't see how any kind of 'empowerment' is possible for any woman as long as even one girl living in prostitution misery exists. That girl negates every moment of strength and confidence Hillary might pretend to.

To further counter women like Platt and Bindman, all you have to do is browse Human Rights Watch. You will find conditions for prostituted women so appalling that you cannot even believe these women are still alive. "Abuses Against Women Sex Workers in Bangladesh": Sold when she was fourteen, a young prostitute, now in her twenties, is doing the best she can. She now has children of her own and every time the school finds out she is a whore, she has to take them out of the school, and move to a different area.

She was taken by the police to a warehouse where eight of them got drunk and raped her all night.

"I am a woman," she says. I have a right to live like other women. No one likes me, everybody hates me." Despised and scorned because she was sold into prostitution at age fourteen and now her children are shunned to punish her even more for the crime of being raped for all these years. The fact that she can say she is 'a woman' like others and deserves the same rights amazes me. What a courageous and beautiful being she must be! If I were treated as she has been, I would be too weak and damaged to assert any rights at all.

HRC interviewed a prostitute who was raped all night by thirty-five men and then, after that, by twenty different men who also beat her. She reports being very weak and later fainting from the abuse. (I don't think it would take me a 'later' to faint. I would have bled to death from the first thirty-five.)

A prostitute raped by a police officer reports he refused to wear a condom because he said, "You are not wife, why should I care about you, you are a bad woman." Another prostitute was raped by a police officer who refused to stop when he hurt her because he denied she could feel pain. As she was being raped, he said to her "you are not a good woman, you cannot feel pain."

Debased, demeaned, degraded, stigmatized, scorned, reviled, hated. Why should any woman have to live like this? Yet this is the reality of the prostitute. This is the reality—underneath the surface—the reality that all the decent women of the world and all the female soldiers who think its fine for the men to use the whores outside the gate—this is the reality they ignore. They see nothing of the true torture that is the life of the prostitute.

Unfortunately, HRC, for all the good they do, calls the girls 'sex workers.' I am dumbfounded that anyone could consider rape by thirty-five men 'work.'

And HRC says the obvious: that these women "suffer many harms, including emotional and physical harms. " Do we really need to say this? I guess maybe we do—since all the decent women of the world do not think that the prostitute suffers any harm at all. She is just a whore for men to use. Period. End of subject. No attention to how she may have gotten into this rape/torture life. Does anyone ever consider that there is something terribly wrong with a girl being 'sold' at age fourteen—or at any age?

I wonder why slavery is so roundly condemned by all these fake civilized people who pretend other human beings should have some rights yet they cannot detect the slavery that lies in selling a girl's body for sex?

Another sample HRW report, this time Kazakhstan and "Police Abuse of Sex Workers" (that abysmally inaccurate term again). It is the same stigma and misery and violence for the poor sold girls.

"Kazakhstan has seen a dramatic rise in the number of sex workers since the dissolution of the Soviet Union…due to unemployment, falling standards of education, and general desperation." You could transfer that sentence anywhere: the Ukraine, Bulgaria, Moldova, any other 'stan' (Uzbekistan)--the fall of the Soviet Union has caused unimaginable sexual damage or a massive scale to women and girls.

In this particular 'stan,' the whore is blamed for the sexual violence against her. So what else is new? It is the same picture in the U.S. A whore is always to blame for the rape inflicted on her.

"Unprotected sex for a miserable $1.33." And the pimps pay off the police by letting the men take free fucks. So what else is new? Burmese girls, just fifteen, just babies practically, trafficked into brutal, high-volume brothels in Thailand—where laborers and soldiers use them and the rape-shit police climb on for their free fucks so they will not say anything about this crime.

Yet nowhere is it considered a crime—whether it be Bangladesh or Burma—or the wholesome wonderful USA—no where is it considered a crime what happens to the bodies of these helpless girls.

I have chosen a losing cause. A cause so hopeless, I gave up long ago. But hopelessness in my coping mechanism and if I don't do something, what is the alternative?

Hopelessness hits hard when I read of Prince Charles visiting a squalid shelter in Nepal where AIDS-ridden discards from Bombay (Mumbai) come home to die in. They come home with what is called the 'Mumbai Disease'—an indication of how widespread is the sale of Nepali girls to India. Prince Charles feels sorry for them so he donates a few of his watercolors to help? Is that all? Then he goes home to his luxuries, his estates, his privilege. That is all? A few watercolors!?

The leader of Nepal is really 'embarrassed' that the Prince saw the Mumbai discards at all.

Their plight is dreadful. As Nina Rao writes in "The Dark Side of Tourism and Sexuality: Trafficking of Nepali Girls for Indian Brothels," "In brothels girls are exposed to brutality, both physical and psychological, such as beating and mass rape to suppress individuality and rebellion…they are forced to live in unhygienic conditions and to consume alcohol and drugs. They have no access to medical treatment and have no freedom of movement."

Corruption at all levels, she says—politicians, police officers, border officials—makes escape and redress almost impossible.

I found a very shocking article called "The Myth of Nepal-to-India Sex Trafficking" by a man named John Frederick. He tries to deny the harsh and unbearable reality of the girls, even though we know that seven-year-old Nepali girls are being forced to have sex with grown men in the Bombay red-light area. He calls it the "Gita Myth" and his approach seems to be as if none of this is happening. "Gita's resistance to sex work and her subsequent rape and torture are routine to the myth," he tells us.

Who would not have a resistance to 'sex work,' I ask? He thinks the brothel should be accepted as a "workplace." He denies those who manage to return to Nepal are damaged when they come back (if they come back). I wonder how he cannot see so much forced sex on a body as doing no damage? And I would ask him if AIDS is a myth as well? At the highest estimate, four out of five Nepali adolescent 'sex workers' in Bombay are infected.

Maybe he needed another article for his academic career and this was it. Scholars always seem to be trying to find new and trendy approaches to prostitution-pain.

I am ashamed that I have at times been part of the academic world. It was necessary to get the Ph.D. to legitimize myself, but I hope I never write about the rape-pain of prostitution in any way that betrays the terrible misery of the girls involved. A seven-year-old Nepali girl in a Bombay brothel. How can one write about that at all?

I also have a lot of trouble with those academics who are so awash in jargon, you never even know, from their descriptions, that physical pain is being inflicted. For example here is Thanh-Dam Truong in her *Sex, Money and Morality: Prostitution and Tourism in Southeast Asia*: "It is necessary to recognize that the sexual act and sexual relations cannot be disconnected from their complex social and historical context. Thus, while sexual intercourse between a man and a woman can occur purely in the existential context of sensuality, intimacy and social significance, the same act can also occur as a form of sexual abuse and violence....When incorporated into market relations, the act of sexual intercourse—whether in the form of erotic art or physical abuse—becomes part of the institution of the brothel..." (53).

How are we to wring any kind of true physical pain and abuse and torment out of such impossible prose? The coldness of the style denies the very rape it struggles to express. She goes on: "Sexual identities are not only created by moral and ideological discourses on sexual behavior but are also formed by processes of production which affect the context in which human sexuality is expressed and experienced." What on earth or in the heavens does this kind of language have to do with the poor Occupation Comfort Girl, terrified, as she is rammed and rammed and rammed and rammed and rammed by twenty-three GI's her first day 'on the job' at a comfort station. What does this kind of prose have to do with her bleeding, scarred insides?

Paola Monzini's *Sex Traffic*: *Prostitution, Crime and Exploitation* is a short excellent introduction to what is going on in the world of prostitution. She describes a girl trafficked into Italy: "She can't go for a walk....She can be subjected at any moment to physical and mental violence, she has absolutely no control over her own existence." Monzini's descriptions of the typical breaking-in process are chilling—the beating, rape, and terror inflicted on the girl. Her description of the utter ruthlessness of the crime syndicates and mafias who do the breaking in are even more chilling. Particularly harsh, she says, is the Albanian mafia. They don't just break a girl but re-break and re-break her. I was sick when I read this. To take an already helpless, pain-ridden creature and inflict even more rape-torture on her. (Amnesty International reports a 14-year-old Albanian sex slave in London being forced to have sex twenty-hours a day.)

What a pattern for our world, I thought, when I read of the re-breaking techniques of the Albanian mafia. The Comfort Women all over again: raped 30-50 times a day by the Japanese and then passed on to the Americans and Aussies and Brits for another dose. Nothing changes on Rape Planet Earth. It just seems to get worse.

Read Monzini's book if you can. It sums up so much of the world of trafficking/prostitution in clear, readable, concise fashion.

Victor Malarek, Canadian journalist and author of *The Natashas: Inside the New Global Sex Trade,* does recognize the terrible harm of prostitution. He is one of the compassionate ones. He sees that these pathetic women are raped, broken, dead 'remnants' of human beings, He points out that we only see the end product—the girl already broken and turned out and ready to be sold.

One of saddest parts of his book: he describes a plump unattractive girl forced on stage in a Bosnian brothel, to strip so the UN Peacekeepers and other multi-national forces can make fun of her. "She was obese and clearly on display for the sport and ridicule of the patrons" (39). Maybe the second saddest part of his book is the description of soldiers putting on a party for one of their mates and a trafficked girl was the 'gift.' She had to submit to rape by all of them.

UN Peacekeepers and other soldiers, like my American ones, causing enormous rape pain to helpless girls—another savage characteristic of Rape Planet Earth that fills me with despair.

I highly recommend Malarek's book. It is full of insights, intelligence, and compassion.

Catharine MacKinnon makes sense to me. She says that the Serbian rape-death camps "comes closest to the experiences of prostituted women, serially raped in what is called peacetime" (176). "Mass rape and serial rape" she sees as "indistinguishable from prostitution. Prostitution is that part of everyday non-war life that is closest to what we see done to women in this war. The daily life of prostituted women consists of serial rape, recognized war or no war. The brothel-like arrangement of the rape/death camps parallels the brothels of so-called peacetime: captive women impounded to be passed from man to man in order to be raped" (188).

She points out that United Nations forces moved in supposedly to bring peace yet their sexual demands and the subsequent massive increase of brothels and trafficking of defenseless girls kept the war on women going red hot. (My phrasing.) Even in peacetime there is no escape from the war on the female body that is prostitution. Only men benefit from war.

She strikes a note with me since I see life as one big rape picture. Fear of being raped rules my every act and every conscious moment of awareness. It has always puzzled me why men don't protect us instead of rape us. The dream and fantasy of my life—never fulfilled—is to find a protective man. A father who will care for me.

One of the most disturbing books I ran across was Maria Laura Agustin's *Sex at the Margins: Migration, Labour Markets and the Rescue Industry.* Even though she includes testimonies of the terribly damaged and is fully aware that girls are forced to serve men, that the pimps take the money, that they break the girls—all of this seemingly has no reality for her—it's all 'media panic' and 'sexual commotion.'

A sample of how she thinks: she makes the amazing claim that when a trafficker says "the cargo change every 10-15 days" he is simply talking in a "disagreeable way" and that this is "evidence of how movers may commodify their clients" (33). For her, the girl as commodity is apparently a 'neutral' fact and all those traffickers who break and burn so cruelly are just 'disagreeable.' I don't think that word is even mildly accurate.

She sees the debt bondage prostitution the girls are trapped in as a way for the girls to earn a lot of money fast. It is puzzling that she ignores the fact the girls is on her back taking 'clients' all day for free so she can pay back an imaginary debt to her enslavers.

Her cold meaninglessly obscure academic jargon phrasings are also a puzzle—for example, "sexual culture can be understood as comprising a continuum of relationships in which sexual labor is present, without differentiating absolutely between marital and extramarital sex" (86). What?

She describes prostitutes who are pimped onto military ships while docked as engaged in one big fun party as they move from ship to ship and sailor to sailor. Serial rape of the body, so she can bring home the money to her pimp, is fun for her?

Quantifying takes the place of heart: in Thailand, she writes, "104,262 employees" are "selling sex" in "7, 758" establishments" (65). No acknowledgement of what that "selling sex" in these apparently neutral venues called "establishments" involves: lack of freedom, debt bondage, very young girls forced by grown-up 'clients,' diseases and physical damage, life-long psychic marring of the girl, hopelessness, resignation, consequent numbness, sometimes even suicide. These 'facts' have been well-documented. This characterizes the Thai sex industry. Even the bar girls, those most free, suffer from fear of violence, disease, low self-esteem, pimp-control.

Back in Europe, she notes that the sex industry in Germany brings in five billion a year. I wonder how she overlooks this simple fact: could you actually find a large enough number of women who would submit, voluntarily, to fucking all those German client/rapists. Are there really that many women willing to fuck the million or so German rapists a day who visit prostitutes? That's a lot of women willing to lay down for rape on a daily basis.

The saddest part of the book for me was this: a 'free' prostitute saying how "the Russians have messed up the job. They do whatever they are asked, anywhere and in front of anyone." How miserable that even the prostitute does not understand. Is any Russian girl going to do "whatever she is asked, anywhere, in front of anyone" without being forced? Absolutely no exploration or understanding on her part of the savage breaking it took to make this girl compliant and docile. Would she really fuck in public, or insert objects inside herself in front of an audience of 'client/rapists,' or 'take on' a group of men and bang them one after the other in front of the others—if she were not forced to, broken to this 'behavior'? Does this 'free' prostitute really believe all Russian women will do anything, without shame, voluntarily? Does she really believe that this self-degradation is natural to all Russian girls turned into whores?

I think I have to return to the comfort women again, just to refresh the mind about what torture doing whatever men ask, in front of everyone, implies. Let me use the Dutch comfort women this time—since I don't think they are any different from their Russian sisters. In their testimonies, they report the same extreme fear and humiliation when raped dozens of times a day, the same destruction of dignity and self-worth, the same crying and shock and dazed minds and bodies and bleeding as do the Korean ones. They describe burning with fear and misery years later—there is no lifting of the mantle of rape once a girl has been tortured in this way. The 'vaginas' and spirits of the Dutch women were no different from those of their Korean counterparts. The vaginas and spirits of the Russian girls who will 'do anything' are no different from those of Western prostitutes. Can anyone seriously believe that Russian girls are actually without shame or feelings or pain when they will 'do anything'? By this point I guess they might be—since you have to numb out completely to be able to 'do anything.' But it is really a matter of the degree of 'breaking.' Of course a deeply and thoroughly 'broken' girl will 'do anything.' After torture, terror, starvation, public anal rape, and time in a 'submissions camp' to 'train' her to endure all kinds of humiliation, what girl will not 'do anything'? The Western prostitute, so 'trained,' would also 'do anything.'

What does this Western 'free' prostitute mean by the Russian girls messing it up for the rest of us? Does she mean that the girls will 'do' anal? Well, not without it being forced on them. What girl wants her body ruined by a dozen or more men a day ramming her butt hole? In what way could this be construed as 'voluntary' on the part of the Russian girls who will 'do anything'? Absolutely astonishing to me that even women cannot see the pain of other women. I have no trouble seeing it at all. I worked as a 'free' prostitute and the amount of numbing and disassociation I had to undergo to shield myself just to have sex with several men a day I did not know was enormous. I would not 'do anything.' I was not forced. But if I had been trained by a criminal group in a submissions camp, if I had been forced to bend over for public anal—till I did not care anymore what happened to me—of course, I would 'do anything.' The poor girl probably cannot tell one man, or rapist, from another, by now.

It is peculiar how values shift. At one time, no one could believe that the" little brown fucking machines"--as the U.S. military so fondly calls all the cute little Asian whores it mass raped—at one time, no one could believe it was not part of their 'culture' to be raped all day. After all, Asian girls were 'natural whores,' weren't they? Now we have the belief that the hundreds of thousands of Russian girls trafficked into Western Europe and Asia are willing "Caucasian fucking machines" with no volition or distaste for their own mass rape? That they gladly do whatever is asked of them, in front of everyone?

Amazing.

It is hard for me to imagine how isolated these Russian girls must feel from the rest of humanity due to the extremes of inhumanity visited on them. As a former prostitute I am always isolated from all the women around me. They are in a different dimension, one way, way over there—on another planet—where I cannot even see them. How much more alone must be these Russian girls feel who have been reduced to such states of terror and 'degradation' that they will 'do anything'—to survive. When they are being forced to do anal in public, I wonder what their thoughts are, of all the other women—those from a different species—those not forced to do anal in public. Can the Russian girls even think anymore, about what is happening to them? Can they even feel the difference anymore, about anything? Doing anal in public pretty much kills everything inside you forever.

Outcast and alone.

Agustin's book is one of the cruelest I read. One of the most insensitive. And that 'free' prostitute must be numb or cruel beyond belief to not see the torture of her rape-dead Russian sisters.

Cleo Odzer's *Patpong Sisters: An American Woman's View of the Bangkok Sex World* gave me some more information about the sex shows that various GI's had already described to me: "pussy write letter, pussy take lit candle inside, pussy smoke cigarette, pussy shoot out banana, pussy open beer bottle," etc.

The dexterous vagina. The public vagina numbed to deal with the humiliation—a girl publicly accessible, in ultimate acts of degradation, to crude jeering rough men. The death of her spirit. Sadness. These are all my thoughts. Odzer's book deals very little with the pain.

She describes places I didn't know about: blow-job bars with girls on their knees, using toilet paper afterwards to clean up with. Depressing.

She gives some insights into what happens when the U.S. fleet comes in for R & R. She says she has seen the drunk American sailors "hollering and staggering." Girls are trafficked into Pattaya to service them. She quotes an article from the *Bangkok Post:* "Pattaya—About 8,000 US servicemen aboard the nuclear-powered aircraft carrier *Carl Vinson* and its seven support ships will begin five days of shore leave in this resort town this morning, and businesses here expect to reap millions of *baht* during the visit" (156).

She describes the "wooden signs [that] staked the spots where liberty boats would land. Each ship had its own Thai fishing boats to ferry boys back and forth. A cloth strung across trees announced WELCOME U.S. NAVY. At the curb, a Bangkok Bank trailer waited for the Americans so that they could change their dollars right there. Very organized" (186).

Overall, Odzer does not stress what leads girls in Thailand into prostitution but she does say this: "A Thai woman's group called Friends of Women had gone to Pattaya to picket the arrival of yet another American fleet, accusing them of bringing AIDS. Bargirls had ordered a counter picket with placards proclaiming: *Ben Ets Dee Kwa Ot Taay* (Better AIDS than Starvation)" (195).

Odzer's description of the drunk American sailors "hollering" made my stomach turn upside down with fear. Those poor bar girls who have to take being roughed up by these drunk crude men.

The U.S. Department of State has come out with some pretty strong statements against trafficking/prostitution: "Few activities are as brutal and damaging to people as prostitution."

"A path-breaking, five-country academic study concluded that research on prostitution has overlooked the 'burden of physical injuries and illnesses that women in the sex industry sustain from violence…or from their significantly higher rates of hepatitis, higher risks of cervical cancer, fertility complications, and psychological trauma.'

"State attempts to regulate prostitution by introducing medical check-ups or licenses don't address the core problem: the routine abuse and violence that form the prostitution experience….Prostitution leaves women and children physically, mentally, emotionally, and spiritually devastated. Recovery takes years, even decades—often, the damage can never be undone." These statements are from official State Department literature on trafficking.

What puzzles me is why the sudden interest by the State Department? They have nothing to gain from opposing trafficking/prostitution. It puts money into their hands indirectly in the form of a hugely lucrative industry and keeps a lot of tourists, locals, and military men happy and fucking along, promoting the patriarchal rape culture that is Rape Planet Earth. The powers-that-be worldwide have nothing to gain from opposing prostitution/trafficking. It must be AIDS that is the concern, not any humanitarian push.

Jennifer S. Butler's "Militarized Prostitution: the Untold Story (U.S.A.)" gives a lot of information about U.S. base prostitution around the world and also information about stop-offs at Pattaya during the Gulf War. I like her succinct analysis of the situation worldwide:

"Military prostitution refers specifically to the establishment of brothels around bases to provide entertainment and sexual 'services' to occupying soldiers. Brothel owners usually either buy women and children from sex traffickers or recruit those who are desperate because of poverty, war, or violence....During war women and young girls who are displaced from land and family support are often forced to sell their bodies to survive.... Sometimes they are the victims of rape during war and deemed unworthy of protection...by a patriarchal culture" (206).

The above information about the 'sourcing' of the girls is useful when we consider that the Filipina and Ukrainian trafficked girls used by the American servicemen in Korea come from such backgrounds, as do the Russian and Eastern European ones trafficked into the sex torture playgrounds of Germany. Since the biggest sex-torture district in Germany and the biggest U.S. base are side-by-side, you can bet that the men are using those tortured bodies and are therefore as guilty of rape as the traffickers and owners who break and exploit the girls.

Phyllis Chesler, in her updated version of her famous *Women and Madness*, sums up in a clear-sighted and elegant way what I call the characteristic Rape Killing Fields on Rape Planet Earth:

"Many men, including HIV positive men, have insisted on unprotected sex with ever-younger women and children in both America and in Third World countries and have infected their female partners with the deadly AIDS virus.

"Male lust and greed continue to drive an unholy worldwide trafficking in girls and women. Rape, including public and videotaped gang rape, became weapons of war in the early 1970's in Bangladesh; in the 1990's in Bosnia and Algeria; and most recently in Rwanda and Sudan, where the women have been previously genitally mutilated and sewn up. This means that gang rape amounts to serious physical torture, which may also have grave medical consequences."

Sheila Jeffreys. Her book on the topic is *The Idea of Prostitution*. Enshrine this woman somewhere. Enshrine her book somewhere—put a big gold light around it, set it on a fluffy cloud. I cannot praise Jeffreys highly enough. She has never been a prostitute but she writes as if she really knows what it is like from the inside. What is even more remarkable is that she is a lesbian and an academic. I never seem to find lesbians who give a damn about what happens to the body of the hetero female. This one does. (Pardon me, Sheila, for my lesbianaphobia: as a rather narrow straight woman, it is a failing of mine.)

And she is completely free of the cold and heartless distancing of most academics. A lot of her book illustrates Kate Millett's view that prostitution is "paradigmatic, somehow the very core of the female's condition." It declares her "subjection right out in the open....It is not sex the prostitute is really made to sell: it is degradation."

Jeffreys goes into problems of word choice: "The word *prostitution* does not include the agents of the abuse, men....*Prostituted woman* is useful in at least indicating that there is an agent involved. But a term which really demonstrates male responsibility does not exist" (141).

She cites the Oslo study about how little choice even girls in the 'civilized' country of Norway have. Average age when they enter prostitution: fifteen. All come from backgrounds of deprivation, poverty, and abuse (153). Extrapolate this to the rest of the world: numerous studies indicate that this is typical of prostitutes worldwide. Given this fact, it is very hard to support any kind of 'normalization' of this institution.

Her view on johns: "They must hold certain ideas about sex and women to enable them to use prostituted women. If those attitudes were to change, then prostitution could not survive" (241).

"Prostitution is male sexual violence." What a clear, succinct phrasing of the truth.

Jeffreys quotes former prostitute Evelina Giobbe: "Prostitution is sexual abuse because prostitutes are subjected to any number of sexual acts that in any other context, acted against any other woman, would be labeled assaultive..." (242).

Jeffreys is the only other writer I know who notes that most feminists don't include prostitution in the category of sexual violence. In fact, I've noticed that when these feminists write on rape—single, gang, date, etc.—the most egregious and frightening kind—prostitution—is absent from their lists.

I go somewhat further in my views in that I don't think most non-prostituted women have a clue as to what prostitution is. I have talked to college girls who are puzzled when I say that the local rape crisis center should be for the truly raped—for all the girls down the street, in the brothel massage parlour two miles from the sacred green precinct of the campus. "But they get paid, how can it be rape?" the college girls tell me. They seem to have no conception, and no curiosity about the origins of the brothel inmates—how they got there, how they are treated. "Would you actually want to do blow jobs all day on any men who walk in?" I ask the college girls. This makes them uncomfortable. I seem to find among these college girls the same dirty-joke blindness about what a prostitute is that the male students have. They snigger and disapprove and show their righteous moral indignation about women who are so shameless as to sell themselves—without having a clue as to the path of abuse and coercion that led to the debt-bondage girl dependent upon her pimp to not beat her anymore with a hanger if only she will beg enough and thank him enough and love him enough for being so wonderful to her. The degradation and death of the spirit we see in the pimp/prostitute relationship is completely beyond these sheltered college girls.

Jeffreys understands—she sees how the prostitute has to accept all this violence as a norm and lie to herself deep inside, where she is all twisted and ruined, so as to endure the unendurable.

Evelina Giobbe understands. She founded WHISPER to help those destroyed by prostitution. One girl she helped says, "I feel like what was taken away from me in prostitution is irretrievable." The Korean Comfort Women said the same thing. "Give me back my life, my girlhood, my womanhood. What was comfort for you was death for me." Torture victims say the same as former prostitutes.

"Prostitution: Buying the Right to Rape" Giobbe titles one of her articles.

"Evelina Giobbe argues that prostitution resembles rape in the shocking similarity of its effects, as revealed in the WHISPER Oral History Project. These effects include feelings of humiliation, degradation, defilement, and dirtiness...difficulties in establishing intimate relationships with men... disdain and hatred toward men. They suffered...nightmares...lingering fears and deep emotional pain that often resembled grieving" (Jeffreys 268).

As I set out to write my own book and to recognize my own past, I did not know that I would find illumination in passages like the above. My own prostitution trauma was relatively mild since I was not trafficked, never beaten or terrorized (except in a couple of rare instances) and had a lot of safety and control over the men I went with and the environment I worked in. But the above list applies partly to me as well, particularly in not being able to find long-term intimacy with men. I have come to realize that I went into prostitution as a way of re-enacting my own gang rape. It was an effort to get rid of an unendurable event in my life by re-living it over and over again. After I left prostitution, and regained some sexual feeling (this took a few years), I preferred brief sexual encounters with men younger than me over any kind of permanence. More re-enactment—going from one man to the next, but this time not for money. I also have been incapable all my life of confronting men for fear of their violence. I have never been able to stay with anyone beyond the first argument—the fear of his hitting me is too great.

I didn't know that I would find confirmation in how I feel about myself in reading about what other prostitutes feel. For example, Giobbe identifies the scarlet letter syndrome: the idea that others can see you have been a prostitute, a being regarded as without value or dignity.

I am hyper-aware, every day, that if the man I am talking to is now polite, that would evaporate if he knew I had once sold myself. He would treat me like a dirty joke. He would not be courteous. Instead, he would become crude and rough.

I don't feel accepted anywhere, or of any value, despite what are called my 'accomplishments'—writing books, getting a Ph.D. All respect for me would evaporate should people know about my past.

Yet, in some odd way, I respect myself more for being a prostitute than I do for being a fake part of the normal world. I have far more value than the men and women who scorn me.

Giobbe gave me some insights into the johns. (I did not use that word—I called the men customers in my head; I think I remember referring to them as 'appointments' when we set up a time to meet.)

"Perpetrators refer to the victims as sluts and whores to justify their violation," says Giobbe (258).

She also tells us that "the johns were so determined to treat the prostituted women they were using as nonpersons that they did not even notice when women were crying as they performed their tricks" (269). This helped me to understand that unthinkable sentence (mentioned elsewhere in this book), the one in Tanaka's chapter on the Occupation Comfort Girls, the sentence, from an American military observer, about how fifty GI's lined up to get at one girl, and how she was 'busy,' as if this were simply a calm, normal, okay activity, and not raping the insides out of the girl. I can also see how the terrified new recruit forced to service twenty-three American soldiers her first day on the 'job' could simply pass by unnoticed, as a human being, by the men. When they rape us to pieces they do not even notice we cry since the sex is so much more important than our pain—or our survival.

It was startling to realize this. When I first read that sentence, I did not have all this other information to help me through the shock and pain of finding out that all GI's, and all men, are rapists. I had not read all these other books back then. It took me weeks to get this sentence out of my head.

Giobbe again: "No other interpersonal, social or work-related type of situation or interaction that elicits these massive traumatic effects…would be condoned."

'The Fifty GI Rapists," as I have come to call them in my head, obviously believed that rape of that small body was not just permissible but a norm—and they would never have admitted it was rape since they disguised it, to themselves, as a financial transaction.

A second haunting sentence, from a U.S. military officer, in the Tanaka book—"these girls desire to stay in this profession because they are homeless and need a way to eat"—is yet another instance of disguise. This time he lies to himself about there being no alternatives. There was a big one. He and all the other men could have set up dormitories for the girls and fed them and made them feel safe and given them blankets to keep them warm during the cold winds of the Tokyo winter that was coming. The same, of course, could be said for the soldiers in Europe—instead of the Italian girl so desperate she will fuck for Spam, and instead of the girls who were put on their backs for the lines of GI's (as one finished up and came out, another went in for his turn)—instead of all this brutality and unpardonable cruelty, the men could have been what men are supposed to be—protective.

Why do men rape us instead of protecting us?

The raped girl is "homeless in her own body" (Jeffreys 274). Homeless in the world at large I would say. To follow Virginia Woolf's train of thought, not only do we women not have a country on Rape Planet Earth, we actually don't have a planet either.

Damage to the vagina, I have discovered, causes severe trauma to the emotions. (I know that damage to mine has caused huge ripples in my whole life. From that first incredibly startling penetration of my virgin body to the use by about 500 different men when I worked as a prostitute—any tearing or bleeding or soreness or fear of male roughness sends me off into trembling and crying and sadness.) Jeffreys describes the ways prostitutes "work out… ingenious and complex systems to protect 'the real self, the personality, from being invaded and destroyed by customers'" (272).

I was really happy to discover that Jeffreys sees the Korean Comfort Women as a norm, not an exception. She says she is "struck by the similarities between what happened to them and what happens to women and girls imprisoned by debt, duty or lack of alternatives, in brothels in many countries around the world. Particularly I am struck by the similarities with the experience of young women used and abused in U.S. military prostitution….But many in the human rights community wish to make a distinction between this latter form of prostitution, which is characterized as 'free,' and that which is 'forced.' Usually terms such as *rape* and *military sexual enslavement* are used for the prostitution which is part of wartime atrocities, so that a clear distinction can be made" (298).

I, of course, hold the position that the Dubai Girl that our navy buys in that city, is identical to the Korean Comfort Women: recruited by deception, broken by humiliation and assembly-line rape. And the "Juicy Girl," as the GI's in Korea call the Russian girls trafficked into the base brothels there—

this girl was brought in by what is now one of the largest and most ruthless and brutal criminal organizations in the world, and they break her with the same cruelty as the Korean Comfort Women knew.

Since the U.S. occupation of Korea began in 1945, Korean girls have been 'trafficked' in every sense of the word—controlled by pimps, enmired in hopeless imaginary debts to their enslavers—and also treated brutally by drunk rough servicemen until years of abuse have rendered them imbecile. Bruce Cumings, an American historian who served in the Peace Corps in Korea in the 1960's, describes how young girls, age twelve or so, are recruited by pimps and turned out as street whores for the GI's and how the prostitutes who have survived the long American Occupation look like diseased broken hags when they are only thirty. He says there is a nightmare street where the old whores live in broken huts and grab desperately at the GI's who go there for a good laugh. Cumings also tells us the shocking news that his fellow male Peace Corps volunteers frequent the brothels—sometimes visiting several in one night. And, to top of his good news about the behavior of men, he says that when he speaks at military academies in the U.S. about our presence abroad, basically all the men want to know about is the availability of cheap "pussy." (You can find his excellent article on prostitution in Korea during the 1960's in *Let the Good Times Roll.*)

Jeffreys points out that "the consequences for the women abused by the Japanese military seem to share much with what we are now beginning to understand to be the common consequences of prostitution."

The distinction between forced/ free, she says, "concentrates attention on the conditions in which the women are abused, rather than on the abusers" (305).

Shocking fact I learned from her book: very young girls, age twelve and thirteen, are forced to take contraceptive pills continuously with no medical supervision so they will not menstruate so they can be available for constant rape. This causes severe physical reactions in the girls, including not being able to stop bleeding once they start. I, for one, cannot imagine how they can live feeling so dreadful since the pills cause nausea and other physical miseries.

Another shocking fact. In the 'casa' brothels of the Philippines girls are treated with such cruel deprivation to keep them broken that a girl did what the client/rapist wanted for free if her would give her some water (314).

I also learned that there are an estimated 30,000 girls serving in bars and brothels around the U.S. bases in Korea.

I found this excellent definition of prostitution in Jeffreys. Prostitution consists of "the mouth, the vagina, the rectum, penetrated usually by a penis, sometimes hand, sometimes objects, by one man and then another and then another and then another and then another" (348). A fittingly and chillingly cold description of a cold, impersonal act.

In light of this definition, it is hard to imagine any girls 'volunteering' for this treatment by men.

I think there is a continental divide between a sensitive, enlightened woman like Jeffreys and ones I read about on military bases around the world. One good example would be Germany, where the largest red-light district in the country is just around the corner from our largest base and the female soldiers and wives and daughters think it just fine for the men to visit the whores—does no one any harm, the men have to get their rocks off, it is what men do, etc., can't deprive a young boy of sex and, after all, it's legal and the girl has a 'right' to make a living this way. I wish some of these ignorant American women would read the accounts of how these girls got into those brothel beds. Don't they realize anything about the coercive nature of this business? (See Inigo's *Stars and Stripes*' article, "Troops Say Proposed UCMJ Change Unfair," for some of these attitudes on the part of American women.)

We have ample documentation of the large numbers of Slavic women trafficked into Western Europe and Asia (particularly China and Korea). In Western Europe, the girls are broken and controlled by the violence of Eastern European gangs. The largest number of girls are now from the Ukraine, where the most helpless and vulnerable are 'recruited' from orphanages by the Russian mafia. In China, about 15,000 Russian girls have been trafficked in to service Chinese men and tourists. In Korea, in just one year, about 7000 E-Visas (those allowing traffickers to bring in girls as 'entertainers') were issued. It would seem that the estimated number of Russian girls (5000) 'entertaining' near U.S. bases is probably more than that—given such a large number of E-Visas being issued in just one year.

A big puzzler for me is lack of enforcement of existing laws or codes or whatever one wants to call them. For example, under the military Code of Honor, it has always, since time immemorial, as they say, been forbidden for any American soldier to buy a prostitute. This has never been enforced or paid attention to in any way. Not even remotely. As I remember one GI in Japan in the 1960's saying to me: "It's a big joke."

So, changes in the UCMJ are not really 'changes.' And will these imaginary 'changes' make any difference? The way the military is phrasing the 'changes' is peculiar: buying a prostitute will now bring the same punishment as being one. Why should she be punished for anything? She is the raped one. That phrasing certainly does not indicate any kind of change of attitude toward the prostitute at all.

William Finnegan's "The Countertraffickers: Rescuing the Victims of the Global Sex Trade" just came out in *The New Yorker*. He is a further source of confirmation. He says the Russian, Albanian, and Ukrainian mafias are now the biggest and most powerful ones in sex trafficking.

He is also a source of information on Dubai, a major destination for trafficked girls and also a major docking port of the navies of the world—a terrible combination fraught with rape for the trafficked girls.

The girls of that sexual rape playground are trafficked from everywhere: in the bars of Dubai, the author found girls from China, India, Bangladesh, Thailand, Iraq, Iran, Jordan, Turkey, Egypt, Vietnam, Kenya, Moldova.

In one bar he says: "The Moldovan was blonde and looked hard-used; she wouldn't tell me much" (57). Maybe he should have substituted 'couldn't.' As a broken, pimp-controlled girl, what exactly could she tell him? To speak might cost her her life.

When the girls get back to Moldova, if they ever do, he says there is almost no reparation, no justice for the girls, and no penalties for those who torture and rape the girls—so what else is new—the picture is no different in the U.S. where a brothel raid will yield a tortured trafficked being who is put in jail, while her customer/rapists are never even considered culpable, and her owners get off with a light penalty—and then she is re-trafficked, or, if she has tried to talk to her other captors (the police), she may be shot by her owners and left in a deserted area. Since she is just a whore, no police force will bother with finding her murderers.

What is greatly lacking for trafficked girls all over the world is protection—and ongoing social services that will replace the jail.

"Many women, having worked as prostitutes, seem convinced that they are incapable of earning a living another way," (49) writes Finnegan. There's a reason for this, Mr. Finnegan. Actually, many. Fear. Even if she escapes her traffickers, there is no where for her to go, and no one for her to talk to. "Once a whore always a whore" applies to us since we can never regain any self-esteem—this is yet another terrible reason women can never really 'escape' prostitution once they have been forced into it.

When you are soft and not tough and feminine, the way I am, the violence of rape damage is permanent. I panic every day now that I am older and know I cannot sell myself anymore. Selling myself is all that I am capable of doing—terrified as I am of it. No matter how many books I write, or how many college degrees I get, I am still in prostitution. It is an environment that never lets you go.

I can't find a country where I can be safe. They all rape us.

The United Nations doesn't seem to care about the fate of whores. In fact, their peacekeepers create a demand for them. Michael Fleshman's "AIDS Prevention in the Ranks" is a good example of the UN attitude—identical to the military one, by the way: only the soldiers matter, and whether they have AIDS—the whores are disposable and negligible—except in so far as they are disease carriers. Fleshman links war, peacekeepers, and 'commercial sex workers,' yet with almost no emphasis on the behavior of men and that there is anything wrong with their buying of women. The cold phrase 'commercial sex worker' cannot in any way express the bleeding sad misery of the girls forced to fuck peacekeepers for food. Forty-five percent of the Dutch peacekeepers in Cambodia engaged in sex with prostituted beings. (I have actually read numbers way higher than this—try 80%--those Dutch guys did not keep their dicks in their pants when massage parlours and adolescent prostitution blossomed as a result of their presence and the desire of pimps to take advantage of this lucrative demand market.) The UN solution to the Dutch presence: hand out condoms. Only token attention to changing the behavior and attitudes of the men, token recognition of the vulnerability of young girls to the military presence.

It is no wonder that these peacekeepers, and their fellow aid workers, are still raping child prostitutes all over the world.

Even the title of this article indicates the emphasis—only the men matter! The attitude seems to be that the men can't control their dicks and, except for AIDS, we wouldn't expect them to, after all, boys will be boys. Only "containing the epidemic" is important—otherwise, it would be rape business as usual—wink, nod.

There is medical care for peacekeepers but none for the prostitutes they infect and destroy. The more I read, the more I think that the only reason not just the UN but the world is paying attention to trafficking is because of AIDS. There is minimal humanitarian emphasis on the in-pain, raped, shredded, destroyed trafficked girl. She only matters because the more men rape her kind, the more they will infect these girls—and then she will pass it on to other rapists. Then those rapists will take it home to the women who matter—the ones called 'decent'—the ones not turned into whores.

Also, I never find anyone in these articles who writes about what is important. Like the way those tiny, tiny Cambodian adolescents must have died, been killed by the pain, when used by all those big Dutch men. How lower abdomen pain was probably intense due to infected uteruses and ruptured ovaries due to the men being too big. The poor little things don't even weigh in at ninety pounds and they have the bodies of children. One Cambodian teenage girl who was trafficked to Europe says her pain was intense in the bottom part of her stomach due to the men being too big for her. Pelvic inflammatory disease, cervical displasia, raw and torn vaginas, all the mess of forced constant intercourse. How come this UN article mentioned none of that? The author pays some attention to women's rights toward the end of the piece but clearly his emphasis is on male bodies, lives, and needs. Women seem incidental to his analysis.

Gordon Thomas' *Enslaved* is useful for his information on the Iraqi military under Hussein. Trucks with girls full of trafficked girls from Thailand were driven to Iraq and into Kuwait. "Crammed into the truck were more than fifty young Thai girls. They had been kidnapped from their villages in northern Thailand by slavers and then brought to Iraq to replenish Saddam's brothels, which had been set up in Kuwait and behind the defense lines of Iraq's army. With a million men under arms, thousands of girls were needed as 'troop comforters.'

"Saddam had ordered that Iraqi women not be used as whores. Instead, many of the hundreds of Filipinas and other Asian women stranded in Kuwait had already been pressed into service" (2). Scary to think of what is going on now in Iraq since so many Iraqi women have been turned into whores. How many of their own soldiers are using them?

Let the Good Times Roll: Prostitution and the U.S. Military in Asia, written by two religious women, Saundra Pollock Sturdevant and Brenda Stoltzfus, is one of the few books that actually interviews prostituted beings. They talk to a Ms. Pak in Korea who is afraid to become a whore for the American soldiers since she is afraid of their big penises. They interview girls working as whores for the American military in the Philippines and Okinawa and everywhere they go what they find are repressive and degrading conditions—like girls being held as virtual prisoners, and being forced to dance naked in bars, and have sex in the corners of the bars, and do blow jobs in public places and be 'three-holers' when 'required.'

It is an invaluable book but I heavily object to the way they call what the girls do 'sexual labour.' That's like calling it 'sex work,' and by now you should know my objections to that despicable phrase.

The authors write: "We really know very little about the physical and spiritual wounds that result from the isolation, the griefs, the denial of human rights, and the breakdown of...human relationships that come...from the selling of sexual labor. From one worker counseling Okinawan women who provided sexual labor to U.S. military men over an extended period of time during the Vietnam War era, Takasato Suzuyo writes about the woman who has ongoing delusions of sexual persecution and becomes greatly agitated and unusually nervous twice a month, on the fifteenth and thirtieth—paydays for U.S. troops. Or the woman who has yet to find a drug that will allow her mind to rest at night and not be filled with images of being raped by gangs of U.S. soldiers, which is what providing sexual labor to twenty or thirty men a night amounts to" (302).

What is described above is of course no different from the anguish that any comfort girl experiences, like my Dubai Girl.

Concerning paycheck-day anxiety, I can attest to a bit of that since when the men at the base where I prostituted myself got paid, more of them would call for appointments with me. Even though I had a lot of control over who I went with—since no pimp or owner ruled over me--still I tried not to turn down the regulars since I was going with them for a reason—they were the more decent lot and I knew they were 'safe' and would not hit me or hurt me. So, I would end up having intercourse maybe six or ten times a day, for several days, until paycheck time died out. It was way too much, by the way. Unthinkable to me how any girl could survive twenty or thirty times a day. My situation was nothing like the beyond pathetic one of the girl described below:

On Okinawa, the authors tell us, about 15,000 girls were enslaved during the Vietnam War, controlled by the *Yakuza*, and used to serve the soldier on R & R from the war. "Control was exercised through physical and psychological terror and intimidation." The girls were held in debt bondage. "One woman who worked in Kin…describes her situation during the Vietnam period:

'Most customers are soldiers from the base…I arrived at this place… seven years ago. I don't know how it worked, but my [debt] never diminished, even though I had twenty or thirty customers a night. Instead the sum increased, because an additional $5 or $10 was added as a fine whenever I had my period or was pregnant and couldn't take any customers'" (307).

I don't think I would have been alive after seven weeks of this pathetic life, let along seven years. Who are these despicable soldier rapists who climbed on this pathetic woman at the rate of 20 or 30 men a night? My former military boyfriends and former military customers did not tell me what they had done in Okinawa and Japan was so beyond horrifying. I had no idea they were mass raping these poor girls as a norm. How did this woman make it? How did she have a mind left after this kind of torture? How could she even speak after years of mass rape? How did she still have a body left after the numbers that mounted her? How did she have a body left after one night, let along seven years? If you do the multiplication, she would have been raped over a hundred times a week, 400 times a month, 4000 times a year (at a conservative estimate). Over those seven years, she would have been raped perhaps 30,000 times? Raped by 30,000 different men. Could she tell the difference anymore, between men? They must have all felt like rapists to her, even the 'nice' ones.

Why is there no rape crisis center for her, I wonder? The good American girl gets all upset if she is raped one time and thinks that this merits a suicide attempt. What about this pathetic whore who never had time to recover from one rape when thousands of others were visited on her devastated body. Left for rape-dead, after R & R. (Where are the other girls, those 15,000? Most are probably dead from those years of rape and abuse. And their rapist/murderers have gone free.)

What I cannot forget is the men who did this to her—men I knew as boyfriends, when I was not in prostitution, and customers, later, when I was. Who are these monster GI rapists who would climb on a near dead-from-pain body, thirty monster GI rapists in a row, night after night? I remember a long time ago reading a poem by an ex-GI, Vietnam vet, about how he climbed on a whore in a tin-hut brothel and how as soon as he came out the next guy unzipped and went in. This GI came home and went to college and became a teacher. I would never want a daughter of mine near him, as a teacher. Did he have daughters of his own? If so, how dare he even be allowed near them, after his rape of that already thoroughly raped little whore girl.

I remember all the ugly stories Vietnam vets brought home—about how you could get the really cheap whores to do a line of your buddies while you took pictures. I was appalled by the sadness and tragedy of this—that any woman could be reduced to this level. The vets just thought it was funny. A dirty joke. I don't understand how these men could have girlfriends and wives and daughters in the States after treating a woman like that in Vietnam. Did it never occur to one of them that it could be their own daughter—treated like that? Degrade one girl and you degrade us all. A man can never be a gentleman or a human being after treating any girl that way. If he rapes one girl, he will rape us all. It is like the soldier in the war in the Congo right now who says he is having fun raping—it's all part of war—and then after the war he'll marry a pure girl and settle down.

He will be a rapist forever. The men who came back from Vietnam who used prostituted girls are rapists forever. No matter how many poems they write about it—to show how 'sensitive' they are. Bullshit to this kind of 'sensitivity,' I say. They raped. No poem with ever erase that.

The world is on the side of the Vietnam-vet rapists. No one cares what they did. The only ones who care are they girls whose lives and bodies they destroyed forever in Vietnam and on Okinawa. And most of these girls are probably dead by now. I hope they are dead—for there is no way they can live with the memories of what was done to their bodies—and their lives.

I cannot be in the same room with a Vietnam vet. Mass raping helpless enslaved little whore girls in brothels. Then coming home and claiming all this PTSD, gotten, I presume because they were forced to rape all these child-size girls.

The hardest thought for me to bear is that my Vic, the man I loved most, contributed to the mass rape of brothel girls in Korea, during that war. The man I loved the most in the world was a monster GI rapist.

I think the military owes reparation to every prostitute our military has ever used. This goes for the girls trafficked into the bars and brothels around our bases now as well.

I learned a lot of other interesting facts from this book. Like how during WWII, 50 million condoms were either sold or handed out per month. (The men obviously didn't use them--given how high the VD rates were.)

One American military study reports that during the course of the war, 80% of single men and 50% of married ones used prostituted bodies. When I read stats like this, I wonder that anyone questions my contention that almost all men are rapists.

Quote from a sailor: "Pussy, that's what the Philippines is all about" (Sturdevant and Stoltzfus 326).

The authors rightly speculate that you must keep prostituted women isolated from decent women--'polarized' is the word they use. Keeping the rape-the-whore system going depends on the 'silence' not only of the prostitute (she has never been considered important enough to listen to) but also the 'silence' on the part of the protected women who chose not to know what is going on (310). Is that ever true. My era, Vietnam, saw massive insensitive denial and ignorance on the part of American women about their heavily raped sisters in Asia. This insensitivity alienated me completely from the women of my generation. I am ashamed to be part of that generation of heartless, vaginaless women.

And, of course, as the authors point out, the military does not want any one to know about what GIs do on leave, on liberty, during off duty hours (315).

Once, I read a comment about one of my articles on the internet that really pleased me. The woman said: "Women like this one have never spoken before, they're not supposed to. It shocks the world."

Next come the three books that changed my life. Reading about what happened to the Occupation Comfort Girls—the girls prostituted to the GI's in Japan after WWII--so disturbed and moved me that I had to do something. So I started writing. This book you are reading, plus five novels which satirize military prostitution, are the result so far. There will be more—one day.

I had powerful, powerful responses as I read these books. I include some of them as comments on the passages I quote.

First, John Dower's *Embracing Defeat: Japan in the Wake of World War II.*

A few wrenching excerpts from his chapter on the Occupation Comfort Girls, the sex slaves recruited to service the American GI's under torture conditions identical to what the Korean Comfort Girls endured:

In a 1947 interview, a prostitute said that once you do this can't ever be accepted again, no other kind of job is ever possible. "You can't trust society. They despise us" (124).

"To the government's surprise professional prostitutes proved reluctant to service the foreigners because they were afraid that the 'oversized sexual organs' of the Americans could injure them."

The Japanese government advertised for the rape prisoners who would occupy the rape factories (my phrasing) in this way: "Seeking the active cooperation of new Japanese women to participate in the great task of comforting the occupation forces." The ads offered housing, food, and clothing. "Most of the women attracted by this advertisement arrived shabbily dressed. Some…were even barefoot. The great majority had had no experience in the 'water trade'" (127).

The procurers who ran the Recreation and Amusement Association (what the brothels were euphemistically called) declared: "We hope to promote mutual understanding between [the Allies occupation forces] and our people, and to contribute to the smooth development of people's diplomacy and abet the construction of a peaceful world."

My comment on this: when does rape = peace for a woman—never. For men I guess it always does. This is Rape Planet Earth and it belongs to them.

On the first day that the first 'rape station' (my term for it) opened, "several hundred GI's quickly found the facility in Tokyo's Omori district, where a small number of mostly inexperienced recruits had been gathered. Neither beds, futons, nor room partitions were available, and fornication took place without privacy everywhere, even in the corridors" (128).

"One naïve recruit to the R.A.A. later recalled the terror of her first day, when she was called on to service twenty-three American soldiers. By one estimate, R.A.A women engaged between fifteen and sixty GIs a day. A nineteen-year-old who had previously been a typist committed suicide almost immediately. Some broke down or deserted. By mid-September, however, this grotesque exercise in 'people's diplomacy' had become more or less routine" (128).

My comment: I am glad that Dower regards all of this as grotesque (it is actually the norm in all war and post-war arenas, by the way) but I do wish he would also write about the brutal, cruel and beyond belief searingly painful torture as the conquerors' penises go in and out and in and out and in and out of the shredded bleeding holes thousands upon thousands of times. This is my history. It is the one I would write if I could, if the world would let me—which it never will. I am not a Dower, a male historian. So my history will never really matter. It is interesting that he uses the word 'routine' in the above passage. It is one I would use as well—to express my idea that rape is simply a norm for the male.

Dower's use of words like 'service' and 'engage' give the impression that this was not a searingly hot and miserable act of rape—it gives the impression that the men were blameless for the rape. And I wish that he would explain how the men could do this if the girls were crying and terrified?

I suppose historians never need to 'engage' this side of history. After all, 'rape diplomacy' is always 'routine.'

He also says that the naïve prostituted girl was 'called upon' to service twenty-three men in one day. What a mild phrase. 'Called upon.' Like in a classroom. To answer a question. I think the girls probably cried and screamed and died and fainted when 'called upon.' It was not a mild, calm act for them. And one day of being so 'called upon,' I know will ruin a girl forever—it will take away her soul and life—to be used by twenty-three men she does not know, in one day. This is far more than being 'called upon.' It is rape-death of the helpless. 'Called upon,' indeed.

"Such 'recreation and amusement' centers expanded rapidly in Tokyo… and spread almost as quickly to some twenty other cities. Not surprisingly, they proved popular among U.S. servicemen. They were, among other things, inexpensive. The price for a short visit with an R.A.A. prostitute was 15 yen, or one dollar—about the same as a half a pack of cigarettes…Two or three times that purchased an entire night of personal diplomacy" (Dower 130).

This paragraph filled me with such hopeless pain and despair that I had to stop reading for a while. Then I reconciled myself, in my thoughts, to the ultimate truth: Rape is an amazingly popular activity all over Rape Planet Earth. Why should it shock me that almost every GI in post-war Tokyo practiced it with gusto—and he got his rape so cheap, too. Who could resist rape at such an economical price?

Reconciled to hopelessness, I continued reading, despite my depression that nowhere does Dower call this rape. Fifteen to sixty GI's a day. Damn, I couldn't even handle half a dozen a day raping me. The big overload of rape I got one day when that half a dozen climbed on and then didn't stop there—they all went again—that day was pure rape hell that I have never recovered from. Once, just once, I was raped as many times as these girls endured for burning months of rape hell. And I didn't survive. How did they? This is the kind of history I want to see written—one that answers this question.

As many others, in addition to Dower, have pointed out "these services did not prevent rape and assault…" (130).

First, I need to say, quite emphatically, that what was taking place inside the 'comfort houses' was a rape hell--one far in excess of the rapes committed on the 'civilian' girls. After all, how can forty rapes a day, inflicted on one body—day after day—even be in the same rape-zone as just one rape on a 'civilian' body? Even one gang rape on a civilian body cannot compare to the daily forty inflicted on the 'professional' whore body—rendered 'professional,' I assume, by continuous violation.

I cried all the way through my second reading of Dower; during my first reading I was so shocked by the facts that I got really cold with fear, and my own rape pain--and then I threw up.

Dower tells us that "despite its popularity and initial support from the victors, the R.A.A. did not survive the early months of the occupation. In January, 1946, occupation authorities ordered the abolition of all 'public' prostitution, declaring it undemocratic and in violation of women's human rights. Privately, they acknowledged that their major motivation was an alarming rise in venereal disease among the troops. By the time the prohibition went into effect a few months later, almost 90 percent of the R.A.A. women tested positive for infection. Around the same time, syphilis was detected in 70 percent of the members of a single unit of the U.S. Eighth Army, and gonorrhea in 50 percent."

My emotional responses to passages like the above are powerful. I am not sure if my fury is a good thing or not. It tears me apart but at least it lets me tell the world that one mind does not consider this situation acceptable. It is outrageous, what was done to these girls—with total impunity. Virgins when they were 'recruited.' This was the typical 'comfort girl' provided to the American troops. A virgin, destitute, very young. So where did the VD come from, I want to know? Where were the GI's raping other prostituted bodies before they inflicted syphilis and gonorrhea on these poor girls? I cannot even imagine the misery of these poor creatures. Virgins. Then having their insides raped out of them day after day; then finding they have these dreadful diseases. And then the U.S. military comes up with a fake pronouncement about 'violating women's human rights' after these girls have had their bodies forcibly invaded thousands of times. All of this in the name of good, clean, GI 'fun.' And then we have some big pronouncement about 'public' prostitution (whatever that is) being abolished for the 'good' of the girls? Well, prostitution continued in even greater force and even greater numbers after all this 'fake' concern for the massively raped girls. Where does it ever end? Never. Sixty years later—no change in attitude: the whore gave all those sweet, wholesome boys diseases. The whore is the blight. Not the rape-shit male soldier. He is 'honored' for being a 'courageous, noble' rape-shit male soldier. The male insanity of the world is beyond anything I can counter—even if I were to write a thousand books.

This is the big mystery for me: what happened to all of these girls? If 90 percent of them were syphilitic and all of them had had the insides raped out of them, everyday, without mercy, where did they go to die? Or to try to continue living—even though I know there is no 'survival' after such torture. 'Prostitution survivor' refers to a raped ghost, not a living being anymore. The aftereffects would have been identical to what the Korean Comfort Women carried with them the rest of their lives: broken bodies and dead spirits. Why is there not one single interview with an Occupation Comfort Girl? Why has not one single girl come forward? I know it is impossible to face the world after your vagina and insides have been destroyed—since that kind of destruction takes the rest of you with it—but is there not even one girl who could speak—the way the Korean Comfort Girls finally did? At least one must still be alive?—in some sense of the word. I puzzle greatly about this—just the way I puzzle that not one brothel whore from Vietnam has ever spoken—or one Italian whore forced to fuck long lines of GI's for that can of Spam. It is a huge mystery—only one group of women, those courageous Korean ones, have spoken.

(A note on terminology: I prefer Korean Comfort Girl, Occupation Comfort Girl, instead of 'Woman' since we are talking about teens here—girls fifteen and sixteen, even younger, mere babies.)

Reasons why girls became prostitutes? According to Dower, it is because they were "war orphans, or…had no fathers." Some were also gang raped by American and Australian soldiers and felt they were worth nothing except to be raped some more. (I definitely recognized this compelling logic: after my own gang rape, there was nothing else I could do except invite more rape in the form of prostitution.)

"Regular force rotations continued to bring in hundreds of thousands of new troops to staff the quarter-million-man occupation army and those who chose the path of chastity during their tour of duty were by all accounts exceptional. By one estimate, almost half of the many tens of millions of dollars that occupation personnel spent on 'recreation' passed through the hands of the [panpans]" (Dower 138).

'Passed through' is probably accurate since it would not have stayed with them. As in all forms of prostitution over the past 3000 years, pimp-coercion and owner- and brothel-control in the form of debt bondage would have taken the bulk of her rape earnings. Few prostitutes ever get to keep any kind of substantial sum--no matter what the era, country, or circumstances.

The second book is George Hicks' *The Comfort Women: Japan's Brutal Regime of Enforced Prostitution in the Second World War.* I learned from Hicks that the Korean Comfort Women were sometimes forced to "continue their role with the American troops." This happened on Okinawa, in Korea, in Burma, and North Borneo. Probably elsewhere as well.

In Tokyo, virgin girls were taken to comfort stations where, Hicks writes, "at night, the American soldiers claimed from them the same sort of service their Japanese counterparts had [from comfort women]. Any girls trying to escape were forced back by Japanese guards…given access to an organised brothel, the Americans may not have thought of what they were doing in terms of rape."

Here are some more passages from Hicks on the pathetic plight of girls given to U.S. soldiers:

"Nine homeless girls in Hiroshima were taken to a "wooden two-storey house. There they were searched by Occupation navy men, covered all the while by firearms…there were suspicions they might be carrying knives to defend themselves. Then they were raped until they lost consciousness."

"Later they were taken to a more permanent comfort station....One at least took her own life."

Japanese authorities and police "made it clear [they] would tolerate the employment of gangs if intimidation were necessary to recruit adequate numbers of comfort women."

"Given the Occupation-induced boom in prostitution, it is not surprising that the first rebuilding from war devastation occurred in red-light districts"

"The question must surely be: Are not all women the victims of wars started by men. Does the abuse and victimisation of women have to be on the scale of the comfort system to become worthy of attention?"

The third book, Yuki Tanaka's *Japan's Comfort Women: Sexual Slavery and Prostitution During World War II and the US Occupation,* is the book, the one with the words that changed my life.

They sit at the top page 155, this passage that set in motion this whole book of mine you are reading. It has haunted and disturbed me. For weeks after I read it, it stayed in my mind like a miserable ache. From this one little section has grown all the pain and outrage of my own words. My novels grew out of it. These are the few words that changed my life: "We had one girl there who served 50 men in one night. She was very busy and the American soldiers stood in line to get at her...."

It shocked me beyond belief to realize that all those ordinary men—all the 350,000 or so stationed in Japan in 1945—were rapists. That rape is the norm. This is what I found so troubling. It is what I cannot rid myself of when I am with men who know nothing about my past—and this means all men since I tell no one who and what I really am—a whore. It haunts me that their politeness would turn to crudeness, maybe even to the roughness of rape—if I were still young enough to be raped as a whore.

I could have been that girl that 50 men lined up to 'get at.' Who was she? Was she raped 50 times every day? Surely, she had the same vagina as the Korean Comfort Girls. Surely, she was damaged just as they were: torn, bleeding vagina; infected and ruptured sex organs. Surely, her mental state was the same as that of the Korean Comfort Girls: dazed, rape-shock, insanity, numbness, unbearable psychological pain. Didn't the American soldiers see all this? If so, why did they keep raping her?

What happened to her? What was her name? I will give her name, Daisy, in despair. I don't know how else to commemorate her terrible pain. I cannot 'comfort' her in any way. But I can give her a name--even if it does her no good so many years later. At least I can think of her as 'Daisy,' to keep her from the complete rape-oblivion that male history has visited on her. She is just a fuckhole that 50 men 'got at' in the male version of history, quoted above from the 'official report' of the period.

"Sex becomes a source of brutality and oppression, instead of one of joy and life, when it is exploited in warfare," writes Tanaka in his introduction. "Military violence involves atrocious abuse of women's sexuality."

"Sex is a beautiful and extremely enjoyable human activity when it confirms…the intimate relationship with a partner. When out of control, however, sex becomes ugly and monstrously abusive" (1).

I am so glad he opens with these kinds of thoughts since one of the painful puzzles of my life is how can such pleasure that the soldiers took on top of me have caused me such pain.

Tanaka is aware of his father's silence on the comfort women of the war, and he is troubled that if he had been in the military would he have also used them? Apparently none of the millions of Japanese men who did this ever talked about it. But, then, neither did the GI's talk about the rape queues they got in—in Tokyo and Palermo and elsewhere.

As Tanaka says, "The U.S. War Department not only distributed massive numbers of condoms and provided 'prophylactic stations' to their troops overseas, but also deliberately kept silent about the military-controlled brothels that their men frequented" (98).

Since the U.S. set up brothels to control VD and improve troop morale—identical to what the Japanese did, "It was therefore quite natural that they were completely unable to discern the criminal nature of the comfort women system" (Tanaka 109)

Tanaka devotes a section to the widespread rape and gang rape on Okinawa during and after the invasion. As an example of a cover-up, I would instance *Teahouse of the August Moon*, a play set during the post-war occupation of Okinawa in which there is not a raped or prostituted body in sight—except for one absolutely voracious and persistent young whore who is determined to corrupt those GI's—no matter what. This is the kind of 'fantasy,' called war propaganda, we are exposed to.

On page 138, there is a terrifying photo of huge numbers of sailors waiting to get into a Yokosuka rape station. This photo made my stomach hurt so much I had to stop and go do something else, to rid myself of squirming with pain. What those poor wretched women must have felt, the cold burning fear, as they heard the noises of men at play, jostling to get in, to get at them. I would have peed with fear, and vomited with fear.

The girls recruited by the so-called Recreation and Amusement Association (your recreation and amusement, my pain and death), were "young women who had become war orphans and young widow who had lost their husbands during the war" (Tanaka 146).

"By the time the occupying forces landed, the RAA had managed to set up only Komachien [which translates as Babe Garden]. As a result this comfort station was flooded with GIs with as early as August 30. There were only 38 comfort women in the station. Given the demand, they hardly had time to rest or have a meal. Shortly thereafter, the RAA recruited new women, managing to increase the number of comfort women at the station to 100. Even then, it is said the minimum number of clients that each comfort woman had to serve each day was 15. One woman was said to have served 60 GIs a day" (Tanaka 147).

If you do the math, these numbers indicate about 1500 men a day were making rape visits to the brothel and that the initial girls were raped about 40 times a day. I don't really see how this is any different from what the Korean Comfort Women endured. This is a war crime on the part of those GI's as vicious as anyone can imagine.

I always wonder why some women are singled out for the worst in abuse. The one who had to 'take on' 60 GI's a day, for example. What made her 'different'—that the men visited such torture on her? It is the same question I would ask myself when I heard Vietnam vets who talked about the 'really cheap whores' that would 'let' the GI's mount them in public—all these rape buddies taking turns on the girl as other guys took pictures. Why should this girl be different from one who is born as a princess and treated as precious and fragile? It makes no sense to me.

Let's take a detour back to the testimonies of the Korean Comfort Girls, to remind ourselves what rape by thirty to fifty men a day feels like—just in case we are tempted to think it was any different for the bodies of the Occupation Comfort Girls. This time the book is *Comfort Women Speak: Testimony by Sex Slaves of the Japanese Military* but it is the same nightmare of shame and torment we have seen. Here are some sections from it:

"I worked from 8 in the morning till 10 at night....I was forced to have sex with 20 to 40 soldiers a day...we all ended up having venereal diseases.... Some girls became hysterical and crazy."

"The most painful thing was continuous, forced sex act with soldiers. Saturdays and Sundays were the worst, facing 30 to 40 men a day I felt like a living corpse. When soldiers came to my room and did it to me one after another, it was done to a lifeless body. Again. And again. And again..." (55).

"I was forced to service sex to…40 to 50 on Sundays. We were exhausted, weakened, and some of us could not even eat meals. We were in the state of the 'half-dead.' Some girls became really sick and could not recover from the ordeal" (50).

"I became ill soon after I became a sex slave and started to bleed severely through my vagina…I frequently thought of killing myself…I had poor health. I was still bleeding, and it became worse when I received many men" (39).

(I would object strongly to the translator's use of the word "received"—as if this were a polite drawing room scene and she were serving tea to the men. Words are important. They need to reflect reality. This is not a drawing room teatime scene. This is a rape killing field. This is not about politeness. This is about massively swollen and in- pain vaginas).

I think the above can help us to do a simple equation: Korean Comfort Girl = Occupation Comfort Girl = Modern Day Comfort Girl in the form of the Dubai one who had a different Pakistani laborer climb on her every fifteen minutes.

Disturbing as the testimonies above are, there was one in this book that bothered me more. A comfort girl said:

"There were some real prostitutes in the building. I was told each of them could take twenty to forty men a night. You could tell them apart…in the public bathhouse. They applied cosmetic all over their bodies after bath. It was because their skin turned dark from abusing drink and drugs" (83).

Amazing! Astounding! Depressing beyond life and belief. Even after being treated like a 'communal sex toilet,' this comfort girl has no sympathy or understanding for the 'real prostitute' who is actually identical to her. How is "could take twenty to forty men a night" any kind of indication of the voluntary? How is this different from what is happening to her? Does the 'real prostitute' have some kind of cast-iron vagina? Is it not obvious that the 'real' prostitute is taking drugs and drinking to bear the pain of sex with 20 to 40 men a night? Does this comfort girl assume that the 'real' prostitute is a different species from her, that she can 'do' huge numbers of men and have it not hurt and destroy her? Amazing.

"Sell your daughters here," said the signs at the edges of the red-light districts of Japan and the girls were caged and continuously raped in order to render them insensible to the disgust and pain of intercourse with many crude ugly coarse filthy men. There is no difference. And there is no difference between any comfort girl and the Dubai Girl, rendered numb and docile and turned into a fuck machine by her mass rape in the Pakistani labor camp.

The above Korean Comfort Girl who thinks she is so different from the 'real prostitute' reminds me of a trafficked girl interviewed in Victor Malarek's *The Natashas*. She is rescued and is in a sanctuary in Italy where she wants to make it clear that she is not one of those 'bad' girls, she is not really a prostitute. She didn't want to do this. Who does? Would the 'bad' girl invite beating, cigarette burns, rape to the point of near death and insanity? These blind idiots—the prostitutes who condemn other prostitutes-- with their deep, deep sexual prejudices keep all of us women in sexual chains.

My disgust at the other women of the world—especially the whores who condemn other whores and the 'respectable' safe women without a clue and the academicians with their tidy, cold, unfurnished minds—these women fill me with such despair and revulsion, that I am just about to violate the basic principle of my life: never give up fighting for lost causes—they are the only ones worth fighting for. (Not an original idea, alas, I wish I had thought of it—I.F. Stone said it first.)

Are these kinds of blind, severely prejudiced, vaginaless, uncompassionate women worth fighting for? I am beginning to think not. As long as we women let these prisons of patriarchal thought and repression twist and pervert our beautiful sexuality, we are doomed. As long as women buy into the idea that there are 'bad' girls out there who deserve to be 'real prostitutes,' it is more than hopeless.

I think the big shock of all my reading in order to be able to write this book was not discovering that all men are rapists. It was my disgust with the women enabling them to be rapists since women condemn their own sisters as whores and sluts and think they 'deserve' what they get. Damn.

Oh, well, all I know is that the life of an Occupation Comfort Girl for even two days would have destroyed me, even if I was on the low-end of the rape scale and only had to 'comfort' fifteen GI's a night instead of sixty.

That one day that I was raped fifteen times almost killed me. In fact, I didn't survive. I am always a raped whore in pain. How could these other girls make it? The fact is, if you look at the testimonies we do have of what mass rape daily does to a girl—those of the Korean Comfort Girls--we see they did not survive either. They say their life was taken from them. I guess it is no wonder that there is not one testimony from an Occupation Comfort Girl. They are probably all dead—in every sense of the word.

To return to Tanaka, we own him such a debt for writing about these poor forgotten ones. He brings in information from a reporter named Mark Gayn of the *Chicago Sun*, who was there on the spot as the comfort station rapes were happening. He describes the RAA delivering a truck load of virgin girls to a unit stationed near Tachikawa—

"Long after night fall, GI's heard the sound of an approaching truck. When it was within hailing distance, one of the sentries yelled 'Halt!' The truck stopped, and from it emerged a Japanese man, with a flock of young women. Warily, they walked toward the waiting GI's. When they came close, the man stopped, bowed respectfully, swept the ground behind him with a wide, generous gesture, and said, 'Compliments of the Recreation and Amusement Association!'" (148).

The sheer ugliness of this picture devastates me. Were they raped into unconsciousness, I wonder?

There were "drunken GI's" who "demanded refunds, claiming the service was poor." I wonder how on earth or in the heavens a man can expect 'good service' from a rape-dead body?

In terms of numbers, the extent of what these rapists did is horrifying: just in one area of Tokyo alone, the prophylactic stations were visited by 10,000 GI's a week (Tanaka 151). The scale of this rape is terrifying.

"For some newly recruited comfort women, who had not been previously associated with the business, it must have been an unbearable experience. For example, Takita Natsue, a 19-year-old girl who had lost all her relatives to the bombing, was one of the new comfort women at Komachien. Only a few days after the opening of the station she committed suicide" (Tanaka 149).

Tanaka draws upon extracts from the diary of Mark Gayn, the Canadian journalist who saw the comfort stations first hand. Gayn writes that due to heavy turnover, men jokingly called the International Palace Brothel in Tokyo "Willow Run" after a Ford factory in Detroit "because…it processed its product on such a huge scale…" (153).

He does an interview with a girl—finally : "She said she was nineteen, and had never been a prostitute until she joined Willow Run five months ago. She now owed the company 10,000 yen (about $660), mostly for the clothes she bought at the brothel store. We got similar stories from the other girls. Most of them had lost their families in the American fire raids." As you can see, the procurers, pimps, and owners are right in there, holding the girls in debt bondage, so that they will die from the rape without even making a cent off of their own pitiful bodies.

As I read Gayn's account, I wondered how he could observe all this without making any attempt to help the girls.

He describes the pitiful cubicles where they fuck—"each tiny room separated by a low partition, and a thin curtain for a door. Each entrance had a crayon-coloured sign reading, 'Well Come, Kimi,' or 'Well Come, Haruko,' those being the names of the occupants."

("Well Come" to her rapists says the girl, in proper Japanese rape-etiquette style: My comment.)

More from Gayn: "Every twenty-four hours a woman 'processed' an average of 15 GI's, each of whom paid 50 yen, or $3.30. Of this amount, half went to the management and the other half was kept by the woman. Out of this income, the women paid for their food, medical expenses, cosmetics and clothes. I did a rapid bit of calculating. Among them, the 250 women 'processed' 3,750 GI's every twenty-four hours. This meant a daily income of $6,200 for the International Palace."

Of which, as we have seen, the girl kept little due to what the brothel charged her for 'expenses.' Concerning the 'processing,' did Gayn in any way know what this word meant as regards the violation of tender female bodies? At the rate of 15 men a day, it meant unimaginable physical damage and mental misery on a level one can never find words for. The other 'comfort girls'—the Korean ones—tried and told us of their bleeding, torn insides and of how many girls didn't make it—they became hysterical, insane, killed themselves. These 'processing' conditions inflicted on the Occupation Comfort Girls are identical to the ones the Korean Comfort Girls endured—and sometimes died from. Where are the Occupation Comfort Girls' stories? I myself could not 'process' half a dozen soldiers a day without severe physical pain—and emotional distress. Fifteen a day would have killed me. Does Gayn in any way realize the sheer disgust these girls must have felt at invasion by 15 men a day they did not know? How does the word 'processing' cover all this? And how does the joking around of the men about this Detroit assembly-line sex make it alright? Did this Canadian journalist also laugh and make dirty jokes as he watched the girls process their 15 men a day? Did he have a wife or sister or daughter back home? Did he see no connection between the unimaginable rape of these girls and what could happen to his own wife or daughter if they were sold into brothel beds? I would of course ask that question of the hundreds of thousands of men who used enslaved girls during the occupation. If usage was almost 100% during the occupation, we have an entire generation of men who are the mass, serial rapists of helpless bodies—and they have never been punished for this unimaginable sexual murder of these girls lives and bodies.

We really need a lot more than this kind of 'processing' coverage of the mass military rape of the female body. And we never get it. The current situation of trafficked girls 'processing' military men around the world is not being described by hardly anyone. We need all female journalists on this story. Right now. In 2009. No more waiting for accurate coverage of Rape Planet Earth. And we don't need anymore 'processing' words used to describe unbearable savaging of the bleeding, raped female body. We need descriptions of the twisted, gargoyle faces girls make when raped; and of the dead blankness in their eyes when they give up and cannot even feel the rape-torture anymore, due to numbness. We need descriptions of how the girls can't walk when the pain comes back. We need everything from now on told from the point of view of the rape-tortured whore body. And I know we will never get it. Female journalists in 2009 have not a clue. They are as blind and callous as the male world they report on and slavishly dote on.

The American higher-ups knew full well what was happening as regards the enslavement of these girls but did nothing since it was necessary for them to have cheap fuck deposit sites for the GI's and these despicable officers had no hearts in them to care with. I quote a Lt. Colonel commenting on the "practice of procuring girls" for the brothels: "The girl is impressed into contracting by...desperate financial straits" (Tanaka 158). He says this and yet has no heart in him to help the girls, even though his own daughter could be one of these pitiful beings, if she were starving and homeless in the ruins of Tokyo. The monster that is the male is beyond my ability to withstand, or understand.

The photographs in Tanaka's book are very disturbing—the whores have deep sadness in their eyes and they look like children beside their conquerors, so tiny, half their size and yet raped anyway. I guess it is natural for men to rape girl children. The helplessness must fill them with great joy at their virility.

Another official document from Public Health and Welfare (PHW) of GHQ of the U.S. military states: "There are many girls who desire to keep on in this business. Most have lost one or both parents in the bombing, and have no funds and no means of livelihood otherwise" (Tanaka 154). "Desire to"? "Desire to"?? "Desire to"??? The men must see the reluctance born of desperation and rape. The men must see that there is another solution—very simple and humane—feed the girls, protect them, help them, don't make them fuck for food. Yet the time-honored historical imperative of man must have his fuck on the helpless defenseless conquered pathetic sad little starving whore reigns supreme. The Rapist Shit Male, in all his despicable brutality, rules the world and all of history. For women, history is only one thing: the necessity to fuck for food in the face of the brutal sex drive of the male.

Tanaka reports that about 10,000 sex slaves for the GI's had been recruited by the end of 1945—since there were 350,000 soldiers needing servicing, this means each woman was being raped about thirty-five times a day. Of course, if the men were getting back in line, as young men tend to do—they want more than one fuck, the girls may have been raped by two or three times this number of GI's.

Rape outside the comfort stations was widespread, particularly gang rape. A 24-year-old maidservant abducted by soldiers in a truck was taken to the "U.S. Barracks in Nogeyama Park. There altogether 27 of the American soldiers violated her in turn and rendered her unconscious…" (Tanaka 121). I would ask: Do the men who did this have fond memories of this event if they are still alive? When they went home in 1946 or 1947, did they go on picnics with their wives and play games with their daughters while thinking what fun they had raping a girl nearly to death in Japan? How did they reconcile such torture inflicted on this girl with being the good, upstanding, noble, fine Christian soldiers that they were? Did they tell the same crude, ugly jokes when they came home as I heard from returning Vietnam vets during my era: these men joked around all the time about the girls they degraded and violated in Vietnam. It was just men having 'fun.' The girls were just 'filth' and didn't matter.

We need, of course, more than just the surface coverage that the journalist/recorder of this incident includes. We need to know who these men are by name and to trace what they did when they went home. Did they ever tell their wives and sisters and daughters about how they rape-murdered a girl's body and spirit one afternoon, just for fun? What we need is to know what happened to the girl after this. Was she insane forever? If just this once she had 27 men inflicted on her, just imagine how much worse must have been the lives of those called 'professional prostitutes,' who were violated like this every day. If these 27 rendered this girl unconscious, were the GI's in the rape-comfort stations climbing on the bodies of unconscious girls as they serially mounted? After all, the girl in the comfort station was no different from this one. She, too, would be rendered unconscious by 27 men climbing on her. We need to ask how all these hundreds of thousands of GI's could climb on the bodies of unconscious women they had paid to fuck and think there was nothing wrong with this. Couldn't they see the girl was unconscious? How could they mistake this for 'consent'? Did it never occur to one of these shit male rapists that it could be their own sister or girlfriend or wife or daughter in that rape-torture bed? Could actually paying to rape in some way make these men think it was not rape? Paid rape is far more vicious than any other kind since the girl is completely helpless due to her status as 'whore.' There is no sympathy for her, no rescue. She is just 'whore,' pure and simple. Is this why it is okay for her to be raped until she is unconscious? Because she is defined and classified as 'whore'? Why are the men who used her not classified as despicable rapists? How could they be allowed to return home as 'noble heroes' after their savage, brutal, rapist binges in Japan?

Just asking. I don't want to be the one to have to ask these questions—but no one else is. It is unbelievably painful for me to even know about the truth of what went on. Apparently the women of America did not want to know—still do not want to know.

What amazes me is that these men can actually be proud of themselves for this—men brag about gang rape—I have heard them do it—my soldier boyfriends and customers bragged about multiple violations of Vietnamese girls. And how can these men dare to go back to America and touch their wives and girlfriends and hold their daughters—after this, how can they dare be allowed to even be in the presence of a woman? Lifelong banishment from our gentle soft selves should be their punishment.

I am also amazed at the continuity of rape. What the fathers pass down to their sons: rape and prostitution-rape were commonplaces of the Vietnam War. In Iraq right now GI's are raping girls. (So, I need to add, are Iraqi men: one girl was used by seventeen different Iraqi men in an American prison in Iraq while American soldiers watched, and then she was returned unconscious to her cell. She stayed unconscious for two days. It is a shame she had to wake up. Death would have been a mercy to her after that. Is she insane now? Why did the American men not stop this? Did they have fun watching? Did they make jokes?)

Both the PHW and military chaplains shared the view that Japanese women were diseased temptresses. "Their own men were seen as clean, innocent and vulnerable to having their high morals corrupted and their health destroyed." Jeeze.

The attitude of the PHW: "It is to be appreciated that among Japanese women no shame attaches to the prostitute whose trade is recognized as honorable and legitimate" (Tanaka). What? What, what, what??? The prostitute in Japan is treated like trash and a toilet—just as she is in every other country in the world. Where does this 'honored profession' myth crap come from? There is no 'honor' or 'respect' involved in prostitution anywhere. If there were, then why do you have girls placed in brothels and outcast from the society of 'normal' women? Why do 'normal' women worldwide scorn girls placed in these rape stations? Why are girls who are held in rape stations by 'owners' and sold to men as if they were just holes with no feelings—why are these girls labeled 'bad' and 'sluts' as they 'allow' themselves to be invaded by shit males they do not know? The whole picture of prostitution is one of scorn for a despised outcast female who is different from 'normal' good girls. I could go on, but why? You aren't going to get even a whisper of sympathy for the whore from the 'normal,' 'decent' women of the world. Blind cruel misconceptions about what constitutes rape is all these 'normal' women understand.

Should even a wisp of understanding invade their narrow brains—should one of them say, "That's awful, that a girl would have to take on 50 men at a time"—should there actually be one small moment of understanding in these 'safe' women's brains—it does no good. The very next moment, they just forget about the poor rape-dead girl and go on with their meaningless activities—writing more papers on Shakespeare, probably.

In 1946, 200,000 VD cases had been inflicted on the Japanese women by the soldiers.

"Some soldiers had 2 or 3 attacks but still continued to have intercourse" (Tanaka). Damn, I say--men just have to keep on fucking and fucking and fucking no matter what, don't they? And I guess the whores just keep on ticking and ticking so matter how much of a fucking they have to take. After all, the whore body can feel no pain, right?

All sorts of 'off-limits' proclamation flew about and all sorts of rhetoric about "emancipating" the women from the "enslaving prostitution business" (with no mention, of course, of who was enslaving them)—but all of this was surface lies. The GI's just kept on fucking and fucking and fucking and VD rates got worse—despite the fact that all these girls were now supposedly "emancipated" from their brothels. What happened, I wonder, to all those grand statements about prostitution being against "women's human rights"? Were they just empty words spoken by liars and hypocrites and men with no daughters or sisters who just needed to keep on fucking and fucking other men's daughters and sisters? When 'man must have his fuck,' there is no mercy for any daughter or sister.

Tanaka notes that the commander of U.S. forces failed to see that the VD rates had anything to do with the behavior of his own men. Again, I am stuck by so many modern parallels—as we have inherited the rape culture of our fathers and grandfathers. It is the whores of the world, now, who are giving everyone AIDS, of course—with a complete failure to note the behavior of men as a major factor. Take the way girls are now forced into prostitution at very early ages, infected, heavily used, and then the soldiers, sailors, businessmen, tourists, local laborers, local police, etc., etc., carry the disease widely out into the population. AIDS studies never, ever, ever mention this forbidden fact—it is all the 'respectable' men of the world who are the culprits and carriers, not those outcast prostitutes.

The big concern in Japan was not the welfare of the prostitutes but a need to hide the VD rates so the media would not pick up this story and tell the women back home what was going on. (I think the women should have been intelligent enough to know that starving girls and horny GI's means mass rape of the girls, but the supreme ignorance of the 'decent' woman in this matter is simply a given.) A memo from an officer to MacArthur in 1946 warned about not wanting any "critical visitors" from back home inquiring about prostitution and temporary wives and fraternization: "their demands for information [must be] anticipated and forestalled" (Tanaka).

The numbers were huge—the 350,000 troops busy raping away and 80% of them acquiring 'temporary wives' and fathering what would be a huge population of abandoned Amerasian children—all of Japan humming away as one big rape factory, one big hot wet crude GI brothel—no wonder there was some concern someone would find out. But, you know, I don't think they really need have worried. American journalists don't give a damn about raped/prostituted bodies—they have conveniently refused to report mass rape of prostituted bodies and unmistakable war-time starvation prostitution for decades—even centuries--no one talked about it during the Civil War—a war which caused the largest increase in the sex 'industry' ever seen. Half of the rape-shit soldiers on both sides had VD from raping prostituted women and girls who has lost their homes and families. The journalists hid it during Vietnam, although they must have seen that Saigon was a rape hell brothel for hundreds of thousands of refugee whore girls. How could they miss this 'fact'? They themselves were probably screwing the insides out of these destitute whore girls. They are hiding it in Iraq—almost completely ignoring the brothels in the Green Zone and the way Iraqi girls are now available, cheap, for sex due to the war.

And American women don't give a damn. They buy into the entitlement-to-rape-foreign-whores-culture so heavily, while pretending it doesn't exist, that they simply don't care. Their insensitive blindness is complete. During my era, the Vietnam one, I could not find one American woman who cared. Even the feminists and war activists totally ignored the hot whore playground of rape hell that was Vietnam. "Fun Fuck Bang in Da Nang, I let you rape me long time!" Jane Fonda and Gloria Steinem had not a clue. Apparently they still don't since the new hot whore hell—Iraq—is not even on their agendas. It's not on anyone's agenda. I don't see Hillary over there uncovering the ruined bleeding raped whores created by our war. She is saying nothing about this topic in Iraq—just as I never heard Fonda or Steinem make one remark about the prostituted and raped women of Vietnam. What kind of feminist could Steinem claim to be if she ignored this?

A big irony of postwar, occupied Japan was that no whore girl could ever be a fit bride—any girl uncovered as a whore for the GI's could never marry one since she was filth. Apparently the thousands of men who made her filth by raping her were blameless and noble and courageous and pure and wonderful. The same policy ruled in postwar Germany: all the starving girls forced to whore were dirty and disposable and could never marry a GI if it was discovered they had been raped thousands of times by other GI's. The sheer rape-craziness of this world stuns me. But I suppose if you have a world in which female sexuality is completely controlled by male notions of what sex is—well, what can you expect? The privileged male will rape and plunder the girls defined as whores and all the 'pure' girls on the other side of the fence will agree that the whore girls deserve what they get. Askew and brutal definitions of female sexuality rule all of us women. No woman can exercise any kind of sexual freedom, no woman can ever express the beauty of her own sexuality---should she ever find it on this sexually savage planet—without being labeled a 'whore' and terribly punished. There is no pure, beautiful, free female sexuality on Rape Planet Earth.

I lived in Japan on military bases in the 1960's when red-light areas were heavily patronized by GI's—in the mid-60's usage of enslaved girls was about 85%--and of course none of the dependent wives and daughters would acknowledge this—and none of the soldiers would speak openly about it to us—but it was known, tacitly, in an underground way, what was going on. I had a lot of contact with the GI's on the base. I would go to movies with them and have milkshakes and French fries with them at the snack bar. They let 'dirty-joke' hints about what they did to the whores slip out—so as to prove their virility and manly bonding. They were polite to me because I was a 'good' girl but I felt great pain at this false distinction being made. I didn't see how they could be nice to me and then go out and hurt one of those girls. We were the same in my mind. If they hurt them, they also hurt me.

Under their comfort system, the Japanese bought tickets and gave them to the girls: "This action," says Tanaka, "encouraged the belief that their conduct was a legitimate, 'commercial transaction.' Whether or not a woman was properly paid by her 'employer'—the brothel keeper—was of no concern to these soldiers, as they had 'paid' for the service. Whatever the misery of her existence, they felt entitled to enjoy the service in exchange for the payment" (174).

Tanaka continues: "The postwar comfort system that the Allied occupation soldiers extensively utilized in Japan was based upon the same fraudulent conception of a business transaction. It is therefore hardly surprising to find the behavior of Japanese soldiers toward Asian comfort women and that of American, British, and Australian soldiers towards Japanese comfort women almost identical. Both Japanese and Allied soldiers held comfort women in contempt, calling them 'a communal toilet' or 'a yellow stool,' yet the soldiers did not hesitate to use the 'service' rendered by these 'cheap whores.'" Tanaka certainly points out very powerfully the cruel inconsistencies in all this: scorn the whore as a 'toilet' but take your 'pleasure' inside her nevertheless. I wonder if it ever occurs to men that the whores they use are beyond value for this 'ability' to give pleasure. They have none themselves, these poor girls—yet think of the thousands of men who take pleasure inside them. One of the cruelest jokes in the world.

Female anatomy is not just destiny but pure misery for the female. Male pleasure means female pain. All the cruel gods of all the patriarchal religions of the world could not have ordered it better—for male domination.

"The commodification and depersonalization of women's sexuality is not unique to the comfort women system. Indeed, it is a universally distinctive characteristic of all forms of prostitution, whether a woman…is coerced or not. She is powerless 'in the sense that the degraded status of the "whore"' dissolves any entitlement to the protection and respect accorded to non-prostitutes" (Tanaka 174).

Tanaka borrows his ideas from Julia O'Connell Davidson in the above paragraph. Bless you, Tanaka, for recognizing that all prostitution is so damaging to us women. You are my hero, Mr. Tanaka.

Compare what you have read above with an official American military report from October 1944. It's called "Report No. 49: Japanese POW Interrogation on Prostitution" and comes from the United States Office of War Information. It describes twenty comfort girls taken prisoner and interrogated in Burma by the Americans. The authorities come to the conclusion that "a 'comfort girl' is nothing more than a 'prostitute' or 'professional camp follower.'" (My comment: the power and lies of misleading language.)

The report says that the Japanese shipped 800 of them to Burma in 1942. It does not say where the other 780 are. We know that sometimes the Japanese killed many of the girls to keep them from talking. And we know that the majority died from the harsh treatment. The few who spoke up in the early 1990's are the rare survivors among the original 200,000.

The report admits the girls were recruited under false pretenses and that they were young and ignorant and uneducated and were sold by their families or relatives and held in debt bondage.

The report goes on to say about the comfort girl: "She 'knows the wiles of a woman.' She claims to dislike her 'profession' and would rather not talk either about it or her family." "She is afraid of Chinese and Indian troops."

"The conditions under which they transacted business were regulated by the Army, and in congested areas…the army found it necessary to install a system of prices, priorities and schedules…as follows:

1. Soldiers--10 am to 5 pm--1.50 yen for 20 to 30 minutes
2. NCO's--5pm to 9 pm--3.00 yen for 30 to 40 minutes
3. Officers--9pm to 12 pm--5.00 yen for 30 to 40 minutes."

"Officers were allowed to stay overnight for 20 yen."

"The soldiers often complained about congestion in the houses…In order to overcome this problem, the Army set aside certain days for certain units."

"Sunday--18th Div. Hdqs. Staff

Monday--Cavalry

Tuesday-- Engineers

Wednesday--Day off and weekly physical exam

Thursday—Medics

Friday--Mountain Artillery

Saturday—Transport."

"Officers were allowed to come seven days a week. The girls complained that even with the schedule congestion was so great that they could not care for all guests."

After purchasing a ticket, a soldier "took his turn in line."

"The girls were allowed the prerogative of refusing a customer. This was often done if the person were drunk."

The report claims girls got half of the earnings, depending on the contract she had signed saying how much in debt she was.

The report admits debt bondage was rampant, with high prices for food, clothing and necessities.

It is hard to know what to make of this fairy-tale surface report, this male fantasy of what happened to the comfort girls, how they felt about it, given that we now have testimony from dozens and they all tell the same story. It is not the story in the above report. And, interestingly, the dozens of testimonies corroborate each other with startling accuracy. All the girls report being virgins when conscripted, being broken brutally by gang rape, being beaten, never seeing any of the money the men paid to rape them—and, of course, most importantly, they all report the exact same devastating pain and rape torture of their bodies—the bleeding and swelling and uterine infections and aching with pain abdomens and the insanity and despair from constant mountings from men—from nine in the morning until midnight—and how they took drugs if they could get them to bear the pain and how the men were dirty and rough and the extreme disgust they felt. And the madness and despair and loss and hopelessness they felt for the rest of their lives.

The above report, instead, says that this 'camp follower' 'knows the wiles of a woman.' That does not seem to have anything to do with what the women say about their lives in the rape stations. They lay on mats all day with their legs open and endured if they could and passed out if they couldn't. They bled. They died inside. They all say they had their lives taken from them. Give me back my girlhood. Give me back my womanhood. Give me back my body. Not one girl reports enjoying this or 'having the wiles of a woman.' Damn. Was the girl flirting while being raped 50 times in a row and bleeding from her womb? What kind of supreme blindness could have afflicted the men who wrote this report?

(The great sacrilege, of course, is that these girls were robbed of that most precious of things, their sexuality.)

The report says that the girls served men from ten in the morning until after midnight—and sometimes the officers all night. This is constant intercourse, something no woman can bear. Here is how the report says the girls responded: "The girls complained that even with the schedule congestion was so great that they could not care for all guests."

The girls "complained" because they were not able to have intercourse with perhaps 50 to 80 men a day? (One comfort girl actually said she was raped 300 times in one day—she had to pee where she lay as the men came inside her every 3 minutes [Ryang].) The girls regarded the men as "guests"? I don't think so. The girls were terrified of the men who were raping them. They cried and curled up in fear and could not walk after so much abuse (Yoshimi).

We also know that they were never allowed to refuse a customer. They were beaten, kicked, starved, and sometimes even bayoneted if they were even slightly 'disobedient' to the men.

The men who wrote this report must have had daughters and wives and sisters. Yet they could not make a simple act of the imagination: they could not imagine a fifteen-year-old daughter of their own not wanting to lie down for twelve or more hours a day, with her legs open, while men entered her? The stance and attitude of the U.S. War Department is unbelievably without mercy or compassion, in this report, for the most brutalized of victims of WWII.

You would think that at least one of the men writing this report would see that even one act of rough intercourse can badly damage a woman. How is it possible these men could think that fifty or more rapes a day shoved into these girls would only result in the girls complaining that they could not service more 'guests' to relieve the 'congestion' of the comfort station. I cannot even imagine the terror these women must have felt as dozens upon dozens of men lined up to rape them, pressed in upon their helpless small bodies to rape them.

I cried deeply when I read this document. I am still crying. There is no hope of ever stopping the rape of our bodies if this is how men regard the rape of these poor comfort women. There was no 'report' from the girls themselves. As we see from the above, the women refused to talk about what happened to them when 'interrogated.' You cannot talk about mass rape of your body when it is fresh. It takes decades for the words to come. The military men apparently saw none of this.

These military men of WWII must have been insensitive monsters beyond our imagination if they could not comprehend mass rape of one girl by 50 men a day as rape. The comfort girl, the report says, "claimed to dislike her 'profession.'" This was no 'claim.' This was no mere 'dislike.' This was revulsion, deep and inexpressible. She was dead because of this 'profession.'

Another horror document that made me cry even more is John Costello's *Love, Sex and War: Changing Values, 1939-45.*

All of the post-war starvation prostitution of women is a crude, cruel joke to him. His chapter called *Yielding to the Conquerors* is subtitled "Liberating Whoredom." He gives the impression that German girls were happy to fuck the GI's for four cigarettes a night: "Germany's female population did not resist the demands of the occupying soldiers....They soon discovered that sex could be traded for food and cigarettes from the GI's."

In the attitude of the U.S.army, he says "sex is a commodity to be traded for the necessities of life. 'In this economic set-up, sex relations...function like any other commodity.'"

"German girls considered 'four cigarettes good pay for all night. A can of corned beef means true love.'"

He is even more jokingly ruthless when he writes about Japan:

"To the delight of the GI's, more than adequate provision had been made for occupying troops."

"The nation that had dispatched medically inspected whores to army bordellos on the Pacific outposts of empire also set up 'rest and recreation' centres for the American army."

"When the first GI's arrived, they found temporary 'Special Recreation Centres' had already been set up in the surviving unbombed factories.... Price-lists for these 'establishments' were posted on the quartermaster bulletin boards in all U.S. Army camps—with the ever-present reminder about the need for prophylaxis to avoid infection:

20 yen—a buck and quarter—for first hour, 10 yen for each additional hour and all night for 50 yen. If you pay more, you spoil it for all the rest. The MPs will be stationed at the door to enforce these prices. Trucks will leave each hour, on the hour. NO MATTER HOW GOOD IT FEELS WITHOUT ONE, BE SURE TO WEAR ONE.'"

At the Yokosuka Amusement Centre, Costello writes there was "a line of enlisted men, four abreast, almost a block long, waiting their turn....MPs kept the line orderly."

His tone is that all of this wartime starvation prostitution is a dirty joke. He makes the sexual misery of women into a cruel dirty joke. He is one of these men who thinks solely with his penis. He does not even seem to have the remotest awareness that war destroys villages, homes, food, crops, takes away support, livelihood, leaves women starving, alone, and desperate. His description of the Korean Comfort Women as "medically inspected whores" in their "army bordellos" is particularly disturbing, given the torture these girls endured. I cried for a long time when I read Costello's words because I thought of the 'other words' I have read—the ones from the Korean Comfort girls themselves, from the 15-year-olds with torn vaginas and infected wombs who tried to kill themselves so they would not have to endure yet another day of 30 rapes.

Costello reports the "delight" of the GI's that "provision" had been made for them—without any mention of the working conditions and state of the girls—which were identical to those of the 'other' comfort women—constant rape, disease, insanity and hysteria, attempted suicide, incredible sexual misery. Is all of this what filled the GI's with 'delight'? That long line of men 'four abreast,' waiting 'their turn'—what were they waiting their turn for? The 'fun' of raping a helpless body? You wonder what the wives and mothers and sisters of these men would have thought, if they saw them 'waiting their turn'? Would it have disturbed these women at all to know that girls were being raped to death by all these 'delighted' GI's?

Does Costello have a wife or a daughter? Would he like to see a long line of men 'waiting their turn' to mount her? The sheer sexual savagery of this—regarded as 'fun' by the men—is inconceivable. Yet a 'norm.' Accepted. What men do. And the girls in the comfort centers are reduced to a state beyond sadness: they will associate sex with misery forever; they will fear and detest sex and men forever---if they survive. All because a line of joking, crude young men have to get their fuck. Male pleasure equals female sexual misery so deep it cannot even be put into words. My despair is so deep at the brutal sexual selfishness of the male that there is no where to go from here. No books I write will help.

Costello reports the dictum issued to D-Day troops--"You will go there as liberating heroes and those women will be eager and urgent in their solicitation of you....The women who will be soliciting your attention are prostitutes of the most promiscuous type." This man and the U.S. military are a perfect match.

I will end this section with a comment by an Australian soldier in Tokyo, September, 1945: "Japan is one big brothel."

More Afterthoughts (Very Wandering Ones)

June 14, 2009

As I do a second edition of *Raped Vagina,* I see constant issues that need commenting on. The situation is similar to the protagonist's plight at the end of *Gulliver's Travels.* This gullible, hopeful hero says (to paraphrase him, Suki-fashion): "Well, I have shown you what is wrong with the world in my books, now why don't you fix it? I notice that the world is just the same as it was when I first wrote my books."

Naïve me assumed that pointing out the problem would lead to action. Some action is taking place in the world, to free the sex slaves. Certainly enough people are writing on this topic. All you have to do is look at the reference section in the back of this book to see just a portion of those giving it their attention.

I think there is enough on the page. We now need to take all the facts and statistics and intentions and plans and use them to actually take the tortured bodies out of the brothel beds.

Since I published this book last year, new events in the world of trafficking have arisen. And I have thought of a few more ideas to enlighten you about prostitution/trafficking. So here is a continuation of my 'afterthoughts.' Sadly, the problem that is prostitution never goes away and there is no respite for the millions of for-sale women being raped—so I must say more. When the last brothel bed is empty and the last whore freed, then I will be quiet.

As I finish up the second edition of this book in June 2009, I note that California has just introduced some possible legislation against trafficking. The pending legislation would increase fines to $20,000 on those convicted of pimping, pandering, or procuring minors; and fifty percent of the money would go to organizations that help minors who have been trafficked. The legislation would also provide for the forfeiting of assets from human trafficking.

I have suggested elsewhere that we should confiscate the earnings of traffickers and use the money to rebuild the lives of the women they have destroyed. The $4-5 billion US that traffickers in Germany bring in per year would be a dandy start. Just think how many trafficked girls that could support! These are idealistic thoughts, and now I find that California may pass laws that would be a step in the direction of taking away money which traffickers have made and applying it to helping their victims. I would like to see the programs funded for adult victims as well.

I look at this legislation and hope it will work if passed. But I wonder if there is a way the traffickers could actually use the legislation to their benefit. I know that a pimp with a 'stable' can make $20,000 in just a few days, so maybe the fine should be $200,000 or two million dollars? I don't see how you can put a pimp out of business with a paltry $20,000 fine if he makes phenomenally more than that off of the sale of bodies?

Legislation tends to work against the weak and the victimized. As a lawyer said to me, prostitutes don't stand a chance in court since they are despised outcasts trying to seek justice in a system where the law favors those in power. The male is the one in power. Currently, prostitutes are arrested and then the court makes money off of them by fining them for being out on the streets, getting raped. If a girl is whoring on the streets and is arrested, she has to pay to get out of jail so she can go out and get raped some more—and have her head bashed against dashboards by sadistic 'customers' as she goes down on her knees in cars to do blowjobs. She has to be punished for 'allowing' this to happen to her through arrest, jail time, and fines. At least, that is the way the system seems to operate and there is no protection for the prostitute. She gets raped on the streets and then raped again by the courts. Is this changing? Will we need radically different attitudes toward the prostituted for there to be significant changes in how she is treated—by the legal system, by the jails, by people in general—who still seem to regard her as an abnormality, a depraved creature, a dirty joke?

Trafficked/prostituted girls can rarely speak for themselves. So if the burden of proof falls on the trafficked/prostituted and she cannot speak against her abusers, due to terror and trauma, how do we construct legislation that will help her? It is a real dilemma. Minors will try to get back to the pimps who have abused them since this is all they know. So beaten down from mistreatment and so needy and lost, the girls have no place else to go. So how can they testify against their pimps—given their mental state? I cannot fully understand what motivates these girl to return to their pimps, but do know that being in prostitution seems to blank out the future. There is no life or world beyond prostitution. It destroys a girl so much that there is nothing left of her to think or feel or dream with. So, maybe the girls return since this is all they can envision for themselves? These are a few problems I would bring up and a few of the questions I would ask about the California legislation—in hopes that it will practical and really help the ones in need, not their oppressors.

I hope the legislation works, if passed. I hope it does not end up being a law that supports more trafficking.

Thus far, the law in general does not seem to be on the side of the prostituted. It seem that when the police set up a 'sting,' if that's what it's called, to bust prostitution rings, it takes them forever—months and months and months, maybe even years—and they see the customers coming and going and coming and going—in and out of the brothels and massage parlours—and they see drunk men going in to party and maybe they see the guys coming back out tucking their dicks in—and it is obvious that girls inside these places are being forced to have sex with men they do not know. Why does it take months and months, maybe even years, for the police or the FBI to actually determine that coercive prostitution-rape is taking place? While they take their months or years, the girls are being raped hundreds or even thousands of times.

Then the bust takes place and the girls have no passports and they are arrested and kept in jail as if they were criminals for letting themselves be raped thousands of times and then they are deported to Mexico or Thailand or Korea or wherever they were trafficked from—to be re-trafficked again, once they reach 'home' (where is home for the girl who has been raped thousands of times? No where). And their exploiters are let off with a bit of a hand slap and a fine since no one could prove 'coercion' since the girls were too mentally and physically broken to speak for themselves. Such is the male system for meting out 'justice' to the prostituted/trafficked girl for 'allowing' herself to have been raped thousands of times.

Prostitution is coercion! How many thousands of times does the prostitute have to be raped by men she does not know for it to be 'coercion'? But such is the definition of prostitution in a male-dominated society that the girl can receive no justice. Not that 'justice' is possible after thousands of rapes. Life is not possible. Best just to give the poor thing a way to euthanize herself.

So, do we now have legislation in California that will bend the system so that it actually benefits the prostituted girl and does not blame her for the mass rape of her body? It would seem that we need to completely revision male/female sexuality in order to do this. Sweden is trying. As is Norway. Their legislation defines prostitution as violation of a woman's rights as a human being. It defines it as sexual exploitation of the female. It says that the men who sell and buy the girls are the criminals. In the USA and in most of the rest of the world, the prostitute is still the criminal. Will the California legislation change attitudes of male/female sexuality? Are the victims still the criminals? If they are not, then why are prostitutes still being arrested all over the USA?

My plan—a plan that will work: recruit the National Guard to go and knock down the doors of all establishments where girls are sold. Take the girls out. Arrest anyone who has made money off the girls. Arrest any men who have used them. Punish the buyers and sellers. Simple. Why should it be so hard to actually physically take a girl away from the men who buy and sell her?

Massage parlour stories on local news stations tend to concentrate on the irrelevant. You have some ambitious 'investigative' reporter making the 'big discovery'—there is sex going on in there. The places may have been there for months or even years—but now we all of sudden are taken by complete surprise that they are really brothels? But there is never any coverage of the relevant part—the girls themselves. Where do they come from, are they held in debt bondage, who trafficked them in, who is taking the money? Would they actually be there performing sex acts with strangers (disgusting!) if they had a choice?

After a massage parlour or prostitution story on the local news, there is a lot of joking around about this 'dirty' topic and the female anchor titters and smirks, as if it were all funny in some way. Would she actually want to be doing blowjobs on these slime men who walk in for their 'massages'? Some guy comes in she has never seen before and she has to take his slime dick in her mouth. Do you know the level of disgust and distancing involved in that act—how far you have to abstract yourself from normal reality so that the disgust will not kill you? Why is there absolutely no understanding, even on the part of other women, of the pain and misery of prostitution? If there were, these 'safe,' privileged female newscasters would not be making smirking jokes about the prostituted.

But, then, all of TV seems unreal to me. The *Today Show* and the *View* and dozens of other programs feature normal, safe people—both men and women—dressed neatly and acting privileged—as if they were totally unaware of the violent rape being visited on millions of female bodies. As if they had some right to be privileged while this is going on. Basically, being prostituted put me in another dimension. When I watch TV, I see a bunch of safe people looking normal because they have not had their bodies raped to pieces. But, then, I also think that it does not take a lot of rapes to make people realize that there is something so vicious and sad and soul destroying about the basic act of prostitution—sex with strangers, usually performed under circumstances of coercion, if not violence itself—it is so obvious that there is something profoundly abnormal and miserable about this act being inflicted on a girl—well, why don't people realize this?

I realized it ages before I was ever raped. I realized it ages before I even had sex. I cannot remember a time in my life when my body did not feel vulnerable. Age four is when I started experiencing my own soft vulnerability, and it is also the age when my memories start to become more detailed. Age three are my first memories but they are very scattered and consist of things like being dressed up as a tiny witch for Halloween and eating a delicious caramel covered popcorn ball that some nice lady put in my trick-or-treat bag. Age four one afternoon a neighborhood teenage boy tried to get at me and I remember he hurt me really bad between my legs and I fought and screamed and he let me go. I had a tough maidenhead so he didn't penetrate me, but I hid in the closet for a long time. Around age seven or eight, a similar incident with another teenage boy holding me down and kissing me and then reaching down to take himself out. Since I didn't know what a penis was, I only realized much later what that reaching down gesture meant. Fortunately, someone came in the house and he let me go. When I was about eleven or twelve a neighbor in his mid-thirties or so pushed me down in the woods near our house and tried to rape me. I fought him and he let me go. He had red-hair so I have always felt faintly sick around red-haired men ever since.

Three attacks before I even had my period. 'Man must have his fuck' reigns across the world. Even a four-year-old is a target. I learned much later that what happened to me is typical—about a third of Western girls are attacked, if not raped, in their childhood. I am sure the numbers must be phenomenally larger for Asia and Africa, where we females are held in even lower esteem. Exploring my past has helped me to understand the sentence that haunts me, a sentence from Yuki Tanaka's book on the comfort women; a sentence in an official WWII American army report about 50 GI's lined up to get at one Japanese prostitute. It is this sentence, in all of its pain and horror, that changed my life and set me off on my big writing journey. From that sentence have come all of my novels and this book you are reading. My quest to understand the reality behind that sentence has guided my life over the past few years. It led me to face prostitution in the world again. After my own time in prostitution, I ignored the subject for decades. I hid from it both inside myself—and out. I have come to realize that the explanation is not complicated—as to how those 50 men could mount one bleeding girl, near-dead from rape-fuck. But it is still horrifying. The explanation is that man must have his fuck. Sex is so overpowering for them that nothing else matters. Just getting the penis inside the vagina is so overwhelmingly important to them that the pain and misery of the girl do not matter. She may be rape-dazed and numb and near-dead from overuse—but the man has to get his fuck—no matter what. No considerations of love or tenderness. Just man must have his fuck.

It is a frightening revelation. The attack on me when I was only four proves my assertion. I did not matter. My life did not matter. It would have been destroyed if he had penetrated me. The only thing that mattered is man must have his fuck. This harsh fact accounts for a lot. All those poor child brides all over the world, girls not even in their teens, getting raped day after day by their middle-aged husbands. Girls in African and Middle-Eastern cultures with two or three babies by the time they are seventeen or eighteen. Bodies and sexualities destroyed because man must have his fuck. Excess children all over the world due to man must have his fuck. I keep hearing about the 30,000 children a day who die from starvation: surplus children, uncared for, because man must have his fuck. The life of every individual child is important. Feed those who are already here. But concentrate on not producing any more. The charitable organizations that feed children around the world need to concentrate on eliminating the 'man must have his fuck' side of the problem. Sterilization, birth control, no girls allowed to marry until age 25, no sex for any girl until she is 25—all sorts of solutions are possible. No overpopulation means no girls to sell and traffic. It means no slave labour, no sweatshops and factories—since there is no surplus population to exploit. It means the end of the rich and privileged exploiting the vulnerable.

I give age 25 as the time when a girl/woman should first have sex because she is then ready for this important event. Teens aren't. A girl must gain knowledge and learn her own emotions and her own body before she has sex. A girl is just turning into a woman around her mid-20's. That is a good time for her to first have sex. Even as old as I am—middle-aged now—I still do not understand the mysteries of sex. How abysmal to force it on young girls whose bodies and emotions are in no way ready for it.

Those attacks on my softness before I even knew what sex was keyed me in that there is something really terrible about male sexual violence. And the way the world normally works. And they keyed me in about how abnormal prostitution-sex is for a woman. No woman invites violation of her body for the sole pleasure of the male. No woman wants to open her legs just a few minutes after meeting a man and let him ram himself into her most vulnerable part, her soft insides. What woman would invite this? I knew all of this from the time I was tiny, even before I knew the details of prostitution.

I had also been 'trained' in soft submissiveness by a rough-mannered father. He taught me that male strength rules the world. He didn't have to hit me much. Just a whack now and then and I was completely submissive. And, oddly enough, I have since discovered that I am one of the fortunate ones. I had enough to eat and a place to sleep and I got to go to school. And compared to some countries where simply beating women and girls is the norm, I only got hit every once in a while. And, since adulthood, I have been able to protect myself: no on hit me when I was a prostitute since I was able to keep away from pimps and pick my customers. I have never been hit by a man since I became an adult. Any man I go with, if we argue or he seems mad, I just leave. This intense fear of male violence has played havoc with my ability to have a 'relationship.' I can't have one—even a small amount of anger on his part and I leave. I am too afraid of male violence to ever even give anyone the slightest chance to hit me. One harsh word or one argument and I am gone. I leave before he might hit me. I am completely incapable of confronting men.

So, I have been trained well. Never confront. Be soft and submissive—or you might get hurt. The small amount of violence I experienced as a prostitute kept me in my place—forever. The physical pain of prostitution so intensified my fear of male strength that it has led to an extreme fear, on my part, of assembly-line sex. Then there is the dilemma of being attracted to the male strength that frightens me. I am criticized for this as if I were to blame in some way. Actually, I see no conflict. Safe, happy sex is only possible for us women if we know that the men will never hurt us—if we know they will stop when we say 'stop, you're hurting me.' The men have to completely control their sexual violence toward us. Only in this way is safe, happy sex possible. Even one trafficked girl being forced—and all safe, happy sex is impossible.

None of the rape or prostitution needed to have happened to me to make me aware of how terrible prostitution is. How abnormal it is for the female. And, apparently, normal for the male who can have sex without feelings while inflicting tremendous pain on the prostituted body. All you have to do is look at my paradigm situation: the 50 GI's lined up to get at one helpless prostituted body in 1945 Tokyo. If that is allowed to happen, even once, then it destroys all female sexuality everywhere for all time and proves that male sexuality—cold, impersonal, brutal—rules all women.

I knew all this when I was really young. Not in words or concepts. But my soft, helpless body told me this. My poor mother's helplessness told me this. She was timid and soft. I always felt terribly sorry for her. I felt sorry for my poor dad, too—he had his own problems in life, his own unfulfillments. He couldn't help it if he was a naturally violent male—the poor guy tried to be loving in his own way. He had a kind side. The problem is his anger and violence kept getting in the way of that. I think he taught me young just how innate and uncontrollable male violence is. Men make war and keep the world in a constant state of misery. It is just built into them to do this. They can't help it.

My own soft, helpless body continues to tell me the truths I discovered at age four—male strength rules; prostitution-sex is abnormal for a woman and viciously brutal on her body; there is no free, beautiful sexuality on this planet. I knew all this in some form from around the age of four. I did not even have to be raped once (let alone thousands of times) to teach me this. Even one rape was too much.

So, why don't other women know this? When I sit in a posh hotel in Paris, with women in neat business suits—all of us at a conference discussing all sorts of useless things—why don't these women beside me know about 'the other reality'? Prostitution is a separate reality, an underground reality, running parallel to the lives of normal, safe women. As we sat in Paris, the abattoir whores were being raped 80 to 160 times a day in the immigrant sections of Paris and cold women sociologists and psychologists and anthropologists were studying the 'specialized houses' of Paris--where girls 'take on' 50 men a day--and making pronouncements about how this was 'hard work' for the girls. I sat there alone, in my separate world of prostitution, different from, highly alienated from this world of protected women in neat suits and did not know how to reach them—or how to show them the dimension I was living in. We sipped that delicious coffee they have in that country and ate those wonderful pastries in that elegant hotel. And I felt miserably guilty that I was now one of the privileged and could do nothing to help the suffering feminine all around me.

Paris is not a city of love and light and joy for the abattoir whore.

Safe protected women seem to regard the prostitute as a woman who belongs to another species. "It takes a special kind of women to do that—I couldn't do that," I heard one 'normal,' safe, non-prostituted woman say. Well, yes you could, easily. Just let a trafficker train you in a 'submission camp' where you 'learn' to allow yourself to be raped all day and you could do it too. Not 'easily,' of course. It is not 'easy' for the girl to allow her body to be raped all day—no matter how many times she has been 'trained' as a part of this rape act. It destroys her—so it is never 'easy'—but she is playing the part allotted to her by 5000 years of human history. It is what the vulnerable female is for: to be rape-fucked. (I learned about these 'submission camps' from a Canadian scholar named Richard Poulin: he says that Balkan girls are 'trained' in them by their traffickers [117].)

I do not know how to tell the scholarly women around me what the true reality of the female is. We have no safety or power or beauty as long as one Balkan 14-year-old is in a rape-torture bed in Greece, being violated 100 times a day. (Another fact that I learned from Poulin.) It is inconceivable that we sit here, ignoring her. It is inconceivable that we teach meaningless classes on useless feminist writers while she exists. We cannot live at her expense. Our privilege and strength do not exist if she exists. Her presence destroys us all. Liberate the prostitutes and you free all of us. Just one girl in sexual slavery and we are all bound with heavy chains. Liberate the prostitute and you finally erase that pernicious distinction between 'good' girls and 'bad' girls that has kept us all in sexual slavery for so long.

The academic world—all closed off and safe—is not the only arena for lies about our femininity and 'strength.' TV seems to ring with jingles and rhymes about the 'goddess within' and how empowered we females all are. Bunch of bunk. I am sure the trafficked girl curses herself that she even has a vagina. The girls held under the worse conditions: the Slavic Girl trafficked into Dubai and 'trained' by being mounted by a different labourer every few minutes; the Balkan14-year-old dying from 100 rapes a day in Greece; the child whores, not even ten-years-old, being raped daily in India and Pakistan, their bodies destroyed long before they are even ready for sex—I am sure there are thousands of other instances, thousands of other examples of desperate women and girls who curse that they were born female if this torture can be inflicted upon them day after day after day.

TV seems like an alien world to me. Commercials about the 'goddess within' and the sacred feminine and the beauty that is woman. The deep, true reality of the 'feminine' world is the abattoir whore and the seven-year-old girl from Nepal in the Bombay brothel having her body ripped apart between her legs every day and the 14-year-old Balkan girl being used 100 times a day by Greek rapist shit males. I think it would surprise these girls to learn that they have a 'goddess within' and sexuality and femininity and beauty. The girl endlessly rape-tortured must curse that she even has a vagina. You can have no 'femininity' when you are age seven and have already had your sexuality completely raped to pieces inside you. What a cruel joke the world of sex must seem to this girl and to the 14-year-old trafficked whore in Greece and to all the abattoir whores in Paris and Morocco and Mexico and wherever else assembly-line sex goes on.

Where is that 'goddess within'? Is it in the pages of *Cosmo* and *Glamour*? It can't exist there, or among the privileged women of the world, since is does not reside in the bodies of the raped. That 7-year-old Nepali girl in Bombay who has had her femininity and sexuality taken completely from her negates all female sexuality all over the world—and exalts the brute rule of male sexuality. All the tender sex that is supposed to come the way of the imaginary *Cosmo* girl safe in the pages of her magazine is an illusion. That magazine is a realm of fantasy sex that has no counterpart in the real world. All the fancy articles about 'naughty sex tricks' and 'the moves men love' are a cruel joke to the body of that seven-year-old girl. All her gods and goddesses died a long time ago. Five thousand years ago, to be exact.

Television. The little box space of the privileged. Imaginary worlds of safety. I am especially struck by all these cosy travel shows with visits to places like Morocco--and tourists eating fancy food in safe restaurants and looking at holy shrines and dropping in on sanitized version of Rick's, while trafficked/prostituted French girls in Morocco are forced to take on a hundred man a day in abattoir brothels and who knows what is happening to the Slavic girls there. Those Slavic girls have been trafficked all over the world. What their men have done to them makes me tremendously ashamed to be part-Slavic. No matter where the tourists go—in India or Asia or the Middle East, there will be Slavic girls, girls broken in rape camps to accustom them to 'customers,' girls whose bodies are being used as rape dumps so that others can make money off of them. So no pilgrimages to shires in Cairo or Cambodia are possible. There are no spiritual sites on Rape Planet Earth. The rape of one female body negates all spirituality.

My philosophy is simple. The privileged cannot exist at the expense of the wretched. One girl being raped anywhere also means I am being raped.

The same principle applies to the other great helpless mass on planet earth, the animals we torture. You cannot sit in a fancy restaurant and enjoy a meal based on having taken the life of another being. That thing called 'meat' on your plate had a life that was as important as yours. If any being suffers, we all do. Anything you might term 'spirituality' is destroyed inside you every time you eat an animal.

If any animal is being tortured anywhere, so am I being tortured. I have been this way since I was a tiny kid. Age four—a year that was revelatory and pivotal in my life. I first start having consistent memories this year and one of the sharpest is seeing a man beating a dog. It made me feel in such deep pain and misery that I ran up and screamed and yelled and kicked the man to stop. For my pains, I was dragged off and spanked.

That dog still haunts me. The fact that I could not help him. And the way I was punished because I cared about him.

Nothing has changed. I have to be punished every day because I feel the suffering of other sentient beings. Sadly, the total brutal mess that is Rape Planet Earth makes me want to turn completely to helping animals and just forget human rights. Maybe no humans deserve any rights. We are too ugly and brutal. The very women and girls I care about are cruel to other women and girls and to animals. I understand the urge animal rights people have to abstract themselves from the human race: many of them despise people for the cruelties they visit on animals. It is an easier way. Just rescue animals and forget about people. I was way, way happier in life when I just cared for animals. I have no idea how to rescue and care for a trafficked girl. Taking in a dog or cat is easy. That rescued animal will do no harm and will be a symbol to you forever that you helped another living being.

Little donkeys in Egypt being given no almost no water and forced to cart tourists all over the place. Donkeys all over the world loaded with bricks that break their bodies and forced to pull carts loaded with half a dozen shit humans. Forget the people. Save the donkeys.

Bear baiting is still going on in Pakistan. De-clawed bears who have had their teeth yanked out are set upon by dogs—for fun and bets. Are prostituted women in Pakistan having fun laughing at the bears? Baby elephants in Thailand are trained through beatings, starvation, terror, torture by fire and nails in their feet—and little Thai girls run around the elephants and laugh. Why should I care if these girls are sold and rape-tortured if they do not care for the helpless elephants? People are beyond despicable. The tourists in Thailand ride elephants that have been broken and 'trained' through beating and torture. All captive elephants are broken this way. They will not submit, or do stupid tricks like kick around soccer balls, without being forced to do so. Same for the whores. You can't really get a girl to lay down and take on multiple strangers without force. Women just don't want to do this. It is big problem with stopping trafficking. You can't get enough 'free' girls who want to lay down and get dicked endlessly without love or tenderness. Given the huge male demand, it can only be satisfied by forcing a girl's body to lay there and get fucked. Man must have his fuck. Since there is no way to stop 'man must have his fuck' and men are stronger than the fragile girls they get their fuck on—well, I guess prostitution will go on forever.

It's hard to feel normal when I watch TV. I enjoy watching tennis, the Grand Slams, like the Australian Open and the French Open and Wimbledon. All the glamorous locations. Strawberries and Cream. I look at all the milling crowds at these events and all the women in jeans and T-shirts, smiling and looking safe and normal. When I ask normal women if they know about the girls in bloody rape-torture beds, as the sporting events roll indifferently on, they look at me as if I have no right to ask this. What is happening to girls in brothels in Melbourne and Paris and London? Why are all of us privileged and safe women not working to help them? Why am I considered unusual because I bring up this crucial fact about female sexuality on our planet? What kind of dignity can you have, to walk around safe, as a woman, in Melbourne or Paris or London, if this is going on? It's hard to imagine sitting comfortably at a tennis match in Paris when an abattoir whore is being raped a thousand times a month, ten thousand times a year? How does one survive that?

So many Slavic girls of all sorts playing tennis. Can they not help all the other Slavic girls around the world who are being sold in India or Korea or China or Dubai? When they play tennis in Dubai, can the Slavic players not call attention to the Slavic girls who have been trafficked there?

It is so puzzling that one Slavic girl is playing tennis while another one might be dying from sexual overuse in Goa, India. As puzzling as seeing a blonde tourist, all cute, in a low-cut skirt, belly button showing, having fun traipsing around Asia and the Caribbean and wherever, all safe and unaware of the pain being inflicted on other girls in sex-tourist destinations, like Bangkok or Amsterdam or Dubai or wherever. It is the great mystery of life. Why is this blonde privileged tourist safe while another girl her age who looks very similar to her is being used 40 times a day until her body and spirit die? No girl can survive that, yet the greater disturbance is the indifference of the safe girl. As she struts around looking all sexy, does the safe girl not realize that someone could take her body and put it in a whore bed and rape-torture it all day—and no one would care?

Of course it is too disturbing to let that kind of reality enter one's life. I realize that. I simply do not know how to keep it out of my life—once I began researching prostitution/trafficking, the extent of the problem overwhelmed me—as did the indifference and blindness and coldness of non-trafficked women.

I don't know how to make prostitution beneficial to the female. The only way would be to disassociate it completely from the norms that rule it: violence, humiliation, social scorn of the prostitute. Since I am naturally very sexual and very sensual, I would love to be able to make my living by selling my beautiful soft femininity in a world that would nurture and praise me. I would love to be able to write a book called *My Posh Life as a Pampered Whore.*

As it is, I understand the need for total, sad numbness of the vagina since mine was overworked when I whored. Not nearly as badly as the poor girls who are used 30 to 100 times a day. Quite mild overwork compared to that. When I first started whoring, I only had a few customers. Toward the end, just before I stopped whoring, I was so worn down and hopeless that I didn't much care what happened to me. So, I could not protect myself very well. At that time, I might go with 3 or 4 guys a night on weekends and get fucked maybe 20 times since the men wanted to go more than once. It was way, way, way too much--even 20 fucks in three days can practically kill you. I had to be numb and dead and sad and hopeless and suicidal to survive it. The thoughts that kept me going were there is no hope, there is no way out of this, I'll die soon and it will be all over with. All of this from being overfucked by men who weren't even being that mean to me. Just kind of careless and crude and joking since I was a whore/dirty joke and didn't much matter. I had no existence. I was a temporary fuck site.

Now, I cannot even imagine how I would have survived if there had been a pimp taking the money and directing the traffic and if I were a piece of property placed in an Eros Centre by an owner who made me take fuck after fuck while he took all the money. Or if I were locked in a room the whole time I was not fucking so I would not run away. Or if I was forced to do anal—one of my hugest nightmares: anal sex. After that one anal rape inflicted on me, I am terrified of even the idea of it. I get really queasy when I see all these porn stars forced to do anal. I get even queasier when I realize that the trafficked girls are forced to do this revolting thing because 'normal,' 'safe' girls won't and men come to trafficked whores so they can degrade them with the pain of anal sex. It makes me sick and sad and beyond hope to think of this. How much more beyond hope must be the girls this happens to?

I wonder what life is like from the perspective of the girl who is used by 50 or a 100 men a day. How does she feel after this? Is she even alive? I would scream and scream and scream if I were raped 50 times a day. And I would pass out and then I would be dead. Forever.

It is interesting that, after WWII, the only 'comfort women' that the Allies paid any attention to were the Dutch ones. It is as if these women had different vaginas from the Korean or Indonesian or Thai ones also being raped 30-50 times a day. When the comfort women—Dutch or Asian—tell their stories—it is all the same pain. The same torn body and the same cold burning fear and misery. The Asian girls curled up in fearful balls when the rough men entered the room—to use them—just as the Dutch ones did. They were terrified. Why were the Dutch ones the only women who were considered possessing vaginas that could be hurt and spirits that could be broken? The same sexuality was taken from the Dutch girls as from the Asian ones. Many of them feared and hated men all their lives. You see, it is the same vagina that all of us women have.

'Sex workers'—women who sell sex and call themselves by this ridiculous phrase and minimize the fact that the majority of sold bodies around the world are coerced—these women criticize me greatly in their writings for the way I express the pain that prostitution represents to me. I would like to ask them if they have had careers that are completely free of the many elements that are typical—to varying degrees—of prostitution: the violence, degradation, scorn by society. Is there any prostitute or 'sex worker' in the world who has always been treated with complete tenderness and respect? Do the women who call themselves 'sex workers' and who fight for 'sex worker' rights have cast-iron vaginas and cast-iron hearts and hides like rhinos that they know no pain from too much intercourse or a client treating them badly? Even the two incidences of violence that clients visited on me scared me to death forever. Of course, I am all for the 'rights' of 'sex workers,' and I wish that those rights would magically spring into being—immediately. I just wonder how you bring them about when the majority of women and girls in prostitution are coerced and held in debt bondage and pimp-controlled and scorned by mainstream society and basically treated like dirt. We have to start with the lowest of the low—the most wretched and mistreated—and free her, before any kinds of rights are possible. We have to immediately take the 14-year-old being raped 100 times a day by 'clients' in Greece out of her prison. If not, no woman who calls herself a 'sex worker' is free in any sense. She could be treated that way as well.

After I left whoring, numbness and hopelessness stayed with me for a long time. It was years before I had sex again. My vagina was an area I wanted to cut out of my body so no man could ever enter it again. When I finally went to some therapy, it helped but I never was able to talk about what really troubled me. It seemed impossible to talk about rape and prostitution in front of these normal people called counselors. They lived on a different planet. So I talked around what really troubled me. But the therapy helped anyway. I finally pseudo-solved my problems with prostitution by simply never thinking about the subject. During the years when I was numb I almost never watched movies or TV or read anything, for fear that something about prostitution would come up. When I went back to college, I avoided the subject and was abnormally sensitive to any references to it in any of my classes or texts. Inside was this knowledge that I was this totally unacceptable thing called a 'whore' and that if anyone around me knew about this, I would be thrown out of school. I felt completely alienated from the women around me.

This mindset carries over to this day. Despite having immersed myself in finding out about prostitution in order to write all my books, I am ready to close down again—forget it forever now that the books are done. It may be the only way to survive since trying to face what has happened to the Dubai Girl--'trained' by letting a different man in to use her every few minutes—this is knowledge I cannot bear to have. And I am still completely alienated from all the women around me. I carry on conversations with them but it is really not me doing the talking. It is a fake me. The real me—the prostitute me—has to stay hidden. I go to a little cocktail party get-together with little canapés and drinks and look at the women around me and they seem to belong to a different species. I do the usual chit chat but there is no 'me' there. Just a ghost or blank space in the air. The women look so 'normal.' All of 'normal' life seems abnormal to me since I can never tell anyone who I really am. I am a prostitute. I will always be one. I can never share this with anyone. The inner misery of never being able to erase all those men who were inside me is what makes the knowledge so painful for me to live with.

I write about it but I will never be able to talk about it with anyone. The words get stuck in my throat. I sound awkward and unsure and clumsy.

I had a big struggle—trying to have sex again after I lost my numbness. (My prose becomes clumsy when I write about this. Reluctant and halting.) It took a few years, but my sex drive finally came back. When I was in prostitution and during the few years after I got out, anything male seemed revolting to me. I hated muscles and all that coarse hair on their arms and the way they smelled. I hated the way they walked and the looks in their eyes. It was almost impossible to watch a movie or a TV show since even two people kissing made me sick. The idea of physical contact with a man made me sick.

All that very slowly passed away. The therapy helped. My body started to feel responsive again and I no longer hated that I had a vagina and the complete numbness between my legs gave way to feeling wet and warm and aching down there again—the way I was before the gang rape and prostitution.

I solved needing men and companionship and arms around me and needing someone inside me by having short-term affairs with men who did not scare me. Really short-term—one night, maybe a weekend. Not frequently. Not looking for someone every night or every week. But every few months I would really feel the need to be held and made love to—and I would go find someone.

I must have chosen well since none of the men hurt me. Most of the lovemaking was routine—kind of ho-hum. And I would always be really afraid at first since you never know what a strange man is going to do to you. A few of the experiences were spectacular. That kind of ecstasy where the world disappears and you live in a few moments of golden light. Then, afterwards, the bed is like a little safe island and his arms make you feel protected.

That's been my love life. I can never have a relationship or anything long-term. The fear is too great. I am sad that life on this planet is such that a woman has to be so afraid of men and sex and love. I am sad that one half of the human race has to be afraid of the other half. I resent that Rape Planet Earth has taken my sexuality away from me. But I do the best I can.

I cannot understand the myth of the powerful female. We are powerless. March 6 is Women's World Prayer Day. We can pray all we want. What good will it do the trafficked? Take all the Lara Croft's and Zena warrior princesses and treat them the way the Slavic girl in Dubai is treated—with a different man let in every few minutes to break her body and spirit—and they have no 'power' left. What a lie is female empowerment. I wonder if, after the few who manage to escape trafficking do—and after they go back into prostitution 'voluntarily' (what an inaccurate word in this context) because this is all they think they can do and they chance to watch a Lara Croft power-woman movie, what a cruel joke this must seem to them. The idea that any woman could have power. Being raped all day takes that notion away from you really fast. It takes away all normality as well. The total abnormality of prostitution for women. What kind of woman would invite this way of life—violence, disease, sex with rough men who think you are a dirty joke, physical damage and psychological misery? Yet there is a total 'normality' of prostitution for men and for non-prostituted women. It seems to be a given of the world that the prostituted woman exists and does not matter. What happens to her is not even regarded as destruction of the female and female sexuality.

I am not an 'empowerment' whore. I am not a 'sex worker.' I am not a feminist. I am a non-empowered anti-feminist who writes literary erotica.

I always look at life from the point of view of the most wretched. There is no other way. 'Empowered' women live in a fake reality. There is no power for women on a planet ruled by rape and brutality. Only a fake privilege for blind women who think they are exempt from the danger. How else can they live with such callousness? Never even giving a thought to the utter wretchedness of the abattoir whore. Assuming their neat stylish suits and silly fantasy magazines like *Glamour* and *Cosmo* will protect them. Put an academic woman or a politician or a feminist in an abattoir whore bed and have her mounted every ten minutes or so by a different male rapist shit and she will bleed and tear and her ovaries will be ruptured and she will die from the disgust and the torture and the nauseating smells coming off the men when they climb on. All the blood under her vagina and butt will negate any 'empowerment' she might have.

I realize that feeling alienated from most academics and feminists and magazine editors is not profitable. We should work together. But I just cannot feel as if I am in the same company with, belong to the same species as, live on the same planet with women who live lives of soft and safe privilege and ignore those who are the most wretched and the most 'oppressed.' 'Sexual oppression' scholars call it, what happens to the trafficked? 'Oppressed' won't do it for what happens to the trafficked, the girls broken in Balkan rape camps, the abattoir whores in Pairs and Morocco. Try something like 'extremes of sexual torture' if you want to find an accurate phrase. What is happening really is a sexual slaughter of the body—and life and spirit of the whore. Sexual murder. Death of the spirit. The experience of the abattoir whore is not on the level of some trivial little 'oppression.' This is not on the level of some sexual harassment infraction—as if a dirty joke or a mild slur deserved all the hoopla in the world—while girls are in rape-torture beds and men they do not even know are climbing on them. I just wonder how some academic or businesswoman in a neat suit would react to the men around her just climbing on her body without any kind of introduction. That goes beyond any kind of 'sexual harassment.' With prostitution, we are talking about extremes of sexual oppression and harassment and conditions beyond rape.

Now I know that the women who style themselves 'sex workers'—in sanitary fashion, to obscure the nature of the 'sex' involved—these women will jump on me for suggesting that prostitution is like trafficking and that it is in any way rape or 'oppression.' Actually it is. There may be a few 'free' prostituted females, but the majority undergo some degree of oppression or coercion—from the mild to the extreme. I could not see how I was 'free' in any way when I worked as a prostitute even though no pimp took my money and I was independent and had some small protection from violence and had almost complete control over who I went with. I will still controlled by a patriarchal world that told me I was a lesser being because I was a whore. I was defined as a 'convenience' and a 'dirty joke.' To this day, many years after I prostituted myself, I will never talk to the average person around me about what I did.

A 'profession' that imposes sex without love or tenderness on a woman and that makes her so ashamed she can never live in mainstream society ever again is no kind of 'profession' at all.

Quite frankly, I am sick of 'sex workers' and 'farangs' and academics criticizing me for daring to speak out against a 'profession' that is full of violence and humiliation for women. I am for 'sex worker' right as much as anyone else—if it could ever really be defined as 'work,' and not as humiliation and oppression.

I could never take the 'sex worker' stance that prostitution is 'normal' for the prostituted. The physical and psychological damage is too great. I would need to see proof from the 'sex worker' camp that prostitution does no harm to the female. The evidence from the opposite side is overwhelming and carries the day. Psychologist Melissa Farley has interviewed over 800 prostitutes all over the world and most of them say the same thing: they are desperate to leave prostitution. There seems to be sameness worldwide: early 'entry' into prostitution (age 13 or 14 in most countries); violence inflicted on the girl; lack of respect from the society around her. How could this do us no harm? It hurts the girl involved—it hurts all women everywhere that even one girl is treated with such disrespect and cruelty.

Maybe academic women really are different. Perhaps they do not regard assembly-line sex with the same horror that I do. Perhaps they could be put in an abattoir brothel and come out unfazed. Simply 'observing' the 100 men a day raping them in tidy, scientific fashion, being good little objective scholars while it is happening. Then going off and writing a tidy, objective, meaningless article about the experience, non-existent, cast-iron vagina and hyper-intellectual mind still intact. Not me. I bleed. I hurt. I look upon the violation of my body with fear and terror and misery. Trembling and shaking.

All of my novels are full of different kinds of prostitutes—from ones who are 'comfort girls'—with tons of men lined up to 'get at' the poor things—to independent whores who can choose their 'customers.' All of my prostituted girls—from the lowest most mistreated 'comfort whore'—the one just like the Korean Comfort Girls—to the most elegant and stylish 'free whore'—are pathetic, to my mind. All are abused by systems that control and define their sexuality in ways that are brutal, patriarchal, and unloving and untender. Of course I recognize the degrees. Far, far better to be a Thai bar girl getting fucked by a dozen or so different men a month than a Thai girl held in debt bondage in a brothel being raped a dozen or more times a night. Far better to be me, with a limited clientele of a bunch of American soldiers—who did not beat me or rough me up—as opposed to the trafficked girls who are broken in rape camps and have anal forced on them. But it is all degradation and control by men. We women are soft and helpless and have no power or freedom or independence.

My novels are not intended as a paean to prostitution.

I think I may be so sensitive to what is happening to Slavic sex slaves all over the world since part of my ancestry is Slavic. That could be me being trafficked. And I am ashamed to be part-Slavic when I see how ruthlessly Slavic men traffic girls all over the world. We are sensitive to that which has impacted us personally. I see my Slavic male relatives as greedy and callous. I know they are the kind of people who would traffic girls. They are worse than the men in *Eastern Promises*. It scares me to know that they might be trafficking me if we were still back in the 'old country.' That which impacts us personally.

I admit it is very difficult for me to talk to any man of my generation because my memories are full of Vietnam vets who came back and made constant dirty jokes about the Vietnamese whores they used and some of those vets raped me and turned me into a dirty joke. It was the war that ruined my life and my body, so I have a permanent aversion to these men. Even now they make dirty jokes about the whores they used. 'Fun Bang in Da Nang' and you put this little slogan on your T-shirts and baseball caps and you ruined the life and body of a starving girl who had to fuck for food. No wonder men like to go to war so much. They are surrounded by girls who have to fuck for food. Men at war can do what comes sexually natural to them--dispense with courtship and tenderness and love and just go straight for the fuck.

Growing up during the Vietnam War and during the era of Flower Power and Free Love of the 1960's and 1970's taught me that man just wants his fuck. There was no Sexual Revolution for Women. The young men around me—the ones who had been in Vietnam, the civilians, the college boys--all of them just wanted their fuck. And once they got it they labeled the girls dispensing 'free love,' whores and sluts—just like they did in the 1950's—and just like they do now.

Vietnam destroyed my life and my body. Vietnam raped me to pieces. Vietnam fills me with such incredible sadness that I cannot even meet people from there without misery in my heart. I would never want to visit the country. I associate it with hell on earth and the rape of my body.

I watch a comedy show called *Whose Line is it Anyway*? for relaxation and most of the time it is a respite from reality, but every once in a while a whore/prostitute joke comes up. Then I see the audience, including the women, just roaring with laughter. Smirks and titters and squeals also come from the women. Don't they realize that they are laughing at the cruelest thing that can happen to a woman? They are making deep sexual cruelty into a joke. Can any kind of legislation succeed if the whore is always a dirty joke and if even women laugh at her pain? As California tries to pass legislation to help the prostituted, will women in California still laugh at 'whore' jokes—as if the girl so treated is dirt and garbage and her suffering is 'funny.' Until we change 'normal' women's attitudes, there is no hope for the prostituted.

For whatever reason, my mind keeps flowing back to that posh hotel in Paris and the protected women scholars sitting around. They seem to me typical of the women of the world, no matter what their status, in that most women are blind and ignorant when it comes to the dreadful reality of the prostituted body, to the misery of her rape-fucked, beyond-rape-fucked shredded body. The normal women of the world just go blindly on their way. A female reporter interviews women outside the goldmine barracks in South Africa: these poor creatures are forced to fuck in the woods around the barracks, on pieces of cardboard. They are forced to fuck their slime-male rapist miner 'customers' for a few cents on these pieces of cardboard. What woman should be reduced to this? Fucking some slime-male on a piece of cardboard for a few cents. But does the female reporter in any way respond to the deep and miserable indignity of this? Nope. She is all cool and collected, as she 'reports' on this. (A situation where 'man must have his fuck' rules to the extreme—no matter what the dreadful degradation of the female.) There is no 'ethics of objectivity' when one reports sexual brutality this deep and this harsh. Any reporter 'reporting' this needs to report the truth: that this is beyond indignity, beyond rape, beyond brutality. Instead, the female reporter walks around in her neat suit, being 'objective.' I would be ashamed of such 'objectivity.' But she, sadly, does not know any better. She has been taught in male schools by male journalists about this imaginary thing called objectivity.

I have absolutely no intention to be objective about the red-hot brutal misery that is prostitution. Women 'reporters' worldwide should be ashamed of themselves for this pretense of objectivity.

Back to Paris—I cannot seem to forget this conference because the women were so smug and self-satisfied and protected and blind. I am sure they were well meaning in their hearts—I am surrounded by academic and professional women who have good hearts and good intentions—so I ask why are their hearts so hardened toward the prostituted? Why is she a dirty joke to them? One woman scholar from Prague made a joke about Shakespeare and how he likened whores to donkeys because both got beat with rods—one on the inside the other on the outside. I asked her if she knew anything about the girls trafficked into brothels in Prague who were forced to fuck 'customers' in front of cameras for porn films. The 'customer-rapists' could fuck the girls for free if they agreed to be filmed for porn. I pointed out that only trafficked whores would 'agree' to be filmed for porn. And they were probably being forced to do anal since 'normal,' privileged, safe women will not do anal. She said she knew nothing about this and did not want to know. It was not her 'field,' to study prostitution. It was their concern, what they did with their bodies, these prostitutes.

I then asked not just her but the other women sitting with me, taking tea and sipping coffee and eating pastries in safety, why it was okay for women scholars to write laudatory articles about a man, Shakespeare, who makes dirty jokes about whores being beaten by rods on the inside the way donkeys are beaten by rods on the outside? No answers. Just blank, blind, smug, stupid, well-educated, objective, learned politeness. Damn, I despise scholars and their shallow, heartless 'scholarship.' I am ashamed to be even tangentially a part of this world.

In the Playboy Forum for June 2009, I came across an article called "A Postcard from Europe" with the long subtitle, "An Acclaimed Croatian Novelist Feels Hope Despite the Fissures Opening as the Economy Sinks." It is by Dubravka Ugrešić, a woman writer who left her country during the war in Yugoslavia and is now living in Amsterdam. She writes: "Ordinary Europeans ooze solidarity. The circulation of human cargo—thanks to the fall of the Berlin wall (Europe celebrates the 20th anniversary this year!) and the benefits of globalization—is livelier now than ever before" (Ugrešić 119). As instances of this 'lively cargo,' she gives Polish plumbers migrating to Spain and Bulgarian women working as maids across Western Europe. In the list, alongside her other items, she gives the following: "Young Moldovan teachers joined western European prostitutes soliciting on every street corner of Europe...Albanians are clever traffickers and pimps" (119). The overall message of her article is about hope in Europe stirred by the hope in Obama's inauguration speech. But I cannot figure out the tone. Is she being ironical about the prostituted/trafficked girls and the selling of 'human cargo' as a 'lively' activity and a 'benefit' of globalization. It is hard to tell from the context of the article. Would the 14-year-old Albanian who is being raped 20 hours a day in a London brothel consider herself as benefiting from her 'globalized' rape? Is the 14-year-old Balkan girl being raped a 100 times a day in Greece feeling the 'benefits' of globalization?

Living in Amsterdam, as she does, Ugrešić must be aware of the situation in her own backyard. Of how legalization has caused huge increases in trafficking and how the few girls who manage to escape their traffickers report the slave-like conditions they work under. There has been coverage of this in the European press—so much so that Holland is re-considering its policies. When the girls in the windows are mostly trafficked foreigners without passports and are 'servicing' 10 to 30 men a day, something is wrong. Ugrešić must be aware of all this. If she is aware, is she trying to be clever at the expense of the trafficked girls being raped all day? Is this an instance of a privileged, intellectual woman joking around about prostitution? Being 'witty' about this terrible cruelty inflicted on the female body.

Surely she must know about the rape camps during the war in her own country. Trafficked girls are also in types of 'rape camps.' How can she make jokes about this? If that is her intention. It is difficult to tell from her tone. Or does she actually think that trafficking 'benefits' the women being trafficked?

That 14-year-old Albanian girl being raped 20 hours a day in London is told about in an Amnesty International report. I am not sure that she would consider the pimps and traffickers who broke her and control her 'clever.' Diabolical and vicious perhaps. Amnesty International also tells us that Slavic girls held in captivity in London are raped up to 40 times a day. (Are British males so incredibly desperate for sex that they must use these bleeding, tortured girls?)

I recently discovered a Canadian scholar named Richard Poulin who has been researching trafficking for twenty years. From him, I learned that adolescent Balkan girls trafficked into Greece are being raped 30 to 100 times a day (111) and that there are 'submissions' camps in the Balkans where girls are 'trained' to be raped (117).

I was so haunted by this new material that I had to do something—so I am writing more 'afterthoughts.' A chance 'fact,' read somewhere, sets me off, since I am so haunted by all this suffering. Not that my writing will help the girls from the Balkans. But what else can I do? I am haunted that this 14-year-old Balkan girl has had her life taken from her when these 100 Greek men rape her every day. She had it taken from her on the first 100-a-day rape. And there is nothing I can do for her. I cannot change the nature of the Greek male. Or the nature of the British male who rapes her counterpart in London. Or—add any nationality—American, Brazilian, Indian, Cambodian, Canadian, Mexican, German—I would have to list all the countries of the world—except maybe Sweden and Norway. From Poulin, I learn that the majority of prostituted beings across Western Europe are trafficked—many of them Slavic girls but there are also ones from South America, Africa, and Asia. So the prosperous, privileged women of Western Europe just go about their business—while the men of Western Europe mass rape enslaved bodies? Utterly amazing. Utterly friggin' fuckin' amazing.

I also recently ran across more material on a website which features Emma Thompson (www.teachers.tv/video/28030). It has information from Poppy and the Helen Bamber Foundation, groups that try to help the trafficked in the UK. Thompson seems sincere in her passion about this cause. She mentions that the men who buy the girls are just 'ordinary.' This is true. But she also says that this is not 'pointing a finger' at anyone. I think we really need to be doing far more than pointing a finger at these men who are raping these bleeding, torn girls every day. If we never punish or censure the rapists, this sanctioned rape of the female body will never end. 'Pointing a finger' would be mild. We need to be chopping off some dicks.

And there is blood involved. These British shit rapist 'ordinary' males are making the girls bleed. I was surprised how much I would bleed from just a few rapes. The blood must be tremendous after 40 or more rapes a day. The 'Journey' exhibit, about sex-slaves, which was in downtown London, showed blood on the filthy sheets where the girl was forced to get fucked. But they did not put enough blood on the sheets. I wish the exhibit could have found a way to express the pain that happens between our legs—this most sensitive part of us is ravaged and the kind of pain involved cannot be put into words. It is different from pain to an arm or a leg. It is sexual pain, which is pain at the center of your being which destroys everything about you. Not to mention that 'unwelcome' intercourse feels like you are being razored to death between your legs. The pain at the tender opening to the vagina feels like fire being applied to a cut.

What kind of man could do this to a woman? An 'ordinary' one apparently. Any man next door to you—or in your household.

Despite more voices and more women and even some sensitive men—like Richard Poulin and Victor Malarek (another Canadian)--actually addressing the rape-prostitution of the female body, trafficking just grows and grows and grows. I think this growth must involve more than how easy it if for the traffickers to trade in flesh and how poor and vulnerable many women and girls are in a world that disenfranchises the female. The root has to be the willingness, ability, and desire of the average human male to rape us. If a man can rape, he will. There has really been nothing in history to stop him thus far. He will rape us soft females because he is stronger, and he can. All the voices out there finally protesting this don't seem to be making a dent in the mass rape of the prostituted body that is taking place daily. Millions of rapes daily. No way to stop it as long as we collectively accept that 'man must have his fuck.' So every 'free,' non-trafficked woman who is not protesting this daily rape is partly responsible for it.

I don't know of any way to stop the natural rape tendencies of the male. I have pondered this since I ran across the one sentence that changed my life and caused me to write seven books. You know the sentence by now, the one revealed by Tanaka (another sensitive male writer) in his material on the Occupation Comfort Girls. It is the sentence about fifty American soldiers lining up to get at one prostituted Japanese body. I have been trying to figure out how this could happen? That one stark piece of rape reality negates all hope. It made me realize that all the men around me are rapists. Take any one of my male friends, lovers, acquaintances and put him in 1945 Tokyo and he would be in line to rape that girl. Almost no men held back: whenever you allow men to rape, they will rape. My former boyfriend Vic, stationed in Korea, says almost every guy there used the whores. It is universal. The rape of the helpless female body by the entitled male. Military or civilian. Given him a space called brothel and he will rape the whore put there for his convenience. Vic said the girls cried when he used them. He felt bad about this but he fucked them anyway. He said pathetic things about the girls—like they looked like they'd been hit by tanks from being fucked so much. Dead eyes, he said the Korean whores had. But he fucked them anyway. Man must have his fuck. Even nice men. Vic was a nice guy.

There is no way we can stop this—this 'man must have his fuck.' We women have no strength. It is because men are so much stronger that they can do this to us—I wonder if the Burmese girls sold into Thai brothels and used by businessmen and labourers and military and police would be there, sore and miserable and diseased, if they had not been forced. Make those girls stronger than the men and there is no way they lay there in rape-misery all day.

Why is this simple fact overlooked? Men are physically stronger. Therefore, they can control our weak softness. The fact that some don't is a miracle we should be grateful for. There are some men who would be ashamed to hurt a woman. But apparently not the millions of customer-rapists around the world. That is a huge number who do not control their strength—and they are using it to destroy us.

I am pure softness. There is no strength in softness or gentleness. I knew I was raped to pieces in some form even under the mild from of prostitution I went through. Just one act of painful intercourse would have made me scared forever. I remember when I lost my virginity. The man was very gentle but the pain scared me to death. The Timid Vagina. The Bleeding Vagina. Being hurt between my legs causes huge repercussions in the rest of my being. It makes the whole world seem terrifying. It makes me feel completely soft and helpless. Fear of assembly-line sex haunts me—it was intensified enormously because I was gang raped. How could any girl take that on a daily basis? How can the girls in the Amsterdam windows survive 10 to 30 rapes a day? Prostitution may be my own private nightmare. Perhaps no other girl in the world minds being prostituted. Maybe their bodies and vaginas are made differently and not at all fazed by 10 to 30 acts of intercourse a day. Even so—even if all other girls in prostitution do not mind being used in this way—my own private prostitution fears are legitimate. It is a legitimate nightmare. As a living being I have the right to safe space on this planet.

I have also come across some new information on Iraq—but it has been hard to come by and very scarce—the forbidden territory: no one wants to talk about the huge number of women and girls prostituted/trafficked/sexually abused because of this war. (By all wars, of course.) The prostitution side of this war is being ignored--as usual. All wars seem to ignore the prostitution side. For me, it is like living through Vietnam all over again: a vast underground of exploited/trafficked/raped/prostituted women and girls almost invisible to the media.

As I sit here writing, I see a commercial on TV for Time/Life and its visual history of Vietnam, claiming it will show me 'the real war'—all the way from the Gulf of Tonkin to the Siege of Khe Sanh and it shows footage of tons of soldiers and sailors but no where do I see the sailors lined up to rape the little whores in the ports where they docked or the GI's lined up outside the brothels set up for them on the perimeters of their bases. No where do I see the despicable South Vietnamese pimps who set up some of the rape facilities. No where do I see the prostitutes shipped into Khe Sanh, along with the Budweiser. What happened to those girls, I wonder? How many were there—for the 6000 Marines at Khe Sanh? Did the girls get raped to death by such large numbers? Prostitutes worldwide say that Marines are the roughest of the American military men. I cannot even imagine not just the vaginal damaging but the bruised bodies of these tiny girls from being laid on by so many rough men. What happened to the girls before they were 'recruited' for Khe Sanh? Were they refugee girls 'recruited' by pimps? Could the girls read or write? Did they even know what was happening to them when so many big solders were raping them everyday? Were they what one fancy female scholar at her fancy university refers to as 'lower-class prostitutes'?

What on earth—or in the deepest hell--is a 'lower class prostitute'? Are the ones in Vietnam who lost their families and homes in the war and ended up homeless refugees abducted or coerced by pimps into 'serving' a dozen GI's a day 'lower-class prostitutes'? Is it because they were helpless and homeless and had to 'take on' so many men that they were 'lower-class prostitutes'? Does the continuous rape of the prostituted body render her 'lower-class' in some way? How many men does a prostituted girl have to be raped by before she qualifies as a 'lower-class prostitute'? Will a hundred do it, or a thousand, or does she have to survive 30,000 or so before she really 'earns' her status as a 'lower-class prostitute'? Did the 'cheap pussy' that my boyfriends told me they bought in Vietnam—the really cheap whores who would 'let' men climb on them while other guys took pictures—and every one laughed and joked around about how much she was getting fucked—is this pathetic creature a 'lower-class prostitute'?

I am ashamed to be part of the academic world.

Where is Time/Life's 'visual history' of all the 'lower-class prostitutes' in Vietnam? Where is the 'visual history' of the girls shipped into Khe Sanh and mounted by all those Budweiser-soaked Marines? Did the girls die at Khe Sanh? Why has no prostituted girl from there ever told her story?

I would have been scared to death if someone shipped me into Khe Sanh and all these drunk men were using me. What kind of lives and rape nightmares did the girls who survived carry with them forever? The things <u>they</u> carried. No one notices this burden of war—the rape memories of the girls. Why am I supposed to feel sorry for the men who raped the girls?

Men go to war—they destroy and rape. They have been doing this forever. Why is this glorious and heroic and noble?

What happened to girls in the 'fancy' brothels in Da Nang? Were the girls held in debt-bondage? Did others take the money from the rape of their bodies? Was it business as usual in these 'fancy' brothels—that is, the 'normal' degradation of being pawed and mounted by drunk men? What was 'fancy' about these brothels for the girls conscripted to serve in them? You see, no overused body enjoys it. She just gets used to it and smiles to survive.

No where do I see the true side of war—which is the rape of the female body. Why doesn't Time/Life tell where those prostituted girls came from, what sort of poverty and hunger drove them to this, who pimped them onto the bases and is taking the money, how many men a day raped them? Why don't we see, in the Time/Life footage, all the soldiers—American, Vietnamese, French—lined up with their dicks out, ready to rape the helpless prostituted body. This is war. (I instance just Vietnam—but I include all wars and all soldiers—for the 5000 years that men have been making war—in my condemnation.)

I am not a 'byproduct' of war. My raped female body is not an irrelevant sideline to the wars you men make. I am not some Hollywood-created bar-girl in a war movie—just a temporary beer-and-bang 'fuck-stop' where you 'let off steam' till you go out and 'heroically' suffer in some futile carnage-ridden battleground of your lost, brutal, ugly, male, war-making souls. I am central to the wars you make. Every prostituted girl in Khe Sanh or Saigon, every rape she endured, was central to the war you men made—the war you inflicted on her.

What you now have, in 2009, is a bunch of vets who still don't talk about the prostituted bodies they raped and who write all these poems and memoirs to show how civilized and sensitive they are—now—after their savage use of helpless girls in war-time. All the poems in the world will never restore the dignity and beauty and life to those young girls they took such terrible advantage of. Yet the men never even admit that they did anything wrong to these pathetic creatures forced to sell their most soft selves due to hunger and war-time desperation. No poem can ever restore the life and dignity you took from this girl. Every use of her prostituted body was rape. You were just one of a long line of rapists who destroyed her. I wonder how you men could buy the really, really young ones? Some pathetic fifteen-year-old who will never even know what life is or what sex is since you raped both of them out of her body.

I cannot feel sorry for the men who make war. They don't have to pick up the guns. For that matter, they don't have to invent the weapons they kill each other with. Since they have been playing this war game so long, they must love it. The big problem is that the majority of causalities in wartime are women and children. Men play their war games at the expense of women and children. War never liberates women. The conquering Allied soldiers who marched into France raped widely—in the name of 'liberating' French women. This is not just one historical instance. It is typical of all wars. While the noble British army did its best to bring its noble civilizing ways to the brown 'heathens' in India, wretched young India girls were forced to go into the barracks and service large numbers of men and the pimping brown 'heathen' shits who sold them were no more civilized than the 'noble' shits who raped the girls.

All men are the same. They rape. They make war. You will never stop war and rape as long as man has a penis. You will never stop prostitution for this reason as well. Man has a penis. He will force it in. It is the way of the world.

I can't seem to get away from the brutality. I just accidentally ran across a song called "Khe Sanh Lyrics" by a man who writes about a soldier taking R & R in Hong Kong , where "there ain't nothing like the kisses from a jaded Chinese princess/I'm gonna hit some Hong Kong mattress all night long." Is this what we are to men: used women (far from 'princesses'—princesses are pampered and cherished) that they buy kisses and fucks from? Sad, bought women that they bang into a mattress all night long? What kind of an attitude is that for men to have toward us? Ugly and brutal. As elsewhere, those girls sold to R & R soldiers in Hong Kong were pimp-controlled and lived in great sexual misery. This image of banging this poor girl into a mattress all night long is absolutely terrifying to me. I hope I never meet the person who wrote this. He would scare me to death. One of the drawbacks of being on the Internet is that you run across information like this—a song called 'Khe Sanh Lyrics' with the sad misery of a prostituted Hong Kong girl in it. The sexual misery of our bought bodies is everywhere. The Internet also tells me that this song was written by an Australian and that it is quite popular with Australian military men. Apparently they like to bang on tables and get rowdy when they hear it. Sad, this roughness, for the prostitutes these men might use in Hong Kong.

Drunk men banging on tables and singing dirty songs about raped whores. What a world of noble 'manliness' we live in.

I don't know how to escape from this male brutal rape world. Where do I go—so they won't hurt me? Where can I go so I will not know anymore about their drunk, rough, terrifying ways? No 'Shire' anywhere to escape to.

There will, alas, never be any coverage of my Vietnam—of the war that destroyed both my life and my body so many years ago.

Left out in coverage of Iraq is the devastating prostitution visited on Iraqi women and girls by this war that is not their war. War is never our war, the female war. It is men making war and damaging us dreadfully. An Iraqi woman writer e-mailed me with some of what she has found out. I will simply quote from her—I asked her permission to use this since anything that is in an e-mail is private. She said go ahead. Please let others know what I have found out. Her name is Ishtar Ennan and here is what she wrote me:

"I finished for the time being writing and publishing articles about trafficking and prostituting Iraqi women in the Green Zone in Baghdad and in Kurdistan, Jordan, Syria, Yemen, Bahrain, and Dubai, as the main destinations for trafficked women. All these places, except Syria, have US military bases. I found that US private security companies have a great role in trafficking of Iraqi women.

"For instance, let's take Dyncorp who was accused of trafficking girls in Cosovo and Bosnia, also trafficking drugs from Colombia, was contracted by the Pentagon to train the Iraqi police, manage prisons , one of them being Abu ghraib,

"I have been following this company since 2003 after reading about its scandals in the Balkans and Colombia.

"After the invasion, kidnapping and disappearance incidents of Iraqi girls and women increased.

"The link to Dyncorp was revealed lately, when it was discovered that the company's manager in Iraq used armoured vehicles to transfer prostitutes to hotels in Baghdad managed by Dyncorp.

"Then the big revelation came when I knew that the top CEOs of Dyncorp were retired US generals who were involved in the destruction of Iraq since 1991.

"This is the BIG CONNECTION. You must have a strong heart to accept this kind of corruption.

"I have followed the trail of Iraqi women trafficking to Yemen which was mentioned early in the report on trafficking by the State Department since 2003, as a destination for trafficked women from Iraq...

"I am an Iraqi fiction writer, activist, and investigative internet journalist. I am living outside of Iraq. I have finished writing and publishing 10 articles about the role of collaborating translators with the US invaders, and 10 articles about the role of the Occupation in trafficking and prostituting Iraqi women.

I have some published books in Arabic, one translated into English and another into Italian.

Ishtar"

End of material from Ishtar.

I simply left Ishtar's English as is—with respect and amazement that she can function in her language and mine, since I would be lost trying to write in her language. I wanted you to hear her words as she wrote them, without any summarizing from me. Ishtar told me she cannot write any more on this now because it is too painful and difficult. This heartened me since I am often criticized for not being able to face the pain of what I write. You can find more information on what is happening in Iraq on Ishtar's blog: ishtar-enana.blogspot.com.

I know from experience that it is tough to come by information about prostitution and rape in Iraq. I no longer come in contact with that many soldiers. Of the few I know who have been in Iraq, I do ask them what is happening. They are very evasive in their answers. I may get an admission that there is prostitution and rape, but they will not go into details. The same for Afghanistan. No definite answers, just eyes looking away, when I ask about Slavic and Chinese girls who are trafficked into that country—or so I have read in various places on the Internet.

It would seem that no matter how many women politicians we have, they still do not pay attention to the sexual destruction of the female body as central to war. I refuse to say as a 'byproduct' of war since the millions of women, girls, and children sexually violated during war and occupation are not a byproduct. They are a central fact—from WWII to Vietnam to Kosovo to Iraq to the Sudan and the Congo. I refuse to regard the sexual destruction of the female body as irrelevant to the male concerns of 'war.'

We really need some women politicians to feel this way. In the news at the moment (June 2009) is a story about how much Nancy Pelosi knew about torture techniques during the Bush administration. Where is her concern for the women and girls currently being sexually tortured in Iraqi prisons? Why are there no front-page pictures of this? Why is only the torture of men important? Why is there still a cover-up of the torture of female bodies during Vietnam? Why do we not have photos and front-page reports of the girls being electrically shocked in their vaginas and on their nipples and of girls being stripped and raped? Why is Amnesty International only interested in the torture of men at Gitmo? Why do we not see what is happening in prisons to women around the world? Where is the coverage of the torture of women—in all wars? Again, only men seem to matter. Only photos of men being sexually humiliated in prison came out of Iraq. Where are the hidden photos—the ones the USA government will not print—the ones of women being sexually humiliated, gang-raped, tortured—in Iraq? The same place the ones from Vietnam are—hidden.

One American woman politician who really seems to care about other women is Barbara Boxer, but I still do not see her taking on the prostitution aspect of the Iraqi war or the women and girls in prisons there being tortured. It's as if this side of war must stay forever hidden.

As I write this, two American women journalists have been arrested in North Korea and now sentenced to labour camps. One of the stories on Yahoo mentioned that the women were investigating the trafficking of North Korean women at the time. Scary. All of the coverage of this event, in both the liberal and conservative media, is characteristically 'macro.' Lots of politics—lots of idea slinging. Some of this is of course necessary. But I wish someone had latched onto what they were investigating and tried to find out if this had anything to do with the arrests. Perhaps it did not. But if it did, it is an indication of how traffickers—whatever their nationality—North Korean, Albanian, German, Columbian—do not want their business interfered with.

On the subject of the media, after all the typical 'macro' coverage of war and misery, I would like to see the 'micro' emphasized. It saddens me to see the 'idea' aspect of media coverage crowd out all else. For the girl on the war-torn ground—whether she be in the Sudan or the Congo or Kenya or Liberia—war is just war to her—all the astute analyses of Western journalists are meaningless to her. She does not know or care about the thousands of male decisions, at high 'political' levels, that led to her plight. Her pathetic plight is her reality. It is the reality of all of us. Self-indulgent debates by the *Capitol Gang* and polite political chit chat on *Charlie Rose* will not change her fate. All sorts of clever comments by hard-voiced, hard-as-nails female journalists contribute to her fate by ignoring her.

When you see a refugee mother running with a baby in her arms—while bombs form the North and bombs from the South and ones from the East and the West explode around her, she doesn't care about all the hard-voiced, self-important, intellectually sophisticated discourse flying about in the Western media. For her, the whole planet is the Axis of Evil. And she is helpless to protect her baby.

All aspects of life are permeated by prostitution for me since that is what I am—a prostitute. Although I have been functioning in academic settings for quite some time now, I feel like an alien beside other academic women. I can have nothing in common with non-whore women so I walk around smiling and being friendly, but with no genuine human contact—since I am a whore. If they knew, they would not speak to me. They would throw me out. After all, what right do I have to say anything? I am just a whore. We have no human rights.

Being an outcast, however, is preferable to the company of those who scorn me.

Being an outcast seems an inevitable part of the whore state, particularly in the blind, ivory-tower academic world. I was glancing though a text book on human sexuality used in one of those fancy college courses with a fancy title about gender and the body and the empowered state of woman, complete with a colon, to show how distinguished the professor of human sexuality was in his thinking when he concocted this title. The text contained one sentence about prostitution and a straggly footnote--as if the most salient fact about women—that we are prostituted in all possible ways and robbed of even the minimum of anything that could be defined as 'our sexuality'--as if the deepest destruction of sexuality known to the human race—the turning of a woman into a 'whore' and the degradation of her entire being--is simply irrelevant to 'human' experience. Amazing.

As I try to finish up this book, in 2009, I struggle with so much that haunts me. My wandering style is an effort to refuse to be part of the traditional academic world—I am ashamed to be what is called a 'scholar' in a world that 'studies' suffering and does nothing about it. My wandering style is haunted and I have no way out other than the Ancient Mariner path of repeating that which haunts me. Not that anyone will listen to my small, insignificant voice. My sheer hopelessness—stemming from what I have learned as I have written and researched this book—the extent of the sexual exploitation in the world is staggering. Trying to do something about it is overwhelming.

I have concluded that there is no way prostitution can be considered 'voluntary' under most circumstances. This seems to be a big point of contention, among scholars—the 'voluntary' aspect, and I think we would be better off if we just stopped arguing about this. This endless, useless debate is not taking the girls out of the brothels. I doubt if girls in brothels have the intellectual leisure to sit around and debate whether their enslavement is 'voluntary.' This is a pastime of the leisured, and the unraped and undegraded. When the attitude that girls in brothels are 'never raped' since the owner/ mama-san has to keep the 'merchandise' in 'good shape' for the ten men a day she has never seen before to mount her—well, you can see that the 'voluntary' debate is futile. Ordinarily, if a girl has 'choice,' she will not invite men inside her she does not know. She will certainly not invite the drunk partying rough shit males who visit brothels to mount her. She won't 'invite' anyone to mount her, in fact, against her will, if she has 'choice.' So, this whole 'voluntary' debate is the self-indulgent, intellectual female doing what she usually does—think in fancy circles around the rape-dead bodies of the prostituted.

When you have a situation where a Slavic Girl is trafficked into Dubai and 'broken' by her pimps letting a different man in to use her every few minutes—and then when you have this same girl sold to businessmen, sex tourists, religious men, military men, students—and she has to fuck whoever comes along—and then she escapes and goes back into prostitution 'voluntarily'—well, that word has absolutely no meaning under the circumstances of this girl's life. (I wonder if all the sex tourists and soldiers and businessmen who use her know of her background? Do they know they are simply next in a long line of rapists? How sad is the word 'intimacy' for the Dubai/Slavic Girl after her heavy use by everyone.)

I know for sure that you can never erase this kind of sexual overuse once it has happened to you. The trafficked girl used 80 times on Christmas Day in London who escapes and goes to college still carries around inside her a depth of sexual abuse that can never be forgotten.

No one is 'okay' after 80 rapes in one day. This is unendurable—for any woman it happens to. (It is not as if the women we label 'whores' have cast-iron vaginas. It astonishes me that 'normal' women think that prostituted women have different kinds of vaginas. We women all have the same body.) No one is ever 'okay' after being treated the way the Dubai/Slavic Girl was. There is simply no healing from this. And there is no 'voluntary' if the girl's entry into prostitution was full of violence and rape. There is no way she can 'go back into it' on her own—even if she 'chooses' to do so. It is not a choice that can in any way be based on what she wants to do. At this point, after so much rape, she is not capable of making choices about her own sexuality.

I am also impatient with those who say—'she knew what she was getting in to.' Boy. Yeah, like I really wanted to have all that humiliation and sexual misery shoved into me by these disgusting drunk men. Until it happens to you, there is no way you can know 'what you are getting in to.' And by then it is too late. It has already destroyed you.

I know for sure that in any act of sex if the woman is not receiving pleasure, it is rape. Prostitution is such a revolting perversion of sexuality. What woman enjoys the overuse of her body? The terrible overuse of her body. If she is not enjoying the sex act, it is rape. Degrees of rape, for sure. The pathetic child whore in a Cambodian or Indian brothel has visited on her the extreme form. But the girl who was 'broken,' escaped her traffickers, and went back into prostitution 'on her own' is also being raped in some way. The breaking trained her to accept the rape. And once having been prostituted, it is practically impossible to leave. Even if you physically leave, somehow, you are still in prostitution. It is hard to explain. There simply does not seem to be any world beyond prostitution. That is the best I can do to explain it.

I know for sure that you cannot be a tourist in Cambodia and go visit a shrine and say 'how spiritual' if even one girl is in some wretched, ugly brothel with her bruised body being used by some despicable Cambodian rapist male or some despicable sex tourist. There is not one single ounce of spirituality in any country where this is happening. You cannot find a shrine to worship at that is 'spiritual' if even one girl is being raped anywhere on this planet.

I know there is no 'Shire' to go back to, no home country to return to, for the prostituted. She has no place of peace on this planet. I know this from the degraded hell that is my own body. What 'Shire' is my home? What stream can I sit by, and have peace?

The norm on Rape Planet Earth is the Japanese girls sold into 'legal' prostitution for over four centuries who were caged and raped continuously to 'fit' them for the 'trade'—the same as in the modern-day 'breaking' submissions camps, where it is assumed that if you rape a girl enough she will not care who uses her. Who thought that one up, I wonder? Certainly not any of the women of the world. What a sick, distorted perversion of sexuality is prostitution.

But maybe the women of the world did have a hand in all this—as complicit in the terrible rape of female bodies. From simply accepting the rapes going on around them everyday—as women in Germany do as they ignore the enslaved girls in their rape prisons called Eros Centres—these 'respectable' women are also responsible. All the American women who ignored the sex slaves created in Vietnam for U.S. military use are also guilty of the rape their men inflicted on these girls. The American women simply regarded the 'whores' in Vietnam as necessary, a norm of war, and as a dirty joke. Not one iota of sympathy or understanding—intellectual or otherwise—did I find during that era among these women, the ones of my generation. They just laughed and smirked if the subject was brought up—and thought these 'whores' got what they deserved if they chose to be 'dirty whores.' Not one thought entered their heads that the girls were largely refugees or homeless and destitute—and more often than not taken over by pimps who exploited them. It never seemed to occur to these 'decent' American women that fucking a whole line of GI's is not fun. It kills everything about you. Even getting fucked by one man a day you do not want inside you will kill you—let alone ten or twenty.

My whole generation of women absolutely sickens me.

The whole dichotomy of women sickens me. Whores cannot afford to have an 'elegance of decorum' since they must become coarse to deal with coarse men. I don't know how you can remain sweet and wholesome when you are being crushed down by crudeness.

I know that as long as we wallow in a world full of surplus children and the insanity of having one child you can't feed—and then producing ten more—there will be the sale of female bodies. Financial desperation and the low status of women over most of the world (in Iran a woman is only 'worth' half a man) and the way girls aren't even taught to read—so they can have no dreams—all of this shows no signs of ending. Or of us even making a beginning to help these girls. More and more and more and more are being born and are being regarded as disposable beings. How does one counter such insanity?

If I see commercials and contests on TV for everyday heroes and all-star people and the such, I wonder how come no whore is ever included in the heroes of the world? She survived (maybe) being a rape dump for men under a patriarchal system that defined her as trash and the men who used her as sexually privileged to buy a body, as if slavery were still okay. I work in academic environments—accessed by my college degrees—but I feel as if I ought to be respected for being a whore—not for having earned degrees from patriarchal institutions called universities that scorn the whore. Maybe I should be respected because I actually survived being turned into sexual garbage and I am now trying to say to a patriarchal world—'you don't have any right to treat any woman like sex garbage.'

With my college degrees, I would like to go teach at some American Universities around the world. But everywhere I go, I will be confronted with trafficked/prostituted girls—and I cannot even do anything about this in my own backyard. There is an American University in Cairo. Slavic Girls are trafficked into that city under E-visas (E for 'Entertainment'). If I teach there, how can I not help them? I can't just sit around safe and privileged. The same if I were to teach in Dubai, or, say, with the University of Maryland in its branches on U.S. bases—say in Germany or Korea or Guam. Everywhere there will be prostituted girls. If I were to teach at the University of Maryland campuses on bases abroad, would they throw me out if they knew I had been a whore? Would the soldiers jeer at me if they knew? Would they treat me like they do the girls outside the gate, the ones they have 'fun' with during off-duty hours? Or would I be fired if I tried to help the whores?

I save my own self from complete hopelessness by believing that the individual life is incredibly important. Helping one girl would do it. Save one soul and you save them all. Except that I tend to see it the opposite way: lose one soul and you lose them all.

Where could I go teach that is free of trafficked girls? Where could I go to vacation, for that matter? If you take a cruise, on some lines, prostituted girls come to the ships to 'service customers.' Any tourist destinations around the word are also sex-tourist destinations. How can I go to Goa, India when I know that trafficked Slavic girls are there? Costa Rica, Belize, Rio, Bangkok—sex tourism is everywhere.

If I were to teach at the University of Maryland campuses on bases abroad, would they throw me out if they knew I had been a whore? Would the soldiers jeer at me if they knew? Would they treat me like dirt?

I watch a show on the Travel Channel about the world's sexiest beaches and one of them is Phuket. The show tells me that Phuket is "sexy because of the sex" and we catch a few glimpses of bar girls with farangs. 'Octopussy' says one sign above a bar. Phuket offers "Thai girls of all shapes and sizes," the show says. This is the same place where a number of prostituted girls died in a fire because they were chained and locked into their brothel and could not escape.

The show also shows us blonde female tourists smiling and having fun. Do these blonde female tourists think nothing of seeing girls for sale all around them? Do they never look below the fake surface smile? What are the conditions under which the prostituted girls work? Do they mind being pawed by drunk partying farangs? Do the Caucasian women tourists interact with the bar girls and ask them anything about their lives? Is poverty the reason the bar girls are here? Are they subjected to any kind of violence or humiliation? Do pimps take their money? If the girls are there due to wanting to have fun and no one controls them and they never have to go with a drunk or unpleasant customer and their lives are much better for this 'profession' of sleeping with sex tourists, I would be very much in favor of sex tourism in Phuket. Or anywhere. But I don't know what the backgrounds of these girls are. Worldwide, mistreatment, sexual abuse, poverty, coercion—all this tends to drive girls into prostitution—very young. It's rarely the desire to party and have fun having sex with strangers. If it were—and the girls were safe and protected while doing this--it would sound like a great life to me. I am very sexual. I would love to sell sex under safe and fun conditions.

Western women who style themselves 'sex workers' and take issue with me for pointing out the misery-and-torture side of prostitution need to ask if most women and girls are in this by choice? If there is even a hint of coercion, there can be no voluntary prostitution. If girls in Amsterdam sex windows are having sex with 10 to 30 men a day, this is assembly-line sex and causes terrible pain to the female body and psyche and cannot be defined as voluntary. If girls in these windows are having sex with that many men a day, it endangers and degrades me as well. There is no way prostitution can be construed as voluntary if there is any sexual pain involved for the female—and sex this many times a day will hurt any female body.

Amsterdam's windows may be a thing of the past. I have been reading that the Dutch are trying to close them down and to reverse the country's legalization policy due to the tremendous increase in trafficking and exploitation that it has brought about. Girls who have escaped traffickers in Amsterdam report being held in slavery-like conditions and being forced 30 or 40 times a day. Surely 'sex workers' who criticize me for writing about the pain of prostitution cannot think that sex this many times a day is voluntary? All they have to do is read about the tremendous physical damage this causes (to the vagina, the cervix, the ovaries) and the psychological damage from entry by strangers. And since the majority of prostituted females in Europe are trafficked, how can there be a voluntary aspect?

Most of the prostitutes in Germany, Italy, Greece, Austria, Turkey, and many other more prosperous countries are what is called 'of foreign origin'—which implies they are trafficked and will do the 'dirty jobs' of anal sex and 'taking on' multiple partners a day which the local prostitutes will not. The girls are trafficked from Eastern Europe and Russia and Africa and Asia and, of course, are not 'taking on' a hundred men a day voluntarily, or welcoming the destruction of their sex organs, anuses, and bodies.

There is an excellent Canadian scholar named Richard Poulin who has been studying trafficking for twenty years. His stats on the Netherlands, a major sex tourism destination, are startling. There 80% of the prostitutes are of foreign origin and 70% of them have no papers, indicating that they are trafficked. This means that almost all of those girls on display in the famous 'windows' are sex slaves, being stared at by the tourists as they stroll along to 'see the sights.' Poulin tells us that these girls "receive between 10 and 24 customers during 12 to 17 hours" (111). (As much as I respect Poulin and think he is a man of both heart and intelligence, I would object to the cool word 'receive.' This is not a refined party where there is a receiving line of guests in evening wear: this is rape. No 'receiving' involved. I would also point out that any prostitute with any measure of say in what happens to her will never 'service' 10 to 24 men a day. I did two or three a day, at the most, and even that made me sore, and sometimes made me bleed. As with the word usage, one needs to be explicit as to what is involved in such horrendous working conditions. At its worst, it sounds as if these girls are being raped two to three times an hour. Would American 'sex workers'—the ones who criticize me for pointing out the cruelty inherent in prostitution—would these women want to take two or three men an hour into their bodies? Men they probably do not even know the names of since the transaction is not like a 'date' and has no vestige of the civilized. Or the tender. If the girls in the windows are trafficked, then the majority of the money is going to the men who own them. Would the American 'sex workers' want to be left with only a small amount of money after all that 'labour'?)

Poulin says that in Austria, 90% of the prostitutes are foreign, indicating another trafficking situation. One of his most depressing statistics is from Greece. In that country minors purchased from the Balkans are "subjected to an average of 30 to 100 sexual contacts a day" (111). These girls can be as young as 14 when they are forced 100 times a day. (I want to comment on the use of the word 'contact' in the above sentence. A 'contact' is a gentle touch on the arm. A contact is a tentative soft approach to a body. It is not the forcing of a 100 men a day on a body.)

It is inconceivable to think of what this must do to a 14-year-old body since the vaginal tissues of young girls are much more friable and fragile than those of grown women. I assume that the ruptured ovaries and infected uteruses typical in such savage forms of prostitution are common among these young Balkan sex slaves in Greece. To have sex with their bodies that ravaged and damaged must be unendurable. I wonder how long they last under these brutal conditions?

If this form of prostitution exists, then there is no free form of prostitution available for any of us. If the majority of prostitutes exists under some kind of coercion—and if the majority enter this 'trade' in their early teens, then I don't see how the women who call themselves 'sex workers' can criticize me for pointing out that almost no prostitutes are really 'sex workers,' in any true sense of the word 'worker.' If violence and humiliation are visited on any prostitute, then no prostitute is free or safe or protected. She could be next. You can't have violence and humiliation be part of the 'job description' and have it really be a 'job.' I would like to know the life stories and working conditions and experiences inside prostitution of all women who call themselves 'sex workers' and who say this is a career choice. If any customer has ever been violent with you or humiliated you, then there is no choice involved. For one, I could be next. Allow men to buy bodies, as if this were still slavery, and allow them to hurt and humiliate the girls, and I could be next. So you cannot 'choose' this as a profession, Ms. Sex Worker, unless we radically change the profession so that no violence, no danger, no disrespect, and no humiliation are involved.

Any time you go with a new man, he could hurt you. This is unacceptable. No prostitution unless there is no danger involved.

Any time you reveal you are a prostitute/whore/sex worker—whatever you want to call yourself—you are in danger of mainstream society rejecting you. This means if you put 'former prostitute' on a resume, you probably will not be hired for the job. This means that all sorts of narrow-minded people will consider you total garbage. Not acceptable. There can only be prostitution if the prostitute is respected—completely—for what she does.

I think it's funny that both 'sex workers' in the USA and 'farangs' in Asia have accused me of believing that prostitution is 'wrong.' 'Wrong'—they throw the word at me--as if I were part of some repressive religious moral majority who condemns sex as sin. Well, I do think that mistreatment of the female body is 'wrong.' I do think that humiliation of the female spirit is 'wrong.' I do think that destruction of female sexuality is 'wrong.' All of this is typical of most forms of prostitution. But as for having some kind of moral/religious slant to my thinking—no way. Religions worldwide repress and destroy female sexuality. Why would I be on their side?

It is a real struggle to write about this subject due to the horrific suffering involved. Being forced sexually is beyond a violation of human rights. My efforts are made far more difficult by 'sex workers' who do not want me to reveal the harsh side of prostitution under which most women exist. If I want the same thing as 'sex workers' do—'human rights' for all women, particular for those of us who sell sex since we have been neglected for so long, then I wonder--Why can't we all work together toward this goal? My job is made a lot tougher by all this opposition and blindness to the cruelty inherent in prostitution.

The very few other prostitutes I've met in person did not look like 'sex workers.' Scars on their bodies. Washed-out eyes. Tough and hardened. Backgrounds that read like a made-for-Lifetime TV movie about runaways and pimps and drugs and incest. Is this typical? I fear so—particularly if the average age a girl 'enters' prostitution in the USA is a mere 14—just a child still. Girls that age should be protected, not climbed on by grown men. It is revolting to think of 'ordinary' American men using these girl children. Do the men go home to daughters the age of these girls?

I was not treated badly at all when I was a prostitute—with a few exceptions: twice men were violent toward me and really scared me and once I was anally raped. Some few customers behaved like real sleazes. But, overall, the majority of the guys I slept with were pretty decent. Hurting a girl, even one called a 'prostitute,' was not high on their agendas. Basically, getting their sex was important and on their minds—not roughing me up or scaring me. It even kind of surprised me that most of these men were nice to me. After all, the military does not exactly instill 'sensitivity' in men, or teach them to respect prostitutes.

Still, despite my experiences, prostitution affected me in very deep ways. Being entered by a lot of different men under frightening and unprotected circumstances is very traumatic. Somehow nothing outside prostitution looks normal or real. It isolated me so much—being entered by so many men I did not want inside me—that I have stayed isolated and outcast from the lives of 'normal' women forever. Such is the response of a prostitute who was treated pretty well. It is really hard for me to imagine the aftermath, the depth of PTS, that girls not so well treated carry around with them. Ones raped multiple times a day and broken by criminal organizations until they are true 'slaves' must not stand any chance of survival at all. No life after prostitution would be possible for women so deeply damaged.

Back to some more information from Poulin. According to him, a prostitute in Germany cannot register in an Eros Centre without her owner. The profits the procurers/owners make off of the girls, he says, are staggering. Each girl in an owner's stable, in Europe, on average earns him about $130,000 US a year. An owner who controls a dozen girls can make about $10,000 dollars a day on them. Russian prostitutes in Germany earn about $9500 a month and the owner/pimp/procurer takes about $8500. Poulin says that the girls are often not permitted to leave the brothels and that the little they earn for themselves is swallowed up in the exorbitant expenses at the brothel for their necessities or for fines they have to pay for having broken brothel rules. This sounds a great deal like imprisonment to me.

Poulin agrees that the Eros centers, no matter if they are covered up by this fancy term, are in essence brothels (118).

(A male friend of mine made an interesting point after I shared the above financial information with him. He said that in cases where the girl makes nothing or almost nothing, he didn't see how you could call it anything but sexual slavery. She is there as a tool to be used by another and she derives no benefit from the deal. Venereal diseases and mental illness from severe sexual abuse will be what she ends up with. How does the girl feel after she has been raped hundreds of times and given her paltry thousand dollars a month—only to have most of it taken away in 'imaginary' brothel debts? I wonder that Germany can allow such a form of slavery inside its 'democratic' borders.)

What I find startling about the information on Germany is that it seems as if legalization has not even given the 'legitimate' (that is, non-trafficked prostitutes—few as they are) any independence either. If a girl (even a non-trafficked one) cannot enter an Eros Centre without a pimp or owner, then I fail to see how any prostitute in Germany is better off because of the legalization laws. It would seem to me that the only way to make prostitution work for the benefit of the girl, in Germany or elsewhere, is to eliminate all the middlemen—procurers/owners/pimps—and to protect her from any interference in terms of others who might take her money. As I understand it, the prostitute in Germany must conduct her business in an Eros Centre and she must rent space to do this—and she cannot rent the space without the presence of her pimp or owner. Even if she had no owner, why would she have to conduct her business only in an Eros Centre if there is, according to the German government, nothing 'wrong' with prostitution? Why can't all girls simply conduct their business out of their homes or flats?

I would appreciate more information from people in Germany who know what is going on there vis-à-vis prostitution.

No matter where you are in the world, it would seem that most prostitution is still a form of slavery. If there is any kind of 'owner' in sight, taking the money, the girl is a sex slave. If there is any kind of owner or pimp managing the girl and controlling who goes in and out of her vagina, then she is a sex slave. The female body is not real estate. A second party cannot sell or rent out a vagina, as if it were not attached to the female, and take the money and have this not be slavery. For that matter, a woman, under the degradation that is now prostitution, on this highly patriarchal planet, cannot rent out her own vagina with any freedom or dignity. She will be in danger of violence and also scorned by society for her choice to do this—so it is cannot be a real 'choice'—under these circumstances of violence and humiliation.

Now, if we completely eliminated trafficking/forced prostitution from the world and replaced it with my version—

In my scheme, no girl under age 25 can be a prostitute. No pimp or owner can take her money. No one can say a disrespectful word to her. The customers have to behave like gentlemen.

One really big problem with completely erasing trafficking, pimps, procurers, owners, etc.—and giving the whores freedom, safety, and independence—is that very few girls will chose to be whores. It is so disgusting—this sex with men you do not know, and so painful if done assembly-line, that girls are just not going to volunteer to lay down and be rammed by ten or twenty men a night. So, we have to change prostitution drastically so that there is no assembly-line. If this happens, what will all those men who have to have their fuck do? I assume that the 40 to 60 men a night who are mounting enslaved Chinese or Slavic girls in London are shit slimes desperate to get their fuck. These shit slimes won't be able to get their fuck anymore, if we take away the sex slave they are getting their fuck on. I mean, what girl would actually choose to work under these conditions?

What puzzles me is that these shit-slime British men aren't being tried as rapists for the sexual murder of this girl's body. I mean, don't the Brits tout themselves as all civilized? So, sorry shit-slime British rapists—and all the shit-slime German men raping trafficked girls—and all the others around the world—you guys won't be able to get your fuck anymore. The only reason you can get your fuck now is the sanctioned rape of the female body called prostitution.

At bottom, the traffickers and procures and brothel owners are just part of the problem. The big problem is the huge demand by 'ordinary' men who must 'get their fuck'—no matter what. I have no idea how those millions of shit-slime rapists around the world we call 'ordinary men' are going to get their fuck once we give women a choice. It is really unlikely that girls will choose to lie down and fuck 40 or 50 or more shits a day.

Even having to fuck 20 or so shits a day—typical, apparently, for the trafficked girls in the Amsterdam windows--is inconceivable. I would invite any 'normal,' 'safe' girl in her privileged little world—say, any one of those female tourists strolling the red-light area in Amsterdam and having fun gawking at the sex animals in their cages—I would invite these girls to take the place of the ones in the windows. Let us have a 'normal' girl go into that space and fuck 20 men in a row that she does not know. What would she feel like at the end of this? Would she feel 'normal' anymore? Would she be insane from the degradation of it? Would she ever be 'normal' again? And would her bleeding vagina ever be the same again? What vicious, indifferent, ugly, blind creatures the 'normal' women of the world are—thinking that it is okay for a 'sex animal' in her cage-window to be raped 20 times a day. I detest the 'normal,' blind, indifferent women of the world. They are complicit in the mass rape of helpless, vulnerable girls and complicit in promoting the 'normalization' of prostitution-rape.

Just as I finish this up, in June 2009, I notice news coverage in Las Vegas of human trafficking. Some locals have staged a march on the Strip against the trafficking in children. Signs read 'Child Sex Slaves in America' and 'Real Men Don't Buy Sex.' The local news reporters tell us that 100,000 children a year are trafficked in America and Las Vegas is a major hub for this. A spokeswoman for the local protestors says that people see the girls on the street and assume they are of age and want to do this. The number trafficked girls can call, the local reporters tell us, is 866-U-ARE-SAFE.

The 'adult' prostitutes are left out of consideration in this coverage. If the average age for a girl to 'enter' prostitution in the USA is 14, then large numbers of the 'adult' girls in the Las Vegas sex industry must have been coerced into the trade when they were underage. It does great harm to make this distinction between child and adult. Both are victims. I have never been able to understand why up until age 17, 11 months, and 30 days, a girl is considered a 'victim' and then when she magically becomes 18 she is now a 'slut' who asks for her fate as a whore on the streets. Where are the adult prostitutes in all this? Why don't the protest signs relate to them as well? (Not that 18 is anywhere near 'adult' range in my estimate. An 18-year-old girl is still very much a defenseless child--in my view.)

As for the sign that reads 'Real Men Don't Buy Sex'—well, millions upon millions worldwide every day buy it by 'forced sale' from females of all ages—as young as six the whores might be, as old as 60. Men buying sex is commonplace. Military men have bought sex in one form or another for 5000 years. American military men have bought sex from millions of vulnerable girls all over the world. Sex tourists are busy buying sex ever day, from Goa to Dubai to Amsterdam. Millions of local men in countries all over the world are buying sex every day. Man must have his fuck. So man buys sex. Man is so desperate for his fuck that he will buy those 100,000 underage sex slaves in America. Men will buy sex slaves of any age anywhere. 'Real men don't buy sex.' The sign is meaningless. Men buy sex. Man must have his fuck.

Until you stop that, you have not a bat's chance in heaven or hell of stopping child or adult sex trafficking. And the penis cannot be stopped. Man must have his fuck.

The mayor of Las Vegas wants to set up a legal red-light district in the middle of the downtown casino area. If he does, how will we know if the girls are trafficked in? If it becomes legal, then this will facilitate the operations of traffickers and of the customer-rapists. Nevada is considering taxing the sex industry. Would this be the kind of 'taxing' we find in Holland, where the State as Pimp is taking money made by raping the bodies of trafficked girls?

As it stands now, the sex industry is already a billion-dollar enterprise in Nevada. A lot of 'real men' must be buying sex. Who are they? Locals? Sex tourists? Where do the tourists come from? The traditional places—Germany and Japan? Or are large numbers of the sex tourists from other American cities?

How are prostituted girls treated in Las Vegas? When the local news covers massage parlours, they never ask if the girls are trafficked in. They never ask where the girls come from at the Golden Lotus Massage Heaven. Do the local newscasters just assume there is some factory on the outskirts of Las Vegas where these Asian toy dolls are manufactured? Without volition built into them? Assembly-line products just delighted to do blowjobs on any sleaze who walks in? Somehow the humanity, the very existence, of the victims, those prostituted, gets completely lost in typical masculine-centric news coverage.

If prostitution/trafficking is big business in Las Vegas, why are the authorities not taking huge numbers of girls out of the brothels and massage parlours and helping them? When a sting does take place it tends to end in the authorities bringing in a verdict of 'no coercion' and the girls are deported. To be re-trafficked? No matter what the conditions the girls work under—filthy rooms, the 'taking on' of drunk customers, no 'coercion' seems to be the conclusion.

Are there any services in Las Vegas to help these girls? If they are not coerced in any way, why are they 'taking on' large numbers of drunk men? Women don't do this voluntarily. Are rape-crisis center services in Las Vegas available to prostituted women and girls?

It is very confusing. It would seem that there is no civilized, humane policy about prostitution in the USA. As for the number girls can call—866-U-ARE-SAFE—I would ask can adult prostitutes call it as well? And how are any prostitutes SAFE if they call this number? Pimps get their property back. And then they hurt that property, for trying to get away.

Even if a girl escapes, she is never safe. Rape nightmares are her fate for the rest of her life. There is no SAFE.

Afghanistan. Destitute women there either beg or sell sex. There are almost 90,000 US and NATO troops there--56,000 from the USA and the rest from 41 different nations. What are the men doing for sex? The situation is the same as we see in all wars: soldiers and hungry women. We know that Chinese girls are trafficked into brothels in Kabul. Who uses these girls? Are Slavic girls being trafficked in for military use? In a 15 June 2009 Associated Press article, "US Gen. McChrsytal Takes Command in Afghanistan," McChrsytal stresses that his policy is "protecting Afghan civilians from all kinds of violence." He is quoted as telling Congress that "the measure of effectiveness will not be the enemy killed. It will be the number of Afghans shielded from violence."

Does he mean sexual violence as well? Does he mean both rape and the sexual violence inflicted on women by the very act of prostitution? Why is what is happening with prostitution in Afghanistan never mentioned in the military reports and stories?

We know that Afghan women have been raped by the Taliban. Are they also being raped by the Allied forces? As in most of the Middle East, girls are married off very young there and forced to have children long before their bodies are even ready for sex. Why is this never mentioned in news stories about Afghanistan?

So much is left out every day. Coverage is 'macro' in all presses, on all websites—except maybe a few feminist ones. Endless coverage of the Pakistani military but nothing about the 200,000 women and girls trafficked from Bangladesh into Pakistan. Are these girls being used to service those soldiers? The sex-slave scene is multinational, goes across borders, and is ignored as an everyday reality since only the news of men and their world is reported.

In Darfur, the biggest torture and violation of women's rights lies in female genital mutilation—commonplace among women of the Sudan. Gang rape receives grudging attention in the media—but nothing about this dreadful shredding of the genitals which takes away all sexuality and sexual rights.

I think we need more news coverage of people like Somaly Mam. If there are others like her? Ask the average person and they don't even know who she is. A child sex slave in Cambodia until she escaped, she now tries to help others like herself. She has received a million-dollar grant to help, plus other funds. You would think that with that kind of money, she could free every sex slave in Cambodia. Why is opposition against her in Cambodia so powerful that she cannot bring about immediate sweeping changes with that kind of money? Her website says that you can buy a 5-year-old in Cambodia for as little as $10. Those who oppose her kidnapped her daughter and they drugged and raped her. I would think that the first thing Somaly should have done with all that money is get her daughter out of Cambodia and someplace safe. I hope she uses some of the money to do this now so her daughter is not a target again. Since the million dollars does not seem to have freed every sex slave in Cambodia, I think there must be something else operating. It is not so much the traffickers that we need to look at but the men doing the buying. Perhaps Somaly can never free the sex slaves because the male demand for bodies—in Cambodia and elsewhere—is simply overwhelming. After all, if there were no 'customer-rapists,' there would be no one for the traffickers and brothel owners to sell the girls to. And the largest customer-rapist base in Cambodia is local men. Sex tourists come there—but their numbers are minuscule compared to the buying of bodies by local men.

Many of the sex slaves in Cambodia are deliberately addicted to drugs to control them and make them docile. This is one reason they have a hard time getting out—no way to deal with the addiction.

I'd like to find out more about the obstacles in Somaly's path as she tries to free the sex slaves in Cambodia. With the million dollars, plus other donations she has received, it would be possible for her to simply hire strong, armed, competent men to go into the brothels and take the girls out. Direct action. I often wonder why this method is simply not applied all over the world. All non-prostituted women and all men who do not buy bodies could simply go into the brothels and stop the enslavement—tomorrow.

Somaly Mam could hire full-time guards—to make sure the girls stay free.

Forty percent of the child soldiers in Africa are girls, conscripted to be raped every night by the men and boys on their 'own' side. These girls are also often controlled through being forced into drug addiction.

Child trafficking, child trafficking, child trafficking. Of course it is important. But where do we hear adult trafficking, teenage trafficking. These females hurt just as much. And when the average age that girls go into prostitution is so young—early teens-- you cannot really draw a distinction between child and adult. The adult is likely to have been coerced into the professions in her early teens—maybe even younger.

I think if I were Somaly, I would use some of that money to hire four ex-Green Berets to protect her daughter—she should be flanked by a guard on all sides of her at all times. If I had a daughter, I would wish I could keep her bodyguarded all the time. It is too dangerous a planet for girls. For women, too. We are all in desperate need of protection by the men who do not use prostituted bodies from those who do. Where are you, men? Why aren't you stopping all the rapes? Protect us.

It is a despicable planet we live on. The whole planet just needs to be wiped out. Just leave the other species and the plants. But rid this planet of this evil thing called 'human.' Without humans, the earth is beyond lovely. We have turned it into an image of our dark selves.

I worry the most about the abattoir whore. Can she even walk after so much rape? Or eat or sleep? Is everything ruptured inside her? *Female Sexual Slavery* says the girls are 'apathetic' after 80 to 160 rapes a day. I think 'comatose' would be a better word. A fuck-dazed dead body with rape-dead eyes. We cannot overstate this extreme of sexual torture. How do you actually fit 160 men a day into one woman? How fast and hard do the fucks have to be to get that many men stuck in her in one day? What do the men think or feel as they mount her? Anything? Is she a dirty joke they laugh at? Do they take pictures, for souvenirs, the way the guys did in Vietnam and Nanking? What kind of male or human mind could actually think up such an extreme of sexual torture as forcing a girl 80 to 160 times a day in the abattoirs brothels of Paris? What kind of city of love and light could do this?

I worry about the battery-cage hens even more than I do about the abattoir whores. They are the only beings on the planet more helpless than the abattoir whores. What kind of dark depths of the human mind could treat helpless animals like this—as a 'norm'?

And I guess that after they finish with their turn on the abattoir whore, the immigrant men of Paris just go home to their wives and girlfriend and daughters—as if nothing had happened? As if it were a 'norm'? *Female Sexual Slavery* tells us that the French police keep order at the gates and joke around, as hundreds of men push to get in. Do the French police then go home to their wives and girlfriends and daughters, as if nothing had happened? Nothing but the 'norm' of unbearable rape? I wonder what the women feel and think as they hear the hundreds of men pushing to get in, when the gates open. Can the women feel or think or hear at all? Maybe they are mercifully unconscious after so many rapes a day. Otherwise, they must be peeing and shitting and vomiting with fear.

I am so terrified of abattoir, slaughterhouse-sex since even the few times I was violated when I was gang raped (about 15 times in a row) killed me forever. It is with deep, deep horror that I think of what I would be today if I had been raped 80 times in a row on that day. I would be nothing. Not alive at all.

So, all the female tourists stroll around Paris, and enjoy the lovely parks and museums and the great coffee—but could they do this if they spent even one day as an abattoir whore? Would there be anything left of them to stroll around?

Normal women and men don't seem to think that prostitution is important enough to discuss or notice. I hold that it impacts all of life. No 'normal' woman can be free or safe or have any dignity as long as even one girl is being mistreated in prostitution. There can be no free, beautiful female sexuality if even one Balkan girl is being raped a 100 times a day in Greece (or London or Paris or India or Korea). Her sexual pain negates all female sexuality. No man can make love to a woman as long as that one girl is being raped. There is no woman for him to make love to. All his tenderness toward one woman cannot take away the rape-misery of the Balkan girl. He can only make love to a woman with beautiful pure sexuality if the raped Balkan girl does not exist. Just one prostituted being on the planet takes away all sexuality from all women.

All of prostitution is rape in some form. I know that many people find this idea disturbing. But use of a prostituted body, under even the most gentle of circumstances, constitutes rape. Any use of a prostituted body is rape. I might as well say it several times since the idea will never be palatable to those who buy women or to 'sex workers' who claim they work 'freely.' I know that some customers are quite nice to the women they buy and these kinds of men would never view themselves as rapists. In some sense, that is true. But the girl is still working under circumstances of coercion imposed upon her by a patriarchal society who defines her as 'whore'—not with respect, but with scorn. So, I would say that even the 'freest' of 'sex workers' cannot escape from this definitional prison. Prostitution will cease being rape when we completely redefine and refashion it as a 'profession' that benefits the female and never degrades or harms her—in any way. To do this, we will need to refashion and redefine all of female sexuality on this planet.

Let's face it. Female sexual oppression and female sexual slavery simply do not matter. They are the lowest items on the human agenda. In fact, the prostitute is not part of the human condition. Visited upon her is one of the greatest destructions a human being can experience—the erasing of her sexuality—in unimaginably brutal ways. Yet all the stories told about her in art and film do not the touch the surface of her reality. From the sugar-coated surface of a Hollywoodish *Waterloo Bridge* to the irrelevance of the two prostituted bodies in *Full Metal Jacket*, her reality and humanity are completely ignored. Vietnam is important—to filmmakers. The men who were there are important—to filmmakers. But the prostituted girls that those men brutalized have no importance whatsoever. The most important destruction in *Full Metal Jacket*—the complete stripping away of all life and beauty from the two prostituted girls—simply has no relevance whatsoever—to life or war—or to Kubrick. These two girls are absent, not just from this war, but from the human condition. Kubrick shows male suffering but he does not go inside the ruined building where all the soldiers take turns on the pathetically fragile field whore pimped for their 'pleasure.' What we see is a mannequin, a doll, a surface. We do not see the misery in her face and eyes as she lays there and is serially raped by a dozen 'customers.' In fact, she wears sunglasses so we do not see her eyes. What kind of terror must be inside her as these men go inside her, taking 'their turn.' Or is she too numb to feel anything in life anymore. The sheer brutal ugliness of the filmmaker ignoring her pain is beyond my understanding. But, then, for this filmmaker and for all others, her pain and humanity simply do not exist.

In fact, the prostitute has no existence. She is completely absent from life, except as an empty fuck-space.

You see, prostitution makes the sexual destruction of a woman complete. It is the greatest hidden horror in the history of humankind. War's huge, dirty secret. Life's huge, dirty secret. All of history's huge, dirty secret.

WWII mattered. But the women sexually destroyed by it did not. The Holocaust mattered. But the women sexually destroyed in the concentration camps did not. You never hear their stories—for the simple fact that the sexual misery of women is irrelevant to the human condition. Only men matter. Only soldiers matter. Only those who glory so disgustingly in the making of war matter.

So, I think the huge difference between my cause and all other causes is that the horrifying destruction of female sexuality that we find in prostitution is simply an accepted norm—no one considers the sexual misery of these women even worth mentioning—except as a dirty joke. The prostitute is a necessary communal sex toilet: horrifying as I find this, apparently all of humankind for thousands of years has considered her to have the function of a sewer—since man must have his fuck, he has to have this 'filth' called the whore to use.

This attitude—the prostitutes as a sewer who has no importance or humanity—is why I despair. I will never be able to even make people see that she is mistreated. The greatest harm on the planet—the complete destruction of female sexuality within prostitution—this leads to the repression of all female sexuality. As long as there is one prostitute in the world, all women will have to fear rape. We are a species whose females have no sexuality—beyond that of a fear of rape.

I wish there were some way I could get rid of the thoughts that haunt me the most—like the ones of the young girls from the Balkans who are being raped a 100 times a day in Greece. Are these young Balkan girls also shipped to India and Asia and the Middle East? Caucasian prostituted girls are shipped into Cairo on what are called "E" visas—meaning "E" for 'entertainment.' Are some of the girls just adolescents? What will happen to them when they are used up and worn out? Do the ones who get used up and worn out in Europe get shipped to even crueler places where women and girls have even less worth and status—like the Middle East? Is that their last place before they die? Why do the lives of these young Balkan girls have to be taken away from them so young? Such a fixation men have on sex with young girls. Because of male need the girls die from rape long before they are even ready for sex—and without ever having lived. How alone do they feel, in Egypt or India, with no one to even give them a kind word? Helpless and alone.

I find all the 'cultures' of the world repulsive since they all promote the rape of women's bodies.

I am always haunted by how ordinary women in, say, Germany, can simply go about their business while they know that over 300,000 women are being held in sexual slavery in their country and that German men are inflicting sexual murder on these girls' already murdered bodies every day, day after day. Doesn't it bother these women in any way? Do they simply take it for granted this certain women have to be raped every day? I could of course apply this to many other countries—except perhaps Sweden. There is seems that the women were troubled by prostitution enough to do something sensible and humane about it: they defined it as exploitation of the female and put the blame on the men who do the selling and the buying. Norway has followed this same path. Denmark is still debating whether to do so. Two and a half sane countries on a rape-insane planet.

I need to move to Sweden.

What do Caucasian Western women think when they are in Goa, India or Dubai or any other sex-tourist destination and they see the trafficked Slavic girls? When the country purports to be 'spiritual,' like India, do the Caucasian women tourists just go off and visit shrines and temples and the like and just ignore the rape scene around them? Since it is a huge sin to kiss anyone in public in India, you would think it would be a bigger sin to rape all those Slavic sex slaves. I guess not. That is permitted, as a 'norm.' But not kissing in public. Amazing.

I really have no desire to understand any culture on Rape Planet Earth. They all permit rape of the helpless. There is not a spiritual spot or space on the whole planet. I will not worship at the false shrines that humans have made to commemorate their raping ways.

Everyday indifference and everyday discrepancies define our insane world. As I wait in line at Target, I see all the smiling safe pampered cover girls on their glossy magazines and wonder why these girls are treasured and given respect and why another girl is subject to a rape camp to make her docile and then her fate is being mounted by dozens of sleaze 'customers' every day and she is now forever defined as some kind of low dirty creature. I used to wonder about this terrible tragedy of 'distance' when I was going to school on military bases. Why did the blonde cheerleader beside me deserve soft, gentle respect from men and why did that GI I talked to last night joke about the whore in Vietnam that he and his buddies used while they all took pictures of the event. Why was she reduced to being filth and why was the cheerleader a treasured being? It never makes any sense to me. If we treated the blonde cheerleader and the safe girls and movie stars on the magazine covers to the same mass rape daily by crude men, would these girls still be treasured?

What makes one girl worth protecting and cherishing and another not? Why is one girl a princess and why is an adolescent girl from the Balkans just a ruined piece of garbage before she is even fifteen because men have mounted her all day? Why this one particular girl ruined? It makes no sense.

I do not mean 'ruined' under our archaic moral systems—as if she has done something 'wrong' by being 'sinful' enough to get her virginity taken away from her and by 'allowing' herself to be fucked all day by men she does not know. Historically, this has been the judgment on the whore—condemned severely for her own rape and for the 'temptation' she offers the men who are the 'victims' of her 'lust.' She made me do it. I had to rape her. She is a whore who tempted me. Religious moral garbage about 'sin' and women as 'bad' still rules our thinking. No, I mean 'ruined' inside in the sense that she has been shredded and destroyed forever. There is no recovery form the unbearable pain and disgust of having had sleaze, garbage men inside you all day.

'V' for victory. The sign of the ages. There is no victory for the vagina. Just 'victors' who destroy it. Victory is purely a male phenomenon on Rape Planet Earth. The irony is that they use the 'triangle' of the vagina to signify it.

Writing this book is never-ending hell since there are no solutions and there is no hope.

I think one of the biggest problems is not regarding prostitution as rape and in many instances it is. At the extreme, we have the case of the Korean Comfort Women. And the Occupation Comfort Girls. What was being done to them was not regarded as rape. By the 'authorities' on both sides—the Japanese themselves and the Allied forces who discovered the girls, they were simply regarded as 'prostitutes.' That meant, by definition, that it was not rape—never mind that what happens to the prostituted body under such circumstances would be regarded as a hyper-from of rape if it were done to a 'normal' girl, that is, one not labeled a prostitute. Can you imagine the girl-next-door being forced to take a long line of men until she bleeds and passes out? And still have it not called rape? Yet the girls conscripted to serve as comfort women were once the girl-next-door. It's funny, in a grim kind of way, to think of the GI's four abreast, in Tokyo, waiting their turn and joking and laughing, if—if it were their sisters or girlfriends in the brothel bed, being mercilessly used. Clearly, what happened to the comfort women then, what happens to 'comfort women' now, is rape although it still does not seem to be regarded as such by most people. A few sensitive souls will beg to differ—but we are practically a non-existent minority. It is now 2009, and almost 20 years after the Korean Comfort Women told their stories, these poor women are still having to argue that it was rape. They are still faced with the attitude, 'oh, yeah, I bet you just loved it,' or 'you sure must have been tough to take on battalions of those men.' Attitudes so ugly they make me cringe, yet quite common among the ignorant, barbaric, brutal, stupid, sexually misconceived masses of inhumanity on Rape Planet Earth.

I think that non-comfort women prostitutes many times still experience their 'servitude' as a form of rape—although perhaps on a much milder level. A bar girl or a prostitute who works without a pimp and controls her own movements and life must still face much of the unpleasantness inherent in the profession, particularly this sex-with-strangers thing. Inevitably, there will be customers who are unpleasant, sleazy, or even downright unpalatable. Just letting them into your private self and softness is awful. I have my own body as testimony for this—and I make no apologies for feeling this way. I still cringe and feel dirty and depressed and sad when I think of a few of the men who used me who were real sleazes. They were in the minority. In your average group of guys—civilian or military—most will be half-way decent human beings (except when the buddy-bonding, brothel-visiting mentality takes them over and their young male-testosterone bodies run wild). But I think even one sleaze male can do real damage to self-esteem and the inner self.

So, even the 'free' prostitutes are sometimes having sex 'against their will'—although in a form far less violent and miserable than what the poor comfort women endure. And, numerically, these 'free' prostitutes are very much in the minority. I am very much in favor of their 'rights' and want to work toward a world where 'sex worker' is a viable, accurate phrase and where no forced prostitution ever exists. Sadly, we are far from that. With the majority of prostituted beings on the planet, 'free' is far from the truth since debt-bondage and coercion in many forms is so prevalent.

The *Pretty Woman* movie has come in for much criticism due to being such a fairy-tale about street prostitution. In many ways, it is quite a soft, unrealistic view of what a real street prostitute in Los Angeles would be experiencing. We have a few glimpses of the harsh world—a crack-whore in a dumpster, allusions to pimps--but Vivian (Julia Roberts) seems to sail right through this dark nightmare and when she ends up in Edward's (Richard Gere) posh penthouse suite, she is relatively unscathed by her past: tough and witty in a cute way, but with no 'baggage' from having sold herself on the streets. A real prostitute would be far more scarred. Leaving all that aside, there is much I like about the movie: the feeling of hope it gives one. Just as Vivian leaves this world, so will her roomie, by implication. And the way Edward treats her is a model for how all 'customers' should behave: not making her feel cheap, giving her respect, and being considerate toward her feelings.

Our attitudes toward prostituted beings have a long way to go before they evolve into anything civilized. Greg Harman's article on the treatment of sex trafficking victims in Texas gives some good examples of the backward state we are in. Bear in mind that Texas is typical of the rest of the USA and the rest of the world (except for Sweden and Norway). He calls the piece "Land of the Lost: Texas Creates Task Force on Sexual Slavery as Bexar County's First Trafficking Case Wraps Up," and you can find it on the *SA Current* site for 18 June 2009.

Harman tells us that in 2007 "San Antonio state Senator Leticia Van de Putte [tried] to push a bill through the state legislature to require sex-trafficking training for all law-enforcement officers....'They just said, "Well, you know. We don't need to be focusing on that. That's not a major crime,"' said Van De Putte."

Harman goes on to tell us of a 16-year-old boy who was trafficked in the Rio Grande Valley and instead of being helped "was charged with prostitution and jailed. Repeated hospitalizations, however, required him to be transported to San Antonio for medical care.

"'It wasn't until the physician examined him and said there was no way this young man sustained these injuries willingly' that the real story came out, said Van De Putte. 'I mean, it was horrible. He had to have his bowel resectioned.'"

The Attorney General's office tells us that "these victims are treated as criminals." The trafficking legislation that Congress passed in 2000 focused on victims trafficked into the USA and now, as of 2008, "domestic victims" are being included in the legislation.

"Three out of four victims of sex trafficking in the United States are U.S. citizens," Harman writes. Aide to Texas Representative Randy Weber, Chara McMichael, "says that 18,000 children enter the sex trade in Texas every year, and that the majority of these are white female runaways between the ages of 12 and 15. The abuse of international trafficking victims in the U.S. is well documented, but the level of violence employed against American kids is even worse, McMichael said.

"'Domestic victims, because they know how to get into a taxi cab and go to a police station and all that, they endure typically significantly more drug abuse, torture, manipulation,' McMichael said. 'They endure significantly more trauma.'"

Miriam Elizondo of the San Antonio Rape Crisis Center tells us that "'once these clients are rescued, they're in this legal system where they have no control....They're stuck. They go from one frustrating, traumatizing situation to a very frustrating, stressful situation....And while they're not being abused and beaten, they still feel they have no control. They're not empowered at all.'

"Fewer than one percent of the Crisis Center's clients identify themselves as trafficking victims, a fact Elizondo credits to the amount of manipulation and abuse that is typically involved in these cases….Without intensive and long-term therapy, trafficking victims are very likely to return to their pimps and old behaviors, McMichael said. 'You almost have to reprogram them how to not be a victim anymore.'"

Another Texan, "Darrell MacLearn, anti-trafficking project manager in Texas for Concerned Women of America….laments the glamorization of pimps, the criminalization of 'whores,' and the normalization of 'johns.' At no time in the history of the country has the sex trade been so deeply enmeshed in popular culture. For that reason, it may be that at no time since Emancipation has the slave trade been this profitable."

Among other activities, MacLearn's group "distributes flyers at truck stops. If sex customers can be trained, the reasoning goes, then just maybe we can save the children.

"'It's economics 101,' said MacLearn. 'If you don't have a buyer for 12-year-old girls, he's not going to try to sell 12-year-old girls'" (Harman).

I think it is certainly interesting that truck stops are one of their distribution places. It is very disturbing to think of some of these truckers using children for sex—as a norm, on the road. I wonder why they are not arrested and charged with all kinds of rape—including statutory. It would seem that 'sex offenders' and 'pedophiles' come in all forms—including the fathers and brothers and husbands and sons that live in our own homes. I wonder why this is never talked about? Is the trucker culture similar to the military and sports culture—what happens on the road—or overseas—is never mentioned when in the presence of your own wife or daughter—and no wonder since some of these truckers are engaged in the horrendous act of buying and raping a child's body—which is what these truckers are doing, when they use 12- and 13-year-old girls. (What are the percentages? How many truckers are doing this, I would like to know.) The 'ordinary' men of the world have a lot to answer for. They outnumber those men labeled 'pedophiles' and they rape far larger numbers of children than do the men called 'pedophiles.' (This is not to in any way exonerate the men we label pedophiles—but to point out that they are not the only ones raping child bodies.) And the ordinary men of the world rape the child prostituted-body with impunity—seemingly. I don't see large number of rape trials involving truckers who have bought the bodies of adolescent girls while they are on the road. We can now prosecute American men who buy underage prostitutes abroad. Why are we not doing this within the borders of the USA? Why are police forces not raiding truck stops and arresting the buyers of adolescent girls? Why is what these truckers are doing not considered rape of the most horrendous sort?

As for trying to educate men not to rape—ha! If these slime-sleaze truckers can use 12-year-old girls and think nothing of it—maybe even consider it a lark, how can you possibly educate them? They go home to daughters the same age and make no connections—between the vulnerable body in their household and the one at the truck stop? Those happy rapist-GI's four abreast in their line in Tokyo, waiting 'their turn' are every man in the world—joking around, considering sexual torture of the female body 'fun.' How can you possibly educate men not to rape when almost all of them are natural rapists? I mention the truckers and the GI's, but I could just as easily point out the million German men who buy sex every day in their country from enslaved girls—and apparently think that this incredible abuse of the body and spirit of a girl is the 'norm.' How could 20 men using one girl in the Amsterdam brothel windows possibly consider that she would invite this level of abuse on her body—yet it is a 'norm' of rape for this to happen to her? No. Nope. No way you can educate men not to rape. Too many of them will rape under circumstances that permit and sanction this act—principally sale of the female body-- prostitution/trafficking—call it what seems appropriate to you. No nation or country is safe or civilized in this regard. You just have some countries that seem even more barbaric in this practice of licensed, accepted rape than do others—places like India where prosperous Bombay ignores the brothelized children with their damaged anuses hanging out of their bodies—like the prolapsed bodies of the helpless all over, battery-cage children—or the brutality visited on the Bangladesh sex slaves in Pakistan.

But take any country and you have rapists—military or civilian. USA news stories criticize India for its child sex slaves but you find them all over America as well. The latest figures (June 2009) from the U.S. State Department and the International Labour Organization are an estimated 250,000 minors trafficked within the USA for sexual purposes and 12 million people trafficked worldwide. The figure within the USA does not mention adult women. What are their numbers?

The story that most affected me, as you know, is the one of all the GI's lined up to get at prostituted bodies in post-war Tokyo and Yokosuka and how these girls were being used 40 times a day and how usage by soldiers was almost 100%--and I have told you how that one sentence about 50 GI's lined up to get at one prostituted body changed my life forever. It turned my perspective on life and sex around so drastically that I have been reeling from it ever since. When I worked as a prostitute, I did not acknowledge to myself that what was happening to my body was rape. I had not been taught to view it in this way. Because the men paid, that made it okay. That meant it was not rape. However, my body knew that it was rape. It told me so all the time—all that pain and soreness and tearing—and even at times when I was feeling okay, just the numbness and lack of 'real' physical response made it a form of rape. I went through the motions and made noises and did what I could to please the man, but it was he who was getting the pleasure, not me.

If the girl is not also enjoying it, that makes it a form of rape. There are lots of degrees and kinds of rape and one kind not recognized at all by the world—the kind I term 'prostitution-rape'—also has degrees and kinds: from the most brutal, hyper-rape inflicted on the comfort women/abattoir whores to the much, much milder form I felt due to being numb and unresponsive inside. Any 'free' whore who likes her 'work' is not being raped—but these types of prostitutes are in the minority. For one, entry into the trade is typically at such young ages, and physical damage so severe, that it would be hard to imagine these really young girls enjoying what is happening to their bodies. Adult women who go in as adults and have no previous sexual abuse and do not work under coercive conditions and enjoy what they do—this is a great picture and I certainly would like to see all prostitution take this form. But it does not seem to in very many instances.

Way back then when I worked as a prostitute, my body was wiser than I was. Much wiser than my mind or emotions. Years later, I am listening to it and it tells me that if I just lay there, unresponsive, even though I pretended for the sake of the man, then I was being raped in some form. And if pain was involved, it was rape for sure.

Despite the opinion of the world, I think that we must define the 15-60 mountings a day that the Occupation Comfort Girls in Japan endured from the GI's as rape—of the most severe and horrendous sort. (Hyper-meta rape.) This is one reason I was so shocked by that sentence about the 50 men all lined up to use one girl. This was horrifying rape being committed as a norm by ordinary men. Since usage was so high in post-war Japan—almost 100% of the GI's indulged—we must conclude that almost all men are Natural Born Rapists. Any man you know—husband, boyfriend, son, father, cousin—could have done this. Place a man in a situation where rape is sanctioned—that is, where he can buy the body of a vulnerable girl—and he will rape. There will be almost no exceptions. I was so haunted by this one sentence—still am—because it meant that almost every man I know would have done this—if you put him back in 1945 Tokyo—or under similar circumstances. Put him on Okinawa, taking R & R during the Vietnam era, and he might be one of the 20 to 30 men a night mounting the poor brothelized girls there. Or he might be buying a 15-year-old sex slave for the night. Put him in Korea in the 1950's and he will be buying pathetic camp-town girls, some of them just adolescents. Put him there now and he will be using the services of Slavic girl trafficked in for him (unless the new Pentagon policy of no use of trafficked girls anywhere in the world by the U.S. military is really taking effect and working).

Put my former boyfriend Vic where he was stationed—in Korea in the 50's, in Japan in the 60's, and on bases in the USA, and he will use prostituted bodies—and he did, everywhere he went since he 'had needs' and they had to be met and he said that all the other soldiers 'had needs' and they all met them in the same way—buy a sex slave. Very few exceptions. Vic said there were times when the whorehouses got really busy and guys did line up and they didn't feel guilty at all. Instead, they 'reveled' in all this partying on whores. It was fun. It was what guys did. It felt good—to fuck a whore and you never thought about it much, what it did to the girl. Even if she cried, you still needed to fuck and you did. He told me that he felt bad about it but that it never really troubled him enough for him to think about it much. He just did it. No regrets either. He 'had needs' back then when he was a young man. Vic was a good guy. Good to me. Pretty kind. But he 'had needs'—so he was a natural born rapist like most of the rest of mankind.

I have a lot of good male friends at this time in my life—and it troubles me deeply that if you put them back in 1945 Tokyo, in the GI lines, four abreast, waiting to get at the whores in the Yokosuka Comfort Stations, almost all these men would have been taking 'their turn'—and maybe even joking around and 'reveling' in it. So, I don't see how you can educate men not to use sex slaves/prostituted bodies/trafficked girls—whatever you want to call the girls. Most men are natural born rapists.

The particular sex trafficking case refereed to in the Texas article above has imposed only very light sentences and punishments on the traffickers. The fact that it is the 'first' in this particular Texas county is also significant since trafficking has been going on forever—there and everywhere. It didn't just spring into being a couple of years ago and now that is why we have the 'first' case to be tried. It would seem that it has simply not been seen as an important enough crime to even pay any attention to—although I cannot think of a crime more significant than the daily rape of the body and the murder of the spirit and life that attends this dreadful torture.

Some kind of enormous blindness must rule us all—since the attitude of Texas law enforcement—this is not a crime that is really 'major' in any way—seems to be typical of us all. I have written quite a bit on the legacy of WWII and the enormous use of prostitutes by the men who made that war. One of my male friends suggested that the WWII generation has 'repressed' this knowledge. It would certainly seem so. The women as well as the men--since we have a whole generation of women who, along with their men from 1945 onwards, simply pretended that the war-time rape and prostitution of huge numbers of women in Asia, Europe, and Australia (as well as some in North Africa) simply did not happen. This 'do it, but don't tell' attitude got passed onto the Vietnam generation—my generation—when those soldiers 'did it' to the helpless girls all over Asia and 'didn't tell'—except that it sure was hard to hide the 'evidence'—all those outcast, surplus, throwaway 'children of the dust.' Nevertheless, we hid the evidence and my generation of women, the Vietnam one, have ignored that it even happened ever since. My alienation from my own generation of women is tremendous because of this. Entire generations of women—mine, my mother's—complicit in the mass rape of other women around the world. Amazing.

Now we have the same cover up in the Iraq generation of war-makers.

What may be the saddest thought of all is that prostituted women in Asia and the Middle East—places where women are still considered second-rate citizens—these women may be treated worse by local men than by the visiting militaries from Western nations, where women have gained some small measure of respect and a few rights.

I see a parallel between the justice system's lax and light sentences toward traffickers and the punishment meted out to those who torture animals. Some poor dog may be beaten and starved and terrorized and even if a humane society manages to take the poor creature away, the 'owner' will get a light fine, maybe a bit of jail time that is shortened. Makes no sense to me. But then it makes no sense to me for any living being to be 'owned' by another—whether it be an animal or a prostitute.

Trafficking legislation, what little there is of it, seems to be focusing on children and teens—what about the adult women?—they are equally victims.

Maybe the most upsetting part of Harman's article is the physician examining the young male who had been raped so much his bowel was terribly injured and the physician concluding that "there was no way this young man sustained these injuries willingly." Who could even possibly think that under any circumstances a prostituted being would 'willingly' allow such damage to his/her body that the bowel has to be reconstructed? I mean who would 'willingly' want his rectum to be all torn to pieces and who would want to be physically and psychologically ruined for life? Where does the word 'willing' even come into this?

I am especially sensitive to this issue of anal rape since the one anal rape I went through has left me with nightmares forever. I detest the idea of anyone touching me near that area and cannot watch anal sex acts in porn because the women look as if they are in pain. Interesting enough, I ran across an article by Suzy McCoppin in the June 2009 *Playboy* called "Bringing up the Rear: The Truth About Anal Sex from a Woman's Point of View." She is not in favor of it either. It heartened me to actually hear this opinion from a woman in a major men's magazine. I shudder when I think of all the trafficked girls who have no choice and whose bodies are so damaged by all this forced anal rape. I wonder if the pain is unbearable all the time or do they numb out after large amounts of damage? Do they ever recover or are their bodies ruined forever? How do the 'customer-rapists' feel about using young girls whose anuses are hanging out of their body due to rape? Does it not bother these 'ordinary' fathers and husbands that it could their own daughters and wives used this way?

Time to wrap up this final section, written in 2009. Time to stop. Even millions of words on the page will change nothing. Still, it was important that I try to say something. My novels on prostitution are alive with both pain and beauty. They are a devastating criticism of prostitution. Even if no one ever reads them, it was important that I turn the pain of prostitution into art since no one else has ever done so—at least, not in the fashion that I do.

I mean for this book, this section, to be something of a hodgepodge—trafficking induces huge amounts of confusion and chaos since it so difficult to do anything about it. Practically ignored for 5000 years as 'incidental' to 'real' history, now that people are allowing the stories of the prostituted to be told—largely because of the remarkable breaking of silence by the Korean Comfort Women in the early 1990's—still there is little done for the prostituted. We even have to call her the 'trafficked,' rather than the 'prostituted' since we are so uncomfortable with the idea of someone labeled 'prostitute' as having any rights or feelings—or being a victim in any way. For centuries, the prostitute has been regarded as inviting the rape of her own body. She still is in most cases. So we have to change her 'tag' to 'trafficked,' so that we can view her as having some humanity—and some right to be a victim. Never mind that large numbers of the 'prostituted' endure the same conditions and miseries that the 'trafficked' do: sexual violence, other kinds of physical violence, humiliation, feelings of hopelessness and despair.

In fact, one reason I wrote this extension to my original afterthoughts is the criticism I have received for daring to speak out against prostitution/trafficking. I have been criticized for asserting that the prostituted and trafficked often 'work' under similar conditions of oppression and abuse and criticized and for daring to say that the majority of prostituted beings have been coerced into this 'profession' in some fashion. This is not to in any way negate the rights of any woman who might choose to sell sex. I am on your side, as I have said. I would love to create a climate and a world in which it was safe to sell sex.

In my writings, I just try to call attention to a few basic and simple things and ask a few basic and simple questions. Like how can a man in the navy who has daughters justify his behavior in ports where the first thing a sailor does is go find a bar with whores, get drunk and 'let off steam.' And then how does the man with daughters justify the dirty jokes he makes about girl whores who could be his daughters—if they were born under less fortunate circumstances. Doesn't he see the connection at all?

I ask why prostitution is taken for granted as a norm when it causes such tremendous female suffering. 'Submission Camps' in the Balkans turn out assembly-whores. These camps, according to Canadian scholar Richard Poulin, are where girls are raped to make them docile and 'willing' to take on 'customers.' No one seems outraged by this treatment of the female. Men and woman all over Europe sit around at cafes or tennis matches and abattoir whores get raped 60 times a day while the privileged are taking coffee or strolling along. Why is there no outrage in Europe over this? How does the girl raped 60 times a day, or a hundred times, survive even one day of this—the pain and bleeding must be tremendous, the tearing and scarring must be tremendous. A girl cannot stroll along and eat an ice cream cone at the French Open or have some strawberries and cream at Wimbledon if she is being raped 60 times a day. Can she even walk at all after this? The Korean Comfort Women tell us that they could not walk after 30 to 50 rapes a day. The damage and infections and rupturing of the sex organs was too great.

So, I point all this out, in my invaluable emotional way, and tell all those strong empowered feminists out there that all one has to do is set them up as abattoir whores, and inflict those 100 rapes a day on them—that's over 20,000 times a year you will be 'entered' by men you do not know and you will have no 'dignity' as a woman. You will have no life. I am a Raped Being. At my center is A Raped Being. At the center of all women on Rape Planet Earth is a Raped Being. The strong powerful feminists are annoyed with me for pointing this out.

I have offended everyone in writing this book.

I have not written the book that needs to be written yet. At the moment, it is not possible to write a 'herstory' of prostitution or a 'herstory' of anything else. The feminine mind has been so stunted and ruined by 5000 years of patriarchal oppression that it is going to take us way more than a few decades to recover. Maybe my ghost 500 years down the road of herstory will be able to write a 'true' herstory of the prostituted woman and a true 'herstory' of, say, WWII—one told from the point of view of all the comfort women—

including all the ones in Europe who have never told their stories. All the ones mentioned by Robert Lilly in *Taken by Force*, about the rapes in Europe by GI's. All the Italian girls who lay in that park in Palermo as the GI's lined up to get at them for a dollar a fuck. Why did these Italian girls never say what happened to them? How come my ghost—500 years in the future—is going to have to tell their story? Apparently the girls in Berlin ravaged by the Russians still are not allowed to tell their story—or have it believed. When one tries, it is condemned as 'lies.' That didn't really happen. This despite eyewitnesses who tell us the girls cried all night as the Russians raped them all night. And then when the German soldiers came back, their response was, "You bunch of whores--letting yourselves get raped like that."

It may be 500 years in the future—so primitive and ugly is our current attitude toward the raped/prostituted female--and my recycled, reincarnated ghost will just have to be patient until her turn comes. As things stand, prostitution is still so accepted as sanctioned abuse of the female body that it would be hard to imagine telling any story that would be meaningful to the trafficked—or that would help her. In the popular culture (and clutter) all around me I find ample proof of my assertion. Just look, for example, at a movie like *Eastern Promises*—clichéd in many ways but at least it does bring up the subject of the sex trafficking of Slavic girls into London. That is enormously in its favor—since the subject seems to be all but hidden from the general London citizen—this despite the fact that I, in another country, can access, on the Internet, groups like Amnesty International or the Helen Bamber Foundation or Poppy—all of whom reveal the sex-torture horrors undergone by these girls in their rape-torture beds in Soho. I think that people in London have access to the Internet, do they not? It is not as if they live with the penguins in Antarctic—I don't know if one can simply click on Internet Explorer down there—with the penguins. But—in the middle of London? And, surely, the tabloids leap on this sort of material don't they? 'Fourteen-year-old sex slave raped 50 times a day!' Meat and bread and butter and potatoes for those famous London tabloids. And I know that the non-tabloid *Guardian* is quite good about carrying trafficking stories. The *Guardian* seems to care about the rape of the female body.

So, how come your average Londoner knows nothing about what is going on? If they did know, would they not be so outraged that they would rise en masse and go get that fourteen-year-old girl out of there?

What is more likely is that, if she is still alive, the *Eastern Promises* scenario will reign: she will somehow escape, pregnant, and stumble into a chemist's, looking for help, and no one will want to help her until she starts hemorrhaging right there, on the clean linoleum floor. Then she will die in a hospital without ever having lived, and her baby girl will be considered future rape fodder for a bunch of shit-males in London who like to climb on 14-year-olds all day. I wonder why the Naomi Watts character could even consider sending this baby back to where her mother came from?

The Slavic Child Sex Slave Girl is now an icon of prostitution culture worldwide. So cheap and abused is she that she is shipped, like Fuck Flesh, all over Europe, not to mention all over Asia and the Middle-East and her blonde child flesh is prized in Dubai.

As in the movie *Human Trafficking*, very little of the horror of her situation is captured in *Eastern Promises*. I spoke once on a blog to a young girl who had been trafficked between Europe and the USA from the time she was 4 or 5 until she was in her early teens. She says that what these movies show is not anything like how terrible it really is for the girl being used. And she too wondered why, when a movie like this came out, or a show on PBS, about *Sex Slaves*, the whole planet tells us, 'Gee, I didn't know that was going on!' Or—'how awful.' Person after person gives us this message—'I didn't know'—you read all this shocked surprise, over and over and over again on blogs/comment sections on the Internet. How could you do not know, is my question?

Human Trafficking shows us a mansion with a bunch of wholesome American boys throwing a party and using trafficked girls who are obviously terrified. One of the girls is being anally raped in public for fun and the look of misery on her face is hard to look at. So sanctioned is the rape of the female body that an entire houseful of partying men can simply ignore the misery of the women and girls brought in for their 'fun'? When one girl tries to escape, no one helps her.

I don't know how one can actually be in the world today, with access to a computer, and not know about the horrors of prostitution/trafficking? What is wrong with all of us, I wonder, that we can ignore this so completely?

I have a personal reason for being so horrified by the fate of the Slavic girls. I have some Slavic ancestry and I think my relatives—male and female—would traffic girls. They are callous and hard enough. I am dreadfully ashamed of my Slavic ancestry, given the modern-day sex-slavery rings that the mafias and crime originations from these countries have created.

The *Eastern Promises* movie gave us a little glimpse into one small portion of this—and how men can compartmentalize: these girls are my daughters so no one gets to rape-fuck them but these other girls are for sale and anyone can rape-fuck them. In the scene where the Viggo Mortensen character rapes the adolescent sex-slave, he tells her to 'stay alive a little longer.' What sad irony—since she will never be alive again. Just that one rape from him killed all her body and spirit—let alone the thousands of others inflicted on her. Male strength truly does rule all. We women stand no chance.

The world seems replete with such painful contradictions. A Shinto sacred feminine life force female deity type entity called 'kami' is supposedly important to Japanese women. Yet in Shinto the worshipping of giant phalluses must be a cruel joke to all the prostituted—all the 'kami's' sacrificed so man can have his fuck. Pilgrims in Thailand take trips to worship at a huge stone penis shrine in this land of the pathetic raped child whore. Anything that has to do with sex must seem like a cruel joke to the girl coerced into prostitution. Who worships her? Can you be 'worshipped' with constant rape? The reality of the world is man must have his fuck and the soft sacred feminine does not matter at all. There are no gods and goddesses for women.

No love goddesses. Just brutal sex goddesses who demand the sexual sale and torture of helpless young girls. No feminine sacred space, no feminine deities that protect us. No stars to wish upon, no hopes—no dreams. All the gods and goddesses died long ago when the little seven-year-old trafficked girl from Nepal got raped for the first time in her Bombay brothel. That rape cancelled them all out.

There is a lovely website called 'Womensspace' and they are sometimes kind enough to print my articles. When I visit this site, I feel at home for a few minutes. Other sensitive women reside in this site. Then I grow embarrassed to be in their company because I am not 'empowered' in any way. I can't answer questions like 'what does it mean to be a woman?' I associate being a woman with sexual pain. I would love to find a place where I do not associate sex with misery.

I try to find solace in fluff movies but every time I see a 'safe' girl in a posh hotel in one of these romantic comedies, it does not seem to blank out what I am trying to escape from. I try to find a few minutes of respite in the sex fantasy-lands of *Glamour* and *Cosmo* where romance and tenderness reign and female sexual satisfaction matters—if only in the illusory pages of such magazines. On occasion, *Glamour* will carry a tiny article about Somaly Mam, the Cambodian former child prostitute who tries to help others of her kind—or an article on how really, really young girls are married off in Yemen and terrified as they are forced to have sex with their older husbands and how a girl of eighteen there is already burdened with several children—way, way before her body is ready for sex—let alone children.

It is admirable that, amidst the fantasies of its illusory world where sexual freedom and safety are actually possible for us women, *Glamour* carries a little article now and then about the way life is for most women on this planet—sexually brutal and very unsafe. (Those Yemen girls are not the exception, in the Middle East, or Africa—where the forcing of mere children into marriage is rampant—and utterly repugnant.) Of course that tiny bit of space devoted to the way the majority of the women and girls on the planet live won't do it—it won't heal the vast sexual misery of our world. But it is a nice gesture.

Ah, Sweden, the promised land.

Another reason I wanted to add another 'Afterthoughts' to the 2009 version of this book is that something rather important is happening in regards to people finally noticing that major sporting events support sex trafficking. It all began when some activists in Europe pointed out that sex trafficking would be an integral part of the World Cup in Germany. No one had pointed that out when the Cup took place in Korea. These same activists mentioned the use of trafficked girls at the Athens Olympics. Now, activists in Vancouver are making efforts to address the trafficking that will be part of the Winter Olympics there in February 2010; South Africa is noticing the problem as regards the World Cup there in the summer of 2010; London is also taking note for the 2012 Olympics there.

What will come of this is uncertain. But Vancouver seems to be at the vanguard of the movement to do something about the sexual exploitation of women at major sporting events. It must go on in far wider venues than just the Olympics and the World Cup. Is it part of major tennis events, like the French Open and Wimbledon? Is it part of horseracing events, like the Melbourne Cup?

Finally, due to those activists in Europe and the ones in Vancouver, something is finally being said about this.

The Olympics—the event that is supposed to celebrate the best in the human spirit-- has an underpinning of 'man must have his recreational fuck on the sex slave trafficked for his pleasure'?

As I finish up writing my wandering afterthoughts, 2009, I am watching Wimbledon. Everything looks so shining and green and clean in that little world. One tennis player is wearing a kind of frilly skirt that looks pleasing and feminine. As if the world had a place for the feminine.

Some of the players are from the Ukraine, the major source of female merchandize for trafficking right now in the world; within that country, half the women are prostituted in some form. With such desperation, and such desperate poverty, controlling the lives of so many, can the women of that country ever recover? Will this sexual misery be their legacy forever?

How could I know, when I was growing up, that I was so fortunate: a place to sleep; food to eat; an education; some protection from sexual molestation—in so far as any girl is safe from that, my circumstances—middle-class military brat—gave me some protection. I wish that I could live in that time of innocence and safety again. Not knowing in this world is the best path.

I am tired of talking and sounding 'academic.' All the authoritative voices in the world ring hollow. No one knows anything. I think I came as close to enlightenment as I am going to get way back when I was age four, that pivotal year. A Marx brothers' movie on TV struck me as symbolic of the whole world—zany, crazy, without sense, so don't try to make sense of it—just enjoy the cosiness of watching a Marx brothers movie. Of course none of this occurred to me as thoughts way back then. Just as feelings. Since I associate the whole world with sexual pain and fear of violence, I need some escapes. The Marx brothers and Tarzan books. Otherwise, the tearing of delicate tissues and delicate softness becomes unbearable. Everyday life is full of allusions to sexual pain, and I feel completely abstracted from the dimension that non-raped women live in. I walk around in a world quite different from theirs. Callous news stories on TV or on the Internet that show not the remotest understanding of what prostitution is, chance remarks around me—like dirty jokes about whores--all can resonate with sexual pain and make me feel queasy and lost. Most days it is really hard to leave the house, since life seems to sexually harsh and abrasive and unforgiving toward the soft.

It is not so much my pain that troubles me. It is minor. It is the lost innocence that finding out about the comfort women has brought about. Like the account of Indonesian prostitutes being conscripted by the Japanese army. When the girls refused to do the numbers required of them, the Japanese tied the girls' legs apart and you could hear the girls crying all night as the men raped them.

When my legs are apart, I feel very vulnerable. I feel cold between my legs, and afraid. When I am with a man for the first time, I always feel this fear, as if my softness could be destroyed by him. Once I relax and he shows me I don't have to be afraid of him, then I feel okay. But why should I have that initial fear? Why should sex involve fear for the female?

I really resent even having this fear. I resent the way living in fear has given me hypochondria and agoraphobia. I should not have to dread stepping out the door. I should not have to dread all this violence that is just beyond the threshold. I should not have to fear my body everyday, with its pains and tremblings.

I have deliberately repeated myself in these 'afterthoughts,' in this book, because talking about prostitution is like taking on the role of the Ancient Mariner. No one listens. You must repeat yourself endlessly. And I am experimenting, in this section, with a more free-flowing way of writing—not one bound by hard logic and hard organization. And the difficulty of speaking about my own past makes me feel as if I am always being publicly raped. What I have written in this book and in my novels needs to be said ten million times. One day in an imaginary future I will write the last novel, *The Freshwater Mermaid.* But only if I am happy and healthy and safe. There is a different book in me somewhere. It may have to wait to come out centuries in the future. I may have to come back as a ghost, or reincarnated, 500 years in the future—to write a book without cruelty. I have to be happy to write again. No more Ph.D. Post-Harlot Depression. No more suffering for anyone in the world. Then I can write that book.

It will probably be 500 years in the future. By then, hopefully, the world will have sorted itself and there will be no need for my book. I don't know how history will make reparation to--commemorate, remember, honor—the Balkan adolescent girl ruined by a hundred rapes a day before she even has a life—or a body capable of sex. Maybe history will figure out some way that we hopeless humans in 2009 have yet to foresee. It is the only hope.

Meanwhile, like Jane Austen, I write on a tiny piece of ivory. She wove her novels from the small world of comfort and folly around her. I weave my novels from the small world of pain and danger around me. Her scrimshaw was called 'family.' Mine is called 'prostitution.' Hers offers the comfort of Jane and Elizabeth, supporting each other, caring for each other. Mine offers beings who have no family and no place in the human condition. My scrimshaw may not be as elegant as Austen's. After all, she seemed to have "the serenity of a mind at ease with itself," as she writes in *Pride and Prejudice*, that humble novel that contains <u>most</u> of the world. My subject matter is too brutal for elegance. Nevertheless, my small piece of ivory is also important.

Once I was walking on Westminster Bridge in London. A typical cloudy/ sunny/rainy/ patchy day. All of a sudden a curtain of rain washed across the bridge and the sun shone through the water and you could see Big Ben and the Houses of Parliament sparkling behind the rain and then a rainbow arc spread out across the Thames—and a seagull squawked at me. A perfect shining moment. With a seagull in the middle of it.

One brief moment of pure beauty.

A moment tucked in the past, where it is safe.

There is a sanctuary for bears in Pakistan run by WSPA (World Society for the Protection of Animals). The poor creatures have been used in the 'fun' Pakistani sport of 'bear baiting'—de-clawed and toothless, they are set upon by trained fighting dogs as men bet on the outcome. One way they are controlled is through pain-infliction: metal rings inserted their noses and lips and yanked on tear them with searing pain if they disobey in any way. The way cattle are controlled, with the rings in their noses—so that torturers can yank their heads in the air—and pour beer down their throats—to create the succulent Kobe beef that fine diners, all dressed up, sit down to at fine restaurants. (Animal torture is the norm on our planet.)

The bears come full of scars and wounds (not just physical ones, dreadful as those are) and with these metal rings in their noses, to the sanctuary. It is full of grass and trees and space for the bears to roam. Once they heal a bit, and the rings are gone, they are free to wander and explore and have a life again.

I don't know if there is a rescue center for the fighting dogs.

WSPA also helps donkeys in Afghanistan—those tiny, spindly little things carrying big loads of bricks.

The only satisfying things I can think to do are save bears and donkeys. And battery-cage hens—the most helpless and mistreated creatures on earth. I can't really help the girls in Afghanistan—all the ones being sold as child brides and all the ones forced into starvation prostitution in this perennially at-war country. All the ones who have babies before they are sixteen—before their bodies and souls and lives are even ready for sex, let alone children. It is hopeless—to try to help the overwhelming number of women and girls living under the sexual oppressions of the world—there are simply too many of them. And it would seem that they will not or cannot stand up and say—'no, I will not marry anyone when I am so young and have had no life yet.' There are quite a few women in the Afghan parliament—89 of them. Can't they do anything to promote sexual rights for the girls of their country? Can't they stop them from being married off so young? Maybe most of the girls in that country are not in a position to have any dreams about a different life. They have not had my advantages. They are probably not literate—so how can they have dreams if they cannot read? I read that most of the girls in Afghanistan are not taught to read. Illiteracy in that country is the norm for the majority of girls. Can the 89 women in the parliament promote education for these girls? Is there any education for them in the rural areas and villages?

Just too many girls everywhere with no opportunities!

So I must try to save animals—just to do one satisfying, meaningful act on this planet. Starting with one chicken. Saving one chicken has immeasurable meaning—on a planet of chaos, with no meaning.

Writing, I have concluded, is not satisfying. I enjoyed writing my novels at first since they are fantasy and science friction, and I could take sexual pain and hide it in an imaginary world. But I wrote this book concurrent with the novels and all the research I did to find out about prostitution/trafficking killed me. What I found out is going on all over the world killed me. It led me to my 'Rime of the Ancient Mariner' technique—trying to say it over and over, to get rid of the pain. It is not working.

Just the act of writing has had value. I never thought I would turn out all these novels or a non-fiction book on prostitution. I discovered that just being creative, as I wrote the novels, gave me a temporary safe space. I could shut out the whole dangerous, frightening planet and just inhabit the fictional world I created.

I discovered that I don't much care about awards and praise for my books but that I want money to protect myself in my old age. If I have a few readers who believe in the books, that's enough. The tough part is how to get money. I don't particularly want anyone to read them, but if no one does, I don't get any money. Money matters. Money means I can live in Big Sur and fund animal sanctuaries. It means I can save bears in Pakistan and donkeys in Egypt and hens all over the world. All the fancy words and concepts of the human world—honor, faithfulness, honesty, love—pretty meaningless—at least between humans. They matter with animals. You love your dog and she loves you back. You take care of your hamster and do your best to be a Hamster Whisperer—you find a middle ground between his little life, solitary and content, and your hectic human one. For the few minutes you are in his world, all is well. You are the best you can be, a Hamster Whisperer.

So, I think it's time to save the bears and the donkeys and the battery-cage hens. And rescue a few hamsters. And to pray to the goddesses of the mountains: Show me the way. I am tired.

Epilogue

Writing this book was extraordinarily painful. Intense and miserable. It destroyed what fragile health I try to hold onto. I hope I never have to write a book that is this much hell ever again.

It was a hopeless task in the service of a hopeless cause.

I tried to put all of the sexual pain in the world into one book, in order to get rid of it. It didn't work.

Sources

This section contains over four hundred sources: both books and articles. I worked on *The Raped Vagina* for two years, from 2006—2008, and during that time I checked the New Books shelf at the local library frequently. I also perused the Internet everyday for pieces on prostitution and trafficking. As a result, many of my sources are 2006-2008 since I kept up with what was currently coming out.

Not all that I read is in the list that follows. I dipped into at least another fifty books, and read hundreds of articles on the Internet that I did not have time to take notes on. The project was becoming overwhelming. The list just got too long.

It is hopeful that there is now so much out there on a subject (prostitution) that was once so hidden. Yet, the pain and suffering of the prostitute still remains largely underground and invisible, despite so much being written.

One reason there are now so many sources I think is that 'trafficking' has become 'trendy.' It is the latest feminist fad: to acknowledge the prostitute in terms of the 'trafficked' being. (Still label her a 'prostitute' and this consigns her again to the category of 'whore' and she disappears once more into invisibility and obscurity.) All these academic women have to get on the 'trafficking bandwagon,' while they never would have bothered with the 'whore bandwagon.'

There is another reason why so much is being written: the link between trafficking and AIDS. Although there may be some slight humanitarian aspect to the uncovering of trafficking, the main impetus is the danger of AIDS. If not for this disease, attention to trafficking, and particularly attention to child prostitution, would be quite minimal. But when you have entire sex industries, such as those in India, Cambodia, and Thailand, dragging hundreds of thousands of children into them, in an effort to provide clients/

rapists with 'fresh, virgin, clean meat'—well, the world will notice—just because the clients/rapists are infecting the little girls at a massive rate. Once her virginity has been sold--sometimes a number of times since owners sew the girls up again, and present them as 'real' virgins—then thousands of more clients/rapists will go at the little girl, and she will be become a raped disease nexus for these men. The next step is taking AIDS home to all those decent, wonderful wives. Can't have that. The wives matter—since they have to make more babies they can't feed. And their husbands have to prove how virile they are by filling them up with more babies they can't feed. It is the basic rule of virility—produce one child to starve, and then add ten more children and let them starve.

'Client-rapists' want 'clean' girls and mistakenly believe that child prostitutes will be uninfected. The opposite of course is true—since children have more fragile vaginal tissues and tear more easily. So, given the sheer numbers of children being sold due to fear of AIDS, someone was bound to notice.

My own personal project is to bring military prostitution into mainstream attention. (My *Raped Vagina* is a step in that direction.)

A word on the MLA style. I used this form because, of the three most popular ones, it is the simplest. The APA style and the Chicago Manual of Style seem more cumbersome to me. I laid out my sources as a traditional MLA 'Works Cited.' Any spacing peculiarities are due to the printers and publishers using their own 'style.' At any rate, the important thing is that you can find where my material comes from—despite any peculiarities or minor lapses in form.

So, here are **The Sources**:

Aaronovitch, David. "Red-Light Reform? Sorry, It's Not That Easy." *Times Online* 19 Dec. 2006 <http:www.timesonline.com>.

Abdool, Karim S.S., and Q. Abdool Karim. *HIV/AIDS in Africa*. New York: Columbia UP, 2006.

Agnew, Vijay, ed. *Diaspora, Memory, and Identity: A Search for Home*. U of Toronto P, 2005.

Agustin, Maria Laura. *Sex at the Margins: Migration, Labour Markets and the Rescue Industry.* London and New York: Zed, 2007.

Alibhai-Brown, Yasmin. "Where Are the Men in this Horrific Story?" *The Independent* 21 Dec. 2006 <http://comment.independent.co.uk/columnists_a_l/yasmin_alibhai_brown/article 2083908>.

Allen, David. "Ban on Drinking in Off-Base Bars on Okinawa, around Iwakuni and Fuji to Be Lifted." *Stars and Stripes* 13 Apr. 2008.

- - -. "Troops Mixed on Anti-prostitution Proposal." *Stars and Stripes,* Pacific Edition 25 Sept. 2004.

Altink, Sietske. *Stolen Lives: Trading Women into Sex and Slavery.* London: Scarlet Press, 1995.

Andaya, Barbara Watson. The Flaming *Womb: Repositioning Women in Early Modern Southeast Asia.* Honolulu: U of Hawai'I P, 2006.

Anderegg, Michael, ed. *Inventing Vietnam: The War in Film and Television.* Philadelphia: Temple UP, 1991.

Anderson, Bonnie S., and Judith P. Zinsser. *A History of Their Own: Women in Europe from Prehistory to the Present.* New York: Harper & Row, 1988.

Anderson, Mark M. "World War II's Other Victims." *Nation* 17 Oct. 2005: 31-38.

Antrobus, Peggy. *The Global Women's Movement: Origins, Issues and Strategies.* London and New York: Zed, 2004.

Anwar, Layla. "An Arab Woman Blues" 2006-2008. Blog. <http://www.arabwomanblues.blogspot.com>.

Apocalypse Now. Dir. Francis Ford Coppola. Perf. Robert Duvall and Martin Sheen. Zoetrope, 1979.

Arkin, William M. "Booze and Broads No More." *Veterans Today* 18 Jan. 2006 <http://www.veteranstoday.com>.

Arthurs, Jane, and Jean Grimshaw. *Women's Bodies*. London: Cassell, 1999.

Atkinson, Anthony B., et al. *Wider Perspectives on Global Development*. New York: Palgrave, 2005.

Baglia, Jay. *The Viagra Ad Venture: Masculinity, Media, and the Performance of Sexual Health*. New York: Peter Lang, 2005.

"Bangladesh--Abuse of Prostitutes." *Human Rights Watch* 2003 <http://hrw.org/reports/2003/bangladesh0803/6.htm>.

Barry, Kathleen. *Female Sexual Slavery*. New Jersey: Prentice-Hall, 1979.

Barstow, Anne Llewellyn, ed. *War's Dirty Secret: Rape, Prostitution, and Other Crimes Against Women*. Cleveland, OH: The Pilgrim Press, 2000.

Bauer, Thomas G., and Bob McKercher, eds. *Sex and Tourism: Journeys of Romance, Love, and Lust*. Oxford: Haworth, 2003.

Beeler, Karin. *Tattoos, Desire and Violence: Marks of Resistance in Literature, Film and Television*. Jefferson, NC and London: McFarland, 2005.

Bekaert, Sarah. *Adolescents and Sex: The Handbook for Professionals Working with Young People*. Oxford and Seattle: Radcliffe, 2005.

Bennett, Catherine. "Why Do So Many Men Still Think the Sex Trade Is Fine?" *The Observer* 20 Jan. 2008 <http.www.swoplv.wordpress.com>.

Bennett, Judith M. *History Matters: Patriarchy and the Challenge of Feminism*. Philadelphia: U of Pennsylvania P, 2006.

Berger, Melody, ed. *We Don't Need Another Wave: Dispatches from the Next Generation of Feminists*. Emeryville, CA: Seal Press, 2006.

Bhaskaran, Suparna. *Made in India: Decolonizations, Queer Sexualities, Trans/national Projects*. New York: Palgrave, 2004.

Biederman, Paul S. *Travel and Tourism: An Industry Primer*. Pearson, 2008.

Billson, Janet Mancini, and Carolyn Fluehr-Lobban, eds. *Female Well Being: Toward a Global Theory of Social Change.* London and New York: Zed, 2005.

Bindel, Julie. "Foul Play." *The Guardian* 30 May 2006 <http://www.guardian.co.uk/germany/article/0,,1785750.html>.

Bishop, Ryan. *Night Markets: Sexual Cultures and the Thai Economic Miracle.* New York: Routledge, 1998.

Blank, Hanne. *Virgin: The Untouched History.* New York: Bloomsbury, 2008.

Boneparth, Ellen, and Emily Stoper. *Women, Power, and Policy: Toward the Year 2000.* New York: Pergamon, 1988.

Bookman, Milica Z. *Tourists, Migrants & Refugees: Population Movements in Third World Development.* Boulder and London: Lynne Rienner, 2006.

Boothby, Richard. *Sex on the Couch: What Freud Still Has to Teach Us About Sex and Gender.* New York and London: Routledge, 2005.

Borenstein, Eliot. "Selling Russia: Prostitution, Masculinity, and Metaphors of Nationalism after Perestroika." *Gender and National Identity in 20 c. Russian Culture.* Ed. Goscilo and Lanoux. DeKalb: NIU P, 2006.

Bosworth, Mary, and Jeanne Flavin, eds. *Race, Gender, and Punishment: From Colonialism to the War on Terror.* New Brunswick, NJ and London: Rutgers UP, 2007.

Brean, Henry. "Love for Sale 101: Brothel Tour Part of College's U.S. Culture Curriculum." *Las Vegas Review-Journal* 11 Apr. 2008: B1+.

Bridenthal, Renate, Susan Mosher Stuard, and Merry E. Wiesner. *Becoming Visible: Women in European History.* Boston and New York: Houghton Mifflin, 1998.

Britton, Patti. *Art of Sex Coaching.* New York: W.W. Norton, 2005.

Brock, Rita Nakashima, and Susan Brooks Thistlethwaite. *Casting Stones: Prostitution and Liberation in Asia and the United States.* Minneapolis: Fortress Press, 1996.

Broken Trail. Perf. Robert Duvall. *American Movie Classics,* 2006.

Brooks, Ann. *Gendered Work in Asian Cities.* Hampshire, UK: Ashgate, 2006.

Brown, Louise. *Sex Slaves: The Trafficking of Women in Asia.* London: Virage, 2000.

- - -. *The Dancing Girls of Lahore: Selling Love and Saving Dreams in Pakistan's Ancient Pleasure District.* New York: HarperCollins, 2005.

Brownmiller, Susan. "Making Female Bodies the Battlefield." *Newsweek* 4 Jan. 1993.

- - -. *Against Our Will: Men, Women, and Rape.* New York: Simon and Schuster, 1975.

Buckley, Cara, and Andrew Jacobs. "The Double Lives of High-Priced Call Girls." *The New York Times* 16 Mar. 2008 <http://www.nytimes.com/2008/03/16/nyregion/a6callhtml>.

Bullough, Vern, and Bonnie Bullough. *Women in Prostitution: A Social History.* Buffalo, N.Y.: Prometheus, 1897.

Bunting, Madeleine. "Acts of Compassion." *Guardian UK* 3 Oct. 2007 <http://www.guardian.co.uk>.

Buszek, Maria Elena. *Pin-Up Girls: Feminism, Sexuality, Popular Culture.* Durham and London: Duke UP, 2006.

Butler, Jennifer S. "Militarized Prostitution: the Untold Story (U.S.A.)." *War's Dirty Secret: Rape, Prostitution, and Other Crimes Against Women.* Ed. Anne Llewellyn Barstow. Cleveland, OH: The Pilgrim Press, 2000.

Byerly, Carolyn, and Karen Ross. *Women and Media: A Critical Inquiry.* Oxford: Blackwell, 2006.

Cachola, Ellen-Rae, et al. "Gender and U.S. Bases in Asia-Pacific." Washington D.C. *Foreign Policy in Focus.* 14 Mar. 2008 <http://fpif.org>.

Cahn, Susan K. *Sexual Reckonings: Southern Girls in a Troubling Age.* Cambridge and London: Harvard UP, 2007.

Callimachi, Rukmini. "Liberian Women Fighting Back: New Rape Laws Urge Victims to Report Crime." *Associated Press* 7 Aug. 2007.

Campbell, Rosie, and Maggie O'Neill. *Sex Work Now.* Devon: Willan, 2006.

Canning, Kathleen. *Gender History in Practice: Historical Perspectives on Bodies, Class, and Citizenship.* Ithaca and London: Cornell UP, 2006.

Capps, Robert. "Crime Without Punishment." *Salon* 27 June 2008 <http://dir.salon.com>.

- - -. "Outside the Law." *Salon* 26 May 2002 <http://dir.salon.com/story/news/feature/2002/06/26/bosnia>.

Carlin, Claire L. *Imagining Contagion in Early Modern Europe.* New York: Palgrave, 2005.

Caryl, Christian. "Iraqi Vice: Porn, Prostitution and Booze." *Newsweek* 22 Dec. 2007 <http://www.msnbc.msn.com>.

Casem, Pfc. Giancarlo. "Army Cracking Down on Prostitution in Korea." *Army News Service* 4 Oct. 2004 <http://www.military.com>.

Castaneda, Xochitl, and Patricia Zavella. "Changing Constructions of Sexuality and Risk: Migrant Mexican Women Farmworkers in California." *Women and Migration in the U.S.-Mexico Borderlands.* Ed. Seugra and Zavella. Durham and London: Duke UP, 2007.

Casualties of War. Dir. Brian De Palma. Perf. Michael J. Fox and Sean Penn, 1989.

Cauvin, H.E. "For Red Light District's Best Brothels, Gold Stars." *New York Times* 2 Nov. 1999.

Chan, Sucheng. *Chinese American Transnationalism.* Philadelphia: Temple UP, 2006.

Chang, Iris. "The Rape of Nanking." *War's Dirty Secret: Rape, Prostitution, and Other Crimes Against Women.* Ed. Anne Llewellyn Barstow. Cleveland, OH: The Pilgrim Press, 2000.

Chase, Anthony, and Amr Hamzawy. *Human Rights in the Arab World.* U of Pennsylvania P, 2006.

Chesler, Phyllis. *Women and Madness.* New York: Palgrave, 2005.

Chirot, Daniel, and Clark McCauley. *Why Not Kill Them All? The Logic and Prevention of Mass Political Murder.* Princeton and Oxford: Oxford UP, 2006.

Christopher, Emma. *Slave Ships and Their Captive Cargoes, 1730-1807.* Cambridge P, 2006.

Churchman, David. *Why We Fight: Theories of Human Aggression and Conflict.* New York: U. of America Press, 2005.

Clark-Flory, Tracy. "Iraqi Women Sell Sex for Survival." *Salon* 29 May 2007 <http://www.salon.com>.

Clift Stephen, and Simon Carter, eds. *Tourism and Sex: Culture, Commerce and Coercion.* London and New York: Pinter, 2000.

Clifton, Allan S. *Time of Fallen Blossoms.* New York: Alfred Knopf, 1951.

Clinton, Catherine, and Nina Silber, eds. *Battle Scars: Gender and Sexuality in the American Civil War.* Oxford UP, 2006.

Cochrane, Kira. "Is Revenge the Best Way to Deal with Rapists?" *Guardian UK* <http://www.guardian.co.uk>.

Cohen, Erik. "Transnational Marriage in Thailand: The Dynamics of Extreme Heterogamy." *Sex and Tourism: Journeys of Romance, Sex and Tourism: Journeys of Romance, Love, and Lust.* Ed. Bauer and McKercher. Oxford: Haworth, 2003.

Coleman, Joseph. "US Military Imposes Curbs in Japan." *Associated Press* 20 Feb. 2008 <http://news.yahoo.com>.

Cooke, John Byrne. *Reporting the War: Freedom of the Press from the American Revolution to the War on Terrorism.* New York: Palgrave, 2007.

Costello, John. *Love, Sex and War: Changing Values, 1939-45.* London: William Collins, 1985 < http://www.heretical.com/costello>.

Cox, David, and Manohar Pawar. *International Social Work: Issues, Strategies, and Programs.* Thousand Oaks, CA: Sage, 2006.

Crary, David. "Human Trafficking Proves Elusive Target." *Associated Press* 30 Oct. 2005.

Crew, Louie. "Assessing the Effects of the U.S. Military Presence in Japan and Korea." <http://adromeda.rutgers.edu>.

The Crime of Human Trafficking: A Law Enforcement Guide to Identification and Investigation. Office of Violence Against Women, U.S. Department of Justice.

Croll, Marie C. *Following Sexual Abuse: A Sociological Interpretation of Identity Re/Formation in Reflexive Therapy.* Toronto: U of Toronto P, 2008.

Cross, Dr Harold H.U. *The Lust Market.* New York: The Citadel Press, 1956.

Crouse, Janice Shaw. "Zero Tolerance for Human Trafficking." *Beverly LaHaye Institute.* Concerned Women for America. 23 June 2006 <http://www.cwfa.org>.

Cudworth, Erika. *Developing Ecofeminist Theory.* New York: Palgrave, 2005.

Cumings, Bruce. *Korea's Place in the Sun.* New York: W.W. Norton, 2005.

Curry, Jennifer, Ed. *Women's Rights.* The Reference Shelf, Vol 77, number 4. The H.W. Wilson Company, 2005.

Curthoys, Ann, and John Docker. *Is History Fiction?* Ann Arbor: U of Michigan P, 2005.

Dalla, Rochelle L. *Exposing the "Pretty Woman" Myth: A Qualitative Investigation of Street-Level Prostituted Women.* Lanham, MD: Lexington, 2006.

Davidson, Julia O'Connell. "Sex Tourism and Child Prostitution." *Tourism and Sex.* Ed. Clift and Carter. London and New York: Pinter, 2000.

Davidson, Julia O'Connell. *Children in the Global Sex Trade.* Cambridge: Polity Press, 2005.

Davis, Sue. "Sexual Exploitation of Iraqi Women: Another Reason to Bring the Troops Home." *Workers World.* 8 Oct. 2007 <http://www.workers.org/2007/world/women-1011/>.

De Jesus, Emmi A., "The Social Cost of US Military Presence." *Asia-Pacific Research Network.* 9 Jan. 2006 <http://www.aprnet.org>.

De la Pedraja, Rene. *Wars of Latin America, 1899-1941.* London: McFarland.

De Leeuw, Hendrik. *Sinful Cities of the World.* New York: Citadel Press, 1934.

DeBonis, Steve. *Children of the Enemy: Oral Histories of Vietnamese Amerasians and Their Mothers.* Jefferson, NC and London: McFarland, 1995.

"Desperate Iraqi Refugees Turn to Sex Trade in Syria." *New York Times* 29 May 2007 <http://www.nytimes.com.2007/05/29/world/middleeast/29syrai.html>.

Dickey, Christopher. "Snapshots of Horror." *Newsweek* 28 Apr. 2008: 57.

Dominelli, Lena. *Anti-Oppressive Social Work Theory and Practice.* New York: Palgrave, 2002.

Donovan, Brian. *White Slave Crusades.* Urbana and Chicago: U of Illinois P, 2006.

Dower, John. *Embracing Defeat: Japan in the Wake of World War II.* New York: W.W. Norton, 1999.

Downer, Lesley, "Slaves to Lust." *Sunday Times, Weekend Magazine.* 18 July 1999.

Druckerman, Pamela. *Lust in Translation: The Rules of Infidelity from Tokyo to Tennessee.* New York: Penguin, 2007.

Ebert, James R. *The American Infantryman in Vietnam, 1965-1972.* New York: Ballantine, 1993.

Edwards, Louise, and Mina Roces, eds. *Women in Asia: Tradition, Modernity, and Globalisation.* Ann Arbor: U of Michigan P, 2000.

Edwards, Tim. *Cultures of Masculinity.* London and New York: Routledge, 2006.

Ehrhart, W.D., ed. *Carrying the Darkness: American Indochina: The Poetry of the Vietnam War.* New York: Avon, 1985.

- - -, ed. *Unaccustomed Mercy: Soldier-Poets of the Vietnam War.* Lubbock: Texas Tech UP, 1989.

Einhorn, Barbara. *Citizenship in an Enlarging Europe: From Dream to Awakening.* Hampshire and New York: Palgrave, 2006.

Eisen, Arlen. *Women and Revolution in Vietnam.* London: Zed, 1984.

Eisenstein, Zillah. *Sexual Decoys: Gender, Race and War in Imperial Democracy.* London and New York: Zed, 2007.

Elfman, Doug. "'Pornstreaming' Is Star's Aim in Las Vegas." Las *Vegas Review-Journal* 8 Apr. 2008: 3A.

Ely, Mike. "More U.S. Rape on Okinawa—Enough!" 22 Feb. 2008 <http://mikeely.wordpress.com/2008/02/22/us-rape-on-okinawa-again-enough/>.

"Emma Thompson on Sex Trade." *Al Jazeera, English* 11 April 2008 <http://english.aljazeera.net>.

"Emma Thompson's Graphic Prostitute Role to Highlight Sex Trafficking Horrors." *The London News.Net* 29 Oct. 2007 <http://www.thelondonnews.net>.

Enana, Ishtar. <ishtar-enana.blogspot.com>.

"Ending Gender-Based Violence." *Women's Commission for Refugee Women and Children*. Sept. 2007 <http://www.womenscommission/projects/rh/ending_gbv.php>.

Engle, Richard. "In Syria, Girls March as Timebomb Ticks." 10 July 2007 MSNBC.

Enloe, Cynthia. *Bananas, Beaches and Bases: Making Feminist Sense of International Politics.* Berkeley: U of California P, 2000.

- - -. *Maneuvers: The International Politics of Militarizing Women's Lives.*

Berkeley: U of California P, 2000.

- - -. *The Morning After: Sexual Politics at the End of the Cold War*. Berkeley: U of California P, 1993.

Fackler, Martin. "Rice Offers Regret After Marine Is Accused of Rape on Okinawa." *New York Times* Apr. 2008.

Falcon, Sylvanna M. "Rape as a Weapon of War: Militarized Rape at the U.S.-Mexico Border." *Women and Migration in the U.S.-Mexico Borderlands.* Ed. Seugra and Zavella. Durham and London: Duke UP, 2007.

Fall, Bernard B. *Street without Joy*. New York: Schocken Books, 1975.

Fang, Bay. "Young Lives for Sale." *U.S. News & World Report*. 24 Oct. 2005: 31-34. Farley, Melissa. *Prostitution Research*. <www.prostitutionresearch.com>.

Farone, Christopher A., and Laura K. McClure. *Prostitutes and Courtesans in the Ancient World.* U of Wisconsin P, 2006.

Farris, William Wayne. *Japan's Medieval Population: Famine, Fertility, and Warfare in a Transformative Age.* Honolulu: U of Hawai'i P, 2006.

Fassin, Didier. *When Bodies Remember: Experiences and Politics of AIDS in South Africa.* Berkeley: U of California P, 2007.

Fennell, David A. *Tourism Ethics.* Toronto: Channel View, 2006.

Ferree, Myra Marx, and Aili Mari Tripp. *Global Feminism: Transnational Women's Activism, Organizing, and Human Rights. New* York and London: New York UP, 2006.

Figueredo, D.H., and Frank Argote-Freyre. *A Brief History of the Caribbean.* New York: Facts on File, 2008.

Finnegan, William. "The Countertraffickers: Rescuing the Victims of the Global Sex Trade." *The New Yorker* 5 May 2008: 44-58.

Firmo-Fontan, Victoria. "Abducted, Beaten and Sold into Prostitution: A Tale from Iraq." *Independent* 26 July 2004 <http://www.countercurrents.org/iraq-fontan260704.htm>.

Fleshman, Michael. "AIDS Prevention in the Ranks." United Nations. June 2001 <http://www.un.org>.

Flowers, R. Barri. *The Prostitution of Women and Girls.* Jefferson, NC and London: MacFarland, 1998.

Foreman, Kelly. "Bad Girls Confined." *Bad Girls of Japan.* Ed. Miller and Bardsley. New York: Palgrave, 2005.

Franco, Jean. "Rape and Human Rights." *PMLA* Oct. 2006, vol. 121, no.5: 1662-1664.

Frey-Wouters, Ellen, and Robert S. Laufer. *Legacy of a War: The American Soldier in Vietnam.* New York and London: M.E. Sharpe.

Full Metal Jacket. Dir. Stanley Kubrick. Perf. Matthew Modine and Adam Baldwin. Warner Bros., 1987.

Gall, Gregor. *Sex Worker Union Organising: An International Study*. Hampshire and New York: Palgrave, 2006.

Gallagher, Anne. "A Question of Bondage." *The Age* 15 May 2008 <http://www.theage.com.au/new/opinion/a-question-of-bondage/2008/05/14>.

Gamel, Kim. "Soldier Gets Expelled from Iraq." *Associated Press* 24 Jan. 2006.

Georgiopoulos, Anna M., and Jerrold F. Rosenbaum. *Perspectives in Cross-Cultural Psychiatry.* Philadelphia: Lippincott Williams & Wilkins, 2005.

Gilbert, Geoff. *Responding to International Crime*. Boston: Martinus Nijhoff, 2006.

Goldenberg, Suzanne. "US Soldiers Accused of Sexual Assaults." *The Guardian* 8 Mar. 2005 <http://guardian.co.uk/world/2005/mar/08/iraq.suzannegoldenberg>.

Goldman, Abigail. "Bewildered Academics Pore Over Sex-Trade Hysteria." *Las Vegas Sun* 31 Jan. 2008: 1-2.

Goodey, Jo. "Sex Trafficking in the European Union." *Transnational and Comparative Criminology.* Ed. Sheptycki and Wardek. London: GlassHouse Press, 2005.

Goodwin, Jan. "I Was Sold for $200 and Now I'm a Sex Slave." *Marie Claire* July 2000.

Goscilo, Helena, and Andrea Lanoux, eds. *Gender and National Identity in 20 c. Russian Culture*. DeKalb: NIU P, 2006.

Greer, Germaine. The Female Eunuch. New York: McGraw-Hill, 1971.

Griffith, R. Marie, and Barbara Dianne Savage. *Women and Religion in the African Diaspora: Knowledge, Power, and Performance.* Baltimore: Johns Hopkins UP, 2006.

Gutmann, Matthew C., ed. *Changing Men and Masculinities in Latin America.* Durham and London: Duke UP, 2003.

Hackett, Elizabeth, and Sally Haslanger. *Theorizing Feminisms: A Reader.* New York and Oxford: Oxford UP, 2006.

Hale, Sondra. *Gender Politics in Sudan.* New York: Westview, 1996.

Hansen, Suzy. "Our Wolves in Uniform." *Salon* 22 Mar. 2001 <www.archive.salon/books/feature/2001/03/22>.

Harman, Greg. "Land of the Lost: Texas Creates Task Force on Sexual Slavery as Bexar County's First Trafficking Case Wraps Up." *SA Current* 18 June 2009 <http://www.sacurrent.com/news/story.asp?id=70254>. Hart, Patricia, Karen Weathermon, and Susan H. Armitage, eds. *Women Writing Women.* Lincoln, NE: U of Nebraska P, 2006.

Hartmann, Heidi. *Women, Work, and Poverty: Women Centered Research for Policy Change.* Haworth, 2003.

Hasting, Michael. "The Opium Brides of Afghanistan." *Newsweek* 7 Apr. 2008: 38-41.

Hayden, H. Thomas. "Presidential Briefing." 7 Aug. 2006 <http://www.military.com/opinion/0,15202,108914,00.html>.

Hayslip, Le Ly, *When Heaven and Earth Changed Places: A Vietnamese Woman's Journey from War to Peace.* New York: Doubleday, 1989.

Heldman, K. "Itaewon, South Korea: On the Town with the U.S. Military." 19 Dec. 1996 <http://www.kimsoft.com/korea/us-army.htm>.

Henriot, Christian. *Prostitution and Sexuality in Shanghai: A Social History, 1849-1949.* Cambridge UP, 2001.

Henson, Maria Rosa. *Comfort Woman: A Filipina's Story of Prostitution and Slavery Under the Japanese Military.* Lanham, MD: Rowman & Littlefield, 1999.

Hentoff, Nat. "Who Will Halt the Raping of Africa." *Associated Press* 5 Dec. 2007.

Herbert, Bob. "Fantasies Well Meant." *New York Times* 11 Sept. 2008: A27.

- - -. "Mayor Puts Spotlight on Industry of the Night." *New York Times* 2007.

Hicks, George. *The Comfort Women: Japan's Brutal Regime of Enforced Prostitution in the Second World War.* New York, London: W.W. Norton, 1994.

Himes, Andrew, ed. *Voices in Wartime Anthology: A Collection of Narratives and Poems.* Seattle, WA, Whit Press, 2005.

Hiroshi, Oseda, and Eric Talmadge. "Diggers Sex, Rape Scandal." *Courier Mail 27* Apr. 2007 <http://www.news.com.au/couriermail/story>.

Hiyashi, Hirofumi. "Comfort Women System Was Obviously Slavery." *Asahi Evening News* 26 Jan. 1997.

Holloway, Pippa. *Sexuality, Politics, and Social Control in Virginia, 1920-1945.* Chapel Hill, U of North Carolina P, 2006.

Hollows, Joanne. *Feminism in Popular Culture.* New York: Oxford, 2006.

Howard, Keith, ed. *True Stories of the Korean Comfort Women.* London: Cassell, 1995.

Human Trafficking. Perf. Mira Sorvino and Donald Sutherland. *Lifetime TV,* 2006.

"Human Trafficking Is Torture by Any Other Name." *Duncan's TV Ad Land* 5 Nov. 2007 <http://www.duncanstv/2007/human-trafficking-is-torture-by-any-other-name>.

Hutton, Fiona. *Risky Pleasures: Club Culture and Feminine Identities.* Hampshire, UK: Ashgate, 2007.

"In Their Own Words: Testimonies of Survivors." *Polaris Project.* April 2008 <www.polarisproject.org>.

"India—the Sex Workers." Dir. Raney Aronson. *Frontline/World.* PBS 2005 <http://www.pbs.org/frontlineworld/stories/india304/aronson.html>.

Ingham, Richard. "From 'Gay Plague' to Global Tragedy: An AIDS Anniversary." 19 May 2008 <http://yahoo.com>.

Inigo, Jessica. "Troops Say Proposed UCMJ Change Unfair in Prostitution-Legal Germany." *Stars and Stripe,* European Edition 27 Sept. 2004 <http://www.military.com>.

"Iraqi Women: Prostituting Ourselves to Feed Our Children." Arwa Damon. *CNN* 15 Mar. 2008 <http://edition.cnn/world.com>.

"Iraqi Refugee Women and Youth in Jordan." *Women's Commission for Refugee Women and Children.* Sept. 2007 <http://www.womenscommission/projects/rh/ending_gbv.php>. "Israel: Human Rights Abuses of Women Trafficked from Countries of the Former Soviet Union into Israel's Sex Industry." May 2000. New York: Amnesty International USA.

Iwao, Sumiko. *The Japanese Woman: Tradition, Image, and Changing Reality.* New York: Free Press Macmillan, 1993.

Jacka, Tamara. *Rural Women in China: Gender, Migration, and Social Change.* Armonk, NY: East Gate, 2006.

Jacobs, Seth. *America's Miracle Man in Vietnam.* Durham and London: Duke UP, 2004.

Jacoby, Mary. "Does U.S. Abet Korean Sex Trade?" *St. Petersburg Times Online* 9 Dec. 2002 < http://www.prisonplanet.com>.

Jaffreys, Elaine. *China, Sex and Prostitution.* London and New York: Routledge and Curzon, 2004.

Jamail, Dahr, and Ali al-Fadhily. "Rape Case Emerges from Shadows." 3 Mar. 2007 <http://www.countercurrents.org/iraq-jamail030307.htm>.

- - -. "Iraqi Women Paying the Price." 24 Jan. 2005. <http://www.dahrjamailiraq.com>.

"The Jamie Leigh Jones Gang Rape Scandal: Halliburton/KRB Employee Gang Raped in Iraq by American Co-Workers Who Cannot Be Prosecuted." *Women's Space* 16 Jan. 2008 <http://womensspace.wordpress.com/2008/01/16/jamie-lee-jones-halliburtonbr-employee>.

"Japan Likely to Drop Marines' Rape Case." *Associated Press* 17 Nov. 2007 <http://www.military.com>.

Jeffrey, Leslie Ann, and Gayle MacDonald. Sex W*orkers in the Maritimes Talk Back*. Vancouver and Toronto: UBC Press, 2007.

- - -. *Sex and Borders: Gender, National Identity, and Prostitution Policy in Thailand.* Vancouver and Toronto: UBC Press.

Jeffreys, Sheila. *The Idea of Prostitution*. Melbourne: Spinifex, 1997.

Jejeebhoy, Shireen J., Iqbal Shah, and Shyam Thapa, eds. *Sex Without Consent: Young People in Developing Countries*. London and New York: Zed.

Jelinek, Pauline. "Anti-Prostitution Rule Drafted for U.S. Forces." *Associated Press* 22 Sept. 2004 <http://www.washingtonpost.com>.

"Johns, Prostitution and Iraq." *Apostate*. 28 Aug 2007 <http://aspotate.wordpress.com/2007/08/28/john-porsitution-and-iraq/>.

Jones, Nicola Anne. *Gender and the Political Opportunities of Democratization in South Korea.* New York: Palgrave, 2006.

Jones, Preston. "We're Still Supporting Slavery." *Christianity Today* 1 Sept. 2004 <http: www. christianitytoday.com>.

Jowers, Karen. "Patronizing Prostitutes Just Got More Costly." *Army Times* 24 Jan. 2006 <http://www.armytimes.com>.

Kalin, Walter. *Human Rights in Times of Occupation: The Case of Kuwait.* London: Sweet and Maxwell, 1994.

Kantola, Johanna. *Feminists Theorize the State.* New York: Palgrave, 2006.

Katsuichi, Honda. *The Nanjing Massacre. A Japanese Journalist Confronts Japan's National Shame.* Armonk, NY and London: M.E. Sharpe, 1999.

"Kazakhstan--Police Abuse of Sex Workers." Human Rights Watch 2003 <http://hrw.org/reports/2003/kazak0603/fromatkkaz2-04.htm>.

Keddie, Nikki R. *Women in the Middle East.* Princeton: Princeton UP, 2007.

Kelpie, Colm. "'America Will Never Leave Iraq,' US Soldier Says." 4 Aug. 2005 <http://www.uslaboragainstthewar.org>.

Kelsky, Karen. *Women on the Verge: Japanese Women, Western Dreams.* Durham and London: Duke UP, 2001.

Kempadoo, Kamala, ed. *Sun, Sex, and Gold: Tourism and Sex Work in the Caribbean.* Lanham, MD: Rowman & Littlefield, 1999.

- - -, ed. *Trafficking and Prostitution Reconsidered: New Perspectives on Migration, Sex Work, and Human Rights.* Boulder and London: Paradigm, 2005.

Kenway, Jane, Anna Kraack, and Anna Hickey-Moody. *Masculinity Beyond the Metropolis.* New York: Palgrave, 2006.

Khan, Shahnaz. *Zina, Transnational Feminism, and the Moral Regulation of Pakistani Women.* Vancouver and Toronto: UBC Press, 2006.

Kimmel, Michael, ed. *The Sexual Self: The Construction of Sexual Scripts.* Nashville: Vanderbilt UP, 2007.

Kirk, Gwyn, Rachel Cornwell, and Margo Okazawa-Rey. "Women and the U.S. Military in East Asia." *Foreign Policy in Focus* <www.fpif.org>.

"Korean Prostitution." <http://www.imjinscout.com/Korean_Prostitution/O1.html>.

"Kosovo UN Troops 'Fuel Sex Trade.'" *BBC News* 6 May 2004 <http://news.bbc.co.uk/2/hi/europe/368173.stm>.

Kristof, Nicholas D. "Do As He Said." *New York Times.* 13 Mar. 2008.

- - -. "The Pimps' Slaves." *New York Times.* 16 Mar. 2008.

- - -. "New York Governor Had Positive Message, Even If He Didn't Follow It." New *York Times.* 15 Mar. 2008.

Kronenberg, Frank, ed. *Occupational Therapy Without Borders: Learning from the Spirit of Survivors.* New York: Elsevier Churchill Livingstone, 2005.

Kuiper, Edith, and Drucilla K. Barker. *Feminist Economics & the World Bank: History, Theory and Policy.* London and New York: Routledge.

Latstetter, Jennifer. "American Military-Base Prostitution." <http://www.wm.edu/so/monitor/spring2000/paper.htm>.

Lay, Mary M., Janice Monk, and Deborah S. Rosenfelt. *Encompassing Gender: Integrating International Studies and Women's Studies.* City U of New York: Feminist Press, 2002.

Lederer, Edith. "Charity: UN Peacekeepers, AID Workers Abusing Kids." *Associated Press* 27 May 2008 <http://news.yahoo.com>.

Lefkowitz, Mary R., and Maureen B. Fant. *Women's Life in Greece and Rome.* Baltimore: Johns Hopkins, 2005.

Lenz, Ryan. "U.S Troops Accused of Killing Iraqi Family." *Associated Press* 30 June 2006.

Leung, Paul. "Sex Tourism: The Case of Cambodia." *Sex and Tourism: Journeys of Romance, Sex and Tourism: Journeys of Romance, Love, and Lust.* Ed. Bauer and McKercher. Oxford: Haworth, 2003.

Leupp, Gary P. *Interracial Intimacy in Japan: Western Men and Japanese Women: 1543-1900.* London and New York: Continuum, 2003.

Levine, Judith. *Harmful to Minors: The Perils of Protecting Children from Sex.* Minneapolis and London: U of Minnesota P, 2002.

Levy, Charles J. *Spoils of War.* Boston: Houghton Mifflin, 1974.

Lewis, David H. *Flower Drum Song: The Story of Two Musicals*. Jefferson, NC and London: McFarland, 2006.

Liddle, Joanna, and Sachido Nakajima. *Rising Suns, Rising Daughters: Gender, Class and Power in Japan*. London and New York: Zed, 2000.

Lie, John, "The State as Pimp: Prostitution and the Patriarchal State in Japan in the 1940's." *Sociological Quarterly* 38, no. 2 (1997): 251-64.

Lifton, Robert Jay. *Home from the War: Vietnam Veterans: Neither Victims Nor Executioners*. New York: Touchstone, 1973.

Lilly, Robert J. *Taken by Force: Rape and American GIs in Europe during WWII*. New York: Palgrave, 2007.

Lindsay, Robert. Blog. 14 Sept 2007 <http://robertlindsay.blogspot>.

Lloyd, Carol. "Survival Sex in Iraq." *Salon* 7 Dec. 2007 <www.salon.com/mwt/broadsheet/2007/07/12/survival_sex/print.html>.

Longstreet, Stephen, and Ethel Longstreet. *Yoshiwara: City of the Senses*. New York: David McKay, 1970.

Loue, Sana. *Sexual Partnering, Sexual Practices, and Health*. New York: Springer, 2006.

Luke, Brian. *Brutal: Manhood and the Exploitation of Animals*. Urbana and Chicago: U of Illinois P, 2008.

Luker, Kristin. *When Sex Goes to School: Warring View on Sex—and Sex Education—Since the Sixties*. New York: W. W. Norton, 2006.

Lyn, Tan Ee, and Jonathon Burch. "Chinese Sex Workers Find Their Way to Kabul." *Reuters* 19 May 2008 <http://in.reuters.com>.

Lyons, Alistair. "Iraqi Refugees Turn to Sex Trade in Syria." *Reuters* 31 Dec. 2007 <http://www.countercurrents.org/lyons311207.htm>.

Mac an Ghaill, Mairtin, and Chris Haywood. *Gender, Culture and Society*. Hampshire and New York: Palgrave, 2007.

MacIntyre, Donald. "Base Instincts." *Time* 5 Aug. 2005 <http://www.time.com>.

MacKinnon, Catharine A. *Are Women Human*? Harvard UP, 2006.

Macleod, Hugh. "Despair of Baghdad Turns into a Life of Shame in Damascus: Young Women Fleeing War and Poverty Fall Prey to Sex Traffickers." *The Guardian* 24 Oct. 2006 <http://www.guardian.co.uk/world/2006/oct/24/syria.iraq>.

Malarek, Victor. *The Natashas: Inside the New Global Sex Trade.* Canada: Viking, 2003.

Malinowski, Bronislaw. *The Sexual Life of Savages in North-Western Melanesia.*

Marcus, Sharon. *Between Women: Friendship, Desire, and Marriage in Victorian England.* New Jersey: Princeton UP, 2007.

Marshall, Lucinda. "Rape in the U.S. Military." *Los Angeles Times* 30 Jan. 2008 <http://www.latimes.com>.

Matsui, Yayori. *Women in the New Asia: From Pain to Power.* Trans. Noriko Toyokawa and Carolyn Francis. Bangkok: White Lotus. Victoria: Spinifex.

London and New York: Zed, 1999.

Matthews, Kymberlie. "The Saving of the Innocents: The *Satya* Interview with Ruchira Gupta, Journalist Turned Activist." *Satya* Jan. 2005 <http://satyamag.com/jan05/gupta.html>.

Mattingly, Doreen J., and Ellen R. Hastings, eds. *Women and Change at the U.S.-Mexico Border: Mobility, Labor, and Activism.* Tucson, U of Arizona P, 2006.

May, Captain Eric H. "X-Rated Iraq: A Tortured Story." 18 Feb. 2008.

Mazurana, Dyan. "Gender and the Causes and Consequences of Armed Conflict." *Gender, Conflict, and Peacekeeping.* Ed. Mazurana, Raven-Roberts, and Parpart.

Lanham, MD: Rowman and Littlefield, 2005.

- - -, Angela Raven-Roberts, and Jane Parpart. *Gender, Conflict, and Peacekeeping.* Lanham, MD: Rowman and Littlefield, 2005.

McCoppin, Suzy. "Bringing up the Rear: The Truth About Anal Sex from A Woman's Point of View." *Playboy* June 2009: 27.

McDonald, Laura S., Robina Bhasin, and Richard F. Mollica. "Project 1 Billion: A Global Modal for Health Recovery of Postconflict Societies." *Perspectives in Cross-Cultural Psychiatry.* Ed. Georgiopoulos and Rosenbaum. Philadelphia: Lippincott Williams & Wilkins, 2005.

McFerson, Hazel M. *Blacks and Asians: Crossings, Conflict and Commonality.* Durham, NC: Carolina Academic Press, 2006.

McKelvey, Robert S. *The Dust of Life: America's Children Abandoned in Vietnam.* Seattle and London: U of Washington P, 1999.

McKenon, Elaine. *The Scarlet Mile: A Sociological History of Prostitution in Kalgoorlie, 1894-2004.* U of Western Australia P, 2005.

MacKinnon, Catharine A. *Are Women Human*? Harvard UP, 2006.

McMichael, William H. "Sex Slaves." *Navy Times* 12 Aug. 2002 <http://www.vvawai.org/general.sex-slaves.html>.

McNutt, Debra. "Is the Iraq Occupation Enabling Prostitution?" *Psyche, Science, and Society.* 11 July 2007 <http://psychoanalystsopposewar.org>.

Meagher, Sharon M., and Patrice DiQuinzio, eds. *Women and Children First: Feminism, Rhetoric, and Public Policy.* Albany: State U of New York P, 2005.

Menon, Elizabeth K. *Evil by Design: The Creation and Marketing of the Femme Fatale*. Urbana and Chicago: U of Illinois P, 2006.

Miller, John. "State, Defense Departments Join Forces To Stop Human Trafficking." USInfo.State.Gov. 23 Sept 2004 <http://usinfo.state.gov>.

Miller, Laura, and Jan Bardsley, eds. *Bad Girls of Japan*. New York: Palgrave, 2005.

Millett, Kate. *Sexual Politics*. New York: Doubleday, 1970.*A Modern Form of Slavery: Trafficking of Burmese Women and Girls into Brothels in Thailand* Asia Watch Women's Rights Project (Division of Human Rights Watch). New York: Human Rights Watch, 1993.

Moffeit, Miles, and Amy Herdy. "Female GIs Report Rapes in Iraq War." *Denver Post* 25 Jan. 2004 <http://www.commondreams.org>.

Molasky, Michael S. *American Occupation of Japan and Okinawa.*

Montgomery, Heather. *Modern Babylon? Prostituting Children in Thailand.* New York: Berghahn, 2001.

Monzini, Paola. *Sex Traffic: Prostitution, Crime and Exploitation.* Trans. Patrick Camiller. London and New York: Zed, 2005.

Moon, Katharine H.S. *Sex Among Allies: Military Prostitution in U.S.-Korea Relations.* New York: Columbia UP, 1997.

Moran, Jeffrey P. *Teaching Sex: The Shaping of Adolescence in the 20th Century.* Cambridge and London: Harvard UP, 2000.

"More on Women Soldiers, Rape and Iraq." *Salon* 19 Mar. 2007 <http.//www.salon.com>.

Morgan, Robin. "Their Bodies as Weapons." *Guardian UK 21* Aug. 2006 <http:www.commondreams.org>.

Morris, Madeline. "Rape, War, and Military Culture." *War's Dirty Secret: Rape, Prostitution, and Other Crimes Against Women.* Ed. Anne Llewellyn Barstow. Cleveland, OH: The Pilgrim Press, 2000.

Moubayed, Sami. "Sexual Repression in Syria." *PostGlobal* 30 Jan. 2007 <http://newsweek.washingpost.com>.

Murata Noriko. "The Trafficking of Women." *Voices from the Japanese Women's Movement*. Ed. By AMPO—*Japanese Asia Quarterly Review*. London: M.E. Sharpe, 1996.

Murdoch, Lindsay. "UN Turns Blind Eye to Use of Timor Brothels." *The Age* 7 May 2007 <http://www.theage.com.au/news/world/un-turns-blind-eye-to-use-of-timor-brothels/2007>.

Nadelson, Theodore. *Trained to Kill: Soldiers at War*. Baltimore and London: The Johns Hopkins UP, 2005.

Neu, Charles E. *After Vietnam: Legacies of a Lost War*. Wheeling, IL: Harland Davidson, 2005.

The New Heroes: "Sompop Jantraka." *PBS* 2006 <http://www.pbs.org/opb/thenewheroes/sompop.html>.

"New Stricter Rules Against Prostitution." *Military.com* 2005 <http://www.military.com>.

Newman, Paul B. *Growing Up in the Middle Ages*. North Carolina: McFarland, 2007.

Niemantsverdriet, Thijs. "Turn Out the Red Light." *Newsweek* 8 Feb. 2008 <www.newsweek.com>.

Norman, Elizabeth M. *Women at War: The Story of Fifty Military Nurses Who Served in Vietnam*. Philadelphia: U of Pennsylvania P, 1990.

O'Toole, Laura, L., Jessica Schiffman, and Margie L. Kiter Edwards, eds. *Gender Violence: Interdisciplinary Perspectives*, 2nd ed. New York and London: New York UP, 2007.

Odzer, Cleo. *Patpong Sisters: An American Woman's View of the Bangkok Sex World*. New York: Arcade Publishing, Blue Moon Books, 1994.

Off Limits. Dir. Christopher Crowe. Perf. Willem Dafoe and Gregory Hines, 1988.

Onishi, Norimitsu. "Japan, Easygoing Till Now, Plans Sex Traffic Crackdown." *New York Times* 16 Feb. 2005: A3.

Oosterveld, Valerie. "Prosecution of Gender-Based Crimes in International Law." *Gender, Conflict, and Peacekeeping*. Ed. Mazurana, Raven-Roberts, and Parpart. Lanham, MD: Rowman and Littlefield, 2005.

Oppermann, Martin, ed. *Sex Tourism and Prostitution: Aspects of Leisure, Recreation, and Work*. Elmsford, NY: Cognizant Communication Corporation, 1998.

Paasonen, Susanna. *Figures of Fantasy*. New York: Peter Lang, 2005.

Padavick, Robert. "The Dark Trade." *Kevin Sites' Hot Zone*. 2007<http://hotzone.yahoo.com>.

Palmer, Elizabeth. "Iraqi Refugees Turn to Prostitution." *CBS News* 31 Dec. 2007 <http://wwwcbsnews.com>.

Park Chung-a. "More Koreans Engage in Sex Trade in US." *American Sex Gazette* 24 Mar. 2007 <http://www.americansexgazette.com/asg/united states>.

Parsons, Jeffrey T., ed. *Contemporary Research on Sex Work*. New York: Haworth, 2005.

Peach, Lucinda Joy, ed. *Women in Culture: A Women's Studies Anthology*. Oxford: Blackwell, 1998.

Pearson, Veronica, and Leung, Benjamin K.P., eds. *Women in Hong Kong*. Oxford and New York: Oxford UP, 1995.

Pennington, Matthew. "Food Crisis Leaves Many Afghans Desperate." *Associated Press* May 2008 <http://news.yahoo.com>.

Perkins, Roberta, and Frances Lovejoy. *Call Girls: Private Sex Workers in Australia*. Crawley: U of Western Australia P, 2007.

Pesek, Jr., William. "One Night in Bangkok Shows the Folly of APEC." *Bloomberg* 22 Oct. 2003 <http://quote.bloomberg.com/apps/news>.

Peterson, Kristen. "Glamour Girls of the Streets." *Las Vegas Sun 4* Dec. 2007: 7.

Pheterson, Gail. *The Prostitution Prism*. Amsterdam UP, 1996.

Phillips, Joshua E.S. "Unveiling Iraq's Teenage Prostitutes." *Salon* 24 June 2005 <http://dir.salon.com/story/news/feature.2006/06/24/prostitutes>.

Platoon. Dir. Oliver Stone. Perf. Charlie Sheen, Tom Berenger, and Willem Dafoe. Orion, 1986.

Platt, Leah "Regulating the Global Brothel." *The American Prospect,* volume 12, no. 12, 2 July 2001. *Women's Rights*. Ed. Curry. The H.W. Wilson Company, 2005.

Pollitt, Katha. *Virginity or Death! And Other Social and Political Issues of Our Time.* New York: Random House, 2006.

Poulin, Richard. "Globalization of the Sex Industry, Violence and Commodification of Human Beings." *Roadblocks to Equality: Women Challenging Boundaries*. Ed.Jeffery Klaehn. Montreal: Black Rose Books, 2009.

Powers, Karen Vieira. *Women in the Crucible of Conquest*. Albuquerque: U of New Mexico P, 2005.

Pratt, Timothy. "Human Trafficking Victims Can Get Help." *Las Vegas Sun*. *Pretty Woman*. Dir. Garry Marshall. Perf. Julia Roberts and Richard Gere. Touchstone, 1990.

"Prostitution in South Korea." *Wikepedia*. Apr. 2008 <http://en.wikepedia.org>.

"Prostitution Ruling Nothing New for USFK." *Stars and Stripes* 12 Jan. 2006 <http://www.military.com>.

Qadiry, Tahir. "Under Wraps: Prostitution Rife in North Afghanistan." *Reuters* 19 May 2008 <http://in.reuteres.com>.

Rao, Nina. "The Dark Side of Tourism and Sexuality: Trafficking of Nepali Girls for India Brothels." *Sex and Tourism: Journeys of Romance, Sex and Tourism: Journeys of Romance, Love, and Lust.* Ed. Bauer and McKercher. Oxford: Haworth, 2003.

"Rape as a War Crime." *America Press.* 13 Oct. 2003. *Women's Rights.* Ed. Curry. The H.W. Wilson Company, 2005.

"The Rape of Iraq." *Women's Space* 8 July 2008 <http://womensspace.wordpress.com>.

"The Rape of Sabrine." *Baghdad Burning.* Riverbend Blog. 26 Feb. 2007 <http://www.countercurrents.org/iraq-burning>.

Raphael, Jody. *Listening to Olivia: Violence, Poverty, and Prostitution.* Boston: Northeastern UP, 2004.

Ray, Audacia. *Naked on the Internet: Hookups, Downloads, and Cashing in on Internet Sexploration.* Emeryville, CA: Seal Press, 2007.

Raymond, Janice G., et al. *A Comparative Study of Women Trafficked in the Migration Process.* Coaltion Against Trafficking in Women.

"Red Light, Green Light: The Global Trafficking of Women." *Feminism and Women's Studies.* 20 Sept. 1994 <http://feminism.eserver.org/gender/sex-work/trafficking-of-women.txt/document_view>.

Regan, Tom. "Report: Sexual Assault of Woman Soldiers on Rise in US Military." *The Christian Science Monitor* 19 Mar. 2007 <www.csmonitor.com>.

Reichert, Elisabeth. *Challenges in Human Rights: A Social Work Perspective.* New York: Columbia UP, 2007.

Reichert, Tom, and Jacqueline Lambiase, eds. *Sex in Consumer Culture.* NJ and London: Erlbaum, 2006.

Reid, Robert H. "U.S. Weighs in on Iraq Rape Case." *Associated Press* 22 Feb. 2007 <http://news.yahoo.com/s/ap/20070222/ap>.

"Report No. 49: Japanese POW Interrogation on Prostitution." United States Office of War Information. 1 Oct. 1944.

"Republic of Korea and North Korea: Trafficking in Persons Report." 2008. U.S Embassy <http://seoul.usembassy.gov>.

"Rescued from Slavery: *48 Hours* Goes Undercover into the International Sex Trade." *CBS News* 23 Feb. 2005 <http://cbsnews.com/stories/2005/02/23/48hours/main675913.shtml>.

Richie, Donald. *The Image Factory: Fads and Fashions in Japan.* London: Reaktion Books, 2003.

Ritter, Karl. "Sweden's Sex Law: Get the Customer." *Associated Press* 15 Mar. 2008 <http://news.yahoo.com>.

Riverbend. *Baghdad Burning: Girl Blog from Iraq.* New York: The Feminist Press at the City U of New York, 2005.

Robinson, Victor (M.D.). *Morals in Wartime.* New York: Publishers Foundation, 1943.

Robson, Seth. "2nd ID Seeks to Curb Lap Dancing in Clubs." *Stars and Stripes.* <http://www.military.com/features>.

- - - ."Soldiers Say Porn Ban May Hurt Morale." *Stars and Stripes* 5 May 2008 <http://www.military.com/features>.

Rogers, Mary, and Paola Tinagli. *Women in Italy, 1350-1650.* Manchester, UK: Manchester UP, 2005.

Rooke, Julia. "Iranian Child Victim of Prostitution." <http://www.flametree.blog-city.com>.

Rosen, Ruth. "The Hidden War on Women in Iraq." *Mother Jones* 13 July 2006 <http://www.motherjones.com/commentary/columns/2006/07/war_women.html>.

Ross, Sherwood. "Rape of Iraqi Women Byproduct of Militarism." *OpEd News* 10 Apr. 2007 <http://www.opednews.com/articles/genera_sherwood_070410_rape_of_Iraqi_women.htm>.

Rostami-Povey, Elaheh. *Afghan Women: Identity and Invasion*. London and New York: Zed, 2007.

Rothenberg, Paula S., ed. *Race, Class, and Gender in the United States: An Integrated Study*, 6th ed. New York: Worth, 2004.

"Rough Cuts--Dubai: Night Secrets--The Oldest Profession in the Newest Playground." Dir. Mimi Chakarova. *Frontline/World*. PBS. Sept. 2007 <http://www.pbs.org/frontlineworld/rough/2007/09/dubai_sex_for_s.html>.

Rowland, David, and Luca Incrocci, eds. *Handbook of Sexual and Gender Disorders*. New Jersey: John Wiley, 2008.

"RSA Lectures: Sex Slavery and Human Trafficking." *Teachers.TV*. <www.teachers.tv/video/28030>.

Ruggiero, Guido. *The Boundaries of Eros: Sex Crime and Sexuality in Renaissance Venice*. New York and Oxford: OUP, 1985.

Rulon, Malia. "U.S. Military Patrols in S. Korea Often Don't Recognize Human Trafficking." *Associated Press* < http://www.highbeam.com>.

Rutherford, Paul. *A World Made Sexy: Freud to Madonna*. Toronto: U of Toronto P, 2007.

Ryan, Chris, and C. Michael Hall. *Sex Tourism: Marginal People and Liminalities*. London: Routledge, 2001.

Ryang, Sonia. *Love in Modern Japan: Its Estrangement from Self, Sex, and Society*. London and New York: Routledge, 2006.

Sanday, Peggy Reeves. *Fraternity Gang Rape: Sex, Brotherhood, and Privilege on Campus*. New York and London: New York UP, 1990.

Sanders, Teela. *Sex Work: A Risky Business*. Devon, UK: Willan, 2005.

Sarhan, Afif. "In Iraq, Sex is Traded for Survival." *Arab American News* <www.arabamericannews.com>.

Sayle, Murray. "Japan's Comfort Women: Theirs and Ours." Mar. 2002 <http://www.jpri.org/publications/critiques>.

Schellstede, Sangmie Choi., ed. *Comfort Women Speak: Testimony by Sex Slaves of the Japanese Military.* New York and London: Holmes and Meier, 2000.

Schissel, Wendy, ed. *Home/Bodies: Geographies of Self, Place, and Space.* U of Calgary P, 2006.

Schmidt, David Andrew. *Ianfu—The Comfort Women of the Japanese Imperial Army of the Pacific War: Broken Silence.* Lewiston, Queenston, Lampeter: The Edwin Mellen Press, 2000.

Seabrook, Jeremy. *Travels in the Skin Trade: Tourism and the Sex Industry.* London: Pluto, 1996.

Secomb, Linnell. *Philosophy and Love: From Plato to Pop Culture.* Bloomington: Indiana UP, 2007.

Seely, Megan. *Fight Like a Girl: How to Be a Fearless Feminist.* New York: New York UP, 2007.

Sen, Krishna, and Maila Stivens, eds. *Gender and Power in Affluent Asia.* London and New York: Routledge, 1998.

Sernau, Scott. *Global Problems: The Search for Equity, Peace, and Sustainability.* Boston and New York: Pearson, 2006.

Seugra, Denise A., and Patricia Zavella. *Women and Migration in the U.S.-Mexico Borderlands.* Durham and London: Duke UP, 2007.

"Sex Slaves." *Frontline. PBS* 2006 <http://www.pbs.org/wgbh/pages/frontline/slaves/needs/malarek.html>.

"Sex Traffickers Target Women in War-Torn Iraq." *Organization of Women's Freedom* 1 Nov. 2006 <http://www.scapa.lv.org>.

"Sexual Violence and Abduction of Women and Girls—Iraq." *Human Rights Watch* 2003 <http.//www.hrw.org>.

Sheptycki, James, and Ali Wardek, eds. *Transnational and Comparative Criminology*. London: GlassHouse Press, 2005.

"Should Prostitution Be Legal Anywhere." Blog. 26 Jan 2007 <http://newsweek.washingtonpost.com/postglobal/2007/01/legalize_prostitution/comments.html>.

Siegel, Deborah. *Sisterhood, Interrupted: From Radical Women to Girls Gone Wild.* New York: Palgrave, 2007.

Sinan, Omar. "Iraqi Refugees Turn to Prostitution." *Associated Press* 25 Oct. 2007 <http://www.countercurrents.org/sinan251007.htm>.

Sinha, Mrinalini, Donna Guy, and Angela Woollacott, eds. *Feminisms and Internationalism*. Oxford: Blackwell, 1999.

Skaine, Rosemarie. *Power and Gender: Issues in Sexual Dominance and Harassment.* Jefferson, NC and London: McFarland, 1996.

Skimmel, Michael. *Manhood in America: A Cultural History*. New York: Oxford UP, 2006.

Skrobanek, Siriporn. *The Traffic in Women*. London: Zed, l997.

Sleightholme, Carolyn, and Indrani Sinha. *Guilty without Trail: Women in the Sex Trade in Calcutta*. New Jersey: Rutgers UP, 1997.

Slim, Hugo. *Killing Civilians: Method, Madness, and Morality in War*. New York: Columbia UP, 2008.

Smith, Clarissa. *One for the Girls! The Pleasures and Practices of Reading Women's Porn.* Bristol: Intellect Books, 2007.

Soldz, Stephen. "The Sex Lives and Sexual Frustrations of US Troops in Iraq." *Veterans Today* 31 Dec. 2005 < http://veteranstoday.com>.

"South Korea: UN Says Sex Industry Employs 5000 Women for GI's." *Human Trafficking* <http://humantrafficking.com/humantraffikcing/client/view>.

Spector, Robert. *World Without Civilization*. Maryland: U P of America., 2005.

Squire, Corinne. *HIV in South Africa: Talking about the Big Thing*. London and New York: Routledge, 2007.

Squires, Judith. *The New Politics of Gender Equality*. Hampshire and New York: Palgrave, 2007.

Staples, Robert. *Exploring Black Sexuality*. New York: Rowman & Littlefield, 2006.

Stetz, Margaret, and Bonnie B.C. Oh, eds. *Legacies of the Comfort Women of World War II*. London: East Gate, 2001.

Stevens, Anne. *Women, Power and Politics*. Hampshire and New York: Palgrave, 2007.

Stoecker, Sally, and Louise Shelley, eds. *Human Traffic and Transnational Crime: Eurasian and American Perspectives*. New York: Rowman & Littlefield, 2005.

Sturdevant, Saundra Pollock, and Brenda Stoltzfus. *Let the Good Times Roll: Prostitution and the U.S. Military in Asia*. New York: The New Press, 1992.

Swanson, Gillian. *Drunk with the Glitter: Space, Consumption and Sexual Instability in Modern Urban Culture*. London and New York: Routledge, 2007.

Talmadge, Eric. "Documents: U.S. Troops Used 'Comfort Women' after World War II." *CNN* 25 Apr. 2007 <http://www.cnn.com/2007/US/1=04/25/comfort.women.ap/index.html>.

- - -. "GI's Frequented Japan's Comfort Women." *Associated Press* 25 Apr. 2007 <http://www.boston.com/news/world/asia>.

- - -. "US Marines Warned of Japan's Anger." *Associated Press* 2 Feb. 2008 <http://news.yahoo.com>.

- - -. "World War II GI's Shacked up with Japanese Comfort Women." *Veterans Today* 26 April 2007 <http://www.veteranstoday.com>.

Tanaka, Yuki. *Hidden Horrors: Japanese War Crimes in World War II.* New York: HarperCollins, 1996.

- - - . *Japan's Comfort Women: Sexual Slavery and Prostitution During World War II and the US Occupation.* London: Routledge, 2002.

Tekola, Bethlehem. *Poverty and the Social Context of Sex Work in Addis Ababa: An Anthropological Perspective.* FSS Special Monograph Series—No. 2.

Thomas, Gordon. *Enslaved.* New York: Pharos, 1991.

Thorbek, Susanne. *Voices from the City: Women of Bangkok.* London and New Jersey: Zed, 1987.

Tijani, Hakeem Ibikunle, ed. *Nigeria's Urban History.* Boulder and New York: UP of America, 2006.

Totten, Samuel, and Eric Markusen. *Genocide in Darfur: Investigating the Atrocities in the Sudan.* New York: Routledge, 2006.

Truong, Thanh-Dam. *Sex, Money and Morality: Prostitution and Tourism in Southeast Asia.* London and New Jersey: Zed, 1990.

Turner, Janice. "Brothels Are Booming, Ban Them." *UK Times Online* 23 Feb. 2008 <http://www.timesonline.co.uk>.

Turse, Nick, and Deborah Nelson. "Civilian Killings Went Unpunished." *Los Angeles Times* 6 Aug. 2006 <http://www.latimes.com/news/printededition>.

Ugrešić, Dubravka. "A Postcard from Europe." *Playboy* June 2009: 119-120.

"United States: The Role of Military Forces in the Growth of the Commercial Sex Industry." *Women's Action.* June 2003 <http://www.equalitynow.org>.

"U.S. Command in Korea Gets Tough on Demand Side of Prostitution." USInfo.State.Gov 24 Sept. 2004 <http://usinfo.state.gov>.

U.S. Department of State. "The Link Between Prostitution and Sex Trafficking." Bureau of Public Affairs. 24 Dec. 2004 <http://www.state.gov>.

"USFK Creates 'Off-Limits' Bars List." *Military.com* < http://www.military.com>.

"US Gen. McChrystal Takes Command in Afghanistan." *Associated Press* 15 June 2009 <http://news.yahoo.com>.

Valenti, Jessica. *Full Frontal Feminism: A Young Woman's Guide to Why Feminism Matters.* Seal Press, 2007

"Valentine's Day." *Las Vegas Weekly* 21-27 Feb. 2008: 24-26.

Van den Anker, Christien L., and Jeroen Doomernik, eds. *Trafficking and Women's Rights.* Hampshire and New York: Palgrave, 2006.

Vandenberg, Marina "Peacekeeping, Alphabet Soup, and Violence Against Women." *Gender, Conflict, and Peacekeeping.* Ed. Mazurana, Raven-Roberts, and Parpart. Lanham, MD: Rowman and Littlefield, 2005.

Vincent, Isabel. *Bodies and Souls: The Tragic Plight of Three Jewish Women Forced into Prostitution in America.* New York: William Morrow, 2005.

Voices from the Japanese Women's Movement. Ed. By AMPO—*Japanese Asia Quarterly Review.* London: M.E. Sharpe, 1996.

Walkowitz, Judith R. *City of Dreadful Delights.* Chicago: U of Chicago P, 1992.

Waller, Marguerite R., and Jennifer Rycenga, eds. *Frontline Feminisms: Women, War, and Resistance.* New York and London: Garland, 2000.

"War Against Women: The Use of Rape as a Weapon in Congo's Civil War." Anderson Cooper. *60 Minutes. CBS News* 13 Jan. 2008 <http://www.cbsnews.com>.

Weaver, Andrew J., John Preston, and Charlene A. Hosenfeld. *Counseling on Sexual Issues: A Handbook for Pastors and Other Professionals.* Cleveland: The Pilgrim Press, 2005.

Weber, Cynthia. *Morality, Politics, and Film.* London and New York: Routledge, 2006.

Wells, Jess. *A Herstory of Prostitution in Western Europe.* Berkeley: Shameless Hussy Press, 1982.

Weston, Burns H., ed. *Child Labor and Human Rights: Making Children Matter.* Boulder and London: Lynn Rienner, 2005.

"What We've Accomplished." 17 Aug. 2007 <http://immorallogic.blogspot.com>.

"Where the Whore's Aren't: Examining the Lack of Prostituted Women's Voices in News Reporting." *Off Our Backs.* 2006. White, Amy E. *The Case for an Uncensored Internet.* Jefferson, NC: McFarland, 2006.

Wildfang, Robin Lorsch. *Rome's Vestal Virgins: A Study of Rome's Vestal Priestesses in the Late Republic and Early Empire.* London and New York: Routledge, 2006.

Wilkinson, David John, Luke Samuel Bearup, and Tong Soprach. "Youth Gang Rape in Phnom Penh." *Sex Without Consent.* Ed. Jejeebhoy, Shah, and Thapa. London and New York: Zed, 2008.

"Will Latest Corruption at Osan AFB Korea Be Covered Up?" *Military Corruption.com* 2005 <http://www.militarycorruption.com/davis2.htm>.

Wilson, Shamillah, Anasuya Sengupta, and Kristy Evans, eds. *Defending Our Dreams: Global Feminist Voices for a New Generation.* London: Zed, 2005.

Wolf, Joerg. "Prostitution in Iraq." *Atlantic Review* 26 Aug. 2007 <http://atlanticreview.org/archives/803Prostitutition-in-Iraq.html>.

"Women, Children and Youth in the Iraq Crisis: A Fact Sheet." *Women's Commission for Refugee Women and Children.* Jan. 2008 <http://www.womenscommission.org>.

Wood, Sharon E. *The Freedom of the Streets: Work, Citizenship, and Sexuality in a Gilded Age City*. Chapel Hill and London: U of North Carolina P, 2005.

Yamaguchi, Mari. "US Airman in Japan Arrested, Accused of Groping Woman." *Associated Press* 2 May 2008 <http://news.yahoo.com>.

Yamanouchi, Yasushi, J. Victor Koschmann, and Ruichi Narita. *Total War and 'Modernization.'* Ithaca, NY: Cornell East Asian Series, 1998.

Yamazaki, Hiromi. "Military Slavery and the Women's Movement." *Voices from the Japanese Women's Movement.* Ed. By AMPO—*Japanese Asia Quarterly Review.* London: M.E. Sharpe, 1996.

Yamazaki, Tomoko. *Sandakan Brothel No. 8: An Episode in the History of Lower-class Japanese Women.* Trans. Karen Colligan-Taylor. London: M.E. Sharpe, 1999.

Yano. Christine Reiko. *Crowning the Nice Girl: Gender, Ethnicity, and Culture in Hawaii's Cherry Blossom Festival.* Honolulu: U of Hawai'i P, 2006.

Yoshimi, Yoshiaki. *Comfort Women: Sexual Slavery in the Japanese Military During World War II.* Trans. Suzanne O'Brien. New York: Columbia UP, 2000.

Zamir, Tzachi. *Ethics and the Beast.* New Jersey: Princeton UP, 2007.

Zeigler, Sara L., and Gregory G. Gunderson. *Moving Beyond G.I. Jane.* Lanham and Boulder: UP of America, 2005.

"The best thing we can do," said Wimsey, "is to look the evidence in the face, however ugly. And I don't mind admittin' that some of it's a positive gargoyle."

--Dorothy L. Sayers, *Clouds of Witness*

"The more I see of the world, the more am I dissatisfied with it; and every day confirms my belief of the inconsistency of all human characters."

--Elizabeth Bennet, speaking in Jane Austen's *Pride and Prejudice*

...industrial society has become paradoxically unlivable, incalculably immoral, and ultimately deadly....We are raised to honor all the wrong explorers and discoverers—thieves planting flags, murderers carrying crosses. Let us at last praise the colonizers of dreams.

--Peter S. Beagle, 14 July 1973 introductory note to *Lord of the Rings*

LaVergne, TN USA
04 August 2010
191873LV00005B/4/P